Papp/Weidi
Licandro/Meir-Hub__, ____

MW01079002

The Handbook of Data Science and AI

Stefan Papp, Wolfgang Weidinger,
Katherine Munro, Bernhard Ortner,
Annalisa Cadonna, Georg Langs,
Roxane Licandro, Mario Meir-Huber,
Danko Nikolić, Zoltan Toth, Barbora Vesela,
Rania Wazir, Günther Zauner

The Handbook of Data Science and AI

Generate Value from Data with Machine Learning and Data Analytics

HANSER

Hanser Publishers, Munich

Distributed by:
Carl Hanser Verlag
Postfach 86 04 20, 81631 Munich, Germany
Fax: +49 (89) 98 48 09
www.hanserpublications.com
www.hanser-fachbuch.de

© Carl Hanser Verlag, Munich 2022
Coverconcept: Marc Müller-Bremer, www.rebranding.de, Munich
Coverdesign: Max Kostopoulos
Cover image: © gettyimages.de/ValeryBrozhinsky
Typesetting: Eberl & Kœsel Studio GmbH, Altusried-Krugzell, Germany
Printed and bound by Hubert & Co. GmbH und Co. KG BuchPartner, Göttingen, Germany
Printed in Germany

Print ISBN: 978-1-56990-886-0
E-Book ISBN: 978-1-56990-887-7
ePub ISBN: 978-1-56990-888-4

Table of Contents

5   Data Management 131

Stefan Papp, Bernhard Ortner

6   Mathematics 153

Annalisa Cadonna

16   AI in Different Industries **453**

Stefan Papp, Mario Meir-Huber, Wolfgang Weidinger, Thomas Treml, Marek Danis

Foreword

"Mathematical science shows what is. It is the language of unseen relations between things. But to use and apply that language, we must be able to fully appreciate, to feel, to seize the unseen, the unconscious." – Ada Lovelace

As Computer Literacy over a generation ago represented a new set of foundational skills to be acquired, Artificial Intelligence (AI) Literacy represents the same for our current generations and beyond. Over the last two decades Data Science has come to encompass the mathematical architecture and corresponding language with which we build and interact with systems that extend our senses and decision-making abilities. Thus, it's no longer sufficient to be able to send point-and-click commands into computers, but rather it's vitally important to be able to interpret and interact with AI-enabled recommendations coming out of computers. Currently, machines, as in computers coupled with sensors (in the broadest sense), are processing an increasingly wide array of data including text, images, video, audio, network graphs and a multitude of information from the web, private industry, and public sector sources. Considering diversity of data, the authors of this book approach Data Science as a key underlying topic for society and do so with great insight, from multiple key vantage points, and in enjoyable style that resonates with novices and experts alike.

To gain value from data is arguably the unifying objective of the 21st century knowledge worker. Even professional areas thought of as classically distant from data such as sales and art, now have data-driven sub-areas such as marketing automation and computational design. For the benefit of readers, the authors bring to bear first-hand experiences and diligent research to provide a compelling narrative on how we all have a role to play when attempting to leverage data for better outcomes. Indeed, the breadth conveyed in this work is impressive, spanning that of hardware performance considerations (e.g. CPU, Network, Memory, I/O, GPU) to that of different team member roles when building machines that can find patterns in data. Moreover, the authors provide important coverage on the ways that machines can now see and read, namely, Computer Vision and Natural Language Processing, with implications across nearly every industry area being profound.

As you read this book, I encourage you to be curious and have on top of mind a set of questions on how your professional journey and society as you see it is currently being impacted by increasingly advanced machines: from the capabilities available on your smartphone to that of how jobs are being refashioned in the marketplace with automation tools. Here are some questions to help you get started:

- How does the ratio of what tasks you spend your time on shift with the emergence of increasingly advanced machines in your job area?
- What are the implications of having machines that have perceptive abilities analogous to your own, as in to see, hear, smell, taste, touch and beyond?

- How as society do we grapple with bias in and trust around data?

- How do we make the building and the use of machines that learn more inclusive?

- What distinctly human abilities can you accentuate to help organizations that you care about to be more competitive and sustainable?

I've been cautious not to use the term thinking machines, or artificial general intelligence, as to be wary about overstatements. What I would like to focus your attention on is the wide applicability of what we're seeing coming out of research surrounding machines that have learning capabilities. From my time in laboratories at Columbia and Cornell Universities, to that of the Princeton Plasma Physics Laboratory, the American University of Armenia and NASA-backed TRISH (Translational Research Institute for Space Health) which is collaborating with TrialX, it's clear that machines can find patterns in data across a tremendously wide range of domains and alert humans in both regular and mission critical contexts. Thus, the impacts to human experience are multi-faceted and Data Scientists have an important role in supporting the design of systems where human interaction with machine output is positive sum. I can't underscore this enough that a zero-sum approach to automation in sub-optimal. Entrepreneurs though tend to find a way toward maximum sum.

With colleagues and through my work at the BAJ Accelerator and Covenant Venture Capital, I support startups to engage in a type of tandem learning: how a rapidly growing company can transform an industry by spotting market gaps to that of how a company's invention can learn and provide new capabilities for customers. For example, in the powerful technology area of Computer Vision that is a mainstay in Data Science, three companies stand out as trailblazing in three very different industry areas: Embodied, Scylla and cognaize in healthcare, security and finance, respectively.

- Embodied's flagship product, Moxie, is a robot that supports the emotional well-being and social development of children. To do so, Moxie must see and communicate with family members in a compelling way, understanding visually as well as via other cues the emotional state of people it's interacting with as to engage in meaningful dialogue. Thus, healthcare providers have a new robotic team member to collaborate with. Embodied has been on the cover of TIME Magazine.

- Scylla enables an organization's security team to be proactive in improving safety. With real-time detection capabilities, camera networks no longer need to be passive and can be transformed to being proactive. Applications are numerous from detecting slip-and-falls in hospitals and stadiums as they happen to improve health outcomes to that of making intruder alerts at manufacturing facilities and office buildings to better protect staff. Scylla has been featured in Forbes.

- cognaize supports financial institutions and insurance organizations process a tremendous amount of unstructured data when making risk determinations. A key insight is considering documents not only as text, but rather also considering visual information: style, tables, structure. In addition, cognaize has a human-in-the-loop whereby colleagues and the system overall continually learn. cognaize has been featured on the NASDAQ screen in Times Square.

In the above three examples of rising unicorn startups, Data Scientists work in close collaboration with engineers, analysts, designers, content creators, domain specialists and customers to build machines that learn and interact with humans in nuanced ways. The result is a transformation in the nature of work: humans are alerted to the most important documents or moments in time and human experience is learned from to improve quality. This is representative of a new shift requiring AI Literacy, where jobs in nearly every facet of the economy will have aspects requiring machine interaction: humans making corrections, learning new skills, reacting to and interpreting alerts, and having a faster response time in helping other humans leveraging machines in support. In the years ahead, I'm excited about the role of Data Science in interface research, new algorithms and how humans can have a force multiplication on their work.

As I co-wrote the first edition of *The Field Guide to Data Science* nearly a decade ago, it's remarkable how much the discipline has advanced both in terms of what has been technically achieved and in an aspirational sense on what is yet to be. The Handbook of Data Science and AI advances the discipline along both of those dimensions and carries the torch forward.

Read on.

Fall 2021
Armen R. Kherlopian, Ph.D.

Preface

"The job of the data scientist is to ask the right questions."
Hillary Mason

Reading the foreword written for our first publication two years ago, I couldn't shake the feeling that some trends essentially stayed the same while others emerged all of a sudden and hit society and companies like an avalanche.

Starting with the changes, that struck society profoundly, it is obvious that the pandemic is one of them. Setting aside the myriad of consequences it had and continues to have on our lives, I want to focus on the facets which relate to the subject of this book: Data Science and AI.

Put simply, the impact there was that entire societies and our whole way of living became data driven in an instant. Key performance indicators like the seven-day incidence rate or forecasts based on pandemic simulations steered our daily life and temporarily even altered basic rights, like the right to leave our homes. This led to discussions and questions, which every Data Scientist with some experience is familiar with and has encountered repeatedly during their working life:

- Can we trust these models and their predictions?
- Is the chosen KPI really the right one for this purpose?
- Is the underlying data quantity and quality good enough?

and so on.

All of these are valid questions and are, just as they were two years ago, fueled by another trend: Digitization. The engine for this is data. On top of that, Data Scientists are still following the same goal:

Giving understandable answers to questions by using data.

Despite all trends, this purpose stays the same and always will be one of the central pillars of doing Data Science.

But this is not the only trend which has remained or become even stronger. The most important, continuing phenomenon is the still massive hype caused by phrases like "Artificial Intelligence" and "Data Science". While these fields are incredibly valuable and powerful, discussions around them unfortunately often evoke false promises and skewed expectations, which in turn lead to disappointment. Some companies already started large, ambitious initiatives in the past, which led to underwhelming results, because expectations were set too high and timelines too short. For example, fully autonomous driving is one particularly challenging problem to solve.

Nevertheless, Artificial Intelligence remains the hope for many companies. Investors perceive it as a general purpose, technology that can be applied almost anywhere. The situation is comparable with the development during the nineties when all things related to the 'Internet' surged. Suddenly, every company needed a web page and significant investments were made to train web programmers. Nowadays, a similar thing happens with everything AI related. Again the investments into AI are enormous and we have a rush of courses on the topic. In the end, the development concerning the 'Internet' led to a vast ecosystem of companies and applications which influence the lives of billions of people in a profound way and it seems that AI follows a similar path.

This explains at least partly another noticeable trend: the further specialization of data science roles with names like "data translator" or "machine learning engineer." It is a somehow natural development as this is a sign that the field is getting more mature, but it also raises the risk of data science responsibilities being scattered across poorly coordinated organizations, and thus, not reaching its full potential. Chapter 14 and 17 go into this in further detail.

Finally, "Trustworthy AI" is emerging as another, highly important movement within Data Science. This is the field of research, which aims to tackle some previously unmet needs, like explainability or fairness. It is therefore included as one of the new chapters in this book (Chapter 18).

Given all these trends in Data Science, one of the reasons for founding the Vienna Data Science Group (VDSG) has become even more important over the last two years: to create a neutral place where interdisciplinary exchange of knowledge between all involved experts can take place internationally. We are still very much dedicated to the development of the entire Data Science ecosystem (education, certification, standardization, societal impact study, and so on), both across Europe and beyond.

A product of the exchange in our community can be found in the 2nd edition of this book, which has been vastly expanded to cover topics like AI (Chapter 9), Machine Learning (Chapter 8), Natural Language Processing (Chapter 10), Computer Vision (Chapter 11) or Modelling and Simulation (Chapter 12) in more depth. To follow our goal to educate society about Data Science and its impacts, a very relevant use case was included in Chapter 12: An agent-based COVID-19 model, which aims to give ideas about the potential impact of certain policies and their combination on the spread of the disease.

To provide our readers with a firm foundation, an introduction to the underlying mathematics (Chapter 6) and statistics (Chapter 7) used in Data Science has been included, and finished with a visualization section (Chapter 13).

Although a lot of content has been added, the goal of this book stays the same and has become even more relevant: to give a realistic picture of Data Science.

Because despite all trends, data science remains the same as well: an interdisciplinary science gathering a very heterogeneous crowd of specialists, which is made up of three major streams:

- Computer Science/IT
- Mathematics/Statistics
- Domain expertise in the industry in which Data Science is applied.

Science aims to generate new knowledge, and this is still used to

- improve existing business processes in a given company (Chapter 16)
- enable completely new business models

Data Science is here to stay and its direct and indirect impact on society is growing at a fast pace, as can be seen during the pandemic. In some areas a bit of disillusionment has set in, but this can be seen as a healthy development to counter the hype. Data Science team roles are becoming more differentiated, and more companies are putting Data Science projects into production.

So, Data Science has grown up and is entering a new era.

Fall 2021
Wolfgang Weidinger

■ Acknowledgments

We, the authors, would like to take this opportunity to express our sincere gratitude to our families and friends, who helped us to express our thoughts and insights in this book. Without their support and patience, this work would not have been possible.

A special thanks from all the authors goes to Katherine Munro, who contributed a chapter to this book and spent a tremendous amount of time and effort editing our manuscripts.

For my parents, who always said I could do anything. We never expected it would be a thing like this.
Katherine Munro

I'd like to thank my wife and the Vienna Data Science Group for their continuous support through my professional journey.
Zoltan C. Toth

When I think of the people who supported me most, I want to thank my parents, who have always believed in me no matter what and my partner Verena, who was very patient during the last months when I worked on this book. In addition I'm very grateful for the support and motivation I got from the people I met through the Vienna Data Science Group.
Wolfgang Weidinger

1 Introduction

"Data really powers everything that we do."
Jeff Weiner

 Questions Answered in this Chapter:

- What makes Data Science, ML, AI and everything else closely connected to generate value out of data so fascinating?
- Why do organisations need a strategy to become data driven?
- What are some everyday use cases in the B2B or NGO world?
- How are data projects structured?
- What is the composition of a data team?

Data Science and related technologies have been the center of attention since 2010. Various changes in the ecosystem triggered this trend, such as

- significant advancements in processing a vast amount of unstructured data,
- substantial cost reduction of disk storage,
- the emergence of new data sources such as social media and sensor data.

The HBR called the data scientist the sexiest job of the 21st century while quoting Hal Varian from Google.[1] Strategy consultants declared data to be the new oil, and there have been occasional "data rushes" where "enthusiasts in data fever" mined new data sources for yet unknown treasures. This book explores data science and incorporates various views on the discipline.

---

[1] https://hbr.org/2012/10/data-scientist-the-sexiest-job-of-the-21st-century

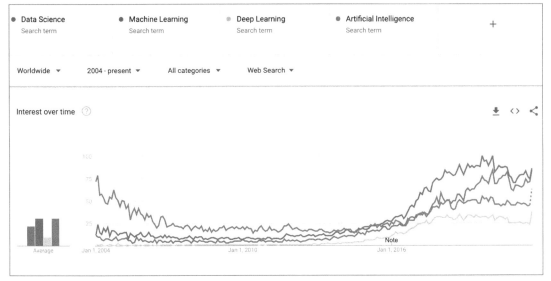

Figure 1.1 Data Science and related technologies on trends.google.com[2]

■ 1.1 What are Data Science, Machine Learning and Artificial Intelligence?

There are many views on data science, and stakeholders in data science projects may give different answers to what they consider data science to be. Representatives address various aspects and may use different vocabulary since businesses and NGOs, for example, pursue different insights from data science applications. Perhaps the one common denominator is this: Everyone expects data science to deliver some value, which was not there before, with the help of data.

Table 1.1 Various views on Data Science

View	Description
Definition from Wikipedia	Data science is an interdisciplinary field that uses scientific methods, processes, algorithms, and systems to extract knowledge and insights from structured and unstructured data and apply knowledge and actionable insights from data across a broad range of application domains.[3]

[2] Data source: Google Trends *(https://www.google.com/trends)*
[3] *https://en.wikipedia.org/wiki/Data_science*#

View	Description
Application-centered view	We collect data and put this into pandas-data frames or data frames in R Studio. We also use tools such as TensorFlow or Keras. Our goal is to use these tools to explore the data.
Platform-oriented view	We create value from the data that we loaded on our SaaS platform in the cloud. Then, depending on the provided data and its structures, we store them in different storage containers, such as blob storage and distributed databases.
Evangelist-oriented view	Data science was the next big thing in 2015. Now, you should look at more specific applications. Looking at the Gartner charts, invest your time exploring cutting-edge trends such as neuromorphic hardware or augmented intelligence.
Management-oriented view	These are the ways of working to bring our company into the 21st century as a data-driven enterprise. During and after our transition, we will penetrate new markets and monetize data as a service.
Career-oriented view	As a senior data scientist at a major company, I can earn a six-digit yearly salary and explore interesting fields in corporate labs.
Use case-oriented view	Tell me your business problem, and we will tell you how we solved it for another customer. From fraud detection to customer retention to social network analysis, feel free to check out our catalog of possible analytics applications.
Entrepreneurial/ Optimistic view	Data Science is one way to change the world. Using Data Science, we can prevent climate change and fight poverty and hunger on a global scale.
Pessimist view	Data Science is one way to change the world. But, unfortunately, power-hungry people will use it to spy on us and suppress us. So Big Brother will be watching you.
Statistician's view	Data Science is just a buzzword. It is just another word for statistics. We might call it statistics on steroids, maybe. But in the end, it's just another marketing hype to create another buzzword to sell services to someone.

The essentials of data science lay in mathematics. Data scientists apply statistics to generate new knowledge from data. Besides using algorithms on data, a data scientist must understand the scientific process of exploring data, such as creating reproducible experiments and interpreting the results.

There are many different terms related to data science. For example, professionals talk about Artificial Intelligence, machine learning, or deep learning. Sometimes experts also talk about related terms such as analytics or business intelligence and simulation. In the following chapters, we will detail and highlight how we distinguish between analytics and data science. We will also highlight various data science applications, such as gaining insights into a text through Natural Language Processing or extracting objects from images via object recognition or modeling railway networks for optimal pathfinding.

Data Science as Part of a Cultural Shift

Suppose you apply for a job as a data scientist in a company. Imagine that, although it is unlikely you will get such an answer, the HR of this company rejects you because your astrology chart based on the data you have provided in your CV does not match the position.

Humans decide on what they believe is right. But, unfortunately, human judgment is flawed through bias[4], and we have mechanisms, such as confirmation bias, which assure us that we cannot err. For example, some people believe in the flat Earth theory or hollow Earth theory, which shows how powerful mechanisms such as confirmation bias can be.

For many of us, it would be disastrous to realize that a comfortable binary view of the world divided into black and white, good and evil, and right and wrong often does not work out. Modern sociological ideas such as constructivism[5] are more connected to data science than many think. The idea is that everyone constructs a reality based on their experience. Within the framework of "our reality", including its rules and conventions, we make decisions. According to studies, it is not uncommon that we are deeply convinced that we are right even if our choices are questionable to others. For example, suppose we have created mental models for ourselves in which we are confident that astrology must be correct. In that case, it is logical to assume zodiacs for personnel decisions will improve the hiring process. At the same time, people with strong religious beliefs might run into conflicts if they ignore what they might call signs or messages from God. Thanks to the biases mentioned above, our belief systems are often hammered into stone.

Data Science is not just a method to extract value from data; it also has the potential to be a method for making decisions that avoids or reduces human bias in the process. However, as will be shown in Chapter 18 on Trustworthy AI, data alone cannot solve the problem, because historical data and the model building process itself are often imbued with the very same biases. With that, business leaders can integrate data science and transparent and non-discriminatory practices, into corporate culture, and this will substantially impact the company's DNA. For example, a bias-aware company will adjust processes. Hiring a new employee is a good example. Many companies enlarge hiring teams that decide on the outcome of the candidate interviews in order to ensure that the bias of a single interviewer will not affect a hiring decision too much. In modern hiring processes, data science can be used to generate predictionsabout candidates to assist the decision-making process. If done with care, these model predictions can help to minimise biases in employment decisions.

[4] https://www.weforum.org/agenda/2018/12/24-cognitive-biases-that-are-warping-your-perception-of-reality
[5] https://www.buffalo.edu/catt/develop/theory/constructivism.html

In the beginning, every judgment is a theory. A theory is neither right nor wrong but inconclusive until it is proven or disproven.

Therefore, the positive effect of hiring personnel using astrological zodiacs would be nothing more than a theory. As long as we cannot prove that an astrological assessment would benefit a hiring process, the statement is inconclusive and, therefore, not recommended to use. Calling astrology inclusive rather than wrong might also make the discussion with believers in astrology less emotional.

Investigating the possible effects of astrology using data science is a perfect introduction to the environment we face in data science projects. Astrology claims to divine information about human affairs and terrestrial events by studying celestial objects' movements and relative positions. In a simplified version, astrology reduces everything to the sun sign, depending on birthdays. Using the simplified model, we could collect data on existing data scientists to determine a correlation between astrological signs and professions. In addition, we could collect the birthdate of a large pool of data scientists. As we need only a birth date and no other personal data, it would even be perfectly legal to collect these datasets from LinkedIn or any other data source containing data scientists' birthdates. Most of the analysis will consist of finding appropriate data sources, collecting the data from the data source, anonymizing it, and preparing it for examination.

Mathematics on the collected data will not leave much room for interpretation of results. Nevertheless, based on analysis, we would conclude a correlation between professions and astrological signs.

There is, however, a more complex form of astrology. Astrological charts include all planets and other celestial objects such as Lilith, the black moon, which does not exist in astronomy. In addition, many constellations are contradictory. An astrologer might call a person impulsive because of Venus or Lilith in Aries or passive because of Mars in Cancer. Finally, an astrologer might claim that readings require intuitive interpretations, which are, of course, not measurable.

Many data science projects might end with the assessment that there is insufficient data for a definite answer, and being unable to prove or disprove a theory might be unsatisfactory for many stakeholders. Yet, exploring data often helps bring clarity to the stakeholders, as at least many learn that achieving objective truth is not as easy as it seems. Therefore, we should be free to differ in personal or subjective beliefs and be cautious about things we cannot verify objectively. Of course, in the end, there is a good chance that we are right with our personal views if we have spent a lot of time exploring a specific field, even if we cannot prove it. Still, as long as we do not have enough data to prove something one way or another, it is a question of academic politeness to highlight inclusive outcomes because of insufficient data when talking with others.

Already as early as 2014, the New York Times[6] wrote about the 80/20 rule. This rule means that the team spends 80 % of their time finding and preparing data for data science projects and only 20 % on analytics. This number may vary enormously by industry. In addition to data modeling, we will also address the preparation and management of data in the chapters to follow. We aim to provide a compact introduction to data platforms and engineering.

In the second part of this book, we assume all the data is prepared and ready and focus on analytics. We will present several ways to generate value from data and cover essential topics such as neural networks and machine learning. We will also cover basics such as statistics.

The third and last part of the book is about the application of data science. Here we cover business topics and also address the subject of data protection.

 Machine Learning and Deep Learning

Starting from Chapter 6, we will detail the differences between these frequently buzzed-about concepts. Still, as using these terms related to data science often creates confusion, we would like to outline them for you here.

In recent years, many companies prioritized processing vast amounts of data. Consequently, scientific processing, such as formulating the working hypothesis, was pushed into the background. Big Data tries to solve problems with a suffi-ciently large amount of computer power and data. This fact creates a productivity paradox: More data and better algorithms do not make us more productive; in-stead, the opposite is often true, as it becomes increasingly difficult to distinguish the signal from the noise. The signal is the information relevant to a question and thus contributes to answering it, while the noise is the irrelevant information.

We attempt to make these signals measurable in the scientific field by measuring he signal detection accuracy and how often algorithms find the signal. The quotient of both measurements expresses the algorithms' accuracy. We describe it as a percentage. A high F1 score means a precise answer, while values around 50 % represent a random result. So if an algorithm has an accuracy of, say, 90 %, it means that 90 % of all information is processed correctly.

This number may sound like a lot; however, data with a large volume is the norm in Big Data. For example, imagine we want to classify comments to find hate speech in social media. Let's say that 510,000 comments were posted per second on Facebook in 2018. Assuming that 10 % were classified incorrectly, we might fail to detect hate speech in 51,000 posts.

To avoid such a situation, deep learning, a group of machine learning algorithms based on neural networks, is currently being applied as an abstract solution to many problems. The advantage of deep learning over classical machine learning is that the former usually scales better with the amount of data and thus provides more accurate results and can be applied to various problems.

---

[6] https://www.nytimes.com/2014/08/18/technology/for-big-data-scientists-hurdle-to-insights-is-janitor-work.html

The disadvantage of some methods in machine learning is that it can be challenging to interpret a prediction because the solution path is not immediately comprehensible. Furthermore, a statistically generated prediction may or may not be correct, as most models usually have less than 100 % accuracy. Additionally, we cannot use statistical forecasts to predict new data that has not been adequately analyzed or has limited usage. This statement may seem trivial, but it is essential since statistical analysis primarily depends on the input data and thus on the modeling skills of the data scientist. It is, therefore, necessary to interpret the result correctly and not to take it as truth.

An excellent example of this is numerical weather forecasts such as the weather report. We know fundamental physical laws in differential equations, but false predictions repeatedly occur due to non-existent or incorrect data or a simplified model. For example, a result of the solved differential equation can be: "Tomorrow the probability of rain is 10 %". Statistically, this means that we have created an analytical model based on historical data and based on all the data we have analysed, in 10 % of the cases with matching input data, it had rained. So 10 % can be a lot or very little; the important thing is to have an appropriate reference amount and relate it to the quantity obtained. In this case, it means that it is quite possible, although not likely, that it will rain tomorrow.

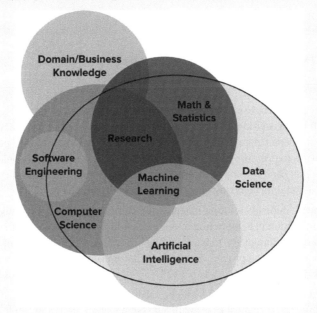

Figure 1.2 Differences *(https://ai.plainenglish.io/data-science-vs-artificial-intelligence-vs-machine-learning-vs-deep-learning-50d3718d51e5)*

Artificial Intelligence

When the common people think of AI, they might think of computers taking over the world such as in Terminator.

Artificial Intelligence is the simulation of human intelligence processes by machines, especially computer systems. There is an overlap between Machine Learning and Data Science, but AI can be seen still separated from both disciplines.

In Chapter 9, we explore Artificial Intelligence in detail. We explain the relation to Data Science and give a brief overview of the history of AI. We also discuss the problems that one may encounter when using Data Science skills to develop AI. In particular, we provide five pieces of advice: Be pragmatic, Make it easier for machines to learn through inductive biases, Perform analytics before creating AI architecture, Watch for the intelligence scaling trap and Watch for the generality trap. In this chapter you will have a chance to learn how to avoid mistakes and how to effectively use your Data Science tools to create AI solutions. After reading this chapter you will understand well where the limitations of AI technology are today and how to cope with those limitations.

■ 1.2 Data Strategy

Some experts say that only companies with a data strategy have a future. We might agree or disagree with this assessment. However, everyone will admit that not every company feels the pressure to become data-driven. Many departments work mainly with pen and paper, in monopolies with no pressure to evolve or optimize processes. The figure below is just one of many models that can be found with web research to highlight different stages of a transformation from a non-data company to an entirely data-driven one.

As data maturity depends a lot on external pressure, companies often migrate in phases. When the competition gets more fierce, the market forces companies to innovate. However, the luxury to resist change due to market pressure can also lead to different forms of stress. Some monopolies face the problem sometimes that no vendor supports the legacy software they used for decades.

Introducing data science in organizations, no matter if it is a business, NGO, or governmental institute, starts in most cases with a mission statement. For example, for a global car manufacturer, a strategy could be formulated as follows:

"Our company aims to be the cost leader in the global supply chain by 2025. This measure enables us to bring electric mobility to the mass market with less cost than our competitors. For us to achieve this, we have to cut our supply chain costs by 20 %."

Other companies simplify the strategy inspired by John F. Kennedy's speech on landing a man on the moon and returning him safely to the earth within a decade.

"Before this decade is out, all of our manufactured vehicles will be driverless."

Figure 1.3 Data Maturity Model[7]

An NGO might have less profit-oriented but no less ambitious goals.

"With the help of our donors, we will use satellite images to explore dry areas in countries to find water points. Using that technology, we hope to be able to decrease the pain of gaining access to water in developing countries."

The recommended practice for companies is to have an owner for data topics. Commonly this is the role of a Chief Data Officer, who needs to ensure that the company can realize its vision with the help of gaining insights from data.

Many companies have established processes to explore the past through business intelligence. For example, in maybe the most classic reference case, retail companies analyze how many products they have sold in the past. As a result, they can learn about which stores did a better or worse job. Based on the insights, leadership can then make changes such as replacing key personnel in poorly performing areas or creating additional incentives for growth in other areas.

Many companies have already reached a high level of optimization through traditional analytics. And it often seems as if conventional methods are at their limits.

Data science often helps to generate new knowledge. In other words, instead of using data science to sell more products, companies often use it to create new products. For example, while traditional analytical methods improve numbers, you get new numbers to work with through data science.

Once a CDO has proposed a strategy to meet the corporate goals, the board will approve the plan and allocate a budget. Using that strategy, the CDO then pools together the various department heads to realize the objective. Then, after a fit/gap analysis of the current situation, they will create hiring plans and plan projects to achieve their goals.

---

[7] *https://www.svds.com/thought-leadership/data-maturity-assessment/*

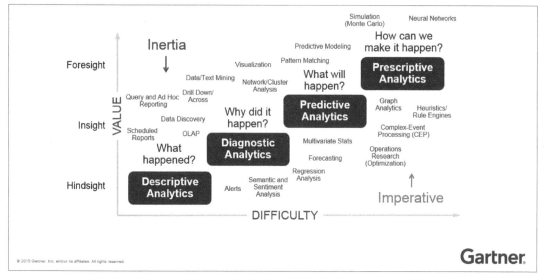

Figure 1.4 The Gartner Analytic Continuum (Source: *https://twitter.com/Doug_Laney/status/611172882882916352/photo/1*)

This position of business also clarifies the role of IT. The CIO is in charge of providing the necessary platforms to enable the teams of the CDO, but IT does not own the data science topic itself. Therefore, the CIO has to assess whether the current IT infrastructure meets the demand of the data strategy and if not, they must come up with a plan to create the required platforms.

1.3 From Strategy to Use Cases

Implementing a strategy defines how a business interprets data and the modeling based on it. Based on the strategy, a company can decide which questions the data scientists must answer. Based on these questions, solution architects can design platforms to host the data and data engineers can determine from which data sources they have to extract data.

Most companies have cross-functional teams for data science projects. They work in an agile team to explore new use cases and methods to apply data science.

Without qualified professionals, a company cannot even begin to implement its ambitious plans. Therefore, we want to look first at how data teams could appear from the project's view. In a corporate world, many of these team members would report to a different department.

1.3.1 Data Teams

We need data professionals to implement a data science strategy or to build up a data-driven start-up. There are two groups of experts in the data world that have evolved.

The first group, people with a statistical background, usually have academic experience and create models to answer the departments' questions. The second group consists of people with an engineering background. They are responsible for fully automating data loading onto the platform and continuously running the developed models' data in the production environment.

In organizations, these two groups have different reporting lines: Business and IT. In most companies, data agendas are a part of the top management board. Therefore, data is associated with the business. Some companies establish the role of a CDO, who directly reports to the CEO and the board. Others create a position, such as Head of Data or Head of Data Science. The authors of this book believe that data should be part of the board. Therefore, we refer to the CDO as the ultimate leader of all data agendas, whereas we refer to the CIO as the position accountable for all IT agendas.

In Figure 1.5 we have many models to describe the different roles per activity and department. Please be aware that we do not cover all roles in detail in this chapter. We cover this topic in more detail in Chapter 14.

Continuum of Analytics Roles and Skills

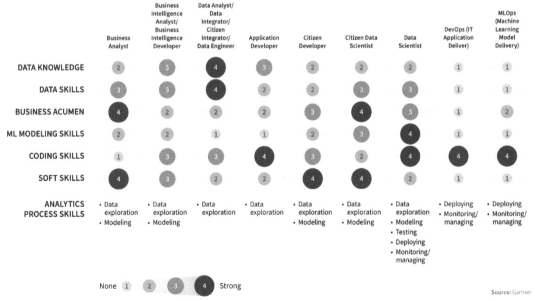

Figure 1.5 Role distribution in data programs (Source: *https://nix-united.com/blog/data-science-team-structure-roles-and-responsibilities*)

1.3.1.1 Subject Matter Expert (Domain Expert)

The SME is an essential person for a data project. Still, this person is often not shown in data teams. A subject matter expert understands, from the inside out, how the company provides its services to its clients inwards-out. They are often also referred to as a domain expert.

An SME is someone who has been performing a day-to-day job for a long time. For example, in a retail organization, a perfect SME might be the person who has been working in a supermarket in different roles for multiple years. They have seen almost every possible imaginable scenario and have a good gut feeling about what clients want. They might also find potential side effects to changes that no one without experience in the field could see.

In some industries, the role of an SME overlaps with an analyst. Finance is a good example. A credit analyst takes all data from a client who applies for credit and calculates the credit risk using a given formula. Unlike data scientists, analysts do not generate new knowledge. However, analysts work with numbers and have a deeper understanding than other types of SMEs.

In an NGO, an SME might be a development worker who fights poverty and plagues in developing countries or works in refugee camps. Therefore, an NGO SME might have a completely different view of what is missing on-site and feasible than those who watch the situation remotely.

SMEs are also often natural authorities in their fields due to their long-term experience. If, for example, a company wants to install a new IT system or new processes on-site, the support of SMEs can be crucial for its successful deployment, as less experienced employees in the field often look up to them.

The actual duties of the SME, therefore, depend on the area of operation but generally include the following activities:

- Provide insights on the existing challenges
- Provide access to possible data sources
- Help formulate goals
- Assist in the release of products and verify their successful outcome
- Guide users towards adopting the new system.

1.3.1.2 Business Analyst

Many projects need a business analyst who acts as a bridge between SMEs and data scientists. The critical skill of a business analyst is to ask the right questions. His job is to find out which activities make sense from a business perspective.

In start-ups, a business analyst helps to formulate the business plan and the value proposition. First, he needs to underline how the business can make profits and measure if we are successful.

Business analysts, therefore, are dedicated to their time to the following activities.

- Write business plans
- Analyze business requirements
- Translate business requirements into work packages for the data team

1.3.1.3 **Data Scientist**

There is a debate about how much statistics a data scientist should understand. Purists claim that you can be only a "real data scientist" if you have a Ph.D. and are acquainted with scientific methods and statistics in and out. They sometimes call everyone else "fake data scientists."

Many modern views differ and see a data scientist as an expert who puts the data into use and creates something new. For example, she can discover a new relationship in the data and build models. It is essential to highlight that good communication and programming skills are helpful to achieve this.

Data scientists should be as versatile as the data they are working with and open to learn about new domains and to collaborate with experts from different fields. For example, working with and analysing imaging data requires specific knowledge in Computer Vision, image processing, machine learning and also specific domain knowledge of differential geometry or medicine. It is important to understand how data are acquired, which false interpretations are possible and also if an expert is required to create a baseline or to evaluate the designed models (for example annotations of a specific tumor tissue in an computer tomography scan by a medical doctor). In Chapter 11 you will get a deeper insight into the field of Computer Vision and how to work with imaging data as a data scientist.

All in all, every data scientist will have some form of understanding of science and statistics. But similar to many examples of autodidactic programmers, who have not studied Software Engineering, many things can be self-taught. It is often the case that a data scientist team consists of people with a diverse skill set. While some of the members are top-notch mathematicians, others complement them with more communication or programming skills but still contribute as much to the outcome as others.

 Mathematics and Statistics

Mathematics and statistics are still the basis of everything we do. Therefore, we dedicate Chapters 5 and 6 to the topics to recap the basics of probability theory, explain a confidence interval, and say that one idea is correct or not mathematically. ∎

The main tasks of data scientists are exciting, sometimes challenging, and highly diverse.

- First, we must prepare our data, often liaising with other departments, such as information systems, and harmonizing various data sources. In many organizations, this is the job of the Data Engineer, especially if these steps need to be automated and have strong SLA requirements.
- Then we engage in exploratory statistical analyses, interpret the results, and use these to gain domain knowledge and conduct further preliminary data investigations.
- Based on these findings, we curate a data set and feed this to a machine learning algorithm, such as those mentioned above, to build a model for a specific task.
- The trained model is tested and fine-tuned to the point where we can use it productively: its outputs, which usually take the form of predictions of a particular output given an unseen test case, will be acted upon by the data science team and other stakeholders in the company.

Of course, this process is not a one-time effort. Data and models must be continuously monitored (and often, continuously retrained) to ensure performance remains at an acceptable level. New research projects must be undertaken based on the company's innovation roadmaps, triggering this process to begin again. We can answer business questions through data, and progress and results must be communicated to various departments, often in sophisticated visualizations and presentations (see Chapter 13, 'Visualisation').

We will describe a lot more about the job of data scientists throughout this book. Data scientists play an essential role in the development of AI solutions (see Chapter 9), but also in the domain of modeling and simulation (see Chapter 12)

1.3.1.4 Data Engineer

Data engineers build and optimize data platforms so that data scientists and analysts have access to the appropriate data. In addition, they load data into the data platform according to the policy set by the architect.

Data engineers implement this activity using data pipelines, load data from third-party systems, transform the data and then store it on the platform. A data pipeline must scale with increasing data volumes and be robust. Therefore, the pipeline must have corresponding fault tolerance. It thus forms the foundation that data scientists and analysts can use to generate knowledge.

Unlike other team members, data engineers must have solid programming skills. Most importantly, a data engineer needs to understand the principles of distributed computation and how to write code that can scale. Thus, the data engineer has a fundamental role in every data science team.

Core activities include:

- Building various interfaces to enable the reading and writing of data
- Integrating internal or external data into existing pipelines
- Applying data transformations to create analytical datasets
- Monitoring and optimization to ensure the continuous quality of the system (and to improve it if necessary)
- Developing a loading framework to load data efficiently

1.3.1.5 DevOps

DevOps is a role that requires a mixture of developer and operational skills. Their task is to operate the data platform upon which the data engineers and data scientists work.

DevOps implement the architectural design for a project or system and address the change requests made by the Data Engineers. With the emergence of cloud systems, DevOps engineers gained popularity and have become a scarce resource in many projects.

Their activities include:

- The scaling of data platforms
- Identification of performance problems in the software
- Automating redeployments

- Monitoring and logging applications
- Identifying resource bottlenecks and problems
- Remediation of issues that occur due to system operations

1.3.1.6 Solution Architect

In the end, someone has to be accountable for everything running smoothly. Only then can the data scientists do their job, and the users can create business value by using the applications developed during the data strategy implementation. In large organizations, this is the solution architect.

Someone must ensure that the proper hardware infrastructure is in place, that the appropriate data management, selecting processing software, can protect data against misuse and theft, and finally, that data scientists and end-users of a system can do their work.

Many organizations have multiple roles for that:

- A **data architect** focuses on data and how data is stored. In addition, she cares about metadata management and the definition of processes to load data into data management software such as databases or object stores.
- A **systems or infrastructure architect** focuses on servers and hardware and ensures the hardware is available. If the company hosts the solution in the cloud, they refer to this role as a 'cloud architect.'
- A **data steward** or **data manager** is responsible for ensuring that the project follows the appropriate corporate policies.
- A **security architect** protects the system against hackers and other intrusion attempts.

In reality, it is hard to isolate those various engineering roles. A data platform must serve multiple purposes and meet multiple functional and non-functional requirements. Without knowing the software, one cannot make a hardware decision, and numerous data platforms have specific hardware requirements. Therefore, there needs to be a generalist who understands everything and can lead other architects to make cost-effective, scalable, robust, and fast solutions.

In large companies, a CIO leads all streams to create standards for every project. Large companies have their frameworks or business units to provide platforms to other departments. A solution architect must often also consider corporate politics as another factor in building the best platform for their project. There are usually fewer restrictions in small companies and more chances to fail with a wrong strategy. Chapter 17, 'Mindset and Community', also explores a risk known as the 'swiss army knife', that might apply to a solutions architect in a small company: Many small companies end up with one person being the single expert for multiple engineering domains.

In many organizations, it often boils down to a situation in which one person with a diverse skill set and broad knowledge is fully accountable for realizing the solution. Although they might be able to delegate responsibilities, depending on the size of a project or company, they ultimately still have to cover multiple roles in other scenarios and thus become a bottleneck.

Typical tasks of a solution architect are:

- As an accountable person for the solution, decide about all parameters or lead the decision-making process. All parameters include, among other things, hardware, operating systems, data management software, data processing, user experience, scalability, and cost-effectiveness.

- Ensure that the project meets all requirements, and the project team has all requirements to build the solution for the ultimate end-users.

- Lead other architects and engineers to implement the solution.

- Ensure that all solutions meet corporate standards for all projects, such as data protection standards.

1.3.1.7 Other Roles

We have not covered BI engineers and Business data owners here. Often in agile teams, we add a Scrum Master to the team.

We will outline in Chapter 16 that data teams might face quite different requirements in different industries. Also, small companies or start-ups have other needs than large enterprises. This diversity means there is no unique definition of how a data team has to be structured. Various roles will exist in one team but not in others.

Data teams in large organizations, especially with regulatory requirements, will incorporate roles such as data managers, security experts, data stewards and more.

1.3.1.8 Team Building

The structure of the team and the operating model depends much on the company's data maturity level. In many cases, some team members have to clear out old legacy systems before creating something new. In some companies, leaders assign individuals to multiple teams.

The success of teams also depends a lot on the corporate culture. We will go more into details on this in Chapter 17, 'Mindset and Community.' Setting up a data-driven organization is the focus of Chapter 14.

1.3.2 Data and Platforms

Company data currently exists in most companies horizontally, in different departments, or vertically, which is fragmented and coupled to various functions and silos. In addition, the proportion of critical information generated outside the usual processes is growing. So then, part of a data strategy is to create a process that can handle various data formats and convert them into a structured and processable format. In this process, we can explore four different properties:

- **Volume:** Describes the amount of data collected through organizations through daily business processes. Volume is an order of magnitudes, such as gigabyte, terabyte, or petabyte.

- **Velocity:** Describes the speed of the data generated during a session or transaction. Sensor data typically has a very high velocity since it often has to be processed immediately. For example, if you detect problems in production with sensors, you want to react within a few minutes.

- **Veracity:** This value describes the trustworthiness or accuracy of the data. For example, we can use data lineage to trace the individual data processing steps and streams. The corresponding signature mechanisms can be confidence-increasing measures. In addition, we can include a watermark to identify which user opened the documents the last time.

- **Variety:** Describes the diverse data formats and data types on a platform. For example, an entire platform must process different data, such as voice data or text data. In addition, it must also have standard connectors to the individual interfaces used in the company to provide the required data efficiently.

Data and Platforms also contain best practices on automating the build of platforms in the cloud or on-premise. There are many non-functional requirements such as durability or availability. One key responsibility of an architect is to find a solution that meets all those requirements.

Chapters 2 to 5 cover infrastructure and data architecture, data engineering, and data management. In Chapter 2, we will look at topologies and hardware. This investigation also includes DevOps-related aspects on how to build data platforms.

In Chapter 3, we look at data architectures in general. We look at solutions on how to store data so that we can access them efficiently. While in Chapter 2, we looked at which hardware we need and how we can automate the creation of platforms, Chapter 3 is about which application platforms provide software to process data in the best possible way.

Chapter 4 covers essential aspects of how to engineer data. Or, more specifically, how to extract data from sources and load it on the platform.

Chapter 11 outlines the necessary routines on how to acquire, store, compress, reconstruct and to process imaging data and their incorporation into Computer Vision systems.

The engineering-related part of this book closes with coverage of data governance in Chapter 5, in which we learn how to set up corporate policies on how to manage data.

1.3.3 Modeling and Analysis

Raw data itself does not yet generate value. Instead, analytical models or algorithms are needed to extract value from the data. Typical use cases are optimization tasks, predictions for the next accounting period, or risk classifications. Thus, leaders must plan how analytical resources, such as personnel or hardware, can be used most efficiently and effectively and thereby have the most potential to generate value.

This initiative must also include automated machine learning model retraining and adaptation to new values still unknown to the system. A possible solution would be, for example, to consider any problems already during the system design or to react to them appropriately during operation.

It is essential to keep the entire end-to-end process in mind, including the users, the complexity of the solution, and the management of the models and the data itself.

As modeling is central to the success of a data strategy, we will explore this already here in more detail.

We will briefly discuss explainable AI strategies on how to make complex computational models interpretable and their decisions and estimations understandable for users. In Chapter 11 explainable AI strategies in Computer Vision for image based models are introduced and it is briefly explained how these can help us humans see what computers and underlying neural networks see.

■ 1.4 Use Case Implementation

Implementing a data science strategy consists of various phases. How the stages look in detail depends on the circumstances. For example, some companies have invested in data platforms, and they have built a scalable data platform that allows the company to deploy new use cases quickly. Other companies have not invested in infrastructure at all and start entirely from scratch.

Figure 1.6 outlines a holistic process that explores the creation of a platform and investigating use cases.

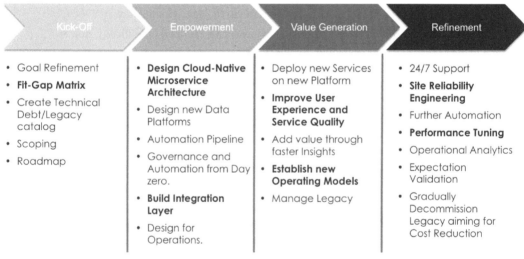

Kick-Off	Empowerment	Value Generation	Refinement
• Goal Refinement • **Fit-Gap Matrix** • Create Technical Debt/Legacy catalog • Scoping • Roadmap	• **Design Cloud-Native Microservice Architecture** • Design new Data Platforms • Automation Pipeline • Governance and Automation from Day zero. • **Build Integration Layer** • Design for Operations.	• Deploy new Services on new Platform • **Improve User Experience and Service Quality** • Add value through faster Insights • **Establish new Operating Models** • Manage Legacy	• 24/7 Support • **Site Reliability Engineering** • Further Automation • **Performance Tuning** • Operational Analytics • Expectation Validation • Gradually Decommission Legacy aiming for Cost Reduction

Figure 1.6 Data platform (provided by *AlphaZetta.ai*)

1.4.1 Iterative Exploration of Use Cases

Data teams can combine two approaches to explore which use cases are most beneficial for business goals.

In the **conceptual approach**, the team aims to find as many new use cases as possible to exploit. Open innovation or design thinking can keep the process as flexible as possible and promote creativity: Design thinking describes finding solutions from the end user's perspective, while open innovation significantly increases the solution space.

In this phase, the team enters a cycle of validation and verification to rule out possible dead ends and non-actionable goals at an early stage.

In the **data-driven approach**, the team explores existing data sources gradually to generate new value. For example, a team can organize workshops such as hackathons to expand the understanding of data. This measure helps with an initial analysis of data sources but is less suitable as knowledge of the data increases.

Independent of the chosen approach, the use case must also undergo a profitability check to determine whether it contributes business value. One way to achieve this is that, after teams digitize existing processes at the beginning of a project, they calculate the costs saved through this measure.

The process starts with a workshop where data and domain experts from different departments and business units determine the potential for optimization. The result of the workshop is a **use case list** that gives an overview of possible explorations. Finally, each item in the list is quantified to determine the feasibility of each use case.

Agile methods such as Scrum are an advantage here. They allow an iterative approach to changing the goal within the development, for example, to align it with new business goals.

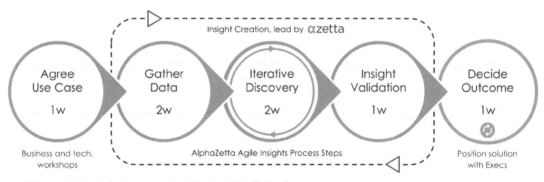

Figure 1.7 Analytical process (provided by *AlphaZetta.ai*)

Figure 1.7 presents an analytical process. Here we can assume that the necessary platform already exists. The analytical process runs as follows:

Table 1.2 Data Science Process

Phase	Description
Agree on Use Case	In this phase, the analytics team agrees on a use case. As a rule, we involve an SME, as she knows which topic is most important for the company.
Gather Data	The team spends two weeks collecting data and reviewing various sources. At this point, the topic of data governance is also essential.
Iterative Discovery	In this phase, data scientists analyze data and gain new insights.
Insight Validation	Once the results are in, you may go back to the Agree on Use Case phase because you came across new insights and data sources during the analysis.
Decide Outcome	In the last step, data scientists evaluate the result, and the team decides whether the project is likely to be a success or failure.

In a positive evaluation, a new phase can follow in which the team brings a use case into production. Of course, the effort required to accomplish this may vary based on the use case complexity. However, the experiences during the discovery phase should indicate what to expect in that step.

 Inconclusive Results

The science in Data Science highlights that we deal with a research-oriented environment. If there were no risk to fail, it is not science. Many organizations setting up data science will also have to learn that there are many reasons why some questions will stay at least partially unanswered.

One reason can be legal problems. For example, sometimes, the team learns that the data they need to solve a problem exists, but they do not have the right to use it. Besides data ownership, privacy protection is a huge topic. If the analysis of various data violated regulations such as GDPR, teams have to stop their investigations. We deal with legal issues in Chapter 15.

Legal problems often go hand in hand with internal misalignments. Especially in a large organization, dealing with governance might delay many projects as settling who owns what might take a while. Discussions on a management level about data projects may result in, for outsiders, intransparent corporate politics. Data professionals often end up waiting for management decisions while the real issues the decision-makers are arguing about are unclear. In historically grown organizations, it often might be just a feud between two or more managers. According to the law of triviality, managers are likely to hack their skulls over unessential details.[8] Chapter 17 addresses how to deal with political topics that may be to a particular extent, also called dealing with irrational behavior.

---

[8] *https://docs.freebsd.org/en/books/faq/#misc*

In many cases, data itself is the problem. The data is available, but the data quality is not sufficient. At other times, the teams might learn that other companies could apply a use case, but that data does not exist for different organizations. Sometimes, an organization also has to realize that the data coming from a supplier is not detailed enough. Negotiating with the supplier to make the data more precise can also be a question of costs. There might also be independent third-party providers of data who sell data at high prices.

Costs, in general, can be a huge issue. For example, when exploring a use case, the team might realize that they need far more computation power or maybe far more engineers to maintain a platform than expected. In addition, managers always have to assess over time if answering specific questions with data is still justified. So, if we learned that it costs, for example, ten times more than expected to solve a problem with data, the value we would gain might not match up.

In general, it is essential to document results in a corporate knowledge base such as Confluence or any other extensive documentation system. An unresolvable problem that exists today might disappear in the future. If the results are not properly documented, a future team might not know that it would make sense to continue past work.

1.4.2 End-to-End Data Processing

In an analysis phase, the data scientists present results to decision-makers and stakeholders and recommend further analysis of additional data sources. In most cases, it is essential that end users can use the analysis results directly, such as in self-service BI tools.

How many results users will leverage also depends on non-technical parameters, such as comprehensibility and usability of the user interface. Some end users might stop using the systems if the data is there but difficult to access. The old UI/UX adage "don't make me think" is still valid, and the more intuitive the handling of applications is, the better.

We can also connect User Experience to the performance and availability of applications. Chapter 3 explains how to design scalable and cost-efficient systems and address various aspects such as when to use on-premise solutions vs. cloud-based solutions.

The implementation of a data strategy includes the following considerations:

- Every business process is a service. The aggregation and analysis of data from all services is the basis for business decisions. These insights help to optimize the service itself and to eliminate weaknesses.

- Companies use a digital channel to communicate with end-users, other services, or partners. In addition, a digital channel allows the application of analytical models.

- Through a data platform, processes and services are managed automatically and are thus always available to the relevant end-user or business unit.

1.4.3 Data Products

Data Pipelines collect data from data sources such as sensors on the physical product (IoT) or social media applications. In the process, analysts can gain insights into how end-users consume a service and use a product. To increase this efficiency of data collection, engineers can transform a product into a "smart product", which can describe its physical state by being equipped with sensors.

Smart products provide additional value to their original value. For example, a smart fridge will still cool the goods inside, but at the same time, this device can notify its owner that certain products are about to run out or expire. As another example, a forklift truck with sensors can autonomously navigate specific locations, react to its environment via sensor data, and avoid accidents.

Product designers can learn how user groups handle a product by integrating end-users and optimizing future versions for various user profiles.

■ 1.5 Real-Life Use Case Examples

After looking at strategy, it is time to explore what companies can concretely do with data science. Chapter 16, 'AI in Different Industries', explores how we can realize applications in specific industries. In that spirit, the following sections describe how a strategy for optimizing the value chain within a manufacturing company might look.

1.5.1 Value Chain Digitization (VCD)

Analytical methods offer application possibilities in production. Examples are supply chain optimization and predictive maintenance.

Supply Chain Optimization

A supply chain of an organization is usually globalized. Different goods and preliminary products are manufactured, produced, or assembled in various locations. By distributing them across several countries, companies can reduce their costs, but at the same time, the number of critical dependencies, and the risk of supply chain interruption, increase. For example, a manufacturer cannot meet their desired production quantities if a supplier fails or if there is a shortage of raw material.

Efficient supply chain management offers a strategic advantage that can accelerate a company's growth. Those who produce products better and faster than their competitors will survive in the market.

Machine learning applications can help to identify problems proactively. For example, if we have access to historical data, forecasting models use neural networks to predict labor strikes or weather problems. Likewise, by simulating a supply chain, various risks can be counteracted, which will subsequently fuel just-in-time production. There is a practical example later in Chapter 16.

Predictive Maintenance

Predictive maintenance is about attempting to predict and minimize machine downtime by analyzing machine data proactively. As a prerequisite for this, sensors are needed that can transmit corresponding data. Data pipelines collect this data primarily from machine sensors, like heat or pressure sensors. For example, one possible result may be the realization that a group of components tends to have a higher defect rate above 100 °C in production. Thus, a production manager can minimize scrap by regulating the temperature. However, even external data, such as air pressure or humidity in the area, are also interesting, as data scientists can incorporate them into the analytical model.

The goal of predictive maintenance is also to send the service employee to fix a fault before it even occurs. This measure leads to reduced costs and increases the quality and availability of services.

How to efficiently collect and analyze mass sensor data is also described later in Chapter 16.

1.5.2 Marketing Segment Analytics

This category measures the effectiveness of marketing efforts and relates them to competitors. The goal is to determine the optimal mix of marketing measures and incentives for specific customer segments to retain and win existing and new customers.

Data Scientists can group data into clusters, such as per geo regions or micro and macro trends. In addition, to learn more about historical data, a good practice is to store data on unsuccessful marketing attempts or processes. In total, a data-driven approach increases the efficiency per marketing campaign and documents which marketing tools, in which situations, have delivered the most success. Scenario Supposelanning, performance, and social media optimization will add even further value.

Suppose campaign managers contrast this data with data collected on competitors' campaigns. In that case, new insights may emerge that can be recycled in future marketing efforts to highlight new and unique selling points.

As a real-life example, obtaining and processing data from various commerce channels through an omnichannel strategy is presented later in Chapter 16.

1.5.3 360° View of the Customer

In this discipline, data scientists analyze customer behavior to understand their needs better. Identifying a *"customer journey"* involves examining historical data and offers insights into factors such as which products customers have consumed, which services they have obtained, and where there were complaints. In automated processes, we can use a *recommender engine* to make a customer the right offer for a service or product at the right time.

Another step is integrating daily data, such as the interaction in the "buy & sell" cycle, and determining the customer's satisfaction with the company by analyzing reviews, inquiries and complaints, and even social media information such as Twitter tweets about the company (see Chapter 10 for a deep dive into how Natural Language Processing makes this possible). Understanding how customers are contacting the company and what they are saying makes it possible to improve services, generate ideas for new products that customers are demanding, and predict possible future interactions and upsell and cross-sell opportunities.

The top priority is to retain the existing customer base, that is, to maximize *customer retention*, and at the same time to advance into new segments. The basis for this can be internal (CRM, ERP ...) and external (social media) data, which are stored in different data silos on a central platform and evaluated with analyses.

We can use *predictive analytics* to help to identify consumer behavior patterns and evaluate them. For example, it is possible to determine when a customer leaves the sales process and why. This insight is the basis for fine-tuning marketing efforts and optimizing all stages of the consumer journey, for example, from improving the in-store shopping experience to revamping the company's online shop.

Also in the medical sector a 360° view of the customer (for example a patient) is highly demanded. The analysis, structured and secure storage of daily routine medical imaging and record data are the profound baseline for medical analysis, patient specific modelling and the prediction of a patient's outcome. The more information we have on a patient, the more it can contribute to solving the puzzle of finding the right diagnosis, assessing the therapy response and possible adaptations.

1.5.4 NGO and Sustainability Use Cases

The aforementioned use cases come from the business world and may give the wrong impression that data science is mostly about using data to reduce costs or increase revenues. However, we can apply data science to support humanitarian causes.

Optimizing a supply chain might also help to improve the logistics of an NGO. And the work of many philanthropists and endowments for NGOs is built upon using data for the greater good. For example, NGOs may use satellite images and machine learning algorithms to detect possible water points in dry areas. Or, they may use data to forecast people's possible movements and predict the number of refugees trying to leave their homelands.

The Paris Agreement signed in 2016 highlights various sustainability goals for the world. However, we are still far behind our plan to reduce carbon emissions. There are many ways to use analytical models to forecast CO_2 emissions and explore ways to reduce them. Chapter 16 explores some of these in discussing the future of data science and AI in the energy sector.

■ 1.6 Delivering Results

The following image is part of a use case library, representing possible use cases that data scientists could explore within a company.

Marketing & Customer

1. Data-Driven Sales Process
2. Marketing Attribution
3. Digital Path to Churn
4. **Digital Path to Purchase**
5. Product Uptake Path
6. Digital Wealth Bots
7. **Location Based Point Of Sale Offers**
8. **NLP Analysis of Credit Dossier**
9. **Money Flow Maximiser**
10. **Path to Profit/Non-profit**
11. **Network Analysis of Customer Portfolio**
12. **Real-time Customer GIS location marketing**
13. **Big Data Cross-Sell Improvement**
14. **Social Network Analysis**
15. **Next Best Action**
16. High Value Lead Customer Generation
17. **NLP Based Lead Generation**
18. Lead Generation from Retail Data
19. Churn Analysis of Customer Balances
20. **Lifetime Value Analytics**
21. Supplier Lead Generation
22. Advanced Card Behavioral Analysis
23. **Predict Complaint/Claim**
24. People Like Me
25. **NPS Optimization**
26. Multi-Channel Customer Engagement
27. **Event Based Customer Lifecycle**
28. Map Out Customer Journey
29. **Real Time Dialogues**
30. Omni-Channel Purchasing
31. **Online purchase patterns**

Risk & Fraud

1. Path to Fraud
2. **Fraud Networks**
3. **Claims Fraud Detection**
4. Collections Analytics
5. **Minimise False Positives**
6. Online Fraud
7. Compromised POS and ATM Detection
8. Application Fraud
9. Anti Money Laundering
10. Cyber Security
11. Employee Fraud
12. Broker Fraud
13. **Risk Scoring Model Improvement**
14. **Risk Affinity Analysis**
15. Guarantee Networks
16. Predict Default Risk
17. **Risk Based Pricing**
18. Credit Risk Uplift Model
19. **Data-driven Customer Verification**
20. Real-time Market and Liquidity Risk
21. **Storm Surge**
22. **Flooding**
23. **Natural Disasters**
24. **Bush Fires**

Operations

1. Sales Compliance
2. **Contact Center Service Efficiency**
3. Automated Email Follow-up
4. **Call Centre Analytics**
5. Data Breach and Leakage Analysis
6. Branch Network Planning
7. Path to Failures
8. Automatic Client Email Routing
9. HR Staff Performance Management
10. Duplicate Customer Records
11. IT Workload Optimization
12. **Improved Customer Onboarding**
13. **Optimise Fee & Commission Collection**
14. **Manual Claims Reduction**
15. **Pricing Optimization**
16. **Telematics Based Pricing**
17. **Location-driven Risk Management**
18. Online Process Failures
19. HR Attrition Analytics
20. Sales & Service Process Failure

Figure 1.8 Index of a Use Case Library (Source: provided by *AlphaZetta.ai*)

Based on each item's title, we can approximately assume what a specific use case does. For example, in 'Digital Path to Purchase', we explore how people use an e-commerce system and interact with users who bought products versus those who did not. Through this, we might discover issues such as a confusing order page on our website, which caused users to abandon their purchases.

We can validate the success of some of the methods listed above, using specific metrics like an increased *return on investment* and a reduced *time to market*. But things get tricky if no such measure exists for our new data science project. How do we measure success, then?

Especially in the beginning, it is almost impossible to measure benefits in numbers. For example, let us assume a company implements its first data science use case. It has to hire a team of people and build up infrastructure, which often involves a steep learning curve. Maybe the investment costs exceed the possible revenues of that use case. But what if the team starts working on a second project afterward and uses all the artifacts created in the first use case?

Departments generate value from their data by solving everyday problems. This measure leads to various prototypes or initiatives that we can turn into a *"digital investment."* A corresponding governance strategy is also necessary to document the data processing steps required to generate the maximum benefit from data and thus the value chain and make the applied actions traceable. In addition, governance increases the level of trustworthiness of the platform, as it is now apparent where the data comes from and where it is stored. Therefore, data governance is also the subject of Chapter 5 in this book.

A Blackbox View

Looking at Data Science from the outside, success depends on asking the right questions and giving the answers that satisfy the audience. Asking the right questions is often not easy. It is often also a question of granularity. However, whether you are a CDO for a government, an enterprise, or an NGO, the question will always be about bringing more value to your clients or improving while you generate value.

Some might oversee that answering questions is a unique field as well. If we have all the perfect answers, but if we cannot communicate them appropriately to our audience, all our work might be in vain in the worst case. Presenting results is a lot about personal development and the ability to communicate. Speech trainers help to accentuate and understand how to say the right things at the right time. Especially people with a technical background are not always aware of the potential benefits of a speaker's training. However, once more data professionals explore how much mirror neurons[9] affect the outcomes of speeches, this might change in a future edition.

While all the questions of how we give a good presentation related to personal development are out of the scope of this book, we dedicate Chapter 13 to Visualisation. Visualization is the core of delivering results to the audience because if we present our results in the best possible way, the results speak for themselves. Visualization is a powerful way of processing data. It helps us to better and faster understand the observed situation. It brings us new information, allowing us to see hidden relationships and representations. It forces us to ask better questions and helps us make better decisions. It tells us a story of yesterday and today, and predicts a story for tomorrow.

As a final point, it is essential to highlight that sometimes the answer in experimental environments is to have learned that there is no satisfactory answer to our questions.

To sum everything up: Becoming a data-driven enterprise is a new form of business in which "data is the new oil." We can use data to generate income through subscriptions or to reduce costs by solving problems. Physical products are now just tools to achieve a goal or address a customer problem,[10] and we aim to generate a continuous cash flow rather than only a one-time income.

Compared to the traditional software industry, the data industry has the following differences:

- A data platform is centralized (data lake or data warehouse) or decentralized (data mesh).
- Customers are co-producers of the solutions or products.
- New solutions and products can be continuously optimized and scaled.

---

[9] https://blogs.scientificamerican.com/guest-blog/whats-so-special-about-mirror-neurons/
[10] https://www.ibsolution.com/academy/blog_en/the-four-steps-on-the-way-to-digitalization

- There are increased requirements for automation and quality assurance due to the amount of data that is processed.
- The organizational form of the people who use Big Data is agile and continuously adapts to the problem. It also allows for making inevitable mistakes while always following the previously defined use cases or the vision.

To summarize this introduction, we will present the topics that a general digitization strategy usually covers for developing a business field.

■ 1.7 In a Nutshell

From Strategy to Implementation

As a rule, a data strategy is derived from the corporate strategy and orchestrated by a CDO. Implementation is usually top-down.

From Questions to Answers

The key to success with data is always to ask the right questions that data should answer. Unfortunately, finding the right questions is not always trivial and might include workshops with stakeholders. On the other end, for an audience, the results of teams exploring data are as good as the team that presents them.

From Use Cases to Values

There are numerous use cases through which companies try to generate value via data science. In data projects, companies explore the possibilities and realize use cases in agile processes.

From Chaos to Platforms

Central for professional data exploration is also to build a platform that matches the requirements of all the data science use cases. For example, various studies show that teams spend 80 % of the time on data preparation in the beginning. A good platform might reduce these efforts for later use cases.

From Individuals to Teams

Many professionals with diverse skillsets work in a data team. To successfully implement a data project, you need people skilled in hardware, networks, operating systems, programming languages, CI/CD, data processing, data analysis, machine learning, reporting, and more. It is almost impossible to find one person that fits into all of these roles.

■

2 Infrastructure

Stefan Papp

> *"Perfection is not achieved when there is nothing left*
> *to add, but when there is nothing left to leave out."*
> Antoine de Saint-Exupéry

Questions Answered in this Chapter:

- Which system environments are necessary for data science projects?
- Why are cloud platforms ideal for experimentation-driven data science environments?
- What is the importance of GPUs and other hardware components for data science projects?
- How are platforms built dynamically with Infrastructure as Code and managed with version management tools?
- What distinguishes a microservice architecture from a monolithic architecture?
- How can Linux systems be used efficiently for Data Science?

■ 2.1 Introduction

The goal of analytical processes in organizations is to gain new knowledge and deeper insights. As a rule, the benefit lies in

- reducing costs,
- making faster decisions and
- penetrating new markets.

There are sometimes decision-makers in companies who hope for results in minimal time. "Quick wins," i.e., situations in which data scientists can already deliver usable insights when exploring the data for the first time – without investing in the preparation of the data – are the exception.

Most companies explored a great deal of innovation using conventional analytical methods. Over the years, perhaps even decades, analysts have already racked their brains over how to optimize revenues and reduce costs. As a result, the use of tried-and-true analytical techniques is no longer likely to yield groundbreaking new insights for many firms. Instead, the hope of many managers lies in newer methods such as **Artificial Intelligence**, **Machine Learning**, and **Deep Learning**. In later chapters the authors will explain the necessary details about Analytics.

In data-driven approaches, data professionals explore enormous amounts of data – up to the petabyte range – structured in particular topologies such as neural networks. Hardware and operating systems are necessary to host and process this data. As a result, we need a scalable and well-performing infrastructure that meets the business requirements for the data science use cases. Figure 2.1. outlines common layers for data architectures.

The term infrastructure is defined by NIST as follows:[1]

> *The capability provided to the consumer is to provision processing, storage, networks, and other fundamental computing resources where the consumer is able to deploy and run arbitrary software, which can include operating systems and applications. The consumer does not manage or control the underlying cloud infrastructure but has control over operating systems, storage, and deployed applications; and possibly limited control of select networking components (e.g., host firewalls).*

The infrastructure for a data platform must meet the following requirements:

- Robust design and redundancy must ensure the lowest probability of data loss (**durability**).
- Security mechanisms must protect data from unauthorized access (**physical security**).
- The data platform must comply with the applicable data protection guidelines (**data protection**).
- The data platform must return results in a reasonable time (**performance**).
- Users must be able to access the platform and its data at any time (**availability**).

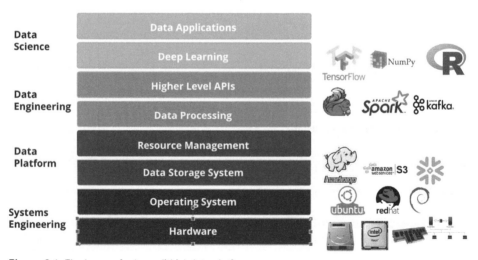

Figure 2.1 The layers of a (monolithic) data platform

[1] *https://nvlpubs.nist.gov/nistpubs/Legacy/SP/nistspecialpublication800-145.pdf*

Few IT leaders have ever doubted that cloud providers, such as Microsoft, Amazon, and Google, can deliver a powerful, robust and secure infrastructure. However, there was skepticism about whether companies should store sensitive data on servers belonging to outside companies. Surveys confirm that today more and more companies are accepting the cloud as the future data platform.[2]

Experts perceive the cloud as a business model[3] and not as a new technology: the goal is to no longer own IT resources but to rent them. In addition, the cloud is also a perfect experimentation lab for data scientists, as they can generate required resources and decommission them dynamically.

Perhaps the most significant benefit of the cloud becomes apparent when business leaders consider the number of experts needed to operate a data platform in a dedicated data center:

- System architects design the solution based on the requirements.
- Operations engineers replace defective hardware.
- Network engineers build the network, including routers and cabling.
- Operating system experts install and configure operating systems.
- Facility managers take care of systems like air conditioning and fire protection.
- Security personnel secure access to the Data Center against unauthorized entry.

Depending on the requirements, we can subdivide individual tasks can even further. In order to guarantee fail-safety, each expert must also have a substitute. In addition, there is a shortage of IT specialists, which makes it challenging to fill vacancies adequately.[4] The cloud significantly reduces the company's personnel expenses.

◼ 2.2 Hardware

Big data platform infrastructures are complex, and mistakes in hardware configuration or procurement can be costly. Below are five real-world examples that illustrate the consequences of the wrong strategy in an on-premises environment.

Example 1: Hardware – CPU

A large international company built a mobile measurement system that collects terabytes of sensor data. One task was to offload the collected data to a central target platform as quickly as possible after a test drive. The transfer to the target platform took place via Ethernet.

[2] https://www.flexera.com/blog/industry-trends/trend-of-cloud-computing-2020
[3] https://medium.com/@storjproject/there-is-no-cloud-it-s-just-someone-else-s-computer-6ecc37cdcfe5
[4] https://employer.it-talents.de/blog/it-fachkraeftemangel

The architects chose the fastest available SSDs for the target platform because they assumed that if several measurement systems write to a target platform in parallel, the physical storage there would become the bottleneck.

When unloading data from the car, users complained that the transfer speed did not meet their expectations. It turned out that all four CPU cores of a measuring system, i.e., the source, were thoroughly utilized during unloading due to the serialization of data. The expensive SSDs of the target platform, on the other hand, had minimum utilization, as multiple data streams wrote in parallel.

Since the client had produced the measuring systems in series, it was impossible to equip the existing measuring systems with more processor cores. Therefore, it was necessary to wait for a new generation that provided more CPU power.

 Example 2: Network

In a Big Data system for transferring data, the network turned out to be a bottleneck. Experts analyzing the problem did their best to solve it via software configurations. One variant they investigated was to enable jumbo packets to increase throughput.

Finally, the team investigated the physical cabling of the network. It turned out that the cabling did not support the expected transmission speeds. Completely rewiring the cluster was expensive and time-consuming. The project was delayed.

 Example 3: Memory

A company promised the customer a Hadoop-based solution for handling data science projects. The team that had to implement the task assumed that only a single query would run in the system. Nobody expected to have to support a high-concurrency environment where multiple users would run queries simultaneously.

When the team presented a prototype to the customer, multiple users were testing in parallel, and crashes occurred because the Hadoop cluster ran out of RAM while running queries. The team could upgrade memory, but it soon became clear that the customer would have to upgrade significantly more than they were willing to spend money on for proper multi-user operation. As a result, the client canceled the project.

Example 4: I/O

In a proof of concept (POC), the client provided the supplier with a cloud system. The client's engineers had installed a Hadoop system that read data from blob storage on this platform. The goal of the POC was to prepare data for an analytical use case, and the managers expected to receive results promptly. However, a complex query with numerous joins took eight hours using Apache Spark as the execution engine. Waiting eight hours for intermediate results meant it was impossible to present and finish the project on time. After tough negotiations with the platform maintainer, the team was able to perform some optimizations. They replaced the file system and switched to Apache Parquet instead of CSV as the file format. In the end, the team could reduce the query time from eight hours to one.

 Example 5: GPU

GPUs are expensive compared to other hardware components. Therefore, to save budget, one company bought only one server with GPUs. However, with multiple data scientists working on projects, delays occurred when too many wanted to use the server simultaneously.

One user suggested dynamically spinning up instances in the cloud for queries and shutting them down after a run. The leadership team rejected this decision as the company had a no-cloud policy. Many data scientists were unhappy with the situation because they could not work efficiently in the existing environment.

The basic knowledge of hardware components of a **Von Neumann Architecture**[5], as displayed in Figure 2.2, is not sufficient for those who set up network clusters themselves to distribute loads to several nodes. The selection of suitable hardware, the positioning of the servers in racks, the cabling, and the operation take up a lot of resources.

Finding the best hardware topology to meet the requirements of business problems is not always easy. In a project, stakeholders may identify new functional and non-functional requirements that the selected topology may not be adequate to support. In addition, the wrong infrastructure strategy can be costly to a business. Some IT departments have to allocate vast amounts of resources to **legacy systems** to keep them alive.

In addition, legacy systems can also affect employee satisfaction in an organization. If there is no opportunity to implement something new in IT, this can also lead to higher staff turnover. Employees are not always willing to work in an environment where there is no room for innovation, and the necessary resources are not available to permanently solve the problems of frustrated users.

The cloud offers companies more flexibility. For example, instead of purchasing hardware themselves, they rent it. Moreover, wrong decisions in the configuration of systems are re-

---

[5] https://www.computerscience.gcse.guru/theory/von-neumann-architecture

versible in the cloud. Research-oriented environments and environments that experience a lot of change thus benefit from the flexibility of the cloud.

 Exercises

- Research on the Internet which GPUs are available for data science applications and how they can affect model building.
- Imagine you are preparing data for analytical modeling. The process takes several hours. Your boss asks you for ways to speed it up. Where do you start?
- Become CompTIA Network+ certified, or if you prefer to work with Cloud environments, pick a network certification of your preferred cloud provider or read books recommended to achieve the certification to learn all you can about various protocol stacks.
- Read the PolarFS paper[6] and understand how PolarFS differs from distributed file systems like the Hadoop Distributed File System (HDFS).

2.2.1 Distributed Systems

Two principles, originally from agile software development, are essential for building data science platforms:

- KISS (Keep it simple, stupid) recommends keeping systems as simple as possible, in line with the quote at the beginning of the chapter. Keeping all building blocks as simple as possible leads to a scalable solution.
- YAGNI (You ain't gonna need it) warns against building something on the suspicion that you might need it later.

Many data science projects failed in the past because the infrastructure did not fit the project requirements. Enthusiasts hope to solve all problems with new technologies. Consequently, engineers often perceive complex technology as an opportunity rather than a threat. Suppose a technology is introduced into the company only because it is new and innovative and not because a preliminary project has established that it solves the current business problems. In that case, this can cause the ambitious project to fail.

The demand for more CPU power is not the only issue; other hardware components must also become more powerful to meet the new requirements. There are two ways to scale when existing hardware is too slow. First, scale up improves the system's performance by replacing one hardware configuration with a more powerful one. However, above a particular load, even the best hardware will not solve a problem. Second, scale out means to distribute the load across more hardware. Here, experts also speak of 'distributed processing' or 'parallelization.'

---

[6] *http://www.vldb.org/pvldb/vol11/p1849-cao.pdf*

At the physical level, the distribution of loads (scale out) can take two forms. In the first variant, operation engineers install multiple components of the same type and a controller within a computer system. Examples of this are RAIDs or multi-core processors.

The operating system ensures that applications can handle the duplication of hardware modules. Those applications can then use threading and multiprocessing to distribute the load internally to several processor cores.

A **Von Neumann architecture** is the basis of a modern computer, as shown in Figure 2.2, and consists of a system that includes a CPU, memory, and an I/O component interconnected by a BUS. Thus, a cluster of computers (commonly called 'nodes') in a server room usually consists of several Von Neumann systems connected via a network.

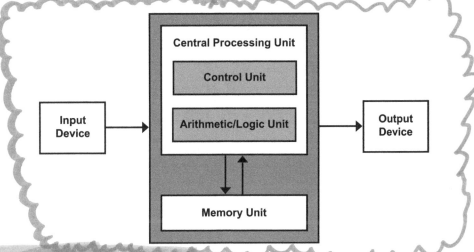

Figure 2.2 Von-Neumann-Architecture[7]

In addition to the hardware modules in a computer system, several computer systems can also be scaled out as nodes in a cluster as a second form of scale-out.

Also, in a cluster, you need software (perhaps the more accurate term would be an 'operating system,' but hardly any engineer uses this term in that context), which orchestrates data processing on multiple machines. This mechanism of managing different devices also includes synchronizing intermediate results and statuses between these processing components. Another task for the software is to react to disturbances, such as a node failure or delayed synchronization.

To illustrate the overhead incurred by parallelization, consider the following example, in which we will contrast local data processing with distributed data processing via Apache Hadoop. When data is processed locally on a single computer, a process loads data into memory. Then, an algorithm is applied to the loaded data to modify it or calculate results from it. These results can be displayed on the screen or saved as a file. If the amount of data to be loaded is larger than the available RAM, delays may occur as the data processing engine needs to swap intermediate results to the local hard disk during processing.

---

[7] Copyright: Kapooht *(https://en.wikipedia.org/wiki/File:Von_Neumann_Architecture.svg)*

Figure 2.3 indicates the additional overhead, using a simplified representation of distributed processing in Hadoop. We have to imagine that in a distributed system, we store all data on different nodes. This mechanism means each node needs to process as much as possible until a framework can collect reduced data on a few nodes. In a local environment, all this preprocessing first on separate nodes and joining later is not necessary.

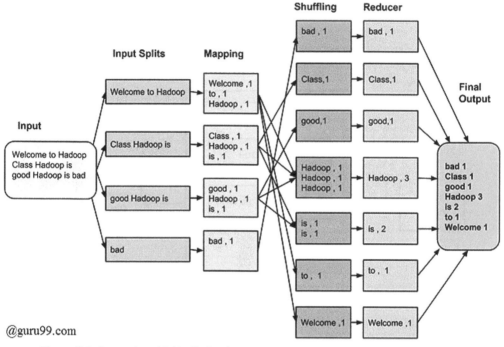

@guru99.com

Figure 2.3 Processing with MapReduce[8]

Developed in Java for the distributed data processing, Apache Hadoop is a software that needs to be installed on your cluster nodes to complete such a task.

In data processing via Hadoop, algorithms are executed first on the data stored on the so-called 'data nodes.' Then, analogous to local processing, processes running on the data nodes load the data into RAM, apply the algorithms, and cache the results. Finally, the intermediate outcomes on the individual nodes are merged centrally in a second step. The details of this process, called **MapReduce**, are described in Chapter 3 and on the Hadoop page.[9] In practical applications, layers abstract this type of processing and provide a unified API. Chapter 4, "Data Engineering," details how frameworks like Apache Spark optimize this flow.

Every engineer should be aware that local processing has a lower overhead. It is always faster if the amount of data is small enough to be processed locally.

---

[8] *https://www.guru99.com/introduction-to-mapreduce.html*
[9] *https://hadoop.apache.org/docs/current/hadoop-mapreduce-client/hadoop-mapreduce-client-core/MapReduce-Tutorial.html*

2.2.2 Hardware for AI Applications

Processors, as devices to perform computations on data, are often divided into CPUs and GPUs. There are also other categories of processors, but these are not relevant to data science and are not discussed in this book.

CPUs are the central controls of a computer and facilitate the calculation of results. Many engineers compare CPUs to a human brain that handles many **different operations**. The key indicator of a processor's strength is **MIPS** (Million Instructions per Second), which tells how many tasks a processor can handle in parallel per second. The first processors from 1951 had 0.002 MIPS; for modern processors, peaks of 2,356,230 MIPS are quoted.[10] If we are not able to provide the capacity required to process enough instructions per second for our data science project, then all processes related to the analysis of data, in particular, will be slowed down.

GPUs are processors designed for graphics processing. The original goal was to free the CPU from the heavy computational load required by 3-D animations. GPUs are optimized to perform many matrix operations well. The Machine Learning chapter goes into more detail about why GPUs are perfect for deep learning applications with neural networks.

GPU processors from manufacturers such as **Nvidia** or **Habana Labs** are installed on numerous data science platforms. In addition, virtualized hardware with GPUs is also part of the standard repertoire in cloud platforms. AWS EC2, for example, uses Habana Gaudi processors and promises to increase the performance of deep learning models by 40 % compared to traditional GPUs.

Figure 2.4 Gaudi – a processor, designed for Deep Learning[11]

Big Data clusters range from 64 GB to 512 GB of **RAM** per node, depending on their use case. These sizes make it possible to load enormous amounts of data into memory. The

---

[10] https://handwiki.org/wiki/Instructions_per_second
[11] https://techcrunch.com/2019/06/17/habana-labs-launches-its-gaudi-ai-training-processor

memory size per node is also a decisive factor for how many users can work with the cluster in parallel.

For a long time, **hard disks** were considered the "bottleneck" in computer systems[12]. We reached mechanical limits fast, and for years the I/O innovation was slower than for other hardware components. With the advent of SSDs, computer systems had new ways to increase performance. For example, cloud providers offer[13] **provisioned IOPS** configurations with up to 256.000 IOPS. They are significantly faster than standard configuration (up to 16.000 IOPS) and therefore explicitly suited for databases with low response time requirements.

In the **network environment**, the Ethernet standard has prevailed over alternatives such as Infiniband. With Ethernet, several standards differ in terms of transmission speeds, among other things. [14] Ethernet is also horizontally scalable via methods such as **link aggregation**.

An optimal server configuration is also a question of cost. The ideal platform covers all requirements at the best possible price. If you ignore infrastructures, you risk paying too much for a platform you cannot use or building a platform that does not meet your requirements. Both variants can have disastrous consequences.

Exercises

- Read more about paradigms such as Moore's Law or Amdahl's Law. A standard work on this topic is the book by Martin Kleppmann, "Distributed Systems." [15]

- Research on the Internet and try to understand what terms like 'PolarDB', 'Paxos', 'Round Robin', 'CAP Theorem', 'BASE' and 'Eventual Consistency' mean.

- Learn to explain the difference between shared-nothing architectures and multi-cluster shared-data architectures.

- Learn how indexes in databases work and how various platforms optimize access through tree data structures. Also, try to understand partitioning strategies and how to work with skewed data.

■ 2.3 Linux Essentials for Data Professionals

We are aware that there is no direct relation between executing commands in a shell and exploring data for many readers. But there are more cases that most people are aware of in which the skills presented in these chapters are essential for data scientists. This section,

---

[12] *https://en.wikipedia.org/wiki/I/O_bound*

[13] *https://aws.amazon.com/ebs/volume-types/*

[14] *https://embeddedgeeks.com/ieee-ethernet-standards/*

[15] *https://www.amazon.com/Designing-Data-Intensive-Applications-Reliable-Maintainable/dp/1449373321*

therefore, summarises some essentials which often are necessary when working with Linux in data projects.

Most data platforms for data science projects are open source, which means they are often run on open-source operating systems. Basic knowledge of Linux is therefore helpful for a member of a data science team. In particular, if you have to prepare demos yourself and can't always rely on systems engineers to set up every system for you, some tips in this chapter can be a lifesaver.

The operation of data platforms, such as Confluent[16], is usually only officially supported on widespread Linux distributions such as Ubuntu, CentOs or SuSE. Especially Linux enthusiasts who love to experiment with more exotic distributions such as Kali Linux or Arch Linux should be aware of that.

 Linux in Business Practice

Enterprise policies for operating systems often dictate a conservative operating strategy. Therefore, many Linux servers running enterprise applications use an older Linux kernel.

However, some modern frameworks require an up-to-date kernel. For example, a user in a Kubernetes environment wanted to use Cilium to enable End2End encryption between Kubernetes services. The servers in the cluster were running on Linux kernel version 4.14, but Cilium required a kernel version 4.19 or later for this functionality.

In another case, system administrators updated a Linux kernel to the latest available version at the time (which was 4.19). However, that specific kernel version was not compatible with a driver for a distributed file system. Thus, a different driver had to be used, resulting in significantly lower data throughput. ■

Terminal Environment

Anyone who works intensively with operating systems must be familiar with the command line. Therefore, the choice of an exemplary terminal environment is mandatory. Those who work with a Mac can, for example, use the application **iTerm2**, which offers more functionality than the standard terminal emulator. Windows users will often use **PuTTY**.

Docker, in turn, is the standard for containers and can be understood as an encapsulated environment within an operating system. A note for Windows users: To execute the following examples, which you will run on a Linux shell, you can also host Linux in Windows installations via Docker. You can download Docker from the vendor's site. After installation, the following command will instantiate a container based on the devenv image:

```
docker run -it stefanpapp/devenv /bin/zsh
```

Programmers who are not familiar with Docker can remember the relationship of images to containers like this: An image is like a class, a container like an object. That's why we like

---

[16] https://docs.confluent.io/platform/current/installation/system-requirements.html

to use the term "instantiation" because it's immediately apparent to any programmer what it means.

Figure 2.5 A Docker container from the devenv image

Once you have executed the command, you will have set up a virtualized environment on his operating system, which encapsulates a mini-Linux.

Shell

If you work with the console, you have to remember many commands. A simple solution is to search for previously used commands in the command line with **CTRL+R**. For example, if you have executed the docker run command, you can activate a search by using the keyboard shortcut **CTRL+R**. If you then type run, it will take you to the last command with run. You can also repeat the keyboard shortcut Ctrl+R to jump to earlier usages of run. You can enhance this searching via hstr[17], which allows you to search through your command history interactively.

It is worth looking at the available keyboard commands to avoid constantly moving the cursor around and saving the navigation keys a bit. Table 2.1 contains the most important of them, but the list of possible commands is extensive. Also, be aware that some shells, such as zsh[18], a Bash replacement, might vary in some details.

Table 2.1 Command line abbreviations for the bash shell

Abbreviation	Command
CTRL+A	Move the cursor to the beginning of the line
CTRL+E	Move the cursor to the end of the line
CTRL+B	Move the cursor back one place
ALT+B	Move the cursor back one word
!!	Rerun the last command; this is especially interesting in the form of **sudo !!**
!ABC	Execute the last command that began with abc.
!ABC:P	Get the last command starting with abc into the command line
!N	Execute the nth command in the history
!$	Last argument of the previous command
!^	First argument of the previous command

[17] https://github.com/dvorka/hstr
[18] https://www.zsh.org/

Sometimes it is helpful to remember necessary commands as aliases:

```
alias lsrec='ls  alhpt | head  n 10' # ls the last ten changed files
alias allscu= 'bind -P | grep "can be found" | sort | awk '{printf " %-40s", $1}
{for(i=6;i<=NF;i++){printf " %s ", $i}{printf"\n"}}'' # all shortcuts in a linux env
```

Another important command is which to located executables.

```
which hive # -> where is the file located that I would call?
```

Package Manager

If possible, you should install software with a package manager. Package managers retrieve repositories that contain software packages that are usable for the respective operating system. You can update these repositories via the Internet.

For each operating system and also for the different Linux distributions, there are various standard package managers. Here is a small selection:

Table 2.2 Package managers for operating systems

OS	Package Manager
Alpine:	apk (*https://wiki.alpinelinux.org/wiki/Alpine_Linux_package_management*)
Ubuntu	apt (*https://linux.die.net/man/8/apt-get*)
CentOS	yum (*https://www.centos.org/docs/5/html/yum*)
Mac OS X	brew (*https://brew.sh*)

You can then install new software via the command line. The following example shows how it works in Ubuntu.

```
apt-get install <package name>
```

You should remember the following minimal set of commands:

Table 2.3 apt commands

Command	Meaning
apt-get update	Update local repository
apt-get upgrade	Update software to the latest version
apt-get install <package name>	Install new software
apt-get uninstall <package name>	Uninstall Software

The commands for operating the package manager apt differ from alternatives like yum. You will find a good overview on the Internet. [19]

If you are familiar with package managers, you will install essential tools for data science yourself. Chapter 4, 'Data Engineering', also introduces the pip tool to install Python libraries.

---

[19] *https://fusion809.github.io/comparison-of-package-managers*

Monitoring and Benchmarking

Data professionals often need to check the utilization of resources. You can use numerous commercial solutions for this. This section presents some open source alternatives.

If you want to know the utilization of resources, you can do this with **htop**. Many data professionals use this command regularly to find out bottlenecks in a data pipeline.

```
htop
```

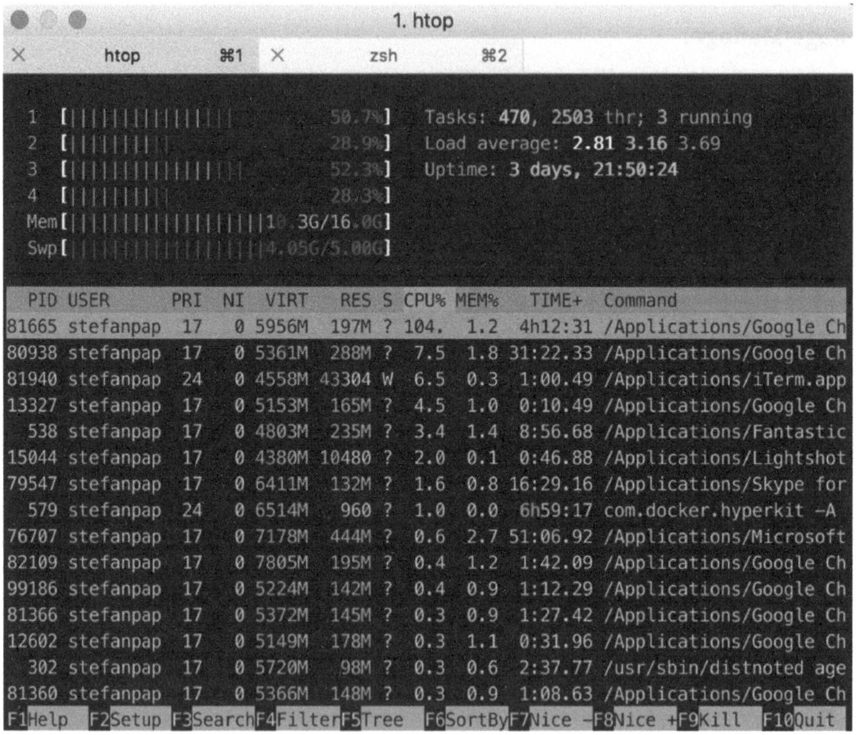

Figure 2.6 The "htop" command as a tool to monitor resources

You can obtain information about the hard disk load via the command du. The -h parameter specifies that the output should be in a *human-readable* format. With this command, you can, for instance, find out if you are about to run out of disk space, which regularly happens if you work with a vast amount of data.

```
du -h #: Disk sizes
```

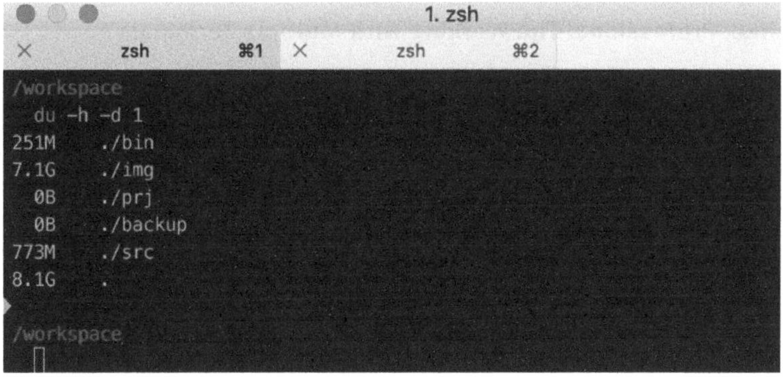

Figure 2.7 The "du" command returns the disk space consumption per directory

If you want to get the information on how much space each mount point uses, type the following command:

```
df -h # Disk free
```

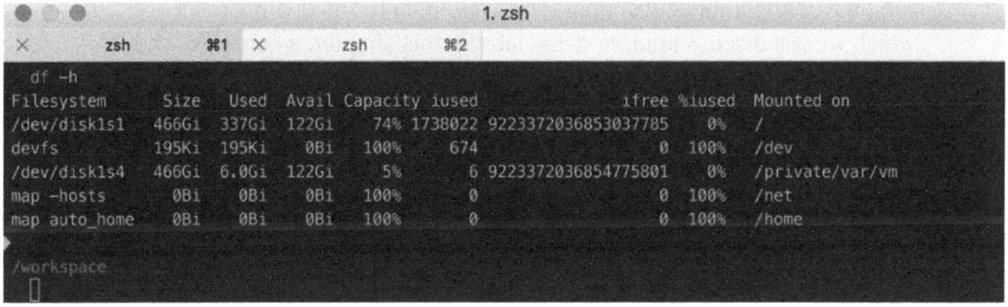

Figure 2.8 The "df" command shows the amount of free space per mount point

Network

It is essential to know your private IP address. You can query this via the command `host-name -I`. You can find out the public IP via the command `curl ifconfig.me`. These are snippets often required to debug the deployment of data applications and can be a lifesaver if you have to present a demo.

Figure 2.9 How to query your IP address

You should ensure that you can connect to various servers using an SSH key without entering a password. For example, you can set up SSH connections using keys as follows.

Linux-Professional-Tip: Working with Multiple Terminals

If you often have to work with several windows in one terminal, you should look at the tool tmux. It is an excellent tool to manage multiple terminals in parallel in the command line. It also offers numerous additional valuable functionalities. [20]

We start two Docker containers in two separate windows:

```
docker run -it ubuntu /bin/sh
```

You can also use the devenv environment to instantiate containers, which is used elsewhere in this chapter. In the devenv environment, however, SSH is already installed. So, to show you how to install OpenSSH, we use images that we set up from scratch.

 Practical Tip for Container Operating Systems: The Smaller, the Better

Containers are encapsulated subsystems embedded in a host environment that run on a configurable guest operating system. In terms of a microservices idea, which we will discuss in more detail later in this chapter, a container should perfectly solve precisely one task.

A Linux distribution for servers or desktops, like Ubuntu or CentOS, includes unnecessary overhead not required in containers, like graphical user interfaces or many drivers.

Therefore, developers created lean distributions for guest operating systems for containers with minimal functionality. Alpine, CoreOS, RancherOS, and others differ in specific details.[21] Those who work a lot with containers will have to delve into this topic.

After that, you should see the following screenshot:

Figure 2.10 Home Screen

First, we install SSH and start the service in both containers. You can do this via the following commands:

---

[20] https://github.com/rothgar/awesome-tmux
[21] https://computingforgeeks.com/minimal-container-operating-systems-for-kubernetes/

```
apt-get update
apt-get install openssh-server
service ssh start
```

Using the root user for routine jobs is not a good idea. It is a security risk, and hence, remote access is often disabled for the root user. That's why we create a user that we want to use for other actions.

```
useradd -ms /bin/bash pontius
passwd pontius
```

We now connect to localhost via SSH and need to enter a password.

```
ssh pontius@localhost
```

Figure 2.11 Enter the password to connect to the target

There are two standard ways to authenticate with SSH:

- With the password
- With an SSH Key

When authenticating with SSH keys, an algorithm matches a private and a public key. If there are no keys on the remote host, you have to revert to enter a password.

We need an SSH key to be able to connect to the target computer without entering a password. You can do this as follows:

```
ssh-keygen
cat ~/.ssh/id_rsa.pub >> ~/.ssh/authorized_keys
```

You can now access localhost via SSH without a password because of registered public and private keys. However, if we want to connect to the second container with SSH, we will re-encounter a password prompt because there is no public key.

First, we look at what IP our target machine has, and then we connect using SSH.

Figure 2.12 Enter the password to connect to the second server

As expected, we have to enter a password. We now distribute the public key to the target computer and try again.

```
ssh-copy-id -i ~/.ssh/id_rsa.pub pontius@<ip>
```

Figure 2.13 Successful connection without password entry

It worked. Please do not forget to set the respective IP addresses correctly.

Being able to connect to a remote system is one essential task when working with networks. But there is more. Often, to discover bottlenecks in your data application, you will also need to explore network performance. For performance tests for networks, the tool iperf3 is a good choice. You install it with the following command:

```
apt-get install iperf3
```

We now need to consider one container as the server and the other as the client. On the server, we execute the following command:

```
iperf3 -s
```

From this point on, the server is a listener; that is, it responds to requests that come from a client.

At the client, we run the following command:

```
iperf3 -c $IP -b 0 -P $PARALLEL -Z -t 20
```

Replace $IP with the IP address of the server. You also need to set a value for $PARALLEL. We use the value four here.

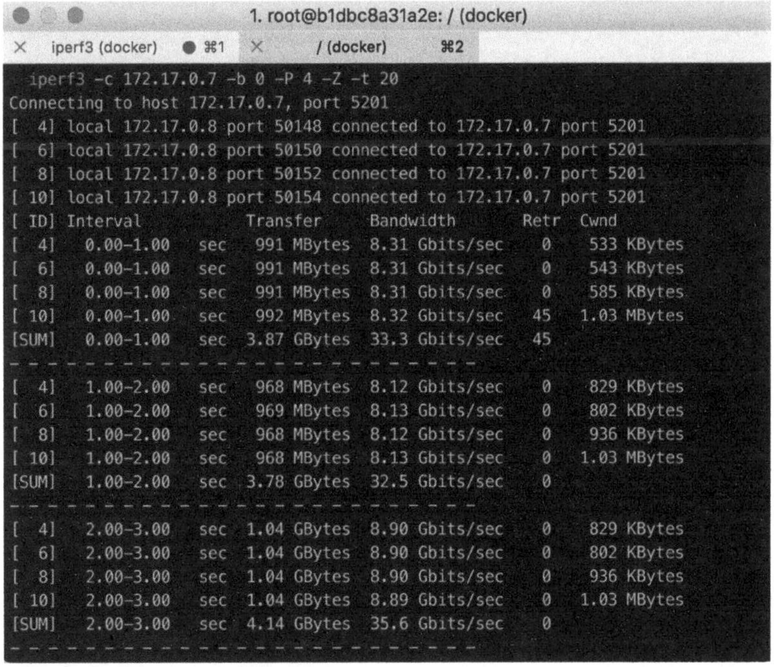

```
● ● ●                        1. root@b1dbc8a31a2e: / (docker)
X    iperf3 (docker)    ● ⌘1    X       / (docker)      ⌘2
   iperf3 -c 172.17.0.7 -b 0 -P 4 -Z -t 20
Connecting to host 172.17.0.7, port 5201
[  4] local 172.17.0.8 port 50148 connected to 172.17.0.7 port 5201
[  6] local 172.17.0.8 port 50150 connected to 172.17.0.7 port 5201
[  8] local 172.17.0.8 port 50152 connected to 172.17.0.7 port 5201
[ 10] local 172.17.0.8 port 50154 connected to 172.17.0.7 port 5201
[ ID] Interval           Transfer     Bandwidth       Retr  Cwnd
[  4]   0.00-1.00   sec   991 MBytes  8.31 Gbits/sec    0    533 KBytes
[  6]   0.00-1.00   sec   991 MBytes  8.31 Gbits/sec    0    543 KBytes
[  8]   0.00-1.00   sec   991 MBytes  8.31 Gbits/sec    0    585 KBytes
[ 10]   0.00-1.00   sec   992 MBytes  8.32 Gbits/sec   45   1.03 MBytes
[SUM]   0.00-1.00   sec  3.87 GBytes  33.3 Gbits/sec   45
- - - - - - - - - - - - - - - - - - - - - - - -
[  4]   1.00-2.00   sec   968 MBytes  8.12 Gbits/sec    0    829 KBytes
[  6]   1.00-2.00   sec   969 MBytes  8.13 Gbits/sec    0    802 KBytes
[  8]   1.00-2.00   sec   968 MBytes  8.12 Gbits/sec    0    936 KBytes
[ 10]   1.00-2.00   sec   968 MBytes  8.13 Gbits/sec    0   1.03 MBytes
[SUM]   1.00-2.00   sec  3.78 GBytes  32.5 Gbits/sec    0
- - - - - - - - - - - - - - - - - - - - - - - -
[  4]   2.00-3.00   sec  1.04 GBytes  8.90 Gbits/sec    0    829 KBytes
[  6]   2.00-3.00   sec  1.04 GBytes  8.90 Gbits/sec    0    802 KBytes
[  8]   2.00-3.00   sec  1.04 GBytes  8.90 Gbits/sec    0    936 KBytes
[ 10]   2.00-3.00   sec  1.04 GBytes  8.89 Gbits/sec    0   1.03 MBytes
[SUM]   2.00-3.00   sec  4.14 GBytes  35.6 Gbits/sec    0
- - - - - - - - - - - - - - - - - - - - - - - -
```

Figure 2.14 Output iperf-results on the screen

As you can see, in this example, four parallel streams had a total throughput of 33.3 GBits per second. We get this high value as we run the test locally without a network. In practice, the value also depends on the Ethernet speed and the number of processes running in parallel, consuming bandwidth.

Table 2.4 Other necessary network commands at a glance

Command	Meaning
nmap	*nmap* is a *port scanner* for networks and hosts. *nmap* sends raw IP packets to all nodes and their ports. The goal is to find out which hosts are available on a network, which services are offered and, if applicable, which OS is installed. You can also get information about packet filters and firewalls via *nmap*.
lsof	The command *lsof* (*list open files*) connects open ports with services. With *grep*, you can filter the output.
netstat	*netstat* shows the contents of individual network-related data structures. You can configure the output. The *man* command lists all options that a user can set in *netstat*.

If you want to try these commands, you can type the following:

```
nmap localhost
nmap google.com
```

Figure 2.15 "nmap" example with localhost and google.com

As expected, the command revealed that Google.com has two open ports: HTTP and HTTPS. Trying to log in there via SSH on port 22 would therefore be pointless. However, the situation is different with localhost, which has opened port 22 for SSH connections.

Use the following command to determine which services exist on the system that listens to port 8080. Use **grep** to filter the output:

```
cat /etc/services | grep 8080
```

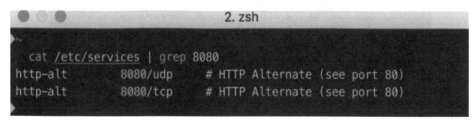

Figure 2.16 With grep as a parameter, all services on port 8080 are filtered.

The following output shows which connections Skype uses, and you can see that some connections are open:

```
lsof -ni | grep Skype
```

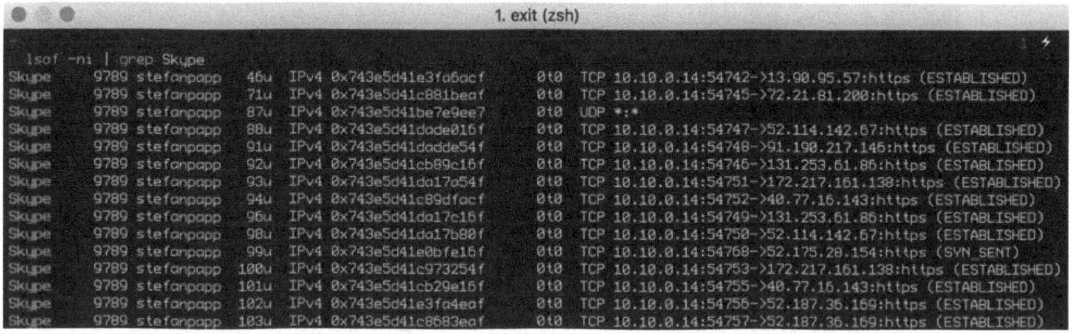

Figure 2.17 "lsof" example revealing all connections to Skype

Finally, we apply **netstat** to look at the address 192.168.1.0 from another side:

```
netstat -an | grep 192.168.1.100
```

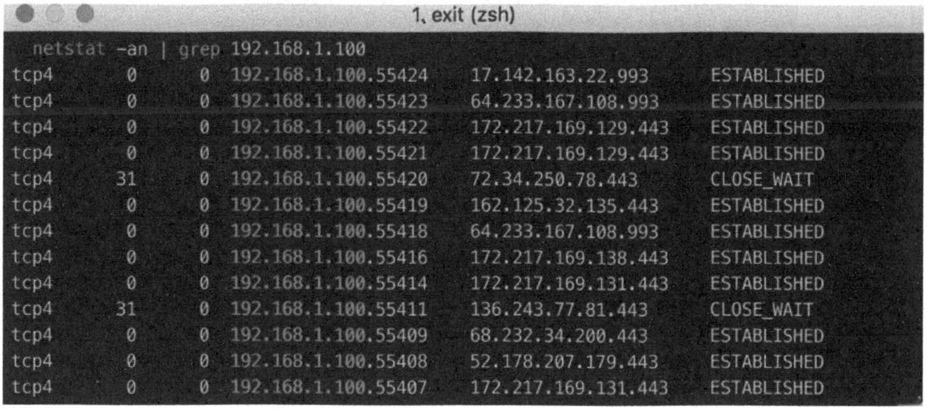

Figure 2.18 "netstat" example showing open connections

nmon

We have now already introduced many monitoring tools, and there are many more. If you do not want to familiarize yourself with a different tool for each area, you can use **nmon**. With this, it is possible to switch between different views.

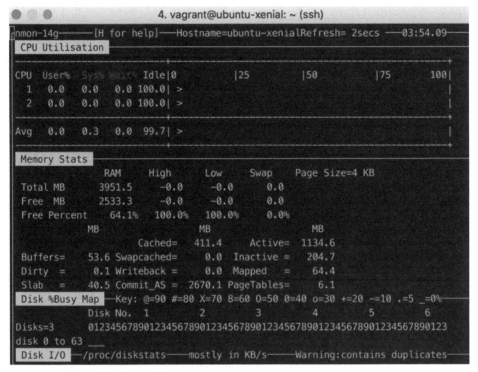

Figure 2.19 Monitoring system environment with nmon

Process Management

Processes also need to be managed. Typically, you would terminate background processes or change their priority.

You can use the ps command to find the currently running processes. With grep, you can filter the output for specific terms.

```
ps -ef | grep Skype
```

This way, you also get the process ID. You can terminate processes with kill.

```
kill <pid>
```

For a developer who deals with Big Data – and thus also with Java-based systems – the command jps is helpful because it displays the currently running Java processes.

The w command tells you who is doing what on a server.

The nice and renice commands adjust the priorities of the processes.

Again someone might ask why a data scientist would need all this. And again, we refer to various situations where data scientists may need to prepare demonstrations and where the ability to handle processes and adjust priorities can be helpful if the demo is not working correctly.

Rights Management

In addition, it is essential to set permissions correctly to ensure that the permissions to access the data meet the specifications of the analytical use case. You should be familiar with commands such as chmod and chown, which change the access rights and file owner, respectively.

It is also helpful to know commands like useradd, passwd, and gpasswd to create users and generate passwords in test environments.

Git

There is a GitHub repository for this book that you can download locally to your computer. For this, you must install Git software. You can install Git with a package manager or download the installation files from *https://git-scm.com*.

The command to install Git via the package manager apt is:

```
apt-get install git
```

The command to load the GitHub repository on the local machine after you have installed Git is:

```
git clone https://github.com/StefanPapp/datascience_handbuch.git
```

You find all Docker images used in this book in this repository.

Familiarize yourself with Git if you haven't already. There are many tutorials on the Internet for this. One advantage of working with Git is to ensure traceability. Changes to files, such as Dockerfiles, can be versioned.

Engineers and data scientists often document results in Git in markdown files (**.md*). **Markdown** is a standard for formatting text with minimal syntax. Unlike LaTeX, a standard well-known in science, markdown is designed for low complexity.

Using a version management system to track changes is essential for all data science projects, as reproducibility and transparency are vital for scientific work.

Vim

A text editor like **Vim** is essential for any engineer dealing with open source platforms since most of the time, you connect to servers via SSH and work on the console.

Many engineers perceive Vim as complex. As a result, some of them prefer IDEs such as Visual Studio Code or IntelliJ.

Bill Joy created vi, the original editor, in 1976. Because, at that time, computer mice and windows-based operating systems were uncommon, the editor excels with a vast amount of keyboard shortcuts to facilitate every action. Bram Moolenaar, a developer from the Netherlands, created Vim, an improved version of this editor. There are also new clones, such as Neovim.

There are numerous "cheat sheets" for shortcuts on the Internet. Once you get used to working with Vim and memorizing the most important shortcuts, you will be faster than using a "windows-oriented editor."

Once you have installed Vim, you can start it as follows:

```
vim <filename>
```

Vim has three modes. We will introduce two of them here: the edit mode and the command mode. In command mode, you can perform various operations. For example, the G key in command mode takes the editor to the end of the file. You can exit the editor and save all changes by entering :x. If you enter :q, you exit and discard all changes. You can use keys such as i (insert) or a (append) to switch to edit mode. Finally, you can exit the edit mode again with Esc.

Once you have mastered the basics, you will soon realize that this is only the beginning. You can combine numerous instructions in command mode. For example, '5dw' deletes five words. 3fe moves the cursor to the third occurrence of 'e'. There are de facto abbreviations and combinations for every command that logically fit together.

In command mode, d always means delete. However, we can use ranges to delete more lines, for example, with :3,7d. This operation would remove rows three through seven. There is an incredible amount of other valuable features, like setting markers to jump forward and backward. It is no surprise that Vim-enthusiasts wrote whole books about this editor to cover all power user tricks.

We would like to mention that Vim is one of those tools where you can still learn something even if you have been working with it for years. Although in large projects, teams will often use IDEs such as Visual Studio Code, IntelliJ, or PyCharm, these IDEs offer plug-ins to integrate Vim functionality.

Data Analysis with System Tools

Every operating system brings standard software for data analysis. Linux is the standard for most data platforms, and it is hard to port them to Windows. Creators of a platform specify the Linux kernels or distributions they support. Therefore, we often use Linux for our examples. macOS users can usually run the examples on their computers as well.

```
apt update
apt install most
cd /var/log/
most dpkg.log
grep -rni error .
grep -c -rni error .
```

With the last two grep commands in the above example, we have already begun exploring data analysis. Filtering the number of occurrences of the identifier error from all log files is a start for error analysis.

The ability to find something out from log files is essential. Additionally, you can refine the grep usage even more. For example, the parameters -B and -A output two lines before and three lines after the error:

```
grep -B2 -A3 -rni error .
```

You can also "tail a file" and filter it by parameters if you want to have live logging. To "tail a file" means to output new entries when processes write to the file. For example, if you run the command below, all logs that meet the search conditions will be displayed in real-time.

```
tail -f /var/log/auth.log | grep 'Invalid user'
```

Theoretically, a data scientist can also use data science tools to analyze logs. For example, you can start R and load the log files into a DataFrame. Then, with packages like DPLR, you can search the content.

In addition, there are command-line tools like *logwatch* and *logcheck* for monitoring log files for more complex scenarios. Still, the standard tools like *grep* and *awk* are sufficient to display essential information. The syntax highlighting in Vim can also be helpful to highlight critical information.

```
● ● ●              4. vagrant@ubuntu-xenial: /var/log (ssh) 🔔
Jul 12 20:19:16 ubuntu-xenial useradd[1036]: new group: name=ubuntu, GID=1001
Jul 12 20:19:16 ubuntu-xenial useradd[1036]: new user: name=ubuntu, UID=1001, GID=1001, home=
/home/ubuntu, shell=/bin/bash
Jul 12 20:19:16 ubuntu-xenial useradd[1036]: add 'ubuntu' to group 'adm'
Jul 12 20:19:16 ubuntu-xenial useradd[1036]: add 'ubuntu' to group 'dialout'
Jul 12 20:19:16 ubuntu-xenial useradd[1036]: add 'ubuntu' to group 'cdrom'
Jul 12 20:19:16 ubuntu-xenial useradd[1036]: add 'ubuntu' to group 'floppy'
Jul 12 20:19:16 ubuntu-xenial useradd[1036]: add 'ubuntu' to group 'sudo'
Jul 12 20:19:16 ubuntu-xenial useradd[1036]: add 'ubuntu' to group 'audio'
Jul 12 20:19:16 ubuntu-xenial useradd[1036]: add 'ubuntu' to group 'dip'
Jul 12 20:19:16 ubuntu-xenial useradd[1036]: add 'ubuntu' to group 'video'
Jul 12 20:19:16 ubuntu-xenial useradd[1036]: add 'ubuntu' to group 'plugdev'
Jul 12 20:19:16 ubuntu-xenial useradd[1036]: add 'ubuntu' to group 'netdev'
Jul 12 20:19:16 ubuntu-xenial useradd[1036]: add 'ubuntu' to group 'lxd'
Jul 12 20:19:16 ubuntu-xenial useradd[1036]: add 'ubuntu' to shadow group 'adm'
Jul 12 20:19:16 ubuntu-xenial useradd[1036]: add 'ubuntu' to shadow group 'dialout'
Jul 12 20:19:16 ubuntu-xenial useradd[1036]: add 'ubuntu' to shadow group 'cdrom'
Jul 12 20:19:16 ubuntu-xenial useradd[1036]: add 'ubuntu' to shadow group 'floppy'
Jul 12 20:19:16 ubuntu-xenial useradd[1036]: add 'ubuntu' to shadow group 'sudo'
Jul 12 20:19:16 ubuntu-xenial useradd[1036]: add 'ubuntu' to shadow group 'audio'
                                                              1,1            Top
```

Figure 2.20 Syntax highlighting with Vim

Anyone who wants to work with distributed systems will not get around using a professional monitoring tool. For instance, advanced admins use tools such as *Nagios*, *Logstash*, or *Prometheus* for this purpose.

System Data – An Unknown Data Source for Data Scientists

Linux provides tons of system data. If you want to try out new data science frameworks and look for test data, you can use monitoring data to populate various algorithms.

This section was just a concise introduction to a few selected Linux commands. Some data scientists, especially those working for small companies that cannot provide system engineers for all teams, will often have to get their hands dirty and fix minor systems issues themselves. You should never underestimate the amount of time data professionals spend on the console to read debug logs, check for performance bottlenecks, or fix connectivity issues. For many people with an Analytics background, handling the system is part of the job.

Below, we sum up some activities for those who want to explore this domain further.

 Exercises

- Learn how to use a Linux distribution. If you have mastered a standard distribution, such as Debian or Ubuntu, you can also venture into a more complex one like Arch Linux.
- Delve into solutions like Cilium and understand how they work.
- Complete a Linux certification of your choice.
- Familiarize yourself with tools like Vim, tmux, and zsh. If you master all the shortcuts, you will work in record-breaking time. Also, visit websites like awesome Vim, awesome tmux, and awesome zsh.
- Understand how to resolve merge conflicts in Git.
- Get busy with Wireshark. Many network professionals recommend the tool to filter traffic efficiently.
- If you want to delve deeper into security to protect data platforms, explore ethical hacking and how to protect systems against attacks. Distributions such as Kali Linux are a good start.
- You can get certifications such as CompTIA+ for networks that will leave almost no question in networks unanswered.
- Subscribe to a Linux podcast. [22]
- Go beyond Linux and explore other platforms, such as FreeBSD, as well.

◾

◼ 2.4 Terraform

A central principle in the data science environment is reproducibility. Thus, a result without the possibility of verification by third parties is not meaningful from a scientific point of view.

Reproducibility in data science projects also means enabling an independent party to create infrastructures to perform experiments at the push of a button. *Configuration drift*, that is the manual modification of existing infrastructures, can influence query results.

Using *Infrastructure as Code*, a system administrator can declare infrastructures in text files. Automation tools will then interpret this declarative language and create this infrastructure on a target platform like AWS or Azure. In this context, we understand infrastructures as building blocks such as virtualized servers, network segments, or storage. The motto is: first, describe your infrastructure as code and let tools create it at the push of a

---

[22] *https://linuxunplugged.com/*

button. Besides the correct interpretation of the blueprint, these tools also catch errors during building the infrastructure and react to them.

One feature of IaC tools, often called provisioning tools, is *idempotency*. Idempotency means that each invocation of functionality leads to identical results. By representing infrastructure as declarative code, system configurations become versionable. As a result, you can store them in version management repositories such as Git.

Each of the three major public cloud providers, Amazon, Microsoft, and Google, has its proprietary product to map infrastructures for its platform as code. However, administrators often prefer a vendor-independent solution. As a result, *Terraform* from Hashicorp has become the standard because it supports AWS, GCP, Azure, and even more exotic providers as target platforms.

Let's imagine what the programming logic would look like if we implemented building the infrastructure ourselves. For example, the following code could be part of a deployment.

```
try:
  CreateNetwork(cidr)
  for i in range(6):
    CreateServerinstance(i)
    else:
  print("Created 6 instances!")
except(PlatformCreationError e):
    print("error")
```

You would have to extend these few lines of code significantly to cover numerous exceptional cases. This excerpt describes only a small part of possible problems during the creation of an infrastructure:

- The cloud provider does not have sufficient resources for new infrastructures, or building the target system would exceed quotas.

- The service account, which you use to execute the automation tool and to create infrastructures, lacks the rights to create individual infrastructures on the target platform.

- Elements that an automation tool wants to create already exist.

Also, tools have to query variables, which describe individual configuration parameters. Below is a small excerpt of such variables:

- The resources (CPU, RAM, disks, etc.) of compute server instances
- The CIDR Ranges of networks
- The configuration of the encryption of data and services
- Firewall rules and access configurations
- Load balancers and their configuration

If you want to program a comprehensive solution yourself, you must write many routines to read in parameters and evaluate them. The complexity of your code would rise exponentially with the elements in your infrastructure. At some point, it would be challenging to read. For this reason, a ready-made solution such as Terraform is a good choice.

For the first tests with Terraform, you must install the application. To do so, you can find the details on the manufacturer's page (www.terraform.io).

In the first example, we download a Docker image and use the heredoc notation.

```
cat << EOF > main.tf
# Download the latest Ghost image
resource "docker_image" "image_id" {
  name = "ghost:latest"
}
EOF
```

If you are using Terraform 0.14 or higher, you also need to add the following file.

```
cat << EOF > versions.tf
terraform {
  required_providers {
    docker = {
      source = "cruiser/docker"
    }
  }
  required_version = ">= 0.13"
}
EOF
```

The next step is to use the declaration just defined as the basis for a rollout. Three commands are essential here: `init`, `plan` and `apply`. You have to execute them in the directory of the *main.tf file.*

```
terraform init
```

After calling the `init command`, Terraform creates a local repository in a subdirectory in the execution directory. Terraform looks in the local folder for a *main.tf file*. In that file, it expects the infrastructure configuration that defines what it needs to build. Terraform also looks for a declaration of a target platform, such as AWS, Azure, or GCP in *.tf files. In our specific case, Terraform will determine the need for Docker. In our example, Terraform will load a provider plug-in for Docker locally into the repository.

```
terraform plan
```

This command verifies that the declarations in the tf files are syntactically correct, and Terraform can execute it. Terraform prepares an execution plan but does not execute commands against a target system yet.

```
terraform apply
```

You can trigger a rollout by calling the `terraform apply` command. Terraform will try to create all required infrastructure elements and return an error if this is not feasible. Figure 2.22 shows a successful rollout. Finally, you can check the status with `terraform show`.

You can use the following command to verify the correctness of the deployment and that we have deployed a ghost image:

```
docker image ls
```

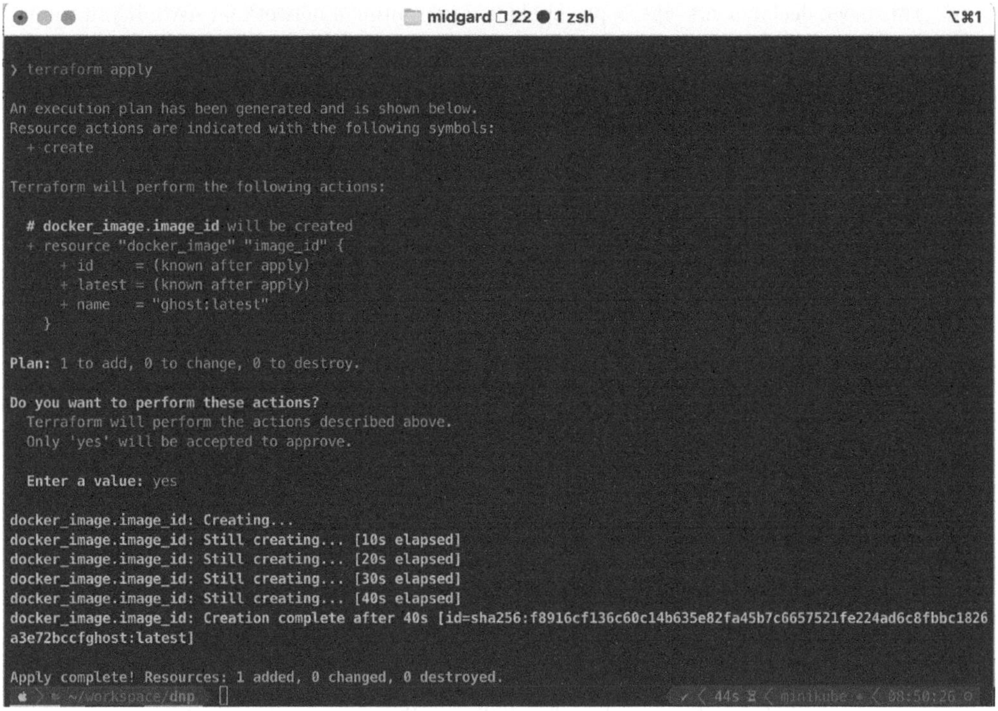

Figure 2.21 Successful execution of terraform apply

If you look at the run directory, you will find the subdirectory `.terraform`, where all loaded provider plug-ins are stored. A plug-in encapsulates the functionality to control the rollout. Alternatively, you can list providers via the following command:

```
terraform providers
```

Blocks in a terraform declaration are always structured as follows:

```
<BLOCK TYPE> "<BLOCK LABEL>" "<BLOCK LABEL>" {
  # Block body
  <IDENTIFIER> = <EXPRESSION> # argument
}
```

Having already declared a Docker image, we declare a cloud resource of the provider plug-in for AWS, as shown below. The block in this example itself is minimalistic. Only one variable determines that a CIDR block is declared. There are many other configuration options for this element. [23]

```
resource "aws_vpc" "main" {

  cidr_block = "10.0.0/16"
}
```

---

[23] https://registry.terraform.io/providers/hashicorp/aws/latest/docs/resources/vpc

This block declares `aws_vpc`, a placeholder representing a network on AWS. If you wanted to reference the resource in other blocks, you could use the label `main`.

In addition to resource types, there are other elements in Terraform, such as variables and outputs. Again, you can find the details in the Terraform documentation.

You can use the following command to delete installations again.

```
terraform destroy
```

In the last part of this chapter, we will create a Kubernetes cluster on AWS using Terraform. This use case is also an excellent practical example to learn more about Terraform.

 Exercises

- Learn about Terraform's modules and understand how to modularize infra-structures.
- If you have a preferred cloud provider, explore the Infrastructure as Code solutions they provide for their platforms, such as AWS CloudFormation or Azure Resource Manager.
- Parallel to Infrastructure as Code; there is also configuration management for application software and services. Learn how to automate software roll-outs like Apache Kafka or Apache Webserver with Ansible, Puppet, and co.
- Take some time to think about how you would update already existing platforms. For example, would you prefer to delete existing platforms and simply recreate a new version? Or would you instead update an existing platform with changes in the infrastructure? We answer parts of this in the Microservices subchapter below.

■ 2.5 Cloud

Many experts see the cloud not as new technology but as an alternative business model to the original idea of procuring and managing hardware. Cloud providers operate huge server farms worldwide and virtualize the hardware. Users can rent these resources.

For the customer, this offer also means relief, as the cloud provider takes care of the management of the IT systems. The cloud has specific requirements. **Elasticity** means, for example, that the available resources for services can be increased and later reduced again depending on current demand.

Cloud providers often advertise the cost benefits of going to the cloud. However, if you purchase expensive hardware and don't use it later, you risk wasting money. For example, a company buys a 40-node cluster for an analytics project, which gets later unexpectedly canceled. But if the IT manager has only rented the infrastructure, they can simply order the services again at the end of the project.

For companies, the cloud significantly reduces operational complexity. They no longer need an operations team to replace defective hardware components and ensure smooth operation. Instead, companies can focus on their core business while someone else takes care of the necessary infrastructure.

Critics of cloud systems see a risk in handing over the infrastructure for managing sensitive data to third parties. As a customer, you don't know what happens to the stored data and whether third parties may access it. Also, company policies in some industries specify that they cannot store data outside of national borders. This regulation is a problem that many cloud providers solve by providing services that guarantee the local processing of sensitive data.

We will take a look at the standard services offered below, listing the cloud provider solutions.

The **XaaS** model describes areas the cloud provider is accountable. The model also specifies which areas remain in the customer's responsibility. The four best-known XaaS are:

- Infrastructure as a Service (IaaS),
- Platform as a Service (PaaS)
- Software as a Service (SaaS)
- Function as a Service (FaaS)

Infrastructure as a Service means renting virtualized hardware resources. The customer gets virtualized servers and decides for themself which operating system they want to use and administer. The cloud provider takes care of the infrastructure. Employees of the provider replace defective hardware, and the provider also guarantees the physical protection of server rooms.

Those who want to go one step further and do not want to worry about the administration of operating systems and applications can use *Platform as a Service*. In this service category, the customer uses pre-configured servers and applications. In addition, the cloud provider ensures that the platform runs and security updates are applied.

With *Platform as a Service*, you use servers and applications. But sometimes, you don't want to manage a platform; you just want to use the software. Think of solutions like Dropbox or Google Drive. It doesn't matter which platform is underneath. *Software as a Service* provides applications for a specific purpose. Examples of data science-specific SaaS solutions from cloud providers include **AWS Sagemaker**, **Azure Machine Learning Studio**, and **Google Cloud AI Platform**.

Function as a Service reflects the trend of serverless computing, which we will discuss in more detail at the end of this section. In addition, they are part of cloud-native architectures.

We can divide cloud solutions into service categories. Table 2.5 lists them.

Table 2.5 Cloud providers and one reference solution

Service	AWS	Azure	Google Cloud
Memory	Amazon S3	Azure Blob Storage	Cloud Storage
Compute	Amazon EC2	Azure VM	Compute Engine
Development	AWS Elastic Beanstalk	Azure Cloud Services	Google App Engine
Container	Amazon EKS	Azure AKS	GKE

Table 2.5 Cloud providers and one reference solution *(continued)*

Service	AWS	Azure	Google Cloud
SQL	Amazon DynamoDB	Azure Cosmos DB	Cloud SQL
DWH	Amazon Redshift	Microsoft Azure SQL	BigQuery
Serverless Computing	AWS Lambda	Azure Functions	Cloud Functions
NoSQL	Amazon DynamoDB	Cosmos DB	Cloud Datastore

For each service, we have listed only one reference solution. A cloud provider usually offers many solutions for one service category. For example, in addition to S3, the object store, AWS also provides services such as **S3 Glacier** (archive storage), **EFS** (distributed file system), or **FSx** (dedicated file system).

Cloud Provider

The August 2020 Gartner Quadrant reflects the state of the cloud vendor market as seen by this globally respected consulting firm. They call Amazon Web Services (AWS) the market leader. Microsoft entered after AWS and has captured a lot of market share with Azure. In addition, Microsoft has a sizable B2B partner network. Some analysts see, therefore, the Redmond company as the leader in this segment. The third is the Google Cloud Platform, which is also well-positioned to gain further market share.

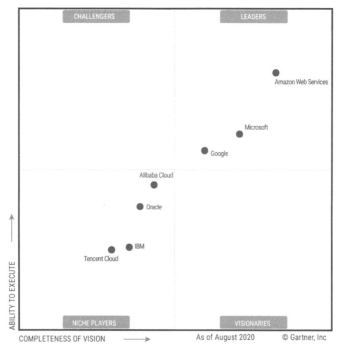

Figure 2.22 Magic Quadrant for Cloud Infrastructure as a Service (worldwide) [24]

---

[24] Copyright: Gartner, Inc *(https://pages.awscloud.com/GLOBAL-multi-DL-gartner-mq-cips-2020-learn.html)*

Challengers like Alibaba Cloud could become more critical in the next few years. They could well catch up via attractive price offers and access to new markets. It is also conceivable that other financially strong players will enter this lucrative market.

2.5.1 Basic Services

Storage Services

Every cloud provider offers a file hosting service to provide customers with unlimited data storage. The core criterion is to keep data availability high and costs low.

Of course, cloud providers intermix storage solutions with other building blocks. For example, for database solutions, the cloud provider may use its storage solution for the physical storage of the data, while the complete database solution also contains a database engine.

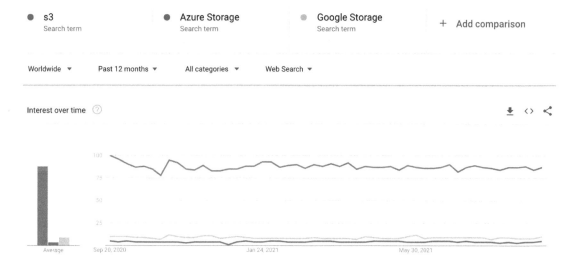

Figure 2.23 Google Trends on Cloud Storage[25]

Perhaps the best-known AWS product is **S3**. Similar to its competitors, AWS bills its clients by consumption.

This durability level corresponds to an average annual expected loss of 0.000000001 % of objects. For example, if you store 10,000,000 objects with Amazon S3, you can on average expect to incur a loss of a single object once every 10,000 years. Therefore, the data is more secure than in any data center as they also mirror the data globally. Files loaded on S3 can be up to 5TB in size. Users can access S3 data via HTTP/HTTPS.

Microsoft and Google also offer the possibility to use the cloud as pure storage. The services for this are **Azure Storage** and **Google Storage**.

---

[25] Data source: Google Trends *(https://www.google.com/trends)*

Companies use storage services to process and also archive data. In any case, the total capacity of file hosting services goes into the exa, maybe even zettabyte range. These are capacities that no company can exhaust.

Security issues are also critical. A private user is not the focus of hackers like a bank or a large company. Especially to comply with GDPR, which is the topic of Chapter 15, a solution provider must ensure that sensitive data is protected. However, the storage services of well-known cloud providers should be sufficiently secure.

It is crucial to know that frameworks like Apache Spark can load and process data from cloud storage services for data science projects. So if you want to analyze your data with data science tools and don't have sufficient storage capacity, you can always load data for analysis from a file hosting service.

Cloud providers also offer file systems that are suitable for particular tasks, such as high-performance computing. The documentation of the cloud providers provides a good overview of these services.

Compute

Users run "compute services" to instantiate virtual servers running an operating system. Then, the compute nodes are optimally networked with the storage systems in a cloud provider's data center to maximize throughput.

You should gear the configuration of the servers towards their application. For example, there are templates for Data Science like GPU-optimized instances.[26]

In addition to the hardware configuration of the servers, DevOps engineers also configure topologies. For example, to optimize network communication, servers can be configured to reside in the same rack physically. Cloud providers charge by the hour or by second. The price depends on the configuration. So, a stronger instance, such as more RAM, a higher number of virtual processors, costs more.

The costs for **EC2** (Elastic Compute Cloud), **Azure VM**, and **Google Compute Engine** can be significant factors for customers deciding which servers to host their applications. However, there is no guarantee that the best initial price provider will remain the cheapest in the long term. Some companies, therefore, also rely on a multi-cloud strategy in which they can switch flexibly between providers.

Databases

Companies can have open source solutions and almost any proprietary software hosted in the cloud. Even former appliances providers – i.e., a hardware and software solution from one manufacturer – such as **Oracle** or **Teradata** advertise that they can now also offer a leading solution in the cloud. Other companies provide their solutions exclusively in the cloud, such as **Snowflake**.

Each of the three major cloud providers also offers its database systems in the cloud. Microsoft's product is MS SQL Server. Amazon has several of its proprietary systems, DynamoDB and Redshift being the best-known representatives. DynamoDB scores with NoSQL capabilities, while Redshift is a data warehouse. Google's solutions are BigTable and BigQuery.

---

[26] *https://trends.google.com/trends/explore?q=Databricks,Oracle,Snowflake*

BigTable is the technology that also gave rise to a famous representative of a database for Hadoop: HBase.

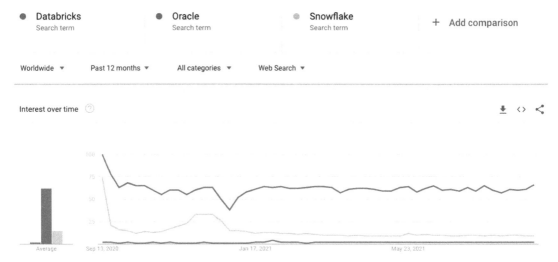

Figure 2.24 Trends in the database sector[27]

The collection of all database systems in the cloud follows the paradigm of polyglot persistence[28]: Specific requirements need specific solutions. As a result, there are individual storage solutions designed to solve one specific use case. Of course, you can apply some of them for other use cases, but this often comes with a price. In extreme situations, a suboptimal storage technology performs ok in test environments but fails to meet various non-functional requirements under full production load. Therefore, understanding which database best solves a particular problem is an essential qualification characteristic of a data architect.

Polyglot Storage and Skiing

You can compare Polyglot Storage with skiing. Skiing has multiple disciplines. Hermann Meier is a retired ski-racer who dominated the world cup in Downhill, Giant, and Super-G at the peak of his career.

You could have asked him to run Slalom as well. As an experienced ski-racer, he would have finished a race, but it is doubtful that he could have reached a performance comparable to a ski racer focused on Slalom.

The heart of a database is its architecture. On-premise solutions often advertise a **shared-nothing** architecture to make the most of existing infrastructure. On the other hand, many cloud providers build their cloud-native database solutions on a **multi-cluster**,

---

[27] Data source: *Google Trends (https://www.google.com/trends)*
[28] *https://martinfowler.com/bliki/PolyglotPersistence.html*

shared data architecture. The second architecture's heart is a layer of super-fast SSD-based disks to replicate data multiple times. Finally, nodes on which query optimizers create an execution plan are located in a separate layer.

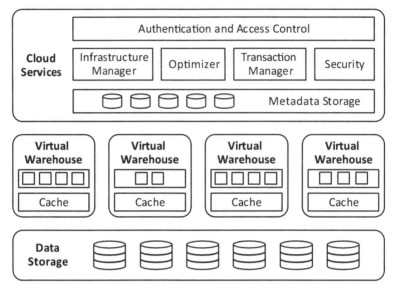

Figure 2.25 Multi-Cluster, shared data architecture
(https://dl.acm.org/doi/pdf/10.1145/2882903.2903741)

Development

The providers also have their proprietary solutions for software development. For example, **AWS Elastic Beanstalk** is a PaaS for Java, Python, Docker, and other platforms at Amazon.

AWS also hosts services that developers can use. These are, for example:

- Simple Workflow Service (SWS)
- Simple Email Service (SES)
- Simple Queue Service (SQS)
- Simple Notification Service (SNS)

In parallel, there are identical solutions from Google and Microsoft.

Directories

AWS Identity and Access Management (called IAM) is a directory service that manages users and resources in an organization on Amazon. You can use IAM to create and group users and control their access to virtually any AWS service, such as EC2 or S3.

Microsoft uses **Active Directory**, and Google uses **Google Cloud Identity** to manage people and groups.

As a data scientist, it is helpful to know that directory services exist and their possibilities to restrict access to resources. You also can limit access to specific models.

Exercises

- Get certified. In preparation for a provider cloud certification, you will learn everything you need to work with the cloud professionally. There are also specific certifications for Machine Learning and other analytics-related skills.

- Study policies, security groups, and firewall settings in-depth. You'll thank yourself when you're pressed for time and need to solve an access problem while you're about to demo.

- Build systems in a cost calculator and get a feel for expected costs in the cloud.[29] Would you recommend a company move its on-premise architecture to the cloud via lift and shift?

- Explore various cloud providers and find out where they have their data centers. Which impact do you think it has when a cloud provider is the first to build a data center in a specific country?

2.5.2 Cloud-native Solutions

Two main architectural building blocks for cloud-native solutions are microservices and serverless architectures.

Microservices

Microservices enforce the following principle: encapsulate all units, let them do only one task, but do it perfectly. Of course, developers already know this idea from the Single Responsibility Principle.

We introduced containers earlier in this chapter. Kubernetes is an orchestration tool for containers. To build microservice architectures, developers have to package atomic functionality in a container. Kubernetes controls the automatic instantiation of containers and the replacement of broken ones. Minikube is a particular version of that software to run the work on a standalone machine for testing purposes. However, if you want to run a production environment, you should always run Kubernetes on a cluster.

Usually, it takes many individual steps to configure details of a Kubernetes installation. This installation can be laborious on an on-premises cluster. Installing Kubernetes in the cloud reduces some steps, but there is no complete automation when configuring Kubernetes via a cloud provider's web interface. The logical consequence is to automate the installation of a Kubernetes cluster via Infrastructure as Code.

For this book, we provide an example of a Kubernetes installation in a Github repository.[30] If you clone this repository locally, you only need to adapt it to your requirements.

---

[29] *https://calculator.aws/#/*
[30] *https://github.com/StefanPapp/terraform-kubernetes-spike*

One possibility is to rename the *terraform.tfvars.template* file to *terraform.tfvars* and fill all values as suggested in the *README.md file.*

The configuration's access and secret keys are used to access your own AWS cluster and must be protected accordingly. Therefore, if you enter sensitive data into the terraform.tf-vars file, you must also ensure that this data does not accidentally end up in a publicly viewable Git repo.

After you have configured everything correctly, you can create the cluster. For this, please execute the following command:

```
terraform init
terraform apply
```

After you created the cluster, the command line tool *kubectl* still needs to be configured so that you can access the cluster from the command line. The following command adjusts the Kubernetes configuration accordingly:

```
aws eks --region eu-central-1 update-kubeconfig --name kube-infra
```

To verify success, query the nodes with `kubectl get no`. Here the "no" is short for nodes.

Presenting Kubernetes in its complete feature set is beyond the scope of this book. In simple terms, the software runs in a distributed manner on several nodes, and there are two categories of services. The control plane manages processes and interactions. So, for example, new requests are received via a Rest API, and the control plane of Kubernetes coordinates appropriate actions. Kubernetes Workers then execute the functionality. A pod is a unit that hosts one or more containers and thus represents a microservice.

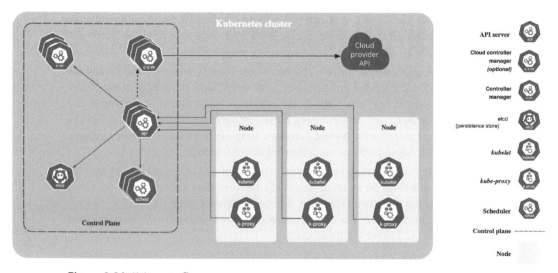

Figure 2.26 Kubernetes[31]

---

[31] Copyright: kubernetes, *https://*kubernetes.io/docs/concepts/overview/components/

Since we do not want to waste resources, we delete the cluster again by calling the following command:

```
terraform destroy
```

Serverless Computing

With serverless computing, software programs run without having to worry about managing servers. Customers only pay for compute time; there are no costs for downtime.

Serverless computing is essential for all use cases that need to be elastic and where the amount of data processed varies greatly. Think of online sports betting providers, for example. A Champions League final means maximum requests and real-time evaluations every second. In comparison, resources would run almost in idle mode at four o'clock at night.

For a data science case, this has its appeal. Instead of compute instances that are manually booted up and down, code is loaded and executed. The corresponding data for this can reside on a file hosting service. No one has to worry about managing servers anymore.

All three major vendors have proprietary serverless systems: AWS Lambda, Azure Functions, and Google Cloud Functions.

 Exercises

- Try Alpine Linux instead of Ubuntu Linux as the operating system for your containers.
- Learn how Pods communicate with each other.
- Understand what a ServiceMesh does and how to configure it.
- Put Secrets in Hashicorp Vault and learn how to use a Secrets Manager with Kubernetes.
- Build in-depth knowledge of Kubernetes and get certified if necessary.
- Delve into Lambda and other serverless applications. There is also a framework for serverless architectures called 'serverless.' [32]

---

[32] *https://www.serverless.com/*

■ 2.6 In a Nutshell

 Infrastructure topics are also crucial for a data team.

Suppose you don't know which hardware requirements are necessary for systems to map specific functional and non-functional aspects. In that case, you'll have a hard time building data platforms that run complex data science applications.

Distributed processing only makes sense if the data is large enough.

If you build a distributed solution for simple problems just because you like to work with an innovative solution, you violate the KISS principle. The unnecessary overhead will harm the project.

Linux is mandatory.

Basic knowledge of Linux helps a user perform many operations essential for Data Science on Linux systems.

Cloud is the future for data platforms.

The cloud is a business model through which IT resources are rented instead of purchased. It makes it easier to work in experimental environments. If you do not find value in the data, you can cancel the infrastructure for the data science project.

Declare your infrastructure.

Creating a platform via a GUI is no longer up-to-date. Architects prefer to declare their infrastructures as infrastructure-as-code platforms.

Polyglot Persistence replaces heterogeneous systems.

No single system for storing data covers all conceivable requirements. Instead, diversity reigns. Objects stores, database systems, and distributed file systems – all have their raison d'être. For some use cases, one solution is ideal; for another, not.

Microservices architectures replace monoliths.

Microservices and cloud-native solutions are leading to a paradigm shift in IT. Similar to how the theory of relativity split physics into classical and modern physics, cloud-native architectures and microservices split IT into classical and modern IT.

■

3 Data Architecture

Zoltan C. Toth

Questions Answered in this Chapter:

- How can we describe the data-maturity model of a company?
- What are the main requirements of a well-functioning data architecture?
- What are the most common file and storage formats used today?
- How do data warehouses, data lakes, and lakehouses differ in their functionality?
- What are the pros and cons of cloud-based vs. on-premises architectures?
- How can lakehouses and Apache Spark provide a scalable platform for data analytics?

■ 3.1 Overview

It is tempting to assume that businesses produce easy-to-use reports, high-performing analytics, and predictive models by simply running sophisticated algorithms on the raw data captured. It is not a well-kept secret that this is seldomly the case. Analytical systems must be backed by a robust, well-functioning, high-performing data architecture to achieve data-driven excellence. In this chapter, we describe the fundamental methodological and technological cornerstones of such architectures.

3.1.1 Maslow's Hierarchy of Needs for Data

You may well be familiar with Maslow's hierarchy of needs, an idea in psychology proposed by Abraham Maslow in 1943, and illustrated in Figure 3.1. This idea outlines the hierarchy of human motivations: The need at each stage must be satisfied within the individual, before motivation can arise at the next stage.

Figure 3.1 Maslow's hierarchy of needs

This concept not only applies to human psychology, but also is directly applicable to the journey of the data science readiness of a company. The outline of such a data needs hierarchy is demonstrated by Figure 3.2.

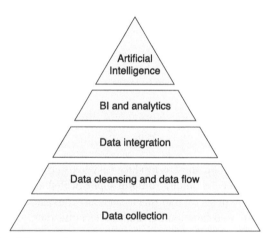

Figure 3.2 Hierarchy of data needs

- You need to get raw data collection right to build meaningful data cleansing and data integration flows.
- Only when clean data is integrated into a data warehouse or a data lake, and relevant data points are interconnected, can a company implement a meaningful Business Analytics (BI) and Reporting layer.
- The business needs to be understood through standard BI and analytics to open the space for Machine Learning and Advanced Analytical use-cases.

All in all, there is no easy way out. You will need to get the basics right in order to build a reliable data architecture that provides maximum business value. The following section sums up the basic requirements for analytical, reporting, and machine learning use-cases.

3.1.2 Data Architecture Requirements

A well-functioning data architecture fulfills the three basic requirements: Reliability, Scalability, and Maintainability [1].

- **Reliability:** The system is expected to keep operating correctly even in the event of particular types of faults. These faults can include hardware faults, software faults, and human error. While even the best-designed system won't be able to cope with every possible kind of fault, reliable data architectures will continue operating correctly – at least to a degree – in certain foreseeable failure scenarios. These can include network outages, hardware failures, system restarts, encountering unexpected data points, and faulty data ingestion or transformation code.

- **Scalability:** Even if a data architecture is working well today, it doesn't mean it will keep working reliably in the future. Businesses grow, and the amount of data collected and processed grows too. A well-functioning data architecture needs to be prepared for incremental growth. Fortunately, most cloud-based data services are created with scalability in mind. On-premises (on-prem) use-cases can also take advantage of scalable solutions; the most popular open-source solutions here are the Hadoop Distributed File System (HDFS) or Apache Spark.

- **Maintainability:** Over time, the complexity of your data architecture is likely to increase. To keep it well-functioning, you will need to put significant effort into keeping it maintainable. As the data readiness of a company improves, this requirement needs to be taken care of in multiple areas: Different developers need to understand the system, implement developments, fix bugs, and operate the architecture continuously.

Good architecture is conceptually simple, easy to operate and to modify. These qualities can be reached through using standard software architecture and software engineering practices.

3.1.3 The Structure of a Typical Data Architecture

Most data architectures share similar workflows:

- **Data ingestion:** Data from various sources are ingested and stored in the infrastructure. These sources include operational log files, CSVs and other data files, third-party applications, and databases.

- **Data cleansing and standardization:** The ingested data gets cleansed. Redundant records are dropped or marked as redundant, data quality issues are noticed and fixed. The cleansed data is integrated into a central place in a standardized format, ensuring that connections between different data points can be established.

- **Data transformation:** The cleansed data is transformed into datasets that can be directly used by business units and serve as a basis for reporting, dashboarding, machine learning applications, and arbitrary analytics.

- **Making the data ready for analytics:** The data is loaded into a storage system performant enough to satisfy the analysts' needs. Necessary permission management is implemented to comply with the business and legal requirements.

A typical data workflow is shown in Figure 3.3. The specific workflow implementations vary use-case by use-case, usually following one of two primary, competing methodologies: ETL (Extract, Transform, Load) and ELT   (Extract, Load, Transform).

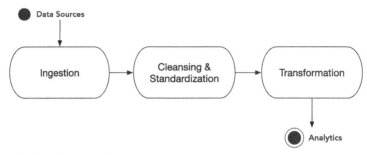

Figure 3.3 A typical data workflow

3.1.4 ETL (Extract, Transform, Load)

Data warehouses are optimized to execute analytical queries on large, well-structured data-sets. Traditional on-prem data warehouses come as appliances (integrated hardware and software solutions); setting them up and maintaining them can get very expensive. The primary motivation behind the ETL methodology is to make sure that only those data points that are directly relevant for analytics are loaded into the data warehouse. One of the primary motivations for this approach is to save costs.

An ETL workflow is shown in Figure 3.4; it implements the following steps:

- **Extract:** The data ingestion step. Raw data is extracted from different data sources and loaded into a staging area, like a local file system or temporary tables in a database or data warehouse.
- **Transform:** The ingested data is cleansed and aggregated, and multiple data sources are connected into a relational format that will be ready for analytics. This operation still happens in the staging area.
- **Load:** The resulting cleansed and interconnected data tables are loaded into the final data warehouse tables.

Figure 3.4 The ETL workflow

3.1.5 ELT (Extract, Load, Transform)

With the advent of cloud-native data warehouses and data lakes, such as Amazon Redshift, Snowflake, and the Delta Lake, data warehouses in the cloud can now store and process arbitrarily large datasets for a reasonable price. Along with these systems getting traction, tools for transforming data on cloud-native data warehouses have emerged. The best known open-source technology for defining these transformations is a tool called The Database Toolkit (DBT)[1]. Technologies like DBT enable companies to implement the ELT pattern, where raw data is directly loaded into a cloud-native data warehouse. Once the data has been loaded, both the data cleansing and the transformation steps take place using SQL, the standard language for data querying and transformation in databases and data warehouses.

Figure 3.5 shows how the ELT pattern implements the following steps:

Extract: Just like with the ETL pattern, raw data is extracted from source applications.

1. **Load:** After the raw data is extracted from source applications, it is loaded into a data warehouse.

2. **Transform:** The data in the data warehouse is cleansed, standardized, and made available for analytics using SQL.

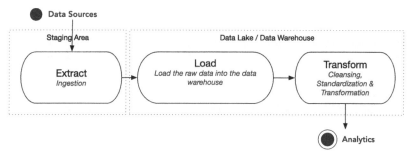

Figure 3.5 The ELT workflow

3.1.6 ETLT

It is crucial to remember that these approaches are only high-level methods to think about your data architecture. They offer best practices that have been proven to work for many companies. However, each use case differs, and businesses need to tailor these concepts to their specific needs. A modern data infrastructure will probably implement ETLT (Extract, Transform, Load, Transform). Using this pattern, after executing fundamental transformations, such as removing personally identifiable information, the ingested data gets loaded into a data lake or a cloud-native data warehouse. Subsequent transformations are then executed in the data lake or warehouse, resulting in datasets ready for reporting and further analysis.

---

[1] *http://getdbt.com*

■ 3.2 Data Ingestion and Integration

Most businesses capture data from a variety of sources. Depending on the sector you work in, these sources can vary widely. Some examples can be raw sensor data in a factory, website clickstream logs in an online business, stock market data for financial institutions, or radiology image data for healthcare facilities. These data sources incorporate different data formats, and data arrives at different velocities. Some data, like image data, may arrive as JPG images, which will be uploaded to a server every night and might only consist of a few hundred images per day. Other sources, like sensor data, can arrive in real-time in a volume of tens of thousands of data points per second. These three factors, Variety, Velocity, and Volume are called the Three Vs of big data.

When building a Data Architecture, our first goal is to capture all the data from these sources and store them in reliable storage systems. Then, in the integration step, we consolidate them and load them into technologies like data lakes and data warehouses, which provide instruments for these data points to be connected and analyzed.

3.2.1 Data Sources

The number and variety of sources from which businesses may capture data is virtually unlimited. Here we will discuss some of the most widely used data source types.

3.2.1.1 REST APIs

Among commercial online services, REST APIs are probably the most common technologies for data exchange. Technically speaking, a REST API is an API endpoint supporting HTTP commands, which help the systems upload, retrieve, and manipulate datasets. An excellent example of a REST API is the API of Twitter. Computer programs can connect to Twitter through this programmatic API to retrieve and publish tweets, and search for hashtags.

Some other popular technologies communicating through REST APIs include:

- **Google Analytics, a website analytics service:** You can retrieve website visit related reports programmatically for your website.
- **Facebook:** Get data about you and your friends, publish status updates, retrieve posts from businesses, and so on.
- **Skyscanner:** Search flights programmatically.
- **Yahoo finance:** Retrieve information about stocks and quotes.

3.2.1.2 Sensor Data – OPC Unified Architecture

In an industrial setting, sensor data is frequently passed around in real-time using the OPC Unified Architecture (OPC UA) protocol. This industrial automation standard offers a secure and open machine-to-machine communication protocol. Sensors and sensor data consumer products (such as Manufacturing Execution Systems) implement OPC UA to have a standard way of real-time communication and sensor data ingestion.

3.2.1.3 Data Warehouses and Databases

Many times, third-party data sources are external databases or data warehouses. In these cases, systems can connect to these databases and extract data using the SQL language. Most databases provide an SQL service endpoint using Open Database Connectivity (ODBC), an open standard for inter-database communication. With the help of ODBC, data platforms can easily connect to external databases and retrieve data.

3.2.1.4 FTP Servers and File Shares

Among the most straightforward data-sharing solutions are FTP servers and other file-sharing solutions. Data providers upload data, such as CSV files, to these services periodically, and data consumers check for new files, download, and integrate them.

3.2.2 Traditional File Formats

3.2.2.1 Plain Logs

Probably the most straightforward data format you will encounter are plain log files. Log files are generated by various applications, including websites, mobile apps, and signal processing components. Log files usually record an event in plain-text form. An example of a log file can be the web server's log, which records every HTTP request sent by the visitors' browser. Here is an example log event from a webserver's log file:

```
22.29.221.79 - - [6/Oct/2021:13:17:10 +0000] "GET /search?term=datascience HTTP/2.0"
200 5316 "https://mywebsite.com/?search?term=datascience" "Mozilla/5.0 (Windows NT
6.1) AppleWebKit/537.36 (KHTML, like Gecko) Chrome/72.0.3626.119 Safari/537.36"
"2.75"
```

As you can see, in this example, the webserver recorded an HTTP request on 6 October 2021 where a visitor searched for the term *datascience* on the website. These events are written to a file, each event in a new line.

Advantages:

- Very easy to capture events: no need to structure the data at the time of writing.
- Easy to read for the human eye.

Disadvantages:

- It is plain text: There is no pre defined structure in the file. If you want to integrate this into a data warehouse, you will need to extract the relevant information from every line.
- As no structure is enforced, this format is prone to errors.

3.2.2.2 CSV

The most common form of storing tabular data is comma-separated value (CSV) files. A CSV file consists of an optional header and a set of columns delimited (usually) by a comma. Here is an example showing registrants of a website:

```
registration_time, email, ip_address, age, country
2021-10-09 15:21:02, registrant1@gmail.com,14.3.221.170,42,AT
2021-10-09 15:24:10, registrant2@gmail.com,132.33.21.154,42,DE
2021-10-09 15:48:47, registrant3@gmail.com,233.0.143.7,42,HU
```

You can see straight away that there are four columns as indicated in the header line, and the records follow in a structured way. CSVs are very popular, yet they also have several shortcomings.

Advantages:

- Probably the most popular format for storing data.
- Virtually every data-processing technology supports CSVs.
- Easy to read for the human eye.

Disadvantages:

- Text-based format: This uses a lot of disk space.
- Prone to errors: As an example, a single value that contains an unexpected comma or new line character can break the entire structure.
- No explicit schema: Even though the column names are usually provided in the first line, the type of the columns, such as whether a column contains numeric or text values, isn't indicated anywhere.
- CSVs can't natively store complex structures, like lists or images.

3.2.2.3 XML

The Extensible Markup Language (XML) – a 25-year-old file format developed to store structured data – is still quite widespread, even though its presence is mostly fueled by old legacy systems. The main goal of XML was to create a file format which can store arbitrarily complex data records and yet is both human- and machine-readable. The XML format stores every data element between a start tag and an end tag, and tags can be nested inside each other. Here is a quick example for storing the registrants of a website in XML:

```
<registrants>
  <registrant>
    <registration_time>2021-10-09 15:21:02</registration_time>
    <email>registrant1@gmail.com</email>
    <ip_address>14.3.221.170</ip_address>
    <age>42</email>
    <country>AT</country>
  </registrant>
  <registrant>
    <registration_time>2021-10-09 15:24:10</registration_time>
    <email>registrant2@gmail.com</email>
    <ip_address>132.33.21.154</ip_address>
    <age>42</email>
    <country>DE</country>
  </registrant>
  ...
</registrants>
```

Advantages:

- Virtually every data-processing technology supports XMLs or has third-party support for them.
- Relatively easy-to-read for the human eye.
- Can store complex data objects.

Disadvantages:

- A very verbose text-based format: It uses a lot of disk space and is slow to process by applications.
- Even though every XML element has its own name, no explicit schema is defined.
- Going out of fashion: Data applications tend to replace XML-based data formats with more modern ones like JSON or Parquet.

3.2.3 Modern File Formats

3.2.3.1 JSON

The JavaScript Object Notation (JSON) is an open-standard file format for storing structured data. It originates from JavaScript, a popular language for web applications, even though the JSON format is language-agnostic. It is a popular format, which is well-supported in virtually every data processing technology out there. JSON offers a straightforward way to store key-value pairs and lists in a text-based format. It is easy to write and read by applications. A sequence of JSON objects – called JSON lines – is usually used for storing multiple records in a single file. A simple example of a JSON lines file would look like this:

```
{ "registration_time": "2021-10-09 15:21:02", "email": "registrant1@gmail.com", … }
{ "registration_time": "2021-10-09 15:24:10", "email": "registrant1@gmail.com", … }
```

Advantages:

- Most data-processing technologies support JSON; it is one of the standard formats of storing data today.
- Relatively easy-to-read for the human eye.
- Able to store complex data objects.

Disadvantages:

- A text-based format: It uses a lot of disk space, and it is slow to process by applications.
- Even though every JSON element has its own name, the JSON format doesn't define an explicit schema.

3.2.3.2 Parquet

Parquet was developed to address many of the disadvantages and limitations of the file formats mentioned above. It is a highly efficient, open-source file format optimized for high-speed data analytics, and works well with large and complex data sets, too. Parquet is widely adopted, and is often considered the go-to format for cloud-native data warehouses, data lake technologies, and big data tools.

Parquet boasts several features which support high-performance analytical capabilities at scale. For example:

- **It has an explicit schema encoded into the data file:** Parquet stores a metadata record in the data file itself, which defines the structure of the data it contains. There is no need to read through a whole Parquet file to infer its schema.

- **Parquet is a compressed format:** Instead of storing the data as text, such as CSV and JSON, Parquet uses data encoding algorithms to store the data in compressed format. Not only does this compression increases processing speeds, but it also decreases cloud computational costs, since many cloud technologies charge based on the amount of data scanned per query.

- **It is a columnar storage format:** The Parquet file stores data in columns instead of rows. This is called the columnar storage format[2]. As a result, querying and filtering data takes less time compared to traditional file formats, as the Parquet reader doesn't need to read through complete rows to extract values for individual columns.

- **Parquet stores internal statistics:** Batches of the data are stored in blocks, and Parquet calculates and stores statistics about the records contained in these blocks. These statistics enable the Parquet reader to skip reading irrelevant blocks of the Parquet file when filtering data.

One caveat when working with Parquet is that you won't be able to manipulate records. The same concepts that make Parquet highly performant for data analytics hinder its ability to update or delete records quickly. However, some solutions, like Lakehouses and the Delta Lake format, mitigate these limitations.

Advantages:

- One of the fastest formats available for data analytics.
- Provides an explicit schema for the data stored.
- Uses little disk space compared to text-based formats such as CSV and JSON.
- Widely supported across data lake tools and big data technologies.
- Supports the storage of complex data types.

Disadvantages:

- No support for updating or deleting records.

3.2.3.3 Delta Lake

The Delta Lake is an open-source technology built on top of Parquet. It stores the data in a set of files called a Delta Table. Delta Tables are extend Parquet files by adding advanced techniques, which mitigate many of the limitations of the Parquet format:

- **Updates and Deletes:** A Delta Table permits updating and deleting records.
- **Schema Evolution:** The schema of a Delta Table can be easily updated.
- **Transactions:** Support for concurrent reading and writing of the data by multiple sources.

---

[2] To learn more about the columnar storage format, visit *https://parquet.apache.org*

- **Time Travel:** With every append, update, or delete, the previous version of the Delta Table is kept in the Delta Lake. This way, no data is lost through accidental deletes or updates, and you can always access earlier versions of your dataset.

Advantages:

- Database-like features and guarantees.
- Many advanced features like Time Travel and Schema Evolution.

Disadvantages:

- Somewhat slower than Parquet when working with small datasets.
- Delta Lake is only supported by two technologies: Apache Spark and Databricks.

3.2.4 Summary

Depending on the use case, you may have a plethora of data sources and file formats to work with. Some of the basic file formats, like plain log files, Excel files, CSVs, or XMLs, are hard to avoid due to their popularity and their frequent use in legacy systems. If you have the freedom of choosing the file formats to use, picking a format that provides a built-in schema and high-performance, like Parquet or Delta Lake, can go a long way. One of the lowest hanging fruits for analytical purposes is to convert the data you ingest into a high-performant analytical format. Pick the Delta Lake if you work with Apache Spark or Databricks and pick the Parquet format if you use other tools. Not only will these technologies make your life easier with schema guarantees and other advanced features, but they can also increase the performance of your data pipeline by a magnitude compared to using formats like CSVs, XML, or JSON for data analytics.

Don't forget that you don't necessarily need to deal with these formats directly. Several technologies exist to help you manage metadata, keep your data organized, or to use SQL to query the file formats discussed in this chapter, like the Lakehouse technologies.

■ 3.3 Data Warehouses, Data Lakes, and Lakehouses

Now that we have discussed the different file formats that fuel today's data analytics technologies, let's look at the modern data warehouse and data lake landscape.

3.3.1 Data Warehouses

You might be familiar with data warehouses (often referred to as DWs or DWHs) as they have been around since the 1960s. Data warehousing is a technology used for reporting and data analytics. The data warehouse is a database that is implemented and organized in a way that enables high-performance analytics. DWHs tend to use column-based storage formats (formats built on the same concepts as Parquet) to enable the highest possible performance for analytical workloads. The storage technologies DWHs use are usually specific to the data warehouse technology, in order to enable tight integration between the storage and the compute/analytics component of the DWH. Data warehouses host tables with complex data types, but they are generally unable to store unstructured data, such as images. The standard language to communicate with a data warehouse is SQL.

A DWH is a specialized technology for accomplishing a single task very well: High-performant data transformation and analytics through SQL. It is probably the best solution to use for reporting and dashboarding purposes; a well-structured DWH can calculate the results of simple analytical queries required for business reports in well under one second. This performance is an excellent fit for business dashboards, where dozens of reports must be displayed within a few seconds.

From an architectural point of view, we can differentiate two dimensions of data warehouses: on-prem versus cloud-based, and cloud warehouses with or without external table support.

3.3.1.1 On-prem vs. Cloud-based Data Warehouses

A traditional data warehouse is a piece of database software that runs either on the computer appliance provided by the DWH's vendor or on commodity computers. The most prominent on-prem data warehouse vendors today are IBM, Teradata, and Oracle.

Advantages of on-prem data warehouses:

- Control: You have complete control over how you configure and operate the DWH. If you use commodity hardware, you have complete control over how much and what kind of storage and compute capacity and memory you provide to your workloads.

- Governance: As you have complete control over the DWH, regulatory compliance is often easier to achieve than with cloud-based solutions. You know exactly where and how the data is stored, and you have total control over both the hardware and the software.

- Speed: As you have complete control over the properties of the DWH servers and the network infrastructure around them, a fine-tuned on-prem DWH solution can have optimal performance characteristics.

Disadvantages of on-prem data warehouses:

- Total Cost of Ownership (TCO): The TCO of an on-prem DWH can outweigh its benefits. You need DWH engineers, system administrators, and network engineers to ensure that the DWH is up and running, well maintained, and up-to-date. Also, you need to purchase and maintain the hardware the DWH runs on.

- Hard to scale: On-prem DWHs run on a fixed number of computers. As the workload or your data grows, quickly adding more storage and computing capacity to the warehouse might be cumbersome; new PCs need to be purchased, which means procurement processes must be passed.

- Upfront cost: To get started, you need to acquire a license from the data warehouse vendor, buy the PCs or the appliances and hire the right professionals to maintain your DWH.

If decreasing upfront cost, getting to a more predictable TCO, or the ability to scale is among your priorities, cloud-based offerings are here to the rescue. Every major cloud provider offers data warehousing services with predictable pricing and great scalability options. The traditional design of a cloud data warehouse is like an on-prem DWH: It consists of a set of computers you rent and pay an hourly fee to use. Most of the cloud-based DWH systems are designed to scale well. They usually incorporate a leader node you connect to and several compute nodes that do the analytics. As the workload increases, you can simply request more compute nodes be added to the DWH cluster. Changing the cluster size takes from a few minutes up to a few hours. You can see the design of such a data warehouse architecture in Figure 3.6.

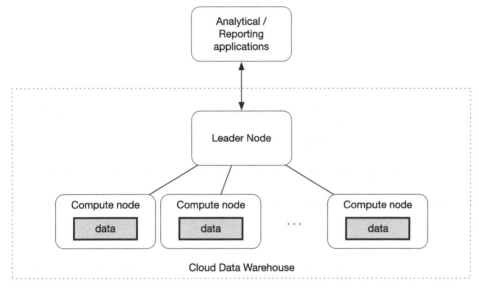

Figure 3.6 Typical cloud-based data warehouse design

Advantages of cloud-based DWH systems:

- TCO: As you usually pay an hourly fee for the computers used, your TCO is easy to calculate.
- Scalability: Scaling a DWH by adding computers comes with a click of a mouse.
- Low maintenance requirements: Cloud data warehouses come with automatic security updates, and they are designed to operate with minimal maintenance work.
- You can start small: It is cheap to start with a single-computer data warehouse instance in the cloud without any hardware investment. You only need to scale the DWH to production size once you are convinced that it satisfies all your requirements.

Disadvantages of cloud-based DWH systems:

- Lack of total control: Even though cloud providers try to give you as much control over your DWH as possible, you don't own the DWHs hardware and you can't fully customize how it works. You have no other option but to rely on the work of the cloud provider's security engineers to keep your data safe.

The best-known cloud-based data warehouse solutions are Amazon AWS Redshift and Azure Synapse Analytics.

3.3.1.2 External Table Support in Data Warehouses

There are some disadvantages of the classic DWH design, regardless of whether it runs on-prem or in the cloud:

- You pay for the compute nodes even if you don't use them. If your data sets are large, you need to rent more nodes to accommodate the volume of data required, even when you don't need the compute capacity of these computers. The same applies vice-versa: If you have a high analytical workload, but the data you manage is relatively tiny, you need to keep paying for a fleet of nodes to match the computational needs, but much of the data-storage capabilities of your DWH can remain underutilized.

- We've seen that cloud solutions offer excellent scalability: you can add or remove computers from the warehouse as needed. However, even this design is unable to react to peak workloads. What happens when you need peak capacity for only a few hours? Adding compute nodes to a large traditional cloud-based DWH might take hours, and the DWH might be inaccessible through parts of the rescaling process.

The solution for overcoming these limitations lies in external tables. The concept of external tables partly decouples the storage component from the compute component in the warehouse. Excess datasets, which can be in any popular format, like Parquet, CSV, or JSON, can be stored in a cloud object store such as Amazon S3 or Azure Blob Storage. . That is, the datasets won't reside on the DWH computers; data volume is stored and scaled completely independently from them. Once you register the excess datasets as external tables, they will integrate very well with the traditional tables of the data warehouse. Practically speaking, you won't see a difference when querying the external tables versus traditional DWH tables.

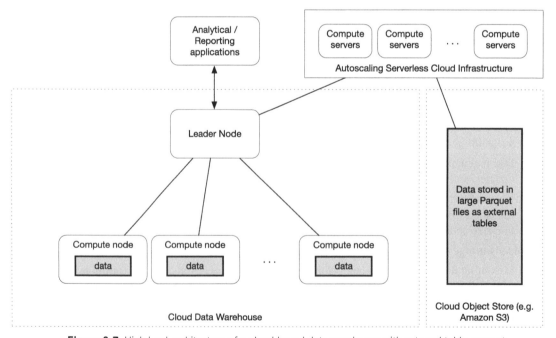

Figure 3.7 High-level architecture of a cloud-based data warehouse with external table support

The trick in these solutions is that most analytical queries executed against external tables are executed on a serverless service independent of your data warehouse. Serverless technologies are fully managed cloud services. The cloud provider manages the infrastructure behind serverless services. You don't need to worry about any of the architecture or the management aspects of the service. In the DHW case, you only pay for the resources you use while your query is running. This way, you can scale your data storage without paying for extra DWH instances. You can also use external tables for managing peak capacity as the processing time of queries executed on external tables doesn't increase as the analytical workload increases. A design of such an architecture is shown in Figure 3.7.

As you see, integrating external tables into data warehouses solves some of the problems traditional DWH solutions encounter. However, they still fall short on processing unstructured or semi-structured data or reacting quickly to peak load for every table. Data lakes and the data lakehouse concept solve some of these problems. We will discuss this in the next chapter.

3.3.2 Data Lakes and the Lakehouse

Data Lakes

As we saw in the previous chapter, storing data in a data warehouse poses a few problems, such as the inability to store unstructured, data-like images. As a response to this problem, in the mid-2010s, the concept of the data lake emerged. To put it simply, the data lake is nothing more than a repository, which can store all kinds of data both in its raw format and in a more cleansed and ready to analyze way, using formats such as Parquet. Practically speaking, you can think of a data lake as a standard file system that scales very well. For on-prem use-cases, the Hadoop Distributed File System is usually used as a data lake. For cloud-based use-cases, the object stores of cloud providers are used, such as Amazon S3, the Azure Blob Storage, or the Azure data lake.

You need to remember that data lakes are merely data storage technologies; hence, unlike data warehouses, they don't have an integrated compute component. This is also an advantage: modern cloud-based data-processing technologies completely decouple the compute component from the storage component. The data is stored in the data lake, and you can scale the number of compute instances independently, depending on your actual workload. This way, if your analytical workload is low, you won't need to pay for many machines. In peak capacity periods, it is effortless to scale up the compute layer to dozens or even hundreds of computers within a matter of minutes. Some solutions, like AWS Redshift Spectrum's external tables or Google's BigQuery, don't even require you to manage compute capacities. The cloud provider takes care of that: the execution of analytical queries is managed internally by the serverless components, meaning they are executed within seconds, regardless of how high the workload on your data lake is. You pay for the number of records scanned while your query was executing. Other data platform offerings, such as Databricks or Snowflake, provide you with the ability to store all your data in a cloud data lake and only use the analytical clusters they provide when you want to work with the data. You are free to decide how big a compute cluster you want to use on both platforms, and you can quickly upscale and downscale these clusters as your workload changes, only paying for the resources you use.

Several solutions integrate with data lakes and offer data warehouse-like services, both using compute instances or serverless technologies:

Technology	Vendor	Description
AWS Redshift Spectrum	Amazon	Amazon Redshift can be extended to work on Parquet files (and other formats) located on S3 through external tables.
Azure Synapse Serverless	Microsoft	Like in Redshift Spectrum, external tables can be created on top of files located on Azure Blob Storage and Azure Data Lake Storage and queried through Azure's serverless component.
BigQuery	Google	Google's serverless data warehouse solution stores the files in its internal data format. You import all the data to BigQuery and analyze it there.
Snowflake	Snowflake	A data warehouse solution that stores the data in an object store (such as Amazon S3, Azure Storage, or Google Cloud Storage) and provides advanced, SQL-based analytical capabilities on top of it.
Delta Lake	Databricks	Databrick's data lake solution uses the Delta Lake format to enable fast analytical capabilities on the object store of every major cloud provider, such as Amazon, Azure, and Google.
Athena	Amazon	Amazon's serverless solution creates external tables on top of files located on S3 and queries them through SQL.
Presto	The Presto Foundation	An open-source solution for analyzing data through SQL. Presto supports multiple data formats, like Parquet, CSV, and JSON, and it supports both cloud-based and on-prem data lakes.
Apache Spark	The Apache Foundation	An open-source solution for transforming and analyzing data and training machine learning models on top of a data lake. Apache Spark supports several file formats and works both on-prem and in the cloud.
Apache Hive	The Apache Foundation	An open-source solution for analyzing data lake data through SQL. It has similar functionalities to Presto and is usually used in traditional Hadoop installations.

3.3.2.1 The Lakehouse

As you can see, there are several solutions to analyze data in data lakes. However, many of the file formats used in these data lakes lack critical features for production workloads, such as data catalogs, fine-grained access management support, transactions, concurrent reads and writes, schema enforcement, and schema evolution. Vendors like Databricks and Snowflake implemented a set of technologies to mitigate these issues. Systems using these technologies are called lakehouses.

The properties of a lakehouse:

- **Cost-efficient storage:** All the data is stored in cloud storage services, providing cost-efficient data storage.

- **Transaction support:** ACID Transactions are supported to ensure consistency between concurrent reads and writes of the same tables.

- **Catalog:** The schema and the location of external tables in the data lake are stored in a Lakehouse metastore to analyze these datasets efficiently.

- **Schema Evolution:** The schema of the tables can be modified without making a copy of the whole dataset.

- **Data Governance:** Fine-grained tools are available for authentication and authorization of data access.

- **BI Support:** Open Database Connectivity (ODBC), a standard API for accessing databases, is provided so various BI tools can connect to the Lakehouse and execute SQL queries against it.

3.3.3 Summary: Comparing Data Warehouses to Lakehouses

At first glance, Lakehouses are just like data warehouses. They manage tables that can be queried through SQL, and they come with transaction support and fine-grained permission management. However, as we saw, the technologies underpinning traditional DWHs significantly differ from Lakehouses, making them suitable for different use-cases.

Advantages of data warehouses:

- They provide tight integration between the data and the compute component, enabling low-latency responses to analytical queries.

- As DWHs store the data in specialized formats, advanced DWH design capabilities like multiple indexes, foreign keys, and many database-specific optimizations are available.

Advantages of Lakehouses:

- The compute and the storage are completely decoupled: You only pay for the storage you need and the compute you use.

- Scalability: As Lakehouses are built on the top of cloud data lakes, they scale exceptionally well and have no problem analyzing massive data sets.

- Elasticity: The compute capacity of the data lakes can be drastically increased or decreased in a matter of minutes. This way, they can react very well to peak workloads.

- They can store any kind of structured or unstructured data: Lakehouses support tabular data, images, voice recordings, videos, and several file formats like Parquet, CSV, and JSON.

All in all, DWHs are great for low-latency workloads, especially for reporting and dashboarding. Lakehouses are great for more general data science and data transformation workloads where low latency is not a priority, but scalability is.

■ 3.4 Data Processing and Transformation

In the earlier sections we saw that several technologies support ingesting, integrating, and storing data. Some of these technologies, like data warehouses, come with built-in data processing components, while others, like data lakes, don't. In most use-cases, you won't be able to avoid using a dedicated data processing technology at at least one stage of your data architecture. Several traditional open-source technologies are available for single-machine transformations and analytics, such as Linux bash utilities, the R language, or Pandas, a Python library for data processing. Running on a single machine makes a data architecture relatively easy to maintain; However, it also comes with several challenges:

- Having all the data processing logic on a single computer makes the workflow prone to errors. The failure of your computer will make the whole infrastructure unavailable.

- As the amount of data grows, you can end up in a situation where you can't scale your computer anymore by adding more CPU or memory. The resources needed by the data transformation jobs might outgrow the data processing capabilities, leading to excessive data processing times.

- Even if you can process all your data on a single computer today and you have a large margin for upgrading the hardware, you might get to a point where you see that you will outgrow a single computer soon. In this case, it can be cumbersome to reimplement all the data processing workflow in a technology that scales well.

Fortunately, a few data processing technologies work very well on a single computer and then effortlessly scale to multiple computers when needed. The most versatile technology for large-scale data processing is Apache Spark, which has become the de-facto scalable data processing technology in the past years.

3.4.1 Big Data & Apache Spark

Apache Spark is a unified analytics engine framework for large-scale data processing. It was open-sourced in 2010, and it has been undergoing very active development since.

3.4.1.1 Architecture

Spark has a multi-layered architecture where several components interact with each other to accomplish large-scale data processing tasks. A simplified Spark architecture is shown in Figure 3.8.

At the foundation of Spark is Spark Core. Spark Core is responsible for supervising the compute nodes, taking care of data passing between the nodes, and managing the execution of distributed data processing algorithms.

One of Spark's "unified" aspects is that it provides you a unified view of different file systems, data lakes, and external databases. Also, it gives you a standard set of commands to work across different formats. Spark supports many file formats out of the box, such as CSV, JSON, Parquet, and plain text files. The supported input sources include local filesystems, HDFS, S3, Azure Blob Storage, HBase, Cassandra, and external databases through JDBC.

Several other file formats and input sources are supported through external libraries, including XML, AVRO, Apache Kafka, Redshift, Azure Synapse, MongoDB, and Elasticsearch.

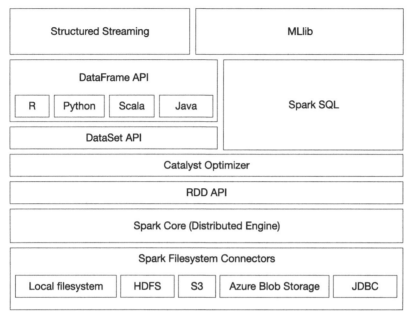

Figure 3.8 A high-level architecture of Apache Spark

There are three APIs for communicating with Spark:

- **The DataFrame API:** As the highest-level of the three, the central concept of this API is the DataFrame, which is a table-like abstraction. The DataFrame API is the most optimized, used and developed API, and should be your standard choice when you use Spark.

- **The RDD API:** Spark's low-level API, which you can think of as the "assembly language" of the system. The other APIs internally use it, but it is hard to use directly and takes much effort to write performant code. If you are new to Spark, you most probably want to stay away from this API.

- **The DataSet API:** This is Spark's data engineering-focused API, which gives you strong type guarantees when you develop Spark applications. This API is only accessible in Scala but not in Python. It is used internally by Spark regardless of your choice of language. Use this API if you need better compile-time error reporting during Spark application development, but only if you are also an advanced Spark user: You need to have an excellent understanding of Spark internals to use this API efficiently.

Using Spark's DataFrame API is the best choice in most use-cases.

Spark provides an SQL API too. With the SQL API, you can write pure SQL code to process and transform datasets. Both the DataFrame API and the SQL API are highly optimized with the help of Spark's internal optimizer, Catalyst.

When it comes to programming language choices, Spark supports four languages out of the box:

- **Scala:** Most of the Spark code is written in Scala, a functional programming language which runs on the Java Virtual Machine, just as Java does. As Scala is the native language of Spark, every Spark feature is accessible through this API. One of the advantages of using Scala is having access to the DataSet API if type guarantees are a priority in your use case.

- **Java:** As Java uses the Java Virtual Machine for executing code, just as Scala does, there are many similarities between these two APIs. You might want to use the Java API if your primary expertise lies in Java and if you don't plan to use Spark for exploratory analysis. Notebook environments used for data exploration, such as Jupyter or Zeppelin, don't support Java.

- **Python:** The Spark Python API is quite advanced. On top of accessing all the features Spark offers through the DataFrame API, the Spark Python API has close integration with Pandas, Python's de-facto single-computer data analytics tool. Through the Python API, you can convert between Pandas DataFrames and Spark DataFrames and execute Pandas functions at scale.

- **R:** Spark natively supports R, one of the major statistical languages. The R API seems to be a bit of an outlier in the Spark ecosystem since, even though it has been closing the gap, it is lagging behind in comparison with the other language APIs when it comes to what Spark functionality it can access.

All in all, if you have a data engineering heavy use-case, you might want to consider the Scala API, and if you are unsure which language to choose or are new to Spark, use Python.

3.4.1.2 Driver and Executors

A Spark cluster consists of two kinds of computers: A single management node, called the driver, and one or more data-processing nodes, called the executors. The relationship between these components is displayed in Figure 3.9.

The driver acts as the manager of the whole cluster. It processes the commands executed by the Spark user and coordinates the distributed data processing of the executors. There is always a single driver node in a Spark application, and it doesn't do any distributed data processing.

The executors are the workhorses of a Spark application. They are responsible for reading and processing the data and exchanging any necessary information to accomplish the distributed computation. The number of executors in a Spark application has no practical upper limit: Facebook reportedly uses a cluster exceeding two thousand computers. The executors consist of cores, which are the basic compute units of Spark. You can think of them as if they were CPU cores on a computer. This architecture provides two parallelization layers: there are multiple executors in a cluster, and each executor has multiple cores. These two layers add up to the total processing capability of your cluster; for example, three executors, each with two cores, resulting in a six-core application. A six-core application means that Spark can execute six tasks in parallel.

Reading from different data sources is also accomplished in a distributed way. Spark will split the input source into partitions and process these partitions in parallel. The default partition size is around 100 megabytes, a conveniently sized piece of data for a single task to process. These partitions are then read one by one by the Spark application cores. If the number of partitions to read exceeds the number of cores available, partitions are put in a queue and processed one after the other. As the processing proceeds, the executors exchange data and statistical information between each other to complete a distributed computation.

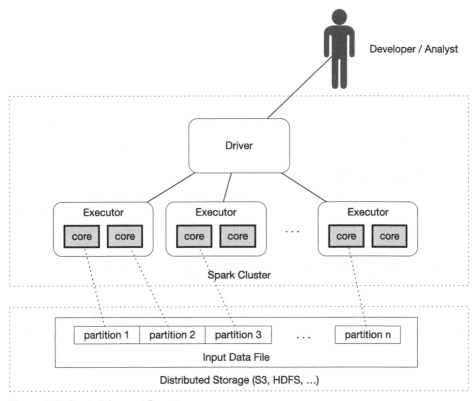

Figure 3.9 Spark Driver and Executors

In a standard setting, the number of executors is determined upfront. When you start a Spark application, you tell Spark how many executors and cores you need. These resources will then be made available for you, and only then will your application be ready to use. However, if you use Spark in the cloud or in a container-orchestration system such as Kubernetes, you can use Spark's dynamic resource allocation capabilities and increase or decrease the number of executors while the Spark application is running.

3.4.1.3 Execution Modes

One of the advantages of Spark is that it runs just as well on a single computer as on a cluster of computers. It comes with several execution modes, which can be organized into four groups:

- **Local mode:** Spark's single-computer mode, in which both the driver and the executors are packaged into one computer process. In this setting, the executors are only simulated. Still, you get a full-featured Spark cluster which you can use on a single computer, like your laptop. This setting is great for development or if your data size doesn't require a multi-node Spark cluster.

- **Standalone mode:** In a standalone installation, you install Spark to a set of computers, and these computers form a cluster. Once the cluster is up and running, you can connect to the master node of your cluster and start a Spark application. If the Spark cluster's resources allow, multiple Spark applications can be executed side by side on the same Spark cluster.

- **Containerized mode:** Spark integrates well with container-orchestration tools, such as Kubernetes, Mesos, or YARN. Using such systems enables you to share the computational resources between Spark applications and other workloads on your cluster.

- **Proprietary Executions modes:** Some companies, such as Databricks, offer proprietary Spark solutions. The main benefit of these is that they have optimizations implemented on top of Apache Spark.

3.4.1.4 DataFrame API

As we discussed earlier, the most common and most optimized API for communicating with a Spark application is the DataFrame API. This API builds on top of the abstraction of the DataFrame, which is a lazily evaluated and immutable data table. A DataFrame has the following characteristics:

- **Data-table like:** A DataFrame is just like any database table. It has a schema, it has records, and it supports the standard data transformations such as selecting, filtering, grouping, and joining data along with several data-manipulation functions.

- **It is lazy:** One of the special features of Spark compared to traditional solutions is laziness: Spark will only read the data and do the processing at the latest point in time possible. When you read from a file, only the file's schema will be read, and Spark will allow you to do all the transformations without reading the file's contents. Once you are finished executing a set of transformations, such as filtering the data and joining it with other datasets, and you want to print the results to the screen or write the results to the disk, only then will Spark read the contents of the data sources and execute the transformations. This feature is essential in a big data processing setting: your datasets might be hundreds of terabytes large, but only a tiny fraction of the input data might need to be read for computing the result of a specific transformation.

- **DataFrames are immutable:** In Spark, you never modify a DataFrame. Applying an operation, such as a filter, always creates a new DataFrame. This concept is harmless because of Spark's lazy nature: DataFrames don't store physical data. Immutability is required for Spark's optimizer: it can review all the transformations to be executed and optimize them before the physical processing starts.

To show some of the capabilities of the DataFrame API, let's use an example of a Python Spark code, which reads a Parquet file, filters it and writes some records back to disk. The example dataset we are using here is the one we introduced in Section 3.2.2.2.

```
01  from pyspark.sql.functions import col
02
03  registrants_df = spark.read.parquet('/data/input/registrants.parquet')
04  above_40_df = registrants.filter(col('age') > 40)
```

```
05   names_40_df = above_40_df.select("registration_time", "email")
06   names_40_df.write.parquet("/data/output/above_40.parquet")
```

Besides its usability characteristics, the main advantage of the DataFrame API is that it comes with Catalyst, Spark's logical optimizer. Before an action is executed, such as the *write* command in the example above, the transformation steps are optimized. Even in this simple case, as we are using the Parquet format, the Catalyst Optimizer can push down the filter condition to the Parquet reader and instruct the Parquet reader to read the age, *registration_time*, and *email* columns only.

3.4.1.5 Structured Streaming

One of the significant components of Spark deals with real-time data. While the basic concepts of working with real-time data are beyond the scope of this book, the general idea is simple: Instead of executing computations in batches, you create a continuously running processing component that ingests, transforms, stores, or reports on the data as soon as it arrives into the system.

Spark tackles the real-time data processing tasks with a component called Structured Streaming. The advantage of this component is that it is fully accessible through the Data-Frame API, and it works using the same abstractions as a static Spark application. This abstraction is called the Streaming DataFrame. A Streaming DataFrame acts just like a DataFrame, but in a real-time setting. You can apply the same set of transformations, such as selecting, filtering, grouping, and joining data. The results of your transformation will be updated in real-time.

Let's assume we have a web application that sends registrant information into a JSON file. We want to read this file, keep only those records with a gmail.com email address and write these emails into a CSV file.

Using static DataFrame code to accomplish this on historical data would look like this:

```
01   from pyspark.sql.functions import col
02
03   registrants_df = spark.read.json('/data/registrants/2021-01-01.json')
04   gmail_df = registrants.filter(col('email').endswith('gmail.com'))
05   only_email_df = gmail_df.select('email')
06   only_email_df.write.csv('/data/output/gmail-registrants.csv')
```

Now let's see the same in a real-time setting, where we read incoming JSON files from the */data/registrants* folder as they appear and we continue writing the processed email addresses to */data/output/gmail-registrants.csv*:

```
01   from pyspark.sql.functions import col
02
03   registrants_df = spark.readStream.schema('email STRING')
04                           .json('/data/registrants/')
05   gmail_df = registrants.filter(col('email').endswith('gmail.com'))
06   only_email_df = gmail_df.select('email')
07   only_email_df.write.csv('/data/output/gmail-registrants.csv')
```

When comparing these two code pieces, you can see that the only difference is in line 7. We specified that we are reading from a stream, and we had to tell Spark which values should be picked up from the JSON file.

Many companies who ingest streaming data implement two parallel data processing pipelines. One for real-time data processing, such as monitoring the number of registrations real-time, and one for static processing, such as calculating the one hundred percent accurate value of daily registrants at the end of each day when late data points have arrived. This approach is the basis of the pattern called Lambda Architecture. As you can see, the similarity between static and streaming processing of data in Apache Spark significantly simplifies the implementation of such an architecture, as most of the code can be shared between the static and the real-time components.

3.4.1.6 Spark MLlib

Even though data transformations and ETL processes can outgrow a single computer quickly, most companies can manage their machine learning needs on a single computer. For those companies that need to scale up their machine learning capabilities, Spark provides a built-in, scalable machine learning component, MLlib. It offers two services:

- MLlib exposes a distributed machine learning framework into which any third-party machine learning software can integrate by implementing their own distributed feature engineering modules, machine learning algorithms, and evaluation metrics.

- MLlib provides a set of built-in machine learning components for feature extraction, transformation, and selection, along with a set of ready-to-use distributed machine learning algorithms.

Here is a summary of the traditional machine learning algorithms and how Spark supports them[3]:

Algorithm	Spark support
- Linear Regression - Logistic Regression - Decision Trees - Random Forests - SVM - Naïve Bayes	Built-in support is available.
Gradient Boosted Trees	Built-in support is available, however, more performant third-party MLlib implementations like XGBoost and LightGBM are available too.
Recommender Systems	ALS implementation natively supported.
Clustering	K-Means, LDA, GMM, PIC natively supported.
Neural networks	Distributed TensorFlow models with Keras are supported through the Horovod project[4].
H2O algorithms	Available through H2O's Spark component, Sparkling Water.
AutoML	Available through H2O and as a proprietary offering in Databricks.

---

[3] For a complete list of the supported algorithms please refer to the Spark MLlib documentation at *https://spark.apache.org/mllib/*
[4] *https://horovod.ai/*

3.4.2 Databricks

It is worth highlighting a software as a service solution, Databricks. Created by the original authors of Apache Spark, Databricks features an optimized version of Apache Spark, integrated into a unified platform for data engineering and analytics. Many of the advanced and high-performance Spark features are offered in Databricks before they are released as open-source Spark code. A screenshot of the Databricks notebook environment can be found in Figure 3.10.

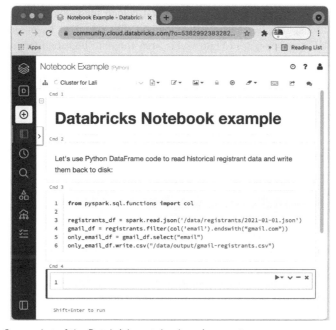

Figure 3.10 Screenshot of the Databricks notebook environment

Databricks offers several features based upon Apache Spark, including:

- An optimized version of Spark and a Spark Cluster management component: Databricks works with Amazon Web Services, Microsoft Azure, and Google Cloud and offers cloud-native improvements of Spark, such as autoscaling, auto terminating clusters, and the ability to use spot instances, a cheaper version of cloud computers.

- A Notebook environment: A full-featured notebook environment is offered with advanced collaboration features like notebook version control, co-editing notebooks, and Google Docs-like commenting.

- A command-line interface and a Python API are provided to interact with Notebooks, Clusters, and Spark Jobs.

- Databricks is the original creator of the lakehouse concept, and it features advanced proprietary Delta Lake features, like the auto-optimization of Delta Tables.

- MLflow, a machine learning model lifecycle management and model registry solution, is tightly integrated into the platform.[5]

---

[5] MLflow is also available as an open-source project at *https://mlflow.org/*

■ 3.5 Workflow Orchestration

Once you have all the tools and capabilities to store, transform and analyze the data, workflow orchestration tools help manage the data flow in your architecture. They connect the pieces from data collection through transformation through to making the data ready for analytics.

The goal of a workflow orchestration tool is to organize both your existing data and any new data you ingest. They ensure that new data is integrated and that every transformation in your data pipeline is executed on a schedule and in a meaningful order. Orchestration tools usually maintain a Directed Acyclic Graph (DAG), which manages the dependencies between different jobs, and they execute the jobs one after the other based on the DAG. An example of a DAG can be seen in Figure 3.11: first, the data ingestion steps are executed, followed by the integration and the warehousing/reporting steps.

Figure 3.11 An example DAG in an Azure Data Factory

Orchestration tools usually come with a built-in scheduler, which executes your DAG regularly. A common choice is a daily execution, which starts after midnight and executes the whole data pipeline. The execution frequency is highly dependent on the business case: While for many use cases, a daily schedule is sufficient, in other cases, you'll want to use more frequent executions to cater to regular reporting updates or data quality checks.

The essential features of an orchestration tool are:

- **DAG support:** As basic as it sounds, supporting a DAG and managing dependencies between jobs is essential for workflow orchestration. You can get away with a purely sequential execution of your data management jobs in the early life of a data architecture. However, as complexity grows, you will face complicated dependencies, which a good orchestrator will help you manage.

- **Parallel execution:** To scale your data workflow, parallel execution of non-dependent tasks is essential.

- **Scheduling:** The scheduler is the core of an orchestration framework. It is vital to be able to set up different schedules for various workflows and to manage historical re-loads of the data.

- **Error reporting:** A functionality with often-overlooked importance is which tools are available when things go wrong. You want to see which job failed, why it failed (i.e., looking at the output and the generated error messages and temporary files), and which other jobs were unable to start because of the failure.

- **Alerting:** When errors happen, you want to be alerted as soon as possible. Most tools come with different alerting capabilities, ranging from sending emails to firing a pager or calling the maintainer over the phone using an automated call provider.

- **Error recovery:** When jobs fail, you will need to re-execute them and execute every other job that depends on the failed job. In many cases, you will need to do this not only for the last execution period but for a longer timeframe. Re-executing all or a subset of your jobs for an extended period is common when errors are discovered days after they occur.

- **Version Control:** As you develop your workflow, and especially if you do it together with other contributors, a good version control integration, such as Git, can drastically simplify the process of tracking changes and reverting to earlier versions of the workflow when needed. Most of the popular solutions come with built-in version control support.

Fortunately, there are several solutions available which check all these requirements. Here are some of the most popular ones:

- **Apache Airflow**[6]: Probably the most widely adopted open-source orchestration tool. It has a rich feature set and many built-in connectors for interacting with technologies such as Snowflake and Databricks. You implement your workflow as Python code, so some coding experience is needed, and you can use a version control system of your preference to track the workflow's Python files. Airflow is open-source and self-hosted, although Amazon Web Services offers a managed version of Airflow. You can see a screenshot of an example airflow DAG in Figure 3.12.

- **Prefect**[7]: A young orchestration framework. Open-source, and just like Airflow, Prefect allows you to implement your workflow in Python.

- **Dagster**[8]: Another fresh orchestration solution. Open source and Python-based, such as Prefect and Airflow.

- **Azure Data Factory**[9] **(ADF):** A fully managed workflow automation solution in Azure. ADF provides a no-code workflow orchestration solution, and it has tight integration with the services available on Azure, such as Azure Synapse and Azure Databricks. You can see a screenshot of an example DAG created in ADF in Figure 3.11.

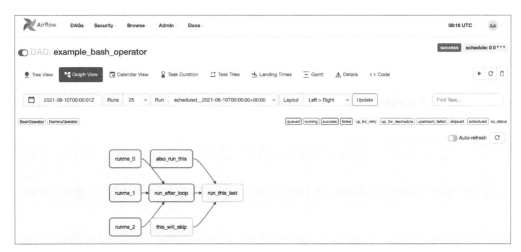

Figure 3.12 Screenshot of the Graph View in Apache Airflow

[6] http://airflow.apache.org/
[7] https://www.prefect.io/
[8] https://dagster.io/
[9] https://azure.microsoft.com/en-us/services/data-factory/

■ 3.6 A Data Architecture Use Case

In the closing section of this chapter, let's go through an example use case that features the architectural components we covered.

The Business Case

A facility automation company provides smart meters to facilities and analytics services for the data generated by these meters. Customers are facility owners and operators interested in different metrics such as water and electricity consumption.

The different roles in these settings are:

- **The facility manager:** A customer who wants to see dashboards of the consumption metrics. They expect the dashboards to be updated every hour.
- **The BI analyst:** A customer with several requirements:

  Monitor the meters via receiving daily email reports.

  Access the same dashboards as the facility manager.

  Conduct analysis on aggregate data both through a BI tool and directly in the data warehouse.

  Investigate and analyze the original record-level data in the data lake.

- **The facility ops team:** The team who takes care of the installation and registration of smart meters.

We work from two primary data sources:

- The facility ops team manages the facility and smart meter records. For historical reasons, they manage this data in an Excel file. Our internal engineering team helped create a small module that uploads this Excel file to an Azure Blob Storage when saved to disk.
- Our facilities send the smart meter data to a Sensor API. This component collects all the metrics in real-time, and it exposes a REST API through which we can download the sensor data for the requested period.

General Architecture

The general design of such an architecture is shown in Figure 3.13. The arrows represent the data flow in the system.

The facility data is available in Excel format and is automatically uploaded to the Azure Blob Storage. A Databricks Notebook is created: it reads the facility data from the Blob Storage and writes it into the Azure data lake in Delta Lake format. This dataset will store the facilities' data and the metadata about the sensors and metrics, but it won't store the actual measurements.

The measurements come from the smart meters installed in the facilities. Every smart meter sends its metrics to the *Sensor API* component, a component that is managed by our operations team. The *Sensor API* exposes a REST endpoint through which we can retrieve the measurements in JSON format.

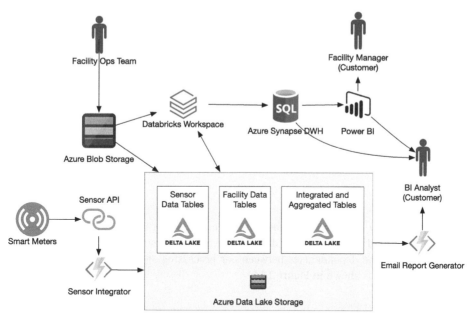

Figure 3.13 High-level architecture and data flow

We implement a *Sensor Integrator* component that connects to the *Sensor API*, retrieves the sensor data for a specified time range, and uploads it into the Azure Data Lake Storage in raw JSON format. Once finished, a Databricks job is executed to cleanse this data and write it back to the data lake in Delta Format.

We use Delta Lake on top of the Azure Data Lake Storage for sensor and facility data. The Data Lake Storage guarantees cross-region replication and high-throughput data read, so our data is kept safe, and our analysis is ready to scale if needed. The Delta Lake provides us with all the guarantees described in Section 3.3.2.2, and automatically keeps the history of the data. This means that if we run into data problems, earlier versions of both the sensor and the facility datasets can be recovered.

Once both the facility and the sensor data are in a Delta Lake format and cleansed, we are ready to join them, enriching the sensor data with facility and meter-related information. We store this final, cleansed and enriched, record-level dataset again in a Delta Table.

On top of our enriched dataset, we apply several aggregations to prepare reporting and high-level analytics. We use Databricks and Delta Lake to ensure that it will scale well even as our data grows.

As a next step, we integrate these aggregates into the Azure Synapse Data warehouse. Synapse is connected to Microsoft's Business Intelligence tool, PowerBI, in which we can create all the necessary reports and dashboards. At this stage, we use a data warehouse instead of Delta Lake because our aggregated data is small enough to use traditional technologies and because DWHs execute queries on small datasets much faster than data lakes do. A fast response time is necessary to make sure our dashboards load quickly.

Finally, we use the Serverless Python Cloud Function to generate an email report based on the aggregated tables in Delta Lake. We send this to the BI analysts once a day.

This architecture would also work well for multiple customers and facilities simultaneously. In such a scenario, we need to take care of permissions:

- Specific records in Delta Lake should only be accessed by their respective owners. You can either set up separate tables for different customers or use record-level permission management in Delta Lake.
- Multiple customers will access the same data warehouse. We can create different tables for each customer or implement record-level permission management.
- Email reports need to be sent out to multiple customers: this should be easy to implement by simply calculating the specific statistics for each customer in the *Email Report Generator.*

Orchestration

Azure Data Factory (ADF) seems a good choice for orchestrating this workflow, as we are using Azure-related technologies for data storage and processing. We create an ADF pipeline that defines the dependencies between our processing steps and schedules the data load. This pipeline is shown in Figure 3.14.

Figure 3.14 Screenshot of the workflow implemented in Azure Data Factory

The first step in the pipeline is a Copy Data activity, where the facility data is copied to the Azure Blob Storage. In parallel, we can already start integrating the sensor data with the Ingest Sensor Data step.

Once the facility data is copied, we cleanse it and integrate it into the Delta Lake. We use a Databricks Notebook as Databricks has a simple-to-use Excel reader. Also, notebook executions are very easy to debug in Databricks in case things go wrong.

Before cleansing and integrating the sensor data, we must wait for all facility data to be integrated. Sensor metrics might reference meters that were recently added to the facility Excel. In this step, we use a Databricks Notebook to read the raw JSON sensor data, cleanse it and store it in a Delta Lake format. At this point, it is essential to use a scalable technology such as Databricks or Apache Spark to make sure we can scale our processing capabilities as the number of measurements increase.

At this point, we have both data sources ingested, cleansed, and integrated into Delta Lake. Next, we create the aggregated tables and write them back to Delta Lake. This step ensures that the BI analysts will be able to read both the cleansed record level data and the aggregated data directly from Delta Lake.

In the last steps, we upload the aggregated data to the data warehouse and call an Azure Serverless Function, which checks whether the daily report has already been sent today. If not, it will read the aggregated data required for the report and send it to the BI analysts' in email.

Having set up our pipeline, we put it under Git version control in ADF's management console. We also create a trigger to execute the pipeline every 30 minutes. This schedule should be sufficient given that our service level agreement requires data to be uploaded every hour. Alerting rules can be set with Azure Communication Services[10] to ensure that our ops team receives both an SMS and an email if a pipeline execution fails.

Requirements Analysis

In Section 3.1.2, we defined the requirements of a data architecture. Let's see whether our solution checks those boxes!

- **Reliability:** All our data is stored in the Azure data lake right after ingestion. The Azure Data Lake replicates our data across various geographical regions to ensure that it is kept safe. Furthermore, Azure Data Factory, Azure Functions, and Databricks are managed solutions with reliability guarantees. We can define restore points for Azure Synapse. We have Git integration set up for ADF to quickly revert to our last working version if we break our ADF pipeline.

- **Scalability:** The number of facilities and smart meters will probably stay relatively small, below the one million record mark, which means we don't need to scale there. However, the number of metrics and data points can quickly grow and accumulate, so we must be sure to use a scalable solution for processing the sensor data. The Azure Data Lake and Databricks both scale well, so they are a good choice for this use case.

  The only bottleneck in this architecture is the Sensor Integrator. Will it ingest all the measurements in a timely fashion? The performance of this component is a risk. However, the problem is not only on the data architecture's side, as the Sensor API is a single machine REST API. We need to have our engineering team scale the API first. Only then can we implement a distributed read of the sensor data with Databricks or another scalable solution.

- **Maintainability:** We work with managed cloud solutions that are famously easy to maintain. ADF and Databricks notebooks have great debuggability and maintainability characteristics. Maintaining Azure Synapse might take some work when we store enormous datasets. However, in our case we only use it for aggregates, so we shouldn't have any problems.

---

[10] *https://docs.microsoft.com/en-us/azure/communication-services/*

■ 3.7 In a Nutshell

 Building a Data Architecture requires several decisions. Do you want to use the cloud or stay on-prem? Are there special governance requirements? How much data do you expect to process in the long term? What data formats do you want to use? What's your fault tolerance level? Let us summarize some of the best practices I've learned when designing and building data architectures:

- **Use the cloud:** Cloud solutions are designed to require zero maintenance and high reliability. Even though your service bills will be higher than the hardware costs when running your on-prem infrastructure, your total cost of ownership can drastically decrease when you use the proper cloud technologies. If you don't have a particular reason, such as governance, to stay on-prem, don't stay on-prem.
- **Use Parquet or Delta:** These modern file formats outperform traditional formats by a large margin. Not only will your data processes finish earlier, but your data will take much less space to store when you use these formats.
- **Use Python:** If you use Spark, try to start with the Python API. Python is the lingua franca of data today, so it is your safest choice.
- **Data lakes and lakehouses scale very well, but they aren't data warehouses:** Although you *can* use a data lake or a lakehouse as a data warehouse, well config- ured traditional DWHs can outperform data lakes by magnitudes when working with moderately sized datasets.
- **Consider the pros and cons of hosted big data services:** Solutions like Data- bricks add many extra performance and convenience features compared to their open-source alternatives, but they come with a relatively high price tag. Know your requirements to see which solutions work best for you.
- **Know your data size:** Are you expecting only a few hundred thousand records in total in the long term? Good for you – you won't need a scalable architecture. You can get away with traditional tools and a single node data warehouse, which will be cheaper and easier to maintain.
- **Keep the raw data safe:** Bugs in the data pipeline can lead to incorrect data and data loss. Sometimes the only option to fix data quality issues will be to re-execute the whole pipeline for an extended period from scratch, starting with the raw data. Storage has become very cheap, so make sure that you save every incoming data point in its raw format.
- **Keep it Simple:** Only use scalable tools and advanced data processing technologies if you need to. They are more challenging to maintain than simple, single-node solutions.
- **Consider single-node solutions for Machine Learning:** Single node machine learning solutions have much better performance characteristics than their distributed peers. Only use a distributed machine learning technology if you must.

References

[1]   Kleppmann, Martin: Designing Data-Intensive Applications. O'Reilly Media, Inc., 1005 Graven- stein Highway North, Sebastopol, CA 95472, 2017

4 Data Engineering

Stefan Papp, Bernhard Ortner

> *"Scientists dream about doing great things. Engineers do them."*
> James A. Michener.

Questions Answered in this Chapter:

- What is data engineering, and how does it differ from other engineering-related domains such as systems and data architecture?
- What is the working relationship between data engineers and data scientists?
- What is a data pipeline, and what is commonly required to load data on a data platform?
- Why do different systems environments enforce distinctive data pipelines?
- How can you serve and update models efficiently?

In the last chapters, we clarified that we need a systems environment and a data architecture to host data. Data engineering is about establishing processes to connect this architecture with the data of real-world applications. This discipline covers various topics, which will be explained in this chapter. Among them, data integration is about ensuring that applications load data on the data platform under defined conditions; another common interchangeable expression for this process is data ingestion. Some companies specify these conditions in a Service Level Agreement (SLA) that defines the minimum non-functional requirements, which would ensure that the system is performing its duties successfully. Another topic is managing analytical models. A data engineer is someone who automates all kinds of engineering-related tasks in data science projects that might take up 80 % of the team's time, including data cleaning. Their goal is to automate all the efforts so that the data science team can focus on their core job: to analyze data.

A data engineer is commonly a computer scientist at their core, yet they should still know about business requirements and analytical processes. They should be a solid programmer, but also possess enough infrastructure-related knowledge required to avoid performance bottlenecks. Although data platforms abstract away a lot of their complexity, a data engineer still needs to understand a lot about workflows in distributed computing, including advanced topics such as high concurrency and low latency scenarios. They also need to understand the internals of database management systems and optimize platforms for fast access, such as through indexing or partitioning.

This chapter describes the requirements, best practices, and common difficulties in developing and deploying data pipelines in production environments to ingest data. We will also address best practices to deploy, update and serve data science models.

■ 4.1 Data Integration

4.1.1 Data Pipelines

A data pipeline is a multi-step process that involves consuming data, processing it, and storing it in an aggregated form to facilitate decision support. It helps to visualize a data pipeline as an abstraction of industrial production processes. Complex products always start with raw materials such as steel, plastic or wood. Then, various production steps transform the raw material into components until they can be assembled into a consumer product. The output of one element in a production pipeline is the input of the next one.

The raw material of a data pipeline is raw data, and end products are analytical models. While in industrial processes, machines and humans transform solid material through chemical and physical processes, algorithms change input data into more refined data sets in data processing systems.

A data pipeline represents a standardized workflow for a dedicated analytical use case. Depending on the business value of a use case, data integration routines address different non-functional requirements, such as performance or robustness.

Data pipelines can work with different storage and processing technologies, and we can also categorize them historically into different eras. The data source and the structure of the data platform somewhat define the best way to design a data pipeline. One thing to consider is whether the platform utilizes a fixed schema (such as a relational database) or is schemaless (as it works with filesystems). In the first scenario, applications need to extract and then transform data before they can load into the data platform (known as "Extract-Transform-Load" or "ETL"). In the second scenario, processes can copy data onto data storage and later transform it into specific analytical data sets if needed (known as "Extract-Load-Transform", or "ELT"). The distinction between ETL and ELT is covered more deeply in Chapter 4.1.1.

Another essential consideration is data delivery. In some scenarios, data is delivered constantly as streams, and in other settings, applications process data as a batch. Streaming scenarios have different requirements than batch scenarios and require additional handling and software components. One example is a scheduling service that starts and stops jobs on demand. Batch processes need a scheduler, whereas streaming technologies can work without them.

Let's explore the different requirements on a historical level. As we do so, notice that computer engineering always abstracts from reality, meaning we can see a model as a computerized version of reality.

File Era

Files can refer to any file type, but office documents such as Word documents or Excel spreadsheets are the most common types for storing business information. Thus, these files were the first abstraction in initial digitization efforts. For example, hand-written or typed letters became documents, or shopping lists became spreadsheets.

The common practice is that applications on a single computer load files from a local hard drive, as the resources of one workstation are sufficient. Generally, a file owner does not create that file to be part of a vast data processing system or systematic querying. Thus, although spreadsheets allow basic filtering, they are not designed for complex queries.

On local file systems, business information is isolated and not accessible for everyone. In addition, files on local systems can get lost, and it is harder to apply governance processes to them. Therefore, companies often want to prevent employees from storing files on their local computers and use a central document management system instead. As an additional benefit, document management systems allow the indexing of documents to make information more transparent.

From a data processing view, business documents are unstructured or semistructured sources. On a central, accessible file system, data professionals can parse and explore them. They are, however, not the common target of data science projects.

 Excel Dilemma

In a perfect world, dedicated database management systems store all business-relevant data. With that, multiple users can query the data, and the IT team can ensure – through efficient backup mechanisms – that data is unlikely to be lost. But, of course, one essential task is also to control who can actually access data.

For many companies, it is still an issue that some users are used to their Excel spreadsheets and rely on Macros they programmed a long time ago and still work. These habits often slow down the adaptation of more systematic approaches to explore data, the likes of which are presented in this book.

■

Database Era

Relational databases were the next logical evolution to enable systems to process data systematically with complex queries. We mainly differentiate into two forms of databases: Transactional and Analytical databases.

Transactional databases were the first generation of databases to abstract the manual processing accounts of bookkeepers. Pioneers such as Edgar F. Codd introduced normalization processes and methods to map reality in data. On a technical level, transactional databases focussed on topics, such as

- providing a generic, Structured Query Language (SQL),
- maintaining ACID (atomicity, consistency, isolation, durability) rules which is a set of properties of database transactions intended to guarantee data validity despite errors, power failures, and other mishaps.
- resolving multiple access conflicts.

While transactional systems focus on the operational aspects of data processing, with analytical databases, we explore aggregated trends. A shop might use transactional databases to manage storage and purchases during business hours in a real-world example. However, a manager is not interested not in complex transactions such as when a company sold item X to which client. Instead, she is interested in aggregated information such as how many items X have been sold over time. Analytics is a different form of processing data. While transactional databases are focused on updating data in rows and keeping data consistent, analytical systems are mostly read-oriented queries in which information gets aggregated. Although some solutions on the market try to establish themselves as hybrid solutions, in most cases, we differentiate between operational databases handling the workload and analytical databases for generating higher-level insights. Both, transactional and analytical databases, can be queried with SQL.

One common task is to extract data from operational systems and load them into analytical databases. Various vendors provide ETL-Tools (see also Chapter 4.1.1) to minimize the impact on operational systems when fetching data, transforming them into data structures for analytical databases and loading them onto the target systems.

Besides relational databases, we also have other database types such as document databases, key-value stores, graph databases, or wide columnar databases. They are commonly referred to as NoSQL databases and architects are often choosing them for particular use cases.

As a rule of thumb, we leverage polyglot storage, which means we have specific database types fulfilling different needs in different scenarios. A data engineer sometimes needs to select the appropriate database type based on the given requirements. For example, some data might have frequent schema changes and it is structured in multiple hierarchies. This use case could indicate that we should store data as JSON objects and keep these objects in a document database such as MongoDB instead of a two-dimensional relational database.

A data engineer often needs to scale out platforms and distribute data. Scalability often comes with a price. The CAP theorem states that three parameters are essential to database systems: Consistency, Availability, and Partitioning. We can have a maximum of two out of three.[1]

 Structured Query Language: SQL

One key advantage of databases is also the standardization of data querying. Although the SQL standard may have various dialects specifically to proprietary database systems, it is still highly standardized, and default queries are the same for every database system.

Some strategists often oversee the impact of using one global standard to model and query data. If there had been multiple competing approaches, evolutions in database systems would most likely have been slower, as the adaptation to these techniques would have been stalled by users needing to learn more standards.

[1] https://towardsdatascience.com/cap-theorem-and-distributed-database-management-systems-5c2be977950e

Data Lake Era

While a database works with structured data and enables us to apply standardized queries to that data, a data lake is a distributed file storage-based platform. Unlike in the file era, when referring to files of a data lake, we refer to constantly produced files such as log files. Even if single log files can be small, they can accumulate to a massive load if there are many of them.

A data lake offers fast data ingest as it is often too time-consuming to convert masses of incoming data into database-compatible structures. You can find more information on data lakes in Chapter 3. In this chapter, we cover the data engineering-related topics.

Queries on raw data in a data lake are commonly slow. The reason is that applications need to determine or validate the schema when reading the data. This principle is also called schema-on-read.

A data engineer's job is to write pipelines to transform this data into data structures that are faster to read. Data pipelines can also help to reduce the noise in data and extract only valuable data from raw data, to be processed later (feature extraction). Data processing often now is performed in iterations.

 Rise and Fall of the Yellow Elephant

Many consulting companies in the mid 2010s advocated Hadoop, which has a yellow elephant as a logo, as an open-source-based alternative to expensive proprietary database management systems. The idea was to push all kinds of data to a distributed file system and run queries resulting in similar quality and performance. Unfortunately, this hype ended in a huge disaster. Companies who hoped to reduce costs by replacing commercial platforms with open-source platforms often ended up paying more.

Many companies could have prevented this negative experience if they understood more about the topics covered in this chapter. For example, they would have known that data lakes lack the design for complex queries in high concurrency, meaning many users use the system in parallel at the same time, scenarios.

Serverless Era

"Serverless" does not so much refer to data storage itself but, instead, to how applications deal with data. Non-serverless applications are running applications that wait for user input to process data. They might also trigger various jobs for cleaning up and monitoring processes. Non-serverless applications are often associated with monolithic applications. In this context, they can be considered black box software packages that manage a whole system entirely.

With the rise of microservices and splitting up responsibilities among various small services, we also experienced serverless databases. The idea is to avoid having a database engine constantly running, waiting for user input. Furthermore, compute power (required for tasks such as processing data) is only needed when a user triggers a request.

Serverless Databases: A Cloud Domain

Serverless databases are usually the domain of cloud providers, as their goal is to minimize idle time. However, the term "serverless" is misleading. You still need infrastructure to accept client requests, who then, in return, trigger the next steps.

■

Data Mesh Era

A data mesh is a decentralized network for processing data in the form of microservices that are divided into data domains. For example, a data domain can be a department or a thematic data collection such as customer data that belongs to a non-technical department.

A microservice is a decoupled data service that provides a type of service, such as user authentication. The services communicate via standardized interfaces and are exchangeable without a tremendous effort as long as their interfaces remain the same.

A service must have an HTTP address (be addressable) that can be assigned to the type of service (be discoverable) via path information in the URL. In addition, the service must provide appropriate security by applying state-of-the-art security techniques. Finally, the data schema must be self-explanatory and trustworthy, which can be ensured by adhering to company or open standards. This measure helps to solve the following three challenges:

1. Clarifying the data ownership: who owns this data?

2. Ensuring data quality: who is responsible for the quality of the data?

3. Avoidance of personnel bottlenecks, since no longer is one individual responsible for data processing, but rather a whole department or team.

The data storage of the microservices is still done either in a local database in the microservice, in the data lake, in the DWH, or a combination of the two (DataLakeHouse).

If the data is stored locally, data synchronization and consistency across different microservices is a problem. The SAGA approach solves this. A saga is a collection or list of local data updates of the respective microservices, which are processed sequentially. If an update cannot be made, the entire saga is canceled and the original state is restored. We can differentiate between two types of sagas:

- **Choreographer-based sagas:** This type of saga allows data to be exchanged directly between the corresponding microservices. A saga can contain several events that result in new events after processing in the corresponding microservice. If all events have been processed correctly, they are confirmed with an Approve event.

- **Orchestration (Message Broker) sagas:** Communication between the microservices is ensured via message brokers such as Kafka. The sagas are sent to the broker as individual messages and stored in the corresponding queue of the microservice. The message describes the steps that have to be executed. Once these have been processed, an Approve event is sent, which is processed by the orchestrator, which decides which message in the queue must be processed next.

In smaller environments, the two-phase commit protocol (2PC) can also be used to synchronize data across microservices. The disadvantage is that the 2PC approach does not scale as well as the SAGA approach for larger amounts of data, since with 2PC the data update blocks the update mechanism until the update is processed.

Polyglot Storage

Suppose we work in a project that leverages multiple data sources and provides data through various channels to other parties. We could have to deal with

- A streaming data source that continuously sends data.
- Batch processes that are triggered by a cron job every day
- A data provider who sends data in JSON format
- Another data provider sends data in custom binary format
- A considerable amount of log files that are generated on the fly

Each data channel could also have different non-functional requirements. Some data must be processed immediately, whereas other data will be only processed on demand.

For each scenario, there is a data storage system that fits best. For example, data provided as a JSON document is best stored in a document database such as MongoDB. Files in a custom binary format might be loaded on a file system and tabular data in a relational database.

 Vendor Selection: An IT Manager's Nightmare

Sorting out various vendors and maintaining multiple technologies to manage data is sometimes the most significant worry factor for an IT manager. Mapping requirements to solutions is often not easy. Sometimes the underlying business requirements are not transparent or are changing. Each vendor promises a plethora of features, and each vendor also has a different cost-benefit ratio. Some vendors also have a reputation on the market that may indirectly affect decision-making processes. In addition, also within an organization, individuals have preferences for one or the other technology and try to evangelize them. It is not always clear how much these individuals are biased.

Having a mix of supported technologies in a data platform that a team can choose from often mitigates this problem. However, if an IT department decided to maintain too many technologies in parallel, it might struggle.

Cynics call some IT managers with tight budgets who have to maintain complex solutions and deal with the emotional distresses and specific requests of stakeholders, sometimes survival experts.

We call the concept of having many different storage platforms available for different requirements also polyglot storage.[2]

To learn more about various options for storing data and using cloud technologies or container orchestration engines such as Kubernetes, please study Chapter 2, "Infrastructure."

---

[2] *https://martinfowler.com/bliki/PolyglotPersistence.html*

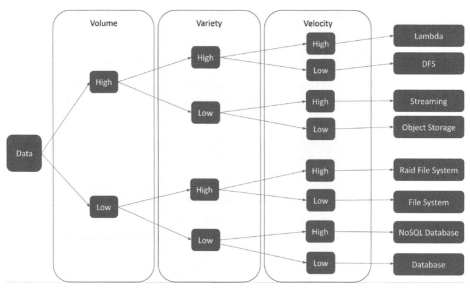

Figure 4.1 Data Storage decision tree

4.1.2 Designing Data Pipelines

To successfully implement a data pipeline we must make various assumptions, from the data delivery to the data platform and its processing.

- **Type of processed data:** Is the data to be processed in real-time, or is it sufficient to process it in batches? Is the data pre-aggregated, or is it unprocessed?

- **Underlying programming language:** In which programming language is the data model or software developed? Is the original language the same as that which is used in the production environment? How does scaling work in this language?

- **Form of the result representation:** Is it sufficient to present the data in aggregated form, or is it necessary to access the raw data? Which data is needed at the end of the processing chain for making decisions?

- **Update frequency and number of models:** How often does a model need to be adjusted and re-trained? Are there many simple models or a few complex ones? How are data science processes built into existing processes?

Once these fundamental questions are clarified, the requirements of a pipeline are defined. It is possible to correct any invalid assumptions later; however, changing them later might require a considerable amount of resources to adapt the existing processes and previous steps accordingly.

Conceptually, most pipelines are similar in design: Data is loaded, transformed, and prepared according to the defined use case. Then, algorithms apply various models to the data, and the results are stored in a database (equivalent to a DataMart in the relational SQL world). The database contains the aggregated data, while the raw data remains in the data lake. The aggregated information is linked to the raw data with a governance process to reload on demand.

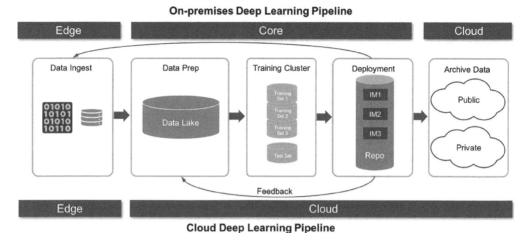

Figure 4.2 An abstract reference data pipeline *(https://netapp.io/2018/09/21/ontap-ai-and-netapp-trident-streamlining-and-simplifying-ai-workloads/)*

Data pipelines, however, differ in details, and they are often also displayed in different granularities. For example, Figure 4.2 is from an article in Software Engineering Daily[3]. It does not expose too many implementation details and focuses on the workflow. This Figure allows discussions on a strategic level. Still, when it boils down to implementing workflows, such a diagram is far too abstract as we miss a lot of details required to get a data pipeline into production.

Satish Chandra Gupta has written an excellent article on Towards Data Science[4]. His data pipeline contains far more implementation details and technologies. Also, it is a good reference model to compare how pipelines might work in the three primary cloud providers.

Still, for the implementation of data pipelines, some details are missing. Therefore, many architects will display further implementation details in more refined architecture diagrams. These diagrams might also contain concrete information on data and more refined workflows on how integration components process data. In addition, these diagrams will incorporate domain language as part of the domain-driven design[5]. Data architects may also include supporting technologies for data pipelines in their designs. They will also integrate observability and information security tools from Chapter 2 and Chapter 5 in architectural diagrams.

In the end, designs for production will contain many details from the domain and specific information on workflow details. As a rule of thumb, if someone can explain a diagram of a data pipeline without understanding the domain and environment, it is not yet concrete enough to be implemented with technologies.

[3] https://softwareengineeringdaily.com/2020/04/30/components-of-modern-data-pipelines/
[4] https://towardsdatascience.com/scalable-efficient-big-data-analytics-machine-learning-pipeline-architecture-on-cloud-4d59efc092b5
[5] https://www.amazon.com/Domain-Driven-Design-Tackling-Complexity-Software/dp/0321125215

A characteristic of data pipelines is that they have the following three properties.

Reproducibility

To make data processing traceable, a corresponding audit trail documents each step, and it is clear how and when the data is processed. It helps to think of the technical part as a "black box" whose content and functioning must be inferred by interpreting the audit trails.

Another requirement for pipelines is that their configurations, input parameters of models, etc., and their code, are managed separately to support error detection. Deep learning models, in particular, do not produce the same results without the correct initial parameters. The results of such models are therefore reproducible only to a limited extent.

Teams use a source code management tool such as Git to achieve reproducibility and storage of older models. The model parameters and the models themselves are managed, for example, in a database or a binary file. In addition, the source code management tool has to support a robust versioning mechanism for rolling back to a previous model if a newer version performs less accurately than the older one.

Consistence

It is difficult to process data consistently because current auditing mechanisms target produced code or models but do not audit the models' data. Consequently, if the data distributions change unexpectedly, new or invalid values arise, or the encoding of the data changes, the model predicts unexpected values or results. Therefore, regular data audits are made so that we can react appropriately to these changes and then incorporate them into the models.

Production Readiness

The goal of any data pipeline is to sooner or later deploy it into the production environment to generate value for the business. Especially in Big Data environments, it is not enough to just produce accurate models or code. One of the main problems is that the developed solution has to scale according to the predefined conditions. This means that the model has to cope with a larger amount of data with a limited resource overhead (runtime, memory consumption) than was required during development.

The model can be trained and improved in the development environment until it reaches a certain level of maturity and then deployed in the production environment.

4.1.3 CI/CD

We need to maintain software versions and also focus on deployment strategies to manage data pipelines. CI/CD (Continuous Integration / Continuous Deployment) has become the standard term for continued governance over the deployment process.

Jenkins is the de facto standard application to create a CI/CD pipeline. It is a build automation server written in Java. Most developers are familiar with the Jenkins web UI and apply configuration settings or trigger builds in their careers.

Jenkins in a Nutshell

Readers unfamiliar with Jenkins can imagine this application as a solution to manage how an organization releases software to its users. In this context, a CI/CD pipeline is a highly customizable sequence of steps to perform quality control on software packages and provide final build outputs to users. Figure 4.3 outlines such a build pipeline.

For example, administrators can configure Jenkins to perform automated unit tests on software. They also can use Jenkins to run modules to create a static code analysis to measure how quality has evolved.

Jenkins has a powerful plugin system with many contributions from open-source engineers, and many plugins can also add features to a step in a build sequence.

Many CI/CD engineers configure Jenkins to trigger builds after a software engineer "pushes a new version to a remote version management system" to validate the software changes.

■

Jenkins itself communicates with numerous subsystems. For example, once connected to a supported version management system, such as Git, Jenkins can track code changes.

In the context of version management, another subsystem is essential. When developers load a new version from the repositories, we compile it with a tool like Maven or Gradle and run unit tests to test that the code works correctly.

In larger software systems, where programmers provide multiple commits per day, Jenkins can create nightly builds that incorporate all changes.

	Prepare Container	Install Gems	Prepare Database	Rake	Security scan	Deploy
Average stage times: (Average full run time: ~14min 34s)	10min 14s	3min 41s	3s	1min 42s	25s	10ms
#20 Aug 04 16:31 — 1 commits	9min 9s	3min 32s	7s	1min 19s	24s	8ms
#19 Aug 04 16:10 — 1 commits	8min 58s	3min 31s	3s	1min 15s	24s	8ms
#18 Aug 04 15:36 — 1 commits	9min 6s	3min 35s	3s	2min 9s	24s	7ms
#17 Aug 04 15:30 — No Changes						

Figure 4.3 Jenkins as an example of a build server[6]

---

[6] Copyright: R. Tyler Croy, *https://www.jenkins.io/zh/blog/2016/08/10/rails-cd-with-pipeline/*

In addition to automating builds, we can implement other processes through Jenkins. For example, static code analysis provides quality metrics, such as whether complexity, indentation, and naming conventions are adequately executed. In larger projects, ignoring these metrics can result in unreadable code. Reference examples of static code analysis tools for Python code are available PyLint and SonarCube.

4.1.4 Programming Languages

There are many discussions about the ideal programming languages for data projects. For example, some programmers argue that Java is the lingua franca for data applications. Their main argument is Java's lengthy leadership of the TIOBE index[7], which is a popularity ranking of programming languages, and the fact that most data frameworks themselves are written in Java.

Other engineers see Scala as the primary language for data applications, especially for Big Data use cases. Scala is functional by nature, which enables us to scale better in a distributed environment[8]. Another argument for Scala is that compilers translate code into a JVM-compatible intermediate language like in Java. On the other hand, critics call Scala too complex compared to Java. As a result, it might be hard to onboard developers who still have to learn the details about Scala.

 Backward Compatibility

Programmers often love new features and more comfort while programming. It is hard to explain to non-programmers, but the ability to solve problems in fewer lines of code than others or more elegantly with specific syntactic capabilities has a substantial positive impact on a programmer's mood.

Suppose you have learned a new programming language such as Rust or Kotlin. You master all the new paradigms these new languages bring, and you finally feel that you can "express yourself more eloquently in code." It feels like a "punch in the face" for some programmers when decision-makers choose an old but established programming language for a new project.

One sad thing about the data industry is that adoptions to new programming languages or even just newer versions take time. Established programming languages cannot break their interfaces to enable backward compatibility. The Python community experienced what may happen if changes become too radical. It took many years to convince some programmers finally to upgrade to Python 3.

There had been a dispute over whether R or Python was the primary language for data scientists. While R is popular within special user groups, especially academia, the industry seems to favor Python. As a result, Python may have become the lingua franca in this

---

[7] *https://www.tiobe.com/tiobe-index/*
[8] *https://www.youtube.com/watch?v=3jg1AheF4n0*

domain. Moreover, Python engineers have tons of analytical frameworks available to them, such as Keras, PyTorch, Scifi, NumPy, and many more.

Python is maintained by the Python Software Foundation[9] and standardized by the various Enhancement Proposals (PEP). Pythonistas claim that Python is perfect for all kinds of data applications and that data engineers and data scientists should only stick to one standard. They also emphasize that Python is more readable than other languages; it is more succinct. In some cases, it takes almost just half of the code to express a routine in Python as compared to Java. Furthermore, unlike other languages, there is no compilation process needed to apply a change and execute an application again in Python.

Various engineers, however, claim that Python code is harder to debug. Especially without compiling, programmers might find problematic code in Python later than in other languages. In addition, an advocate of different languages may consider that it is harder to maintain large software projects with Python as programming languages such as Java enforce a clear structure. Or in other words: "Python allows you to create a mess if you want, while the Java compiler forces you to correct every syntax error." Another argument is performance. The default interpreter CPython is often slower than other programming languages, and in addition, Python has language-specific bottlenecks such as the global interpreter lock (GIL)[10] for multithreading. It is a mutex (or a lock) that allows only one thread to hold the control of the Python interpreter and which slows down multi-threaded applications.

The main reason why Python is so prevalent in the Data Science community is, perhaps, that it is easy to populate data structures for analytics. For example, in the Figure below, we just need two lines to load a custom data structure in a pandas data frame, which is a versatile data structure for all kinds of algorithms to analyze data.

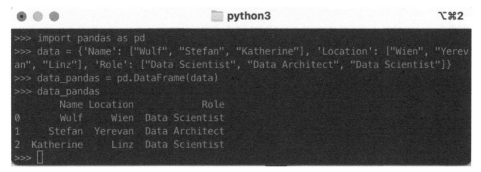

```
>>> import pandas as pd
>>> data = {'Name': ["Wulf", "Stefan", "Katherine"], 'Location': ["Wien", "Yerev
an", "Linz"], 'Role': ["Data Scientist", "Data Architect", "Data Scientist"]}
>>> data_pandas = pd.DataFrame(data)
>>> data_pandas
        Name Location            Role
0       Wulf     Wien  Data Scientist
1     Stefan  Yerevan  Data Architect
2  Katherine     Linz  Data Scientist
>>>
```

Figure 4.4 Sending data to pandas.

Unrelated to the first example, the code snippet shows that, unlike other programming languages, getting a CSV file into a data structure is a one-liner. If you compare this to Java, in which you had to write tons of boilerplate code to be able to get even started, it might be clear why Python is so popular in scenarios where conciseness is essential.

```
pd.read_csv(my_csv_file)
```

---

[9] https://www.python.org/psf/
[10] https://realpython.com/python-gil

One Real Deciding Factor for a Programming Language

Many companies have trouble finding software engineers with knowledge of specific languages. Lastly, the skillsets of programmers depend strongly on the curricula of their schools and universities. Although solid software engineers are supposed to be multilingual, sometimes it can get harder to staff teams once a solution scales if the programming language is exotic.

Many IT managers resort to the most logical decision to have one programming language as standard and enforce to use it for every new software. This circumstance highlights why modern programming languages like Kotlin, which would be a perfect fit for many data projects, are rarely used.

Many experts also recommend conventions for git repositories to use a programming language efficiently, as outlined below. The more projects follow the same routines, the easier it is for a new developer to be onboarded.

.github/workflows	Don't fail when releasing an existing version (#126)
data	add data_files example
src/sample	Removed blank lines
tests	26 added simple module and test module
.gitignore	have the tests we're including actually run and pass
.travis.yml	Remove Python 3.5 and add 3.9 (#132)
LICENSE.txt	Add a LICENSE.txt file
MANIFEST.in	Remove Python 3.5 and add 3.9 (#132)
README.md	119 updated python logo (removed some other code from my own fork)
pyproject.toml	Implement PEP 518 and opt into PEP 517 builds
setup.cfg	Drop support for EOL Python 2
setup.py	Remove Python 3.5 and add 3.9 (#132)
tox.ini	Remove Python 3.5 and add 3.9 (#132)

Figure 4.5 Python sample Project Structure[11]

A README.md file contains documentation in markdown format. Among these files, we store dependencies or package management configurations. Thus, the README is essential to manage all files necessary to allow a build server to generate executable solutions.

In src, a developer finds the source code. Each project also contains tests such as unit or integration tests.

---

[11] *https://github.com/pypa/sampleproject*

4.1.5 Kafka as Reference ETL Tool

In Chapter 3, we introduced ETL from a process view. But it also helps to understand how ingestion tools work. Apache Kafka has become the standard for a toolchain to load message-sized data to a data platform.

 Size Matters

When we talk about message-sized data, we refer to all kinds of data that we could load as a data set into a database row. However, plain old file copy processes do a better job of ingesting blob data, such as files.

Apache Kafka is an open-source distributed event streaming platform used by thousands of companies for high-performance data pipelines, streaming analytics, data integration, and mission-critical applications. There are commercial versions of Kafka available, most famously the Confluent platform. The confluent platform adds a lot of enterprise features on top of the Kafka core.

At its core, Kafka is a distributed commit log. A so-called "broker" is a service to provide the functionality to process incoming messages. By scaling brokers, we can also increase the load able to be processed by Kafka. Kafka distributes data on so-called "topics." We can imagine a topic as a mailbox with an address into which we can post messages at any time. To ensure that no message is lost, we can ensure that we replicate messages over multiple brokers. Many messages often have one attribute that functions as key. Unlike database keys, which aim to be unique, we pick keys in messages to provide an optimal data distribution. Imagine you have datasets of customers with registered home addresses all over the country. If you put them all in one queue, we have to process all data in one queue. If the load increases, we might run into performance problems.

The knowledgeable data engineer defines a partitioning strategy. He might use, for instance, the zip code as a distribution key. With that, we can distribute the load. Assuming we have ten partitions to use all zip codes starting from zero to nine, we can process incoming data on ten different brokers on different machines.

Other factors for choosing the best possible decision factor include expected querying strategies. These are out of this book's scope, but interested readers can look up the following links.[12,13] Choosing a good key for partitioning will increase the performance in processing distributing data.

In Chapter 2, we showed how to use Docker. We can use the script below to deploy a mini Kafka image on a local computer using docker-compose up.

```
version: '2'
services:
  zookeeper:
    image: confluentinc/cp-zookeeper:latest
```

---

[12] *https://medium.com/event-driven-utopia/understanding-kafka-topic-partitions-ae40f80552e8*
[13] *https://newrelic.com/blog/best-practices/effective-strategies-kafka-topic-partitioning*

```
    environment:
        ZOOKEEPER_CLIENT_PORT: 2181
        ZOOKEEPER_TICK_TIME: 2000
    ports:
      - 22181:2181

    kafka:
      image: confluentinc/cp-kafka:latest
      depends_on:
        - zookeeper
      ports:
        - 29092:29092
      environment:
        KAFKA_BROKER_ID: 1
        KAFKA_ZOOKEEPER_CONNECT: zookeeper:2181
        KAFKA_ADVERTISED_LISTENERS: PLAINTEXT://kafka:9092,PLAINTEXT_HOST://
localhost:29092
        KAFKA_LISTENER_SECURITY_PROTOCOL_MAP: PLAINTEXT:PLAINTEXT,PLAINTEXT_
HOST:PLAINTEXT
        KAFKA_INTER_BROKER_LISTENER_NAME: PLAINTEXT
        KAFKA_OFFSETS_TOPIC_REPLICATION_FACTOR: 1
```

After the Kafka service is online, we can verify that using the following command.

```
nc -z localhost 22181
```

We can then use the Kafka binaries from the Kafka client[14], which can be downloaded from the vendor's site, to use some commands to create topics and load data into them.

```
./bin/kafka-topics.sh --bootstrap-server localhost:29092 --create --topic test
--partitions 1 --replication-factor 1
./bin/kafka-console-producer.sh --broker-list localhost:29092 --topic test
```

We should focus on these commands. The first tells Kafka to create a topic. The second opens a console window to collect user input. This user input is then sent as a message to the topic test. Suppose we imagine a physical mailbox and hundreds of letters coming in. In such a case, it might make sense to distribute the letters into multiple mailboxes to avoid overflowing one mailbox. As long as we remember which letter is in which mailbox, everything is fine. If we again think of a physical mailbox, one partition strategy could be to have one mailbox for each house inhabitant so that, for instance, Mum and Dad have separate mailboxes. Figure 4.6 outlines this.

Partitioning can be easily confused with replication. Partitioning will increase performance, as Mum always goes to "Mailbox.Mum" to receive her letters, while Dad goes to "Mailbox. Dad". But what if some vandal burns down "Mailbox.Mum"? All her letters would be lost.

With replication, we ensure that every letter delivered to "Mailbox.Mum" is duplicated and stored in the other mailboxes. So, to sum it up: We use Partitioning to increase performance by splitting messages by keys; replication ensures that no message is lost.

---

[14] *https://kafka.apache.org/*

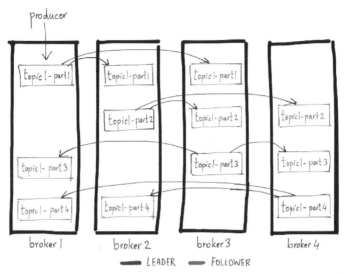

Figure 4.6 Replication of message across multiple Kafka brokers (*https://www.confluent.io/blog/hands-free-kafka-replication-a-lesson-in-operational-simplicity/*)

We can then also read from a topic again.

```
kafka-console-consumer.sh --bootstrap-server=localhost:9092 --consumer.config=config/
consumer.properties --topic test --from-beginning
```

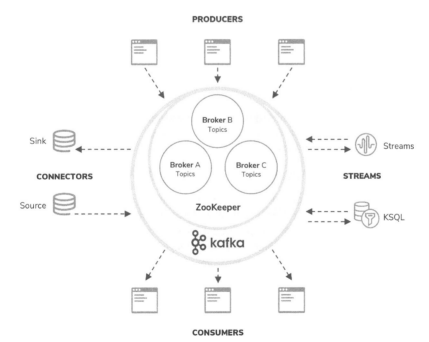

Figure 4.7 The essential Kafka Actors. Source: *https://coralogix.com/blog/a-complete-introduction-to-apache-kafka/*

We introduced Kafka through one of its core functionalities as a message broker. Messages are sent to various topics and received from consumers. This strategy allows us to qualify the first actors in a publish-subscribe system. A producer is an entity which pushes messages to a topic; a consumer is an entity which loads messages. A producer can be a command-line tool or code embedded into an application, such as

```
from pykafka import KafkaClient

client = KafkaClient(hosts="localhost:9092")
topic = client.topics['test'.encode()]
with topic.get_sync_producer() as producer:
    producer.produce('test message'.encode())
```

A deployment of Kafka in production usually contains many more services. As one example, Kafka Connect is a service for importing or exporting data from an external data source. You might, for instance, create a MongoDB-Connector. Once a producer pushes a new message into a Kafka topic, a connector automatically syncs it as a JSON object in MongoDB. Or you might consider connecting to a file system as a source. A user might copy a file there, the connector picks it up and pushes it into Kafka.

But what if, by mistake, a user copies an incorrect file to the source? Components such as the Kafka Schema Registry validate the schema of each message. If the message does not represent an intended form, the Kafka Schema Registry rejects it.

To manipulate and process data in transit, we have Kafka Streams. This framework allows us, while Kafka messages are in transit, to manipulate or query them.

There are many more services in a possible Kafka deployment. For example, there are UIs to manage Kafka or to monitor its workload.

The core feature of Kafka is to allow everything to scale. The LinkedIn engineering team created it to manage the workload for LinkedIn when they got into danger of not being able to handle that amount of load anymore. While it was impossible to increase the load with existing messaging systems, by using Kafka, it became just a matter of acquiring new hardware to meet new load requirements.

Data Engineers often need to harden a deployment with encryption and advanced authentication methods. This topic is beyond the scope of the book.

 Why Engineering also Matters for Data Scientists

Many data scientists may now argue that the internals of technologies such as Kafka might not be relevant to them and wonder why we present technical details here. Some people compare a data team with a soccer team with different roles. Defenders might be systems engineers, midfielders are the data engineers, and often, all the fame goes to the strikers who are supposed to score. But, we can assume it is clear with whom we compare strikers in this analogy.

Some people want to be strikers because of their fame. Who would deny that shooting an essential goal in a match lets a player stand out, even if defenders contributed a similar amount to the success by preventing goals of the foreign team?

There is also an archetype of a striker who only thinks about scoring goals. The media often calls them lazy, as they do not want to help out much in the defense when needed. On the other hand, outstanding strikers do not just wait for midfielders to pass a ball and head towards the goal. Instead, they make themselves essential for the overall gameplay.

As the archetype of the "lazy striker" who just waits for the ball from other players to score, there are also archetypes of data scientists who wait to receive data to score. They do not care about the rest; all they want is to apply algorithms and impress the audience with the insights they generated. Needless to say that in many companies, this archetype does not have a good reputation. To make it short: To excel as a data scientist, it is also essential to understand the whole game you are playing

4.1.6 Design Patterns

Design patterns are templates or strategies for well-known problems that occur regularly, such as standardized data loads or machine learning applications. Different design patterns are available for various problems. These include the current state of the industry concerning security and legal requirements.

Depending on the relationship and type of data and transformation, a different pattern may be applicable. Following are a selection of frequent design patterns used in data engineering.

Dispatcher and Adapter Pattern

In the dispatcher pattern, a function splits a data stream into different streams based on a characteristic or property of the data. The resulting streams have a lower volume or frequency than the original stream. A use case of this pattern is separating data or providing different data granularity.

The adapter pattern is the inverse of the dispatcher. It can receive data from data sources of different types and then provide them in a uniform output format. The difficulty here is to consider the various properties of the sources and then integrate them. Thus, we use a separate adapter for each source.

Protocol Converter

Protocol converters convert the data from one format to another. Usually, the data is not changed; the transformation exchanges just the format. In this step, content metadata such as the system load timestamp or a unique identifier to help detect and handle duplicates later is added.

The goal of the protocol converter is to standardize different data to make later steps easier. Therefore, this pattern is often combined with the adapter pattern since the data is merged in a platform in the next step.

Complex Event Processing

Complex Event Processing is a method to filter out "special" data from a data stream. "Special" data differs from the rest concerning one or more properties, such as error cases or fraudulent behavior in data transfers. Such cases are called "events." One property of events is that they tend to occur infrequently compared to the rest of the data. Therefore, we must store the affected data permanently to draw any conclusions or document their occurrence.

This pattern can also be extended by data science models, for example, to make real-time predictions.

4.1.7 Automation of the Stages

Since individual automation methods differ from each other, different approaches are necessary for automation. Furthermore, not all stages are currently automatable. Consequently, we focus here on the description of the automatable steps. For example, the loop data cleaning, exploration, and modeling, described above, can only be efficiently performed manually due to the different types of input data.

4.1.8 Six Building Blocks of the Data Pipeline

Figure 4.8 shows how various data processing steps of a pipeline are interconnected. Specifically, it depicts the Exploration – Data Cleansing – Modeling loop, which iteratively improves the generated model. The modeling process will execute individual steps several times. During the iteration, the focus of the previous iteration can change significantly due to discoveries arising within the data.

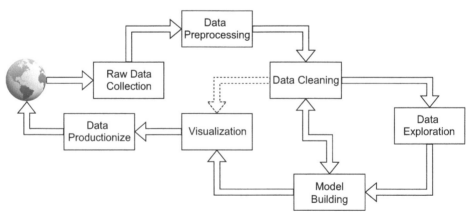

Figure 4.8 Data Science Process

In this reference example, we build a data pipeline with the following six stages.

Stage 1: Data Collection

The source data is loaded into a designated place in the data lake. In most cases, engineers need to prevent operational systems from being blocked during data export. One of these methods is Change Data Capture (CDC), where transaction logs are used as a basis to load data to a lake.

It is imperative to load data fast with a minimum number of transformations. At this phase, algorithms sometimes prepare data for parallel processing by adding loading timestamps, bucketing, and partitioning information.

In the data environment, the following typical data loading scenarios usually arise:

- Reading flat files such as JSON, CSV, or HTML.
- Fetching data through Database interfaces from data-warehouses such as Oracle or Teradata.
- Receiving Streaming data like Kafka or RabbitMQ.

We introduced Kafka as a reference technology for data integration. A Kafka connector is a module that connects Kafka brokers to a specific data source. For example, if we configured a Kafka connector to a file source, new files copied to a specified directory would be automatically ingested.[15]

It has also been common to use microservices for jobs to trigger batch jobs to collect data. For example, cron jobs or orchestration tools such as Airflow or Kubernetes provide functionality for schedulers.

Many companies run large batch jobs to load data to an analytical platform at night to ensure that operative systems are not affected during business hours.

Stage 2: Data Cleaning and Preparation

"Data cleaning is the process of preparing data for analysis by removing or modifying data that is incorrect, incomplete, irrelevant, duplicated, or improperly formatted."[16]

Cleaning data may also mean bringing data into a uniform encoding format. One common problem is that similar data attributes have different encodings. For example, some may use the 'yyyy-MM-dd' date format, others a structure such as 'dd-MM-yyyy.' Furthermore, cleaning processes can help standardize data units. Therefore, data provided in units of length in the US system, such as in feet and inches, might be converted to a metric system or vice versa.

Data cleansing also deals with missing values, a common challenge when building a machine learning model. In the article "How to Deal with Missing Data"[17], the author recommends options to deal with them. We can either remove them or impute them. As imputation method, the author recommends

- Mean, Median and Mode
- Time-Series Specific Methods
- Last Observation Carried Forward (LOCF) & Next Observation Carried Backward (NOCB)

---

[15] *https://www.baeldung.com/kafka-connectors-guide*
[16] *https://www.sisense.com/glossary/data-cleaning/*
[17] *https://www.mastersindatascience.org/learning/how-to-deal-with-missing-data/*

- Linear Interpolation
- Seasonal Adjustment with Linear Interpolation

Data Cleaning may also have an organizational aspect. For example, if we receive bad-quality data from external data providers, we sometimes can negotiate with them to improve the quality. Data providers can use, for instance, better sensors when collecting data. We might also balance out inaccuracies using machine learning if we have labeled datasets with correct data.

 Data Cleaning in Practice

For telcos, it is sometimes difficult to get accurate geographical positions of a person using telecommunication data. Many aspects affect the determination of an exact location, such as signal strength or the position of a person in a building. However, through triangulation, this data can be improved and made more accurate.

Automotive companies get a lot of data from sensors to improve their autonomous driving capabilities. As the data quality received from Lidar and other sensors is essential for building these capabilities, lousy quality in data can give feedback to the team producing the sensors to improve the hardware.

Suppose a company uses satellite images to predict fires in dry areas or to manage agricultural processes. They might realize that some photos are too inaccurate for various explorations. So they might explore using drones instead.

Some companies also use data cleaning to anonymize data and ensure that a platform for analytics never contains PII data.

Many companies keep data cleaning and data preparation separate. They see data cleaning as a process to improve quality, data preparation as a process to prepare data for analytics after the data has been cleaned.

Data preparation aims to prepare data for machine learning algorithms and other methods to analyze data. In this step, individual, sometimes different data sources are consolidated and merged into one analytical dataset.

In many projects, this is a collaborative and experiment-oriented process. Data Scientists create analytical datasets, create some models and analyze the results. If the results are not good enough, teams can integrate the feedback into the next iteration of data preparation. So with time, the analytical datasets get more purposeful and targeted towards specific algorithms, and the team's understanding of the data improves.

From a technological point of view, we can use Kafka Streams or KSQL commands to transform data into our target structure. Another option is to use Apache Spark that has been introduced in Chapter 3.

The data is called an "analytical data set" at the end of the data cleansing process. We can use it with machine learning algorithms. They look like a large table which has the following characteristics:

1. There is a column in the table that represents a uniquely identifying key.
2. All attributes are encoded in the same way.
3. Query and exploration are supported using a query language.
4. Columns with missing values have been removed or imputed.

Stage 3: Exploration and Visualization

Parallel to data cleaning, the data is visualized and exploratively evaluated. For this purpose, various display types such as box plots, histograms, scatter plots, and so on are often used. The aim is to find a sufficiently precise correlation or covariance between one or more variables. To interpret and "explore" the data correctly, a certain amount of domain knowledge is necessary.

Notebooks, such as Jupyter or Colab, are used for data exploration and prototype development. These applications abstract the technical problems by setting up the environment via kernels. A kernel contains a programming language or interfaces to proprietary products, such as Matlab or SAS, and it is used with the plug-and-play principle. This feature makes it possible to try out different solutions tailored to the problem and end-user.

The notebook itself provides a graphical WYSIWYG interface similar to Microsoft Word. In addition, a user can embed mathematical formulas and visualizations in continuous text. The image below shows the Lorenz Equation example from the Jupyter Notebook collection[18]:

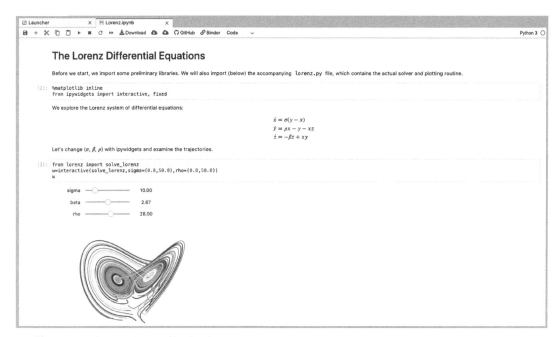

Figure 4.9 Example Jupyter Notebook

---

[18] *https://jupyter.org/* (This sample can be recreated by clicking on "try it" in the browser)

The grayed-out area is source code executable via the play button. The notebook inserts visual elements such as graphics at the appropriate points. This feature actively supports data exploration and storytelling.

Stage 4: Modelling

Based on the prepared data, models are built and trained. Then, different models have to be tried out and compared based on some predefined criteria. A typical evaluation criterion is cross-validation. We divide data into similarly sized sets, one of which is used for testing and validation while the rest are used for training the models. This process is repeated using a different test set until each set has had a turn at being the test set. Sometimes, the overall results will be compared to another model using A/B testing. We cover these procedures in detail in Chapters 5 and 8.

Stage 5: Interpretation

When interpreting the results, data professionals put individual elements into a more appealing, presentable form. Thus, even laypeople should be able to compare facts.

One possible type of visualization that shows the advantages and disadvantages of a machine learning model is the Confusion or Error Matrix. In this visualization, the data classified by the model is compared to the actual data, which helps depict the strengths and weaknesses of the model. One recognizable feature is that the diagonal of the matrix usually shows the highest number of correctly classified data, while numbers deviating from the diagonal represent misclassified data. Figure 4.10 shows a simplified version of a confusion matrix.

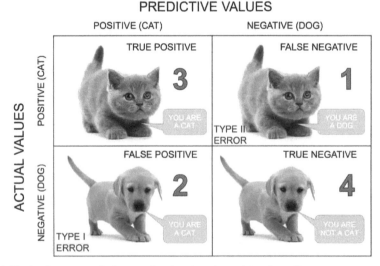

Figure 4.10 A reference confusion matrix taken from keytodatascience[19]

---

[19] *https://keytodatascience.com/confusion-matrix/*

Stage 6: Delivery to the Production Environment

Compared to the previous stages, the main difference is that the production environment contains considerably more data. The data must be processed after a specific time to address any company service level agreements concerning quality and reliability. In addition, someone must think about the update process of individual models or parameters. New data creates a model drift[20], and we need to retrain our models on new data. Consequently, models need to be regularly maintained and occasionally replaced.

The more a department learns to apply data science, the more they will automate and decrease the total time for deployments. Ideally, the final goal should be full automation, that is, "end-to-end" automation.

■ 4.2 Managing Analytical Models

We need a predefined process with defined parameters to deploy a data pipeline into a production software environment. This process is based on Continuous Delivery (CD)[21], a multiphase software delivery process. The goal is to deliver the current software to production at any time. CD is a collection of best practices, tools, and techniques that support this goal as automatically as possible.

We introduced DevOps in Chapter 2. It is a process improvement approach that allows for the most efficient and effective software delivery into production. Analytics Operation, AnalyticsOps or DataOps for short, is a further development of DevOps to manage ML-specific topics and data lifecycles.

Quality Assurance and Testing

Development teams validate software quality with tests that ensure that the software functions according to the previously specified requirements. We divide these requirements into component, module, and integration tests for individual parts of the software. CI/CD pipelines commonly trigger tests every time the code is changed and ensure that the software's core functionality is maintained even if relevant parts are changed. Integration testing is more challenging to implement in a Big Data environment because it requires a test environment.

One metric to make code quality quantifiable is to measure the code coverage. This metric tells us how much code is covered by unit tests. This ratio should be high to eliminate as many sources of error as possible during creation.

Quality Assurance Instances

There are resources in the company that perform quality assurance. Based on the result, the produced software is revised another time, or the delivery process is started. Adapted to Big

---

[20] *https://towardsdatascience.com/model-drift-in-machine-learning-models-8f7e7413b563*
[21] Further reading: *https://continuousdelivery.com/*

Data, it is also essential that the models' predictions are tested, for example, by comparing the accuracy matrix, confusion matrix, ROC, or cross-validation scores. It is also vital to test the input data, for example, by replacing or varying it. In this way, tests execute the model on entirely new data. Unfortunately, this step can currently only be insufficiently automated.

 *Ops

Someone who studies blogs and participates in discussions about AI should have observed the large number of new terms ending with Ops. MLOps, DevSecOps, AIOps, DataOps, and many more expressions are used interchangeably within the data science community. One blog entry even tries to list and classify them.[22]

As the terminology is still evolving and the community is still deciding what in detail various Ops-variants are supposed to do, we do not stick to a fixed expression to reference the discipline of managing analytical models. This might change in future editions of this book.

■

4.2.1 Model Delivery

In the model development process, the requirements for the final model may change: It has to work autonomously and without human interaction until it is replaced or superseded. In addition, it should deliver controlled results and has to be monitored.

Currently, there are two different ways to use data science models. Either an additional program operates the model, and the development is executed separately from the driver program, or the model is operated in a container, i.e., containerized, and then applied to the data. Containerization describes an approach in which the model is encapsulated in a container. With both types of use, manual deliveries to the production environment are not recommended since manual processes usually introduce further errors. Consequently, this means that the models should come from a version control service, like Git, and be (semi-)automatically deployed via a build server (Jenkins) in the appropriate environment.

Typically, three different environments are used, depending on the maturity of the software.

Development

The development environment contains the current state of the software and is updated frequently. The goal is to support the development cycle and to try out new ideas or fix problems.

---

[22] https://datakitchen.io/why-are-there-so-many-ops-terms/

Test

In the test environment, the software is tested before it is rolled out. To accomplish this, system and integration tests validate the interaction of the software with other components and processes. Therefore, it is essential to test how the software functions under conditions as close to reality as possible.

Production Environment

The software is installed in the production environment during periodic release cycles if the test phase is successful. Only then does it achieve added value for the company.

4.2.2 Model Update

Before we describe the two update types in more detail, we will briefly discuss the difference between R and Python models, as these are currently the most common data science languages.

Models in R

R has its origins in the academic world. Various research institutions maintain it as an open-source project. As a result, new models are often first implemented in R before being adapted in other languages. The R language is kept concise and combines various concepts to make it very flexible and extensible.

R Data pipelines are usually delivered in a container to avoid the conflict between different concepts and versions of the libraries. However, one disadvantage is that a complete environment always has to be built in the container. This dependency means if we have multiple full environments running in parallel, we waste resources. Another problem with R models is that there is no efficient library management. Teams can also circumvent the conflicts with the container approach. Additionally, Spark supports the execution of R code using data processing engines like Spark.

Models in Python

Similar to R, Python is also concise and promotes an easy-to-read programming style. In addition, due to the focus of Big Data companies on Python, current machine learning libraries are available or preferably implemented in Python. Thus, engineers can use them directly without sacrificing the convenience of modern development environments.

These development libraries have the advantage that Python contains standard development tools such as library management. According to the Tiobe index, Python is the most popular programming language.[23] This popularity underlines the number of resources available for it.

---

[23] *https://www.tiobe.com/tiobe-index/*

Apache Spark contains a Python interpreter, enabling us to write code that runs in distributed environments. To learn more about Apache Spark, please explore the section on Spark in Chapter 3.

Independent of the model serving approach, a containerized model can be adjusted or replaced with the rolling update of Kubernetes. This step sequentially replaces all existing pods with new pods containing the latest changed models. As a result, two potentially different versions are active for a short time.

As an alternative to this scenario, a team can choose a solution via a driver program. Here, the program that processes the data calls an interface in the container or embeds the model natively into the data-processing code.

This interface between the containers and the code is usually a web interface that responds within a specific time in a particular format; otherwise, latency in the further processing chain will arise. The driver program is a Big Data framework, such as Spark or Flink, that calls the appropriate endpoints and enriches the web response before the engines process data in the chain. Thus, it strictly separates the data science model from the code that processes most of the data.

Suppose we want to port a model from the development environment to production. We can store it in a standardized format and import it into the production data pipeline with appropriate interfaces with the corresponding model language. Thus, we use fewer resources than with the previous approach, but incompatibilities between versions may occur, for example, if a particular algorithm is not supported. In addition, there may be scaling problems since the authors of some libraries did not design them for parallelized operation.

4.2.3 Model or Parameter Update

If we want to exchange a model or parameter, but the actual code of the model remains the same, we can update the corresponding file or database entry. Suppose we want to exchange a parameter during operation. In that case, we can add an intermediate layer between the model code and the actual model, for example, with PMML or ONNX. This layer ensures that the individual models remain portable. Parameters of the unique models must also be portable since we must ensure that they work optimally with the update. We can store parameters in JSON or XML, for example.

Regardless of how the model parameters are changed or made available, a model should scale with the number of calls.

4.2.4 Model Scaling

If we scale modelsupdate in production, we need to expose the model first to the corresponding data sets. As a result, various problems may occur, such as resource problems or, in the worst case, the models are calculated on incorrect training data or encoded differently. Quality assurance aims to avoid these errors early by considering different aspects of Big

Data during creation and modeling. The goal of scaling is to run the previously developed model efficiently, that is, with as few resources as possible.

If a model is scaled horizontally, i.e., calculated over several computers, the problem may arise that the model only calculates a partial solution and not a globally unique solution. In the next step, the individual partial solutions must then be processed into an overall solution. This method means that the amount of data is distributed equally among the available computers, and then per computer, the model performs the data processing. Once this is complete, the overall solution is calculated.

This process contrasts with vertical scaling, which focuses on upgrading the hardware. With more physical resources available to the computer, the calculations are more efficient. The overall solution is then computed on one computer. The disadvantage is that this type of scaling is only feasible if the workstation has enough hardware resources.

4.2.5 Feedback into the Operational Processes

An operations lifecycle must also reflect updating or replacing of models. The model and the model's corresponding input data provide essential starting points for further improvements. As an approach for delivered models, we should again use the black box view since these models cannot be changed and must still have an indicator of the status.

Consequently, in addition to the parameters of the old model, we should track operational metadata such as time required, memory available, and so on, to enable an analysis of the performance.

Incorporating models into the operational processes gives an impression of which parameters, variables, or features significantly influence the model's quality or behavior. Then, if necessary, the influence of the parameters on the model can be simulated and iteratively improved to remove less important features and parameters based on their predefined criteria. This approach aims to make individual models more performant, smaller, and thus more efficient.

◼ 4.3 In a Nutshell

 Data Engineers build data pipelines to load data onto data platforms.

Data pipelines add and deliver value for companies by (semi-)automatically applying models to data. The greater the degree of automation, the higher the added value achieved. There are different channels for ingesting data into a platform.

Automation is the key.

Just as important as a high degree of automation is the need to consider how the created model is exchanged and updated. In the update process, the model must remain portable. Otherwise, the pipeline can be interrupted in the worst case, especially if the development environment and programming language are very different from the production system.

Kafka is a standard for messages-based data.

There are many data ingestion tools on the market. However, Kafka is maybe the most powerful open-source framework to ingest data into a data platform.

Don't confuse a data pipeline with a ci/cd pipeline.

One is to transform raw data into models, the other to transform source code into deployments.

◼

5 Data Management

Stefan Papp, Bernhard Ortner

> *"Without a systematic way to start and keep data clean, bad data will happen."*
> *Donato Diorio*

 Questions Answered in this Chapter:

- What is Data Management, and how does it relate to other "data disciplines"?
- What is Data Governance, and what is needed to establish governance rules for companies?
- Why do we need to address regulatory requirements, and which consequences might we face if we ignore them?
- What is data modeling, and what is its correlation to data management?
- How can a data catalog help us to understand more about what we know?
- How should you address master data management correctly?
- How can you share data suitably, and which standards exist for that?
- What is information security, and what do I need to know to have a basic understanding of that domain?

We highlighted in the last three chapters that setting up an environment for data science projects is a precondition for getting started to work with data professionally. Without infrastructure and data platforms, we cannot store data in databases and run computation to extract value from data. Therefore, after learning about infrastructure in Chapter 2, we focused in Chapter 3 on showing how to build a data platform using architectural designs such as a data lake. Finally, in Chapter 4 we loaded data onto a data platform with technologies such as Apache Kafka.

If a data science project is like building a house, we could say that we have now covered how to build the foundation, such as a cellar, and can now start "building our living space." We should be able to focus on doing what many experts associate with the essence of data science and AI, such as analyzing data sets, running machine learning algorithms, and impressing an audience with our newly generated knowledge. However, there is one item still missing to complete our "foundation."

Suppose you build a data platform and load random data sets onto it. And let us further assume that you found the data in various data sources within an organization. After you load this data onto the platform, you ask your data science team to explore the data. In this scenario, things could still go wrong. For example, some of the data you provided might contain Personal Identifiable Information (PII), meaning it might be illegal to process them without the consent of the individuals who can be identified in that data set. Especially in the EU, violation of the General Data Protection Regulation (GDPR) can be costly[1] and ignoring privacy could ruin a company's reputation. Chapter 18 deals more with AI and ethics issues such as this.

Since data has value, some companies introduced the concept of data ownership. Like using photos from the internet, we might not be allowed to generate insights from data available to us without asking the person who owns it for permission first.

Some industries, such as the finance industry, are heavily regulated. For example, if regulated enterprises do not transparently process data and follow the regulators' standards, they can face fines. The Sarbanes Oxley Act[2] is maybe the most famous reference for such a regulation.

But data governance is not just about legal issues. For example, imagine one of your team members has built a complex data pipeline to ingest specific data sets from an operational data store. She invested a lot of effort to make this pipeline, which fetches data from the source and pushes it into the data platform, production-ready. In Chapter 4, we showed that such an undertaking is not always trivial, and might take some effort. Now imagine you learn that an engineer of a different department has already done the same thing before you: suddenly your IT has two artifacts – both of which do the same thing – to maintain, unless a decision-maker decides to retire one solution.

Lastly, you might want to explore the company's data lake to see what data might be available that could help you generate more value. As your company is enormous and multinational, you learn that many people loaded data into the data lake over the years. Suddenly, you understand why some colleagues call your enterprise data lake a "data swamp." Of all the terabytes of information contained in that lake, the purpose of much of that data is unclear. Suppose for some other data sets, a colleague has documented the purpose she had been loading the data onto the platform. But maybe she has not explained in that document what the data represents. In some cases, you might just see data in a column with a non-descriptive column header and you would have to guess what the values could mean. Not only do you not know who owns the data, but also you wonder whether the data is still valid. If no one takes care of methods to manage data processing in a large organization, chaos will emerge. Thus, a data platform will be useless in time if team members cannot look up which data it contains.

Strictly speaking, the term "data managementd covers a lot of more than just organizing data[3]. By its formal definition, it would also cover data integration, which we discussed in Chapter 4. However, in this book, we use "data management" in the sense of the remaining effort required to provide the proper processes to ensure that data is processed systematically and transparently.

---

[1] https://www.tessian.com/blog/biggest-gdpr-fines-2020/#:~:text=Under%20the%20GDPR%2C%20the%20 EU's,financial%20year%E2%80%94whichever%20is%20higher
[2] https://en.wikipedia.org/wiki/Sarbanes%E2%80%93Oxley_Act
[3] https://en.wikipedia.org/wiki/Data_management

We cover data governance as an overall process to apply corporate rules and company policies to comply with regulators. We also introduce concepts such as quality, that have a direct relationship with exploring data.

Information security explains how to protect information from a technical point of view. We will explore the basics of encryption and secret management in the context of data science. For those who are interested in legal aspects, we cover them in Chapter 15.

■ 5.1 Data Governance

In his book "Non-Invasive Data Governance," Bob Seiner describes the term as follows:

> *"Data governance is the formal execution and enforcement of authority over the management of data and data related assets."* [4]

The author further adds:

> *"By including the term, 'governance,' data governance requires the administration of something. In this case, data governance refers to administering, or formalizing, discipline (behavior) around the management of data."*

Consequently, data governance is a collection of processes that define legal and internal company requirements for company data. Data ownership is one of these processes. A company establishes procedures to assign data to persons who thereby become liable for the appropriate processing of the data under their charge. Thus, "data owners" will be held accountable if they are negligent in protecting the personal data entrusted to them.

Data governance is a procedure that gives companies control over how project teams and processes handle data. Enforcing liabilities can also increase the trust among the users of a data platform.

There is no unique, globally accepted definition of data governance in all respects. A simple Google search for "data governance framework" will return many different interpretations that may overlap in details. Figure 5.1 shows one model for a data governance framework.

The efforts required for maintaining effective data governance may vary depending on the organization. A minimum set of rules is helpful for any company, but commonly the larger the company, the more effort is needed to govern it. Perhaps more than with other chapters in this book, the information in this chapter will be more or less useful for different readers, depending on the company they work for. Members of a startup might want to jump right to the topic of information security, whereas employees of a large organization might want to read this entire chapter multiple times.

---

[4] Seiner, B.: Non-Invasive Data Governance: The Path of Least Resistance and Greatest Success. 2014.
  https://www.amazon.com/dp/B00N3259RG/ref=dp-kindle-redirect?_encoding=UTF8&btkr=1

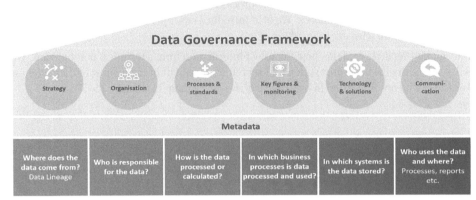

Figure 5.1 The data governance framework of btelligent *(https://www.btelligent.com/en/ portfolio/data-governance/)*

 Glossary

Many people who have not worked much in large enterprise environments are unfamiliar with terms such as "policy", "compliance", "governance" or "regulators".

Studying a glossary while reading this chapter can help to understand content easier. The page datagovernance.com[5] has a good overview of the most common expressions and can be an excellent companion to this chapter.

5.1.1 Data Catalog

A data catalog captures the metadata generated during operational use of data, such as the time of collection, the source- and destination-folders, configurations, duration of the processing, and so on. The goal of the data catalog is to support operational processes. We can classify data catalogs into two categories:

- **Active data catalog:** The synchronization between the data catalog and the operational data is active; each interaction triggers a data catalog update. Experts recommend this procedure for batch processing, since the additional resources required for updating the data catalog have no impact on performance.

- **Passive data catalog:** In the passive data catalog, we maintain data ourselves. This strategy has the advantage that the data catalog process is "detached" from the operational process and hardly affects it.

Depending on the type of operational metadata stored, we can use a data catalog to verify input data by evaluating historical process data and comparing it to current data.

---

[5] *https://datagovernance.com/the-data-governance-basics/data-governance-glossary/*

Data catalogs can provide two functionalities:

- They are required for meeting the requirements of regulators who force businesses to keep track of how they manage data.
- They are also deeply integrated into data exploration processes, which is often the first step in modeling.

In Chapter 3, we introduced a product called Databricks. Like Databricks, many additional, powerful commercial platforms compete to become the leading data platform in the cloud.[6] Such vendors often highlight their diverse features for advanced data exploration. A data catalog is one of these features.

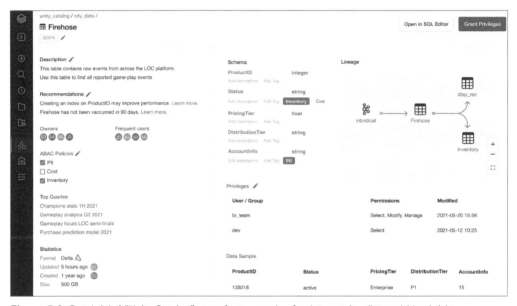

Figure 5.2 Databricks' "Unity Catalog", a perfect example of a data catalog *(https://databricks. com/wp-content/uploads/2021/05/unity_catalog-1-min.png)*

Figure 5.2 contains a screenshot of Databricks' "unity catalog", which perfectly outlines the capabilities of a data catalog. Other large platforms such as Snowflake also offer their own versions. A data catalog allows us to retrieve information such as:

- standard statistics, like format, last updates, creation date, and size
- privileges, such as who is allowed to do what to data
- lineage graphs
- schema of data, its descriptions, and tags
- statistics on common queries and users who access the data
- important policies, such as those revolving around PII
- data owners.

---

[6] *https://databricks.com/blog/2021/03/04/databricks-named-a-leader-in-2021-gartner-magic-quadrant-for-data-science-and-machine-learning-platforms.html*

We can see data catalogs as the successors to traditional database management UIs for database administrators to manage database objects. They add a lot of context information to data, increasing the transparency of an organization's information assets.

We can even use data catalogs for data exploration. For example, a common first step in data science projects is to apply supervised learning mechanisms, such as outlier detection or clustering, to data. Many data catalogs can provide this information out of the box.

 Open Source vs. Commercial Software

In Chapter 16, we outline open source vs. commercial software in more detail. But, first, let's summarize the situation: vendors often establish black box solutions that incorporate many features. Unfortunately, this "one box to bind them" approach also leads to vendor lock-in.

The open-source community instead tries to separate functionalities into clearly distinct services. If a development team decides to discontinue an open-source project, other developers can build an alternative service. The success of the open-source community depends on clearly separated and well-defined interfaces.

Amundsen is an open-source data catalog.[7] You can connect it to many potential data sources and collect a lot of metadata. You then can democratize data by allowing various users to add tags or descriptions.

Prometheus[8] is a tool that has become the de facto standard for observability. It allows an application to expose metrics through a standardized interface and client libraries, and Prometheus itself is a service that can be configured to scrape the exposed data of its target. As a result, Prometheus is an excellent way to collect operational metadata. Meanwhile, Grafana is a well-established visualization tool used to display Prometheus data in dashboards.

5.1.2 Data Discovery

Data discovery is all about establishing a structure in data and creating relationships between one or more data sets. This process enables us to identify structure in existing raw data, gain new insights, increase data quality, or verify or falsify working hypotheses.

Data discovery also enables us to establish a common language within the company and across different departments. For example, technical and business data modeling are two methods of data discovery.

---

[7] https://www.amundsen.io/amundsen/
[8] https://prometheus.io/

5.1.2.1 Technical Modeling

Technical data modeling aims to capture the schema for a given source of raw data before it is modified or combined with other data.

By processing raw data, we can also detect errors at the beginning of the processing chain, and thereby detect common inaccuracies in data sources earlier. Other advantages are that we can use the data already for model building, and that data discovery can be supported by actively tracing the processing chain. For example, the image below shows Apache Atlas, a tool that automatically traces this chain depending on the data processing steps of the respective person.

Figure 5.3 Example of a Lineage in Apache Atlas
(Credit: ext Spline OSS, *https://absaoss.github.io/spline/2019/01/24/Atlas-Support-Is-Back.html*)

Tools like Atlas collect technical metadata, such as file or database names, field names, field types, encoding, length of fields, and so on. In this step, we enrich data with a timestamp to mark the creation time, and a unique identifiable attribute (UUID) to identify the record in the system. This step helps us to find possible errors or deviations in the delivery and to react semi-automatically if necessary. Technical modeling is also the basis for generating appropriate data quality metrics then.

5.1.2.2 Business Modeling

We may provide the same raw data to different departments without giving them any context. Consequently, this also means that various recipients may interpret data differently.

To solve this problem, we can accurately establish standards in interpreting the data from a broad, high-level business perspective. In contrast to technical modeling, the main goal of business modeling is to solve business conflicts, such as the ambiguity of concepts or the different use of the same KPIs. We represent these relationships as a directed graph with edges that have "consists of" or "has a" annotations. For example, Figure 5.4 represents a reference data model taken from a tutorial on modeling data.

Business departments also model business data, in order to create a shared understanding of that data. When the common understanding exists, we transfer it into a corresponding model in the data catalog.

PHYSICAL DATA MODELING

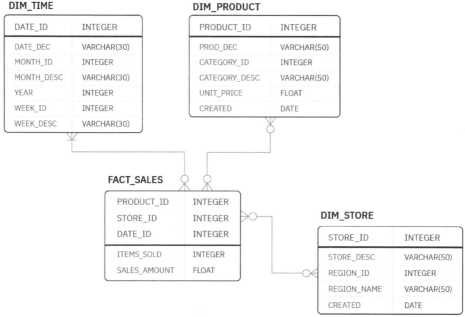

Figure 5.4 A Reference Physical Data Model[9]

5.1.2.3 Roles and Responsibilities

Now that we have explained how to model data, we should also explore who can be responsible for these processes from a company's perspective.

Data steward is commonly a role within an organization whereby the role-holder is responsible for data maintenance, data collection, and modeling. This role tends to be business-oriented. Employees who work as data stewards have to have the appropriate domain knowledge to correctly model the facts around the data. Companies like Experian recommend hiring data stewards[10] to improve data quality.

Smaller companies often cannot hire a full-time employee as a data steward. Thus, subject matter experts, analysts, and data scientists may also share the duties of a data steward.

There are three ways in which we can embark upon the subject of data modeling:

1. **Data modeling started with a problem in the respective department or subject area:**
   The underlying problem is that two previously independent departments need to find a common language and exchange existing definitions and concepts. As soon as they establish a common understanding, they can document their agreements and knowledge

---

9 https://www.ibm.com/cloud/learn/data-modeling
10 https://www.experian.co.uk/business/glossary/data-steward/

appropriately. This approach follows the top-down approach, as data is modeled with a bird's eye view.

2. **Data modeling is created based on a technical necessity:** The data is collected specifically for an operational process and managed locally by the person who develops the corresponding software. As soon as we transform the data, we also capture the data model changes. This process follows the bottom-up approach, as it works from the "bottom-up" perspective.

3. **Dedicated organizational departments or staff units take care of data modeling:** People from outside the department model that department's data. The approach includes a systematic walk-through of all departments, and is rarely applied because the appropriate knowledge of how departments use the data is often missing.

Data Governance Council

The Data Governance Council is a decision-making board formed by department heads to coordinate and control data modeling efforts. Their goal is to define the requirements of the companies' data and the strategies and implementation framework for the entire company. This is achieved through various activities:

1. The council defines the framework for data governance, that is, how teams should model, standardize and collect data. This practice includes providing an appropriate forum, such as a community, where data stewards can exchange and discuss ideas. Typically, they develop new policies, standards, and guidelines collaboratively. The result of the exchange is then prepared and made available to the stakeholders in a suitable format.

2. The Data Governance Council also defines the tools by which the data modeling happens, aiming to standardize the toolset for the whole organization. In addition, the goal is to have a standard business glossary with commonly defined and shared terms. The regular updating of this dictionary is also an activity of the council.

3. The council controls data modeling projects from a macro level (in comparison, data stewards work at the micro-level). Consequently, the board identifies possible potentials, sets up projects for this purpose, and monitors their progress.

4. Finally, the council also ensures that data governance is implemented correctly in all company departments, and that all projects adhere to the appropriate framework.

It is uncommon for smaller organizations to establish a data governance council. Still, larger organizations, especially multinational organizations[11], benefit from this structure. For example, global organizations such as the UN, IAEA, or WHO can use a data governance council to facilitate their work when dealing with different interest groups.

 ■

---

[11] *https://www.epa.gov/data/data-governance-council*

5.1.3 Data Quality

We need to determine metrics if we want to ensure data quality successfully. However, as with data governance, there is no universally accepted definition of data quality, and many consultants are creative in designing their slides with different attributes.

In Figure 5.5, we outline the metrics taken from a research project called "Big Data Quality Dimensions: A Systematic Literature Review" published in 2020[12].

Yet this is only one view, and it can also help to compare it with other perspectives. For example, another research[13] highlights an almost identical list of metrics: Completeness, Accuracy, Consistency, Validity, Timeliness, and Integrity.

Figure 5.5 Data Quality Attributes

Let's define common attributes in quality frameworks and outline what they mean:

- **Accuracy:** Imagine a real estate agent wants to reach out to some of his customers with offers for luxury departments. Suppose the customer rating is incorrect due to inaccuracies while collecting the income, and thus this offer also goes to customers who cannot afford a luxury department. Clearly the accuracy of the data was too low.

- **Completeness:** Suppose the real-estate agency has entered all their clients into a customer database. But when they want to reach out to them, they realize that e-mail addresses and phone numbers are missing for some datasets. Such data would score poorly for completeness.

---

[12] https://www.researchgate.net/figure/Data-Quality-Dimensions-adapted-from-DAMA-2013_fig1_341650593
[13] https://www.cloverdx.com/blog/6-data-quality-metrics-you-cant-ignore

- **Consistency:** Data has to represent the correct status, at any time, reliably. If you have different systems, you may have different information about a user; any shared attributes within this data cannot be allowed to differ. An example of this would be a user who has "January 30, 1981" as their date of birth in one system, but a different date of birth – perhaps caused by confusion regarding date formatting – in the other.

- **Integrity:** Data integrity is the overall accuracy, completeness, and consistency of data.

- **Relevancy:** For any given use case, the data collected has to serve that use case genuinely. For example, suppose we want to understand what types of customers buy luxury cars. A customer's shoe size would hardly affect purchasing behavior and would not be relevant in this sense.

- **Timeliness:** Data has to be available when it is needed. For example, if you give purchasing recommendations on the stock market and your model evaluates the data too late, it will deliver false recommendations. In the stock market environment, fluctuations are possible within a few seconds, and consequently, a delay of several minutes often means that you are no longer on time.

- **Uniqueness:** Imagine you collect the data of all company employees in a database, and there are multiple records to one or more individuals. Additionally, you might have one or more departments using a different database to process the same data. Only one record or one database gets updated at some point in time, and people using the other record or database have outdated information. Therefore, if data are unique, it ensures transparency, and companies can avoid confusion or conflicts.

- **Validity:** Imagine you look up an event calendar and read about an event you want to visit. You show up, but nobody is there. Soon you learn that you had an old calendar that contained some outdated – and thus, invalid – information.

All quality attributes have to be measured individually, and KPIs may vary. For example, the term "real-time" specifies a system that delivers a response within a certain, guaranteed time. Suppose system A has real-time requirements of two hours and system B of two seconds. If data for system A is available in one hour and thirty minutes and for system B in three seconds, data for system B fails to meet the SLAs, even though it is, in fact, available more quickly.

5.1.4 Master Data Management

Master data represents "data about the business entities that provide context for business transactions"[14]. Therefore, it must be unique across the enterprise (for example, there should be only one record on a specific individual).

A golden record is a "single, well-defined version of all the data entities in an organizational ecosystem." In this context, a golden record is sometimes called the "single version of the truth," where "truth" is understood to mean the reference to which data users can turn when they want to ensure that they have the correct version of a piece of information. The

---

[14] DAMA-DMBOK: Data Management Body of Knowledge. Data Management Association. 2017. ISBN 9781634622349.

golden record encompasses all the data in every system of record (SOR) within a particular organization"[15].

In B2C scenarios, we can compare the hunt for a golden record in companies with searching for the holy grail: Many hope it exists, but it is nowhere to be found. Why is it so complex? Let's consider an example. According to Statista[16], we have 38,313 people named "James Smith" in the US, making it the most common name. So, we can assume that we will find a multitude of James Smiths, with the same birthdate, living in different or even the same city. This means the James Smith registered on 285 Fulton St, New York, NY 10007, USA, might be the same person as the one registered with 1 Telegraph Hill Blvd, San Francisco, CA 94133, United States some years ago. But it may be difficult to know this for sure, without additional attributes. Even if we have those extra attributes, we may need to deal with typos, name alterations, or even fake data, which can occur if someone does not want to provide their actual information.

Luckily, *james.smith@gmail.com* or *https://www.facebook.com/james.smith/* are unique identifiers. And although a "real James Smith" may use different email addresses and use various social media accounts, there is a good chance that the information we get through linking social media accounts may identify that person better than just through standard data such as name, address, and birthday. Of course, we rarely call Facebook or Gmail "identity providers" in the first place when we talk about them, but we should be aware of their impact in the B2B world if they are the missing link between people using different systems.

5.1.5 Data Sharing

Data sharing describes principles for how a company can share data effectively and add value outside of the company. It is the ability of an organization to distribute its data within a defined group of people without inconsistencies in the data or problems occurring during transmission. Different entities can share data but usually follow the value chain of the business departments. Depending on the purpose of data sharing, there are four scenarios:

1. **Data sharing to make the company more efficient:** Departments can share data with other business units to generate new ideas and improve processes or products.

2. Data sharing to eliminate data silos: Data managers can counteract historically grown data silos with data sharing, and increase the collaboration between different teams. In doing so, they increase the flow of information and knowledge, and further enhance the effectiveness of collaborating teams.

3. Data sharing as a product: Companies can sell data directly. In this case, the data is the end product.

4. **Data sharing as product differentiation:** Service providers of B2B companies can publish this data and establish themselves as an ecosystem. "Data as a Service" leads to new revenue streams, and companies receive added value through improved data services.

---

[15] *https://whatis.techtarget.com/definition/golden-record*
[16] *https://www.statista.com/statistics/279713/frequent-combinations-of-first-and-last-name-in-the-us/*

Data sharing creates a "win-win" situation, as the value of the data increases with its use. In addition, this willingness to open up can lead to new revenue streams, as the shared data is used to develop new products or services.

One way to share data is to make it available for a larger audience. Organizations can provide open data free of charge in a machine-readable format, such as JSON or CSV. An open license allows sharing and processing of the data without restrictions. The goal is to generate added value via:

- **Traceability of decisions based on Open Data:** Because the basis of the findings is open, we can understand the effects accordingly.

- **FAIR Principle:** Another synonymous principle that extends Open Data, the FAIR principle emphasizes discoverability and interoperability with minimal human impact. It aims to improve the processing of data via automation.

To support processing, we must add a globally unique persistent identifier to the dataset. The record must also remain available even if someone deletes the dataset. Instead of physically deleting it, the system marks the dataset as deleted. The metadata of the dataset contains all relevant information, as well as references to other datasets. The data is in a recognized format, such as XML. Furthermore, the metadata has to be indexed by a search engine and actively support discoverability. The open format of Open Data then allows practical reusability and thus increases the added value of the data.

■ 5.2 Information Security

We can differentiate between *platform security* and *information security*. Platform security aims to block potential intrusion attempts, using tools such as firewalls, secure authentication, and intrusion detection software. Consequently, the Center for Internet security (CIS) benchmarks[17] define best practices for hardening operating systems, orchestration engines, or cloud platforms. System engineers can use them as a checklist to make a platform more secure, and turn to them for advice about deactivating various unused services and adding encryption mechanisms.

Cloud providers advertise many services to measure the security level in the cloud against hacking attempts. In addition, all cloud providers also promote a "shared responsibility model"[18,19,20]. It emphasizes that while the cloud provider can provide strong platform security, it is still the customer's responsibility to protect the information in the cloud.

Similar to platform security, information security has standards. In addition, some organizations act as representatives for information security. For example, in the EU, it is ENISA.[21] These organizations promote best practices for information security. One of these recom-

---

[17] *https://www.cisecurity.org/cis-benchmarks/*
[18] *https://aws.amazon.com/compliance/shared-responsibility-model/*
[19] *https://docs.microsoft.com/en-us/azure/security/fundamentals/shared-responsibility*
[20] *https://services.google.com/fh/files/misc/gcp_pci_srm__apr_2019.pdf*
[21] *https://www.enisa.europa.eu/*

mendations is Privacy by Design.[22] Ann Cavoukian created these principles to have a common standard to protect an individual against data misuse. In this section, we give an overview of how to safeguard information based on these standards.

5.2.1 Data Classification

Let's first answer one question in detail: what do we have to protect? Every organization has public information, and some public content does not need protection. So, how do we define which data is confidential?

Data classification defines a confidentiality level of data sets and categorizes them into security classes. There is no unique standard accepted worldwide that specifies these levels. Therefore, institutions create their own classifications. We have provided some examples in the table below.

Standard	Classification
GitLab[23]	Classification into labels from red to green.
Carnegie Mellon University[24]	Classification into "restricted", "private", and "public"
Berkeley[25]	Classification into four levels from P1 to P4

In most cases, companies will use common classification standards and adjust them for their needs. Some may call sensitive data confidential; others may use terms such as "secret" or "top secret". The standards are also adapted to company-specific requirements and can vary from organization to organization, since each organization may have fundamentally different data to others.

Most important of all, data classification standards have to be unambiguous. A data professional needs to immediately understand how information needs to be classified based on its content. The classification has to be clear without any interpretation of how to handle the data and who should have access to it. A good data classification standard also describes the impact of data misuse. Some guidelines even outline possible consequences which may be applicable if there is a data exposure, or "leak."[26]

Privacy by Design[27] defines the fundamental principle that we assume data is private if not otherwise specified. Privacy by Design also recommends eight Privacy by Design strategies. We cover the techniques Inform, Control, Enforce and Demonstrate with a data catalog. The other four attributes describe how a company can ensure that access to data is restricted:

- **Minimize:** Personal data should be restricted to the minimal amount possible (data minimization).

---

[22] *https://www.enisa.europa.eu/publications/privacy-and-data-protection-by-design/at_download/fullReport*
[23] *https://about.gitlab.com/handbook/engineering/security/data-classification-standard.html*
[24] *https://www.cmu.edu/iso/governance/guidelines/data-classification.html*
[25] *https://security.berkeley.edu/data-classification-standard*
[26] *https://www.angelo.edu/administrative-support/information-technology/it_policies/dataClassificationStandard.php*
[27] *https://www.enisa.europa.eu/publications/big-data-protection*

- **Hide:** Personal data and their interrelations should be hidden from users working with data.
- **Separate:** Personal data should be processed in a distributed fashion, in separate compartments whenever possible.
- **Aggregate:** Personal data should be processed at the highest level of aggregation and with the least possible detail by which it is (still) useful.

The key to optimal security is always to apply privacy principles to their maximum. A system should provide users only information that is relevant to them. A vigilant information security department must also perform regular audits to ensure that users are following required standards.

Based on the respective classification of the data, we can also create an authorization structure. Here, the data owners define which user groups can read which data.

From practice: Be the devil's advocate, but not the devil himself.

We can compare a day-to-day job of an infosec employee with the employees in a legal department: An infosec employee always has to expect the worst and articulate possible consequences if things go from bad to worse.

Sometimes there is friction in a company. For example, enthusiasts in a company visualize what an organization can do and would love to overhaul the company strategy with new data monetization strategies and new business models. These employees with a revolutionary mindset often perceive an infosec department as a massive concrete wall that obstructs the profitable path to a new future. Frustrated innovators may even argue that companies can sabotage themselves by being overly protective.

In large organizations, infosec employees may become bureaucrats. However, some cynics claim that ambitious infosec employees can be even more dangerous. It sounds far-fetched, but many engineers have at least one war story in which they had to explain to a larger audience why their system did not work, and often superiors blamed them for adding a new bug or not testing the rollout. Sometimes the root cause actually comes down to something like a member of an infosec department closing a port or restricting access to a system without announcing this properly. Once the security engineer reopens the network port, the application runs again. Therefore, one metric to measure the effectiveness of infosec departments is purposeful and transparent actions. And to close ports to improve some numbers in a security dashboard alone should not be the goal, if this could affect project teams.

5.2.2 Privacy Protection

No individual user should be identifiable in a data set unless they have given their consent (Chapter 15 will explain the legal background for this). However, a company can generalize user information from a data set, and it is more difficult to detect a person once the details are gone. We could replace a birthday with birth year, a name with initials, and a residential address with the person's hometown. Data scientists can use the data as soon as it becomes improbable that one could identify a person from that data set.

Attribute	Unaggregated	Aggregated
Name	William Henry Gates III	BG
Home Address	1835 73rd Ave NE, Medina, Washington	Washington
Birthday	October 28, 1955	Age between 60 and 70
Marital Status	Divorced	–

Ensuring that people are not identifiable in a dataset requires an understanding of statistics. It depends on many factors, such as the number of people in the data set and the prior-knowledge that a viewer of the data could have. For example, if we know that Bill Gates is in a specific hospital and precisely one person in the aggregated hospital data set has the initials "BG" and is aged between 60 and 70, we will be able to identify him.

If we had more multiple patients that matched the aggregated data set, it would be more difficult. Still, suppose a diagnosis is attached to every person, and we had detailed insights into Mr. Gates's history of illnesses. In that case, we might again at least speculate about the reasons for his presence in the hospital. As a rule of thumb, the smaller the data set, the more we need to generalize in order to achieve anonymity.

The exact anonymization process required comes down to purpose. For example, assuming we want to study various illnesses and just need medical data, the person's initials or home addresses might not matter; a randomly generated, unique ID would be enough as a unique identifier of a data row. On the other hand, if we have a theory that some illnesses are more frequent in certain regions, the home address might be relevant as a column.

There are data anonymity techniques such as k-anonymity, l-diversity, and t-closeness. These statistics offer various methods to measure the chances to identify people in a data set. Chapter 15 provides more details, in its section on anonymity.

 Telecommunication Use Cases as a Reference

A Telco is an excellent example of how much privacy by design matters. Each Telco has the technologies to track its users. In a country without any privacy rules, sales departments could send users in supermarkets messages about products at any time. One benefit of data protection laws such as the GDPR is that people are also protected from being spammed in such a manner.

Still, aggregated user data is valuable for telecommunications. Chapter 16 shows how we can monetize generalized data to gain insights about customer segmentation in geographical areas. Many data scientists will spend a lot of time planning aggregation strategies to ensure that it is impossible to identify individuals in data, and that the data sets are nevertheless still valuable.

5.2.3 Encryption

Encryption is about more than just hiding data from a user's plain view on an application screen. (In fact, secure applications do not display data at all, if it is not relevant for users and the current use case). Instead, encryption is one of the core pillars of information security. For example, there exists a risk that hackers can intercept data on its way from a sender to a recipient. Thus, we use encryption in transit to ensure that they would not see messages in plaintext. Furthermore, thieves can steal hardware, but a thief might not be able to use the information on a stolen hard drive, if it has been encrypted. We call this topic encryption at rest. In Chapter 15, we will provide more details on these processes.

Bruce Schneier outlines the process of encryption. He introduces two approaches[28]: Symmetric and asymmetric encryption.

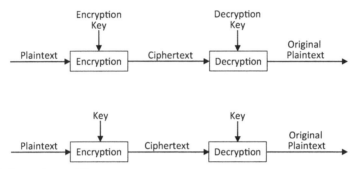

Figure 5.6 Encryption workflows

In symmetric encryption, data is encrypted and decrypted with the same key. By contrast, in asymmetric encryption we use one key for encrypting a message and another to decrypt it.

Figure 5.7 outlines a reference case in which a user wants to retrieve data from a secured environment. To do so, she needs to authenticate. Suppose she is authorized to view the item. In that case, the data store returns the data first encrypted. Next, a service user will request access to the encryption key and decrypt the message with the key in plain text. Lastly, the data will be sent to her via HTTPS.

---

[28] Bruce Schneier, Applied Cryptography, John Wiley & Sons Inc, 2015.

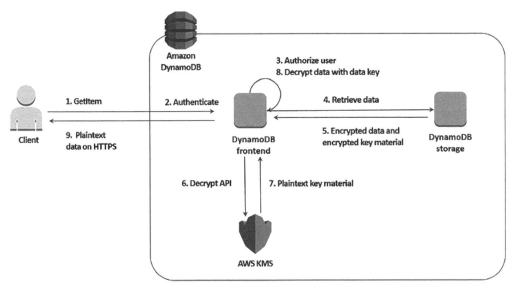

Figure 5.7 A reference workflow of retrieval using a key management service
*(https://aws.amazon.com/blogs/database/understanding-amazon-dynamodb-encryption-by-using-
aws-key-management-service-and-analysis-of-api-calls-with-amazon-athena/)*

 Transport Layer Security (TLS)

TLS has become the leading standard for encryption in transit. It is a crypto-
graphic protocol to provide communication security over a computer network.
While security departments manage details such as TLS certificates in large
companies, a minimum awareness of TLS is always necessary for data
scientists. In addition, data scientists working for startups or small companies
may also provide their solutions through web portals. It would create a negative
impression if web portals that present confidential insights have outdated TLS
certificates or no TLS enabled on the platform. In addition, many consumers
would be mistrustful of a company providing sensitive information over an
unencrypted channel.

Chapter 4 contains an analogy of data scientists as soccer players, in which
one waits for opportunities to be delivered to them, similar to an archetypical
football striker who just waits for other players to provide passes. Similarly,
some data scientists might expect to receive a link to a JupyterHub notebook
and to simply be able to work from there without any need to talk about
infrastructure and TLS details. Yet many companies expect data scientists to
be hands-on, if needed. The first test is when you sit data scientists in front
of a terminal window, pass them some credentials and ask them to set up a
passwordless ssh connection to a remote server. This experience can lead to
the kind of moment in which a person's face expresses more than a thousand
words (and not all of them are pleasant)!

5.2.4 Secrets Management

With the key management system in Figure 5.7, we already touched on having single services that hold confidential information. In a KMS, the encryption key is this confidential information. Key management systems also have additional key rotation policies to ensure that keys are changed within specific periods.

Secret managers, often also called vaults, are services to store confidential information. Passwords are the most common type of information we want to protect, because they provide us with a mechanism to fetch sensitive data. But all kinds of confidential information, such as certificates or secret memos, can be stored there.

Hashicorp Vault and Ansible Vault are two examples of secret managers. Nearly all data scientists will be confronted with these technologies at some point in their career, and need to be able to master them. Figure 5.8 shows the fundamentals of Hashicorp Vault. The critical success of a key manager is to provide strong authentication methods to ensure data is safe and has good integration into diverse systems and technologies.

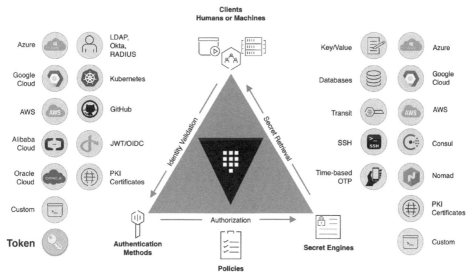

Figure 5.8 Hashicorp Vault
(https://learn.hashicorp.com/tutorials/vault/getting-started-intro?in=vault/getting-started)

For this book, a detailed description of these services is out of scope. Hashicorp Vault[29], however, provides excellent tutorials for the interested reader.

---

[29] https://www.vaultproject.io/

5.2.5 Defense in Depth

Defense in depth is a concept used in information security in which multiple layers of security controls (defense) protect an information technology (IT) system.

Figure 5.9 shows the castle Hochosterwitz in Austria. As we can see, this castle has various layers of defense.

Figure 5.9 Castle Hochosterwitz (Source: Rollroboter, CC BY-SA 4.0, *https://en.wikipedia.org/wiki/Hochosterwitz_Castle#/media/File:Hochosterwitz_%C3%9Cbersicht.jpg*)

The defense is oriented so that if an enemy attacker breaks through one fortification, they still have to fight through other walls and towers. With that, a castle is harder to take.

Defense in depth in a computer security environment also contains many layers. For example, even if an attacker breaches a firewall, they may not be able to cause any damage if, for instance, data has been encrypted.

In Figure 5.7, we outline a secure access workflow to fetch confidential data. If we study this picture in more detail, we will see multiple layers of security.

- The clients themselves need to authenticate against a user directory before they can even trigger a request.
- The clients must authenticate against a service, and the service will reject them if they cannot perform read operations on the target.

- The service user running the front end must authenticate against the key management system to fetch the encryption key.
- Lastly, from the frontend to the user, there is another encrypted communication via HTTPS.

Now that you understand how to structure and secure data, it is time to jump into analytics. The next chapter will present the essentials: Mathematics and Statistics.

■ 5.3 In a Nutshell

How much Data Governance matters to you may depend on the organization you work in.

Some organizations require a lot of control over their data, others less.

Data Catalogs are the new democratized versions of old tedious database administration UIs.

Looking at Data Catalogs, they already give a lot of insights into the data structures of a company.

InfoSec matters to us all.

We can be the most brilliant data scientists in the world, but a project will likely fail if we do not protect our information security.

Aim to master standard security tools.

SSH, TLS, and Vaults can be part of your daily job. Some companies expect you to master them, even if you are a data scientist.

Golden Record

Sometimes the same entity is represented in different data. Finding out which data belongs together enables us to get deeper insights.

■

6 Mathematics

Annalisa Cadonna

> *"We will always have STEM with us. Some things will drop out of the public eye and go away, but there will always be science, engineering and technology. And there will always, always be mathematics"*
>
> Katherine Johnson

Questions Answered in this Chapter:

- What are the topics in mathematics that are needed to understand machine learning models and algorithms?
- What are matrices and vectors?
- How does matrix decomposition work and how is it used in data science?
- What is gradient descent and how does it work?
- What is constrained optimization?
- How can we incorporate uncertainty in machine learning?
- What is a random variable?
- What is the difference between continuous and discrete random variables?
- When are two variables independent?

Machine learning algorithms have become readily accessible in the last few years thanks to easy-to-use software libraries, where low-level details are not shown to the practitioner. Such accessibility allows a growing number of applications to exploit the potential of machine learning and artificial intelligence. However, it also poses a risk: the practitioners might not understand fully the inner workings and limitations of the algorithms they use. While skilled in programming languages and computation, data scientists with a background in computer science and software engineering might lack the mathematical foundations to deeply understand some machine learning models and algorithms.

The goal of this chapter is to make the reader familiar with the four mathematical fields which constitute the basis of machine learning and artificial intelligence: linear algebra, calculus, optimization, and probability theory. The first three fields are deterministic, meaning they do not leave room for uncertainty. Probability theory, on the other hand, provides us with tools to account for uncertainty, which is key in data science.

Of course, a chapter is not enough to explain all the mathematics at the base of data science! We have omitted the topics that are not crucial for the understanding of the next chapters of this book. If you are familiar with any of the topics covered in this chapter, feel free to skip the relative section. If you are new to the topics, this chapter will equip you with the skills to understand the foundations of most models and algorithms employed in data science. You should be able to follow along even without a quantitative background. However, we assume that you are familiar with the set of real numbers and its properties.

In Section 6.1 we outline the foundations of linear algebra; Section 6.2 presents a few topics in Calculus and Optimization. Section 6.3 introduces the reader to probability theory. Finally, Section 6.4 concludes by summarizing the key concepts presented in the chapter.

■ 6.1 Linear Algebra

Vectors and matrices, the building blocks in linear algebra, are at the basis of many models and algorithms that we use in data science. Here, we mention only a few:

- Structured data come in the form of matrices, which have observations on their rows and variables on their columns. Such matrices are used in multiple linear and logistic regression, among other methods.
- Sentences can be represented as vectors.
- Principal Component Analysis and other techniques for dimensionality reduction are based on matrix decomposition.
- Images can be represented as tensors, which are a generalization of matrices to a higher dimension.

6.1.1 Vectors and Matrices

In the next pages, you will often see the notation $\mathbb{R}^2$, $\mathbb{R}^3$, ... $\mathbb{R}^n$. What do these symbols mean? $\mathbb{R}^2$ is the set of all ordered pairs of real numbers, or 2-tuple of elements of $\mathbb{R}$. This concept can be generalized to $\mathbb{R}^n$, which is the set of all n-tuples of elements of $\mathbb{R}$. Such n-tuples of elements of $\mathbb{R}$ are called **vectors** in linear algebra. Another way to think of vectors is as arrays of numbers.

We indicate vectors with a lowercase bold letter. When we want to write a generic vector, each element is written lowercase and is identified by one single index. Moreover, we use by default the so-called column vectors format, in which the elements of the vector are placed under each other in a column. As an example, we write:

$$\mathbf{a} = \begin{bmatrix} a_1 \\ a_2 \\ \vdots \\ a_n \end{bmatrix}.$$

Vectors live in a structured space called (finite) vector space. Loosely speaking, a vector space is any space which contains mathematical objects that can be multiplied by scalars and added together, resulting in an object of the same type. In linear algebra, a scalar is an object that scales the elements of a vector space: in our case, a scalar is simply a number. According to this definition, $\mathbb{R}^n$ is a vector space.

As mentioned, adding two vectors of the same length results in another vector, which is obtained by element-wise addition. When we multiply a vector by a scalar coefficient we obtain a scaled vector, where each element of the vector is multiplied by the scalar.

Example: Addition of two vectors of the same length

Let $\boldsymbol{a} = \begin{bmatrix} 2 \\ 4 \\ 1 \end{bmatrix}$ and $\boldsymbol{b} = \begin{bmatrix} 4 \\ 1 \\ 1 \end{bmatrix}$, we have that $\boldsymbol{c} = \boldsymbol{a} + \boldsymbol{b} = \begin{bmatrix} 2 \\ 4 \\ 1 \end{bmatrix} + \begin{bmatrix} 4 \\ 1 \\ 1 \end{bmatrix} = \begin{bmatrix} 6 \\ 5 \\ 2 \end{bmatrix}$.

Example: Multiplication of a vector by a scalar coefficient

Now, let us consider a scalar $\lambda = 10$. We have that $\lambda \boldsymbol{a} = 10 \begin{bmatrix} 2 \\ 4 \\ 1 \end{bmatrix} = \begin{bmatrix} 10(2) \\ 10(4) \\ 10(1) \end{bmatrix} = \begin{bmatrix} 20 \\ 40 \\ 10 \end{bmatrix}$.

■

The second type of object at the foundation of linear algebra is a matrix (plural '**matrices**'). A matrix is a rectangular object with rows and columns. We usually denote a matrix with a bold capital letter and denote each element of the matrix with a capital letter with two indexes, one for the row number and one for the column number. For example,

$$A = \begin{bmatrix} A_{1,1} & A_{1,2} & A_{1,3} \\ A_{2,1} & A_{2,2} & A_{2,3} \end{bmatrix}$$

is a *2-by-3* matrix. Of course, when doing practical calculations, we replace the generic elements with real numbers.

As we did with vectors, we can define the addition of matrices as element-wise addition and the multiplication by a scalar coefficient as the operation that returns a matrix with every element multiplied by a scalar. To add two matrices, they must have the same dimension, that is, the same number of rows and columns.

Example: Addition of two matrices with the same dimension

Let $A = \begin{bmatrix} 1 & 2 \\ 3 & 2 \\ 1 & 5 \end{bmatrix}$ and $B = \begin{bmatrix} 5 & 3 \\ 2 & 4 \\ 2 & 6 \end{bmatrix}$. Let us calculate the matrix C as:

$$C = A + B = \begin{bmatrix} 1 & 2 \\ 3 & 2 \\ 1 & 5 \end{bmatrix} + \begin{bmatrix} 5 & 3 \\ 2 & 4 \\ 2 & 6 \end{bmatrix} = \begin{bmatrix} 6 & 5 \\ 5 & 6 \\ 3 & 11 \end{bmatrix}.$$

Example: Multiplication of a matrix by a scalar coefficient

Let us now consider $\lambda = 3$ and calculate λA: $\lambda A = 3 \begin{bmatrix} 1 & 2 \\ 3 & 2 \\ 1 & 5 \end{bmatrix} = \begin{bmatrix} 3 & 6 \\ 9 & 6 \\ 3 & 15 \end{bmatrix}.$

■

When doing calculations that involve matrices and vectors, we often encounter the concept of the **transpose** of a matrix. The transpose of a matrix is the matrix with its rows and columns inverted. This means that the number of rows becomes the number of columns in the transpose, and the number of columns becomes the number of rows. The transpose of A is denoted with A^T.

An important consideration to make before we proceed is that a vector is a matrix. Specifically, a column vector of length n is a matrix with n rows and one column, and a row vector of length n is a vector with one row and n columns. Hence, the transpose of a column vector is a row vector with the same elements, and vice versa.

 Example: Transpose of a matrix

Let $A = \begin{bmatrix} 1 & 2 \\ 3 & 2 \\ 1 & 5 \end{bmatrix}$, we have that $A^T = \begin{bmatrix} 1 & 3 & 1 \\ 2 & 2 & 5 \end{bmatrix}$.

Let $C = \begin{bmatrix} 1 & 2 \\ 3 & 5 \end{bmatrix}$, we have that $C^T = \begin{bmatrix} 1 & 3 \\ 2 & 5 \end{bmatrix}$.

Example: Transpose of a vector

Let $a = \begin{bmatrix} 1 \\ 3 \\ 1 \end{bmatrix}$ be a column vector, the transpose of a is the row vector $a^T = \begin{bmatrix} 1 & 3 & 1 \end{bmatrix}$.

An important class of matrices in linear algebra are the so-called **square matrices**, which are matrices where the number of rows is the same as the number of columns. The most popular square matrix is the **identity matrix**, which has ones on the diagonal and zero elsewhere. We denote the n-by-n identity matrix with I_n. As an example, we write the *3-by-3* identity matrix as

$$I_3 = \begin{bmatrix} 1 & 0 & 0 \\ 0 & 1 & 0 \\ 0 & 0 & 1 \end{bmatrix}.$$

The identity matrix plays the role of the number one in linear algebra: each square matrix multiplied by the identity matrix results in the original matrix itself: that is, $AI_n = A$. This will become clear once you know how matrix multiplication works. We will get there in Section 6.1.2.

The identity matrix allows us to define the **inverse** of a matrix. Specifically, if there exists a matrix B for which it holds that $AB = I_n = BA$, B is called the inverse of A and denoted as A^{-1}. When the inverse of a matrix exists, the matrix is called 'invertible' or 'nonsingular'. When the inverse of a matrix does not exist, the matrix is called 'noninvertible' or 'singular'. If a matrix is invertible, its inverse is unique, which only one inverse exists. When A^{-1} exists, there are several algorithms to calculate it analytically. However, in data science, we rarely calculate the inverse directly, mostly because of computational limitations. Nonetheless, the inverse is important for two main reasons:

- we need to know if a matrix is invertible when solving linear systems, and

- we use the inverse notation when writing mathematical models or explaining operations involving matrices.

Among the square matrices, an important subclass is that of matrices with non-zero values on the diagonal and zero otherwise: such matrices are called square **diagonal matrices**. As an example,

$$D = \begin{bmatrix} 4.2 & 0 & 0 \\ 0 & 3.5 & 0 \\ 0 & 0 & 1.9 \end{bmatrix}$$

is a *3-by-3* diagonal matrix. While the most popular diagonal matrices are square, we can have also rectangular matrices that are diagonal, if the only elements different than zero are the ones with the same column and row index. Other important square matrices are triangular matrices. A square matrix is lower triangular if all the entries above the diagonal are zero, while it is upper triangular if all the entries below the main diagonal are zero.

Another linear algebra object worth knowing, which could make your calculations easier, is the **trace**. The trace is the sum of all the diagonal entries of a square matrix. For an *n-by-n* matrix A the trace is denoted as $tr(A)$ and defined as

$$tr(A) = \sum_{i=1}^{n} A_{i,i}.$$

The trace operator allows us to manipulate operations involving matrices by using two useful properties:

- the trace operator is invariant to the transpose, $tr(A) = tr(A^T)$, and

- the trace operator is invariant to multiplication obtained by taking the last element of the product and placing it in the first position. This means that $r(ABC) = tr(CAB) = tr(BCA)$.

Before proceeding to describe the operations between matrices and vectors, we want to make the reader aware of the existence of **tensors**, which can be seen as a generalization of matrices to a higher dimension. Tensors play an important role in fields where structured data has more than two dimensions. For example, a red-green-blue image can be represented as a three-dimensional array. The first and second dimension indicate the pixel, and the third dimension contains the red, green, and blue values for each pixel.

6.1.2 Operations between Vectors and Matrices

In Section 6.1.1, we saw how both matrices and vectors can be multiplied by a scalar and added to each other. Now, we explain a few other operations involving matrices and/or vectors.

Matrix Multiplication

Let us consider an *m-by-n* matrix A and an *n-by-p* matrix B. The product AB is defined to be the *m-by-p* matrix C, with entries in row i and column j given by

$$C_{i,j} = \sum_{r=1}^{n} A_{i,r} B_{r,j}. \hspace{3cm} \text{Equation 6.1}$$

In words, Equation 6.1 says that the entry in row i and column j of C is computed by taking the i-th row of A and the j-th column of B, multiplying the corresponding entries, and then summing up.

 Example: Matrix multiplication

Let us consider two matrices. A is a *3-by-2* matrix and B a *2-by-4* matrix:

$$A = \begin{bmatrix} 1 & 2 \\ 3 & 2 \\ 1 & 5 \end{bmatrix}, B = \begin{bmatrix} 5 & 3 & 3 & 2 \\ 2 & 1 & 4 & 1 \end{bmatrix}.$$

The product of A and B results in the following *3-by-4* matrix C:

$$C = AB = \begin{bmatrix} 9 & 5 & 11 & 4 \\ 19 & 11 & 17 & 8 \\ 15 & 8 & 23 & 7 \end{bmatrix}.$$

Two facts are very important to remember about matrix multiplication:

- We can multiply two matrices only when the number of columns of the first matrix is equal to the number of rows in the second matrix.
- Matrix multiplication is not commutative, which means that AB does not necessarily equal BA, even when both products are defined, such as in square matrices.

Vector Multiplication

When we deal with vectors, we encounter two types of products.

1. The **inner product**, also called dot product or scalar product, is obtained by summing the products of corresponding entries in the two vectors. The inner product results in a scalar and is only possible between two vectors of the same length. We denote the inner product between a and b as $a \cdot b$ or $a^T b$.

2. The **outer product** between two vectors is obtained by multiplying each element of the first vector by each element of the second vector, and it results in a matrix. If the two vectors have dimensions n and m, the resulting matrix is an *n-by-m* matrix. We denote the outer product between a and b as $a \cdot b$ or ab^T.

 Example: Inner product

Let us consider two vectors of length three:

$$a = \begin{bmatrix} 2 \\ 4 \\ 1 \end{bmatrix}, b = \begin{bmatrix} 1 \\ 3 \\ 1 \end{bmatrix}.$$

The inner product between a and b is

$$a \cdot b = 2(1) + 4(3) + 1(1) = 2 + 12 + 1 = 14.$$

Example: Outer product

Let us now consider the vector a from before (of length three) and a new vector d of length four:

$$a = \begin{bmatrix} 2 \\ 4 \\ 1 \end{bmatrix}, d = \begin{bmatrix} 2 \\ 3 \\ 1 \\ 2 \end{bmatrix}.$$

The outer product between a and d is

$$a \cdot d = \begin{bmatrix} 2(2) & 2(3) & 2(1) & 2(2) \\ 4(2) & 4(3) & 4(1) & 4(2) \\ 1(2) & 1(3) & 1(1) & 1(2) \end{bmatrix} = \begin{bmatrix} 4 & 6 & 2 & 4 \\ 8 & 12 & 4 & 8 \\ 2 & 3 & 1 & 2 \end{bmatrix}.$$

■

Matrix-vector Multiplication

To define matrix-vector multiplication, it is useful to think of a vector as a matrix. As we saw before in the case of matrix multiplication, the number of columns of the first element needs to equal the number of rows of the second element. Hence, we can multiply a row by a matrix, or a matrix by a column vector.

 Examples: Matrix-vector multiplication

Let us consider a *3-by-2* matrix and a vector of length two:

$$A = \begin{bmatrix} 1 & 2 \\ 3 & 2 \\ 1 & 5 \end{bmatrix}, a = \begin{bmatrix} 1 \\ 3 \end{bmatrix}.$$

We can multiply A by a because the number of columns of A equals the number of rows of a. We obtain

$$Aa = \begin{bmatrix} 1(1)+2(3) \\ 3(1)+2(3) \\ 1(1)+5(3) \end{bmatrix} = \begin{bmatrix} 7 \\ 9 \\ 15 \end{bmatrix}.$$

Now, let us consider a vector of length three:

$$b = \begin{bmatrix} 2 \\ 4 \\ 1 \end{bmatrix}.$$

Clearly, the multiplication Ab cannot be done. However, we could pre-multiply A by the transpose of b, obtaining

$$b^T A = \begin{bmatrix} 2(1) + 4(3) + 1(1) & 2(2) + 4(2) + 1(5) \end{bmatrix} = \begin{bmatrix} 15 & 17 \end{bmatrix}.$$

■

6.1.3 Linear Transformations

Matrix-vector multiplication allows us to write a system of linear equations in a compact form. Most of us are familiar from high school with systems of linear equations and how to solve them. Here is an example of such a system:

$$\begin{aligned} 2x_1 + 3x_2 + 5x_3 &= 1 \\ 4x_1 - 2x_2 - 7x_3 &= 8 \\ 9x_1 + 5x_2 - 3x_3 &= 2 \end{aligned}$$

Equation 6.2

We can write the system in Equation 6.2 in a more compact form as

$$\begin{bmatrix} 2 & 3 & 5 \\ 4 & -2 & -7 \\ 9 & 5 & -3 \end{bmatrix} \begin{bmatrix} x_1 \\ x_2 \\ x_3 \end{bmatrix} = \begin{bmatrix} 1 \\ 8 \\ 2 \end{bmatrix}.$$

In general, a system of linear equations can be represented as

$$Ax = b,$$

Equation 6.3

where $A \in \mathbb{R}^{m \times n}$ is a known matrix, $b \in \mathbb{R}^m$ is a known vector and $x \in \mathbb{R}^n$ is a vector of unknown variables. The system can have one solution, no solutions or infinitely many solutions. Yes, there are never more than one and less than infinitely many solutions! Often, we write the solution of the system as $x = A^{-1}b$. Clearly, we need to say something more about A^{-1}, as we know it does not always exist. For A^{-1} to exist, the system needs to have exactly one solution for every value of b.

We do not show the details here, but simply say that a necessary condition for the inverse to exist is that A is a square matrix. This condition however is not sufficient, as the columns of the matrix also need to be linearly independent.

Let us try to look at this from a different perspective. A solution of the system in Equation 6.3 exists if and only if b can be obtained by a linear combination of the columns of A. In this case, we say that b is in the column space of A, where the column space of a matrix is the set of all the linear combinations of the columns. Intuitively, if b cannot be obtained by any combination of the columns of A and hence is not in its columns space, the system has no solutions. If we want to make sure a solution exists for any b, then the column space of A must contain the whole $\mathbb{R}^m$; that is, it needs to have at least m independent columns. The requirement that the matrix has exactly m linearly independent columns enters into play when we want to make sure we have one and only one solution to our system, for each b.

Linear dependence is an important concept in data science: two linearly dependent variables contain the same information as is contained in one variable. Equivalently, if a variable is the linear combination or two or more other variables, then the variable is redundant, and is not adding signal for us to discover, but only noise.

6.1.4 Eigenvalues, Eigenvectors, and Eigendecomposition

Eigenvalues and eigenvectors reveal important information about a matrix. The eigenvectors of a matrix are the directions along which applying the linear transformation induced by the matrix results simply in scaling (and/or flipping the sign). The factors the eigenvectors are scaled by are called 'eigenvalues'. In mathematical terms, this concept is represented via the eigenvalue equation: a non-zero vector v is an eigenvalue of A if it satisfies

$$Av = \lambda v \qquad\qquad \text{Equation 6.4}$$

for some scalar λ.

In general, when we find one eigenvector of a matrix, any vector that is a multiple of the eigenvector satisfies Equation 6.4 and hence is an eigenvector itself. To simplify things, one usually considers the unit eigenvectors, which is simply an eigenvector whose Euclidean norm is one.

A matrix whose eigenvalues are all positive is called 'positive definite', and a matrix whose all eigenvalues are negative is called 'negative definite'. If there are some zeros amongst the eigenvalues, we talk about 'positive semidefinite' and 'negative semidefinite'. The concept of a positive definite matrix is central in linear algebra, as positive definite matrices are usually "nice" matrices to work with.

The product of the eigenvalues of a matrix is the **determinant**, denoted as $det(A)$. The determinant is a number, and its absolute value can be interpreted as the scaled factor by which applying the linear transformation induced by A expands or contracts volumes. If the determinant is one, then A preserves the volume. If the determinant is zero, the volume is completely lost. When the determinant of a matrix is zero, the matrix is not invertible. A useful property of the determinant is that $det(AB) = det(A)det(B)$.

Let us assume that a matrix A has n eigenvectors with corresponding eigenvalues. Let us consider a matrix V, whose columns are the eigenvectors of A, and a diagonal matrix Λ, whose diagonal contains the eigenvalues of A. The **eigendecomposition** of A is given by

$$A = V\Lambda V^{-1}. \qquad\qquad \text{Equation 6.5}$$

We also say that a matrix A is diagonalizable if it is similar to a diagonal matrix. In mathematical terms, being similar to a diagonal matrix means that there is an invertible matrix V such that $V^{-1}AV$ is diagonal.

Not every matrix can be decomposed using eigenvalue decomposition, and for some matrices the eigenvalues and eigenvectors can be complex. In data science, we usually have to decompose real symmetric matrices, such as the covariance matrix. Real symmetric matrices are very likable, as they have real-valued eigenvalues and eigenvectors. Moreover, their eigenvector matrix Q is orthogonal, which means that $Q^T = Q^{-1}$. The decomposition for real symmetric matrices always exists and Equation 6.5 becomes $A = Q\Lambda Q^T$.

We arrange the eigenvalues in the diagonal Λ in descending order. Under this convention, if the eigenvalues are unique, then the eigendecomposition is unique. The eigenvectors corresponding to unique eigenvectors are linearly independent.

Principal Component Analysis (PCA) is a very well-known machine learning algorithm which is based exclusively on linear algebra and specifically on the eigendecomposition. PCA is largely used in data science for dimensionality reduction. Often, PCA is a step used to reduce the dimension of the data before processing with classification, regression, or clustering.

The goal of PCA is to find a low-dimensional representation of the data that maintains as much information as possible. This is equivalent to capturing the largest amount of variance in the data. It can be shown, by following an iterative approach, that the eigenvectors of the covariance matrix are the directions of maximum variance. The variance of the data projected on each eigenvector is then equal to the corresponding eigenvalue.

6.1.5 Other Matrix Decompositions

Matrix decomposition is useful in data science for various reasons. First, it allows us to look at the data from a different perspective. Second, it enables dimensionality reduction, while retaining most of the signal present in the data. Third, decomposing a matrix can facilitate computation. In fact, it allows to decompose matrices into simpler parts, making it easier to carry out complex matrix operations.

In this section we look at three additional matrix decomposition methods: LU decomposition, singular value decomposition (SVD) and Cholesky decomposition.

LU Decomposition

LU decomposition is often used to efficiently solve systems of equations without having to calculate the inverse. It consists in decomposing a matrix in the product of a lower triangular matrix, L and an upper triangular matrix, U. That is, we can write $A = LU$.

Let's see how can solve the system in Equation 6.2 using LU decomposition. First, we replace A with LU: the system becomes $LUx = b$. Now, we can solve this system in two steps:

- first, we solve $Ly = b$ for y,
- second, we solve $Ux = y$ for x.

Each system is straightforward to solve because the matrices involved are triangular and we can use forward substitution and backward substitution, respectively.

Singular Value Decomposition (SVD) and Pseudo-inverse

Singular value decomposition (SVD) is a way to decompose the matrix into singular vectors and singular values. The SVD is more general than the eigendecomposition, in that every real matrix has one, including non-square matrices. Let consider an *m-by-n* matrix A. Its SVD can be written as the product of three matrices as $A = UDV^T$, where U is an *m-by-m* matrix, D is an *m-by-n* matrix and V is an *n-by-n* matrix. The matrices U and V are orthogonal matrices, and D is a (not necessarily square) diagonal matrix. The elements on the diagonal of D are called singular values, while the columns of U and V are the left-singular vectors and right-singular vectors.

SVD allows us to partially generalize matrix inversion to non-square matrices by using the **Moore-Penrose pseudo-inverse**. We have seen that the inverse of a matrix is defined only if the matrix is square. However, we can solve linear systems involving non-square matrices. The Moore-Penrose pseudo inverse is defined as

$$A^+ = \lim_{a \to 0}(A^T A + aI)A^T.$$

Equation 6.6

We can write the pseudo-inverse in Equation 6.6 though a decomposition as

$$A^+ = VD^+U^T,$$

Equation 6.7

where V and U are the matrices in the singular value decomposition of A. D^+ is obtained by the diagonal matrix D in the singular value decomposition by replacing the non-zero elements with their reciprocal and then taking the transpose.

Going back to our system of equations in Equation 6.2 with a non-square matrix A:

- If A has more columns than rows, through the Moore-Penrose pseudo-inverse we obtain one of the infinitely many solutions. Specifically, we obtain the solution with the smallest Euclidean norm.

- If A has fewer columns than rows, there are no solutions. In this case, the Moore-Penrose pseudoinverse provides a solution such that Ax is the closest to b in the Euclidean norm.

Cholesky Decomposition

The Cholesky decomposition is considered the square root for matrices. As the square root of a number allows us to decompose the number into two identical components, the Cholesky decomposition splits a matrix into two components, which are identical except that one is the transpose of the other. The Cholesky decomposition can be applied only to symmetric, positive definite matrices, and looks like $A = LL^T$, where L is a lower diagonal matrix with positive diagonal elements. L is unique and is called the 'Cholesky factor' of A.

Since the covariance matrix is a symmetric positive definite matrix, the Cholesky decomposition is often used in statistics and data science. For example, it is used for efficiently generating samples from a multivariate Gaussian distribution, and to perform linear transformations of random variables. The Cholesky decomposition is also useful to efficiently calculate the determinant of a matrix. In fact, triangular matrices have the property that the determinant is the product of the diagonal elements. This, together with the fact that $det(A) = det(L)det(L^T)$, makes it straightforward to calculate the determinant.

■ 6.2 Calculus and Optimization

The goal of most machine learning algorithms is to find the optimal model configuration with respect to a technical or business metric, given the data. To achieve this goal, an objective function is maximized or, alternatively, a loss function is minimized. Optimization plays a crucial role in machine learning and understanding the basis of optimization provides the data scientist with useful tools. Many machine learning algorithms aim to optimize an objective function by finding an optimal combination of parameters. To find the optimal solution methods based on derivatives and gradients are used, such as the popular gradient descent method. The branch of mathematics that deals with derivatives and gradients, among other things, is called calculus.

The central concept in calculus and optimization is that of **function**. A function is an object that receives something as an input and returns an output. We usually denote a generic function with f and write

$$y = f(x),$$ 　　　　　　Equation 6.8

where x is the input and y the output. The input and output of a function can be numbers, vectors, or matrices. In many applications in machine learning, $x = x$ is a vector in $\mathbb{R}^n$ and y is a real number. In this case, we say that the function f maps $\mathbb{R}^n$ to $\mathbb{R}$.

6.2.1 Derivatives

If you have worked with machine learning algorithms, it is likely that you have heard multiple times the term 'gradient'. The gradient is a generalization of the derivative to a multivariate setting. Let's quickly review the concept of derivative before moving to the gradient and other more interesting objects. The derivative of a function measures how much the output is sensitive to a change in the input. Consider a univariate function (x), which is well-defined in the neighborhood of a number a. The derivative of f in a is defined as the following limit:

$$f'(a) = \lim_{h \to 0} \frac{f(a+h) - f(a)}{h}.$$ 　　　　　　Equation 6.9

When such a limit exists, the function f is said to be differentiable in a.

Example: Derivative

Consider the function $f(x) = x^2$. We want to find the derivative in $a = 3$, we have that

$$f'(3) = \lim_{h \to 0} \frac{f(3+h) - f(3)}{h} = \lim_{h \to 0} \frac{(3+h)^2 - 3^2}{h} = \lim_{h \to 0} \frac{h^2 + 6h}{h} = \lim_{h \to 0} h + 6 = 6$$

We can apply the derivative transformation for each possible value of the input x, in which case we obtain another function, called the 'derivative function' or simply 'derivative'.

Using the definition in Equation 6.9, we can calculate most derivatives. However, it is useful remember a few cases and rules that make our life easier:

- the derivative of a polynomial $f(x) = x^n$ is $f'(x) = nx^{n-1}$,
- the derivative of the exponential function $f(x) = e^x$ is the exponential function itself, that is, $f'(x) = e^x$.

Example: Derivative function

Consider again the function $f(x) = x^2$. By applying the derivative of a polynomial, we find that $f'(x) = 2x$.

If we are interested in the value of the derivative in 3, we can plug in the value 3 and obtain $f'(3) = 2(3) = 6$, which is the same value that we obtained from the definition.

There are then a few rules for derivation, including the famous chain rule. The main rules of derivation are the following:

- **product rule:**

  fxgx'=f'xgx+fxg'x,

- **quotient rule:**

$$\left(\frac{f(x)}{g(x)}\right)' = (f'(x)g(x) - f(x)g'(x))/g(x)^2,$$

- **sum rule:**

$$\left(f(x) + g(x)\right)' = f'(x) + g'(x),$$

- **chain rule:**

$$\left(g(f(x))\right)' = g'(f(x))f'(x).$$

The geometric interpretation of the derivative is that of the tangent to a function. When we calculate the derivative at a specific point $x = a$:

- if the derivative is greater than zero, the function is increasing in a,
- if the derivative is smaller than zero, the function is decreasing in a,
- if the derivative in a is equal to zero, a is considered a stationary point. A stationary point can be a maximum, minimum or a saddle point.

When we talk about maximum and minimum, we need to distinguish between local and global:

- a local maximum is a point where the function is larger than all its neighboring points, but is not the largest globally,
- a local minimum is a point where the function is smaller than all its neighboring points, but is not the smallest globally,
- the point in which the function is the largest is called the 'global maximum', and
- the point in which the function is the smallest is called the 'global minimum'.

Sometimes we are also interested in a derivative of a derivative, which we call the 'second derivative'. The second derivative gives us information on how the derivative changes as we change the input to our function. The second derivative measures curvature:

- if the second derivative is positive, the function curves upwards,
- if the second derivative is negative, the function curves downwards,
- if the second derivative equals zero, there is no curvature.

In Figure 6.1 we can see an example of a function with a local maximum, a local minimum and saddle point.

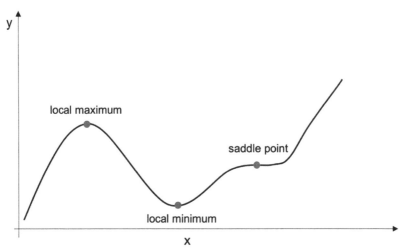

Figure 6.1 Example of a function with local maximum, local minimum, and saddle point

6.2.2 Gradient and Hessian

In machine learning, we often deal with functions that take multiple inputs and return a univariate output. For simplicity, let us consider the case in which f takes in input two variables, that is $y = f(x_1, x_2)$. We can find the derivative of the function with respect to each of the two variables, while keeping the other constant: each one of these derivatives is called partial derivative. The gradient, denoted as $\nabla_x f$, is the vector that contains the two partial derivatives.

 Example: Gradient

We want to find the gradient of the function $f(x_1, x_2) = \left(x_1^2 + x_2^3\right)^2$.

We start by finding the two partial derivatives using the chain rule for each derivative:

$$\frac{\partial f(x_1, x_2)}{\partial x_1} = 2\left(x_1^2 + x_2^3\right)\frac{\partial}{\partial x_1}\left(x_1^2 + x_2^3\right) = 4\left(x_1^2 + x_2^3\right)x_1 = 4x_1^3 + 4x_1 x_2^3$$

$$\frac{\partial f(x_1, x_2)}{\partial x_2} = 2\left(x_1^2 + x_2^3\right)\frac{\partial}{\partial x_2}\left(x_1^2 + x_2^3\right) = 6\left(x_1^2 + x_2^3\right)x_2^2 = 6x_1^2 x_2^2 + 6x_2^5$$

and the gradient is then

$$\nabla_x f = \left[\frac{\partial f(x_1, x_2)}{\partial x_1}, \frac{\partial f(x_1, x_2)}{\partial x_2}\right] = [4x_1^3 + 4x_1 x_2^3, 6x_1^2 x_2^2 + 6x_2^5].$$

Instead of considering two inputs, we can consider n inputs and write them in compact form as a vector $\boldsymbol{x}$: we have then the function $f(\boldsymbol{x})$, which maps $\mathbb{R}^n$ to $\mathbb{R}$. We can think about the gradient as the derivative of a function with univariate output with respect to a vector. The product rule, sum rule and chain rule apply not only to each partial derivative separately, but also to the gradient itself.

Important to remember is that in the case of a function with multiple inputs, the stationary points are the points where all the elements of the gradient are equal to zero.

In Section 6.2.1 we learned of the importance of the second derivative. As the gradient is the generalization of the first derivative, the generalization of the second derivative is the Hessian matrix, denoted with $\boldsymbol{H}$. The Hessian matrix contains all the second order derivatives. We can have:

- the derivative with respect to x_i of the derivative with respect to x_j, keeping all the other x's constant, which we denote as $\dfrac{\partial^2 f}{\partial x_i \partial x_j}(\boldsymbol{x})$,

- the second derivative with respect to x_i, keeping all the other input variables constant, which we call the 'partial second derivative' and denote as $\dfrac{\partial^2 f}{\partial x_i^2}$.

The Hessian matrix looks like

$$\boldsymbol{H} = \begin{bmatrix} \dfrac{\partial^2 f}{\partial x_1^2}(\boldsymbol{x}) & \dfrac{\partial^2 f}{\partial x_1 \partial x_2}(\boldsymbol{x}) & \cdots & \dfrac{\partial^2 f}{\partial x_1 \partial x_n}(\boldsymbol{x}) \\ \dfrac{\partial^2 f}{\partial x_2 \partial x_1}(\boldsymbol{x}) & \dfrac{\partial^2 f}{\partial x_2^2}(\boldsymbol{x}) & \cdots & \dfrac{\partial^2 f}{\partial x_2 \partial x_n}(\boldsymbol{x}) \\ \vdots & \cdots & \ddots & \vdots \\ \dfrac{\partial^2 f}{\partial x_n \partial x_1}(\boldsymbol{x}) & \dfrac{\partial^2 f}{\partial x_n \partial x_2}(\boldsymbol{x}) & \cdots & \dfrac{\partial^2 f}{\partial x_n^2}(\boldsymbol{x}) \end{bmatrix}.$$

How can we use the Hessian to determine what type of stationary point we are looking at? We can check the following:

- if the Hessian is positive-definite (all eigenvalues are positive) at the stationary point, then the stationary point is a (local) minimum,

- if the Hessian is negative-definite at the stationary point (all eigenvalues are negative), then the stationary point is a (local) maximum,

- if the Hessian has both positive and negative eigenvalues, then the stationary point is a saddle point,

- in all the other cases, we cannot say.

6.2.3 Gradient Descent

Gradient descent is the most well-known algorithm used in machine learning to find the optimal configuration of parameters of a model, given the data. It is very popular and has been extended to be computationally efficient in specific applications. Combined with the backpropagation algorithm, it is widely applied to train neural networks. The goal of this chapter is to lay the foundations so the reader is equipped with the tools to understand machine learning algorithms on her own, so we will only explain the simplest versions of gradient descent. Refer to other chapters

Again, consider our function $f(x)$ which takes as input a vector and returns a univariate output, and assume that our goal is to minimize it. The goal could also be to maximize the function $f(x)$ but in this case, we can simply change the sign and minimize. In machine learning problems, $f(x)$ is often the loss function of our model and x is the set of model parameters. Notice that usually the set of parameters is denoted with θ, so as not to confuse it with the dependent variables. The loss function is denoted with L. Hence, you will have to find the minimum of $L(\theta)$, but the procedure does not change.

We indicate with x^* the input vector which minimizes $f(x)$. How can we find x^*? In some cases, we can find x^* in closed form, that is, analytically. However, in most machine learning algorithms, the closed form solution either does not exist, or it exists but is too computationally expensive to calculate, or when we replace the solution formula with numbers, we encounter numerical problems.

Imagine a valley: our goal is to get to the lowest point in that valley. Intuitively, when we start, we will want to move downhill. If we want to move downhill fast, we will take the steepest route. We might stop every few meters, re-evaluate what the steepest direction is and adapt our path. When we cannot go downhill anymore, we stop, and we say we have arrived. The distance between re-evaluations is an important aspect: if we stop to re-evaluate too often, it will take us a long time to get to the bottom. If we don't stop often enough, we will not adapt to the ever-changing slope. Not only that, we will risk overshooting the lowest point. This is the concept behind gradient descent: the goal is to minimize a function by iteratively moving in the direction of steepest descent. The step size done before re-evaluating the gradient is called the 'learning rate'.

We outline here a simple gradient descent algorithm to find the minimum of $f(x)$. The gradient descent consists of many iterations. We denote with x^i the value taken by the inputs at iteration i. We do the following steps:

- we start with a guess x^0, and then
- we iterate according to $x^{i+1} = x^i - \gamma\left(\nabla f\left(x^i\right)\right)^T$ where Y is the step size or learning rate, and $\nabla f\left(x^i\right)$ at the current step,
- we stop when we are not really moving anymore, or we have completed a predefined maximum number of steps.

For appropriate step sizes, the algorithm converges to a local minimum. Choosing an appropriate step-size is thus very important. If the step size is too small, convergence might be too slow. If the step size is too large, gradient descent can overshoot and even diverge. Some extensions of gradient descent adapt the step size at each iteration. The convergence of the gradient descent, in general, might be slow and have a zig-zag behavior. An extension to gradient descent called 'gradient descent with momentum' introduces a term that remembers what happened in the previous iteration. This makes the gradient updates smoother, in a moving average fashion.

Computing the gradient can be computationally very expensive. For this reason, it is sometimes preferable to calculate an approximate gradient and use the approximate gradient to decide which direction to take next. **Stochastic gradient descent** is a stochastic approximation of gradient descent which is widely used in machine learning. The loss function is constructed as the sum of many terms, such as one term for each data point. The loss function in this scenario looks something like

$$f(x) = \sum_{i=0}^{n} f_i(x).$$ Equation 6.10

Remember that the gradient is a linear operator, which means the gradient of a sum of functions equals the sum of the gradients of each function. So, the gradient of the function in Equation 6.10 is

$$\nabla f(x) = \sum_{i=0}^{n} \nabla f_i(x).$$

Evaluating all the n gradients can be computationally very expensive. As an alternative, we could calculate at every iteration the gradient only for a subset of the terms $f_i(x)$ in the sum in Equation 6.10 . We could also randomly pick only one term in the sum. If we choose the terms randomly, we are basically using a random subset of the data to calculate the gradient. Under mild assumptions and an appropriate learning rate, the stochastic gradient descent converges to a (local) minimum. Not only is the stochastic gradient descent faster, but, because it is noisier, it sometimes helps us avoid getting stuck in some bad local minimum. Stochastic gradient descent is very popular in large scale machine learning algorithms, such as deep neural networks, combined with backpropagation.

Gradient descent is a first-order optimization algorithm. We could also add second order information, which is contained in the Hessian matrix. The most popular second-order optimization algorithm is the Newton's method. Netwon's method is not often used in deep learning and in big data settings because it is computationally and memory intensive. Some alternatives to Newton's method (so called 'quasi Newton' methods) are based on approximating the inverse Hessian.

A big question arises whenever we talk about optimization: can we be sure that our algorithm converged to the best solution? Optimization algorithms can ensure convergence to global solutions only under some assumptions on the form of the function that they are trying to minimize. If the function we are trying to optimize is nonlinear, one way to find a good solution can be use different starting points and take the smallest value amongst the minima the algorithm has found. In the specific case of deep learning, the situation is much more complicated, as the underlying loss function is highly nonlinear. Not only are the algorithms not guaranteed to converge to a global optimum, but they could converge to points which are not even local optima, as there are regions in the domain in which the gradient is very small. Machine learning researchers have developed some partial solutions to these issues.

6.2.4 Constrained Optimization

In Section 6.2.3, we considered the problem of finding the minimum of a function $f(x)$. In some machine learning problems, we are interested in finding the minimum only over a specific set of values of x. This branch of optimization is called 'constrained optimization'. We can write a constrained optimization problem as

$$\min f(x)$$
subject to $g_i(x) = 0$ Equation 6.11
subject to $h_j(x) \leq 0$

where $g_i(x)$ for $i = 1,\ldots,I$ are I equality constraints and $h_j(x)$ for $j = 1,\ldots,J$ are J inequality constraints.

A way of solving a constrained optimization problem is by using duality. Duality in optimization refers to the idea of converting the problem into another optimization problem with a different set of parameters, which is easier to solve. The solution can then be converted back to the original optimization problem. A very general approach is the Karush-Kuhn-Tucker (KKT) approach. For each constraint we introduce a variable, called the 'KKT multiplier', and we write the so-called 'generalized Lagrangian function' as

$$\text{Lag}(x, \lambda, \alpha) = f(x) + I\sum_{i=1}^{I} \lambda_i g_i(x) + \sum_{j=1}^{J} \alpha_j h_j(x).$$ Equation 6.12

The KKT multipliers are contained in the vectors λ and α. Instead of the constrained optimization problem in Equation 6.11, we can now solve the following unconstrained optimization problem: $\max_{\lambda} \max_{\alpha > 0} g(\lambda, \alpha)$, where $g(\lambda, \alpha) = \min_{x} \text{Lag}(x, \lambda, \alpha)$ is the Lagragian dual function, which is always convex.

If there are no inequality constraints, the method is called method of the Lagrange multipliers.

An inequality constraint is said to be active when the solution is on the boundary of the area defined by the constraint, that is, $h_j(x)$ is active if $h_j(x^*) = 0$. If an inequality has no influence on the solution, the relative constraint is said to be inactive, and its corresponding KKT multiplier is set to zero.

Some machine learning techniques that use constrained optimization and the trick to move between the primal and the dual formulation are support vector machines (SVMs) and regularization methods, such as Lasso and Ridge regression.

■ 6.3 Probability Theory

Probability theory is the mathematical field that deals with uncertainty and randomness. It provides data science practitioners with tools to make statements about how confident they are about their predictions, classifications, and conclusions in general. Most branches of computer science and engineering deal with deterministic quantities, and as a result, many data scientists struggle at the first encounter with uncertainty. However, there are many sources of uncertainty when we deal with data:

- measurement errors,
- the randomness of the underlying generating process itself,
- the fact that we do not observe everything we would need to in order to make certain statements,
- models that are not complete, for privacy or computational reasons.

The concept of probability for simple and repeatable tasks is straightforward. If you toss a coin many times, you expect to obtain a head about half of those times. Hence, you can say that the probability of flipping a head is 50 %. According to this definition, called a 'frequentist' definition, the probability is the number of times you observe an outcome (in our example, obtaining a head) divided by the number of times you execute an experiment (tossing the coin).

This kind of definition, however, is not always applicable. Imagine you hear your friend Jane say that with 80 % probability your friend John will not come to the party. Did Jane come to her conclusion after repeating many times the same party and counting how many times John showed up? Clearly not. Jane used a probability to express her belief about John's behavior. This interpretation of probability is called 'Bayesian probability'.

While there is an ongoing debate between frequentists and Bayesians, we will not wade into it here. In data science, you will encounter some problems where a frequentist approach is the most appropriate, and others in which a Bayesian approach is required in order to be able to estimate the parameters of your model.

6.3.1 Discrete and Continuous Random Variables

Uncertainty is introduced in machine learning models through objects called random variables. Imagine you are rolling a die. The number you roll is a random variable: it can be "randomly" any of the numbers between one and six. Now, imagine you are watching a football match and a player kicks a ball; the distance the ball will cover is also a random variable. What is the difference between the two random variables? The number we obtain when rolling a die is a discrete random variable as it can take only discrete values. How far a football player kicks a ball, expressed in meters, is a continue random variable, as it will take a real value. Clearly, the number we obtain by rolling a die and the distance covered by a ball follow different behaviors. How do we express the behavior of a random variable?

Discrete Random Variables

For discrete random variables, we assign a probability to each value that the random variable can take. The function that describes such probabilities is called the **'probability mass function' (pmf)**. We usually denote random variables with a capital letter and the values the variable can take with small letters. Let X be a discrete random variable and let $x_1, x_2, \ldots$ be the possible values that X can take, the pmf is denoted as p and we write $p(x_i) = P(X = x_i)$, where $P(X = x_i)$ is the probability that X is equal to the value x_i.

In the example of rolling a die, we say that the random variable follows a discrete uniform distribution because all the values between one and six have the same probability. The pmf becomes

$$p(k) = P(X = k) = \frac{1}{6} \text{ for } k = 1, 2, 3, 4, 5, 6.$$

A pmf must satisfy the following properties:

- each probability is a number between 0 and 1, included, and
- the sum of the probabilities associated with each value must be one.

Let's go back to the example of flipping a coin. The outcome of the experiment can be either head or tail. When we have a random variable which has only two possible values, such a variable is called 'binary'. We typically code the potential values as one or zero and we call arbitrarily $X=1$ a success, and $X=0$ a failure. The behavior of a binary random variable is described by the **Bernoulli distribution**.

We denote the probability of success with p, and write the pmf as

$$p(1) = P(X=1) = p,$$
$$p(0) = P(X=0) = 1-p.$$

The flipping the coin experiment can be modeled though a Bernoulli distribution, with parameter p = 0.5.

Now, imagine that you flip 100 coins and count the number of heads. You repeat this experiment many times. Each experiment consists of 100 flips, which are called trials. What is the distribution of the number of heads? The number of heads follows the so-called **Binomial distribution**. The parameters of the binomial distribution are the probability of success and the number of trials in each experiment. In this specific example, the parameters of the Binomial distribution are 0.5, which is the probability of flipping a head for each coin, and 100, which is the number of flips for each experiment. Generalizing to a probability of success p and n trials, we can write the pmf of a Binomial random variable as

$$P(X=k) = \binom{n}{k} p^k (1-p)^{n-k} \text{ for } x = 0, \ldots, n,$$

where $\binom{n}{k}$ is called the 'Binomial coefficient'. The Binomial coefficient comes from a branch of mathematics called combinatorics, which we will not discuss here.

The last discrete distribution you should know as you start your data science journey is the Poisson distribution. The **Poisson distribution**, like the Binomial, is used to model count data. While in the case of the Binomial distribution there is a maximum number of successes one can obtain, hence an upper limit to the count, this is not the case with the Poisson. The Poisson distribution has only one parameter, called the 'rate parameter', and the pmf is

$$P(X=x) = \frac{\mu^x e^\mu}{x!} \text{ for } x = 0, 1, \ldots,$$

where μ is the rate parameter, e is the Euler number and ! is the factorial operator. The Poisson distribution is used to model the number of occurrences in a unit of time. For example, it can be used to model the call per hour in a call center, so that staffing can be planned.

Continuous Random Variables

The concept of continuous random variables is harder to grasp than the concept of discrete random variables. Unlike a discrete random variable, a continuous random variable X almost never takes an exact prescribed value x, but there is a positive probability that the value of X will lie in a very small interval around x. This sounds rather complicated but using continuous random variables should come naturally to you if you are familiar with real numbers. In fact, the support of a continuous random variables is either all $\mathbb{R}$, or a subset of $\mathbb{R}$.

We describe the distribution of continuous random variables through the so-called 'probability density function' (pdf). Let us consider a variable which follows a **uniform distribution**, that is it can take values uniformly in the interval $[a,b]$. Its pdf will be

$$p(x) = \begin{cases} \dfrac{1}{b-a} & \text{if } a \le x \le b, \\ 0 & \text{otherwise.} \end{cases}$$

If we are interested in the probability that the random variable will have a value between c and d, with c larger than a and d smaller than d, we have that $P(c \le x \le d) = \dfrac{d-c}{b-a}$. This is illustrated in Figure 6.2.

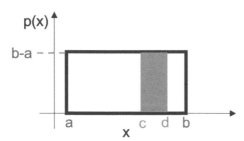

Figure 6.2 Pdf of a uniform random variable

The pdf satisfies the following properties:

- it is always nonnegative, that is, $p(x) \ge 0$, for all the x in its domain,
- the area under the curve and above the x-axis is equal to one, and
- the probability of taking values in an interval is the area under the curve, above the x-axis, in that interval.

All the above properties can be easily verified for the pdf of a uniform random variable in Figure 6.2. Now, imagine making $c=d$. Clearly, we obtain an area under the curve of zero for the point $c=d$. This is an intuitive way to show that the probability of a continuous random variable to take an exact prescribed value is equal to zero.

The most popular continuous distribution is the **Gaussian distribution**, or normal distribution. The distribution of many variables, such as age, height, and IQ, has been found to follow approximately a Gaussian distribution. The pdf of a Gaussian distributed random variable is

$$p(x) = \frac{1}{\sqrt{(2\pi\sigma^2)}} e^{-\frac{1}{2\sigma^2}(x-\mu)^2}, \quad \text{for every } x \text{ in } \mathbb{R}. \qquad \text{Equation 6.34}$$

The Gaussian distribution has two parameters, μ and σ, which are the mean and the standard deviation, respectively (we will see a general definition of mean and standard deviation in Section 6.3.2). When $\mu = 0$ and $\sigma = 0$, we say that the variable is a standard normal variable.

The importance of the Gaussian distribution in statistics and machine learning is due to many reasons, but two stand out:

- The first reason is the **Central Limit Theorem (CLT)**. The CLT states that the sum of independent and identically distributed random variables converges to a Gaussian distribution as the number of variables involved in the sum increases. This is valid regardless of the distribution of such variables, and it holds also for discrete variables.

- The second reason is that most of the time the errors in statistics and machine learning models are assumed to follow a Gaussian distribution. Placing a distributional assumption on the errors allows us to test the significance of the parameters, and to build prediction intervals.

Figure 6.3 depicts the popular bell curve, specifically the pdf of a standard normal variable. Shaded in blue, you can see 95 % of the area under the curve. If you are familiar with testing, you will know that this corresponds, on the x-axis, to the interval [-1.96, 1.96]. This means that a standard normal variable will take values in such an interval with a probability of 95 %.

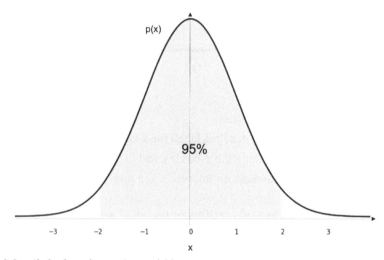

Figure 6.3 pdf of a Gaussian random variable

6.3.2 Expected Value, Variance, and Covariance

Expected value and variance are very useful for describing properties random variables. The expected value, or mean, of a random variable is the value that we expect the variable to take on average. This, of course, depends on the distribution that the random variable follows.

The **expected value** of a function $g(X)$ of a discrete random variable X with pmf $p(x)$ is given by

$$\mathbb{E}_X[g(x)] = \sum_{x \in \mathcal{X}} g(x)p(x)dx, \qquad \text{Equation 6.13}$$

where $\mathcal{X}$ is the set of possible values that the random variable X can take. When we consider the identity function $g(x) = x$, we obtain the expected value of the variable itself.

For continuous random variables the sum in Equation 6.13 is replaced by an object called an 'integral'. We will not explain what an integral is here, but you can find it in any introduction to calculus book. For now, you should just be aware that the integral is "like the sum", but for probability density functions.

While the expected value gives us information on the center of the distribution, the **variance** gives us information on the spread. The variance of a random variable X is

$$\mathbb{V}_X[x] = \mathbb{E}_X\left[\left(x - \mathbb{E}_X[x]\right)^2\right].$$

Equation 6.14

An alternative expression to Equation 6.14 is $\mathbb{V}_X[x] = \mathbb{E}_X\left[x^2\right] - (\mathbb{E}_X[x])^2$.

Notice that unit of the variance is the square of the unit of the variable X. The **standard deviation** is the square root of the variance, and it has the nice property that it is expressed in the same unit as the random variables. For example, if our random variable is height expressed in cm, the variance will be expressed in cm^2 and the standard deviation in cm.

Let us now consider two random variables X and Y, each with its own expected value and variance. We can describe the linear association between the two variables thought the covariance. The **covariance** between two random variables X and Y is defined as

$$Cov_{X,Y}[x,y] = \mathbb{E}_{X,Y}\left[\left(x - \mathbb{E}_X[x]\right)\left(y - \mathbb{E}_Y[y]\right)\right].$$

The unit of the covariance is the product of the unit of X and that of Y. The variance and covariance also depend on the size of the values that the variables can assume. It would be nice to have a quantity that expressed the association between two random variables and did not depend on the units or the size. Luckily, this quantity exists and is called **correlation**. The correlation between two random variables X and Y is defined as

$$Corr_{X,Y}[x,y] = \frac{Cov_{X,Y}[x,y]}{\sqrt{\mathbb{V}_X[x]}\sqrt{\mathbb{V}_Y[y]}}.$$

Equation 6.15

The correlation is a number between minus one and one. The correlation is one when the two variables are perfectly positively correlated, which means Y is always equal to X. The correlation is equal to minus one if the two variables are perfectly negative correlated, which, similarly, means Y is always equal to minus X. If the two variables are independent, then the correlation between them is zero, while the opposite is not always true. To get a better understanding of correlation, you can play a few rounds on *http://guessthecorrelation. com*. It is important to say again that covariance and correlation capture linear associations between variables, and no other types of association. To be exhaustive, we need to mention that the correlation in Equation 6.15 is called Pearson's correlation, and other types of correlation exist which we will not cover here, such as Kendall rank correlation, Spearman correlation, and Point-Biserial correlation.

While we have introduced the definition of mean, variance and covariance for random variables, in real life we do not observe the variables themselves, but a sample of their realizations. Sample mean, sample variance and sample covariance are key in statistics, and are the 'realized' versions of the quantities described in this chapter.

6.3.3 Independence, Conditional Distributions, and Bayes' Theorem

Consider the event $A=\{My\ favorite\ movie\ is\ being\ shown\ on\ TV\}$ and the event $B=\{It\ is\ my\ birthday\}$. The two events A and B are independent because the occurrence of one does not influence the occurrence of the other. Similarly, two random variables are independent if the value that one takes does not influence the other, in the sense that it does not change the other's pdf or pmf. In other words, two random variables X and Y are independent if knowing the value that X took does not change what I know about Y, and vice versa. The concept of independence is a fundamental one in probability theory and beyond. Many statistical and machine learning models make independence assumptions and the conclusions we can draw are based on these assumptions.

Before writing the formula for independence of two random variables, the concept of a joint probability distribution needs to be introduced. The joint probability distribution, denoted as $p(x,y)$, describes whether two variables vary together, and is the extension of probability distribution to multiple random variables. Now, if two variables are independent, the joint probability distribution is simply the product of the probability distributions of each variable.

Two random variables X and Y are **independent** if for any of the values they can assume, we have that $p(x,y)= p(x)p(y)$, where p is either the pdf or the pmf, depending on the type of variables.

Consider now the event $A=\{It\ is\ raining\}$ and the event $B=\{I\ am\ going\ to\ the\ beach\}$. Clearly A and B are dependent. Knowing whether it is currently raining or not will affect the probability that I am going to the beach. The concept can be extended to random variables, and we can have the probability distribution of a variable depend on the realization of another variable. We denote this conditional probability distribution as $p(x|y)$. If two variables are independent, then $p(x|y)=p(x)$.

Another concept you will encounter in your data science journey is that of conditional independence. Now, we introduce a third random variable Z and we say that if we know the value of Z, then X and Y are independent. How can this happen? Let's consider the number of chimneys in a Nordic town and the number of babies that are born in the town. The higher the number of chimneys, the higher the number of babies born in that town. What could make the two events independent? The size of the city. The number of chimneys and the number of babies are not independent, but they are independent conditionally on the size of the city. Of course, this is assuming we are considering towns with similar winter temperatures. In formulas, we have that $p(x,y\,|\,z)=p(x\,|\,z)p(y\,|\,z)$.

where p is either the pdf or the pmf, depending on the type of variables.

Before ending this chapter and talking about statistics, we need to explain **Bayes' theorem**. Bayes' theorem is extremely useful and will appear in various forms during your data science journey, as it allows us to update probabilities based on existing and new information. Provided we know $p(x|y)$, $p(x)$ and $p(y)$, Bayes' theorem allows us to calculate $p(y|x)$ as follows.

$$p(y\,|\,x) = \frac{p(x\,|\,y)p(y)}{p(x)}.$$

Equation 6.16

While you may not have seen Bayes' theorem expressed as in Equation 6.16, you might have seen its version for events, that is

$$P(A\,|\,B) = \frac{P(B\,|\,A)P(A)}{P(B)}.$$

Let's use Bayes' theorem with an example. Consider a test for a disease that is 90 % *sensitive*: if a person with the disease takes the test, there is a 90 % chance the test is positive. The test has a lower *specificity*, only 80 %, meaning if it is taken by someone without the disease, the test will be positive with a probability of 80 %. Assuming 0.5 % of the people who take the test have the disease, what is the probability that a person has the disease if they test positive? We apply Bayes' theorem and find that

$$P(\text{disease}\,|\,\text{tested positive}) = \frac{P(\text{tested positive}\,|\,\text{disease})P(\text{disease})}{P(\text{tested positive})}.$$

The denominator can be found with the so-called law of total probability:

$$P(\text{tested positive}) = P(\text{tested positive}\,|\,\text{disease})*P(\text{disease}) +$$
$$P(\text{tested positive}\,|\,\text{no disease})*P(\text{no disease})$$
$$= 0.8*0.005 + 0.2*0.995 = 0.203.$$

The probability that a random person has the disease if they tested positive is then

$$P(\text{disease}\,|\,\text{tested positive}) = \frac{0.8*0.005}{0.203} \approx 0.02.$$

This means that the probability of having a rare disease is still low even after taking the test and getting a positive result. Such a situation is common in medical tests because it is crucial to identify people with the disease. Giving a positive result to someone without the disease has in fact a lower cost than giving a negative result to someone with the disease.

◼ 6.4 In a Nutshell

Loss Function

The goal of most machine learning algorithms is to minimize a loss function. It is important to know what the loss function looks like. To minimize a loss function we need to know calculus and optimization.

Matrices and Vectors

Being familiar with matrices, vectors, and the operations amongst them is key to understanding how machine learning algorithms work.

Matrix Decomposition

Matrix decomposition is key for various reasons. It can be used for dimensionality reduction, and also helps make some algorithms computationally more efficient and numerically feasible.

Gradient Descent

Gradient descent is an iterative algorithm based on a simple concept: at every iteration, we follow the direction in which the gradient of the loss function is steeper.

Constrained Optimization

Sometimes we need to minimize a loss function subject to some constrains. To do so, we can move to a dual representation of our optimization problem.

Probability Theory

Uncertainty is crucial in machine learning, as it allows us to express how certain we are about a conclusion. To be able to understand uncertainty, one needs to be familiar with the basics of probability theory.

Random Variables

Random variables are variables which can take different values according to a specific probability function.

Bayes' Theorem

Bayes' theorem allows us to update our predictions when we receive new information.

7 Statistics – Basics

Rania Wazir, Georg Langs, Annalisa Cadonna

> *"All models are approximations. Assumptions, whether implied or clearly stated, are never exactly true. All models are wrong, but some models are useful. So the question you need to ask is not 'Is the model true?' (it never is) but 'Is the model good enough for this particular application?'"[1]*

Questions Answered in this Chapter:

- How can we classify different types of data?
- What is the difference between regression and classification?
- What is linear regression? How do we interpret the parameters in a linear regression model?
- What is logistic regression? How do we interpret the parameters in a logistic regression model?
- What performance metrics do we use in regression and classification?
- What are cross-validation and bootstrapping?

A question often arises when one approaches data science for the first time: what is the difference between statistics and machine learning? You will hear a multitude of different answers to this question, which can be encapsulated in one statement: the difference between statistics and machine learning is their purpose.

Statistics focuses on doing inference about relationships between variables. Statistical models allow us to predict new observations, but this is not the focal point. The purpose of machine learning, on the other hand, is to make predictions about new observations as precisely as possible.

Simple models like linear regression or logistic regression are often considered statistical models. This is particularly the case if we are testing to understand whether a predictor has a significant effect on the response, or if one model is better than another one. Statistical models are interpretable, meaning we can understand the role of each parameter in the model. On the other hand, when machine learning models are used, one often does not care about interpretation.

Assume a business problem was defined and all the necessary data collected and organized. Data scientists usually go through three phases before they decide which model should be put into production.

---

[1] Box, G. E. P.; Luceño, A.; del Carmen Paniagua-Quiñones, M. (2009), *Statistical Control By Monitoring and Adjustment*

- In the first phase, the data is explored. We ask ourselves questions such as: are there missing or wrong data points? Are there outliers? What kind of attributes are there, and how many of them?

- In the second phase, the data must be prepared. We ask ourselves the following questions: how should we handle missing data? How and how do we recognize erroneous data? How do we deal with outliers? Are they important to the decision process or should they be removed? Depending on the models we will try out, the data may also need to be normalized.

- Finally, the third phase consists in experimenting with various statistical and machine learning models.

The three phases described above are not executed once in a data science project, but multiple times. Why is this the case? Well, for example, we might observe that the model results depend strongly on the way we handle outliers and missing values, and choose to prepare data in a different way. Or we might realize that some features could be better engineered.

This chapter is organized as follows. Section 7.1 describes different types of data. In Section 7.2, Section 7.3, and Section 7.4 we look at simple linear regression, multiple linear regression, and logistic regression. Finally, Section 7.5 introduces a few models to evaluate how accurate a model is.

■ 7.1 Data

Data can come in various forms depending on the application and the collection mechanism. The first distinction we can make is between structured and unstructured data. A simple example of structured data is a spreadsheet: each row of data denotes an observation, each column refers to a variable. Unstructured data, on the other hand, are for example text or image data. In statistics, we usually deal with structured data.

In the case of structured data, it is important to understand what type of variables we are dealing with. Variables can be divided into quantitative and qualitative variables:

- **Quantitative variables**, also called numeric variables, can be measured and take numeric values. Examples of quantitative variables are age, income, value of a piece of property, and temperature. Quantitative variables can be discrete or continuous. Usually, we are dealing with a discrete variable if its value answers the question "how many?", as in, "How many students are in a class?" or "How many rooms does a house have?" Discrete continuous variables can have decimals in their value. Usually, the number of digits depends on the precision of the measurement instrument. For example, one thermometer could record 37.1°C, another one 37.12°C. A trick to understand whether a variable is discrete or continuous is to ask if adding a decimal makes sense. Can we say we have 5.5 (alive) elephants? No? Then the number of elephants is discrete.

- **Qualitative variables**, also called categorical, take values in a limited number of categories: satisfaction ratings in a survey ("very", "enough" "not at all"), age groups, or the brand of a product purchased are just some examples. Qualitative variables can be ordinal or nominal. Ordinal variables are variables with a "logical", well understood order. If we consider the results of a competition, for example, we can say that a second place is better than a third place. If we consider t-shirt sizes, there is a well understood order: S – M – L – XL. Nominal variables, on the other hand, do not have an order. Eye color is an example of a nominal categorical variable. One might like brown eyes more than green eyes, but we cannot say that brown eyes are better, or higher, or bigger than green eyes.

Statistical machine learning models can be of two types,, depending on the available data:

- Some models are used in cases when we can observe both the independent and the dependent variables. This is known as "supervised learning". We can classify such a model further:

    Regression models are used when the dependent variable is quantitative, and the goal is to predict a quantitative value.

    Classification models are used when the dependent variable is qualitative, and the goal is to predict a class.

- Other models are used when we do not have a dependent variable, or our data are not labeled. We talk in this case of "unsupervised learning". The most popular method in this context is clustering. Clustering algorithms look for similarity groups in a data set without knowing exactly what the underlying "true" groups are. This is useful, for example, in a market segmentation problem in which we want to group customers and rank them according to similar behavior patterns, without having a categorization in advance. If you would like to see an example, in Chapter 10, Section 10.3.2, you can find an explanation of document clustering using the K-Means algorithm.

■ 7.2 Simple Linear Regression

Many methods used in data science are generalizations or extensions of linear regression. Since linear regression is one of the easiest and most widely used methods, it offers us a quick entry point to learn about statistical models.

Let's start by investigating the relationship between two variables. First of all, we make the simplifying assumption that this relationship is linear.

A simple linear regression model looks like

$$Y = mX + n + e,$$ Equation 7.1

where m is called the "slope", n is called the "intercept", and e is an error term, centered at zero, whose variance does not depend on X. Introducing the error term means we assume that our data will not follow a perfect straight line, and will instead be spread around it.

How can we interpret the intercept and slope parameters?

The intercept is the expected value of the dependent variable when the independent variable is zero. If the value of the intercept m is exactly zero (which is to say, X has no effect on

Y), then we would be left with $Y=n+e$, resulting in all the data points being spread around the intercept. The slope parameter has the following meaning: if we were to change X by one unit, we would expect a change in Y of m units. This type of change is called "absolute change". The effect of X on the expected value of Y is linear, and it is positive when m is positive, and negative when m is negative. Notice that the expected value of Y, conditioned on X, is $mX+n$: this is the regression line that we are trying to estimate. In other words, we want to find the optimal value of the parameters such that the regression line is as close as possible to the data.

In linear regression, the goal is to minimize the sum of the squared distances between the regression line and the data points. That's because the distance between each point and the regression line is an error, and we want to minimise the sum of these errors. The main reason why we use the square distance in this calculation is that if we didn't, the positive and negative distances would "cancel each other out", resulting in a small total distance, even when the distances may in fact be large. Hence, we square each distance, so that all quantities are positive, before we add them up. A second reason is that by using the squared distance, data points that are more distant from the regression line will have more weight than data points that are close to the regression line. A third reason, or consequence, of using the square, is that our loss will be "nice" to work with.

In linear regression, the goal is to minimize the sum of the squared distances between the regression line and the data points. The main reason why we use the square distance is that positive and negative distances would "cancel out", so we want to add up positive quantities. A second reasons is that by using the squared distance, data points that are more distant from the regression line will have more weight than data points that are close to the regression line. A third reason or consequence of using the square, is that our loss function will be "nice" to work with. To review what a loss function is, please refer to Chapter 6, Section 6.2.

Let us consider N data points: for the i-th data point X takes value x_i, and the response variable Y takes value y_i. We can write our loss function as:

$$L = \sum_{i=1}^{N} (y_i - mx_i - n)^2 \qquad\qquad \text{Equation 7.2}$$

The loss function in Equation 7.2 is called **quadratic loss function**. The values of n and m, which minimize the quadratic loss function, are denoted with m and n and are defined as

$$\hat{m} = \frac{S_{xy}}{S_{xx}}, \text{ and}$$

$$\hat{n} = \bar{y} - \hat{m}\,\bar{x}.$$

In the above equations, $\bar{y}$ and $\bar{x}$ are the sample mean of the y-values and of the x-values, respectively, s_{xy} is the sample covariance matrix, and s_{xx} is the covariance matrix of the independent variable. These quantities are calculated as follows:

$$\bar{y} = \frac{\sum_{i=1}^{N} y_i}{N}, \bar{x} = \frac{\sum_{i=1}^{N} x_i}{N}, s_{xx} = \frac{\sum_{i=1}^{N}(x_i - \bar{x})^2}{N-1}, s_{xy} = \frac{\sum_{i=1}^{N}(x_i - \bar{x})(y_i - \bar{y})}{N-1}$$

With the tools covered in Chapter 6, you should be able to analytically derive the formulas for the optimal m and n.

Once the parameters have been estimated, we can evaluate the model performance using a metric. In regression, the Mean Squared Error (MSE) is often used. The MSE is calculated as

$$MSE = \frac{1}{N}\sum_{i=1}^{N}(y_i - \hat{m}\, x_i - \hat{n})^2$$

Alternatively, instead of the MSE, the Root Mean Squared Error (RMSE) may be used. As the name suggests, the RMSE is the square root of the MSE. One advantage of the RMSE is that it is expressed in the same units at the dependent variable. For example, if Y is measured in meters, then the MSE is measured in square meters, but the RMSE is measured in meters.

Let's now implement a simple linear regression. The Python library Scikit-learn [1] provides many statistics and machine learning algorithms. Scikit-learn also contains some datasets. To run the following lines of code, install Python 3, for instance from *https://www.python.org* and then then run: pip install -U scikit-learn. Below, we import the Boston Housing dataset, which contains data relative to housing in the Boston area. We use MEDV, the median value of a house in $10000, as dependent variable.

Listing 7.1 Simple linear regression 1: Import data and libraries

```
# import the required libraries

from sklearn.linear_model import LinearRegression
from sklearn.model_selection import train_test_split
from sklearn.metrics import mean_squared_error, mean_absolute_error, r2_score
from sklearn import datasets as ds

import pandas as pd
import numpy as np
import matplotlib.pyplot as plt
import seaborn as sns

# load the Boston Housing dataset, which is part of the sklearn datasets
boston = ds.load_boston()
print("Type of imported object: " + str(type(boston)) + "\n")
print("A bunch is a special kind of Python dictionary. \n The key values of the
boston record are: " + str(boston.keys()) + "\n")
print("The short description of the record: " + str(boston.DESCR))

Xarray = boston.data
Y = boston.target
X = pd.DataFrame(Xarray, columns = boston.feature_names)
```

With the head(), describe() and info() methods we get a better overview of our dataset and how it is structured. The method head() will show us the first few lines, describe() will give us some summary information, such as max, min and sample mean, and info() will tell us which type the variables in the dataset are.

Listing 7.2 Simple linear regression 2: Explore data set

```
print(X.head())
print(X.describe())
print(X.info())
```

Please run Listing 7.1 and Listing 7.2. We have 506 observations in total, and all our variables are numeric. Let's quickly see how many missing values are in the data set.

Listing 7.3 Simple linear regression 3: Search for missing data

```
# To figure out the missing values
missing = len(X.index) - X.count()
missing
```

There are no missing values in this dataset. This will rarely happen in real life applications.

Before we go any further, let's visualize our data. We use INDUS, the proportion of non-retail business acres per town, as the independent variable.

Listing 7.4 Simple linear regression 4: Data visualization with two variables

```
plt.scatter(x = X.INDUS, y = Y, alpha = 0.3)
plt.xlabel("INDUS (in %)")
plt.ylabel("MEDV (in $10000)")
plt.show()
```

The scatter plot can be seen in Figure 7.1. The relationship between the two variables does not appear to be completely linear. However, a decreasing trend can be seen in the data.

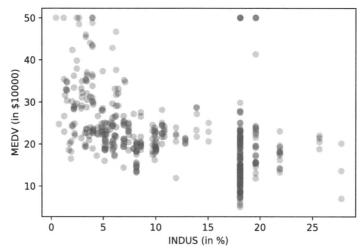

Figure 7.1 MED vs. INDUS

Taking a close look at the graph in Figure 7.1, we notice that it shows a few peculiarities:

- First, the vertical line at 18 % INDUS catches our eye. There are many observations with INDUS = 18 %, and at that value of INDUS, MEDV takes many different values. One should investigate the reason behind this with the relevant experts.

- Second, we note two outliers at 50 MEDV and 18 % and 20 % INDUS. The y-value of these data points differs strongly from the y-value of other points with the same or similar x-value. Are these two outliers due to randomness or is there a story behind it? We usually need to dig deeper into outliers to know how to deal with them, but we will not investigate this further here. However, we need to keep in mind that the outliers will affect our loss function, which treats them as any other data point.

■ A final observation is that at MEDV = 50 the points form an almost horizontal line. Could it be that this data set was cut at MEDV=50? How to deal with these values would also need further exploration.

Before moving on, we split our dataset into training data and test data. This is an essential part of any data science project and will help us to evaluate the performance of our model. We set the size of the test set to 20 % of the entire sample size.

Listing 7.5 Simple linear regression 4: Split into training and test data

```
# Now, let's split the data into train and test sets:
X_train, X_test, Y_train, Y_test = train_test_split(X, Y, test_size = 0.2, random_
state = 18)
oneX_train = X_train.INDUS.values.reshape(-1,1)
oneX_test = X_test.INDUS.values.reshape(-1,1)
```

Let's keep going with our simple linear regression.

Listing 7.6 Simple linear regression 6: Simple model calculation

```
# Just do it! Run the linear regression now.
lin_reg = LinearRegression()
lin_reg_model = lin_reg.fit(oneX_train, Y_train)
Y_predictions = lin_reg.predict(oneX_train)
lin_params = {"slope": lin_reg.coef_[0], "intercept": lin_reg.intercept_}
print("And this is how our straight line looks like: y = %.2fx + %.2f" %(lin_
params["slope"], lin_params["intercept"]))
```

And this is how our linear line looks now: y = -0.65x + 29.65. This means that when we increase INDUS by 1 %, we expect a decrease in MEDV of $6500. Let's lay the regression line over the data to obtain the plot in Figure 7.2. Notice that this is an absolute change in the dependent variable, and the percentage is the unit.

Listing 7.7 Simple linear regression 7: Visualization of the fitted model

```
plt.scatter(x = oneX_train, y = Y_train, alpha = 0.5)

plt.xlabel("INDUS")
plt.ylabel("MEDV in $10000")
plt.title("Training Data Results")

plt.plot(oneX_train, Y_predictions, color='blue', linewidth=3)

plt.show()
```

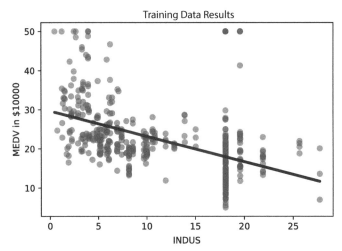

Figure 7.2 Simple Linear Regression INDUS vs MEDV, training data

Now that we have calculated our simple linear model, we also need to check how well it is performing.

First, we evaluate it on the training data.

Listing 7.8 Simple Linear Regression 8: Evaluating the Model on Training Data

```
# Check the results:
lin_mse = mean_squared_error(Y_train, Y_predictions)
lin_rmse = np.sqrt(lin_mse)
lin_mae = mean_absolute_error(Y_train, Y_predictions)

medY = np.median(Y_train, axis = 0)
maxY = np.max(Y_train, axis = 0)

print("The linear regression with one dependent variable has a training RMSE of " +
str(lin_rmse) + ",")
print("and a training MAE of " + str(lin_mae) + ".")
print("Compare this to a Y median value of " + str(medY) + " and a Y maximum value of
" + str(maxY) + ".")
```

The linear regression with two variables has achieved a training RMSE of 7.98. Compare that to a median of 21.20 and a maximum of 50.00 of the dependent variable. This doesn't look very good, as the RMSE makes up just under 40 % of the median value. Notice that the model almost always performs better on the training set than on the test set, as it has already seen the data it is trying to predict. So, how is the performance on the test set?

Listing 7.9 Simple Linear Regression 9: Evaluating the Model on Test Data

```
Y_predictions = lin_reg.predict(oneX_test)

# Check the results:
lin_mse = mean_squared_error(Y_test, Y_predictions)
lin_rmse = np.sqrt(lin_mse)
lin_mae = mean_absolute_error(Y_test, Y_predictions)
r2 = r2_score(Y_test, Y_predictions)
```

```
print("The linear regression with one dependent variable has a test RMSE of " +
str(lin_rmse) + ",")
print("and a test MAE of " + str(lin_mae) + ".")
print("Compare this to a Y median value of " + str(medY) + " and a Y maximum value of
" + str(maxY) + ".")
print("The coefficient of determination is " + str(r2) + ".")
```

The linear regression with two predictor variables achieved a test RMSE of 8.28. Anyone who has followed the preceding calculations to some extent will notice that we calculated not only the RMSE, but also the MAE. MAE stands for Mean Absolute Error, and it is one of the metrics we can use to evaluate the performance of our model. The MAE is calculated as

$$MAE = \frac{1}{N} \sum_{i=1}^{N} |y_i - \hat{m} x_i - \hat{n}|$$

The MAE calculates the sum of the absolute distance of the predictions from the real values, and is less sensitive to outliers than the RMSE. The test MAE for this model is 5.82.

We also calculated the coefficient of determination, also called the R-squared. The R-squared tells us how well the predicted values of y explain the variation in the observed values. In contrast to MSE and MAE, a model is "better" if the test R-squared is larger. In this case, the R-squared is 0.23. This will be relevant in Section 7.3, when we talk about multiple linear regression Figure 7.3 shows the regression line overlaid on the test data.

Listing 7.10 Simple linear regression 10: Model visualization

```
plt.scatter(x = oneX_test, y = Y_test, alpha = 0.5)
plt.xlabel("INDUS")
plt.ylabel("MEDV in $10000")
plt.plot(oneX_test, Y_predictions, color='blue', linewidth=3)
plt.show()
```

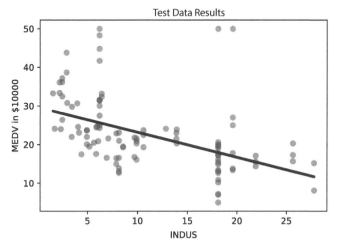

Figure 7.3 Simple Linear Regression INDUS vs MEDV, test data

One last exploration method we can use is to look at plot of the residuals in Figure 7.4. The residual plot is a graphical representation of the deviation of the predicted data from the observed data. The vertical axis always shows the difference between the predicted and observed *y*-values. The horizontal axis indicates the *x*-value for a simple linear regression, and the predicted *y*-value for a multiple linear regression (see Section 7.3). The residuals plot shows us that we have outliers in the residuals, but no other clear pattern is visible.

Listing 7.11 Simple Linear Regression 11: Residual Plot

```
# calculate the residuals
res = Y_test - Y_predictions
plt.scatter(x = oneX_test, y = res, alpha = 0.5)
plt.show()
```

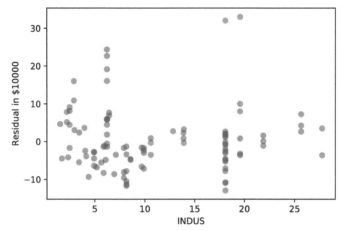

Figure 7.4 Residuals Plot

If you would like to view more statistics for evaluating datasets and models, such as p-values for the coefficients or the F-statistic, you should use the Python *statsmodels* [2] package.

It should be noted that the linear regression has not totally failed in this case, but we are still far from a good result. We could try in further runs to remove the outliers and possibly also the observations where MEDV is close to $500000. We could also add in the other variables to do a multiple regression, and we might want to consider using other methods besides regression. We will now try to build a model that predicts MEDV based on more than one independent variable.

■ 7.3 Multiple Linear Regression

Multiple linear regression extends simple regression to consider more independent variables $X_1, X_2, ..., X_k$, while there remains always just one dependent variable. Other terms used to refer to the independent variables are "covariates", "predictors", "regressors", or "features", while for the dependent variable you will hear "response variable", "target variable" or "outcome". A multiple linear regression model is described by the following equation:

$$Y = m_1 X_1 + m_2 X_2 + \cdots + m_k X_k + n + e. \hspace{2cm} \text{Equation 7.3}$$

In In Equation 7.3 n is the intercept and $m_1, m_2, ..., m_k$ are the parameters relative to the predictors $X_1, X_2, ..., X_k$.

How do we interpret the parameters in a multiple regression setting? Since we have more than one regressor, we have a slightly different interpretation: the parameter relative to a regressor is the expected absolute change in the response variable when we change that regressor by one, while keeping all the other regressors constant. Notice that this interpretation is valid only for dependent variables that appear in a linear fashion. If we have second order or higher order terms, such as a squared predictor, or an interaction, this interpretation does not hold. To understand why the interpretation does not hold in the presence of nonlinearities, imagine we take, for example, $X_2 = X_1^2$. In such case, we cannot change X_1 without changing X_2.

For each data point we have a set of one dependent variable and k independent variables. That is, for the i-th data point we have $(y_i, x_{i1}, x_{i2}, ..., x_{ik})$. The loss function is defined as

$$L = \sum_{i=1}^{n} (y_i - m_1 x_{i1} - m_2 x_{i2} - ... - m_k x_{ik} - n)^2.$$

As we did in the simple linear regression, we can find the values of the parameters that minimize the loss function. The solution can be found analytically using differential calculus. However, data scientists usually rely on software like python to find the estimates of the parameters. Let's now fit a multiple linear regression model to our Boston housing dataset.

Listing 7.12 Multiple Linear Regression Model 1

```
# Run the multiple linear regression:
lin_reg_mult = LinearRegression()
lin_reg_multmodel = lin_reg_mult.fit(X_train, Y_train)
Y_mult_predictions = lin_reg_multmodel.predict(X_test)
```

How sure are we that some parameters are not equal to zero? To answer this question, we need to assume a distribution on the error, usually a Gaussian distribution, and perform classical hypothesis testing. In the case of multiple linear regression, we must also consider the F-statistic. We will not go into detail here, but the interested reader will find the appropriate formulas for this in any statistics textbook.

We now want to compare the simple linear regression model with the multiple linear regression model. To do so we could, for example, compare the R-squared or R-square adjusted, which is the R-squared penalized for the number of predictor variables. Another way is to evaluate how well the models are doing in making predictions on the test set.

Listing 7.13 Multiple Linear Regression 2: Evaluating the Model on Test Data

```
# Check the results:
lin_mse_mult = mean_squared_error(Y_test, Y_mult_predictions)
lin_rmse_mult = np.sqrt(lin_mse)
lin_mae_mult = mean_absolute_error(Y_test, Y_mult_predictions)
r2_mult = r2_score(Y_test, Y_mult_predictions)
print("The multiple linear regression has a test RMSE of " + str(lin_rmse_mult) +
",")
print("and a test MAE of " + str(lin_mae_mult) + ".")
print("The coefficient of determination is " + str(r2_mult) + ".")
```

The multiple linear regression has a test RMSE of 5.26, and a test MAE of 3.63. Both the RMSE and the MAE are lower for the multiple regression model!

The coefficient of determination (R2) is 0.69, which is much larger than in the simple regression model. Yet this metric should be used with caution, because if the number of independent variables in the regression is increased, the coefficient of determination automatically increases as well. To counter this, the adjusted coefficient of determination is often used, which penalizes for the number of independent variables in the model. To calculate the adjusted coefficient of determination, have a look at the *statsmodels* [2] documentation.

How sure are we that some parameters are not equal to zero? To answer this question, we need to assume a distribution on the error e (usually, a Gaussian distribution is assumed) and perform classical hypothesis testing. In the case of multiple linear regression, we must also consider the F-statistic. We will not go into detail here, but the interested reader will find the appropriate formulas for this in any statistics textbook.

Problems with Linear Regression

What problems can occur with linear regression?

- **Nonlinearity:** while it seems obvious that a straight-line equation is not appropriate for a nonlinear relationship, one is often misled by the ease and ubiquity of this model to see everything as "linear enough."

- **Outliers:** these are observations or data points whose y-value is far from they-values of the other observations with similarx-values. Sometimes these observations are legitimate points, but often they are a sign of errors or anomalies in the data set.

- **High Leverage Points:** these are observations that have unusualx-values. These can be very problematic as they often have an excessive impact on the model. Therefore, it is important to identify them and, if necessary, eliminate them.

- **Collinearity:** this problem is present only in multiple regression and describes the situation in which two or more independent variables are correlated with each other. Collinearity introduces noise to the model and lowers the confidence in our conclusions.

- **Heteroskedasticity:** this refers to situations where the variance of the residuals is unequal over a range of measured values. Regression assumes that the residuals are drawn from errors with the same variance. One way to try and mitigate heteroscedasticity is to apply a transformation, such as the logarithm, to the dependent variable. If this does not help, an extension of linear regression called weighted regression can help.

- **Overfitting:** this problem occurs when the prediction line follows too closely the training data because there are too many parameters. Overfitting causes poor predictive performance on unseen test data.

■ 7.4 Logistic Regression

Despite the name, **logistic regression** is a method for classification. In fact, logistic regression is used when the target variable is binary, although it can be extended to account for target variables with multiple classes.

Logistic regression is a natural extension of linear regression to binary data. However, it is also a building block of Neural Networks (NNs, discussed in detail in Chapter 8 and 10). For our purposes, it is sufficient to know that logistic regression can be seen as the simplest NN; that is, a neural network consisting of only one neuron.

Simple Logistic Regression

Let us go through an example of logistic regression using an iconic dataset [3]. The iris dataset contains 150 observations from three iris species: setosa, versicolor, and virginica. There are four independent variables: sepal length and width, and petal height and width.

Since we want to build a binary classifier, we start by building a classifier that identifies whether an iris flower is of the setosa variety. We create a binary variable which is one if the flower is an iris setosa, and zero if it is not setosa. For now, we use only the petal width as an independent variable: this model is called simple logistic regression.

In this example, we do not split the data into training and test data, as the goal is simply to illustrate logistic regression.

Listing 7.14 Logistic Regression 1: Import Iris Data

```
# import the required libraries
from sklearn.linear_model import LinearRegression, LogisticRegression
from sklearn import datasets as ds
import pandas as pd
import numpy as np
import matplotlib.pyplot as plt
iris = ds.load_iris()
X = iris.data[:, 3:] # Use only "petal width" as feature
# The classes have been coded as numbers:
# 0 = setosa 1 = versicolor, 2 = virginica

Y = (iris.target == 0).astype(np.int) # 1 if setosa, 0 otherwise
```

Since linear regression was so easy, why don't we try modeling our data with a straight line again? What it looks like for our iris dataset can be seen in Figure 7.5.

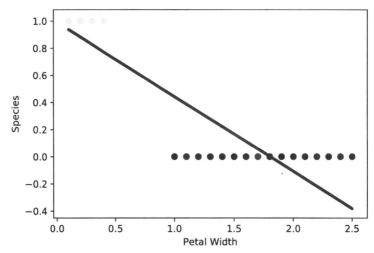

Figure 7.5 Linear Regression with the Iris dataset: Petal width vs Species

A probability should have a value in the interval [0,1] and the values of a straight line clearly do not.

Ideally, we would want our model to predict the probability that a flower is an iris setosa. Then, one can say that the flower is predicted to be an iris setosa if this probability is greater than 0.5, for example.

To achieve our goal we use a logistic transformation. The logistic function should be familiar to anyone who wants to work in data science. It is also used as an activation function in neural networks. The logistic function looks like

$$p(X) = \frac{e^{mX+n}}{1+e^{mX+n}} \qquad\qquad \text{Equation 7.4}$$

The interpretation of the parameters in Equation 7.4 is not as immediate as in linear regression. If m is positive, the probability of $Y=1$ increases with X and if m is negative, the probability decreases with increasing X. Moreover, the strength of this influence depends on the size of m. When X is binary, one way of looking at the parameter m is that of log-odds ratio. The odds ratio is defined as the ratio of the odds of a success when the binary variable is one and the odds of success when the binary variable is zero.

Since we are now working with probabilities, the MSE is no longer as useful as a loss function. Instead, we want to maximize something called the log-likelihood function. Doing so, we find the parameter values that, when plugged into the model, are most likely to have generated the data. Considering the observations $(x_1,y_1),...,(x_k,y_k)$, the log-likelihood function is defined as

$$L = \sum_{i:y_i=1} \log\big(p(x_i)\big) + \sum_{j:y_j=0} \log\big(1-p(x_j)\big)$$

How to optimize this function to the parameters m and n cannot be explained in detail in this chapter, but we can at least try to understand the result. So let's fit a logistic regression.

Listing 7.15 Logistic Regression 2: Calculate Iris Model

```
log_reg = LogisticRegression()
log_reg.fit(X, Y)
Y_log_pred = log_reg.predict(X)
print(log_reg.coef_)
```

We obtain a coefficient of -4.53. This can be interpreted as: the larger the petal width, the lower the probability that the flower is an iris setosa.

Multiple Logistic Regression

To address a somewhat challenging dataset, we downloaded U.S. Census data from *https://github.com/jbrownlee/Datasets/blob/master/adult-all.csv*.

We want to use the data to predict people's annual income. This variable has only two categories: income greater than 50K and income smaller or equal to 50K. We convert the target variable Y into an indicator variable, so that Y=1 if the income is greater than 50K and Y=0 if the income is smaller or equal to 50K.

A logistic regression with multiple independent variables looks like this:

$$p(X) = \frac{e^{m_1X_1+m_2X_2+\cdots+m_kX_k+n}}{1+e^{m_1X_1+m_2X_2+\cdots+m_kX_k+n}}$$

The interpretation of a parameter relative to a predictor is the same as in the simple logistic regression model when the other predictors are kept constant. Like in logistic regression, this is not valid in the presence of nonlinearities in the independent variables.

Listing 7.16 Logistic Regression 3: Import and Summarize U.S. Census Data

```
# Import the libraries needed
import os
import pandas as pd
import numpy as np
# Other libraries we will need
import seaborn as sns # for creating a heatmap of correlated variables
import matplotlib.pyplot as plt # for creating plots of the data
from sklearn.linear_model import LogisticRegression
from sklearn.model_selection import train_test_split
from sklearn.metrics import confusion_matrix, roc_curve, roc_auc_score
import itertools

# The dataset is in the Data folder
DATASET_PATH = 'Data/'
# Read the data from the CSV file
data_path = os.path.join(DATASET_PATH, 'adult-all.csv')
censusData = pd.read_csv(data_path, na_values = ["?", "?"], encoding = "utf-7")

# Because the CSV doesn't contain any header, we add colum names
# using the description from the original dataset website
# Get to know the data with head, describe, and info methods
censusData.columns = ["Age", "WorkClass", "FnlWgt",
        "Education", "EducationNum", "MaritalStatus",
        "Occupation", "Relationship", "Race", "Gender",
        "CapitalGain", "CapitalLoss", "HoursPerWeek",
```

```
        "NativeCountry", "Income"]
print(censusData.head())
print(censusData.describe())
print(censusData.info())
```

Logistic regression can work with categorical attributes, but to do so, these must first be converted into "dummy variables". Here, we will consider only the numerical variables.

Next, we plot at the correlation matrix. You can see this matrix in Figure 7.6. The correlation matrix simply gives us an idea on the correlation between variables. Looking at the correlation matrix is important to identify if some independent variables are highly correlated with each other. However, the correlation matrix will not show more when one variable is a linear combination of two or more other variables. Here, we will consider only the numerical predictor variables.

Listing 7.17 Logistic Regression 4: Calculate U.S. Census Data Correlation

```
newData = censusData.select_dtypes(['number']).assign(Income =
                              censusData.Income==">50K")
X = newData.drop(["Income"], axis = 1)
Y = newData.Income.astype(np.int)
corr = newData.corr()
%matplotlib inline
sns.heatmap(corr, annot = True)
```

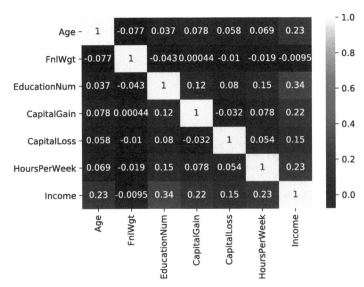

Figure 7.6 U.S. Census Data housing correlation matrix

And now we are ready to go. We start by splitting the data into train and test sets and fit the multiple logistic regression model.

Listing 7.18 Logistic Regression 5: Compute U.S. Census Data Model

```
# Now, lets split the data into train and test sets:
X_train, X_test, Y_train, Y_test = train_test_split(X, Y, test_size = 0.3, random_
state = 18)

# Instantiate Logistic Regression
log_reg = LogisticRegression()
log_reg.fit(X_train, Y_train)

coefs = {X.columns[i]: log_reg.coef_[0, i] for i in range(len(X.columns))}
print(coefs)
```

We obtain the following estimates of the parameters:

```
{'Age': -0.007655848296448912, 'FnlWgt': -3.61671491989561e-06, 'EducationNum':
-0.0017782912826572424, 'CapitalGain': 0.0003465194114016101, 'CapitalLoss':
0.0007733636767756606, 'HoursPerWeek': -0.008348455224276595}
```

The code has calculated for us the coefficients of the independent variables. From these coefficients, we can see how great the influence of each feature is, and whether it has a magnifying or reducing influence on the target variable.

Evaluation

How can classification model be evaluated? The starting point for the valuation is the so-called **confusion matrix**. Let us define as positive the observations for which the dependent variable is one and negative the ones for which the dependent variable is zero. True Positives (TN) are the positive observations which are correctly predicted as positive, and True Negatives (TN) are negative observations which are correctly predicted as negative. On the other hand, False Positives (FP) are negative observations that are predicted as positive, and a False Negatives (FN) are positive observations that are falsely predicted as negative. Keeping this in mind, we can build the confusion matrix as follow.

		PREDICTED LABELS	
		Positive	Negative
ACTUAL LABELS	Positive	TP	FN
	Negative	FP	TN

With the help of the confusion matrix, we can define the following metrics to evaluate a classifier:

- The success rate or **accuracy** is calculated as the number of observations correctly identifies as positive or negative, that is $TP + TN / (TP + FN + FP + TN)$.

- **Sensitivity** is the percent of positives that were also predicted to be positives, that is $TP / (TP + FN)$. It is also called True Positive Rate or **Recall**.

- **Specificity** is percent of true negatives detected as such by the algorithm, that is $TN / (TN + FP)$. It is also called True Negative Rate.

- **Precision** is the percentage of true positives out of all observations predicted to be positive, that is $TP / (TP + FP)$.
- And finally, the F-score, which seeks to combine the information from Precision and Recall into one number: $F\_score = 2 * Recall * Precision / (Recall + Precision)$.

We now predict the class of the observations in the test set and plot the confusion matrix in Figure 7.7.

Listing 7.19 Regression 6: U.S. Census Data Prediction and Confusion Matrix

```
Y_pred = log_reg.predict(X_test)
cnf_matrix = confusion_matrix(Y_test, Y_pred)
sns.heatmap(cnf_matrix, annot=True, fmt="d")
```

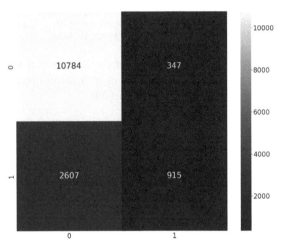

Figure 7.7 Logistic regression, confusion matrix

Notice that by using the predict() method, we will directly obtain the predicted class. When we estimate the parameters of the logistic regression, however, we have access to even more detailed information: the probability that the sample belongs to the positive class. If we want to obtain this probability, we will need to use predict_probs(). The predict() method by default uses a threshold of 0.5, which means that every observation with a probability above 50 % of belonging to the positive class will be assigned to that class.

In many applications, not all errors are to be valued equally, however: for example, in a medical diagnostic procedure, one might prefer to have one more false positive than a false negative, as the latter means missing a true positive diagnosis. In such cases, one could reduce the "cost" of a false positive. For classifiers that calculate probabilities, as for logistic regression, this can be done by moving the classification threshold to account for the cost of false positives and false negatives. Yet we can never really minimize false positives and false negatives; there is always a tradeoff. To understand why, perform the following thought experiment. Imagine an algorithm that classifies all observations as positives. You would have 100 % true positives, but also 100 % false positives. On the other hand, imagine that you classify all events as negative. This would result in 0 % false positives, but also 0 % true positives.

The **Receiver Operating Characteristic (ROC)** curve is quite useful to illustrate the compromise between True Positives and False Positives. A ROC curve is a graph with the True Positive Rate on the y-axis, and False Positive Rate on the x-axis. Going back to the two algorithms above, the ROC curve connects the two points (0,0) and (1, 1). A good model has a ROC curve that comes as close as possible to the left corner, that is the ideal situation (100 % True Positives, 0 % False Positives). We can move along the ROC curve by changing the threshold that we use to assign observation to the positive class. We can then choose the threshold based on what error costs more in our application, and how much more.

Let's calculate the ROC curve of our logistic model and plot it. The ROC curve can be seen in Figure 7.8.

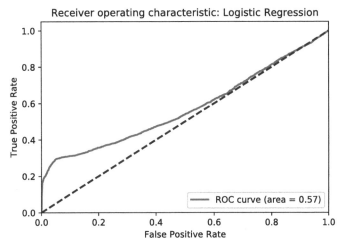

Figure 7.8 Logistic regression, ROC curve

Listing 7.20 Logistic Regression 7: U.S. Census Data ROC Curve

```
# We need the classifier predicition probabilities to compute the ROC Curve:
Y_prob = log_reg.predict_proba(X_test)

# The roc_curve metric returns the False Positive Rate (FPR), the True Positive Rate
(TPR),
# and the Thresholds (the cutoff probability for determining the class), which we
don't need here.

FPR, TPR, _ = roc_curve(Y_test, Y_prob[: , 1])
ROC_AUC = roc_auc_score(Y_test, Y_prob[: , 1])
# we could also use the more generic ROC_AUC = auc(FPR, TPR)
plt.figure()

# set the line width to 2
lw = 2

plt.plot(FPR, TPR, color='red',
        lw=lw, label='ROC curve (area = %0.2f)' % ROC_AUC)
plt.plot([0, 1], [0, 1], color='darkblue', lw=lw, linestyle='--')
plt.xlim([0.0, 1.0])
```

```
plt.ylim([0.0, 1.05])
plt.xlabel('False Positive Rate')
plt.ylabel('True Positive Rate')
plt.title('Receiver operating characteristic: Logistic Regression')
plt.legend(loc="lower right")
plt.show()
```

We can calculate one more metric for the logistic regression model: the **Area Under the Curve (AUC).** The area under a curve is a measure of how well a classifier is performing compared to classifications which were generated randomly. If the AUC is close to the 45° line (dark blue dashed), the AUC is only 0.5 and the binary classifier is not better than simple guessing. The more the curve tends to the top left corner, the closer the AUC is to 1. The AUC for our model is 0.58.

■ 7.5 How Good is Our Model?

We have seen from the previous examples that every algorithm needs an internal loss function which it tries to optimize using the training data. What kind of model is developed depends essentially on the selected loss function. As we have seen in linear regression, the MSE or RMSE are very often used as performance metrics in regression problems, although the MAE is also a popular criterion.

If one speaks of a classification and requires from the algorithm only the class membership, then the accuracy is often used as the deciding metric. The confusion matrix, on the other hand, gives much more accurate information about the performance of the model. Before tuning the threshold of a classification model, one might choose the best model based on the AUC.

But how can we decide how well an algorithm has worked on the data at hand? If we use the value of the loss function on the training data, we run the risk of evaluating our model too optimistically. After all, the loss function was optimized specifically for the selected data!

So we need to test our model with other data that we've never seen before to get a feel for how well our model will then perform "live". And that's why we split our dataset into training and testing data. In machine learning, the data is often split into training, validation, and test sets. The validation set is used during development to tune the hyperparameters of the model, which are parameters that are set by us and not estimated by the algorithm. For example, in binary classification problems, the threshold can be considered a hyperparameter. Hence, we fit the model using the training data, fine tune the threshold using the validation data, and then obtain the final performance metric on the test set.

Often we want to use a more robust approach. The most popular approaches are **cross-validation** and **bootstrapping**. There are different possibilities of cross-validation, but we will concentrate on the zz-fold cross-validation and set for convenience zz = 5. Thus, the training dataset is divided by random sampling into five subgroups of approximately equal size. Imagine a large pizza divided into five pieces, and mark the top piece as 1, and further clockwise as 2, 3, 4, and 5. In the first pass, take data group 1 as validation data and train with the remaining data (groups 2, 3, 4, 5). In the second pass, the second data group is set aside for validation and the algorithm trains with the other data groups (1, 3, 4, 5). One continues in such a way until all five data groups have served exactly once as validation data. Then you have five test metrics (for example AUC for classification and RMSE for regression) which can be used to compare the different algorithms. In bootstrapping, you take the training data via random sampling with replacement. Thus the same observation can be drawn several times, and other observations may not appear in the training data at all. This statistical fact is exploited by bootstrapping: We continually draw samples from the training data until we have a new training data set of the same size. The observations which were never drawn in this procedure go into the validation data set. The validation results are used to compare the different algorithms. To reduce the variance of the validation results, cross-validation or bootstrapping is often performed several times, and the mean of the performance metrics over each trial is used to evaluate the model. Regardless of whether bootstrapping or cross-validation is used, after the best algorithm has been selected, training is again performed on the entire training data. The model is then tested on the test data to make a statement about how well it works in general.

■ 7.6 In a Nutshell

Types of Data

Data can be categorized as structured (tables) or unstructured (test, images, etc.). Structured data contain variables that can be quantitative or qualitative.

Linear Regression

In linear regression, the dependent variable is quantitative. The interpretation of the parameter relative to an independent variable is the expected absolute change in the dependent variable when we change the independent variable by one unit. The MSE, RMSE and MAE are metrics used to evaluate how good a linear regression model is.

Logistic Regression

In logistic regression, the dependent variable is binary, that is takes only two values, often coded with zero (negative) and one (positive). The interpretation of the parameters is not as immediate as in linear regression but gives an indication of the effect of the independent variables on the response. AUC gives an idea of how good a model is. Depending on the importance of the classification errors in the specific applications, other metrics are used.

Cross-validation and Bootstrapping

Cross-validation and bootstrapping are two techniques to obtain a more robust measurement of the performance of a model. Both consist in calculating many metrics on subsets of the training data. The final performance metric is then calculated on the test set.

■

References

[1]   Pedregosa et al. Scikit-learn: Machine Learning in Python (2011), *JMLR 12*, pp. 2825-2830

[2]   Seabold, Skipper, and Josef Perktold. statsmodels: Econometric and statistical modeling with python. *Proceedings of the 9th Python in Science Conference* (2010)

[3]   Fisher, R.A. The use of multiple measurements in taxonomic problems, *Annual Eugenics* (1936), 7, Part II, 179-188

8 Machine Learning

Georg Langs, Katherine Munro, Rania Wazir

Questions Answered in this Chapter:

- What are the principles and key concepts of machine learning?
- Which machine learning techniques exist and what are their capabilities and differences?
- What is supervised and unsupervised machine learning, and what are corresponding applications?
- What is deep learning and what are the key models and learning approaches in this area?

■

■ 8.1 Introduction

Machine learning is a branch of artificial intelligence that follows an interesting approach: Instead of implementing sets of rules and walking through them using static algorithms, rules or models are learned from examples. For example, instead of designing a decision tree by hand that determines the logical voting behavior of people based on characteristics such as their place of residence, income, age and the make of car they own, a large number of examples are collected, for each of which the place of residence, income, age, make of car and voting behavior are known. This data is the training data, with the aid of which learning algorithms generate models. Presented with a new example, such models provide a prediction of what the most likely voting behavior is. In this context, we call the result of the model a "prediction", even if it does not necessarily concern an observation in the future.

The basic building blocks of machine learning are observations such as images, measurements, texts, laboratory values or sound signals, and a target variable that each observation is connected to and that a model is supposed to predict. Target variables can be discrete categories (colors, party, diagnosis) or continuous values (temperature, size, monetary value). In the first case we speak of a classification model that maps observations to classes, in the second case of a regression model that maps observations to continuous values.

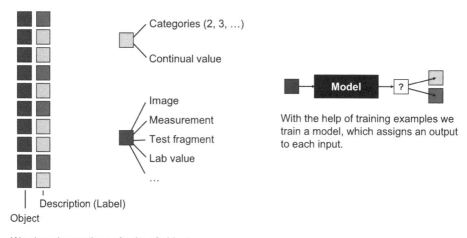

Figure 8.1 Machine learning models are trained with examples, each of which consists of a pair of input (e.g. a photo of an animal) and correct output (e.g. the object category "cat")

Research and development of models and learning algorithms that turn a large number of examples into prediction machines has been around for a long time. The prediction engines can get very complex, but the underlying principle is often similar: how do you compare observations and draw conclusions about an example without a label from those examples for which you do know the label?

If the weather report records rain in all of the surrounding districts, you don't need to look out the window to make a likely correct forecast that rain will fall here as well. We call this the nearest neighbor classifier, and it is one of the simplest, but surprisingly successful, mechanisms for using observations to make predictions. George Chen and Devavrat Shah provide an excellent discussion about the power of this approach tracing it back to the 11th century[1] Today it is experiencing a renaissance, as it delivers surprisingly good results, especially with very large amounts of data. It is therefore a good starting point for establishing models and characteristics.

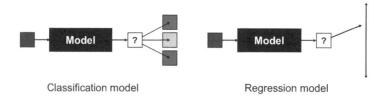

Classification model   Regression model

Figure 8.2 Classification models map inputs to discrete categories, regression models to continuous quantities

[1] Chen, George H., and Devavrat Shah. "Explaining the Success of Nearest Neighbor Methods in Prediction." Foundations and Trends in Machine Learning 10.5-6 (2018): 337–588.

■ 8.2 Basics: Feature Spaces

Sometimes observations consist of very clearly defined characteristics, such as water temperature, air pressure, course, direction or size. In many cases, however, observations are more complex – such as a photo of a person – and usable features must first be extracted before they can be processed by a model.

We are here speaking of "feature extraction", meaning the conversion of observations into feature vectors that contain the relevant properties in order to provide the prediction model with information. The prediction model then maps these feature vectors onto the target variable in the target space. The target variable can either be categorical (classification model) or continuous (regression model). This concept is illustrated in Figure 8.3.

 Example: Classification of Objects in Images

- **Observation:** whole picture
- **Features:** Result of filtering the image with a wavelet filter bank consisting of a vector of numbers
- **Target variable:** Object category: car, pedestrian, tree, street

■

Feature extraction is one of the critical components of successful prediction, and for a long time, work on improving feature extraction has been one of the most important areas of research in pattern recognition and machine learning. An important part of the improvement of prediction models occurred in this area, and one of the most influential steps – similar to the step from manually creating rules to training, with the aid of examples – was the step towards algorithmic selection of features (discussed below) and finally, learning algorithmically how to extract feature based on the training data.

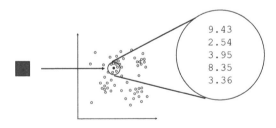

Feature extraction

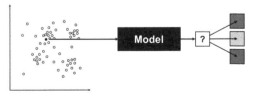

Prediction model

Figure 8.3
Feature extraction: An observation is converted into a feature vector. The vector is a point in a feature space and prediction models only work on this representation. They can be thought of as mappings from a feature space to a target space.

Three Strategies for Feature Extraction

1. **Hand crafted features:** The design of feature extractors that turn observations into feature vectors is carried out by experts. Features should on the one hand contain sufficient information for the prediction model and on the other hand do not contain any information that could have a disruptive effect. This is especially relevant in models that are unstable if irrelevant information is making up substantial parts of the features used as input. In scenarios in which there are precise hypotheses regarding the relationship between observation and target variable, using this knowledge is an excellent strategy to construct or select features. Hence, domain knowledge based feature construction continues to be relevant when there are reasonable expectations about the predictive value of certain characteristics. A rule of thumb: if you know of a meaningful relationship, you should use it.

2. **Algorithmic feature selection:** Instead of specifying a narrow set of carefully selected features, selection is performed by an algorithm. It is provided with a set of features – many of them possibly worthless or spurious – and selects features that have predictive power. Algorithmic feature selection can either be univariate, when each feature is assessed in isolation from the others, or multivariate, when the features are used and assessed as part of a larger whole. One example are bagging classifiers such as random forests (see section 8.3.2), which as part of classification model training also assess features with regard to their multivariate predictive power and only use those that actually contribute to the accuracy of the prediction.

3. **Algorithmic generation of features:** Instead of specifying a repertoire of features and selecting predictive features through a selection mechanism, feature extractors are learned on the basis of training data. This leads to the elimination of the restriction of the feature vocabulary to a predefined set. However, typically it requires much more training data. One example are convolutional neural networks, which learn filters that represent the training data in a compact manner and at the same time can be used for the prediction goal. These will be discussed in Section 8.5.1.

The three dominant strategies for feature extraction were presented in the box above. The progress from initially manual design to automatic feature selection and finally to learning feature extractors is closely related to the development of predictive models in general.

Imagine a nearest neighbor classifier (NN classifier) that is supposed to determine whether a car is a truck or a passenger car based on latitude, longitude and height. With a few hundred training examples, the classification probably works well, since the two classes, with rare exceptions, fill characteristic regions in the feature space. If we take color instead of length, the NN classifier collapses, since the distances are dominated by a worthless variable, and the height – although informative in itself – only has a comparatively small share in the signal. The selection and scaling of the features becomes a question that we must answer before using predictive models.

Classifiers such as nearest neighbor classifiers and, to a certain extent, Support Vector Machines (SVM) suffer from sensitivity to too many non-informative features. This has resulted in an enormous amount of effort put into the design of features for such algorithms.

A major step that improved the accuracy and reliability of classifiers and regression models was the development of methods that can cope with a substantial number of non-informative features. Examples of this are boosting models (AdaBoost)[2] or bagging models (Random Forest)[3]. As part of the training process, both model families assess the contribution of each individual feature to the correct prediction and select the final features accordingly. This can mean that different features can be used for different subsets of training examples. The trick for both model types is to use a large number of very simple so-called "weak learners" that only have access to part of the training data and part of the overall feature set during training. It is a very different strategy from using a single complex model that works with all examples and characteristics at the same time. After the training has been completed, all weak learners can be used to predict a new observation, and their respective predictions can be summarized as a voting result. This has a fascinating effect: weak learners who can't do anything with the new example because they haven't seen anything comparable during the training produce a comparatively even – random – distribution of votes. Those weak learners who cast correct votes tend to agree with each other – which typically leads to an often gentle but reliable win in the correct class.[4]

Some methods go one step further, in that they don't even select from a set of provided features, but rather, learn to extract features themselves from the input data. Deep learning methods such as convolutional neural networks (CNN) belong to this type of model. On a certain class of data for which neighborhood relations are important (such as images, in which objects are made of clusters of neighboring pixels), CNNs learn feature extractors in the form of filters, which on the one hand are particularly well suited to capturing the variability of the data and on the other hand result in filter responses that contribute to the prediction of the target variable.

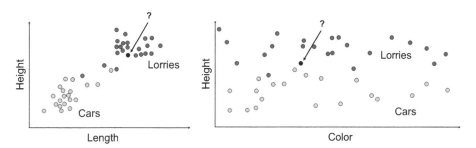

A new example can be classified based on the labels of its neighbors in the feature space.

An NN classifier can be rendered useless by uninformative features, since they disturb neighborhood relationships.

Figure 8.4 Nearest Neighbor Classifiers assign new observations – that is, feature vectors – to a category based on the categories of the closest neighbors in the feature space. This method is sensitive to features that contain no usable information or any scaling of feature sizes.

[2] Rätsch, G., Onoda, T., & Müller, K. R. (2001). Soft margins for AdaBoost. Machine learning, 42(3), 287–320
[3] Breiman, L. (2001). Random forests. Machine learning, 45(1), 5–32
[4] Bühlmann, P., & Yu, B. (2002). Analyzing bagging. The Annals of Statistics, 30(4), 927–961

■ 8.3 Classification Models

The mapping from a feature vector to a categorical target variable is called "classification", and the corresponding models, "classifiers". The following is a brief overview of some of the most important classifiers, highlighting their properties and limitations. Your selection depends on the task, the number of available training data and expectations of the distribution of the training data in the feature space.

8.3.1 K-Nearest-Neighbor-Classifier

K-Nearest-Neighbor-Classifiers (k-NN-Classifiers) convert the mapping from a feature space to a categorical target variable by evaluating the known labels of the closest neighboring training examples in the feature space. Each example – each observation, we want to classify – is represented by a feature vector. This vector is a point in the feature space (see Figure 8.5). For the training set of examples, we know the positions in the feature space, and the label. Training the model consists of simply storing the feature vectors and labels of training examples, often via an efficient coding (such as a socalled "kd-tree").

When the classifier is applied to a new example, first features are extracted to form the feature vector of the new example. We don't know the label yet, and so we look at the labels of stored training examples in close proximity to make a judgement. Practically, we evaluate the labels of a certain number (typically denoted as k for a k-NN-Classifier) of the closest neighbors in the feature space, and assign the label corresponding to the majority vote of this set to the new example.

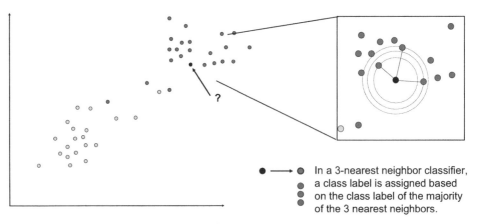

In a 3-nearest neighbor classifier, a class label is assigned based on the class label of the majority of the 3 nearest neighbors.

Figure 8.5 k-NN classifiers carry out a classification by "voting" on the closest neighbors of a point in the feature space. The example shows the decision on a point (shown in black) with an unknown class, based on a 3-NN classifier.

On the one hand, the method is very simple to implement, and while the rapid retrieval of the nearest neighbors is a challenge with large training data sets, computational power, and effective data structures such as kd-trees have solved this to some extent. This has recently led to a renewed increase in their relevance. However, a limitation illustrated in Figure 8.4 remains: k-NN-Classifiers depend on a meaningful distance to determine the closest neighbors. In feature spaces that represent diverse characteristics such as height, length, color, or speed of cars, it is difficult to decide for a correct scaling of the different coordinate axes in the feature space. Is speed more or less important than height when classifying between a car and a lorry? Non-informative features can lead to a complete failure of the classifier. Hence, the dependence of k-NN-Classifiers on informed and careful feature construction and selection guided by expert knowledge.

8.3.2 Support Vector Machine

Support Vector Machines (SVM), similar to k-NN-Classifiers, assume a relatively dense distribution of training examples in the feature space. Instead of using all examples to classify a new one, SVMs identify so-called support vectors (SV) during training. These are vectors that are close to the class boundary in the feature space. Support vectors are chosen in such a way that the distance between the points of the two classes has the maximum distance to the separation area. The interface is a so-called "hyperplane" (it has one dimension less than the feature space). Through their position and a kernel that determines their area of influence – or the analogous distortion of the feature space – they define the class boundary.

When a new example is classified, only the coordinates of these SVs have to be used. SVMs have been around for a long time and in some cases are still widespread in applications ranging from the analysis of seismic signals to proteins. Again, an important limitation on their use relates to the choice of features. SVMs are substantially affected by interfering features and therefore careful design and choice of features is important analogously to k-NN-Classifiers. This reduces their applicability, since it often requires resources for feature design that are not necessary with other methods, such as the ensemble methods described later in this chapter.

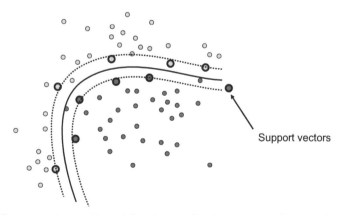

Figure 8.6 Support vector machines define the boundary between two classes in the feature space using support vectors.

8.3.3 Decision Tree

A decision tree is a different type of classifier. It is based on a series of decisions – a path through the branching points of the tree – that encode the features of an observation. Each branching of the tree corresponds to the observation of a feature, for example the color of a car, which can be divided into categories (green, blue, red). After all features have been queried and the decision tree has been run through accordingly, a leaf is reached. A leaf has no further bifurcation, and the leaf label determines the class label of the example. Decision trees thus differ somewhat from the two previous classifiers, which operate in continuous vector spaces.

Decision trees initially treat each feature as a quantity that can be broken down into discrete categories that drive the decisions at its bifurcations. During the training, a tree forms branches, and examples travel along the branches guided by decisions made at each bifurcation. The decision at each bifurcation is determined by a feature. If the feature is categorical, each category results in a branch starting at the bifurcation. If the feature is scalar, we use a threshold value, so that an example goes one or the other way, depending on whether the corresponding observed feature is larger or smaller than the threshold value.

During training, training examples "travel" along branches chosen based on their observed features and the corresponding decisions made at each bifurcation. Each example will end up in one of the branches, resulting in a set of labels in each branch. If this set only contains a single label, we turn the branch into a leaf and assign it this very label. If the set contains multiple labels, we attach a new bifurcation to the end of the branch, and let a different feature further separate examples with different labels. This continues until we have either only leaves, or until we have reached a certain allowed depth of the tree. In the latter case the last level of branches is turned into leaves, but some may contain examples with different classes. There, the ratio of examples with a certain class can be treated as a probability of this class being present in the leaf.

The so-called CART algorithm is a method to train decision trees using examples for which binary labels are known.[5]

When we use a trained decision tree to classify a new example, for which we don't know the label, we let it travel along the bifurcations, routed by its features, and assign the label of the final leaf it reaches. The category of the leaf is output as the final classification result of the decision tree. We can use decision trees for regression tasks as well. Then instead of assigning the example a discrete categorical label, we assign the average of the target values observed in the training set examples that reach the particular leaf.

Decision trees are sensitive to the risk of so-called "overtraining". This means that from a certain branching level the decisions continue to separate the training data better and better, but this separation might work only on the training data. On new data it might actually deteriorate the classification accuracy – the agreement between the true labels, and the output of the classifier. This is called "overtraining". The result is that new data are not sorted as correctly as the training data when running through the decision tree. One means of preventing this is so-called "pruning", which means simply pruning the decision tree (by removing leaves and nodes) to a branching level that is stable and generalizes well. The

---

[5] Breiman, L., Friedman, J. H., Olshen, R. A., & Stone, C. J. (1984). Cart. Classification and Regression Trees; Wadsworth and Brooks/Cole: Monterey, CA, USA

success of such an approach can be tested using cross-validation methods. In Section 8.6 we will look into more details of evaluation methods. Another, usually more successful, method is to use decision trees as elements in ensemble methods such as random forests. This is discussed in detail in Section 8.3.

Note that we briefly mentioned the transformation of a continuous variable (a number) to a categorical variable (A or B) before. Let us look at this in a bit more detail. There are more or less elegant ways to turn a continuous variable into a categorical one or vice versa. We can threshold a scalar to turn each observation into one of two categories (smaller or larger than the threshold). We can also lign categories up, for instance A – B – C – D, and treat this as a continuous variable. While this is possible, careful attention must be paid to the implicit assumptions. For example, a vector space contains a structure that results from distances, which is to say that the phrase "point A is between B and C" makes sense and also means something. This is not necessarily the case with categorical variables. If you turn a categorical into a continuous variable, it can happen that you encode properties that are not contained in the data or their relationships. For example, if you convert red – green – blue to 1 – 2 – 3, you may be encoding a sense of order which is not present in the original data. In the next section we will see a successful way of creating very powerful classifiers by converting continuous classification problems in vector spaces to categorical decisions in many decision trees.

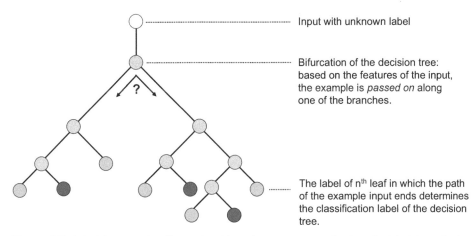

Figure 8.7 A decision tree classifies an input based on a sequence of categorical decisions. Each bifurcation routes the example along one of its branches based on one specific feature. The labels of the leaves determine the label assigned to the input example.

■ 8.4 Ensemble Methods

Ensemble methods perform classification or regression not through a single complex model, but through an ensemble of many relatively simple models. Often each of these models is only trained on part of the training data, or it only has access to a selection of the features available in the data. The resulting classifier (or the regression model) applies all of the simple models (known as "weak learners") and processes their individual predictions into an overall result, which is often created through simple vote, such as taking the mode of the output predictions (known in ensemble modelling as the "majority vote"). Ensemble models have very interesting properties and are characterized in particular by their robustness against noise in the features and very good generalization behavior to new data. In the following we will first discuss two important statistical terms that help characterize the advantages of ensemble methods, and then explain an example, Random Forests, in detail.

The development of ensemble methods such as bagging and boosting was motivated by an effort to improve two core characteristics of classification or regression models: bias and variance.

8.4.1 Bias and Variance

Bias and variance are two quantities that are relevant in the context of machine learning and predictive models in general. They describe the capacity of a model to make repeatable predictions on the one hand (low variance) and on the other hand to be close to the truth with these predictions (low bias). An excellent discussion of these quantities in the context of ensemble methods was given by Geurts et al. in 2006[6], and by Geman et al. in 1992[7].

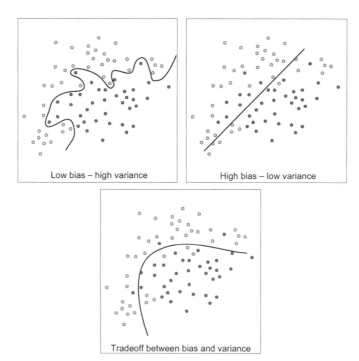

Figure 8.8 A schematic representation of bias and variance

[6] Geurts, P., Ernst, D., & Wehenkel, L. (2006). Extremely randomized trees. Machine learning, 63(1), 3–42
[7] Geman, S., Bienenstock, E., & Doursat, R. (1992). Neural networks and the bias/variance dilemma. Neural computation, 4(1), 1–58

When training a model, the aim is on the one hand to represent the distribution of the training data in the best possible way with the model by optimizing the model parameters, such as the support vectors in a support vector machine. At the same time, we know that the training examples are only a finite limited sample from the actual distribution. Therefore, blindly aiming for perfect separation on the training data can lead us At the same time we want to make sure that the model can also be generalized to new data, that is, it also reflects their distribution, even though the new data were not available during training.

As shown in Figure 8.8, a good example of a trade-off between bias and variance can be achieved by controlling the complexity of a model. A very complex model that is trained on too little data can represent the distribution of this data optimally, producing a classification error rate on the training data of 0, but the generalization to new data suffers. When the model is used to predict new data, there is high variance in the predictions that is independent of the variance in the training data. This situation is called overfitting. It is characterized by low bias and high variance. The opposite happens when the model is too simple. In this case, the bias is high because the distribution of the training data is not reproduced well, but at the same time the variance is low and the error rate for new data that was not available during the training will be roughly the same as the error in the training data set. This situation is called underfitting.

 Bias and Variance

The estimation error of a model in predicting target variables from new observations that were not part of the training data can be broken down into two components in two ways:

- **Bias:** An incorrect estimate of the model parameters such that they do not reflect the actual distribution of the sample data.

- **Variance:** The variance of the prediction that arises when the model reproduces the distribution of the training data well, but the generalization to new data suffers.

- **Over-fitting:** The model follows the distribution of the training data to an extent that reduces its accuracy on new data.

- **Under-fitting:** The model does not adequately reflect the distribution of the training data.

■

8.4.2 Bagging: Random Forests

Random Forests (RF), introduced by Leo Breiman, are one of the most prominent examples of an ensemble method.[8] These powerful and complex classifiers, which are part of a class of so-called "bagging classifiers", are not trained on all data at once during training. Instead, a large number of so-called "weak learners" are trained. These are each simple: for

---

[8] Breiman, L. (2001). Random forests. Machine learning, 45(1), 5–32

example, they may simply make a decision based on a threshold value of a feature (such as considering all vehicles longer than 4 meters a truck, and all vehicles up to this length a car). The training accepts that each of these weak learners cannot provide a reliable or precise classification result on their own: Only the combination of their predictions becomes interesting. In order to make this possible, each of the weak learners is trained on a subset of the entire available training data set, and at the same time they can also use only a part of the characteristics, or even only a single characteristic, for the classification. This leads to a large number of simple models, each of which uses only a selection of the available features.

In the case of a random forest, the weak learners are decision trees (see Figure 8.9) – hence the name. Each of the decision trees is trained on a subset of the training data set. At each branch, a random set of features are made available to the decision tree, and the training algorithm selects the feature that leads to the maximum gain in purity of the two data sets resulting from the decision at this decision branch. Here, purity is used in the sense of how many different labels are contained in a data set. A data set with examples having the same label would be pure compared to a set of examples with many different labels. This means that the decision – for example based on a threshold value of a feature at a branch – leads to two sets of examples that result from the branch (cars longer or shorter than 4 meters). These amounts are typically not varietal, but should be more varietal than the amount before branching. This mechanism continues until each lot (each leaf) is sorted; that is,, i.e. the training data set used for this decision tree is perfectly classified.

When training a random forest, the decision trees are each trained using a randomly selected subset of the training data. This means that each decision tree "sees" only part of the data and can consequently only work well with data whose characteristics are represented by this set (we will come a little further on in this section to an interesting effect that results from this). At the same time, the features that are available to each of the decision nodes – each branch – in each of the decision trees is randomly selected from all the available features. Only on this subset of features does the algorithm look for the feature that leads to the most correct separation of the classes at this branch.

A random forest consists of a large number of decision trees that have been trained using various examples and features. In order to classify a new observation, all decision trees are first applied and thus cast their "vote", so to speak. This can be given in the form of a vote for a class, if the decision trees have been trained up to leaves containing only samples of a single class. Or it is given as a probability that corresponds to the ratio of the classes in the leaf, if the training of the tree was stopped while leaves still contain examples with different labels. The final classification result is given by the mode of votes, the label, that obtained the majority consensus of all weak learners.

Why are the two key ingredients – examples and features – chosen at random? This creates robustness, every decision tree works well on part of the data, which improves the capacity of the final random forest classifier. When classifying a new observation in the form of a feature vector, trees that have already "seen" similar things tend to be correct. In contrast, the trees for whom this observation does not come close to any of the examples they have already seen, react more randomly. The correct class wins due to the fact that the trees that tend to be correct also tend to agree in this case, contributing to a majority, while the others produce random noise. Random forests are among the most robust and best classifiers available, and require very little adjustment and fine-tuning during training.

Types of Ensemble Methods

Ensemble methods learn several so-called "weak learners" on the basis of different subsets of the training data drawn at random (with replacement). Bagging and boosting are two methods that differ in the way the random subsets are drawn. Ensemble methods have the goal of reducing the variance by repeatedly drawing the training sets at random and at the same time increasing the bias as little as possible. The key aim is to make the errors of weak learners cancel each other out, so that aggregated predictions have lower variance, while not creating bias based on prior assumptions.

- **Bagging:** The subsets of training examples are drawn randomly and independently of each other.

- **Boosting:** The subsets are drawn with weighted probabilities, whereby the weights of one subset can depend on the training result on another subset.

- **Weak learner:** A classifier or regressor that only weakly reflects the actual relationship between input and output variables of the training set. This means that, in contrast to a strong learner, a weak learner behaves only slightly better than a random decision.

■

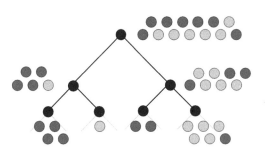
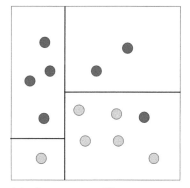

Figure 8.9 A decision tree corresponds to repeated splitting of the feature space. When a new example with an unknown class is routed through the decision tree, it ends up in one of the leaves that correspond to one of the regions in the feature space.

Before discussing the advantages of the random restriction of the features, let us introduce a second very central ability of random forests: the algorithmic selection of relevant features. Each time a decision tree performs a branching, the training data is separated following the decision rule. This allows us to measure and compare the purity of the labels in the set before the branching decision and the two sets after the decision (Fig.8.9). We measure the purity of labels in the form of the so-called "Gini Impurity", which essentially records how evenly the two classes are distributed in a set. If both classes appear equally often, this leads to a high Gini impurity. On the other hand, if there is only one class, the Gini Impurity is zero. This gives us a tool with which to record the decrease in Gini Impurity each feature has contributed to throughout the Random Forest. It results in the Gini Importance of a feature. The Gini importance is high if it has often contributed a lot to improve class separation, and vice versa.[9]

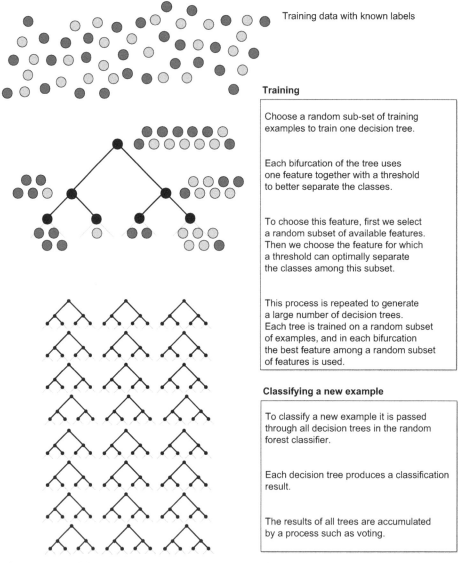

Training data with known labels

Training

Choose a random sub-set of training examples to train one decision tree.

Each bifurcation of the tree uses one feature together with a threshold to better separate the classes.

To choose this feature, first we select a random subset of available features. Then we choose the feature for which a threshold can optimally separate the classes among this subset.

This process is repeated to generate a large number of decision trees. Each tree is trained on a random subset of examples, and in each bifurcation the best feature among a random subset of features is used.

Classifying a new example

To classify a new example it is passed through all decision trees in the random forest classifier.

Each decision tree produces a classification result.

The results of all trees are accumulated by a process such as voting.

Figure 8.10 Training and applying a random forest classifier

The simple observation that the training mechanism tends to select informative features, while not using those that do not contribute to a correct classification, leads to the interesting property of random forests of being very robust against worthless features. They are either never used, or the trees which rely on them tend to lose out in the final voting.

---

[9] Breiman, L. (2001). Random forests. Machine learning, 45(1), 5–32

Gini Importance gives us the option of looking for features with a – multivariate – relationship to the target variable in the case of complex classification issues. Sometimes, as in functional brain imaging, that's even the primary goal. The random selection of subsets of features plays a role here insofar as it means that even closely correlated traits have high Gini importance values, since they can occur independently of one another in different trees. Without random restriction of the respective features, only one of the correlated characteristics would be used, which would lead to a loss of robustness and the "disappearance" of potentially informative features.

8.4.3 Boosting: AdaBoost

Boosting is an ensemble learning technique similar to bagging, based on multiple weak learners. However, instead of randomized and independent training of the weak learners such as in random forests, boosting creates a cascade of simple classification models during training. A prominent example is adaptive boosting, or AdaBoost which won the Gödel Prize in 2003[10] A cascade of weak learners can be trained as follows. First we draw a random subset of training examples to train the first weak learner. For the second weak learner we select part of the training examples randomly, and part of the training examples for which the previous weak learner performed poorly. We repeat this for all further weak learners, always sampling further training examples for new learners based on the performance and disagreement of the previous ones. This strategy leads to a coverage of the training examples by a set of weak learners.

One of the key differences between bagging and boosting is the selection of individual training sets for the weak learners. Both select sub-sets from the overall available training examples. However, while bagging selects the sub-sets randomly and independently, the cascade approach of boosting makes these sets dependent on each other. The training data for one weak learner is not independent from those of the others.

■ 8.5 Artificial Neural Networks and the Perceptron

The last classifier we discuss is a technique that sounds very simple at first: the perceptron[11]. It is motivated by biological neurons and works with two very simple mechanisms: the merging of many input values and an internal nonlinear function that maps the resulting value to an output. The input values are scaled by weights, then summed up, and the result is mapped to the output value by a nonlinear function. This very simple mechanism enables both continuous mapping, and classification. Figure 8.11 illustrates a perceptron.

---

[10] Freund, Yoav, and Robert E. Schapire. "A decision-theoretic generalization of on-line learning and an application to boosting." Journal of computer and system sciences 55.1 (1997): 119–139

[11] Rosenblatt, F. (1958). The perceptron: a probabilistic model for information storage and organization in the brain. Psychological review, 65(6), 386

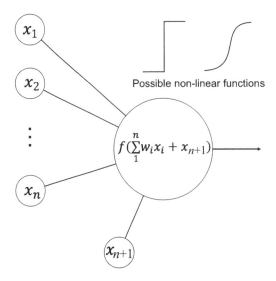

Possible non-linear functions

Figure 8.11
A perceptron processes input from multiple other units that might be observations, or the output of other perceptrons. The processing consists of a weighted sum of the input values and a subsequent nonlinear function.

The weights are factors with which each input is multiplied before all of them are summed up. Another way of viewing them is as weights of the connections that scale the values while they are transmitted from the output of one perceptron to the input of the receiving one. In addition to the weights applied to the incoming values, each perceptron has an additional additive value, the so-called bias. This is added independent of the input values.

During the learning process, the weights and the biases are changed and optimized in such a way that with a given input feature vector, the output of the perceptron corresponds to the desired class label of training examples or achieves this in as many cases as possible.

The perceptron serves as a building block in larger artificial neural network architectures, when the output of one layer of neurons is used as the input of the next layer. Such networks are also called multilayer perceptrons, a form of artificial neural networks (ANN), because they consist of several layers. We divide these layers into an input layer with input units, a number of hidden layers with hidden units and a final output layer with output units. In the case of the multilayer perceptron, all of the units are perceptrons, and often we refer to them as neurons.

When moving to higher layers, the number of perceptrons can be increased or decreased. Later in Section 8.5.4 we will see how this change of layer widths can be used to force a network to learn about the inherent structure in a large number of observations.

In this framework, a classification process is typically modeled as a multilayer perceptron which, in its last layer, contains a number of perceptrons equal to the number of classes. To classify an input feature vector, its values are entering the multilayer perceptron in its first layer. Here, the number of perceptrons is equal to the number of features. From there the values are passed forward through the networks and its perceptrons, until they reach the last output layer. The output neurons are used as indicator function, to determine the class the network predicts. Each is assigned a value by the forward pass of the input values through the networks, and the output perceptron with the highest value determines the class.

To train a multilayer perceptron we use a set of training examples with known feature vectors, and known labels. During training, feature vectors are the input to the network, while labels determine the desired output. We pass the feature vector through the network, obtain the class prediction of the network by determining which output perceptron has the highest value, and compare this label with the desired label known in the training set. For instance, for a five dimensional feature vector (1.3 0.3 2.5 1.2 5.1) the correct label among four possible labels is '3'. The desired output of the network would therefore be (0.0 0.0 1.0 0.0), but the actual output of a not-yet-perfect network may be (0.3 0.5 0.3 0.2). We would like to change the weights so that ultimately the correct class "wins", as would be represented by an output vector such as (0.2 0.4 0.8 0.3), where the largest value is in the third position. We can perform training using an algorithm called backpropagation[12]. This algorithm uses the difference between the desired and current network output (for example, comparing (0.3 0.5 0.3 0.2) and (0.0 0.0 1.0 0.0)) to adjust the weights throughout the network. This is achieved by starting from the output layer and translating the difference between the delivered and desired vectors to gradients in the parameter space of a layer. The parameter space consists of all the values we can change during training. Here these are the weights of the connections and the biases of each perceptron. This is repeated until the input layer is reached, and then repeated again with a new training example.

While an immense variety of models can be implemented with this architecture, neural networks initially suffered from the very slow convergence of the optimization algorithms with which they were trained, which also made it almost impossible to train very deep networks. This even led to a time of relatively low activity in AI research: the so-called "AI winter"[13]. In Section 8.5 we will come back to this architecture and discuss how several methodological advances are now rendering the use of this architecture for a set of classes of problems feasible.

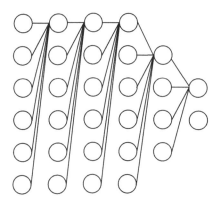

Figure 8.12 A multilayer perceptron consists of several layers of perceptrons. The illustration shows the connections to the top perceptron in each layer as an example. During the training, the weights of these connections are optimized using training examples in the form of pairs of input and output values.

[12] Hecht-Nielsen, R. (1992). Theory of the backpropagation neural network. In Neural networks for perception (pp. 65–93). Academic Press
[13] Schank, R. C. (1991). Where's the AI?. AI magazine, 12(4), 38–38

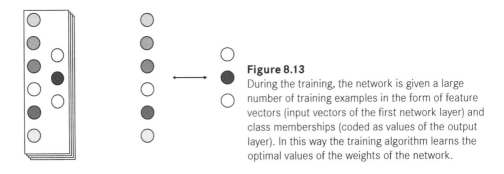

Figure 8.13
During the training, the network is given a large number of training examples in the form of feature vectors (input vectors of the first network layer) and class memberships (coded as values of the output layer). In this way the training algorithm learns the optimal values of the weights of the network.

■ 8.6 Learning without Labels – Finding Structure

Sometimes we don't know what we are looking for in the form of labeled training examples. Instead we are aiming at identifying structure in unlabeled training data. This structure can have the form of similarity relationships between examples that amount to a so-called manifold (see Section 8.4.2), or a grouping of examples into subsets so that within each subset the similarity of examples is high, while the similarity between examples in different clusters is low.

More generally, unsupervised learning typically aims at gaining an explicit or implicit representation of the underlying distribution of the training data. We assume that the training examples do not stem from an absolutely random distribution – such as random pixel values forming images – but instead are samples of a more or less narrow distribution in the space of possible observations. Figure 8.14 illustrates this general idea.

8.6.1 Clustering

One of the simplest approaches towards unsupervised learning is clustering. Here we identify clusters of examples that are more similar than examples in other clusters. The two key ingredients of clustering are a similarity function that captures relevant characteristics of the data, and an algorithm to assign examples to clusters based on this similarity function. A similarity function tht enables the comparison between any pairs of examples. Sometimes we can use a distance measure in the feature space, such as the Euclidean distance between two points representing two examples. The clustering algorithm then has to use these distances to identify groups of examples so that examples are close by to each other within the group, while the groups are far apart. The k-means clustering method is one example in the family of so-called expectation maximization methods to perform clustering[14]. In k-means

---
[14] Do, C. B., & Batzoglou, S. (2008). What is the expectation maximization algorithm?. Nature biotechnology, 26(8), 897–899

clustering, first a random sub-division of training examples into initial clusters is defined. This is independent of their features or distances, and we call it a random initialization. In the second step, the mean of each cluster is formed, and all examples are re-assigned to clusters based on their proximity to these means. Each mean determines the cluster membership of the examples. In the third step, the means are recalculated based on the new subdivision of the training data. Step two and three are repeated until the means and memberships converge, that is if new iterations don't change anything or so little, that we determine the clustering as being finished. For a detailed description of using k-means clustering for text classification, see Section 10.3.2 in Chapter 10.

8.6.2 Manifold Learning

In manifold learning, we are not necessarily interested in grouping data, although that can be a secondary step. Instead we tackle the question of learning a meaningful metric capturing the relationships in the training data in the first place. Remember, we would need such a metric for k-means clustering, but sometimes we don't have it from the beginning. Often, we are only able to determine a similarity or affinity between a sub-set of pairs of the overall training data. A similarity measure between all pairs is either not initially available, or we might be doubtful as to whether it is meaningful.

An example is the Euclidean distance between two points on the earth's surface. The Euclidean distance is what you measure if you span a tape measure between two points in a straight line. If we are interested in travel time by plane between two points, then this Euclidean distance is only informative for close by points. For points far apart it represents the distance of drilling through the earth – exciting, but not a travel experience we are after. Therefore, let's trust that the small distances between points correspond to travel time, but that we are only interested in traveling within a narrow band around the surface, or on the surface on which these points are situated.

This surface, is a so-called manifold, and within it, locally the Euclidean distance makes sense. There is a more formal definition of a manifold, but that it is a Euclidean space only locally is the key aspect. Manifolds are a tremendously helpful tool for thinking about our world and representing the relationships between observations.

In the case of the earth the solution to our problem, is to realize that the manifold that captures the relevant distance as a sphere. On this sphere, we can use the geodesic distance along the surface to plan for optimal routes. The sphere is the manifold we are traveling along. In other learning scenarios we might not know the shape of the manifold a priori. Here, manifold learning translates a set of pairwise distances into a metric, so that we gain a representational space in which the Euclidean distance represents meaningful travel distances within the manifold. This is particularly relevant if we are observing networks, which can be thought of as a large number of pairwise relationships. Manifold learning approaches include isomaps[15], diffusion maps[16], or methods we will discuss later in this chapter, such as autoencoders.

---

[15] Balasubramanian, Mukund, et al. "The isomap algorithm and topological stability." Science 295.5552 (2002): 7-7
[16] Coifman, Ronald R., and Stéphane Lafon. "Diffusion maps." Applied and computational harmonic analysis 21.1 (2006): 5–30

To be useful for subsequent clustering and analysis, manifold learning approaches typically transform all the points that make up the manifold into a new so-called embedding space. In this embedding space, each point is represented by a point, but now the Euclidean metric within the entire space represents the metric within the manifold, or an approximation thereof. This is what geographical maps are: an embedding of the geodesic distance on the earth's surface, into a two-dimensional embedding space, so that we can use a ruler to measure the travel distance on the earth's surface.

8.6.3 Generative Models

Generative models, illustrated in Figure 8.14, are another approach in the area of unsupervised learning. The aim is to create models that can actually generate realistic new examples resembling those observed in the training data. Generative models are trained on examples without labels, and assume an underlying but unobservable distribution of these data. An explicit density model estimates this underlying distribution based on the training data, and typically results in a parametric representation of this estimate, such as a Gaussian Mixture Model (GMM). Training approaches for this type of model are, for instance, based on maximum likelihood[17]. Alternatively, we may train a model that is able to generate examples that are hard to discriminate from the observed examples stemming from the training distribution. This would be referred to as an implicit density model.

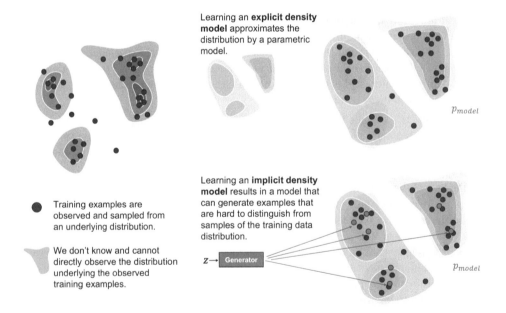

Learning an **explicit density model** approximates the distribution by a parametric model.

p_{model}

Training examples are observed and sampled from an underlying distribution.

We don't know and cannot directly observe the distribution underlying the observed training examples.

Learning an **implicit density model** results in a model that can generate examples that are hard to distinguish from samples of the training data distribution.

$z \rightarrow$ Generator

p_{model}

Figure 8.14 Generative models are trained from a set of unlabeled examples, and learn either a parametric estimate of the underlying distribution, or a process to generate samples that resemble the characteristics of the training examples well.

---

[17] Le Cam, L. (1990). Maximum likelihood: an introduction. International Statistical Review/Revue Internationale de Statistique, 153-171

■ 8.7 Reinforcement Learning

In the previous sections we discussed supervised and unsupervised learning for machine learning models. Both of those assume that all training data is available from the start of training, and exists independently of the model itself. Reinforcement learning (RL) follows a different approach, in that at least part of the training data is generated by the model itself, while it is trained.

We often think of RL models as agents. The agent still needs to create its own training 'examples'. It needs to act and observe how the environment responds to its actions, in order to generate data for its own further training. The agent adjusts its behavior according to the response it gets for its actions, makes more actions, receives more responses, adjusts its behaviour again, and so on. This "learning by doing" has many parallels to biological processes: for example, humans are never told that they will earn points by eating, or lose points by touching hot objects. Instead, our ability to feel pain is an effective reward function which we learn and then use to avoid injury in a vast variety of situations. Thus, we learn even from a young age that if we touch something hot, it hurts, and if we eat when we are hungry, we feel good.

In formal terms, the key components of RL are the agent, its current situation or state, its environment, the actions it performs and a reward that is used to inform the agent whether an action given the current environment is "good" or "bad". A policy determines the agent's next action given its current state. A reward is determined by the agent's action within its environment. Sutton and Barto provide an extensive tutorial on the concepts of reinforcement learning in their book.[18]

Now that we have introduced some key terms, let us dive into reinforcement learning in more detail. The environment in RL is often modelled in terms of Markov decision processes (MDPs), a common framework for modeling decision making in situations where an outcome is only partly influenced by a decision maker, and partly by an external random effect – the environment. We use S to denote the set of possible environments and states in which the agent finds itself and A the set of the agent's possible actions. For example, in the case of an autonomous vehicle, the state S would be described by the position of the car relative to the centre of the lane and the distance from the car in front. The set A would represent actions including acceleration, braking, turning left, or turning right.

The RL agent interacts with the environment in time steps. At each timestep t, the agent has a state s_t, and a selection of actions a_t to choose from. Having chosen, the decision maker will be moved into a new state s_{t+1} influenced by the chosen action and the current state, together with a random element. More formally the new state is decided by a probability function whose distribution is determined by current state and chosen action. At the same time it is given a reward r_{t+1}, based on the transition (st, at, st+1). The probability of moving into the new state, given the current one and the chosen action, is denoted by a state transition function $P_a(s, s')$. This probability is conditionally independent of all previous states and actions, given s and a.

[18] Sutton, R. S., & Barto, A. G. (2018). Reinforcement learning: An introduction. MIT press

As in real life, the immediate reward for an action is not the full story. Our aim is often to train an agent so that it accumulates rewards over time, instead of only getting the biggest possible reward right now, at the cost of possibly larger rewards later. For instance, imagine you were an agent being trained to get from A to B in a city as fast as possible. We design a reward function in which the reward is high for any timestep (or, more specifically, for any move within a timestep) which reduces the distance to B. You will learn to navigate a city on foot, using paths as straight as possible and always in the direction of B. That's fine, but what if, a few steps in the opposite direction to B, there was a bus stop with connections straight to B? How can you make an agent learn to utilise such possibilities, too?

The key idea in RL is thus to optimize the policy for rewards accumulated over a number of steps in the future, instead of only a single step, assessing the value of states and the value of actions given a specific state.[19] To venture onto paths that do not bring immediate reward, but accumulate reward over time, training has to involve trade-offs between the *exploitation* of an agent's current policy ("go for the immediately largest reward") with *exploration* of actions that do not bring immediate optimal reward ("lets see what happens later"). While training is running with this trade-off the agent records the accumulated gain of pairs of states and actions – the policy – and thereby learns to take those actions with the optimal long-term value. A more extensive explanation can be found in the book "Machine Learning" by Tom Mitchell[20] which is available on the authors web page at Carnegie Mellon University [21]. The topic is still an area of very active research[22], and deep reinforcement learning has furthered the capability of this family of approaches[23].

We will finish this section with a prominent example which illustrates how reinforcement learning overcomes the challenges of previous approaches, specifically, learning policies via supervised learning. AlphaGO is a deep learning model that made headlines by playing the game "Go" as well as, or better than, the best human players.[24] During a game of Go – in contrast to chess – the number of possible moves a player can make increases. RL is the only feasible approach to train an agent to play the game. In the AlphaGo model, the state is the current board position, and the action is the move the agent makes. You should recognise from the introduction above that we still need a policy, which is usually a probability distribution of making a certain move, given a certain state. In the case of AlphaGo, the policy is actually a policy network that determines the next move (See Section 8.5 for an explanation of artificial neural networks, and Section 8.9 for an explanation of deep learning). It was in learning this policy network for AlphaGo that RL was able to shine, where supervised approaches failed.

Before work on reinforcement learning began, the policy network for AlphaGo was initiated by supervised learning, resulting in a supervised learning (SL) policy network. Data for supervised learning was generated by simply downloading 30 million board positions and the corresponding next moves by human players from the popular KGS Go Server. The SL

---

[19] Watkins, C. J., & Dayan, P. (1992). Q-learning. Machine learning, 8(3–4), 279–292
[20] Mitchell, T. (1997). Machine learning
[21] *http://www.cs.cmu.edu/~tom/mlbook.html* (last accessed November 2021)
[22] Liu, Q., Yu, T., Bai, Y., & Jin, C. (2021, July). A sharp analysis of model-based reinforcement learning with self-play. In International Conference on Machine Learning (pp. 7001–7010). PMLR
[23] François-Lavet, V., Henderson, P., Islam, R., Bellemare, M. G., & Pineau, J. (2018). An Introduction to Deep Reinforcement Learning. Foundations and Trends in Machine Learning, 11(3–4), 219–354
[24] Silver, David, et al. Mastering the game of Go with deep neural networks and tree search. nature, 2016, 529. Jg., Nr. 7587, S. 484–489

policy network was trained to predict the next move of a human given a board position. It predicted expert moves with an accuracy of slightly more than 55 %, which was at that time already better than the state-of-the-art. But then, AlphaGo's developers began experimenting with a new, RL-based approach: letting different, intermediate versions of the SL policy network play against each other, to keep the pool of policies in the training diverse. The reward function was surprisingly simple: 1 if the move wins the game right now, –1 if the move loses the game right now and 0 for all other moves. The RL policy network weights were then updated at each time step to maximize the expected outcome of the game. Finally, a value network was trained to estimate a value function of a state (that is, a board position), as the expected outcome of the game if the agent were to play perfectly from that point on.

The policy network was initially trained on a huge number of state-outcome pairs. However, this did not work well when sampling from real data: the board positions were so similar to each other the model experienced overfitting, which is to say that the number of actually independent training examples was far lower than the samples board positions. Thus, instead of using real games, the developers generated training data by letting the RL policy networks play against each other, generating about 30 million different positions sampled from different games. The result was a fairly well playing policy network, and a value network that could judge board positions, in terms of the probability of winning, quite well. In the last step, these two networks were combined, to improve the policy network even further.

The story of AlphaGo clearly demonstrates that the ability to simulate data is key, and that often simulated data outnumbers data available in the real world, and can even supersede its value for training, due to its diversity. Consequently, the following year the authors went a step further: they did away completely with any initialization based on observing humans, instead using RL for generating the entirety of their training data.[25]

■ 8.8 Overarching Concepts

In the previous sections, when describing various classifiers, we encountered a number of concepts that several of these classification methods have in common and that play a role in deciding which of the methods to use for a specific problem. We'll review these again here and contrast them with one another to get an overview before we dive into the next big topic.

All of the methods discussed so far use a feature representation that brings the observations into a processable form. The construction of these features is done by rules that are established once and then applied to all observations. A key consideration in the development of feature extractors and classifiers relates to understanding the problem and the aspects of the data that contain relevant information. That is, if you know characteristics that are related to the target variable, you should typically use them. It means that you bring in knowledge and understanding of the mechanisms or laws of the data that cannot be made available to the learning algorithm or can only be made available with the help of a large number of training examples. So, in feature construction, follow the motto: "You know a feature that makes sense? Use it."

---

[25] Silver, David, et al. Mastering the game of go without human knowledge. Nature, 2017, 550. Jg., Nr. 7676, S. 354–359

But what should be done with other aspects of the observations, of which one does not understand in advance whether and in what combination they can serve the prediction? With many of the aforementioned methods, such as bagging or boosting, the best choice is often to generate features – even if it is not certain whether they are useful – and leave it to the algorithm to learn which features to use.[26]

We will get to know a completely different level of feature creation in the next section: the algorithmic construction of features using neural networks.

■ 8.9 Into the Depth – Deep Learning

Research on neural networks increased again around 2010 for three reasons. The amount of available computing power had increased enormously and in particular hardware architectures such as those used in graphics cards turned out to be optimal computing hardware for training neural networks. Second, some algorithmic advances had been made that were nearer to solving the problems one had faced prior to the onset of the AI winter. For example, new methods to train networks without being hindered from the progress of the optimization by vanishingly small gradients during backpropagation had been developed. And third, the availability of data, especially image data, increased dramatically. This led to the ability to effectively train actually deep multilayer perceptrons on a large amount of data. A rapidly growing field dealing with deep learning had emerged.

8.9.1 Convolutional Neural Networks

One of the first and most successful architectures of the new deep learning era was the Convolutional Neural Network or CNN. CNNs are multilayer perceptrons with an architecture that leaves out a relatively large number of connections between the layers. The CNNs' own connection pattern results in a behavior of the layers that corresponds to a filtering of the input layer below. CNNs typically assume spatially structured inputs, such as images. You need this property to make sure that the neighborhoods the filter is considering are actually relevant. Here, the bottom layer can be thought of as simple edge filters. The second layer works on the output values of the first layer and thus filters the filter responses to the input - typically an image - according to the first filter bank. Each layer is connected with the one below in such a way that the weights of the connections result in a series of filters that are applied one after the other, each on the previous layer. In Chapters 8 and 10 CNNs are discussed in the context of image processing and language processing.

The capability of CNNs to learn efficiently from large numbers of training examples rests on several assumptions about the real world, and advances in the training strategy of artificial neural networks. The first assumption is an observation about the visual world that surrounds us. CNNs and the repeated filtering – and downsampling – of input values reflect an

---

[26] Langs, G., Röhrich, S., Hofmanninger, J., Prayer, F., Pan, J., Herold, C., & Prosch, H. (2018). Machine learning: from radiomics to discovery and routine. Der Radiologe, 58(1), 1–6

observation that can best be described as compositionality. That is, we are surrounded by objects and observations made up of components that occur in different configurations. For example, a table with a vase is not fundamentally different from a table with a plate. Both overall objects share sub-objects (the table). The second assumption is that a filter – a component in the lowest layer of a CNN – that works on one part of an image, might work equally well on a different part of the image. You don't have to learn how to detect edges in the lower left corner or in the upper right corner of an image independently. You can just assume that you need an edge detector in your filter repertoire. Since you are adjusting weights when training an artificial neural network such as a CNN, the strategy of learning such a filter only once, and reusing it across the input image, amounts to weight sharing. Finally, the decision of approaching the mapping from an input image to a label such as "cat" via the use of filters exploits the assumption that neighborhood matters, and that the input filters only need to be connected to a relatively small portion of the image, as long as we apply them analogously across the image – like a parsing of the image with a filter. These three assumptions essentially reduce the number of connections for which weights have to be trained, in contrast to a fully connected network. This reduces the parameters, and accordingly makes training based on a set number of examples, in a set amount of time, easier.

In a train of thought similar to the bagging strategy, CNNs invest the computing power not in a single, very complex layer of perceptrons, but in the stacking of relatively simple filter banks. While lower levels learn to respond to more primary visual properties such as contrast, edges or light frequencies, layers above learn how to deal with compositions of these elements. Thus, on the one hand CNNs can represent the visual variability present in the training data, and on the other hand they become very good at mapping this representation to the correct class affiliation.

8.9.2 Training Convolutional Neural Networks

In general the training of artificial neural networks aims at minimizing a loss function that reflects how well the network performs. Typically, this is measured by how close the output of the network comes to the desired output, when training examples are processed for which input and output are known. Imagine the loss function as a landscape with hills and valleys. The position coordinates of this landscape are the parameters of the network – the weights we want to optimize. The height at each point of the landscape could then indicate the average error the network makes, the loss. To train a model means to search for the deepest point in the landscape, the coordinates of this point are the optimal parameters of the network. In real training situations we never see the entire landscape, but only a tiny neighborhood around the current position (which is defined by the current network parameters). In each training step, we update the parameters based on one training example so that we travel downhill in this tiny neighborhood, and then draw the next training example. In a landscape – or more formally a function $l(x)$ over the coordinates x, the gradient at each position x is the direction in which $l(x)$ increases most. We go the other way to move a smaller loss value, and thus this type of optimization is called gradient descent optimization.

The training of CNNs, as it is done today, addresses a problem known as the vanishing gradient problem. If a training algorithm for a CNN adjusts weights by for instance backpropagation it compares the output of the CNN with the desired output given in the training data.

The difference between the two is used to update the weights in the last layer of the network. Next, propagating the output back to the second-last layer again creates a difference between output at that layer and desired output. This difference is again transferred into a gradient, which is used to determine the degree and direction with which to update the weights in this layer. This process is repeated until the first layer of weights is reached. In theory this strategy converges at a good solution, but in practice the gradient vanishes as it is propagated back through the layers. That is, the gradient – the weight updates – get too small to converge in any reasonable time. Correspondingly training in a limited time frame becomes infeasible. Training CNNs can address this issue by initiating training in a layer-wise fashion. In this approach, layers of the CNN are trained successively each with the objective of representing the variability delivered by the previous layer when it processes a lot of training examples. Only after layers are initiated this way, is supervised training for the output labels performed on this pre-trained network.

This is a strategy has proven to be successful in different contexts: "first learn to represent the variability of the training data, and then learn to link it with the desired target variables". It has led to an extremely useful approach called transfer learning. In transfer learning parts of ANNs trained to solve one problem are reused as initialization for ANNs that are trained to solve a different problem. In image processing it has turned out that lower layers are surprisingly transferable across problems.[27]

A contrary problem to vanishing gradients is that of exploding gradients occurring in RNNs. This occurs when gradients accumulate and result in very large updates to weights during training, and a correspondingly unstable behavior of the network. Aside from revisiting the network architecture itself, one strategy to remedy this is gradient clipping, where if a gradient becomes too large, it is scaled down. Exploding gradients are relevant in the training of recurrent neural networks (see section below) where long short-term memory (LSTM) is one of the strategies to counter them.

Overall, CNNs have led to an enormous increase in the performance of classifiers and regressors, which are particularly successful in areas where data with spatial structure is processed.[28]

By now a wealth of CNN-based architectures exist, that enable scaling and improving this type of models beyond the initial results. Early examples are LeNet introduced by LeCun in 1998[29], and AlexNet by Khriszevsky in 2012 that yielded outstanding results at the image net competition at that time[30]. To achieve larger models with more and wider layers, sparse CNN structures were approximated with a dense construction and so-called inception modules, parallel, alternative convolution layers in architectures such as the GoogLeNet.[31] Res-

[27] Yosinski, J., Clune, J., Bengio, Y., & Lipson, H. (2014). How transferable are features in deep neural networks? Advances in Neural Information Processing Systems, 27, 3320–3328

[28] Krizhevsky, A., Sutskever, I., & Hinton, G. E. (2012). Imagenet classification with deep convolutional neural networks. Advances in neural information processing systems, 25, 1097–1105

[29] LeCun, Y., Bottou, L., Bengio, Y., & Haffner, P. (1998). Gradient-based learning applied to document recognition. Proceedings of the IEEE, 86(11), 2278–2324

[30] Krizhevsky, Alex, Ilya Sutskever, and G. E. Hinton. "ImageNet classification with deep convolutional neural networks. Advances in Neural Information Processing Systems 25 (NIPS 2012)." (2012): 1097–105

[31] Szegedy, C., Liu, W., Jia, Y., Sermanet, P., Reed, S., Anguelov, D., Erhan, D., Vanhoucke, V., & Rabinovich, A. (2015). Going deeper with convolutions. In Proceedings of the IEEE conference on Computer Vision and pattern recognition (pp. 1–9)

Nets were proposed to counter the vanishing gradient problem by using residual connections or skip connections that bypass layers, and transport the gradient to lower layers, without getting diluted.[32] DenseNets advance the concept of ResNets and connect all layers with all other layers by skip connections, while each layer is relatively narrow, adding only a small feature set to the resulting collective models. The final classifier then has access to all feature maps across the entire model.[33]

8.9.3 Recurrent Neural Networks

Recurrent neural networks (RNN), depicted in Figure 8.15, are a family of network architectures that are particularly well suited to processing sequential data such as speech, writing or sound signals. Like the previously discussed architectures, an RNN consists of input units, hidden units and output units. In the case of RNNs, each input at each timestep is used to calculate an output for that timestep, but the output is not only based on the input word: the hidden state of the previous calculation based on the previous input is also used. This means that, as processing progresses, the hidden state builds up a representation of the entire sequence processed so far. Consider the example of translating the sentence "Die Hauptstadt Österreichs ist Wien" into "The capital of Austria is Vienna". By the time the RNN begins processing the input word "Vienna", the "context" of the previous words can already provide a good predictive contribution to the translation of that word into its German equivalent, "Wien". Successful areas of application are language processing, translation or any processing of sequential data whose individual components or points in time are related to one another. Sequence to sequence learning is explained in the context of language processing in Section 10.3.3.

How do we represent words? The two most common approaches are to use "one hot" or "distributed word vectors" representations. In a one-hot representation, a vector is used with a length corresponding to the number of words in the training vocabulary. That is, every word from every training document has a place. A word is encoded in such a vector by marking a 1 in the slot for that word and a 0 for all other word slots. Distributed word vectors, such as word2vec[34], are an alternative and very effective representation that has become more and more widespread recently. They are created by embedding words in what is known as an embedding space, in which the distance between word vectors reflects their semantic relationship.[35] Thus, words with similar meanings will be clustered together, whereas those with completely unrelated meanings will be spread further apart. Apart from creating a meaningful distance in the representational space, it has several other advantages over a one-hot representation that are explained in Section 10.2.1 in this book.

---

[32] He, Kaiming, Xiangyu Zhang, and Shaoqing Ren. "Deep Residual Learning." Image Recognition (2015)

[33] Huang, G., Liu, Z., Van Der Maaten, L., & Weinberger, K. Q. (2017). Densely connected convolutional networks. In Proceedings of the IEEE conference on Computer Vision and pattern recognition (pp. 4700–4708)

[34] https://www.tensorflow.org/tutorials/representation/word2vec

[35] Mikolov, T., Chen, K., Corrado, G., & Dean, J. (2013). Efficient estimation of word representations in vector space. arXiv preprint arXiv:1301.3781

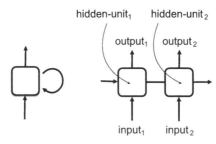

Figure 8.15 Recurrent neural networks: In each step, the output is determined on the one hand by the current input and on the other hand by the previous "hidden state" of the network. Hidden states can be understood as a memory that contains information about previous calculations and inputs. Since the architecture is always the same, the network can be visualized as shown on the left, while the representation on the right is often referred to as "unfolding", which is only possible in full in the case of a finite RNN.

In principle, RNNs can also be used in cases that do not contain an obvious sequence, such as when processing images. Here, identifying the sequence becomes one of the training tasks, like an RNN reading house numbers and learning how to sequentially control the visual attention to accomplish this task effectively.[36] A good and critical overview of RNN architectures is given by Lipon et al. 2015.[37]

8.9.4 Long Short-Term Memory

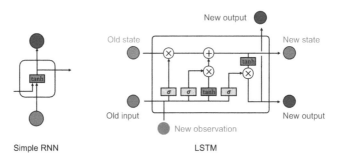

Figure 8.16 LSTM architectures control the contributions that are made to the cell status in a more differentiated manner than RNNs without LSTM components. During execution, they allow an old status to be forgotten and the contributions of the new observations to be controlled.

Standard RNNs, like other architectures, suffer from the problem of the vanishing gradient during training. Recall that this means the corrections that change the weights in the network during learning, when comparing the network result with the desired target value through backpropagation, become smaller and smaller the deeper one goes back in the

[36] Ba, J., Grosse, R., Salakhutdinov, R., & Frey, B. (2015). Learning wake-sleep recurrent attention models. arXiv preprint arXiv:1509.06812

[37] Lipton, Z. C., Berkowitz, J., & Elkan, C. (2015). A critical review of recurrent neural networks for sequence learning. arXiv preprint arXiv:1506.00019

network. In the case of RNNs, this makes it more difficult to learn relationships over longer periods of time: The influence of earlier inputs is "forgotten", the further one progresses through the input sequence.

One technique to improve this behavior and to use both short-term and long-term memory in the network consists of so-called long short-term memory (LSTM) cells (Figure 8.17).[38] The LSTM architecture is found today in a large number of applications that solve language processing or translation problems. The idea here is not just to simply take over the cell status and link it to the new observation, but to control its change and influence in a more differentiated manner and to learn this control with the help of the training examples. The cell status is carried over from the previous step and the current observation. Together with the old output, it controls the forgetting of this status by multiplying it by a number from 0 to 1. The new observation then in turn contributes to the change in the cell status and only then are the cell status and new observation used together in order to calculate the output at the current point in time.

A very good explanation of the architecture, upon which Figure 8.17 is based, comes from Christopher Olah[39].

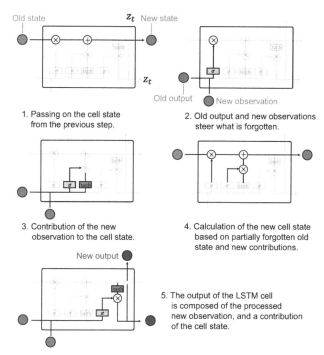

Figure 8.17 The components of an LSTM cell. The change in the cell status is controlled by three aspects: by a new observation, by forgetting the old status, and by the influence of the status itself on the new output of the cell. (Illustration based on C. Olah: "Understanding LSTM Networks", 2015)

[38] Hochreiter, S., & Schmidhuber, J. (1997). Long short-term memory. Neural computation, 9(8), 1735–1780
[39] Olah, C. (2015). Understanding lstm networks. *http://colah.github.io/posts/2015-08-Understanding-LSTMs/last accessed Nov 2021*

8.9.5 Autoencoders and U-Nets

We have learned about CNNs that translate an input image to an output target that might be either just a single label, or a short representative vector. A different approach is based on the idea of autoencoders.[40,41] There, input data is passed through a number of encoder layers to finally result in a low-dimensional representation of the input. The right-hand side of the network, also depicted in the right side of the autoencoder in Figure 8.18, is composed of decoders that map this low dimensional representation back to data resembling the input. The network is trained based on a loss function that penalizes differences between input and output. The constraint that the network has to pass the information through a narrow bottle neck layer fosters an efficient representation of the variability in the training data. Similar to CNNs, this principle can be applied to image style data, where encoders and decoders consist of convolution and deconvolution layers.[42] This architecture can serve two purposes. First, it can be used to create a low dimensional embedding of the training data, that itself is the desired result of the training. In many examples the need to represent variability efficiently leads to an embedding in the bottleneck layer, whose neighborhoods relationships are meaningful: Examples that are close by share feature characteristics. These representations could then be used for clustering as described in Section 8.4.1. The second use of this type of architecture is to map input images to an image representation such as a label map. This is the kind of usage applied in image segmentation. Here, the training is not based on single images, but on images paired with the known label maps in the training set.

In practice the latter type of mapping led to workable but fuzzy mappings, as the level of detail that was transported through the autoencoder suffers. To counter this, there are two strategies that are now wide-spread and have led to a tremendous expansion of the role of these image-to-image type mapping models in practice. First, the loss of detail can be countered by skip connections, which connect layers in the encoder and decoder part of the network. The input is parsed through the usual sequence of convolution: down-sampling, deconvolution, and up-sampling layers that learn common structural elements on different levels. At the same time the signal is also passed on directly to the opposite layer. This enables the preservation of detail, as the direct input from the skip connection and the input coming from previous deconvolution and up-sampling layers are combined (Figure 6.18). This class of networks, called U-nets due to the typical visualization of the layers, was published in the context of labeling microscopy imaging data.[43]

The second component of strategies to train models that map from inputs to complex outputs such as label maps or images concerns the training, and is described in the next section.

---

[40] Hinton, Geoffrey E., and Ruslan R. Salakhutdinov. "Reducing the dimensionality of data with neural networks." science 313.5786 (2006): 504–507

[41] Baldi, P. (2012, June). Autoencoders, unsupervised learning, and deep architectures. In Proceedings of ICML workshop on unsupervised and transfer learning (pp. 37–49). JMLR Workshop and Conference Proceedings

[42] Masci, J., Meier, U., Cireşan, D., & Schmidhuber, J. (2011, June). Stacked convolutional auto-encoders for hierarchical feature extraction. In International conference on artificial neural networks (pp. 52–59). Springer, Berlin, Heidelberg

[43] Çiçek, Ö., Abdulkadir, A., Lienkamp, S. S., Brox, T., & Ronneberger, O. (2016, October). 3D U-Net: learning dense volumetric segmentation from sparse annotation. In International conference on medical image computing and computer-assisted intervention (pp. 424–432). Springer, Cham

8.9.6 Adversarial Training Approaches

In the previous section we briefly touched on the issue that a loss function – the criterion with which we train an artificial neural network – can have trouble capturing all we want the network to learn. If we penalize the sum of all differences between the input and the output of an autoencoder, we might end up with a model that generates the coarse image, but that skips small details, because in terms of the loss function and the resulting gradient they do not have a big impact. At the same time, if we create a loss function that specifically captures small details, the training might have trouble learning anything at the very beginning. In short, adapting the loss function while we are training is a strategy worth looking at.

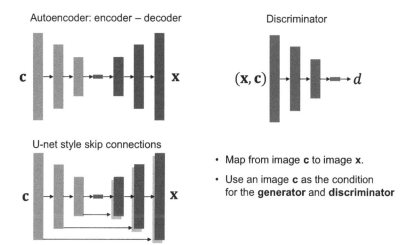

Autoencoder: encoder – decoder

Discriminator

U-net style skip connections

- Map from image **c** to image **x**.
- Use an image **c** as the condition for the **generator** and **discriminator**

Figure 8.18 Autoencoders map images to images. They consist of an encoder and a decoder connected by a low-dimensional bottleneck. U-nets contain skip-connections that map directly from encoder to decoder circumventing this bottleneck. Training of this type of networks can either rely on the difference between input and output or on an adversarial discriminator.

Adversarial training is such an approach. Instead of using the difference between the actual output and the desired output as a means to steer the gradient during training, we train an adversary to the mapping network. The adversary is a discriminator that determines whether the output is an actually observed training example, or an output generated by the model. As we train our main model, we also update the adversary, so that while the main model becomes better at generating output that resembles real data, the adversary becomes better at discriminating between model-generated output and real examples. Thereby, it can provide a useful gradient throughout the training, while both model and discriminator become better. Figure 8.18 illustrates this scheme. The autoencoder or U-net maps from an input image c to an output image x. The training of this model can either be driven by a loss function capturing the difference between the output x and the desired output sampled from the training data or by a more sophisticated mechanism based on an adversarial discriminator. In adversarial training, the discriminator learns to discriminate between a generated output x, given input c as a so-called "condition", or a genuinely observed desired output sampled from the training pairs in the form of c and x. Adversarial training has led to impressive models translating images to label maps, or even the other way around.[44]

8.9.7 Generative Adversarial Networks

For a long time a limitation of deep learning approaches was the lack of generative models that could capture the variability in real world data, and at the same time work with low dimensional representations in the generator space. Autoencoders are to some degree usable, since, after training, the decoder in principle maps from a low dimensional generator to the actual observation space of images.

A leap in capability came when generative models met adversarial learning in the seminal work of Goodfellow and colleagues, who proposed Generative Adversarial Networks (GAN).[45] Figure 8.19 illustrates the scheme of GAN training. For imaging data, one can imagine the generator as a forger that is working on generating realistic images, by sampling vectors z out of a uniform distribution in the latent space, and running these vectors through a deconvolution and upscaling network that is the generator. At the same time we train a discriminator to correctly classify an image into two categories: real example, or generated example. You can imagine this as the police, trying to catch the forger. The reward function of the generator is determined by the discriminator, by penalizing the generation of examples that are correctly detected as forgeries by the discriminator. While training progresses, both generator and discriminator get better. The generator defines the model distribution implicitly through the examples it generates. If generator and discriminator models are differentiable – that is if we can formulate a gradient function as explained in Section 8.5.2, this can be implemented in a very efficient fashion. Training progresses in two gradient steps: updating the discriminator to get better at detecting forgeries, and updating the generator to get better at fooling the discriminator. One can view this training as a game between generator and discriminator, with a solution reached in the so-called Nash equilibrium where each player wishes to minimize the cost function that depends on parameters of both players while only having control over its own parameters.

---

[44] Isola, P., Zhu, J. Y., Zhou, T., & Efros, A. A. (2017). Image-to-image translation with conditional adversarial networks. In Proceedings of the IEEE conference on Computer Vision and pattern recognition (pp. 1125–1134

[45] Goodfellow, I., Pouget-Abadie, J., Mirza, M., Xu, B., Warde-Farley, D., Ozair, S., ... & Bengio, Y. (2014). Generative adversarial nets. Advances in neural information processing systems, 27

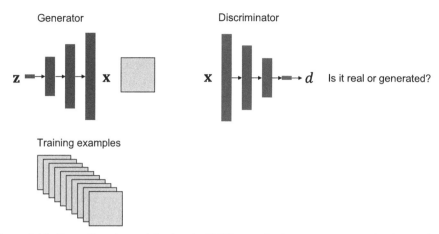

Figure 8.19 Generative adversarial networks (GAN) are trained to generate examples that are indistinguishable from real world training examples. The cost function they are trained with is based on a discriminator that learns to discriminate between generated ("fake") examples and real examples sampled from the training data. As training progresses, both improve, until they reach a so-called "Nash equilibrium".

Not unlike in the case of the autoencoder, this leads to useful properties of the representations in the latent z-space. One example is that we can perform vector arithmetic such as adding and subtracting vectors in the z-space and obtain seemingly meaningful results in the observation space.[46]

GANs have turned out to be very powerful in representing rich variability in the training data. Thus, one application of GANs is anomaly detection, where a GAN is trained to generate medical imaging data of healthy anatomy, and the residual between the genuinely observed new images, and the best approximation generated by the GAN, is used as a marker of anomalies potentially linked to disease.[47] Another application area is the translation between different observational spaces such as text and images[48] or even languages[49].

Training GANs can be difficult, and a number of new approaches to facilitate this training have recently emerged. One of the possible limitations of GAN training is a situation resembling a catch me if you can game called mode collapse. In this case, the generator becomes very good at generating one particular example, and then when the discriminator catches up, the generator switches to a new example and repeats this strategy. Mode collapse is easy to recognize, as after training the generator can only generate a few different examples, and traveling in the latent space does not lead to a continual transition between generated im-

[46] Radford, Alec, Luke Metz, and Soumith Chintala. "Unsupervised Representation Learning with Deep Convolutional Generative Adversarial Networks." arXiv e-prints (2015): arXiv-1511

[47] Schlegl, T., Seeböck, P., Waldstein, S. M., Schmidt-Erfurth, U., & Langs, G. (2017, June). Unsupervised anomaly detection with generative adversarial networks to guide marker discovery. In International conference on information processing in medical imaging (pp. 146–157). Springer, Cham

[48] Zhang, H., Xu, T., Li, H., Zhang, S., Wang, X., Huang, X., & Metaxas, D. N. (2017). Stackgan: Text to photo-realistic image synthesis with stacked generative adversarial networks. In Proceedings of the IEEE international conference on Computer Vision (pp. 5907–5915)

[49] Conneau, A., Lample, G., Ranzato, M. A., Denoyer, L., & Jégou, H. (2017). Word translation without parallel data. arXiv preprint arXiv:1710.04087

ages. One learning strategy which reduces the risk of mode collapse, as well as tackling vanishing gradients in GAN training, is to replace the discriminator with a critic, that instead of only penalizing falsely classified cases, provides a critique, that also provides a gradient to the training if a correctly classified image is generated. The theory for this approach was proposed in Arjovsky, Martin, and Léon Bottou[50], and its applications to GANs was proposed in Arjovsky, Chintala and Bottou[51]. It has also been used to improve anomaly detection in medical imaging data.[52]

8.9.8 Cycle GANs and Style GANs

Methods based on GANs have advanced rapidly, and here we discuss two particularly relevant examples. Cycle GANs are an approach to learn a mapping between domains, even if no paired examples are available.[53] Cycle GANs can learn to map between imaging characteristics of different scanners in medical imaging, even if no paired imaging data is available. Such a situation is realistic in practice, since studies scanning patients multiple times in different scanners for the sole purpose of model training are rare and often limited.[54] Applications reach beyond imaging data to, for instance, language translation models trained from large so-called corpora of language data but without any ground-truth sentence pairs (known as parallel corpora).[55] The intuition of cycle GANs is that even-though no paired examples are available, the structure in the two domains is similar enough that a representation of their variability can be essentially aligned. Imagine two languages, and the use of words in the context of other words: If we define neighborhood relationships based on the co-occurrence of words in close proximity in texts, the resulting representation of the overall structure of the language might exhibit sufficient similarity to align these manifolds.

The second hugely influential extension of GANs are so-called Style GANs. These networks split the generation into two steps, first a mapping from a latent space into an intermediate space, and then a mapping from this intermediate space to the final actual observations. The second step injects the intermediate values to different layers of the synthesis network, and thereby enables a more independent steering of different aspects of the generator compared to standard GANs. Style GANs allow for the control of the generator at different levels of

---

[50] Arjovsky, M., Bottou, L. "Towards principled methods for training generative adversarial networks." arXiv preprint arXiv:1701.04862 (2017)

[51] Arjovsky, M., Chintala, S., & Bottou, L. (2017, July). Wasserstein generative adversarial networks. In International conference on machine learning (pp. 214–223). PMLR

[52] Schlegl, T., Seebóck, P., Waldstein, S. M., Langs, G., & Schmidt-Erfurth, U. (2019). f-AnoGAN: Fast unsupervised anomaly detection with generative adversarial networks. Medical image analysis, 54, 30–44

[53] Zhu, J. Y., Park, T., Isola, P., & Efros, A. A. (2017). Unpaired image-to-image translation with cycle-consistent adversarial networks. In Proceedings of the IEEE international conference on Computer Vision (pp. 2223–2232)

[54] Seebóck, P., Romo-Bucheli, D., Waldstein, S., Bogunovic, H., Orlando, J. I., Gerendas, B. S., Langs, G., & Schmidt-Erfurth, U. (2019, April). Using cyclegans for effectively reducing image variability across oct devices and improving retinal fluid segmentation. In 2019 IEEE 16th International Symposium on Biomedical Imaging (ISBI 2019) (pp. 605–609). IEEE

[55] Lample, G., Conneau, A., Ranzato, M. A., Denoyer, L., & Jégou, H. (2018, February). Word translation without parallel data. In International Conference on Learning Representations

detail corresponding to layers in the generator. To some extent this enables the decoupling of different characteristic levels, as long as they correspond to layers in the generator. [56]

8.9.9 Other Architectures and Learning Strategies

In addition to RNNs and CNNs, there are a large and rapidly growing number of different network architectures and their corresponding learning strategies including transformers described in Section 10.3.4 of this book. Primary sources for keeping up to date are the Neural Information Processing System Conference (NeurIPS)[57], the International Conference of Machine Learning (ICML)[58] or the International Conference of Learning Representations (ICLR [59]. Almost all publications can be accessed with Open Access and algorithms are typically implemented very quickly in the common libraries or made available in other ways.

Learning strategies can particularly focus on the number of examples, and the transfer of structure from comparable domains is resulting in a diverse set of approaches gaining interest. What these approaches have in common is that they tackle situations of limited training data. They include families of techniques such as few-, one-, or even zero-shot learning.[60]

■ 8.10 Validation Strategies for Machine Learning Techniques

Validation of machine learning models is a key activity when developing, training, and deploying models. It has to be part of the planning of development from the start, since it involves the management of data. A key aspect is the careful separation of data used for the development of models, their training, their intermediate evaluation during successive improvements to the models, and the final evaluation of the models' performance. This is critical, since the high number of parameters of these models poses the risk of overfitting, and consequently an overoptimistic assessment of model capabilities, if the validation data was at all touched during the method development.

A typical strategy is the following. After receiving the data, we split it into a development and a test set. The test set is locked away, and can never be assessed during development. This separation has to be complete before development commences, and the selection of the two data sets has to be randomized, except in situations we will discuss below.

---

[56] Karras, T., Laine, S., & Aila, T. (2019). A style-based generator architecture for generative adversarial networks. In Proceedings of the IEEE/CVF Conference on Computer Vision and Pattern Recognition (pp. 4401–4410)

[57] *www.nips.cc*

[58] *www.icml.cc*

[59] *www.iclr.cc*

[60] Kadam, S., & Vaidya, V. (2018, December). Review and analysis of zero, one and few shot learning approaches. In International Conference on Intelligent Systems Design and Applications (pp. 100–112). Springer, Cham

During development we further split the training data into a training and validation set. Training data is used for the training of models, and validation data is used for their intermediate validation, decisions regarding model architecture, design, and parameters, and parameter tuning. If data is not abundant, instead of a fixed split into training and validation data, we can perform cross-validation. For instance, in the case of five-fold cross validation, we split the development data into five equally large subsets. We can either select them randomly or stratify them based upon their properties, such as labels, or data sources. Then, during cross validation we cycle through the five folds, and in each cycle, we use one of them as validation data, and the remaining four others as training data. Thereby every example is used for validation once, but for each run, there is no overlap between training and validation data. The finel cross validation results can be a good approximation of the capability of the model and serve as a good source to select parameters, or perform design decisions. Further subdivisions can be done if enough data is available. For instance, one can keep the validation set fixed, but instead of using it for parameter optimization of a particular model, we perform parameter optimization in a cross-validation fashion on the data, excluding this validation data.

Finally, after design and parameter optimization is finished, the model's capability is reported based on results on the test set. This is necessary since even if the validation set is not seen during the training of a particular model variant, the observation of validation results by the developer and subsequent design decisions will still lead to overfitting on this data.

In the health care area it has become common practice to require validation on an "external validation set", which comes from a different source than the data used for the model development. This is motivated by the insight that models can pick up particularities of individual clinical centers, and therefore generalize only poorly to other centers. An excellent overview of this topic is given by Glocker and colleagues[61].

Further consideration during validation are matters such as fairness, biases and non-causative factors that might enter the model training, leading to undesirable replication of sub-optimal decisions that are present in the training data, but not linked to actual relationships we want to model. An example are biased treatment decisions, based on uneven knowledge regarding the effectiveness of treatment in different sexes, which we don't want to perpetuate via the use of machine learning models. Here, the first step is to identify these biases with careful validation designs, and then to develop strategies to counter them in machine learning models.[62]

---

[61] Castro, Daniel C., Ian Walker, and Ben Glocker. "Causality matters in medical imaging." Nature Communications 11.1 (2020): 1–10

[62] McCradden, Melissa D., et al. "Ethical limitations of algorithmic fairness solutions in health care machine learning." The Lancet Digital Health 2.5 (2020): e221-e223

■ 8.11 Conclusion

This chapter dealt with the basics of machine learning relevant to data science. Both classification and regression can be viewed as a mapping of input values to target variables. The two most important components of the applicable algorithms are feature extraction and the prediction model, which maps the feature vectors to a target variable.

We got to know models like nearest-neighbor classifiers, which operate according to a simple principle: if the feature vector is similar, the target variable must also be similar. Support vector machines are more complex models, able to approximate distributions in the feature space with fewer training examples. However, both suffer from the limitation that features that contain no information can substantially worsen the result.

In addition to classifiers, which require carefully selected features in order to perform well, models that select features independently (such as random forests) or can even learn feature extractors themselves (such as RNNs and CNNs) are becoming increasingly important.

Current research is increasingly concentrating on the field of deep learning and the construction of ever more powerful architectures that can learn complex relationships from very large amounts of data.

■ 8.12 In a Nutshell

Machine Learning

A family of techniques that create models for prediction, classification or estimation based on training examples instead of hard-coding a set of rules during development

Supervised Machine Learning

Machine learning based on training examples in the form of pairs consisting typically of an input and the corresponding output. During training the model learns to predict the output for new inputs.

Unsupervised Machine Learning

Machine learning based on training examples without known output. Here, the aim is to find structure in the data in the form of groups of examples, or relationship networks.

Deep Learning and Artificial Neural Networks

Models consisting of deep artificial neural networks with a large number of layers. These models can be designed in a wide variety of architectures. They range from classification networks such as convolutional neural networks, to networks that map between images such as autoencoders, and generative models such as generative adversarial networks.

9 Building Great Artificial Intelligence

Danko Nikolić

"We propose that a 2-month, 10-man study of artificial intelligence be carried out during the summer of 1956 at Dartmouth College in Hanover, New Hampshire. The study is to proceed on the basis of the conjecture that every aspect of learning or any other feature of intelligence can in principle be so precisely described that a machine can be made to simulate it. An attempt will be made to find how to make machines use language, form abstractions and concepts, solve kinds of problems now reserved for humans, and improve themselves. We think that a significant advance can be made in one or more of these problems if a carefully selected group of scientists work on it together for a summer."
John McCarthy, Marvin Minsky, Nathaniel Rochester and Claude Shannon in 1955

Questions Answered in this Chapter:

- What is AI and how is it different from simply creating machine learning models?
- What does it take to create a great AI product?
- What are the common traps when designing and developing an AI, and how can you avoid those traps?

9.1 How AI Relates to Data Science and Machine Learning

You may be asking yourself, what is the function of a chapter on Artificial Intelligence (AI) in a book on data science? Often, AI is understood as just a fancy name for machine learning models, models that data scientists build anyway as part of their job. If that were the case, AI would simply be a part of data science and there would be no need to write a separate chapter on AI as the rest of the book is all about that technology. Well, this is not exactly correct. Although it is true that one of the most important – and perhaps most juicy – parts of AI is in the machine learning models, there is a lot more to AI than just machine learning. There are a few critical considerations that one needs to keep in mind when developing an AI product; considerations which you will not normally find covered in a typical data science book, or indeed, even in other chapters of this book. Critically, if you make a mistake in one of these areas, your final product may disappoint. For example, you may run into a situation in which everything seems fine early in the process of creation, but the final product is underwhelming and does not satisfy the needs and expectations of the end users.

Let us first see which kind of machines we consider today as being examples of AI. What may immediately come to mind is perhaps a robot. However, not just any robot. Most robots are not very intelligent. Robots consist of mechanical components such as arms and actuators. And then there are batteries and sensors. But those alone are not enough to describe a robot as having AI. There are many robots that are quite useful to us but are plain dumb. Examples are vacuum cleaner robots at homes and industrial robots on factory floors. What makes a difference to whether robots will receive the title of being "artificially intelligent" or not is what they can do autonomously with all their hardware. Only a smart robot, one with capabilities far exceeding the plain programming of movements, will be worthy of the honor of being called an AI. We are here looking for a robot that can exhibit a variety of different behaviors, or be able to find its way in a complex environment, or accomplish tasks in a variety of novel situations. For example, think of an anthropomorphic robot capable of clearing up a table full of dirty dishes, then manually washing these dishes and finally, drying them and putting them into the cupboard – and all that without breaking anything! Robots with such a level of skill do not yet exist.

To begin creating such a robot it may soon be clear that training deep learning models will not be enough. One may choose to rely on deep learning to a high degree and yet, the robot will need a lot more than what deep learning can offer. To foster the required intelligence in the robot, we will need to create and use technologies much broader than what machine learning can offer – and also, much broader than what data science covers. Still, data scientists will play a critical role in developing such robots. Hence, you find yourself reading this chapter.

One type of a robot has obtained significant attention from the industry and also a great deal of investments: our cars. A lot of money has been poured into making cars capable of driving by themselves and thus into turning them into intelligent robots. The problem of autonomous driving is not an easy one, especially not if the vehicle is driving in the "real world" and not a controlled test environment. The variety of different situations that the vehicle may encounter is huge. Hence, such vehicles present a great challenge for the technology. Perhaps the autonomous driving problem is as difficult as cleaning up a table with dishes. The pressure for the quality of the solution, that is, not making an error, is high too. While our manual dish-washing robot may in the worst case break a few glasses or plates, a car robot carries a much bigger responsibility; it is responsible for human lives. This is an additional reason that makes a successful self-driving car a tough goal. Nevertheless, there has been quite some progress in this domain. Arguably, autonomous vehicles are the smartest, most intelligent robots which mankind has built so far. And yet, there is still work to be done. The question is then: What did it take to make those machines intelligent? And which intelligence related problems and hurdles do these machines still face? Is it all simply the data science of building bigger and smarter models, or is there more to it?

To address these questions, let us first establish that AI does not equal a machine learning model. To understand that, it helps to make a distinction between a product and a critical component necessary to build a product. A product is a lot more than just its critical components. A knife is more than a blade, although a blade is its critical component. A monitor is more than its critical component, the screen. A memory stick is more than an SSD chip. A bicycle is more than a pair of wheels and pedals. In all these cases we note that a product is more than its critical components.

We can appreciate this difference in the example of a car. A car suitable to sell on the market and thus suitable to produce value for the customer is more than an engine placed on four wheels. For a car, one needs a steering wheel and brakes. Yet, this is still not a complete product. A full product also requires headlights for night driving, a windshield, doors, windows on those doors, wipers on the windshield. One also needs a full cabin with seats. Then one needs a heating system, air-conditioning, and an entertainment system. All this needs to be packed into a beautiful design which is pleasing to a human eye. Only after putting all of this together, are we beginning to have a full product called a car.

An AI is like a full product. It is a machine that does some service for a human and in order to get this service done in a satisfactory fashion, the machine has to be complete. One must create a full product. So, a machine learning model may be a critical component for an AI, maybe the equivalent of what an engine is for a car. Importantly, however, we have an AI only after we have built a product around that (machine learning) engine.

In practice, as a bare minimum, creating a product will require putting the model into production and establishing an interface for acquiring inputs that will go into the machine learning model and then also generating some form of output. Often, there is a lot more required to create a useful product. As we have seen in the case of the autonomous vehicle, there is a lot of hardware needed to create a complete car.

But it is not only "non intelligent" components that one needs to add to machine learning models in order to create an AI. A deeper reason why machine learning alone is not enough for AI is that AI solutions are often a lot more complex than what could be achieved by a single machine learning model. For example, let us consider a chat bot. Let's assume that all we need to create, outside of the intelligent component, is a minimal interface consisting of text fields to enter users' questions and print the machine's answers. One may conclude, then, that it should suffice to place in-between these two components a large, well-trained machine learning model to do the chatting with a human user. Unfortunately, this is not how it works. Every elaborate intelligent chatting assistant (think of Alexa, Siri, Cortana, etc.) is a lot more complex than relying on a single deep learning model.

Below is the architecture of the original Watson AI solution – a machine that made history in 2010 for winning the game of Jeopardy against the top human players in that game. It is clear that the organization of this AI was a lot more elaborate than a single machine learning model. In fact, many of its components do not even rely on machine learning and yet, they nevertheless contribute to the overall intelligence of Watson. It is necessary to understand that only the machine as a whole is an AI; no single component alone is one. Much of this overall intelligence comes from the architecture – how the flow of computation is organized and how it is decided which component will be executed when. Thus, it is not only the weights in the machine learning models that contribute to the overall intelligence. There is a lot more, including the rules by which different models mutually interact and help each other. Only the full combination of all the parts, the Watson, is a full product and is an AI.

Something similar holds for the intelligence of autonomous vehicles. The internal architectures of the algorithms driving the cars are not any simpler than that of Watson. Moreover, over time, as cars become smarter and better drivers, the number of components and the internal complexity of overall AI solutions tends to increase.

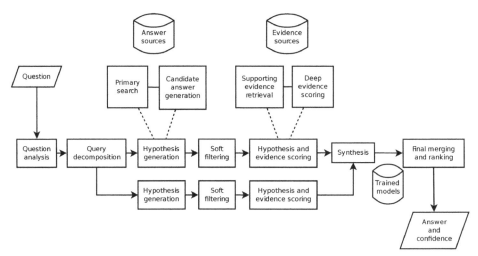

Figure 9.1 The architecture of the original Watson AI that won the game of Jeopardy against the best human competitors *(https://en.wikipedia.org/wiki/File:DeepQA.svg)*

Importantly, many of the components of such solutions are also not machine learning models, but employ some other algorithms. These other components may involve searches through databases, brute-force approaches to finding optimal solutions, pure scientific calculations, rule-based decision making, and so on. Again, all those components jointly contribute to the overall intelligence of the AI.

Finally, there is one more reason why machine learning and AI are not the same thing. Machine learning is often used for purposes other than building intelligent machines. Machine learning has uses that exceed what AI is meant to do. In particular, machine learning is often used as a tool for data analysis. The author of this chapter has extensively used machine learning tools as a means for analyzing how the brain stores sensory information. We trained machine learning models to read information from brain signals. Critically, what interested us was not to build a product. Rather, we asked questions about the brain, for example, how long does the brain hold information about an image that we briefly presented on the screen? Or, how fast can this information be erased by a newly presented stimulus? In this way, we generated numerous insights on how the brain maintains sensory information [1-3]. For pure engineers, such a use of machine learning may come as a surprise. However, for a data scientist, this should not be so unexpected. No scientist should hesitate from using machine learning algorithms as analytics tools. There are great benefits from such uses of machine learning, especially in situations in which the data are complex and insights are difficult to achieve with traditional analytics methods.

To understand the relationship between machine learning and AI, it is common to draw Venn diagrams, like those depicted in Figure 9.2. The Venn diagram on the left is the one which can often be seen in AI literature. But the one on the right is more correct, as it also takes into account the fact that machine learning can be used for purposes other than AI.

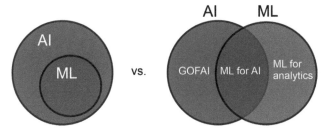

Figure 9.2 The relationship between AI and machine learning (ML). Left: the relationship as commonly depicted in the literature. Right: A more realistic depiction, showing that machine learning can be used for purposes other than AI, such as analyzing data. GOFAI stands for 'Good old-fashioned AI', which does not employ machine learning.

■ 9.2 A Brief History of AI

To appreciate the fact that AI does not need to exclusively rely on machine learning, it is best to take a look at its history. Notably, the history of AI is longer than that of machine learning. In fact, roughly speaking, AI had two major stages. The first stage focussed on the development of algorithms that had nothing to do with machine learning. Instead, these early algorithms relied solely on machine knowledge that was manually fed into the machine – by humans. For example, during this first stage, a large, rule-based decision tree would be considered a state-of-the-art algorithm for AI. Characteristic of this form of AI is that it did not store its knowledge in the form of numbers and did not make conclusions by applying equations to those numbers. The reason was simple: It would have been very hard for humans to feed number-based knowledge, such as the connection weights of artificial neural networks, into a machine. Instead, most of the knowledge was stored in a symbolic form – a form understandable to humans. For example, a knowledge item could use symbols to represent "if fever, then flu". Inferences were made by applying logical rules on those symbols. The rules were again human understandable.

We often refer to this stage of AI as *symbolic* AI (see also Chapter 10). Another commonly known term is Good-old-fashioned-AI, abbreviated as GOFAI. Research on symbolic AI began already in the 1950s, with the official birthplace being the historical Dartmouth conference in 1956. The organizer of this conference, John McCarthy – the person who formulated the term "Artificial Intelligence" – also introduced the first programming language to help computers achieve symbolic intelligence: LISP. The two-letter abbreviation 'AI' did not come into widespread use until after Steven Spielberg's, "A.I. Artificial Intelligence", from 2001.

Machine learning entered the field of AI only later, ushering in its second – and still current – stage. In fact, it wasn't until the 1970's that machine learning really caught on, although some of the algorithms existed a lot earlier. The reason for the delay was that it took time to realize that symbolic AI had limitations and that another approach was needed. One problem was that symbolic AI could not effectively learn on its own; the knowledge needed to be spoon-fed by humans. This produced a huge bottleneck as often the amount of knowledge needed to be manually set up was too overwhelming. Therefore, the GOFAI approach to increasing the intelligence of machines became unsustainable. As a result, many projects failed to reach the level of usefulness, not moving much further from the initial proof-of-concept; what worked well on a small scale did not materialize on a larger, more useful scale.

Today, in the second stage, we overwhelmingly rely on machine learning algorithms to feed knowledge into machines, transforming it from large datasets into matrices of model parameters. These algorithms provide a great relief from manual work. All that humans need to do is provide examples of intelligent behavior. The machine is then able to extract the rules by which this behavior is being made.

Obviously, this way, we have achieved a great advancement in our ability to increase machine's intelligence. However, it is incorrect to assume that the world has moved away from symbolic AI and that GOFAI algorithms are history. Not at all. The symbolic approach is still alive and well. Every complex AI solution created today is a mash of machine learning and GOFAI components. Symbolic AI is no less important a part. It is only that GOFAI components are not being advertised, which has more to do with the current hype and marketing strategies than with the facts on how the machines work under the hood. Symbolic AI is all over the place. Often it is GOFAI who decides which deep learning algorithm to run next. Other times, GOFAI receives outputs from machine learning models to make the next decision. In other approaches, machine learning assists GOFAI in finding an optimal solution. And so on. Often, the two components are nested: a symbolic algorithm calls machine learning model which in turn calls another GOFAI component for help, going back to machine learning and so on. The possibilities are limitless. Watson could not win a game of Jeopardy without GOFAI components. Without using a GOFAI, in 2016 alphaGo could not have won the game of go against the world champion, Lee Sedol (the score was four to one for the machine). An autonomous vehicle cannot drive without old-fashioned AI components. Alexa, Siri and co. cannot engage in a conversation with you without symbolic parts of their overall intelligence architectures. And so on.

What does it all mean for a data scientist today who is tasked with developing an AI product? Very likely, your solution will need to involve a lot more things than just a machine learning model. There will be a lot of engineering needed outside of machine learning. It will be difficult to avoid symbolic components. This means you will have to make wise architectural decisions about the entire solution and these decisions will include a lot more than just machine learning. Moreover, to create an effective product, you may even need components that lie outside of engineering. A good design of the interface for your AI may be as critical for its success as will the performance of the underlying model. Much like one needs to add an ergonomic handle to a blade to make a good knife, or needs to provide comfortable seats to make a great car, your AI will need to evolve in many different dimensions in order to present a great product. Machine learning models will be just a part of the entire result and thus, only a part of the entire customer experience.

■ 9.3 Five Recommendations for Designing an AI Solution

On the way to creating an AI solution, a data scientist will need to make a number of decisions. You, as a data scientist, will necessarily have to create an architecture combining components of different types, interacting and jointly bringing the intelligence to your machine. Perhaps you will draw this architecture with multiple boxes and arrows, like the drawing of the Watson architecture in Figure 9.1. The question is then: Which strategies can you use and what should you look for to avoid certain common mistakes?

9.3.1 Recommendation No. 1: Be pragmatic

In the previous chapters of this book, you have seen various recipes on how to solve data science problems. This is all presented to you as individual pieces; for example, as individual machine learning algorithms. Also, the pieces are shown in an idealized world, independent from real life. When you design a real AI – a complete product – you will need to think about how to pick algorithms for an imperfect world. You will need to think about how to combine them. Also, you will need to find and use algorithms not described in this book. It is important not to stick with one set of algorithms just because they worked for you in the past, or just because this is what you know. Expand your knowledge, as you need it. Pick the algorithms based on their suitability for a given problem, not based on convenience. Keep in mind that your new problem will always be slightly different from anything else that you have seen in the past. Be eclectic in selecting the tool to solve the tasks. Choose from the widest selection that you possibly can. Do not limit yourself.

Also, stay pragmatic. Your first concern should be achieving the goal. You do not always need to use the latest algorithms, the hottest and most-hyped tool. Rather, take whatever works best for the problem at hand. I have seen data scientists falling "in love" with certain types of models and then playing favorites. But success in data science does not come when you play favorites. I have seen people trying to solve every problem with the same approach. There are individuals who expect that everything must be solved with deep learning. I have also seen die-hard fans of Bayesian approaches. Sure, both Bayesian and deep learning methods are charming and have some attractive features, giving them unique "super-powers". However, both also have disadvantages. In fact, any approach you pick will have some advantages over others, and necessarily also some disadvantages. Your job is to consider both sides and weigh the pros and cons in order to make a good choice.

It is paramount to be aware of both advantages and disadvantages of any given method or algorithm. Disadvantages may be harder to learn about because authors who publish papers about their new methods tend to focus on the positive aspect. The rosy pictures are what motivates them to perform the research and write papers in the first place. So, we should have some understanding. Nevertheless, one still needs to acquire a skill for "reading between lines" and detecting possible limitations and pitfalls. An experienced data scientist will be able to smell possible disadvantages of a new method, even if they are not as clearly spelled out as are the advantages. Develop such a skill, as it will give you a lot of powers for making good design decisions for your AI architectures. The goal is to acquire knowledge about a lot of algorithms, models, and optimization techniques.

The pool of tools to pick from is huge. A single person can probably never have a full overview of the data science field. Acquiring comprehensive knowledge on machine learning methods and AI algorithms requires life-long learning. And you are never finished. Moreover, the pace with which new algorithms are being proposed is increasing rapidly as more and more people work on the topic, universities open new AI and data science departments, and governments funnel more money towards research in the AI. Keeping up with everything that is going on is a challenge. You should never stop learning but also never expect to know it all.

What helps in navigating this ever-growing forest of new works is a thorough understanding of algorithms. You will be more efficient in understanding a new algorithm if you already have a deep understanding of a related, existing one. Superficial understanding of methods is not nearly as powerful. Proper understanding of several different algorithms, each belonging to a different category, is probably the best strategy one can undertake towards mastering the field of data science. New algorithms are often related to the existing ones. Rarely, researchers come up with an entirely novel approach to solve a machine learning problem (although occasionally they do exactly that). If you understand deeply one algorithm, then it becomes easy for you to quickly grasp the essence of its cousins – they become a variation on the theme. In contrast, if you only superficially understand an algorithm in the first place, a variation of this algorithm may be a mystery for you, and you may have difficulties deciding whether this new variation will be helpful for your new problem or not.

One can always try the algorithm on the data and see what happens. There are also tools for trying multiple algorithms automatically and picking the best one (referred to as autoML). But this cannot get you far. You cannot develop an autonomous vehicle by randomly trying different architectures. By building AI, you will have to do good old human thinking – and a lot of it. In this case you want to minimize decision making by trying the algorithms on your data. Sure, you will have to do that at some point, there's no doubt about this. However, what makes a difference between an experienced AI developer and an inexperienced one is that the former can achieve the task with more thinking and less trying. Experienced people can sift through possibilities in their heads, without having to train the algorithm on the data. The extended knowledge allows them to detect that something is not going to work well even before they try to make it work. This saves a lot of time.

What else can help you make good decisions? A good idea is to draw your future architecture before you start coding. Specify the details and try doing mental simulations of the flow of data throughout the system. At each step ask yourself a question: Do I see a reason this step would fail or have difficulties? If you do see possible problems, address these problems immediately. Pragmatic is to address the weakest points first. Do not hope that a miracle will happen after you spend time working on the easy part.

There is a common belief that with enough computational power and a sufficient amount of data, anything is possible: that anything can be learned by a machine. Although there is some truth to this statement, there is also quite a bit of falsehood there, too. Some of these issues I will address later within this chapter. The bottom line is that blindly following a strategy of more-data-with-more-computation-power is almost guaranteed to bring you problems. It is much better to thoroughly clean up your algorithms by using your understanding of statistics, machine learning and AI in general. Keep the faith in big data and computational power as your last resource.

Certainly, you will need to try out different designs. And you will need to use the results of these trials as feedback. They will guide you on how to improve. It is vital to realise that your iterations will be much quicker and much more effective if you understand more deeply what you are doing.

Thinking is comparatively hard. Coding and running models is comparatively easy. Still, not shying away from doing the hard part will likely give you the competitive advantage that you will need to create a product that the market needs and enjoys.

Finally, do not forget that one person does not know everything. Build a team of people with different topics of expertise. Have everyone contribute; everyone should have a say. Make sure you get everyone's talent used towards your final product.

9.3.2 Recommendation No. 2: Make it easier for machines to learn – create inductive biases

There is one simple truth about machine learning algorithms: Some learn faster and better than others. In some cases, it takes just a few examples to reach high performance. In other cases, millions of examples are needed. While there are many reasons for these differences, there is one reason which you have the power to control: One factor that determines the learning efficiency of an algorithm are its inductive biases. Inductive bias is like a piece of knowledge added into an algorithm, enabling it to skip some learning steps and walk quicker and more confidently towards the end. Literally, inductive biases enable algorithms to jump to conclusions. And if you have inserted the right inductive biases, your algorithm will jump to the right conclusions, too.

So, what is an inductive bias? It is a predisposition towards finding (i.e., inferring, inducing) a certain relationship in the data. Inductive biases help the algorithm find a certain relationship even if the evidence is very weak and would otherwise require going through millions of data points. Inductive bias is a sort of prejudice to detect a given type of pattern in data.[1] For example, if your mathematical model is made from sine and cosine functions and you fit mostly the parameters of such functions (e.g., amplitude and phase of a sine), then your model will likely be able to fit such functions in the data, even with small amounts of data. In other words, the model will have a bias towards finding a sine wave.

What tricks people into ignoring the importance of inductive biases is that one can in theory use the same type of sine-based model to approximate functions other than sine waves. You could combine millions of sine waves to accurately approximate a power-law function. But this is much harder. You will need a bigger model – that is, one with a larger number of elementary sine waves and therefore, a larger number of parameters – and you will need more data for training.[2] This relationship holds for any model and for any data. You can

---

[1] Inductive biases have nothing to do with biases in the data, which is an entirely different problem.
[2] Fourier Transform is a tool to assess how complex a sine-wave-based model is needed for a time series. Time series that are periodical and resemble the shapes of sine-waves can be approximated by simple models. Others need complex models and many parameters.

approximate almost anything with large enough deep learning algorithms. And you can achieve similar feats with large enough decision trees (see Section 6.2.3 for decision trees). There is even a mathematical theorem, the Universal Approximation Theorem[3], which proves that an artificial neural network with only one hidden layer can approximate any mathematical function provided enough neurons are available in the hidden layer [4]. So, what is the problem then, if we can approximate anything? Why would we worry about adding inductive biases if models can approximate any function without them? I have already hinted at the most obvious problem: If the inductive biases of the model do not match well with the data, you need a lot of data and a big model and a lot of computation. This also means more CO2 released into the atmosphere during the training and production of the model. None of that is good news.

On the other hand, if you add the correct inductive biases, you can reduce the model size. You can then train it with fewer data points as this leaner model does not fall easily into the local minima of overfitting[4]. The advantages of inductive biases are the reason that we have so many different models. Every problem is a little bit different from any other problem and can be thus more optimally tackled with a more specialized set of equations. Every problem has, in theory, a most optimal possible model specialized for just that problem. Hence, we will never run out of space for inventing new models. The list of all possible models is infinite; we will never reach the end of this list.

I learned about the power of inductive biases in practice on one occasion where my team and I wanted to induce overfitting in deep learning neural networks. Our end goal was to test an algorithm that reduces overfitting in a situation of one-shot learning, and our approach was as follows: generate an unlimited amount of data for training the one-shot learning algorithm (see Chapter 10)[5,] induce overfitting on this dataset, and then 'save' the network from overfitting, using our new algorithm. My idea was to create our 'unlimited data' using one deep learning network with a random set of weights, and then train another naive deep learning network to learn the same random mappings. We were confident that we could create overfitting this way, but were proven decisively wrong: We kept reducing the size of the training data set, but the new network did not want to overfit. The performance on the test data remained good, sometimes with as little as 10 or 20 data points. At first, my colleagues and I were puzzled. How was that possible? These were supposed to be very hard data to learn, with complex random relationships in a multi-dimensional space. How could the network learn these relationships with only a small number of examples? This learning was efficient even when we changed the architecture of the network, the number of layers and the sizes of each. The ability to efficiently learn the data was robust.

It took a few days for us to realize that the model which we hoped would overfit was 'doomed' not to, as it had perfect inductive biases for the data. We used the same ReLu and sigmoid transfer functions for generating data and for the model that was learning the data, which basically made the learning model's job very easy. This illustrated to me how powerful inductive biases can be: the same network may need a million examples to learn something counterintuitive for its inductive biases, such as recognizing a flower on a photograph, and only ten examples to learn something that is highly complex for any other model but is

---

[3] *https://en.wikipedia.org/wiki/Universal_approximation_theorem*
[4] *https://en.wikipedia.org/wiki/Overfitting*
[5] One can learn here about one-shot learning: *https://en.wikipedia.org/wiki/One-shot_learning*

perfectly intuitive for this particular network. This is because the network has exactly the right inductive biases.[6]

Inductive biases give us a lot of possibilities to play with when developing models. The game is two-dimensional. One dimension relates to the type of inductive biases: Should we use ReLu or sigmoid transfer functions, or should we use tangent or even sine waves? This way we are changing which assumptions the model makes about the world. We can replace one assumption for another, and by doing so, we change the inductive biases. A linear model makes a specific assumption about a linear relationship between data. A decision tree makes yet another assumption. And so on.

The other dimension along which we can play with inductive biases is, how tight are the assumptions we want to make? We can make a more relaxed set of assumptions, which basically means having a model with more parameters. We can also make a stricter model, with fewer parameters. By adding more units (neurons) to a neural network, we are relaxing its assumptions. Models that are well suited for a given problem, i.e., have exactly the right set of inductive bases, can often do great work with only a handful of parameters. The biggest models today have billions of parameters. These models are quite relaxed: There are a whole lot of different things that they can possibly learn.

As we mentioned, this has direct implications on the amount of data needed to learn. A strict model will be able to learn from only a few data points of course, provided that the inductive bases are correct. If the inductive biases are incorrect, then a small model will never fit well, no matter how many data points you give it for training. Your only two options for improvement are either increasing the size of the model (with a corresponding increase in the data set size), or getting your inductive biases right. Therefore, even with bad inductive biases you can fit data well; all you need is enough parameters and enough data. Deep learning falls into this latter class of models, not specialized, having relaxed assumptions, and requiring a lot of data. See Figure 9.3 for the relationship between the number of data required (expressed as 'Training effort') and the strictness of the model (expressed as 'Specialization'), across different types of models. The strictest models are the laws of physics. For example, $E = mc^2$ has only one parameter to fit, namely c. Then one can use the 'model' to predict E from m.

---

[6] Later I learned that someone made the same mistake as we did and published a whole paper without realizing the inductive bias issue that we discovered, thereby making the incorrect conclusion that neural networks are not susceptible to overfitting [5].

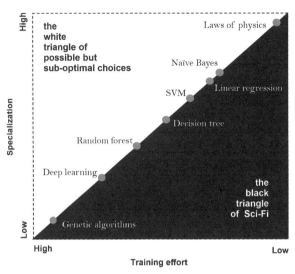

Figure 9.3 Different models have different abilities to learn. Some require a lot of data and a high training effort. Others can learn quickly with only a few examples. A model is used optimally if it lies somewhere on the diagonal: In this case, the right model has been chosen for the task. If the amount of data you need and the training effort are too large for the given level of specialization, then you are doing something wrong even if your model is performing well (the white triangle). It is impossible to have a well-performing model that is both generic and requires a small amount of data to learn. This can only happen in fantasy and sometimes, naively, data scientists hope to find such a model.

So, how can you take advantage of this knowledge about inductive biases? You can introduce such biases into your models to help those models learn better and quicker. This will allow you to make models smaller, faster and more reliable. You just need to find the right inductive biases. Sometimes, you will need to do the opposite, increase the size of the model and thus, relax its assumptions. You have to find out what the right approach is for your problem. In fact, if you have ever performed hyperparameter tuning[7], then you have already had your first experience in adjusting models' inductive biases. If you have well-structured validation and train data sets, then you have the chance to find a more appropriate architecture of a model for your data, and thereby improve the inductive biases of your model.

But you can do even more. Nothing is stopping you from creating original, new inductive biases that nobody ever has created before and that are exactly suited for your problem. You may be thinking, "but this is not what people do". You would be wrong. New inductive biases are created every time a new machine learning architecture is introduced. Practically every research paper on deep learning that proposes or tests some novel architecture is in fact proposing or testing a new set of inductive biases. Why would they need to do this? We have already mentioned the Universal Approximation Theorem, which states that a network with a single hidden layer can approximate anything. So, why wouldn't we use such vanilla deep learning for everything? The problem is that it would require exorbitantly many data points. To reduce these demands, researchers come up with more specialized models designed for specific purposes. This is how the 'deep' part of deep learning was born, which

[7] https://en.wikipedia.org/wiki/Hyperparameter_optimization

means stacking more layers to a neural network: Researchers looked for ways to introduce good inductive biases. Adding more layers did the job. For example, convolutional layers create great inductive biases for the processing of images. Images tend to have a lot of local correlations and weak correlations across long distances (see Section 6.5.1), and this is what convolution takes advantage of. Deep Learning with long short-term memory (LSTM) cells makes assumptions about temporal dependencies within the input data (LSTMs are described in Section 6.5.3). And so on. Here too, the rule holds: these inductive biases will make your model more specialized, and it will be applicable to a smaller range of problems. For example, if your data have long-range correlations, convolutional models will not be able to pick up this information. This is often exactly the case with natural languages, where meaning can be determined by words which are quite distant from one another. Therefore, for problems such as language modelling, we cannot use convolutional networks but instead, certain other architectures that have inductive biases more suitable for the structure of language (Natural Language Processing is covered in Chapter 10). Every good inductive bias that you can come up with will be a blessing for your model. Just keep in mind that you are making your model more specialized for a specific class of problems.

Some of the most elegant inductive biases exist in the equations used in physics, which we call then 'the laws of physics'. Chemistry is also not doing too badly. Scientists throughout history have made enormous efforts to find perfectly fitting, simple models, as I explained above with regards to Einstein's famous formula. In data science, we cannot hope to achieve that in real life outside of basic science. Still, we can try to approximate it as much as possible. The rules of logic, which are a part of GOFAI, can help us move towards this goal. Therefore, combining GOFAI with deep learning can be a lot more productive than either of the two alone. This is also why we need to build complex architectures for AI. A well-designed architecture introduces inductive biases into the overall AI solution.

There is one more common activity in data science that is intimately related to inductive biases. This is feature engineering (explained in Section 6.1). When you perform feature engineering, you usually think of it as transforming the data to work better with a machine learning model that you are feeding the data into. However, in effect, you are introducing inductive biases. To understand that, think about a combined model, one that is formed by merging your routines for data transformation with the model to which you feed the data. The two together form a super-model. This super-model has more stringent and more suitable inductive biases than the original deep learning model alone. In other words, you may use an off-the-shelf model that is general and then you add a data transformation algorithm to it to make a new model that is more specialized. This is why feature engineering is so useful.

Many other tricks to improve the performance of your model are in fact, introducing inductive biases. Various regularization techniques such as ridge, lasso or dropout[8] all introduce specializations into models, each through a slightly different inductive bias. But this nature of regularization is also why these tools do not always work, and why their advantages tend to be visible only with a small number of data points. They may have negative effects on performance with larger amounts of data. Sometimes, it is better to leave the model not regularized. This is because the inductive biases made by regularization are not the perfect ones; they are only roughly approximating some data properties. An unrestricted model can

---

[8] *https://en.wikipedia.org/wiki/Regularization_(mathematics)*

learn more fine relations than what regularization can offer, but again, the price is the amount of data required.

Sometimes, data scientists are not quite aware of these dependencies between inductive biases, model performance, and amounts of data required. Sometimes, they naively hope that one could have it both ways: a general algorithm that can learn nearly anything, and do that with small amounts of data. This is mathematically impossible. Such a super-algorithm is something like a perpetuum mobile of data science; intuitively it seems possible, but only once we look into the laws of machine learning we realize that it is, in fact, impossible. Don't make this mistake because you will waste a lot of time trying to achieve the unachievable.

Understanding your problem well is the best route towards effectively building useful inductive biases. The effort needed to invest in understanding the problem will always be a trade-off between the amount of data you have (and the amount of computational power you require), and the degree to which you understand the problem. The more data (and computation power) you have, the less you will need to understand the problem and still be able to create a well performing model. The more your data shrinks, the more you must think.

9.3.3 Recommendation No. 3: Perform analytics

One cannot understate the importance of analytics. The worst thing you can do after getting hold of your data is directly jump into feeding it into a model. You need first to understand your data. You will need to interrogate the variables and the relationships between them. I don't have in mind only the basics, such as descriptive statistics, histograms and correlations. I am referring to analytics that will help you decide which model is best for the problem at hand. Analytics is the best way to come up with great inductive biases for your data.

I want to give another example from my own experience. At one point in my career, I was tasked with building a model that monitors the market of crypto-currencies and proposes an optimal portfolio – i.e., an ideal combination of crypto currencies – for reducing risks as much as possible. In such models the goal is to minimize the ratio between the gain won and the risk taken. A naive approach to this problem would be to attempt to train a deep learning model or some other off-the-shelf machine learning model. One reason that this would not work in my case was that the amount of available data was way too small. The entire history of the crypto market was only a few years old and there was simply not much data in existence. Moreover, much like every other market, the properties of the crypto market change over time. So, whatever regularities you extract during one period, tend no longer to hold any more in the next. We needed the right set of inductive biases. What made much more sense is to do something similar to what is being done in classical markets: develop a good theory of how the crypto-market behaves and describe this in a few simple equations. These equations would serve as our inductive biases. Luckily, we already had a good starting point: The classical stock market concepts already existed, such as the Sharpe ratio, efficient frontier, capital allocation line, and others [6].

We performed an extensive analysis of the existing data from the crypto market, with the goal to investigate the degree to which the rules of the classical financial markets still applied there. We literally went step-by-step through an introductory book in financial mathematics [6] and tested for each testable property of the stock market, whether it also held true for the crypto-markets. We found that, while many things were similar across different markets, the crypto market had its own unique properties. For example, in crypto markets, volatility of volatility turned out to be important. Based on these insights, we created an AI solution that was partly based on novel algorithms that we invented. We created a whole new type of inductive biases and hence, a whole new type of a model. And the effort paid off. Our first version of the model already performed well, behaving stably throughout all the turbulences of the crypto market. The AI occasionally made unexpected choices. Each time something like this happened, we resorted to analytics to check how and why the decision was made. Each time it turned out that the AI made a correct decision. The market was 'crazy' and the AI needed to act accordingly. It kept doing everything right. Over time, we were able to show that our AI performed better than a major index of crypto-currencies.

For me, this was a great example of building a model based on analytics and the consequent introduction of inductive biases. The blind trial and error we see in, for example, the aforementioned AutoML, cannot beat analytics and careful thinking about the problem. This is especially true when the amount of data is small.

However, analytics is also useful when you have a lot of data. Analytics can help you decide which type of model would be the best and can help you engineer good features for it. Here is an example. In one case my team needed to build a model that would predict when a coffee machine is likely to fail and need to be serviced. As inputs, we had the logs on a day-by-day basis containing information from various sensors placed into the machines. Before we trained any models, we performed analytics about the correlations between various variables (we used advanced forms of correlation such as 'scaled correlation'[9]), which led us to discover that cumulative variables had a great predictive power. Thus, we created cumulative time series simply by summing up all the values until that time point in the original time series. This also made intuitive sense: The cumulative values represented the amount of wear and tear in the machines. And sure enough, after we made the appropriate feature engineering steps and fed the cumulative variables into a neural network, we got a well performing model. Had we not done the analytics first, we would likely have missed the opportunity of transforming the data in such a way.

It is important to note that exploring your data can require even more advanced methods than financial analytics or correlation structures. As I mentioned earlier, machine learning needs not be used only for creating high-performing models, but also as an analytics tool. I described our own use of machine learning to investigate how the brain stored information. Similarly, you can train simple machine learning models on subsets of data to get a feel for how the data respond, and to assess which inductive biases they like. In fact, every analysis performed on data implicitly fits a model to those data. For example, if you compute a correlation, such as Pearson's coefficient of correlation, you are not only measuring the degree of association between two variables, but also fitting a linear model to those data. The resulting degree of association indicates how well a linear model describes the correlated variables. The same holds for other types of analyses. Statisticians long ago recognized the fact that, with virtually everything you do, you are fitting a model. In fact, this is why they created a Generalised Linear Model (GLM) on the foundation of which countless

---

[9] This is an invention of mine about which one can read on Wikipedia here: *https://en.wikipedia.org/wiki/Scaled_correlation*

other procedures have been developed (like ANOVA, regression, and factor analysis, just to name a few).

Use this insight to your advantage. There are numerous ways in which you can fit small models to subsets of data and get useful insights. For example, you may test different assumptions (different inductive biases). Or you may want to gradually reduce or increase the number of variables to observe how your predictive power changes. You may gradually increase the amount of data you feed your model, to observe how the performance is affected. This can give you an idea of how much more data you may need or whether you are close to reaching a saturation point with the given model. You can gradually add to your data noise that resembles real life, in order to observe the problems that the model may encounter out in the real world. And so on. Make a note in the research papers that you read of how the authors themselves tested the model performance. Copy them. Sometimes, you will need to be creative. There is an infinite world of interesting tests that one can do with a data set.

The insights you get from such analyses will sometimes be invaluable. They may give you a critical idea on how to improve your AI architecture. They may tell you under which conditions your autonomous vehicle will work well and under which it will struggle. This may help you prevent disasters before they happen. It may even assist you in ways I myself have not yet conceived of. As I said, the importance of analytics cannot be understated.

9.3.4 Recommendation No. 4: Beware of the scaling trap

There are a few traps lurking behind the mathematical complexities of machine learning problems. Data scientists may fall into those traps and confidently build expectations about how their model, or more often, their AI solution, will work in the future. You have been caught in a trap in the past if your project looked all good and promising during the proof of concept, and if, on the basis of this good performance and by applying a basic logic about how to create a full product, you (or your company) went on and invested significant effort and resources only to discover that the full product did not work nearly as well as it should have, based on the initial plans. In the worst cases, the project needed to be abandoned. In less bad cases, the approach to the problem needed to be changed. Nevertheless, the expected time of completion needed to be significantly extended.

Such traps, consisting of a deceivingly rosy picture in the beginning, happen in all types of engineering projects. Yet AI seems to have more than its own fair share. Consider, for example, how often the Tesla corporation has been delayed in their development of fully autonomous cars. The first expectation was 2017, then the deadline kept moving. At the time of writing this book (2021), the performance is still not satisfactory.[10] It always seemed like one more big step was needed, but then the result did not work to all stakeholder's satisfaction, and a next step was needed, which again proved unsatisfactory, and so on. Another example was IBM's ambitious attempt to create AI for health care, or an AI-physician, if you will. This had many troubles and again, what engineers and data scientists expected to work, did not, or was realized only after significant additional resources had

---

[10] *https://en.wikipedia.org/wiki/Tesla_Autopilot*

been invested. There is still no well-performing "Watson for Oncology".[11] The majority of such 'failed' projects are likely not being advertised, and hence we will never know the true extent to which they occur in the world of AI.

The trap of seeing too rosy a picture of the future is not a recent phenomenon. The history of AI is packed with failed predictions made by the most prominent AI minds at the time. Even Alan Turing, arguably the smartest person ever to work in AI, predicted in 1950 that "... around the year 2000, computers will be able to answer questions in ways identical to those of human beings". Now, 20 years after his proposed turning point, we are still far from achieving that. In 1958, Herbert Simon, a Nobel Prize winner and a leader in AI and cognition, together with his colleague Allen Newell, predicted that "Within ten years a digital computer will be the world's chess champion". In 1965, Herbert Simon also stated that "machines will be capable, within twenty years, of doing any work a man can do." In reality, a ten-year prediction about chess turned into 40 years of work, as it was only in 1997 that IBM's Deep Blue beat Garry Kasparov. And, as mentioned, we are still not at the point of machines fully replacing human work. It seems that this human-level intelligence is something that particularly inspires AI researchers and traps them into making overly ambitious predictions. For example, Marvin Minsky, widely regarded as one of the fathers of AI, said in 1970, "In from three to eight years we will have a machine with the general intelligence of an average human being." Historically, the next step in AI always turned out to be harder than what it seemed to the biggest and best minds at the time.

I believe that we can identify today two types of thinking traps which lure people into making ambitious promises, and that we can educate ourselves about them. If we understand these two traps, we will be less likely to make AI promises that we cannot keep, and our projects will be less likely to fail.

The first trap is what can be called a 'scaling trap'. This occurs when everything works well on a small scale, in terms of the amount of data and the size of the model, and we then have to repeat exactly the same thing on a larger scale, with more data and bigger models. The intuition is often that, if we made it work on a small scale so well, it should not be too hard to scale the same approach up to a much higher intelligence. If it took just one month to teach a robot to avoid two types of obstacles, it should not take much longer to teach it to avoid hundreds of obstacles. We should expect some sort of acceleration effect over time whereby, after having already learned so many different obstacles, some generalization should take place and learning should go quicker for new obstacles. This is what intuitively makes sense. Similarly, if it took 100,000 example images to train my deep learning model to accurately distinguish ten categories of objects in photographs, imagine what we can do with tens of million images. Perhaps, the model should be able to reliably distinguish everything we practically need. Again, some sort of benefit of learning at scale and some effect of generalization makes intuitive sense: Later, the new objects and items should be added quickly into the model. There should be a point at some scale of the model at which everything tremendously accelerates.

This is a question of how well the intelligence of machines scales. Increasing the accuracy or keeping the accuracy but increasing the number of categories distinguished both result in increasing the intelligence of our AI. So, the question of scaling intelligence is a question

---

[11] https://spectrum.ieee.org/how-ibm-watson-overpromised-and-underdelivered-on-ai-health-care

of how many resources we need to add in order to increase the intelligence of the machine to the next level. To double the intelligence, do we also need to double the resources? That is, do we need to roughly double the amount of data and the size of the model?

Previously, researchers did not have answers to those questions. Today, we can derive clear answers from experiments that have been performed with models and data sets of different sizes [9]. Unfortunately, the answers are not good. While intuitively, we expect the effort to go down as we increase the proportions of the models and the amounts of data, the opposite is in fact true. The amount of effort needed to bring a model to the next level increases with the magnitudes of the models. It takes a lot more effort to increase accuracy of an already accurate model than of an inaccurate one. Similarly, it takes a lot more effort to add one more category (and not lose classification accuracy) to a machine learning model that already knows many categories than to a model that knows only a few categories. Increasing the intelligence of machine learning models is a staircase in which every new step is higher than the previous one.

This is a hell of a trap for those who do not keep this fact in mind every time they try to improve the performance of a model. Our intuition will always tell us: there must be some sort of an easy trick, I just need to find it.

Unfortunately, your mind is misleading you. The intelligence of machine learning models does not tend to scale that way. Rather, demands on resources for creating intelligent machines tend to explode. These demands will often grow as per the power law: If you need to double the intelligence of your deep learning model, it will not be enough just to double the resources. You will need much more. You may need to raise your needed level of intelligence to some exponent. The truth is that the demands on resources grow with the demands on intelligence. And this exponent is larger than one, a lot larger than one.

So, here is the scaling trap in a nutshell: i) our small-scale model works well. ii) our minds compel us to assume approximately linear scaling properties of the problem, iii) we make rule-of-the-thumb predictions about the resources required to achieve a full product, iv) we get to work according to these estimates, v) after significant time and effort, we realize that, although the model can do a lot more than before, its overall value and quality is miles below what was expected. We have fallen into the scaling trap.

Let us look at some evidence. MNIST[12] is a popular data set for training and testing models to distinguish ten categories of hand-written digits. To achieve 88 % accuracy on this dataset, it is enough to use a linear model with about 100,000 parameters [7]. However, it is also possible to achieve about 99.9 % accuracy on MNIST, which is just over a 10 % increase in accuracy. How? If your suggestion would be to increase the number of parameters in the model also by about 10 %, you would be mistaken. In fact, the number of parameters needed is much larger and also, a great deal of additional inductive biases are required. The best performing model at the time of writing is 99.87 % accurate but requires about 1.5 million parameters, a whopping increase of 1500 %, and this is a result of 20 years of research into inductive biases for these types of problems.[13] Obtaining the last percentages in accuracy is increasingly hard. A very small improvement requires a huge effort, not only in the model

---

[12] *https://en.wikipedia.org/wiki/MNIST_database*
[13] *https://paperswithcode.com/sota/image-classification-on-mnist*

size and the training time, but also in data enhancing and in human thinking on how to improve the overall architecture.

We have made great progress in AI in recent years, but we have also had to increase the demands of our machines. The sizes of our models grew tremendously over the years. In fact, they exploded. In Figure 9.4, we see how the computation needs of various models have grown since the year 1960.[14] Note that the scale on the y-axis is logarithmic. This means that a linear curve in the plot indicates exponential growth in the computational demand. Moreover, the graph shows two exponential trends: the one before about 2012 roughly follows Moore's law, which tells us how fast the computational power of our hardware grows. In particular, Moore's law states that the computational resources double roughly every two years.[15] The other slope, after 2012, has a much steeper growth, with resources increasing tenfold every year. In other words, the exponent of the curve increased in recent years. We are clearly building ever more gigantic models – models that do not follow Moore's law. The demands that we request from hardware are much larger than the speed with which the "bare metal" of the electronics improves. As a consequence, in recent decades the execution of model training had to shift first from CPUs to GPUs of single computers, then from GPUs to farms of GPUs in computational centers. The latest trend is to build computational centers dedicated just to deep learning models.

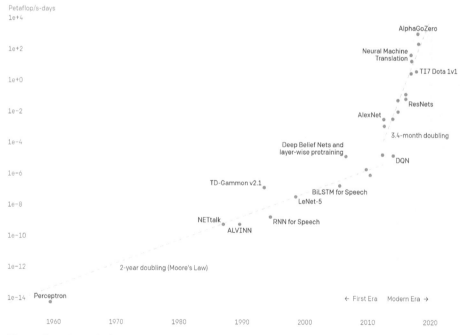

Figure 9.4 An analysis made by openAI about the amount of computation needed to train a model and the year in which the model appeared (reproduced from: *https://openai.com/blog/ai-and-compute/*)

[14] *https://openai.com/blog/ai-and-compute/*
[15] *https://en.wikipedia.org/wiki/Moore%27s_law*

While we are building these gigantic models, the question is whether their intelligence equally gigantically increases. Do they become tenfold more intelligent every time we increase their size by a factor of ten times? According to a study by Bianco et al [8], this does not seem to be the case. In Figure 9.5, we see the relationship these authors obtained between the accuracy of a model on the ImageNet dataset[16] and the model's demands on resources, expressed as the number of floating-point operations required to compute the model. The relationship is similar to that which we saw for the MNIST dataset: We have to undergo large increases in model sizes only to increase their performance relatively little. This is not encouraging.

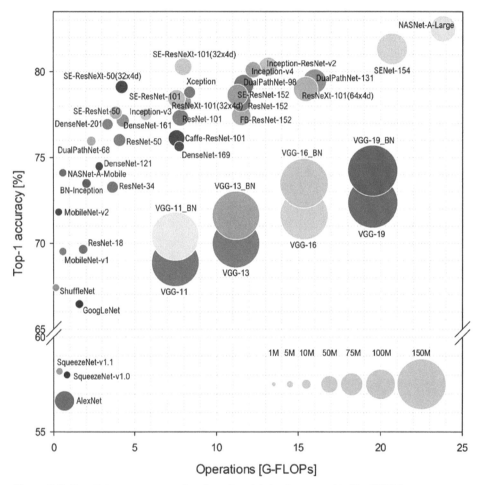

Figure 9.5 Growth in accuracy as a function of model size (expressed in GigaFLOPs). Circle size indicates the number of parameters in the model. (Reprinted with permission *https://arxiv.org/pdf/1810.00736.pdf*)

---

[16] *https://www.image-net.org/*

This problem of the increase in intelligence with the increase in resources has been most thoroughly investigated by openAI [9]. A core idea of their research has been to extend the sizes of the data and models, to scales never seen before, and then plot the relationships. Using loss on the test data set as their measure of intelligence (lower loss indicates higher intelligence and is covered in Section 5.2), openAI researchers asked how the loss reduces as a function of resources. They explored different forms of resources: computation in floating point operations, the size of the training data set, and the number of parameters in the model. And for the first time they went to huge scales. They investigated what happens at over one petaFLOP, over one billion parameters, and at billions of data points in the training data set. What they found was always the same relationship – a power law[17]. The demands on resources kept growing at the same pace that the demands on the models' intelligence increased.

In the original paper, the authors focused on the positive side: that intelligence keeps increasing. The models never stop becoming better. However, another side to this finding, of which we also must be aware, is that there is never a point at which the power law-driven demand in resources stops. There is no point at which the model becomes so smart that it no longer requires ever more resources for every additional step of increasing its intelligence. Therefore, the situation is as follows: Yes, we can grow the intelligence of deep learning models indefinitely. However, this comes at a price: we need a power law growth in resources. In practice, then, it seems that we in fact cannot grow intelligence indefinitely. The indefinite growth in intelligence is only 'in theory', only if we had unlimited resources. But our resources are limited. Hence, we will have to stop at some point. These findings from openAI tell us that it will likely be impossible to grow the intelligence as far as we would like to.

We already see clearly how our dependency on ever-increasing sums of resources is depriving us from using the AI solutions in practice. While state-of-the-art models from only a few years ago could be implemented and trained on individual computers and even at home, the best models of today can be played and experimented with only by an exclusive club of organizations, those that can afford 10s or even 100s of millions of dollars in hardware and data. This problem is also visible in the technology for self-driving cars. Automotive companies are able to deploy much more accurate AI solutions for self-driving cars on gigantic super-computers than what they can do with the relatively miniscule computational units which will fit under the hoods of individual cars. A part of the challenge of creating truly autonomously driving vehicles is the power law discovered by openAI: intelligence requires a disproportionate increase in resources. This is true for training data, computer memory, and computational power.

Therefore, although the intelligence of deep learning can be scaled, it does not scale well. And if you are not aware of this problem, you may fall into a trap. The next question is, then,

---

[17] The power law is slightly less explosive than exponential functions and yet, still poses ever-accelerating growth in demands on resources. An example of an exponential function is b^x, where b is the fixed base and x is the variable, such as the time passed since we started building computers. So, for example, if we double the computational power every year, b = 2. A power law function would be x^n, where n is the fixed exponent. For example, if we solve relationship problems for x objects in a 3-dimensional space, then the computation time will scale proportionally with x^3. They both "explode" because their derivatives explode: the derivative of an exponential function is another exponential function; the derivative of a power function is another power function.

what can we do in practice to prevent falling into that trap? Also, are there remedies to this problem of scaling?

First and foremost, do not ever promise that you will develop a large-scale functioning product based on a small-scale demo. Before you make such a promise, you have to have addressed the scaling problem. You must ask the question: can I scale it well enough? Is the power law going to destroy me, or will I have enough resources (data, memory, computational power)? Be wise about scaling the intelligence.

You may need to do some thinking and analytics before you will know whether your problem will be able to scale. You can:

1. Assess the exponent of your power law,

2. Reduce your ambitions,

3. Reduce the exponent.

To assess the exponent of your power law, you can do an analysis on a small scale to see how well your model and data work together. Then you can extrapolate the obtained results to a larger scale. The extrapolation will give you an assessment on whether you will have enough resources to achieve the levels of intelligence that you seek. An analysis on a small scale will include stepwise creation of models of different sizes (or different data sets sizes, or different accuracy levels) much like openAI did in their analysis. You can then plot these relationships. You will also need to define intelligence. openAI has used loss as a proxy for intelligence, which was a convenient measure. Depending on your problem, you may need another measure. If your goal is not to reduce loss but to increase the total number of categories that your model is able to distinguish while keeping the loss unchanged, then the intelligence may need to be defined as the number of categories successfully distinguished (where 'successfully' means at a pre-defined loss). If these estimates tell you that you will have enough resources to boost your model to the level you desire, then go straight for it. Collect your data, get your computational power and start training. But if the estimates tell you that the total amount of resources exceeds what you can afford, then perhaps there is no point even in trying. You have just computed that this is doomed to a failure. We do not want to do 'mindless' boosting of our resources without first doing such research. Instead, we want to be smart like openAI was: They performed such research to help develop their famous GPT-3 model[18].

Reducing your ambitions is another sensible step. For example, you may decide to build a level 2 autonomous driving, not level 4 or 5.[19] This will be then what you will promise to your stakeholders and to your customers. That way, you will ensure that your AI project does not fail.

Finally, you can also reduce the exponent of your machine learning algorithm. This is probably best thing you can do. How does one reduce an exponent? The answer is always the same: We insert appropriate inductive biases. As mentioned already, research on different versions of machine learning models is nothing else but attempts to find inductive biases for a given class of problems. Effectively, what successful attempts do is reduce the exponents of the power law for a given problem. Therefore, research is what can help you tremen-

---

[18] *https://en.wikipedia.org/wiki/GPT-3* or see Chapter 10, NLP.
[19] See here for different levels of autonomous driving: *https://www.aptiv.com/en/insights/article/what-are-the-levels-of-automated-driving*

dously reduce the explosion rate with which the demands on your resources grow. Importantly, sometimes it will not be enough to read the literature and pick from there whatever the state-of-the-art is. You may need to do your own research. The reason for this is that your problem is likely unique and nobody else has really encountered it. Therefore, the inductive biases that will help you the most are probably the ones that you need to discover on your own.

To understand that it is sometimes better to invest effort into your own research of inductive biases than in brute-force training of models, consider the graph in Figure 9.6. The two curves depict the total resources needed for two different models. One model already exists and hence does not require any initial research; we can start scaling it immediately. However, unfortunately, this model does not scale well – the exponent is too high – and this hurts us only later, after we have already spent much money and time on building a bigger model. Only later do we realize that we will not be able to achieve our goals with this approach. Another model requires high initial costs into research of inductive biases, and hence, it does not seem attractive at the start. However, the research effort reduces the exponent of the power law, which then has a cumulative effect over time. Furthermore, only with this approach are we able to build a model that reaches the needed levels of intelligence with acceptable costs. Therefore, although this approach initially seems too expensive and a waste of time and resources, in the long run, this is the only way that works. A great thing is that there are ways to decide based on quantitative analysis which of the two strategies we should choose: If an extrapolation of our initial analysis of exponents indicates that the demands on resources are too high, we'd better choose the research route. Otherwise, we chose the route of scaling the existing model.

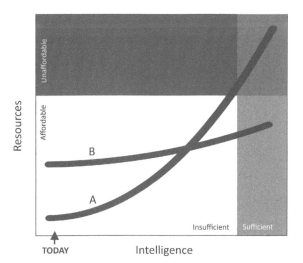

Figure 9.6 Two models, A and B, for which the demands on resources grow with the power law. Model A has low initial costs but high costs later. Model B has high initial costs due to the research needed to find the proper inductive biases, but these in turn reduce the exponent of its power law. Model B thus gives us a better return on investment.

In our (re)search for inductive biases, it is allowed to go beyond deep learning. Deep learning has inherent limitations that will always follow the aforementioned power law, no matter how wisely we create the architecture of the network or how effective is the learning algorithm we build. New deep learning approaches will reduce the rate of demand growth but, nevertheless, this growth will still have an exponent a lot larger than one. If we want to get rid of power law entirely, we have to get rid of deep learning. This is often possible in some components of the overall AI solution but in many cases, deep learning is still the best we can do.

To understand why and how we could possibly get rid of the unfortunate power law in machine learning algorithms, it is necessary to understand where this power law comes from in the first place. And for that we have to resort to Lego bricks. Everyone who has played at some point with Lego will intuitively understand why it is impossible to make a perfect sphere out of Lego bricks. A brick is a cuboid that has six sides and 12 edges, and its shape is not suited for making the smooth surface of a sphere. What one can do is combine a number of bricks to make an approximate sphere. The result will be an approximation with some error. As Figure 9.7 shows, however, the sphere will still be rough under our fingers.

The roughness of the sphere will depend on the number of bricks used. With fewer bricks, the sphere will be quite rough; with many bricks, the roughness will reduce. We can make quite an accurate parallel to deep learning models by taking Lego bricks as a model of a sphere, the number of bricks as representing the number of parameters in the model and the shape that we make out of the bricks as representing a trained model. Finally, the roughness of the surface is our loss.

So, the question is: How does the needed number of bricks (the resources) increase with the reduction in loss (the intelligence)? If you plot this dependence, you will get the same result as openAI got for deep learning models: the relationship is a power law. Moreover, the exponent of this power law is exactly 3, because we are building a 3D object.

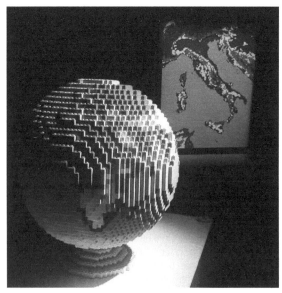

Figure 9.7 A sphere approximated by Lego bricks illustrates the problems machine learning models face when approximating real-world phenomena. More bricks will make the approximation smoother but never perfect; as we increase the smoothness, the number of bricks grows as power law.

This parallel illustrates quite accurately where deep learning models struggle. Elementary computation functions such as ReLu and sigmoid functions play the same role as the cuboid bricks in Lego models. The real world, be it written or spoken language, or images taken by a camera of an autonomous vehicle, is not made out of ReLu and sigmoid functions. These functions only approximate the real world, and this poor fit between the two sides is the ground for a power law relationship. Whenever you have a general elementary component that can approximate almost anything, be it a Lego brick or deep learning ReLu function, you will necessarily observe a power law.

That is, unless your elementary component just happens to fit perfectly into the real-world problem. If you need to approximate another cuboid with Lego cuboids, then the approximation smoothness will not suffer from the mentioned limitations. Quickly we will come to the point where the approximation is perfect and smooth – no improvement needed. In the case of deep learning, we have seen something similar in the case when the 'real world' is created by another deep learning network; in that situation there is the needed perfect fit. So, all we need to do is create a model whose elementary units fit the real world better. This is sometimes the case with for example, decision trees. There are data that can be nearly perfectly fitted by a decision tree while at the same time are difficult to approximate with deep learning.

The most powerful approach is to create your own model, one that is suited exactly for the data you are dealing with. I have given the example of a model specialized for crypto currency markets. We can build one for anything. All we need to do is a) understand the nature of the problem, and b) describe this nature in a form of mathematics or logic. This is all.

The parallel to playing with Lego pieces is using pieces of brick other than cuboids. Lego started with cuboids but soon after started producing pieces of other shapes. For example, there are Lego wheels. With cuboids, it is difficult to approximate wheels. So, to enable children to build cars, they manufactured specific pieces in the shape of wheels. This is what you need to do with your model. Find out which 'shape' is needed and then 'manufacture' it. The process of finding out what is needed is analytics, the process of manufacturing is the formation of inductive biases.

If you do that process well, you can escape the power law. You can create a model that is perfect for your data. I have personally been lucky enough to have been trained during my PhD in building such models for data obtained in neuroscience and behavioral science. The fields of computational neuroscience and mathematical psychology are in desperate need for building such models.

9.3.5 Recommendation No. 5: Beware of the generality trap (there is no such a thing as free lunch)

As you will frequently need to come up with new ideas for inductive biases in your models, you will likely be tempted to reuse something that already exists out there in the literature. Someone has already gone through a similar process, tried out an idea and reported that it was working for them. Why not reuse it for your project?

There is no problem in reusing, except that you need to be wary of one more trap that is lurking for you. This is the trap of apparent generalization. When you observe how seemingly effortlessly this new method works on all the various examples the authors of the paper show, you will find it hard to resist the idea that it must work for you, too. After all, the logic of the idea seems solid, and the results show excellent performance on a variety of tasks. Moreover, it seems that also the intelligence scales well on the data used by the authors. What could go wrong?

At first it may even appear that the new method finally presents a solution you have been looking for all your life, a panacea for all your machine learning challenges, something that works well always and for all problems. Not only will this magical solution help you now, but also from now on, for all your problems. Certainly, given the way some research papers are written, there is nothing to suggest otherwise. Often, there is no mention of cases in which the said method does not work, and nothing is written to indicate that you may be looking at a method with narrow applicability.

An unfortunate truth of machine learning is that it is mathematically impossible to create an ultimate algorithm that works for all possible problems. As we have seen above, an algorithm cannot generalize to a wide variety of problems and be effective at the same time. Now we must expand this wisdom: For every machine learning algorithm exists some data that the algorithm cannot even possibly learn. I am not talking here about poor scaling. Rather, I am talking about a total inability to achieve any performance above the chance level.

It may be obvious that a sine wave cannot describe a square shape, or that a linear equation cannot describe a circle. However, it is not clear that there is something that a deep learning algorithm cannot learn. The limits of complete AI solutions that rely on deep learning can be obvious. For example, alphaGo can only play the game of go. Watson can only play Jeopardy. Neither of them can drive a car. A car-driving AI cannot play Jeopardy or go. However, aren't we told that an artificial neural network with many ReLu functions can approximate any mathematical function? It is enough to have just one hidden layer and a machine can approximate anything given enough data and enough units in the hidden layer (see footnote 3). How can I then say that it is not possible to create a panacea algorithm? Deep learning in a way seems to be just that. Unfortunately, this is not true.

To understand why no algorithm can do it all and why this applies to deep learning too, let us go back to our Lego pieces. Are there things in the world that cannot be approximated by Lego bricks? Sure, you can approximate any solid object, a house, bridge, tree, shape of a person and so on. But there are a few things that you cannot approximate on any satisfactory level. We already mentioned wheels that kids love to have on their toy cars. A rolling wheel simply does not work with bricks. Another example is a squishy sponge. In general, Lego does not work with states of matter other than the solid state. It cannot do fluids, gases, or plasma. Also, generic Lego bricks are not enough to implement electric circuits as they isolate but do not conduct electricity, not to mention impossibility to have light bulbs or electric motors. Therefore, although Lego bricks are able to approximate some aspects of reality, sometimes with poor scaling capabilities but recogniseable nonetheless, there are parts of reality they cannot address.

Similar problems hold for deep learning. Consider for example a pseudo random number generator such as Mersenne Twister[20]. You cannot implement such a generator using deep learning in any satisfactory way. Mersenne Twister has a simple algorithm; the number of operations is ridiculously small in comparison to any deep learning algorithm and yet, it generates random numbers practically indistinguishable from true randomness. So, can we just use Mersenne Twister to train a deep learning network with one hidden layer and achieve about the same? Unfortunately, no. The Mersenne Twister algorithm is so much different from ReLu and sigmoid functions that the problem is about as difficult as creating a wheel or fluid out of Lego bricks. You could not even overfit Mersenne Twister and have deep learning memorize its sequence. A computer of the size of our Milky Way galaxy would probably not be enough.

There will always exist problems for machine learning algorithms that they cannot tackle. Even a most general form of deep learning – a single hidden layer – is not general enough. The limitations are then even larger for more specialized models that have more than one hidden layer and have other inductive biases to make them perform better on specific data.

There is even a mathematical theorem proving that this will always be the case: You cannot create a machine learning algorithm that can work for all possible problems. This proof is popularly called a "no free lunch theorem".[21] The implication of the theorem is basically that there is no free lunch in machine learning: If you change the inductive biases of your model to gain something, you will necessarily have to pay the price; you will at the same time lose something. What you will lose is exactly the opposite of your inductive bias. If you assume ReLu transfer function, you will make it more difficult to learn everything non-ReLu; if you assume sine waves, you will have difficulties with linear functions. And so on. Also, if you create a more elaborate model that combines sine waves and ReLu, you will still lose something. You will reduce the capability to learn and hence, you will need more data due to the larger number of parameters. And so on. This is a game in which you can never win. There will never exist such a thing as a truly 'general' learner algorithm.

This property of machine learning forms a trap for the reason that it is counterintuitive. Our intuition tells us that, if we think hard enough, we should be able to come up with an algorithm that can do the magic: learn fast and under all conditions. Unfortunately, both the math and practical experience tell us that is not true. Such a magic algorithm would again be a form of a machine learning perpetuum mobile – and if we try to build one, we will just be wasting time.

So, what can we do to protect ourselves from this trap? How do we suppress our seductive intuition? First, we must stay aware, regularly reminding ourselves that there are no free lunches in machine learning. A good way to do this is not to ask questions like "Which powerful idea can I come up with that will solve all the problems?". Instead, we should ask something along the lines of "Which trade-off can I make; what am I ready to give away and what can I hope to obtain in return?" The latter type of questions may guide you to make more realistic design decisions for your AI architectures.

---

[20] *https://de.wikipedia.org/wiki/Mersenne-Twister*
[21] *https://en.wikipedia.org/wiki/No_free_lunch_theorem*, *https://machinelearningmastery.com/no-free-lunch-theorem-for-machine-learning/*

A common trap is in the published work. When we read papers on fresh new algorithms, the papers often present only one side of the picture. They tell you how well the algorithm works on their data. But what they typically fail to do is to explain which price they had to pay for their lunch. Usually, this part is entirely skipped, and one is left with the impression that the new algorithm only brings benefits and there are no disadvantages to it. As a minimum, we have to be wary of that fact. We have to read between the lines and detect by ourselves the price for the lunch being offered. We have to then know whether we are willing to pay this price – or whether we are at all in the position to make the payment. It is better to ask this question immediately, while reading the paper, than discovering the same answer the hard way – after several months of effort with trial and error in unsuccessful attempts to make the method work for you (although, sometimes there is no other option but trying things out the hard way).

One thing that helps a lot to encourage such thinking is getting good training in traditional statistics. Traditional statistics is based on assumptions such as the Gaussian distribution, linear relationships, independence of sampling, homoscedasticity and so on. These assumptions are the inductive biases of statistical methods. For example, GLM is biased to find linear relationships. By stating assumptions, as is a tradition in statistics, one is basically stating the conditions under which the method works. The assumption is the price to pay: your data need to meet the assumptions. In other words, the authors of the paper in statistics say: If your data do not meet these assumptions, nobody knows whether and how well the method will work for you. In statistics, there is even a whole sub-field of investigating how robust statistical methods are on any violation of assumptions. Statisticians are quite disciplined about the prices being paid for lunches. Learning statistics means being trained in thinking this way.

But we don't have this type of discipline in deep learning. The published papers usually get away without pointing out limitations. And this is somewhat understandable. Machine learning problems are mathematically so much more complex in the background than the mathematically elegant models of statisticians. It is much more difficult to track what is going on behind the scenes. But this is also unfortunate and can create an ugly trap for us.[22]

The history of machine learning algorithms is packed with examples of methods that everyone got overly excited about at the beginning, only to later realize that these methods are not a cure-all and that they are, instead, just one of the many tools that you may try to use. For example, people are now a lot less excited about long short-term memory (LTSM) networks (see Section 6.5.3) than when they were first proposed. Back then, it was almost expected that these networks would solve all our problems with time series and temporal dependencies within data. Today, they are only one of many tools available.

Another example is the Adam optimizer[23] – a learning algorithm – which at the beginning seemed like a solution to all our gradient descent-based problems [10]. Over time, it became clear that one is paying a price, the lunch the optimizer provides is not free. Today, Adam optimizer is just one of the many tools that we can use to train our deep learning models, and it keeps improving [11]. What can help you judge whether an algorithm is suitable for

---

[22] It would be nice if all the machine learning articles were required to have a section somewhere towards the end entitled something like "The price paid for the lunch." I bet many people would read this section first, in a way people sometimes read the menus in restaurants starting from the right side.

[23] https://machinelearningmastery.com/adam-optimization-algorithm-for-deep-learning/

your data is understanding the inner workings of the algorithm. They describe its inductive biases. If you know these inner workings, you can mentally simulate them and try to think whether they seem likely to work on your data. You can do that with multiple learning algorithms and then pick the one that seems the best. However, sometimes, we simply must try out various options to discover which is the most appropriate.

Learning algorithms are generally an interesting topic when it comes to the lack of free lunches in machine learning. One must keep in mind that deep learning does not constitute only the transfer functions like ReLu and the network architectures. A critical component is the learning algorithm that sets up the weights of the network. As a rule, these algorithms are quite limited. We usually rely on some form of gradient descent (see Section 5.2), but gradient descent requires that data have certain properties, and has its own inherent problems, the most notorious being the fact that it tends to get stuck in local minima and usually does not find the global minimum. This means that our learning algorithms almost never find the best solution possible. An interesting fact is that we have an algorithm that can find the best solution (the global minimum) and this algorithm is even simple to code into a computer program. The algorithm relies on a brute-force search of all possible states of the parameters. The only problem is the lunch price that needs to be paid: the computational time would be way too long. For real, practical problems, we are talking here about age-of-the-universe long. Therefore, we have to undergo trade-offs and get thinking, using our human intelligence to come up with some smart way of learning with an affordable price.

It would be naïve to think that one could train a deep learning network to act as a learning algorithm. We have to do something else, something outside of deep learning. To understand that, let us go back to our Lego world. In Lego, the equivalent of learning is the process of arranging Lego pieces into the form of the final object that we want to build. Normally, it is a human child or adult who would do the arranging process (adults also love to play with Lego even if they don't want to admit it). But consider a situation in which you need to create a machine to arrange Lego pieces. For example, you may give the machine a photograph of an object and ask the machine to build such an object. Now comes the key question: can you stay loyal to Lego and use Lego bricks to create the assembly machine? There is a problem right there. For one, Lego bricks don't even remotely have the capability of doing something like robotic manipulation of pieces, as would be required.[24] Similarly, in deep learning, you have to jump out of the ReLu and sigmoid functions to train ReLu and sigmoid functions. The learning algorithm must know how to do exactly the things that the ReLu does not know how to do.[25]

And this brings us to our final and perhaps ultimate thought about how to defend ourselves against the no-free-lunch-theorem. We have to use our minds to do great engineering. We must add pieces of algorithms that jump out of the world of the other algorithms that we are already using. In the end we will have, as I already stated multiple times, an elaborate machine containing multiple pieces. Some of them will rely on machine learning. Others will be best described as GOFAI. You need both and you will have both. Finding a good solu-

---

[24] The reason my comparisons with Lego bricks work so well in this text is because I am not merely making a metaphor here. Lego is as much a model of the world as is any other mathematical model. I am hence comparing two equals: Lego base model to deep learning based model.

[25] For those who want to go deeper into the issues of assembly machines and what would it take for machines to assemble themselves without human help, I suggest reading about the theory of autopoiesis (meaning something like 'self-assembly') and the theory of practopoiesis (meaning 'assembling by acting').

tion that works for your customers will partly require you to use your knowledge on existing algorithms and partly it will be a work of art. And, as always, we need a pinch of luck as we cannot control everything. I wish you good luck.

■ 9.4 Human-level Intelligence

Finally, being myself a brain scientist, I feel compelled to make a few comments about human intelligence and the efforts to make machines as intelligent as humans are. Currently, our machines are far from being a match for a human. Sure, they beat us in many specialized tasks, ranging from multiplication of many-digit numbers to searching quickly through millions of images to find one with an airplane in it. Still, we understand the world, we creatively find new solutions and flexibly adjust to new situations. The ultimate goal of the AI research field is to create machines that match humans in all these aspects.

So, what does it take to get there? The answer is that we do not know. Neuroscience does not have an answer on how the biological brain achieves its capacity to be creative, to understand the world around itself and to be conscious. This is an area of intensive research. Unfortunately, no breakthroughs are coming for now. We are still largely fumbling in the dark.

If brain science is not helpful, then many AI researchers say: 'Heck, I am not waiting. I am doing research on my own.' This is how we arrived at the topic generally called 'Artificial General Intelligence,' or AGI. AGI is an attempt to develop algorithms, approaches, strategies, and philosophy that will lead to the next generation of AI, one more like our own, human intelligence.

Much like brain science is having a hard time, the AGI field is equally tapping in the dark. Here and there one can see a paper stating in the conclusions something like '… perhaps our work can pave the way towards AGI', which may produce some excitement, if only temporary.

What I would like the reader to bring with them is the knowledge that these research efforts often forget to ask the two critical questions that we discussed above. These questions are:

1. "Is our new idea still subjected to the power law?"

2. "How do we cope with the no-free-lunch theorem?"

In other words, the authors often do not assess how much resources their new AI idea will require for it to scale in intelligence to the level of humans. They also do not ask themselves, what is it that their method cannot do, and which price did they have to pay to achieve whatever they have demonstrated in their paper?

The scaling question is the trap many fall into, and AGI researchers do not seem to be an exception. I am yet to see a single proposal that shows the possibility to be, on the one hand, a general enough learner to be remotely similar to the human brain, and on the other hand, specific enough to learn from a small number of examples. The human brain found a successful way to balance these two aspects which tend to otherwise exclude each other. The brain found for itself the right spot of fast learning and general enough capabilities. I do not see AGI researchers recognizing this fact and trying to find the right spot for their machines.

Similarly, we are still yet to find an AGI paper that acknowledges the existence of the no-free-lunch-theorem and designs its research efforts around this. The human brain must be paying some price for the intelligence it gains. So must any AI approach that mimics this intelligence.

Cognitive science knows very well a few (expensive) prices that we, the owners of the human brain, get invoiced for on a daily basis. For example, our short-term memory (a.k.a., working memory) is notoriously incapable of memorizing more than a handful of pieces of information. Try to memorize a random sequence of 12 digits in a single trial. If you haven't been specifically trained for such tasks, you can't do it. For machines, of course this is trivial. This inability to memorize random information is the price we pay for the intelligence we have. The reasons for this lie in the fact that our minds rely heavily on concepts. Another example of the price we pay is that we easily get distracted. Machines can stay focused within their for-loops until the tasks are finished. Our minds cannot do that.[26] Therefore, if you see a proposed AGI approach that does not have a similar price list as the human mind, perhaps this is not really going in the right direction.

I haven't yet seen an approach towards achieving human-level intelligence that would satisfy these criteria – one that would be able to deal with the power-law scaling problem and would consider the no-free-lunch-theorem.[27] This leads me to conclude that the word 'general' within the term AGI is an unfortunate choice. From what we have seen before, there could exist no such thing as 'general' intelligence. If you want to get somewhat general, you have to pay the price for having to train the algorithm with vast amounts of data. And it is impossible to be absolutely general due to the no-free-lunch theorem. An example of the price paid for some generality is one of the most advanced deep learning models for natural language processing, called GPT-3 (see Chapter 10). The amount of data on which this model was trained is probably a million times bigger than the amount of language exposure a human person gets in their life[28]. And yet, humans can be more creative in using language than can GPT-3. But we also pay a price for it: we cannot store into our memory the vast amounts of information that GPT-3 can. We also cannot generate texts even close to the same number and speed as the machine can. We are slower. We have to think. Having to take the time to think is also one of the prices that our brains pay for its intelligence.

GPT-3 is somewhat general too – in some ways a lot more general than the human mind. Still, this deep learning monster cannot do basic things that the human mind can. Therefore, using the term 'general' for an AI approach that has the ambition to mimic the human brain is misleading: It gives the researchers the idea that they should be looking for some sort of algorithm that is general and can learn anything. But this is

1. mathematically not possible due to the no-free-lunch theorem,

2. not sustainable due to the power law increase in resources, and

3. clearly not how the human brain works.

---

[26] More information on the differences between human and artificial intelligence can be found in this talk of mine: *https://bit.ly/3tIyScg*. Also, a talk on my two cents on what we need to pay attention to in the brain: *https://bit.ly/3hzA9h4*

[27] One more issue that needs to be resolved when achieving human-level intelligence is the problem of the generated variety of responses, which I did not discuss in this chapter but one can read about in [12].

[28] GPT 3 was exposed to some 260 billion tokens. In contrast, there are only about 20 million seconds in a person's lifetime.

I think that, considering the power law and the no-free-lunch theorem, it is clear that whoever is looking for a general algorithm is looking for the equivalent of a perpetuum mobile in machine learning. General intelligence seems intuitively possible, but unfortunately cannot exist. Don't get lured into this trap during your own efforts when creating an AI product. You are guaranteed to end up at a dead end. There is no such thing as general intelligence and likely will never be. This also means that we humans do not possess a general intelligence: We are good at solving certain types of problems and horrible at solving many other types of problems.

■ 9.5 In a Nutshell

Building an AI product requires much more than training a machine learning algorithm. Namely, one has to think a lot.

The five pieces of advice listed in this chapter require you to i) be pragmatic, ii) make it easier for machines to learn by creating inductive biases, iii) perform a great deal of analytics, iv) be aware of the scaling trap and v) be aware that there is no such a thing as a free lunch in machine learning.

If there is one single thing to remember, then the reader is advised to keep the following picture in mind (Figure 9.8), which is the devil's cycle that will always haunt them while creating AI products.

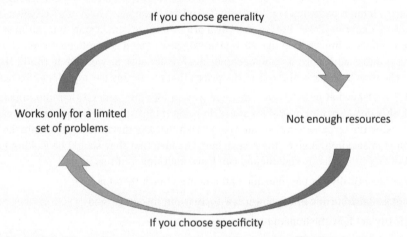

Figure 9.8 This devil's cycle is what makes machine learning difficult and each successful AI product a piece of art

References

[1]   Nikolić, Danko, et al. "Distributed fading memory for stimulus properties in the primary visual cortex." PLoS biology 7.12 (2009): e1000260

[2]   Nikolic, Danko, et al. "Temporal dynamics of information content carried by neurons in the primary visual cortex." NIPS. (2006)

[3]   Lazar, Andreea, et al. "Visual exposure enhances stimulus encoding and persistence in primary cortex", PNAS, (2021)

[4]   Hecht-Nielsen, Robert. "Kolmogorov's mapping neural network existence theorem." Proceedings of the international conference on Neural Networks. Vol. 3. IEEE Press New York, 1987

[5]   Lawrence, Steve, C. Lee Giles, and Ah Chung Tsoi. "Lessons in neural network training: Overfitting may be harder than expected." AAAI/IAAI. 1997

[6]   Bodie, Zvi, and Alex Kane. "Investments." (2020)

[7]   LeCun, Yann, et al. "Gradient-based learning applied to document recognition." Proceedings of the IEEE 86.11 (1998): 2278-2324

[8]   Bianco, Simone, et al. "Benchmark analysis of representative deep neural network architectures." IEEE Access 6 (2018): 64270-64277

[9]   Kaplan, Jared, et al. "Scaling laws for neural language models." arXiv preprint arXiv:2001.08361 (2020)

[10] Bae, Kiwook, Heechang Ryu, and Hayong Shin. "Does Adam optimizer keep close to the optimal point?." arXiv preprint arXiv:1911.00289 (2019)

[11] Kingma, Diederik P., and Jimmy Ba. "Adam: A method for stochastic optimization." arXiv preprint arXiv:1412.6980 (2014)

[12] Nikolić, Danko. "Why deep neural nets cannot ever match biological intelligence and what to do about it?." International Journal of Automation and Computing 14.5 (2017): 532-541

10 Natural Language Processing (NLP)

Katherine Munro

"As beautiful and informative as computers can be, their algorithms can also lead us down some strange, potentially scary paths." – Text generated by a neural network language model[1] in response to the prompt, "Can computers ever understand language?"

Questions Answered in this Chapter

- What is NLP and why is it currently receiving so much attention, in both academia and industry?
- What are the common steps in the "NLP Pipeline", used to prepare data for analysis and machine learning projects?
- How can you practice these steps yourself, using popular NLP libraries?
- What are some common tasks in NLP, and how are they achieved?
- How has the field of NLP developed over the last decades, from rule-based approaches to neural networks and the Transformer?
- What are the latest developments in NLP, and what implications does this have for the future?

■ 10.1 What is NLP and Why is it so Valuable?

Natural Language Processing is a discipline with two broad goals: using computers to process and analyze natural language data, and developing diverse, language-based technologies. The first goal – processing and analyzing text data – is valuable in the same way that any data science field is valuable: for gaining actionable insights. For example, a commercial entity might use language data to improve their business intelligence or identify consumer trends, while a linguist may use it to research fundamental questions about human nature and how we understand and use this incredible and unique gift, language.

The second goal – developing language-based technologies – is valuable because people *want* to communicate. Of course this is true in our interactions with other humans, in which case NLP technologies such as voice dictation, machine translation, and real-time confer-

---

[1] *https://app.inferkit.com/demo*

ence captioning are all vital. Yet it is even true with our interactions with other tools: Gone are the days when we adapted ourselves for "the machines", such as formulating our web search queries in a way we thought the browser would understand. Today, we talk to our mobile phones, our smart home devices, and even our cars, and we expect them to communicate effectively back.

The push for better language-based technologies has given rise to two new sub-disciplines of NLP (which now exist in addition to the broad spectrum of traditional NLP tasks, such as classification and information retrieval). These two new sub-disciplines are **Natural Language Understanding** (NLU) and **Natural Language Generation** (NLG). NLU involves bringing structure to raw text sequences, such that that structure can be mined for information required to complete a certain task. NLG does the inverse, producing human-like text from a prompt or a structured information object.

Let's clarify the difference between NLU and NLG with an example: using your voice to request something from your smart home speaker device. First, **Automatic Speech Recognition** converts your words to text. Then, in the NLU stage, the following three steps take place:

- **Domain detection** determines the domain of your request, such as online shopping or media playback.

- **Intent detection** determines your desire, such as to add an item to your shopping list, or to play a song.

- **Slot filling** identifies the important information within your utterance, which the device will need for executing your request. The slots could include things like the name of a product and a quantity to buy, or the name and artist for a specific song.

Note that these three steps need not occur in this order and can happen simultaneously, with the output of one step assisting another.

Having retrieved all of these important details, the software powering the digital assistant can act on them, such as by passing them to the API of the relevant app. The API's response may be tuned into natural language text: if so, this would be an example of NLG in action. Finally, this text may be "spoken" aloud to you, thanks to **speech synthesis**, or "speech-to-text".

NLP, the discipline which makes all of this possible, is a combination of methodologies from linguistics, data science, and AI. In this chapter, we will examine some of the most common tools and techniques used in NLP, following a historical timeline in order to demonstrate the decades of exciting research which have brought us to where we are today. As you are reading, look out for the grey boxes explaining how these concepts are applied in various NLP applications: you may be surprised at how many you interact with on a daily basis.

■ 10.2 NLP Data Preparation Techniques

10.2.1 The NLP Pipeline

Across the world, more and more data are being produced, every single day, at an ever-increasing pace. But it's not all contained in nicely prepared spreadsheets and databases: A lot of it is an unstructured mess, and text data is a huge contributor to the chaos. For example, just think of all the different styles of websites which exist now and are newly created every day: there's a wealth of information to be found, but it's in different formats, languages, styles, and often contains encoding errors, spelling errors, hashtags instead of sentences, emojis instead of words, and so on.

In order to get value from text data, we need to first bring structure to it. This section will introduce you to some of the many techniques which can help in this data preparation step. Data scientists, business analysts and computational linguists generally pick the techniques which are appropriate to their end goal, and then string them together in a so-called "pipeline". It is called this, because each technique modifies the text data before passing it onto the next step. The final result is a new dataset which has been cleaned and structured in a systematic way, making it suitable for further applications such as analytics, information extraction, linguistic research, and machine learning.

Gathering the Data

Whether you want to analyze language data to gain new insights, or you want to use machine learning to solve a specific, language-related use-case, you're going to need a lot of data. This can take many forms. For example

- A collection of documents which humans have classified according to some schema, such as news articles labelled by topic
- Text sequences in which individual words have been annotated with lexical and/or grammatical characteristics
- Highly unstructured information from diverse web pages on the internet
- Images or audio recordings of writing and speech

And so on.

If you simply want to practice NLP techniques, popular text processing libraries such as the Natural Language ToolKit (NLTK) [1][2] contain diverse datasets and excellent tutorials in their documentation on exploring them. For other applications you may need to capture your own language data, and you can do this as you would any other kind of data: from conducting surveys and interviews to crawling information from the internet.

Throughout this chapter, we will use NLTK to practice implementing the NLP pipeline. NLTK can be installed on a Mac or Unix device using:

```
pip install -U nltk
```

---

[2] See also, for example, spaCy (*https://spacy.io/*) for NLP in Python and Stanford Core NLP if working in Java (*https://stanfordnlp.github.io/CoreNLP/*)

For installation on Windows, the NLTK providers recommend you follow the instructions at *https://www.nltk.org/install.html*.

In order to follow along with the practical NLP pipeline steps in this chapter, please download and import the following packages:

```
import nltk
nltk.download("punkt")
nltk.download("wordnet")
from nltk.stem.snowball import SnowballStemmer
from nltk.stem import WordNetLemmatizer
from nltk.corpus import wordnet, stopwords
```

Next, we will define a small text, which we will use for processing:

```
biography = "Julia Gillard is an Australian politician and Australia's only female
prime minister, serving from 2010 to 2013. She grew up in Adelaide and attended the
University of Melbourne, graduating with a Bachelor of Laws degree. During that time,
she was president of the Australian Union of Students. Gillard first worked as a
partner at the law firm Slater and Gordon, specializing in labor law. She later joined
the Labor Party and became its chairwoman."
```

Cleaning and Case Normalization

Cleaning refers to removing unwanted characters, such as punctuation marks or HTML remnants from scraped web text. Case normalization simply means converting the text to use only one case (usually, lowercase).

Tokenizing and Sentence Tokenizing/Sentence Extraction/Sentence Boundary Detection

Tokenizing, sometimes called "tokenization", means splitting the input text into individual words, or "tokens". This is not as simple as splitting sequences by whitespaces or a punctuation mark. Some languages, such as Mandarin, don't always use such symbols to indicate word boundaries (see the discussion in Part-of-Speech Tagging, below, for further examples). Even in languages which do, there are edge cases: for example, "New York", "Beyonce Knowles-Carter" and "12.345", might all be better treated as one token, depending on the use case. Thus, commonly available tokenizers are either based on complex rule sets or trained machine learning algorithms.

Sentence tokenizing, known also as sentence extraction or sentence boundary detection, is simply the process of identifying the individual sentences in a text. Again, this may not be as simple as splitting a text on a punctuation mark.

You can perform tokenizing and sentence tokenizing in NLTK, and display the output, using:

```
biography_tokens = nltk.word_tokenize(biography, language="english")
print(" | ".join(biography_tokens))
biography_sents = nltk.sent_tokenize(biography, language="english")
for sent in biography_sents:
    print(sent, "\n")
```

Part-of-Speech Tagging (POS Tagging)

This step takes care of automatically assigning the grammatical roles, such as "noun", "verb", or "adjective", to each word in the sentence. Special tags are used for each part of speech, and the system of tags used by a given POS tagging tool is called its "tagset". Figure 10.1 shows an example generated by another NLP library, Stanford Core NLP [2], using the Penn Treebank tagset [3].

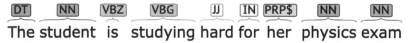

Figure 10.1 Demonstration of POS tagging a sentence

The tag labels in this sentence (there are many more in the full tagset) correspond to the following parts of speech: DT = Determiner, NN = noun (singular), VBZ = verb (3rd person, singular, present), VBG = verb (gerund or present participle), JJ = adjective, IN = preposition, and PRP$ = possessive pronoun. You can also retrieve information about this tagset in NLTK using:

```
nltk.help.upenn_tagset() # Describes all tags
nltk.help.upenn_tagset(tagpattern="VB") # Describes a specific tag
nltk.help.upenn_tagset(tagpattern="VB*") # Describes any tag beginning with VB (i.e.
all kinds of verbs)
```

And finally, you can generate a list of tuples of (token, tag) using:

```
biography_tokens_and_tags = nltk.pos_tag(biography_tokens)
```

If this is the first time you are reading about POS tagging, you may think the concept (if not the practice) is rather simple. For English, it may be, but this is certainly not a universal. Many languages feature much more complicated grammatical roles and syntactic functions than English. Furthermore, while English tends to use separate words to represent individual units of meaning, many other languages 'compose' words out of individual morphemes, which makes learning one POS tag per word impossible.

Consider the following example (reproduced from [4]) from the North American Indian language, Chinook. The single word "ačimluda" actually contains the meaning of an entire phrase: "He will give it to you." That is, it contains the elements a- (indicating the future), -č- (meaning "he"), -i- (meaning "him"), -m- (meaning "thee", an archaic form of "you"), -l- (meaning "to"), -ud- (meaning "give") and -a (again indicating the future). This is an example of an **agglutinating language**, as are Turkish, Finnish and Japanese, among others. For such languages, we often require **morphological disambiguation** to first identify the units of meaning within each word (conceptually this is similar to tokenization), followed by **morphological tagging**, as opposed to POS tagging. These techniques are beyond the scope of this chapter, but we encourage you to perform your own research, if you would like a fuller understanding of just one of the ways multi-lingual NLP can be both challenging and fascinating.

Stemming

Stemming uses algorithms based on rules (often derived from statistics) or machine learning to strip the endings from words, leaving only the word stem. This stem may not always be a grammatical word. For example, converting plural nouns to singular can be done by removing the suffix "-s", but this won't work for irregular English nouns. Thus we get "dogs" → "dog", but "countries" → "countrie", and "women" → "women". Similar problems arise in other languages, too. For example, in German many plural nouns can be converted to singular by removing the suffix "-en" or "-er", but irregular nouns pose problems, too. Thus we get "Frauen" → "Frau" ("Women" → "Woman"), which is correct, but "Bücher" → "Büch" ("Books" → "Book", where the latter should actually be spelled, "Buch").

This may sound like a serious problem, but it doesn't have to be. At least for statistical machine learning projects, creating stems which are also correct words is not particularly important: what *is* important is that each individual word is stemmed consistently and at inference (test) time, the new data is stemmed in the same way.

For analysis projects, particularly linguistic research, the creation of non-words via stemming may be more problematic. In that case, lemmatization offers a solution. Before we discuss it, let us perform stemming on our biography_tokens:

```
snowball = SnowballStemmer(language="english")
biography_stems = [snowball.stem(token) for token in biography_tokens]
print(" | ".join(biography_stems))
```

Lemmatising

Lemmatising, or "lemmatization", generally relies on dictionary lookup to convert each word to its standard form. Again an example could be reducing plural nouns to singular, but with lemmatizing, the result should also be a complete word, recognized in the given language as the official standard form of the given input word. This accuracy may come at the cost of being slightly slower than a stemming algorithm, however, modern machines and methods largely negate this cost. A more significant problem is the need for language-specific dictionaries, which require considerable manual work in their creation, and thus tend only to be available for a few of the world's thousands of languages.

Another problem for lemmatizers is that they cannot handle novel words, such as "twerking" or "vaping", which have only officially entered the dictionary in recent years. In contrast, stemming is often able to handle novel words, as they tend to follow the same morphological inflection rules as other words of the same grammatical Part-of-Speech (see Part-of-Speech Tagging, above) in the same language. For example, if you are an English speaker and encounter a new verb like "vape", you already know that it can be inflected as "vaped" or "vaping", depending on the context. Similarly, German speakers will automatically know that the past tense of "twerk" is "getwerked", however odd it may sound! This fascinating property of language is referred to in linguistics as "productivity" and can be useful in defining rule-based NLP applications, such as stemmers. This is demonstrated in the code below:

```
wordnet_lemmatizer = WordNetLemmatizer()
novel_words = ["twerking", "twerks", "twerked", "vaping", "vapes", "vape"]
print(" | ".join([snowball.stem(t) for t in novel_words]))
```

```
print(" | ".join([wordnet_lemmatizer.lemmatize(t) for t in novel_words]))
```

Now let's continue processing our biography text, using:

```
biography_lemmas = [wordnet_lemmatizer.lemmatize(t) for t in biography_tokens]
print(" | ".join(biography_lemmas))
```

While the above code will work, the WordNetLemmatizer actually performs better if given the part of speech that corresponds to each token. Unfortunately, the tagset used by this lemmatizer differs to the Penn Treebank tags used by NLTK's POS Tagger. Thus, in the below code, we take our list of tuples of (token, tag) and convert the tags, first.

```
def upenn_to_wordnet_pos(tag: str):
    if tag.startswith("V"):
        return wordnet.VERB
    elif tag.startswith("J"):
        return wordnet.ADJ
    elif tag.startswith("R"):
        return wordnet.ADV
    else:
        return wordnet.NOUN
biography_tokens_and_wordnet_tags = []
for tok, pos in biography_tokens_and_tags:
    new_pos = upenn_to_wordnet_pos(pos)
    biography_tokens_and_wordnet_tags.append((tok, new_pos))

biography_lemmas_improved = [wordnet_lemmatizer.lemmatize(word=token, pos=pos) for
token, pos in biography_tokens_and_wordnet_tags]
print(" | ".join(biography_lemmas_improved))
```

 Uses for Stemming and Lemmatization

Stemming and lemmatization reduce the size of the vocabulary that needs to be processed, while ensuring that all words are represented in a consistent way. For analysis purposes, this can help us identify more general trends in the data. For example, much of the initial work on stemming and lemmatization was born from research into information retrieval. Meanwhile, for statistical machine learning tasks, making the vocabulary smaller and the individual word representations more consistent reduces our feature set (and therefore model size), while providing more training examples for each generalized version of the word than there would have been for its original variations. Both of these factors can improve the model's performance.   ■

Stopword Removal

Languages contain many words which occur frequently but add little meaning, such as articles and prepositions. Consider the sentence, "the dog bites the man". If we remove the article, "the", we end up with, "dog ... bites ... man". While no longer grammatical, most of the meaning is preserved. Thus, "stopwords" don't contribute much to textual analyses. Nor do they help statistical machine learning models such as classifiers, since they appear in all contexts. Hence, they are ignored in some classification and, particularly, information retrieval tasks. Domain-specific stopwords may be removed, too. For example, if certain tokens appear frequently and in all contexts in your domain, you may wish to exclude them.

NLTK contains stopwords in various languages. The code below shows how to display the English stopwords, and remove them from a text:

```
stopwords_en = set(stopwords.words("english"))
print(" | ".join(stopwords_en))
biography_no_stopwords = [l for l in biography_lemmas_improved if l.lower() not in
stopwords_en]
```

Note, however, that stopwords can be crucial for NLU. For example, the word 'not' (and it's equivalent in other languages) is often included in stopword lists, and yet 'not X' has a very different meaning to 'X'. Furthermore, each individual employs stopwords with a certain style, and this information can be used for tasks such as author profiling: identifying the speaker or author of a text, which can be used for purposes from historical linguistics (see, for example, the controversy over who really wrote some of Shakespeare's plays) to forensic linguistics (identifying criminals in online chatrooms, for example).

Named Entity Recognition (NER) and Noun Chunking

NER is the process of assigning labels like "person", "place", "organization", "date/time", "event", "number", and so on, to relevant words in the sentence. Sometimes, special affixes to the labels will indicate whether the label is at the beginning or inside of an entity. For example, the word "Angela" in Figure 10.2 would be labelled "B-Person", while "Dorothea" and "Merkel" would both be labelled "I-Person". All words with no color highlighting would be labelled "O", indicating they are outside of any entity. This is referred to as an "**IOB**" or "**BIO**" labelling schema.

Figure 10.2 Demonstration of entities which could be extracted using Named Entity Recognition

Noun Chunking is like a simpler version of NER: we are not interested in what kind of "thing" an entity is, we simply want to extract it from the text.

The code for extracting noun chunks and Named Entities is virtually identical in NLTK, differing only in the value of the "binary" argument:

```
# Extract noun chunks
biography_binary_entities = nltk.ne_chunk(biography_tokens_and_tags, binary=True)
print([i for i in biography_binary_entities if type(i) == nltk.tree.Tree])
# Extract Named Entities
biography_labelled_entities = nltk.ne_chunk(biography_tokens_and_tags, binary=False)
print([i for i in biography_labelled_entities if type(i) == nltk.tree.Tree])
```

Notice that the output of NLTK's noun_chunk() function is the entire sequence as an nltk.
tree, a class for representing hierarchical language structures. Every recognized noun
chunk within that tree is, itself, represented as a tree. This is why the code above checks for
trees in the output, and prints them.

 Uses for POS Tagging and Named Entity Recognition

POS tags and Named Entities are often used as input features for solving NLP
tasks with statistical machine learning. Note that, interestingly, POS-Taggers
and Named Entity Recognizers are themselves often built via statistical machine
learning.

Other use-cases include annotating data for linguistic research and performing
rule-based information extraction by retrieving the Named Entities or words
with a certain POS-Tag, such as "Noun".

◼

Custom Pipeline Steps

Depending on your use case, you may add other steps to your text data preprocessing. Imagine, for example, that you have a statistical model whose job will be to classify each word in
your input as a certain label (such as a POS tag, in the case of training a POS-tagger). In this
case you will wish to create features which describe each token. These could include, for
example, any combination of the first or last n characters, the previous or next word, or the
word shape (which could be represented as an "X" for a capital letter, an "x" for a lowercase
letter, a "0" for a digit and a "." for a punctuation mark).

10.2.2 Converting the Input Format for Machine Learning

If you are using your text data for a machine learning project, you will likely need to convert
it into a format the training algorithm can understand. This could be a data frame (as shown
in Figure 10.3), a dictionary of words and their features, or some other input structure. In
the following, we will introduce just some of the possible and common techniques. We will
hold off on our discussion of word embeddings, another popular method, until Section
10.3.4.

word	lemma	shape	pos_tag	...	first_three	last_three	prev_word
Merkel	merkel	Xxxxxx	NNP	...	mer	kel	dorothea
is	be	xx	VBZ	...	is	is	merkel
the	the	xxx	DT	...	the	the	is

Figure 10.3 Example representation of part of an input sequence after performing custom feature
extraction for a statistical machine learning model

Bag-of-Words (BOW) Input Representation

Most statistical machine learning algorithms require input text to be converted into consistently structured, numeric sequences called "vectors", via a process called "vectorization". A simple means of vectorization is to take the vocabulary of the entire dataset and then represent each document as the number of times each vocabulary word appears in that document, completely ignoring word order. We call this kind of representation a "bag of words."

As an example, if you wanted to classify emails as "spam" or "not spam", you would have a collection of emails represented as feature vectors as per Figure 10.4. Each row (vector) represents one document, and each column represents a feature which can be expressed in words as "number of times vocabulary word W appeared in this document". Even from this small example, it's easy to guess that document 001 is not spam, but 002 probably is.

Doc. ID	Hi	Jane	How	are	you	...	Hurry	big	reward	credit	card
001	1	1	1	2	2	...	0	0	0	0	0
002	1	0	0	0	3	...	2	1	1	3	3

Figure 10.4 Example bag-of-words encoding for two documents

Term-Frequency Inverse-Document-Frequency (TF-IDF) Input Representation

The bag-of-words method counts how often a word appears in a document. Yet, as stopwords show us, many highly frequent words don't contribute much to a document's meaning. Conversely, rare words may have a powerful impact. The TF-IDF vectorization method takes this into account by computing a *score*, rather than a frequency, for each word in the vocabulary.

We first calculate the term frequency (TF), which is a term t's frequency in a document d, normalized by dividing by the length (in words) of the document:

$$\text{TF}(t,d) = \text{count}(t) \text{ in } d \text{ / number of words}(d)$$

Next, the document frequency (DF) counts the number of documents in which t is present, normalized by dividing by the number of documents N in the dataset:

$$\text{DF}(t) = \text{count}(t \text{ in } N) / N$$

The inverse document frequency (IDF) measures how important a term t is for differentiating between documents. The more documents in which t appears, the less useful it is for helping us differentiate: that is, we have an *inverse* relationship. For example, stopwords will appear in most documents but assist us very little. Hence, we calculate:

$$\text{IDF}(t) = N / \text{DF}$$

The IDF may explode for large datasets, which is why we may take its logarithm instead. At test time, if a document contains a word not in the original vocabulary, its (inverse) document frequency will be zero. Since division by zero is not possible, we "smooth" the count by adding 1. Finally, we multiply these components to calculate the TF-IDF score. The complete formula is thus:

$$\text{TF-IDF}(t,d) = \text{TF}(t,d) \cdot \log\left(N / (\text{DF} + 1)\right)$$

The TF-IDF score for a word enables us to find those documents which best match that word. This is the basis of searching, document clustering, and many other information retrieval tasks.

Truncating and Padding

Neural network (NN) approaches tend to require less preprocessing than statistical machine learning ones; in fact, they rarely utilize features like POS tags, learning instead from the (vectorized) text itself. However, some NNs do require each input sequence be the same length. In this case, we may truncate sequences to some maximum length, and "pad" shorter sequences by adding some dummy token vectors.

■ 10.3 NLP Tasks and Methods

What powers NLP tools and processes? The drivers can roughly be grouped into three categories, each of which arose as new resources became available and new methods were developed to overcome the shortcomings of old ones. Thus, this section will introduce these categories and their techniques in roughly chronological order according to their popularity of use, to help you contextualize each one. The categories are rule-based processing (see Section 10.3.1), statistical machine learning (Section 10.3.2), neural network approaches (Section 10.3.3), and approaches which take advantage of the benefits of transfer learning (Section 10.3.4). Each category is introduced below with a selection of typical tasks and the techniques which may be used to solve them. Some advantages and challenges for each category are also presented.

Challenges of Working with Natural Languages

As just noted, each category of NLP methods, from rule-based to neural, features its own unique advantages and challenges. Yet one of the frustrating and fascinating things about natural languages is that they all pose problems which are consistently difficult to solve. So, if you are considering specializing in Natural Language Processing (which I highly recommend), then be warned.

Natural languages are

- **infinitely creative:** you can say the same thing in many, many different ways, making it almost impossible to codify meaning using rules, and equally difficult to capture sufficient training data for any machine learning-based NLP approaches.

- **inferential:** meaning is often implied from what is *not* explicitly communicated. For example, if I say, "it's cold in here", and you are sitting beside an open window, you might offer to close it. That kind of social knowledge would be incredibly difficult to encode or to 'teach' a machine, as would phenomena like jokes and sarcasm.

- **lexically and syntactically ambiguous:** some words and sentence structures can be interpreted in multiple ways, requiring human common sense for disambiguation.

- **context-based:** understanding often relies on the surrounding words and even the world-views of the communicating parties.

- **negatable:** a simple change can reverse the meaning of an entire sentence. For example, "Writing rule-based language tools is really easy - not!".

- **idiomatic:** most languages feature phrases whose meaning has nothing to do with the words it contains. You can understand the difficulty of this as soon as you try to tell a non-German speaker, "That's not quite the yellow of the egg!"

- **multimedia based:** this is increasingly becoming an issue, as more people communicate via hashtags and emojis. For example, some humans can decode "👁 🐑 🍁 🐑"* but writing rules for this would be virtually impossible!

*I bee leaf ewe → I believe you.

10.3.1 Rule-Based (Symbolic) NLP

Machine Translation

Rule-based machine translation usually involves translating individual words and phrases via dictionaries, and then, if the target language requires it, reordering those words using hand-written word-order rules. For example, in this translation from English to German, the words are first translated using a dictionary, and then reordered:

Yesterday – I – read – a – wonderful – book

Gestern – ich – habe gelesen – ein – wunderbares – Buch

Gestern habe ich ein wunderbares Buch gelesen

Unfortunately, long-distance dependency relations between words, such as the relation between "habe" and "gelesen" above, make writing phrase-based rules difficult. This is particularly true in long sentences with nested structures, such as we get when we add the adverb clause "during my train trip" to our above example:

Gestern, während meiner Zugfahrt, habe ich ein wunderbares Buch gelesen.

Lexical and syntactic ambiguities, which occur when a word or phrase could be interpreted multiple different ways, also cause problems. For this reason, rule-based machine translation has all but been replaced by statistical machine learning and neural network approaches, which we will see later in this section.

Grammar Parsers

Grammars are sets of rules which attempt to describe all possible sentences in a language. Parsers are algorithms capable of building a data structure from an input. In the 1950s, computational linguists attempted to write grammars and create parsers to process them, in order to automatically identify syntactic structures in texts. The goal of such work was to add rules to rule-based machine translation systems which incorporated these automatically identified structures (the code example below shows you how to extract and view one kind of syntactic structure yourself). Such rules could assist with the ambiguities problem referred to above.

Developing rule-based grammar parsers is a challenge in itself, though, which is why they are no longer common. However they can still be useful in certain cases. For example, imagine you would like to perform entity extraction for entity types which are not recognized by commonly available Named Entity recognizers (see "Named Entity Recognition and Noun Chunking" under Section10.2.1 for some common entity types). You could build a grammar parser to perform this extraction. Furthermore, you could even use this parser to create data to train your own entity recognizer, perhaps automatically extracting a shortlist of training examples first, then reviewing them and throwing away any false positives, and finally, training your NER model from there.

The following code snippet defines a grammar for a noun chunk, then uses NLTK's regular expressions parser to identify chunks in some data we prepared under "Part-of-Speech Tagging" in Section 10.2.1.

```
grammar = r"""
    POSS: {<DT>?<NN|NNP><POS>}
    PP:{<IN><NN|NNP>}
    NP: {<POSS|DT>?<JJ>*<NN|NNP>+<PP>*}
    """
parser = nltk.RegexpParser(grammar)
biography_noun_chunks = parser.parse(biography_tokens_and_tags)
print([i for i in biography_noun_chunks if type(i) == nltk.tree.Tree])
```

The example might take a little explaining. The variable "biography_tokens_and_tags" contains a list of tuples of (token, POS tag). The grammar consists of the following components:

- **POSS:** Zero or one determiner (DT) followed by a noun (NN) or proper noun (NNP) followed by a possessive marker, "'s"

  Example: This would recognise "The girl's" in "The girl's laptop".

- **PP:** A prepositional phrase, consisting of a preposition (IN) followed by a noun or proper noun

  Example: This would recognise "on the table" in "The book on the table".

- **NP:** A noun phrase, consisting of zero or one instances of either a possessive (as defined above) or a determiner, followed by zero or more adjectives (JJ), followed by at least one noun or proper noun, followed by zero or more prepositional phrases (as defined above)

  Example: This would recognise even complex noun phrases such as "the boy's red tennis racquet" or "the University of Vienna" or "Jane's shiny new convertible in the carpark at her office", and so on.

This grammar may look complex, but it is, in fact, too simple. For example, it would fail to find complex noun phrases consisting of a coordinating conjunction such as "and", as in, "The School of Arts and Sciences". In other words, we have a **recall** problem. If you like, you can try to adjust the grammar accordingly (hint: the POS tag for a coordinating conjunction is "CC". I recommend you create a new component called "CC", like we did for POSS, and include it in the final rule). But beware, your **precision** may suffer as a result, as your grammar may begin to attribute too much linguistic content to individual noun phrases. Thus, in the sentence, "The boy washed the dishes and the girl raked the lawn", your grammar may erroneously identify as a noun phrase the words, "the dishes and the girl", when these should in fact be two noun phrases, "the dishes" and "the girl". This difficult balancing act is known as the "**precision-recall problem**," and does not only affect building grammar parsers: as Chapter 9, "Artificial Intelligence", and the following sections show, all kinds of symbolic approaches to NLP and AI can suffer this dilemma.

Symbolic Meaning Representations

Computational linguists in the late 60s and early 70s focused on representing meaning in a structured way that could be input to a computer. The representations would contain limited vocabulary and concepts, and simple systems were developed to process this data, such as to answer questions about it. Unfortunately, the need to manually-encode semantic knowledge made all of these systems too limited, and work in this area slowed significantly. However it never fully ceased: in fact, recent years have seen some researchers call for re-introducing symbolic representations even into more complex architectures, such as those based on machine learning and neural networks. Proceedings of The International Workshop on Designing Meaning Representations [5] are a testimony to the ongoing interest in this field.

Advantages and Challenges for Rule-Based (Symbolic) NLP

The benefit of rule-based NLP techniques is the human knowledge that goes into making them, producing some highly accurate results. However, this knowledge comes at significant resource costs, as experts are required to define, maintain and improve rule-based systems. Thus, it is also difficult to scale such systems to handle language beyond highly specific use-cases. New experts may even be required, with highly specialized knowledge, such as linguists who are experts in the new language to be processed. As a result, adapting rule-based systems to new domains or other languages poses a considerable problem.

 Uses for Rule-Based NLP Systems

Despite the difficulties rule-based systems pose, they are still used in a number of situations. For example

- when the domain and variability of inputs are restricted: such as in simple, template-based chatbots

- when the input data is highly structured: for example, for categorizing IT-support tickets, or summarizing information into simple texts, like weather and sports reports

- when the available data is small: such as machine translation for low-resource languages

- when it can improve more complex systems: for example, rule-based lemmatization can be used to prepare text data for a statistical language processing system.

10.3.2 Statistical Machine Learning Approaches

If writing language rules is so hard, how do infant humans acquire their native grammar so effortlessly? They learn from exposure to language data: hearing other humans talk. This is also the idea behind statistical machine learning approaches to NLP, which came to prominence in the late 1980s to 1990s. These work by making probabilistic decisions about the most likely output for a given input, based on frequencies collected from previously observed data.

In this section, we will observe statistical machine learning tasks and techniques together, in the context of real-world examples, to aid your understanding. This list is not exhaustive: some of the other algorithms introduced in Chapter 8, for example, could also be applied to text data once it is converted into the appropriate input format (for example Support Vector Machines, introduced in that chapter, can be used for tasks such as document classification or information extraction). However, this list should provide you with a solid foundational knowledge of common approaches.

Text Classification (Task) with a Naive Bayes Classifier (Technique)

Given a dataset of labelled documents, text classification is the task of assigning new documents to one of those label classes. Examples include **spam detection** for emails, document categorization for business documents such as customer inquiries, and **sentiment detection**. The latter involves identifying the sentiment expressed in texts, such as positivity and negativity and the strength thereof, and has multiple purposes (see "Uses for Text Classification", below).

A commonly used algorithm for text classification tasks such as sentiment detection is the **Naive Bayes** Classifier (see also the extensive discussion in Chapter 6). Imagine we want to label movie reviews with the labels "positive", "negative", and "neutral":

"Titanic is a great movie. I love the acting and love the soundtrack too!" = Positive

"Titanic is not a great movie. It's a terrible one." = Negative

"Titanic is a movie from 1997." = Neutral

A Naive Bayes classifier uses the so-called "Bayes rule" (see Section 6.3.3) to define $P(c|d)$, the probability of class c given a document d. In real words, given a movie review, it tries to calculate how likely it is that that review is positive or negative, using:

$$P(c|d) = \frac{P(d|c)P(c)}{P(d)}$$
Equation 10.1

Let's walk through this together. Imagine the document is a very simple review, d=['Excellent', "movie'], and the class is c=positive. $P(d|c)$, called the "likelihood", means "How likely is this review, given that we know its class is positive?" $P(c)$, the "prior", asks, "of all our training documents, what percentage of them are positive?" We multiply these, then divide the result by a normalization constant, $P(d)$, which will ensure that all results are within the range [0,1] and that the final probability distribution sums to one.

The algorithm learns these probabilities from the training data (which will have been vectorized in some manner, such as using a bag-of-words encoding (Section 10.2.2)). So to learn the "likelihood", $P(d|c)$, we:

1. Take the first word in d and count how often it appeared in the dataset in a positive document: that gives us $P(word_1|c)$.

2. Repeat this for all n words in the document.

3. multiply all the $P(word_x|c)$s together and replace $P(d|c)$ with that value, i.e. $P(word_1, word_2, ... word_n|c)$.

The remaining probabilities, $P(c)$ and $P(d)$, can be directly counted from the data.

Equation 10.1 could theoretically be used to create a "Bayes Classifier". However, given the infinite ways words can be combined, it becomes impractical to calculate probabilities for all possible combinations. Thus we make some *naive* assumptions, which give this classifier its name. First, we assume that word order does not affect meaning (though of course, it does). This enables us to care only about *which* words are in a document and treat "Great movie. Loved it!" and "Loved it! Great Movie!" as one combination. Second, we assume that $P(word_1|c)$, $P(word_2|c)$, and so on are independent (though of course they are not, since the likelihood of any word is affected by what comes before it). This "conditional independence assumption" means the term $P(word_1, word_2, ... word_n|c)$ from earlier can be expressed as $P(word_1|c) * P(word_2|c) * ... * P(word_n|c)$, which is much easier to calculate. Effectively, instead of training a huge number of parameters that would require a lot of data, we simply calculate them from another smaller set of parameters whose estimates require smaller amounts of data. Thanks to these assumptions, a Naive Bayes Classifier will have far fewer parameters than a Bayes Classifier and will learn much faster.

 Uses for Text Classification

- Spam filtering and automatic email categorization
- Directing customer service queries, e.g. IT support tickets
- Getting consumer feedback, e.g. performing sentiment detection on Twitter tweets to gauge consumers' reactions to a new product
- Finding areas for service improvement, e.g. hospitality providers like hotels and restaurants may use online reviews to assess and improve their performance
- Automatic content filtering, e.g. detecting and censoring hate speech on social media platforms
- And many more

Text Clustering (Task) with K-Means (Technique)

We saw that text classification involves learning to assign documents to different classes according to a given schema, such as "positive or negative." But what if we don't know that schema? For example, what if we want to identify trends in the search queries coming into our website, or identify areas for improvement in the online reviews of our hotel or restaurant? We want to cluster the texts according to these themes, but we don't know what the themes are. Since we have no training labels, we need an *unsupervised* learning algorithm. For text clustering, *K*-means is often a good choice. (Note that this should not be confused with the K-Nearest-Neighbors algorithm (see Chapter 8), which is a *supervised* algorithm for classification and regression: That is, like all supervised learning algorithms, with K-Nearest-Neighbors our target variables are available as labels and the model can learn to predict them).

The goal of the *K*-means algorithm is to group data into *K* clusters of similar data points. That is, it tries to identify *K* central points, or centroids, around which the nearby points are similar to each other, but different from the other groups.

The process is as follows:

1. Randomly initialize *K* starting centroids in the dataset vector space.

2. Assign each data point to its nearest centroid.

3. Calculate the distance between each centroid and the points assigned to it, and move the centroids to the mean (centre) of the closest points.

4. Repeat steps 2. and 3. until either we reach some predefined max iterations, or until the position of the groups doesn't change anymore (or at least, doesn't change more than a predefined threshold).

Note that when we refer to a point being "near" the centroid, we are referring to Euclidean squared distance. Consider, for example, the vector space illustrated for the K-Nearest-Neighbors algorithm in Chapter 8, Figure 8.4. In such a Euclidean plane, imagine some point p is located at the (x,y) coordinates (-1,-1), while another point q is located at (1,1). The Euclidean distance is the diagonal line between them, which we calculate using:

$$d(p,q) = \sqrt{(q_1 - p_1)^2 + (q_2 - p_2)^2}$$

In our example, this works out to be:

$$d(p,q) = \sqrt{(1-(-1))^2 + (1-(-1))^2}$$
$$= \sqrt{(2)^2 + (2)^2}$$
$$= 2.82$$

For optimization problems, it is often desirable to omit the square root and retain the squared Euclidean distance, as this is a convex function which allows convex analyses to be used. Fortunately, minimizing the squared Euclidean distance is equivalent to minimizing the Euclidean distance, but easier to solve. Thus, in the K-Means algorithm, we are concerned with the sum of the squared distances between the centroid and the points assigned to it:

$$d^2(p,q) = (p_1 - q_1)^2 + (p_2 - q_2)^2 + \dots + (p_n - q_n)^2$$

The goal of the K-means algorithm is to minimize this sum.

In this example, we are measuring distances between points in two-dimensional space. In order to apply this to texts, which are collections of words, we must convert those texts into numeric vectors. This can be done using a vectorization method such as TF-IDF (see Section 10.2.2), which will necessarily represent the texts in a much higher dimensional space (the exact dimensions will be based on the size of the vocabulary of the dataset on which the vectorizer was fit). But the fundamental concept remains the same.

By finding those centroid locations which minimize the sum of squared distances to the assigned points, the K-Means algorithm will identify K groups of related data points. In text clustering, these will be clusters of documents which are similar in some way. Thus, it can be useful for discovering themes and trends in text data, or topics which can be handled with specific business logic. However, note that we must first choose K ourselves, based on our intuitions about the data, and our choice of K may not produce the optimal solution for our purposes (though we may not even realize that a better solution is available). By this I mean to say that, given a different K, the algorithm will find a new way to classify the documents, which may turn out to be more informative or useful for us. Thus, we often need to explore the results under different values of K, in order to arrive at a sensible one. Alternatively, we may have to choose K based on our end goal: for example, we might only intend to automatically handle five kinds of consumer queries to our website, so we have no choice but to use $K=5$ to cluster those queries.

 Uses for Text Clustering

- Identifying trends and insights from free (that is, unstructured) text
- Search engines and document retrieval: which document cluster best matches this query?
- Summarizing information: what are the key topics?
- Product recommendation systems: so-called "content-based filtering" revolves around understanding characteristics of the product or media being recommended; this can be extracted from product descriptions

Part-Of-Speech Tagging (Task) with a Hidden Markov Model (HMM) (Tool)

For sequence labelling problems, where the goal is to label each word in an input sequence, we can use **stochastic approaches**. These predict possible outcome sequences weighted by their likelihoods, according to an (often unobservable) process whose outputs depend on previous outputs.

Recall from Section 10.2.1 that POS tagging requires assigning a part of speech, such as "noun" or "verb", to every word in a sequence. We *could* solve this probabilistically by calculating the most frequent tag assigned to each word in some training dataset, and then using those probabilities to tag future sequences, but this can lead to problems. Consider the following training set:

01	*Pronoun*	*Verb*	*Adjective*	*Noun*
	I	run	every	weekend.
02	*Pronoun*	*Verb*	*Adverb*	*Adverb*
	I	run	very	fast.

03	Article	Noun	Noun	Verb	Adverb
	A	morning	run	is	fun
04	Pronoun	Verb	Determiner	Noun	
	I	enjoyed	my	breakfast	

Given this training set, and the following test sequence, we would incorrectly tag "run" as a verb, when it is actually a noun in this case. (As a side tip, note the use of the asterisk in this example, which in linguistics means, depending on context, either "This is incorrect" or, "There are no records for such a usage"):

01	*Pronoun	Verb	Possessive Adjective	Noun	Verb
	I	enjoyed	my	morning	run

Clearly, performing POS tagging using only the most common tag per word is not appropriate. A common approach instead is to use Hidden Markov Models (HMM). As stochastic processes, HMMs are useful when we can observe a sequence, such as a POS-tagged sentence, but we cannot observe the process of hidden states which created that sequence. That is, we cannot observe the grammar.

Let's tag 5. properly, and add it to our training set as Example 6:

01	*Pronoun	Verb	Possessive Adjective	Noun	Noun
	I	enjoyed	my	morning	run

Now consider the simple hidden Markov model in Figure 10.5:

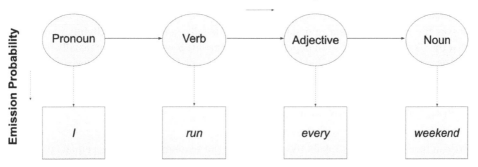

Figure 10.5 A simple Hidden Markov Model for Part-of-Speech Tagging

The POS tags represent hidden states, and the **transition probabilities** are likelihoods of transitions between hidden states, such as $P(\text{Noun} \rightarrow \text{Verb})$, which is the likelihood that a verb follows a noun. The **emission probabilities** are likelihoods that each word really could be output from the indicated hidden state. For example, $P(\text{Verb} \,|\, \text{"I"})$ should equal zero in English, as "I" can never be a verb.

Our tiny training set has 17 transitions, and the word "run" appears four times. So the transition probabilities would include*:

$P(\text{Noun} \rightarrow \text{Verb}) = 0.06$ (occurred in 1/17 transitions)

$P(\text{Noun} \rightarrow \text{Noun}) = 0.12$ (occurred in 2/17 transitions)

... and the emission probabilities would include* (*but not be limited to):

$P(\text{"run"}=\text{Verb}) = 0.5$ (occurred 2/4 times)

$P(\text{"run"}=\text{Noun}) = 0.5$ (occurred 2/4 times)

Once all of these probabilities are learned (counted) from the training set, they can be used to calculate the likelihood of sequences 7. and 8., below. This is done by multiplying the transition and emission probabilities at each time step (individual word) together. So although "run" appears equally often as a noun and a verb, and thus the emission probabilities are the same for this word for both parts of speech, once we also consider the transition probabilities, we find the most likely (and correct) sequence is 8.:

```
01   *Possessive Adjective    Noun        Verb      Verb     Adverb
     My                       morning     run       is       fun
02   Possessive Adjective     Noun        Noun      Verb     Adverb
     My                       morning     run       is       fun
```

For longer sequences, these probabilities become much more complicated to calculate. But algorithms such as the Viterbi algorithm [6] can be used to efficiently find the output sequence which maximizes the likelihood of the model.

Statistical Language Modelling (Technique)

A simple concept, which is yet fundamental to the remaining statistical and neural NLP techniques in this chapter, is language modelling. This is the task of learning probability distributions for all sequences in a language, such that for any given sequence of any given length, m, we can assign it a probability $P(w_1, \ldots, w_m)$. Of course, it is not tractable to learn a probability for all of the infinite possible sequences in a natural language (Chapter 9 discusses the scaling problem in detail). Thus, we usually make the simplifying assumption that the likelihood of one word depends only on the last n words, where n usually = 1, 2, or 3. The resulting model is called a uni-, bi- or tri-gram language model, respectively. An n-gram language model will assign the probability for a sequence of length m as follows:

$$P\left(w_1,\ldots,w_m\right)=\prod_{i=1}^{m}P\left(w_i\mid w_1,\ldots,w_{i-1}\right)\approx\prod_{i=1}^{m}P\left(w_i\mid w_{i-(n-1)},\ldots,w_{i-1}\right)$$

We can read this as: the probability of observing the sequence $(w_1, \ldots, w_m)$ equals the product of the probabilities of observing the ith word w_i after the preceding $i - 1$ words. This is approximately equal to the probability of observing w_i in the smaller context window of the preceding $n - 1$ words. For example, below we see uni- and bi-gram model representations of the probabilities for a simple sequence. Note that "BOS" stands for "Beginning of Sequence" and "EOS" for "End of Sequence". As discussed in the section on Naive Bayes Classifiers, these probabilities can be ascertained using counts in a training dataset:

$P_{\text{uni-gram}}(w_1, w_2, w_3, w_4, w_5) = P(w_1) * P(w_2) * P(w_3) * P(w_4) * P(w_5) = P(\text{BOS}) * P(\text{"I"}) * P(\text{"like"}) * P(\text{"pizza"}) * P(\text{EOS})$

$P_{\text{bi-gram}}(w_1, w_2, w_3, w_4, w_5) = P(w_1) * P(w_2 \mid w_1) * P(w_3 \mid w_2) * P(w_4 \mid w_3) * P(w_5 \mid w_4)$

$= P(\text{"I"} \mid \text{BOS}) * P(\text{"like"} \mid \text{"I"}) * P(\text{"pizza"} \mid \text{"like"}) * P(\text{EOS} \mid \text{"pizza"})$

A trained statistical language model is useful for disambiguating between multiple possible interpretations of an input, in cases of syntactic or lexical ambiguity. For example, there's nothing in the English grammar to prevent the phrase "the chicken is ready to eat" from meaning the chicken is waiting for a meal. But we already know this interpretation is un-likely, even absurd, and our use of language would reflect that. A language model's proba-bilities will, too.

 Uses for Language Modelling

Many NLP applications benefit from knowing the relative likelihood of different language outputs. Some everyday examples are listed below:

- Automatic Speech Recognition, also known as "speech-to-text", and the inverse, "text-to-speech"
- Search bar hints on websites and internet browsers
- Spelling and grammar check in word processing programs
- Next word prediction and "Swype text" on a mobile phone

■

Statistical Machine Translation (Task)

Statistical machine translation came to prominence in the 1990s with the idea of taking a dataset of bi-lingual text and, from it, learning $P(e|f)$: the probability that a string f in the source language could produce e in the target language. Note that this task relies heavily on statistical language modelling, as discussed above. Using Bayes Theorem, the task can be represented as follows:

$$P(e|f) \propto P(f|e)P(e)$$

Equation 10.2

Here $P(f|e)$ is called the "**translation model**" and represents the probability that the French source string is the translation of the English target string. $P(e)$ is the "**language model**": a model of the target language, English, from which we can ascertain the probability of seeing that target language string.

Let's clarify that with an example. $P(e|f)$ is, as we know, the probability of seeing e, given f. In terms of statistical machine translation, it is the probability of a source string (say, the French phrase, "le chat") producing a specific target language string (in this case, the English phrase, "the cat"). This $P(e|f)$ is proportional to the probability of "the cat" translat-ing into "le chat", multiplied by the probability of seeing "the cat" in English. For any given f, the best translation $\hat{e}$ is that which maximizes:

$$\hat{e} = \arg\max_{e \in e^*} P(e|f) = \arg\max_{e \in e^*} P(e|f)P(e)$$

Equation 10.3

In early, word-based machine translation, algorithms were trained on parallel language corpora – pairs of sentences translated by humans – and learned to predict the most com-mon translation of individual words. Unfortunately, such datasets are costly and difficult to produce. Furthermore, languages often contain phrases whose meaning is different from the meaning of the individual words, making this an inappropriate approach. For example, "*real estate*" should definitely not be translated to "*domaine nouvelle*" in French, or "*echter*

Nachlass" in German. For this reason, **Phrase-Based Machine Translation** was introduced. The process is as follows:

1. Split texts into individual tokens (unigrams) and "phrasemes" of two or three tokens (bi- and tri-grams). For example:

   "real" (unigram), "real estate" (bigram), and "real estate agent" (trigram).

2. Translate the phrasemes probabilistically using word and phrase alignment tables. Such tables consist of pairs of words or phrases paired between the source and target language; the tables themselves are usually automatically detected as an intermediate step in the overall process (see, for example, [7]). In the following example, the first translation would be chosen, as its probability is higher than that of the second:

   $P(\text{"}der\ Immobilienbranche\text{"} \mid \text{"}real\ estate\text{"}) > P(\text{"}echter\ Nachlass\text{"} \mid \text{"}real\ estate\text{"})$

3. Reorder the translated phrases (also probabilistically, based on learned orderings), if required.

4. Select the most probable translation, using a model trained with an expectation-maximization algorithm like that in Equation 10.3.

Phrase-based machine translation produces more accurate and natural-sounding translations than previous statistical techniques, and was the dominant approach until 2016, when Google introduced neural machine translation (see Section 10.3.3, Neural NLP). Yet it is still used by Google, and no doubt many other translation services, for certain phrases. In fact if you search for a polysemous word (a word with multiple meanings) in Google translate, you can view frequencies for the various possible translations.

Advantages and Challenges of Statistical Techniques

An advantage of NLP tools based on statistical machine learning methods is that they perform well on majority cases; that is, on the most common usages and variations of language. This alleviates some of the burden of hand-writing rules, where one faces a precision-recall tradeoff between majority and edge cases, and thus allows researchers to dedicate more time to augmenting statistical systems with special rules specifically for those edge cases. Statistical models are also quite robust to unknown words and "noisy" input, such as spelling errors, for which one cannot write rules.

Another advantage is that statistical models can produce multiple outputs along with the likelihood of each. This means they can even be incorporated into larger systems which select from the offered outputs. Finally, statistical models can usually be made more accurate by adding more data. This became a huge benefit in recent decades, as the introduction of the internet and social networks rapidly increased the amount of text data available to train on.

But all these benefits don't come for free (a fact also discussed in the "No Free Lunch" section in Chapter 9). First, the effort required to prepare clean, structured, and labelled data for *any* data-driven method should not be underestimated. Statistical machine translation, in particular, requires a high-quality, paired language dataset, which is hard to come by. We may try to mitigate this by automatically labeling our text data using other components in the NLP pipeline – for example, a Part-of-Speech tagger may be used to annotate data for a Named Entity Recognition model – however such components usually introduce their own errors, as they are usually also built using statistical machine learning. Thus, they can put a maximum threshold on the accuracy we are able to achieve.

Secondly, statistical machine learning models require careful feature extraction and selection: curating those aspects of the input data which will be most useful for the model (see the discussion on feature extraction strategies in Chapter 8). This still requires time, manual effort by data scientists, and much experimentation. A similar amount of effort is required to select appropriate machine learning algorithms, and to train and test models.

10.3.3 Neural NLP

Convolutional and Recurrent Neural Networks, and Long-Short-Term Memory Networks

Despite having been invented far earlier, it was in the early 2000s that we saw the rise of using Neural Networks (NNs) for NLP. Early attempts were with **Convolutional Neural Networks** (CNNs), which had previously been used for image processing.

Chapter 8 describes CNNs in detail, so I will here simply summarize a typical CNN-based architecture for image processing, before drawing a parallel to using the same architecture for language processing. The architecture I am referring to is built upon CNN layers with local pooling. In such a setup, input is processed via sliding windows in a CNN layer, whose output representations for each window are then combined in a process known as "pooling", before being fed to the next CNN layer, and so on. What makes this possible is the fact that a unit in a higher layer does not need to see the entire lower layer: a representation of a small window will suffice.

The effect of this pooling is that representations from the input are aggregated into ever-more abstract concepts. More concretely, a window in a lower CNN layer might observe only a few pixels, which are pooled in a higher layer to form a representation of a line, which is pooled with other representations in yet-higher layers to form a representation of some shape, such as an ear in a facial recognition model. A CNN for language processing works similarly. The lowest-level window might observe single characters (unigrams), making this a "character-level CNN". Or it might observe two characters (bigrams) or three (trigrams) or individual words (making this a "token-level CNN"). Intermediate pooling layers will combine these representations into something like words, and still-higher layers will pool them into phrasemes, and eventually, whole concepts. The trained CNN can use these concepts to complete the task for which it was trained.

We have seen that one of the challenges of natural language data is that long-distance contexts influence meaning. The following German to English translation illustrates this:

Wir gingen den ganzen Tag den Berg hinauf

We were going up the mountain all day

Wir gingen den ganzen Tag den Berg hinunter

We were going down the mountain all day

CNNs struggle to take such contexts into account, leading to errors. Thus, they were soon overtaken by **Recurrent Neural Networks** (see Chapter 8), which maintain a representation of hidden states at previous time steps (input tokens) in addition to the current token. This representation acts like a memory, which can be useful in cases of long-distance dependencies. Unfortunately, classic "vanilla" RNNs must propagate their losses through each of their network layers per time step to calculate a gradient. This makes them prone to the **vanishing-** or **exploding-gradient problem**: a situation in which, due to backpropagation over very long sequences, the loss value either becomes so small that the loss essentially stagnates, or so large that it results in large updates to the model, making it unstable. For this reason, vanilla RNNs were eventually replaced by **Long Short-Term Memory Networks** (see Chapter 8). These can learn to balance how much near and distant context they retain, which can help avoid vanishing- and exploding gradients and improve performance, even in cases of long-distance dependencies.

Sequence-to-Sequence Learning with an Encoder-Decoder Architecture

The neural networks outlined above are undoubtedly powerful, but they suffer a significant drawback: they require input and output sequences of a known, fixed length. Since natural language utterances vary in length, one solution when using such networks is to truncate sequences to some maximum length, and pad sequences which are shorter than this. But this leads to throwing away useful information on the one hand, and unnecessarily storing empty tokens on the other.

A better solution is sequence-to-sequence models (see Figure 10.6), introduced and named "Seq2Seq" by Google researchers [8]. As will be explained below, these architectures use an end-to-end approach to map an input sequence to an output one. When training a part-of-speech tagger, for example, the input would be a series of tokens making up a sentence, and the model should learn to map this to a series of part-of-speech tags. A Named Entity recognizer would learn to map the same input sequence to a series of Named Entity tags in the BIO (begin-inside-outside) schema (recall this from the explanation of Named Entity Recognition in Section 10.2.1). Another use case would be slot filling, which was introduced in the beginning of this chapter as the means by which a digital personal assistant, such as that in your mobile phone or smart speaker, can understand and execute your requests. Slot filling is also a sequence labelling task which typically follows the BIO schema, but rather than naming entities, the labels name crucial pieces of information the digital assistant requires to execute your request. If your device has detected that you wish to book a flight, for example, then slot labels will be entities like "B-departure-city", "I-airline", and so on. Finally, in using a sequence -to-sequence model for language translation, input would be a source language sequence, and the model would learn to map this to a target language translation. Whatever the task may be, sequence-to-sequence learning with an encoder-decoder architecture is achieved using two neural networks trained in the following, end-to-end manner:

Encoder: First, the so-called "encoder" neural network encodes an input sequence $X = (x_1, ..., x_{Tx})$ into a single vector representation, called the **context vector**, denoted c. The encoder works one time step (input token) at a time: at the first time step, it generates a hidden state representing the tokens processed so far (that is, just the first token), and passes this on. At the second time step, it uses that generated representation to produce a new hidden state after processing the new token. Of course, this is also passed on, and the process continues for all time steps.

Now that you have an idea of how the encoder works conceptually, let us look at the process mathematically. A hidden state at time t is represented as

$$h_t = f(x_t, h_{t-1})$$ Equation 10.4

This formula indicates that h_t is derived by applying the nonlinear function f (which is typically some kind of RNN, such as an LSTM), to the current token, x_t, and previous encoder hidden state, h_{t-1}. The context vector, c, is generated by applying another nonlinear function, q, to the entire series of generated hidden states:

$$c = q\left(\left\{h_1, ..., h_{T_x}\right\}\right)$$ Equation 10.5

The encoder information flow is represented in the left half of Figure 10.6, where, at time step "C", for example, the network receives the vector for "C", plus the hidden state for "B", which itself will have been influenced by the hidden state for "A". Encoding stops once the encoder has processed the "EOS" token (recall from our introduction to statistical language modelling that this stands for "End of Sequence"). The final encoder output will be a representation of the entire input sequence, with dimensions equal to the number of hidden units in the final encoder network layer.

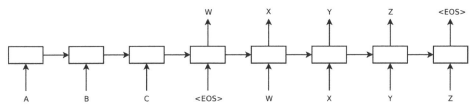

Figure 10.6 The original representation of a sequence-to-sequence model

Decoder: The "decoder" neural network takes the final encoder state and, also working one step at a time, begins generating an output sequence based on learned conditional probabilities for combinations of possible outputs. Importantly, the hidden state representations of the decoder's own predictions at each step are fed back into the decoder, such that it can use them for context while continuing to generate output predictions. This can be seen in the right half of Figure 10.6: when the network outputs "W", this is fed back into the network to aid in predicting "X" (remember "X" could be anything, such as a POS tag or NER label, an output word in a target language, or something else we want to map an input sequence to). This use of previous predictions as clues for generating new predictions is highly relevant for text processing, as language, (and so by extension the tags we may use to annotate language) is contextual: For example, certain POS tag sequences are more or less likely, or even impossible, and knowing what was just predicted is very useful.

Let us again look at this process mathematically. The decoder is typically trained to predict the next output $\hat{y}_t$ given c and all the previously predicted outputs, $\{\hat{y}_1, ..., \hat{y}_{t-1}\}$ (which could be, for example, POS tags, Named Entity labels, or target language tokens). It does this by learning a probability over the output y = $(y_1, ..., y_{Ty})$, using

$$p(y) = \prod_{t=1}^{T} p(y_t \mid \{y_1, ..., y_{t-1}\}, c)$$ Equation 10.6

That is, the probability of the target language sequence equals the product (π) of the conditional probabilities of all output tokens, each which are determined given the previous outputs and the context vector. Practically, each of these conditional probabilities are modeled as

$$p(y_t \mid \{y_i, ..., y_{t-1}\}, c) = g(y_{t-1}, s_t, c)$$
Equation 10.7

where g is a nonlinear function, such as a (possibly deep) RNN, which outputs the probability of y_t, and s_t is the RNN hidden state.

The original Seq2Seq model was used for performing neural machine translation. A four-layer LSTM was used to encode an input sequence, such as "*I like pizza* EOS", into one representation, before a similar LSTM, conditioned on that representation, then computed the probability of the sequence "*Ich mag Pizza* EOS". You can think of these two sequences as replacing the "A B C" and "W X Y Z" examples in Figure 10.6, but note that in their implementation, the decoder was actually made to read the input in reverse: "C B A". This was a clever trick which was found to improve performance, most likely because it reduces the average distance between an input token and its corresponding output token (depending on the two languages and their word order rules, of course). In later improvements, **bi-directional** LSTMs were used. These consist of two LSTMs, one processing the input in a forward direction, and the other, working backward; the outputs of both are combined in some way before being passed on to the remaining layers of the network, such as a final activation layer. The benefit of so-called "bi-LSTMs" is that they can learn from context both before and after the current token, which is beneficial in many languages.

In addition to impressive translation performance, a practical advantage of such end-to-end models is that intermediate steps like word alignment and language modeling are no longer required.

Neural Attention

Despite their early successes, sequence-to-sequence models faced a problem when processing long sequences: the need to compress the entire sequence into a fixed-sized context vector, making it an information bottleneck. Furthermore, information about early tokens will be progressively lost, as new tokens are encoded. This is especially problematic in the case of long-distance dependencies.

Neural attention was introduced to resolve this. Let us explore it by walking through the so-called "Bahdanau attention" architecture, [9], which was first applied to an encoder-decoder model for neural machine translation.

The encoder stage is as previously discussed, with the encoder progressively encoding all input tokens, including the final "EOS" token, into hidden states, which are non-linearly combined into a vector c. Importantly, note that this vector is allowed to be of a variable length.

In the sequence-to-sequence model with attention, the decoder re-defines the conditional probability from Equation 10.6 as

$$p(y_i \mid y_1, ..., y_{i-1}, x) = g(y_{i-1}, s_i, c_i)$$

Again, here x is an input sequence, g is a nonlinear function, and $y_1, ..., y_{i-1}$ are the previous predictions. But now we have s_i, which is the decoder RNN hidden state for time step i, and we have c_i, which is a distinct context vector for each target word y_i. What does this mean? Recall from Equation 10.5 that in a typical sequence-to-sequence model, c (just c, not c_i) is created by applying a nonlinear function to a series of encoder hidden states. Similarly, in a model with attention, each c_i depends on a sequence of so-called "annotations" $(h_1, ..., h_{Tx})$, which contain the encoder's representation of the entire input sequence. The crucial difference is that c_i includes a particular emphasis on the input token i and its neighbors. How is this emphasis achieved? Instead of using a forward RNN to encode each h_i, input is processed by both a forward- and backward-RNN, both of which produce a series of hidden states, which are then concatenated. Thus, each h_i summarizes both the tokens preceding and following i, which is a huge benefit for natural languages, given that both contexts can heavily influence meaning. And since RNNs represent recent inputs better than older ones, each annotation h_i will be focused on the corresponding x_i and its neighbors.

Returning to the context vector c_i, it is computed as a weighted sum of these annotations h_j. The weight is determined by an "alignment model", a, which takes the current input annotation h_j and the previous decoder hidden state and computes a score for how well the inputs around position j and the outputs around position i are aligned. In other words, in the alignment model, a_{ij} reflects the probability that y_i is aligned to (that is, is a translation of), x_j.

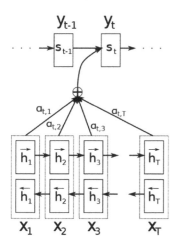

Figure 10.7
An encoder-decoder model producing the *t-th* target word, y_t, given the source sequence $(x_1, x_2, ..., x_T)$ [9]

Thus, the alignment model learns to align words in a manner similar to the word and phrase alignment tables used in earlier, statistical machine translation (see Section 10.3.2). Each a_{ij} reflects how important h_j is with regards to the hidden state s_{i-1} in generating the next hidden state, s_i, and the output, y_i. For example, in Figure 10.8 on the left we see a learned alignment based on attention. The gold standard alignment is shown on the right.

The alignment model is a fully connected **Feedforward Neural Network** (FNN): a simple architecture in which all neurons in one layer are connected to all neurons in the next layer. This FNN is trained jointly with the model and produces an output for the current time step. This is of course a practical benefit, as the historical, intermediate step of creating word alignments, whether by hand or statistically, is no longer required.

Note that this section has described only one possible attention architecture. The interested reader may wish to compare it with another proposal from the same period, known as "Luong attention" [10]. Later, we will also see an example of attention in the famous "Transformer model".

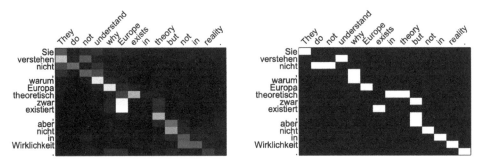

Figure 10.8 Word alignments learned by an attention mechanism (left) with the gold standard alignments (right) [10]

Advantages and Challenges of Neural Network Approaches

Like statistical machine learning algorithms, neural networks can produce highly accurate, robust results, when given enough data. But unlike many statistical machine learning approaches, neural networks can essentially perform their own "feature selection", since the features are the input tokens and the networks learn for themselves how to utilize them. In neural language modelling, for example, the only feature engineering required is to pad and truncate all input sequences to a single length. This saves some time and effort compared to statistical machine learning approaches, although it is of course still essential to properly clean and structure your data before beginning a neural network-based NLP project.

Another benefit of neural NLP techniques is the ease with which we can divide individual tokens into character n-grams, allowing the model to learn sub-word generalizations which can help when handling future, **out-of-vocabulary (OOV)** tokens. Finally, sequence-to-sequence models and the end-to-end learning of higher-level tasks (such as question answering) have another advantage: they reduce our reliance on NLP preprocessing pipelines of individual statistical machine learning-driven components. As we have previously noted, such components can introduce their own errors to the overall pipeline.

Yet the kinds of neural network architectures I have described here also come with drawbacks. While being excellent at the task for which they were trained, they do not always generalize well to new domains. And training a new model for a new task requires a significant amount of in-domain data, compute power, and training time. Thus, many practitioners either turn back to simpler statistical machine learning approaches or look forward to new techniques, including transfer learning and the use of Transformer-based models.

10.3.4 Transfer Learning

Non-Contextual Embeddings (Word2Vec, GloVe, and more)

Transfer learning refers to the technique of **pre-training** a model on one data set and one, usually generic, task (such as language modelling), with the intention to continue training the model on another data set and target task. The reason for pre-training is to transfer knowledge from the initial data set to the later data set. Transfer learning is thus typically performed when the data for the target task are insufficient: We can take advantage of a related, much bigger data set, after which it becomes much easier to train the model on the smaller data set.

Before we move on to transfer learning in the sense with which it is now commonly meant in NLP – unsupervised language model pre-training on large, unlabeled datasets – we should examine an earlier transfer learning approach, which is still used today: dense vector embeddings.

The problem with the simple statistical approaches for NLP outlined earlier in this chapter is that linguistic features such as word counts and POS tags are high dimensional and sparse. For example, if you consider the simple bag-of-words encoding presented in the section on film review classification (Figure 10.4), but imagine each vector is actually the length of the entire dataset vocabulary, you will understand how such vectors end up very large and consisting of mainly zeroes. This is impractical, as the information density considering the amount of storage required is low. Another issue with some of these approaches is that input words are treated separately, thus failing to take advantage of common relations between words and the meaning they lend one another.

For these reasons, NLP practitioners began using dense vector representations of the input, called embeddings. The input may be sliced into individual characters, character n-grams (sub-words) or individual words, giving rise to the terms **character-**, **sub-word-** and **word-level embeddings**. We will stick to word-level embeddings for our explanation.

Word embeddings are numeric representations of words, which have been arranged in **distributed, semantic space** according to characteristics of each word and its neighbors. The arrangement follows the "distributional hypothesis", which says semantically similar words should appear in similar contexts, and dissimilar words should not. For example, the vectors for "tiger" and "lion" should be more similar than those for "tiger" and "spoon".

Word embeddings can be learned jointly with a model for a specific task, to maximize their utility for that task. In this approach, the vectors are initialized randomly and thereafter updated – via updating the weights in a neural network – to better reflect a mapping between the input and output signal. Unfortunately, this requires a significant amount of labelled data and can limit the model's generalizability to new tasks and domains. Thus, it is more common to use pre-trained word embeddings, which can be trained on masses of readily available, unlabeled data. The pre-trained embeddings are used to encode the input for the NLP task at hand, simply by looking up the existing embedding for each input word in the training data. The benefit of this is that the existing embeddings transfer their pre-learned syntactic and semantic knowledge to the new task; thus, this is an early example of transfer learning in NLP.

Two kinds of non-contextual word embeddings which were and have remained rather popular, are Word2Vec and GloVe.

Word2Vec

Word2Vec [11] are among the earliest pre-trained word embeddings. They are learned using simple neural networks in one of two architectures: continuous bag-of-words (CBOW) and skip-gram (Figure 10.9). The CBOW model is trained to predict a target word given a k-sized context window of past and future words around it, without considering word order. Conversely, the skip-gram model has to predict a k-sized context window given an input word. After each prediction, the word embeddings vectors are adjusted based on the prediction error until the model learns to encode semantic and syntactic relationships.

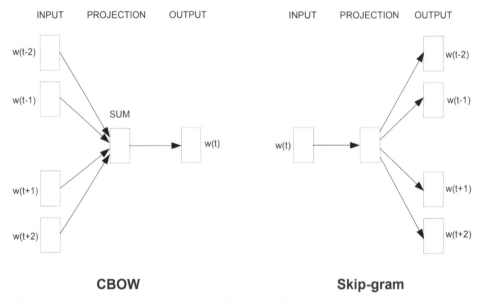

CBOW   **Skip-gram**

Figure 10.9 The two architectures proposed for learning Word2Vec word embeddings: continuous bag-of-words (left) and Skip-Gram (right)

Word2Vec was highly successful and popularized the use of pre-trained embeddings for NLP tasks. Yet the use of a small, local context window could limit the subtlety of learned word meanings and even cause semantically opposing words with similar typical contexts, such as "good" and "bad", to be clustered together. Thus, Global Vectors (GloVe) embeddings were proposed.

Global Vectors (GloVe)

While Word2Vec implicitly distributes its output vectors in semantic space, GloVe [12] makes this an explicit goal. GloVe embeddings are trained by first building a word-word co-occurrence matrix which counts how frequently different words occur adjacently in a training dataset. The ratios of these co-occurrence probabilities are purported to contain the information GloVe vectors must encode. Since these probabilities are derived from the entire dataset, the context used is said to be *global*. As an example, in a dataset consisting only of "It was the best of times, it was the worst of times", a co-occurrence matrix as depicted in Figure 10.10 will be created. It shows that "it" appeared zero times with "it", but twice with "was", while "the" appeared zero times with "the", but twice with "was" and once with "best" and "worst", and so on:

	it	was	the	best	of	times	worst
it	0	2	0	0	0	0	0
was	2	0	2	0	0	0	0
the	0	2	0	1	0	0	1
best	0	0	1	0	1	0	0
of	0	0	0	1	0	1	0
times	0	0	0	0	1	0	0
worst	0	0	1	0	0	0	0

Figure 10.10 Example co-occurrence matrix for tokens in a simple, one sentence dataset

Next, a log-bilinear model is trained with a weighted least squares regression objective to produce word vectors as follows:

$$J = \sum_{i,j=1}^{V} f\left(X_{ij}\right)\left(w_i^T \tilde{w}_j + b_i + \tilde{b}_j - log X_{ij}\right)^2$$

where

- V is the size of the training set vocabulary
- X_{ij} is the number of times word i occurs in the context of word j
- w_i and b_i are the word vector and bias for i
- $\tilde{w}_j$ and $\tilde{b}_j$ are the word vector and bias for j
- $f(X_{ij})$ is a weighting function which should assign relatively low weight to both very rare and very frequent co-occurrences.

The final vectors will have the property that the dot product of any two words' vectors will equal (or be close to equal with) the logarithm of their co-occurrence probability; that is, the goal of the regression objective is to minimize this difference. Since the logarithm of a ratio equals the difference of logarithms, these logarithms of ratios of co-occurrence probabilities can be directly related to vector differences in semantic space.

A problem with both GloVe and Word2Vec (at least in their original implementation) is that word-level embeddings fail to take advantage of morphological and word shape information, such as suffixes and capitalization, which could be useful for tasks like Part-of-Speech Tagging or Named Entity Recognition. This also means that, since it is not feasible to store embeddings for a language's entire vocabulary (or miss-spellings), they cannot handle OOV words (out-of-vocabulary input words will be represented as zeroed vectors or in some other principled way, such as using the mean of the known words' vectors). This is a barrier for generalization and real-world usage, such as in general web- and particularly social-media text.

A greater problem, though, is that GloVe and Word2Vec are **non-contextual**: each word only ever receives one embedding, regardless of its usage in various contexts. Thus, we cannot model **polysemy** – when one word has multiple different, possible meanings – and use this knowledge to resolve semantic ambiguities. This can make even cases as simple as the following, rather tricky:

1. "She likes *to* box" versus "She likes *the* box".

2. "He likes *to* cook" versus "He likes *the* cook".

In Sentence 1., if we were to look only at the non-contextual embedding of "box", it would be hard to know whether to translate this into German as "boxen" (the substantive verb) or "Box" (the noun). Of course, the surrounding context will help the model disambiguate, but there may be other cases where this is not so clear. A similar ambiguity arises in Sentence 2.: should we translate "cook" into "kochen" (the substantive verb) or "Koch" or "Köchin" (the male and female versions of the noun, respectively)? Contextual word embeddings dramatically assist in these situations, as we will see with the ELMO model, below.

Language Model Pre-Training

Just as, earlier, we introduced statistical language modelling before diving into some statistical machine learning approaches, we must now turn to neural language modelling as a foundation for the tools and techniques we are about to discuss. Recall that statistical language modelling is the task of learning a probability distribution over possible sequences in a language. As noted in the statistical NLP (Section 10.3.2), this knowledge of sequence likelihoods can be highly beneficial in tasks which require natural language understanding and generation. Luckily, we can also harness the power of neural networks for this task.

As a simple example, the GPT (Generative Pre-Trained Transformer) [13] model, which will be discussed in more detail later, uses a language modelling objective during pre-training. Taking a context window k, and a corpus of tokens $U = \{u_1, ... u_n\}$, it aims to maximize the likelihood:

$$L_1(U) = \sum_i log\, P\big(u_i \,|\, u_{i-k}, ..., u_{i-1}; \theta\big)$$

by modelling the conditional probability P using a neural network with parameters θ. We will discuss the specifics of this implementation later, in the GTP section. For now, a simple approach to building a language model could look as follows:

1. A context-independent token representation is computed using token embeddings or a character-based CNN.

2. These representations flow through L layers of forward LSTMs, each of which output a context-dependent representation for each token.

3. These top-layer outputs are softmax normalized and used to predict the next token, given the previous tokens. Note that the softmax function, which is often used as the final activation function in a neural network, ensures that all output values are between [0,1] and sum to one.

4. The loss between the predicted and true token is backpropagated through the network, and parameters are updated accordingly.

These steps actually describe a forward language model. A backward language model works similarly, but predicts a previous token given its future context. While both forward and backward contexts can be useful for encoding a word's meaning, it is clearly more desirable to use both. Thus, in the following sections, we will see multiple architectures (ELMO, BERT, and GPT) implementing bi-directional language modelling. In fact, language model pre-training has become almost the standard transfer learning approach in NLP, as the pre-trained models encode some kind of linguistic "knowledge" which has proven immensely beneficial for learning downstream tasks. Furthermore, the language modelling can be based on large, readily available unlabeled data, which can reduce the amount of data, compute power, and time required to learn the downstream task. This is particularly beneficial for tasks and domains where labelled data are scarce, such as low-resource languages.

Contextual Word Embeddings (ELMO – Embeddings from Language Models)

At the time of its release, ELMO [14] set a new state-of-the-art for many common NLP tasks. This was mainly due to its introduction of deep, contextualized embeddings, and its being trained on a then-uncommonly large dataset.

ELMO uses character-level representations and whole sentence contexts in order to learn a different embedding for each word in each of its contexts, and to be able to represent OOV words by understanding subword units. Additionally, its three-layer architecture enables it to capture non-linear relations between inputs and to create deep representations, which can help in disambiguating polysemous words. The training process is as follows:

1. We start with a large, unlabeled text dataset, and use n-gram convolutional filters to calculate context-insensitive character embeddings. Recall from our discussion on Word-2Vec and GloVe that "context-insensitive" means each n-gram receives a single embedding, regardless of the various contexts in which it appears.

2. The character embeddings are fed to L stacked bidirectional LSTMs (biLSTMs), which calculate context-dependent word representations by jointly maximizing the log likelihood of the word sequence both forward and backward. The LSTMs get their bidirectionality by concatenating the features of two unidirectional (left-to-right and right-to-left) models into a bidirectional language model (biLM):

$$\sum_{k=1}^{N}\left(\log p\left(t_k \middle| t_1...,t_{k-1};\theta_x,\vec{\theta}_{LSTM},\theta_s\right)+\log p\left(t_k \middle| t_{k+1},...,t_N;\theta_x,\overleftarrow{\theta}_{LSTM},\theta_s\right)\right)$$

$$\sum_{k=1}^{N}\left(\log p\left(t_k \middle| t_1,...,t_{k-1};\theta_x,\overrightarrow{\theta}LSTM,\theta_s\right)+\log p\left(t_k \middle| t_{k+1},...,t_N;\theta_x,\overleftarrow{\theta}LSTM,\theta_s\right)\right)$$

where t_k is a token at time step k, θ_x is a token representation and θ_s is a softmax layer.

For each token and L biLSTM layers, $2L+1$ representations are generated (the final architecture used a value of $L=2$).

3. The contextual word representations from the intermediate layers of the biLM are then collapsed to one vector using a learned, task-specific weighting of all LSTM layers. This act of combining the internal layers into one is what makes ELMO's embeddings "deep";

Prior to this, it was common to simply take representations from the top layer of a (bi) LSTM language model.

To use these learned embeddings in a downstream task, the collapsed vectors are concatenated with the original input vectors and fed to a task specific RNN. The latter learns the best linear combination of these representations for the task at hand. This method of freezing the model weights to feed to a downstream, task-specific architecture is known as a **feature-based approach** to language model pre-training. That is, the pre-trained representations act as features for the downstream model. It is also a kind of **semi-supervised learning**, as an unsupervised language modelling stage is followed by supervised learning for a specific task.

The Transformer

The Transformer [15] was designed to solve sequential data tasks, such as NLP, while handling long-range dependencies. While many variations exist, this section describes the original architecture, starting with the overall plan and then detailing the Transformer's implementation of neural attention.

Input: Input sequences are represented numerically (such as via byte-pair encodings [16]) and fed to the model along with positional encodings. The latter are required for making use of word order, since the Transformer architecture is non-recurrent (contrast this with an RNN, which processes the input sequentially and implicitly maintains that order throughout). So for learning a task like German to English translation, the encoder will receive the German sentence (embedded in some preparatory, numeric manner) and positional embeddings. The decoder will receive the English translation (and positional embeddings).

Encoder: The encoder consists of $N=6$ stacked, identical layers, each of which contains a multi-headed self-attention mechanism and fully connected Feedforward Neural Network (FNN). The attention mechanism generates an encoding for each input token, which, in our translation example, means generating a numeric vector for each token in the German input sequence. This output undergoes layer normalization [17] before being fed to a fully connected Feedforward network. The FNN output is normalized again and then fed to the next encoder layer. This process generally repeats for all $N=6$ encoder layers, however, note that residual connections around the self-attention mechanism and FNN allow either one to be skipped at any point.

Decoder: Like the encoder, the decoder also consists of $N=6$ decoder layers, each containing a self-attention layer and fully connected FNN. Again, residual connections are deployed around each sub-layer and layer normalization is applied thereafter. The difference from the encoder is that each decoder layer features an *additional* sub-layer, the "encoder-decoder attention layer", which performs multi-headed attention over the entire encoder output (in our example, the encoded German sentence).

In the final decoder output layer, the FNN projects the incoming vector into a "logits" vector of dimensions equal to the training data vocabulary size. A softmax probability is generated for each possible output token, and then for whichever index in the vector has the highest probability (the argmax), the corresponding token in the vocabulary is taken as the final output. In our example, this would be the English word the Transformer has predicted as coming next in the translation. The loss between this token and the true next word is then calculated and backpropagated through the entire network, and training continues.

In Detail: Transformer Attention: Calculating Transformer attention begins with linearly mapping the input tokens to three matrices: the queries (Q), keys (K), and values (V) matrix. Then, each input token in query matrix Q will be compared, simultaneously, to all keys within key matrix K and value matrix V. Each comparison between a query and a key results in a similarity value, and softmax is applied afterward to all of these similarity values (recall that the softmax function scales values to the range [0,1] and ensures that they sum to one). The resulting scores will tell the model how much to attend to the corresponding value for each key. For example, if we are encoding the sequence "The student passed her physics exam because she studied hard for it", then the token "student" is highly relevant to encoding "she" (and should thus receive more attention), while "exam" is relevant for encoding "it". Having calculated these scores, we multiply them with V to produce a final vector as the output of this attention layer.

Note that even from the first pass, the Q, K & V matrices will have been embedded as random, numeric vectors. As with any neural network, the purpose of training is to repeatedly adjust these embeddings until they represent each token's semantics under different syntactic and semantic contexts.

Scaled Dot-Product Attention: The formula for Transformer attention is denoted:

$$Attention(Q,\ K,\ V) = softmax\left(\frac{QK^T}{\sqrt{d_k}}\right)V$$

Putting this into words, the Transformer takes the matrix product of Q and (a transpose of) K and scales this via multiplication with $\frac{1}{\sqrt{d_k}}$, which should prevent the softmax gradient from becoming vanishingly small. This value is normalized via the softmax function and finally multiplied by V.

Self-Attention: In the encoder self-attention layers, the Q, K, and V matrices are all derived from the previous encoder layer. This enables the encoder to attend to all positions from the previous layer for generating an encoding. The decoder self-attention layers work identically, taking the output from the previous decoder layer. The additional encoder-decoder self-attention layer within the decoder works slightly differently, performing multi-headed attention over the entire encoder output: It does this by taking its queries from the previous decoder layer (that is, the queries are the previously emitted English tokens), and taking its key and value matrices from the output of the *encoder* stack. Additionally, a small change is made in calculating the scaled dot-product attention here: future tokens are "masked", by setting the inner products at those positions set to -∞, so that the decoder cannot peek at future tokens when producing its output.

Multi-Headed Attention: The role of a single attention head is to project its input into distributed semantic space (see the discussion on non-contextual embeddings, Section 10.3.4) using a learned, linear transformation. The role of multi-headed attention is to provide the attention layer with multiple "representation subspaces", in which to represent subtle differences of meaning based on context. Thus, each encoder and decoder layer features a multi-headed attention layer with $h=8$ attention heads. The attention function is calculated in parallel for each of these (as per the "Scaled Dot-Product Attention", above), resulting in h value matrices V. These output values are concatenated and multiplied with a trainable output matrix, thus summarizing those h output matrices into a single matrix.

The Impact of Transformers on NLP

The Transformer was the first sequence-to-sequence model to do away with convolutions or recurrence and instead rely entirely on self-attention. This enables parallelization, which can decrease training time while still preserving impressive performance: when the Transformer was first presented, it set a new state-of-the-art on English-to-German and English-to-French translation. In fact, the Transformer spawned a wave of variations which continued (and still continue) to set new records in diverse tasks: first in NLP, and more recently even in other challenges such as image and audio processing. In what follows, I will outline two of the more famous Transformer "spin-offs", BERT and GPT.

Bidirectional Encoder Representations from Transformers (BERT)

As one of the earliest and most successful Transformer-based models, BERT [18] arrived with a number of properties which aided its astonishing results.

By far BERT's biggest contribution is its use of **self-supervised pre-training** followed by a supervised **fine-tuning approach**. In order to understand the benefit of this, let us compare it with ELMO, which (you may recall) is intended to be used in a feature-based manner. That is to say, ELMO's learned embeddings will be added as input features for an entirely new, task-specific architecture. While this enables the transfer of learned meaning from ELMO to new tasks, it requires that an entirely new architecture be built and trained per new task. This can be a barrier to generalization and changing domains. By contrast, with BERT

1. We first pre-train the model in a self-supervised manner using a large, unlabeled (and thus more easily available) dataset. Various training tasks may be used for this step and will be touched on below.

2. After pre-training, BERT's learned parameters and embeddings are fine-tuned: we simply continue the training using a smaller set of new, labelled data, thus further improving all parameters end-to-end for the downstream task. We can even switch from sequence-to-sequence pre-training to classification task fine-tuning, simply by adding a final classification layer and computing a standard classification loss. This dramatically increases the speed and convenience with which we can adapt the model to new tasks and domains.

In addition to the practicalities of BERT's pre-train-then-fine-tune approach, a number of other features helped it achieve impressive performance in a wide variety of NLP tasks.

Firstly, its 30,000 WordPiece [19] vocabulary addresses the OOV-word problem, by deriving "word pieces" from the input words and learning to embed these, too. For example, from the words "walk", "walks", "walked" and "walking", the word pieces "walk", "## s", "## ed" and "## ing" would be derived. This can help with novel words, spelling errors, and learning conjugated forms of rarer verbs.

Secondly, BERT's inputs can be manipulated to allow for training on a wide variety of tasks. One option is to feed input as sentence pairs (along with a learned token embedding representing to which sentence each token belongs), which enables BERT to learn word relations across sentences. This is beneficial for tasks such as question answering and entailment (determining whether one sentence implies another). Another possibility is to prepend each input sequence with a "CLS" token, whose final hidden state can be used to represent the entire sequence for classification tasks, such as sentiment analysis and intent- and domain detection. Recall from the introduction of this chapter that the latter two tasks are undertaken by your phone or smart speaker to understand the domain and nature of your request, such as "domain=shopping, intent=make an online purchase" versus "domain=weather, intent=query the weather for the weekend".

Finally, for cases when the (pre-training) task is language modelling, BERT's creators proposed two new methods for achieving bidirectionality. Standard conditional language models are necessarily unidirectional, as bi-directional conditioning over multiple layers would allow the model to indirectly see the tokens requiring prediction (see the discussion on ELMO, above, for an example). BERT's creators showed that deep, bi-directional relations were more powerful, and they achieved bidirectionality using two novel pre-training techniques on large, unlabeled data: **Masked Language Modelling** (MLM) and **Next Sentence Prediction** (NSP). In Masked Language Modelling, a percentage of input tokens are randomly masked or replaced by other tokens and the model must predict the missing token. Conversely, in Next Sentence Prediction, the model must classify whether the second sentence in a sentence pair follows the first or is a random replacement. The benefit of both techniques is that the model can use the entire bi-directional context around each token, to build that token's context-aware embedding.

BERT's was also bigger than the original Transformer: for example, the small version, "BERT Base", featured $L=12$ encoder-decoder layers and $H=12$ attention heads, while in "BERT Large", $L=24$ and $A=16$. Altogether, its novel features and innovative training regime helped BERT set a new state-of-the-art in various NLP challenges. Furthermore, the code and pre-trained models were open-sourced, allowing BERT to become a great democratizer of the power of AI for NLP.

 Uses for Transformer-Based Models

The state-of-the-art in many NLP tasks is rapidly changing, thanks to Transformer models and, in particular, BERT and the BERT-inspired models which followed it. So rather than pinpoint a current "best architecture" or "best performance", let it suffice to say that Transformer-based models have excelled in many standardized NLP challenges. These include

- **Natural Language Inference:** Given a pair of sentences, predict whether the second sentence entails, contradicts, or is neutral regarding the first.

- **Question Answer Retrieval:** Given a question and Wikipedia passage containing the answer, identify the text span containing the answer.

- **Question Answering:** Construct a well-formed answer given a question and text.

- **Question Pairs:** Determine whether two questions from an open-domain question forum are semantically equivalent.

- **Common Sense Inference:** Given a statement and four possible next statements, choose the one which most logically follows.

- **Linguistic Acceptability:** Determine whether a given word sequence is linguistically acceptable.
- **Textual Similarity:** Score how semantically similar two statements are.
- **Boolean Question Answering:** Given a passage and a question, provide the correct ("yes" or "no") answer.
- **Causal Reasoning:** Given a premise and two choices, determine either the cause or the effect.
- **Reading Comprehension:** Given a paragraph and related question, determine which of a set of given possible answers are correct.
- And many more

■

Generative Pre-Trained Transformer (GPT)

As a precursor to understanding GPT, let us first introduce two important terms: **generative versus discriminative modelling**. A discriminative model is a *supervised* machine learning model which makes predictions based on conditional probabilities. Also referred to as a "conditional model", it can be used for logistic regression and classification tasks, such as sentiment analysis. This kind of model requires labelled data, which usually comes at a significant cost. A generative model learns a probability distribution over a dataset and uses this to return the likelihood for a given output, such as a token sequence in language modelling. This can be done in an *unsupervised* manner using easily available unlabeled data, such as text scraped from the web.

The aim of the original GPT model was to use generative unsupervised pre-training (with a language modelling objective) to learn a universal representation of language, then follow that with discriminative fine-tuning. This should ease the data scarcity problem, while still offering the benefits of transfer learning, where the general pre-training can provide a performance boost for downstream tasks. In fact, this proved highly successful: on numerous NLP tasks, GPT outperformed discriminatively trained models with architectures specifically designed and trained for those tasks.

Let us examine this process in a little more detail. In Section 10.3.4, under "Language Model Pre-Training", we saw how GPT uses a standard language modelling objective to conduct its unsupervised pre-training. The language model itself consists of a multi-layer Transformer *decoder*: that is, the decoder's multi-headed self-attention and Feedforward Neural Network Layers are used to produce an output distribution over all possible output tokens. The model itself is trained via stochastic gradient descent. The fine-tuning stage requires a labelled dataset C, which consists of input tokens $x_1, \dots x_n$, and a corresponding label y. The input tokens are passed through the pre-trained model, and the final Transformer block's activations are fed to a linear output layer with softmax activation to predict an output label y. Language modelling is introduced again as an auxiliary objective during fine-tuning, as this was found to assist generalizability and accelerate model convergence.

What is interesting about this entire process is how it takes inspiration from the various other architectures outlined above. For example, it follows BERT's approach of using unsupervised pre-training plus supervised fine-tuning, yet is similar to ELMO in the sense that

ELMOs representations are fed as inputs to a new architecture. However, unlike ELMO, it uses Transformers and self-attention rather than BiLSTMs. And again, like BERT, GPT's inputs can be adjusted to handle sentence pairs (and even triplets), in order to solve a variety of tasks such as textual similarity and multiple-choice question answering.

GPT was first introduced in 2018. In 2019, GPT-2 was announced as a bigger and dramatically more powerful version, capable of producing realistic-sounding, human-like texts. It also excelled at **zero-shot learning**: a machine learning task in which a learned model must make predictions for inputs that were never seen at test time (see also Section 10.3.4). In fact, GPT-2's creators, OpenAI, declined to open-source the project, citing concerns over the potential for it to spread false information and clutter the web with textual noise. After significant controversy over this decision, however, the model was eventually publicly released.

In 2020, OpenAI announced GPT-3, which gained immediate attention thanks to the staggering 175 billion parameters of the full version. While GPT-3 exceeded the high-performance benchmarks set by its predecessor, this came at a much greater compute cost. Once again, the model was not released publicly, instead being made available first only to subscribers and then exclusively to Microsoft. This, too, attracted some criticism, as it goes against recent trends for open sourcing these incredibly powerful, pre-trained models.

 Uses for GPT: Natural Language Generation (NLG) is just the beginning.

GPT is renowned for its ability to generate realistic-sounding prose. This could be used in many ways: any industry where text is produced and consumed is a potential use-case. However, in the near term it will more likely be used to help automate the creation of simple, repetitively structured texts, such as sport and weather reports. Ideally, this will free up content creators to focus their unique human intelligence on more challenging creative tasks.

More recently, GPT-3 has also been used for non-NLG tasks which capitalize on its extensive language model pre-training. While many of these are still in an early experimentation stage, they point to an exciting road ahead for GPT and NLP in general, with applications like

- Translating text to programming code
- Explaining code as text
- Creating website designs based on written commands
- Retrieving images based on a description
- Summarizing results from customer surveys
- Handling more conversational style search queries
- And many, many more.

◼ 10.4 At the Cutting Edge: Current Research Focuses for NLP

Recent years have seen a surge in interest and progress in NLP, driven by the successes of neural network methods and, in particular, the introduction of the Transformer. Initially, this produced a race for the state-of-the-art, as record performances on diverse NLP benchmarks were repeatedly and rapidly set, broken, and set again. More recently, attention has shifted somewhat away from record-breaking, to producing NLP systems, which are more efficient, ethical, and easier to deploy. This section highlights some current, key focuses in the field.

Transfer Learning from Fewer Examples

As discussed in Section 10.3.4 it is common to take a large, pre-trained language model and then fine-tune it on a supervised, task-specific dataset, updating the weights to create a final, fine-tuned model. Unfortunately, the new data set usually still needs to be substantially large, and if it is not large (or diverse) enough, the fine-tuned model may not be able to generalize well beyond test cases which resemble the training ones. Thus, much research currently focuses on learning from fewer examples.

In **few-shot learning**, no weight updates are allowed. Instead, during inference time, which is when a trained model is actually used to produce an output, we simply demonstrate the new task a small number of times first. The way this looks in practice is: we provide a simple task description such as "Translate German to English", plus a few examples of an input context – the German sentence – and an expected output – the English translation. Finally, we provide a single prompt – a German sentence – and the model outputs a translation. **One-shot learning** works similarly, except that only one context-output pair is provided. In **zero-shot learning**, as you may have guessed, we provide only the task description and no examples. This is the most similar to the way humans perform tasks: usually we are excellent "generalizers", able to complete new tasks using our prior knowledge and without needing any kind of new schooling. However it is also the most challenging, as even for humans it can sometimes be hard to understand an instruction without any examples.

While learning from few or no examples is very exciting, it comes at a cost: without fine-tuning, all knowledge must come from the original pre-trained model which must necessarily be huge (containing millions or billions of parameters). Furthermore, the demonstrations still need to be hand-engineered. Hence, research is going into making this more efficient: possible approaches include using smaller models, for which fine-tuning is more tractable, and generating prompts automatically [20]. Alternative work concentrates on only updating small subsets of the model parameters, such as [21].

Making Models Smaller and More Efficient

Recent years have shown quite clearly that training larger and larger models on more and more data tends to produce better and better results. However, it also drives up the costs of training, in two ways. First, computation is usually done over a large number of high-performing GPUs (Graphics Processing Units), which are expensive to buy or rent. This excludes all but the largest and wealthiest organizations from contributing to research in the field. Second, the energy needed to run these GPUs is significant, thus increasing the carbon footprint for each model produced [22]. And while these costs tend to be increasing rapidly, the rate of improvement we are seeing is slowing down. Furthermore, it can be impractical to work with large models, even when they have been pre-trained for us.

Various techniques are being developed to tackle this problem. Some focus on reducing neural network model sizes. For example, **pruning** involves removing parameters (weights or entire nodes) [23], while **quantization** reduces the precision of neural network weights, which in turn reduces the memory and computation footprint [24]. Other approaches aim to make the training itself more efficient (the available methods are too diverse to list here, but see [25] for an overview). Meanwhile, there has been a general push for researchers to report the size and training costs of their models, aided by new tools which can help calculate the energy requirements for their experiments [26]. This has even led to new, efficiency-related benchmarks.

Scaling down and making models more efficient should help to democratize NLP technologies: the reduced need for data and compute power will reduce barriers to entry into the field, while smaller models are ultimately more practical to deploy in real-world applications.

More Sophisticated Evaluation Metrics

Despite the impressive performances by state-of-the-art NLP models such as GPT, we are still far away from models which truly understand and use language the way humans can [27] (if indeed, this is possible at all). Many NLP tasks have traditionally been measured with metrics such as accuracy, which don't reflect those limitations. Thus, some researchers are pushing for more fine-grained evaluation metrics which can help us probe into what current models are capable of. Others are focusing on testing on problematic cases, for example by filtering out examples for which a model has already demonstrated success.

As a result, new benchmarks are being established to test architectures where they are known generally to be weaker. For example, while the Transformer performs well by being able to observe relations between all tokens in a sequence, it's speed decreases and memory requirements increase as sequences get longer. Google's "Long Range Arena" [28] was thus developed to test Transformer-based models under long-context scenarios, up to the thousands of tokens.

Multilingual Models and Benchmarks

Recently, state-of-the-art NLP models such as BERT have been trained for languages other than English. There has also been work on "massively multilingual machine translation", which involves training one model to translate between many different language pairs. A prominent example of this is Facebook's M2M 100 [29], which can translate between 100 different languages and, unlike similar approaches, does not require English data.

This has given rise to new benchmarks for multilingual models, such as the Cross-lingual TRansfer Evaluation of Multilingual Encoders (XTREME) benchmark, designed to test on 40 languages and nine tasks [30]. Existing benchmarks have also been recreated for other languages: for example, the Cross-lingual Question Answering Dataset (XQuAD) [31] consists of questions translated from the Stanford Question Answering Dataset (SQuAD) [32]. All of this is important work, as many languages are underrepresented and under-researched, and multilingual NLP should make it easier to build NLP applications in languages other than English.

■ 10.5 In a Nutshell

 The Aim and Value of NLP

NLP is a combination of methods from linguistics, data science and AI. Its predominant goals are extracting valuable insights from language data and building language-based technologies which people use every day.

The NLP Pipeline

An NLP practitioner must choose which techniques to apply to prepare her data for NLP projects. The combination of these transformations is referred to as the NLP pipeline. Libraries such as NLTK and spaCy exist to assist with this; this chapter provided some code examples using NLTK.

The Evolution of NLP Techniques

Like many branches of AI, NLP has seen a progression of popular methods, from rule-based (symbolic) approaches, to approaches based on statistical machine learning, followed by neural networks and deep learning. Transfer learning and pre-training models, especially Transformer-based models, have recently and rapidly advanced the state of the art, and continue to do so.

NLP Tasks and Methods

The tasks in NLP are as exciting as they are challenging. They can be clustered under the umbrella of big, broad goals, as in Natural Language Understanding and Natural Language Generation, or they may be more specific tasks, often used as pre-processing steps for a larger task. This chapter provided diverse examples and clarified them via descriptions of the methods commonly used to achieve them, such as Part-of-Speech tagging with a Hidden Markov Model (a preprocessing task), or Slot Filling (a Natural Language Understanding task) with an encoder-decoder neural network.

The Future of NLP

NLP is currently experiencing a surge in interest, from academia to industry. This chapter concluded with a discussion of current research directions, and the implications for the future. In any case, the way ahead is bright!

References

[1] Bird, Steven, Edward Loper and Ewan Klein (2009), Natural Language Processing with Python. O'Reilly Media Inc

[2] Manning, Christopher D., Mihai Surdeanu, John Bauer, Jenny Finkel, Steven J. Bethard, David McClosky. "The Stanford CoreNLP Natural Language Processing Toolkit." *Proceedings of the 52nd Annual Meeting of the Association for Computational Linguistics: System Demonstrations*, 2014, *https://aclanthology.org/P14-5010*

[3] Santorini, Beatrice. "Part-of-Speech Tagging Guidelines for the Penn Treebank Project (3rd revision)." *Technical Reports (CIS).* University of Pennsylvania, Philadelphia, 1990, *https://repository.upenn.edu/cgi/viewcontent.cgi?article=1603&context=cis_reports*

[4] "Agglutination." Encyclopædia Britannica. Encyclopædia Britannica, inc. *https://www.britannica.com/topic/agglutination-grammar*

[5] Xue, Nianwen, William Croft, Jan Hajic, Chu-Ren Huang, Stephan Oepen, Martha Palmer, and James Pustejovksy. "Proceedings of the First International Workshop on Designing Meaning Representations." In *Proceedings of the First International Workshop on Designing Meaning Representations.* 2019

[6] Forney, David. "The Viterbi Algorithm." *Proceedings of the IEEE* 61 (3), 1973, *http://dx.doi.org/10.1109/PROC.1973.9030*

[7] Pal, Santanu, Sudip Kumar Naskar, and Sivaji Bandyopadhyay. "A hybrid word alignment model for phrase-based statistical machine translation." In *Proceedings of the Second Workshop on Hybrid Approaches to Translation*, pp. 94-101. 2013

[8] Sutskever, I., Vinyals, O., Le, Q.V. "Sequence to Sequence Learning with Neural Networks." *Advances in Neural Information Processing Systems*, 2014, arXiv:1409.3215

[9] Bahdanau, Dzmitry, Kyunghyun Cho, and Yoshua Bengio. "Neural machine translation by jointly learning to align and translate." arXiv preprint arXiv:1409.0473 (2014)

[10] Luong, Minh-Thang, Hieu Pham, Christopher D. Manning. "Effective approaches to attention-based neural machine translation." arXiv:1508.04025 (2005)

[11] Mikolov, Tomas, Kai Chen, Greg Corrado, Jeffrey Dean. "Efficient Estimation of Word Representations in Vector Space." arXiv preprint, arXiv:1301.3781 (2013)

[12] Pennington, Jeffrey, Richard Socher, and Christopher D. Manning. "Glove: Global Vectors for Word Representation." *Proceedings of the 2014 conference on empirical methods in natural language processing (EMNLP)*, 2014, *https://aclanthology.org/D14-1162.pdf*

[14] Radford, Alec, Karthik Narasimhan, Tim Salimans, Ilya Sutskever. "Improving Language Understanding by Generative Pre-Training." Preprint, 2018, https://s3-us-west-2.amazonaws.com/openai-assets/research-covers/language-unsupervised/language_understanding_paper.pdf

[15] Peters, Matthew E., Mark Neumann, Mohit Iyyer, Matt Gardner, Christopher Clark, Kenton Lee, Luke Zettlemoyer. "Deep contextualized word representations." arXiv preprint, 2018, arXiv:1802.05365v2

[16] Vaswani, Ashish, Noam Shazeer, Niki Parmar, Jakob Uszkoreit, Llion Jones, Aidan N. Gomez, Łukasz Kaiser, Illia Polosukhin. "Attention is All You Need." *Advances in neural information processing systems*, 2017, *https://proceedings.neurips.cc/paper/2017/file/3f5ee243547dee91fbd053c1c4a845aa-Paper.pdf*

[17] Sennrich, Rico, Barry Haddow, Alexandra Birch. "Neural Machine Translation of Rare Words with Subword Units." arXiv preprint, 2105, arXiv:1508.07909

[18] Jimmy Lei Ba, Jamie Ryan Kiros, Geoffrey E Hinton. "Layer Normalization." arXiv preprint, 2016, arXiv:1607.06450

[19] Devlin, Jacob, Ming-Wei Chang, Kenton Lee, Kristina Toutanova. "Bert: Pre-training of Deep Bidirectional Transformers for Language Understanding." arXiv preprint, 2018, arXiv:1810.04805

[20] Wu, Yonghui, Mike Schuster, Zhifeng Chen, Quoc V. Le, Mohammad Norouzi, Wolfgang Macherey, Maxim Krikun et al. "Google's neural machine translation system: Bridging the gap between human and machine translation." arXiv preprint, 2016, arXiv:1609.08144

[21] Gao, Tianyu, Adam Fisch, Danqi Chen. "Making pre-trained language models better few-shot learners." arXiv preprint, 2020, arXiv:2012.15723

[22] Houlsby, Neil, Andrei Giurgiu, Stanislaw Jastrzebski, Bruna Morrone, Quentin De Laroussilhe, Andrea Gesmundo, Mona Attariyan, Sylvain Gelly. "Parameter-efficient transfer learning for NLP." *International Conference on Machine Learning*, 2019, *http://proceedings.mlr.press/v97/houlsby19a. html*

[23] Schwartz, Roy, Jesse Dodge, Noah A. Smith, Oren Etzioni. "Green AI". *Communications of the ACM* 63, (12), 2020, *https://doi.org/10.1145/3381831*

[24] Blalock, Davis, Jose Javier Gonzalez Ortiz, Jonathan Frankle, John Guttag. "What is the state of neural network pruning?" arXiv preprint, 2020, arXiv:2003.03033

[25] Han, Song, Huizi Mao, William J. Dally. "Deep compression: Compressing deep neural networks with pruning, trained quantization and huffman coding." arXiv preprint, 2015. arXiv:1510.00149

[26] Tay, Yi, Mostafa Dehghani, Dara Bahri, Donald Metzler. "Efficient transformers: A survey." arXiv preprint, 2020, arXiv:2009.06732

[27] Henderson, Peter, Jieru Hu, Joshua Romoff, Emma Brunskill, Dan Jurafsky, Joelle Pineau. "Towards the systematic reporting of the energy and carbon footprints of machine learning." *Journal of Machine Learning Research* 21, 2020, *https://www.jmlr.org/papers/volume21/20-312/20-312.pdf*

[28] Bender, Emily M., Alexander Koller. "Climbing towards NLU: On meaning, form, and understanding in the age of data." *Proceedings of the 58th Annual Meeting of the Association for Computational Linguistics*, 2020, *https://aclanthology.org/2020.acl-main.463*

[29] Tay, Yi, Mostafa Dehghani, Samira Abnar, Yikang Shen, Dara Bahri, Philip Pham, Jinfeng Rao, Liu Yang, Sebastian Ruder, Donald Metzler. "Long range arena: A benchmark for efficient transformers." arXiv preprint, 2020, arXiv:2011.04006

[30] Fan, Angela, Shruti Bhosale, Holger Schwenk, Zhiyi Ma, Ahmed El-Kishky, Siddharth Goyal, Mandeep Baines et al. "Beyond english-centric multilingual machine translation." *Journal of Machine Learning Research* 22, (107), 2021, *https://www.jmlr.org/papers/volume22/20-1307/20-1307.pdf*

[31] Hu, Junjie, Sebastian Ruder, Aditya Siddhant, Graham Neubig, Orhan Firat, and Melvin Johnson. "Xtreme: A massively multilingual multi-task benchmark for evaluating cross-lingual generalisation." In *International Conference on Machine Learning*, pp. 4411-4421. PMLR, 2020

[32] Artetxe, Mikel, Sebastian Ruder, and Dani Yogatama. "On the cross-lingual transferability of monolingual representations." arXiv preprint arXiv:1910.11856 (2019)

[33] Rajpurkar, Pranav, Jian Zhang, Konstantin Lopyrev, and Percy Liang. "Squad: 100,000+ questions for machine comprehension of text." arXiv preprint arXiv:1606.05250 (2016)

11 Computer Vision

Roxane Licandro

"Vision is the art of seeing what is invisible to others"
Jonathan Swift – Irish Writer [30.Nov.1667–19.Oct.1745]

Questions Answered in this Chapter:

- What is Computer Vision?
- What is imaging data and how are these acquired and processed?
- How can we understand and extract information from imaging data?
- What are the application fields and future directions of Computer Vision?
- How can we make humans see what computers see?

■ 11.1 What is Computer Vision?

Computer Vision is one out of three major disciplines in visual computing, beside computer graphics and image processing (cf. Figure 11.1). In contrast to computer graphics, which focuses on creating scenes or visualizations of objects based on descriptive components, Computer Vision has the contrary aim: retrieving a description of visual data (image, video), which makes it processable and analyseable in a digital way. In other words, to *make machines see.* Computer Vision aims to understand and reproduce human vision processes – including object recognition and tracking, motion analysis or text recognition, to name a view – in reality. The third component in visual computing and also a closely connected field to Computer Vision is image processing.

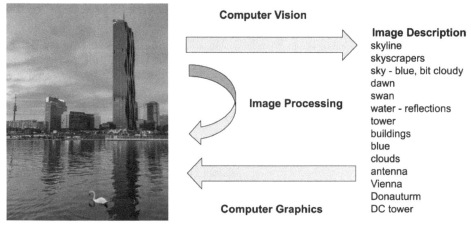

Figure 11.1 Visual Computing – An interplay of three major disciplines: Computer Graphics, Computer Vision and Image Processing. (Image courtesy Roxane Licandro)

Related techniques work on image level to process images in such a way – that they are more interpretable for a specified Computer Vision task. Image processing requires as input an image and provides a processed image as output using techniques like:

- **image enhancement:** saturation or brightness correction, noise reduction,...
- **image compression:** JPG compression (lossy), PNG compression (lossless),...
- **feature detection:** edge or interest point detection,...
- **image combination:** image panorama stitching, multi-modal image registration,...

Image processing supports the extraction of suitable image descriptors for Computer Vision related tasks and processes.

The applications of Computer Vision are for example...

- **industry related image processing systems:** recognition and identification of objects on a conveyor.
- **clinical systems:** tumor delineation and size measurement in medical images for surgery and treatment planning.
- **identification systems:** mobile phones using face recognition for the owner's identity verification to unlock the phone.
- **image based retrieval systems:** to retrieve similar images from a database which match a query image.
- **systems in the research field of artificial intelligence:** robot and computer systems, which can perceive, understand and consequently interact with their environment like self-driving cars.

In this chapter we will first introduce the versatile image acquisition techniques and underlying physical models (Section 11.2). Since Computer Vision focuses on developing and investigating techniques to reproduce human vision, we will also have a closer look at cases when this system fails. We will talk about how images can be perceived differently by humans (optical illusions) and we will have a closer look at how computers can be tricked in the image capturing and analysis processes. In Section 11.3 we will provide a brief overview of image processing techniques, which are frequently used to support Computer Vision techniques. Image compression routines and computational photography techniques, are also discussed. In Section 11.4 we will have a closer look at Computer Vision applications and future directions in this research area and in Section 11.5 we will conclude with a discussion on how the *cycle of vision* closes, by briefly introducing techniques to make humans understand what computers see to solve Computer Vision tasks.

■ 11.2 A Picture Paints a Thousand Words

A picture paints a thousand words. What do we, as humans, actually see in a picture? The objects? The color? The interaction between objects? The fine details caused by the brush stroke? In most cases it depends on what is visible in the picture, on how well our eyes see, on what we are looking for and where our attention lies. We recommend to read David Marr's book *Vision* [1] to get insights into this from a technical but also philosophical point of view. He was a pioneer in investigating human vision and the corresponding neurocognitive and psychological processes.

But coming back to Computer Vision: How does a computer see? Or how can we make a computer see? In a first step toward answering this, will have a closer look at how the human visual system 'captures' images of the world. Understanding the processes of human vision will help us to actually reproduce them, in order to develop Computer Vision systems.

11.2.1 The Human Eye

The eye is an organ which reacts to light stimuli and enables the human to see. If visible light arrives in the eye, information from the environment is perceived. The visual system consists of several components which are depicted in Figure 11.2: The lense of the eye is used to get a focused image of the environment, which is further projected up-side down onto the light sensitive membrane (retina) at the back of the eyes. The retina consists of photoreceptors which are excited by light and trigger the generation of neural impulses by chemical and electric processes. Subsequently, these impulses are transmitted to brain areas for further processing. The retina consists of several layers of neurons, which are connected via synapses. There are two types of light sensitive photoreceptor cells: rods (~100 million) and cones (~5 million). Rods work at a low level of light (night vision), cannot distinguish colors, but make us see grayscale images in low-light conditions, i.e. are responsible for monochrome vision. The cones are not as light sensitive as rods and are involved in the color seeing process. Three different types of cones exist (trichromatic vision), which respond to different wavelengths of the visible light (long-wavelength (L cones)): 564–580 nm, middle-wavelength (M cones): 534–545 nm, and short-wavelength: 420–440 nm (S cones)) and are seated around the fovea centralis.

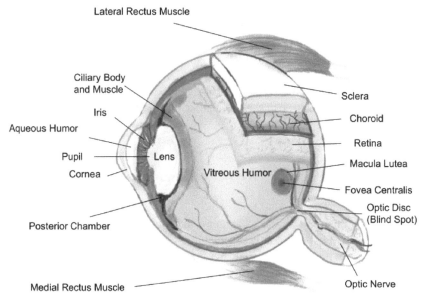

Figure 11.2 Schematic illustration of the human eye and its components. (Image courtesy Roxane Licandro)

Color is perceived through the combination of stimuli of cone cells and the difference in the signals received from the cone types. This process ensures color constancy, which results in the effect that under varying illumination conditions, color is perceived relatively constantly. The luminance perception of the human retina uses M and L cone cells combined during daylight vision, which are most sensitive to green light. The fovea centralis lies in the center of the macula lutea, the sharpest area of vision. Around 50 % of nerve fibers propagate impulses exciting at the fovea to the corresponding brain areas, the remaining 50 % of fibers forward impulses from retinal receptors [2].

When the Human Vision System 'Fails' – Optical Illusions

The human vision system is not perfect. Optical illusions, double interpretations as well as inconsistencies show the fallibility of it. Figure 11.3 provides some examples of optical illusions: On the left side we see some optical illusions regarding length (called a Müller-Lyer Illusion). The purple and blue lines appear to be shorter in the first row in comparison to the lines in the second row, although all lines have the same length [3]. On the right we have an Ebbinghaus Illusion. The purple circle has exactly the same size, although the right one is perceived of as bigger, which is triggered by the size and position of the surrounding circles [4]. Humans can also be tricked in their perception of grayness levels. In the middle of Figure 11.3 we see an example of how gray values are perceived of in relation to the background brightness. The left side of the square in the middle of the image seems darker in comparison to the right side, although it has the same gray value.

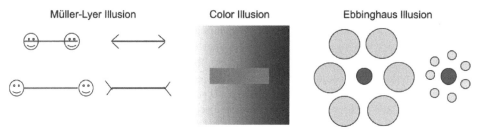

Figure 11.3 Examples of optical illusions: Illusions regarding the length (*left*), regarding the gray value (*middle*) and regarding the size (*right*). (Image courtesy Roxane Licandro)

These are only a few examples of optical illusions, which make the human vision system fail or interpret images incorrectly (Please see [*https://michaelbach.de/ot/*] and [5] for more interpretations and examples). This raises the question: Do we want machines to see like humans? Thus, when creating Computer Vision systems, we have first to reflect on the question: what should a machine see? And how can we make it see that? And which input does the machine understand? Therefore, in the next chapter we will have a closer look at how to capture images from the environment and what should be paid attention to in the imaging process.

11.2.2 Image Acquisition Principle

The development of the pinhole camera (camera obscura) in the 13th century was one of the inventions which led to photography. At the time, painters used it to obtain a 2D projection of a real world object or scene on a paper, which was geometrically correct, to be able to paint more details. In Figure 11.4 on the left the basic principle of a pinhole camera is visualised, which consists of a closed dark room with a pinhole on the front side and an image plane on the opposite side. Light beams originating from an object point (apple), which go through the pinhole, are linearly projected onto the image plane as a smaller up-side down image of the visible scene. By using flipped mirrors the position and orientation of the image on a piece of paper on a glass surface is adjusted [3].

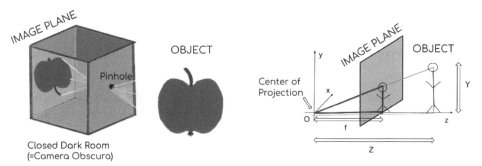

Figure 11.4 The ideal pinhole camera model for perspective projection. (Image courtesy Roxane Licandro)

The underlying model of the ideal pinhole camera describes the mathematical relation between a three dimensional point and its corresponding projection onto the two dimensional image plane. Since no lense is used, the camera aperture overtakes the role of focusing the light and can be denoted as a point O. This camera obscura is the simplest acquisition device, which reflects the geometry of perspective projections exactly. This model is used for the simple approximation of the projection of a 3D scene to a 2D image. The following assumptions are made for the introduction of the equation for perspective projection: (1) The center of projection O overlays with the origin of the camera coordinate system, (2) the optical axis is oriented along the z-axis of the camera, (3) the image plane $I(x,y)$ lies in front of the center of projection to avoid a flip of the image. The schematic illustration for these assumptions are provided in Figure 11.4 on the right. The focal length f denotes the distance between the image plane and the center of projection (in digital cameras this would be the distance between the lense and the photo sensor). The optic axis is the line going through O, orthogonal to the image plane. Z denotes the distance between O and the object in z direction, X the distance in x direction and Y in y direction respectively. The perspective projection of the 3D point $P(X,Y,Z)$ to the two dimensional coordinates x and y on the image plane $I(x,y)$ can be computed using the triangular relations visualised in Figure 11.4 on the right, resulting in the following Equation 11.1 for perspective projections:

$$x = f/Z * X \text{ and } y = f/Z * Y \hfill \text{Equation 11.1}$$

The perspective projection has the following properties: it is a non-linear projection, where in general the three dimensional information gets lost. It is defined as a one to n mapping, since several 3D points can be mapped onto the same position on the image plane, three dimensional lines are projected onto two dimensional lines (exceptions are lines parallel to the optical axis), distances and angles are not preserved and parallel lines are not projected onto parallel lines (exceptions are lines parallel to the image planes) [3].

Image Sharpness

For being able to obtain a sharp projection, the pinhole would have to be as small as possible, leading to less light being able to pass through. This consequently would require an increase of exposure time, which in reality is not feasible. To overcome this, lenses and lense systems are used to improve the imaging quality, but consequently lead to a more complex projection. Rays from an object are refracted by the lense and collimated into a single focal point. If the object lies at a defined distance u away from the lense, a focused image is projected behind the focal point at a distance v on the image plane. In Figure 11.5 these relations are visualised on the left. It can be expressed by the simple lense equation:

$$1/u + 1/v = 1/f \hfill \text{Equation 11.2}$$

According to the definition of Equation 11.2, object points only with a specific distance v from the camera/lense are imaged in a sharp way, while the rest is blurred. In reality this distance is a range (also called Depth of Field (DOF)), which is defined by the distance between the closest and farthest object points which can be sharply visualised. The DOF is influenced by the resolution of the camera sensor, the thickness of the lense and the size of the aperture. The aperture lies in front of the lense, and is a circled opening which determines, depending on its diameter, the angle between rays and the image plane. The smaller the diameter, the fewer rays hit the image plane, the darker is the image for a given exposure time, the higher is the DOF. Beside the aperture, the lense also influences the DOF: the bigger the lense is, the higher is the amount of rays of an object point which hit the image plane. Neighbouring object points outside the DOF range are visualized as overlapping circles, which consequently lead to an unsharp image. Thus, the range in which a sharp image can be created is decreasing with increasing size of the lense, since the size of the overlapping circles increases with increasing lens size. The resolution of the sensor also influences the DOF. The higher the resolution of the sensor, the better the unsharp circles can be imaged, this means the DOF becomes smaller. Also with an increasing focal length of the lens, the DOF decreases.

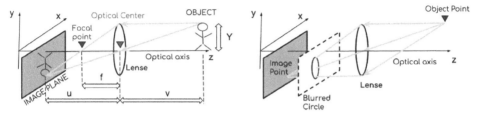

Figure 11.5 Schematic illustration of the projection principle for cameras with an ideal lens (*left*) and visualization of the depth of field effect (*right*). (Image courtesy Roxane Licandro)

Digital Image Resolution

The term "image resolution" is used to express the achievable grade of detail in an image. Four different kinds of resolutions can be defined:

- **Radiometric resolution:** This determines the system's ability to differentiate between brightness levels and is defined by the number of gray levels or Bits (8 Bits ~2^8 = 256 gray levels). The human is capable of differentiating around 120 gray levels.

- **Sensor resolution:** This is determined by the number of image elements (pixels) in a sensor and is denoted as the number of pixels in a row times the number of pixels in a column (e.g. 640 x 480).

- **Spatial resolution:** This resolution describes the ability of the sensor system to separately capture neighboring object structures. In the field of optics and photography it is denoted as lines per millimeter (L/mm) and describes the minimal distance between two neighboring features or the minimal size of a feature.

- **Temporal resolution:** It describes how many images per second can be captured (e.g. 100 frames per second (FPS)).

In digital cameras with a limited resolution, a conversion of the analog signal (continuous function of time, spectrum or space) to a digital signal (a discrete function of time, spectrum or space) has to be performed. The resolution limit is computed by the Nyquist-Shannon Sampling Theorem, which says that an analog signal can be reconstructed from a digital one by setting the sampling rate at least two times higher than the maximum occurring frequency in the original signal.

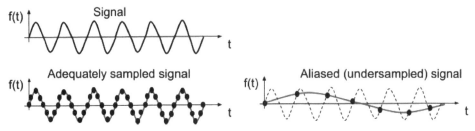

Figure 11.6 Schematic illustration of the Aliasing effect occurring in the case of an undersampled signal. (Image courtesy Roxane Licandro)

If the sampling rate chosen is smaller than this frequency, that is, the signal is undersampled, the so-called "aliasing effect" occurs. This is where the original signal is falsely represented as a low frequency signal. An example of this effect and a well sampled signal is given in Figure 11.6.

Image Color in Photography

In digital photography an image sensor is required to convert an optical image into a digital signal. There are two dominant groups of pixel sensors: (1) Charge-Coupled Device (CCD) and (2) Complementary Metal-Oxide-Semiconductor (CMOS). CCD pixel sensors record light as a small electrical charge in every photo sensor, which subsequently is converted to voltage one pixel at the time of reading from the chip. An additional analog digital converter is applied to obtain a digitized image in a linear way. CMOS consists of photosensors with extra circuitry to each, which convert the light energy to a voltage. The resulting output is in comparison to CCD sensors non-linear, since every pixel is independent from its neighbors.

For obtaining a colored digital image, three strategies are possible: The Field Sequential technique, the three CCD and the Color Filter Array (CFA).

The *Field Sequential Technique* was developed by Prokudin-Gorskii in the beginning of the 20th century.

He applied color filters to filter out red, green or blue specific light wavelength ranges, so only specific rays hit the sensors and produced gray scale images on glass negatives. Figure 11.7 displays examples of Prokudin-Gorskii's red, green and blue filtered images of a scene (scan of 1910 published glass negatives).

A colored image is created by combining the three obtained filter images with the lantern projection scheme he developed. Therefore, a concave mirror was placed behind a light source to direct the light through the three glass plate negatives (also called "lantern slides") of the color filtered images separately, onward into a lens at the front of the projector. For every "color filtered" glass plate negative, a separate projection unit was used. The output of every unit was projected through a filter and superimposed exactly on a screen by additively synthesizing the original range of color.

An improved color separation is achieved with the *three CCD technique* which uses a prism to splitter beams into a red, green and blue component, each of is projected onto a separate CCD sensor. This results in a higher light sensitivity, since the sensor captures most of the light entering the aperture.

Filter Specific Images   **Color Image**

Figure 11.7 View of the city of Perm from the railroad bridge across Karma. (Images taken from the Prokudin-Gorskii Collection at the Library of Congress, published in 1910, Creator Prokudin-Gorskii [1863 – 1944], *https://www.loc.gov/pictures/collection/prok/*).

The most popular technique for acquiring color images uses a *Color Filter Array (CFA)* (also called Color Filter Mosaic (CFM)). Here, the pixel sensors have a collection (mosaic) of small color filters which are positioned in front of these sensors. Since photo sensors detect light intensity only, the filters enable the specification of the wavelength range (color) of the light hitting the sensors. The most common filters used are Bayer filters, which were invented by Bryce E. Bayer of Eastman Kodak. A Bayer pattern consists of 50 % green light range sensitive filters and 25 % red and 25 % blue light range sensitive filters. That is, every sensor pixel has either a red, green or blue filter and is therefore capable of recording one color only. The imbalance between the proportion of sensitivity per color is necessary due to the increased sensitivity of the human eye to green light.

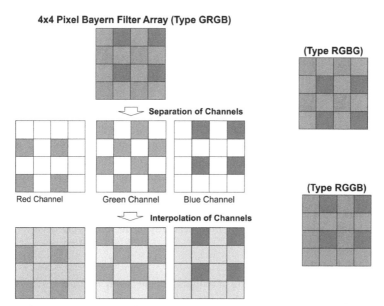

Figure 11.8 Schematic illustration of the demosaicing procedure of Bayer pattern based color image acquisition. (Image courtesy Roxane Licandro)

In Figure 11.8 schematic examples of Bayer pattern types are visualised, while for the pattern GRGB the corresponding demosaicing routine is shown in detail. In the first step the color channels (red, green, blue) are separated and subsequently in a second step the missing information is obtained by a defined interpolation scheme, which varies upon different camera manufacturers [6].

11.2.3 Digital File Formats

After light rays (which may be filtered or unfiltered, depending on the acquisition procedure) hit the sensor, the signal is digitalized to obtain a quantized value for every pixel (in 2D) or voxel (in 3D). A pixel/voxel is the smallest individual element in a 2D/3D digital image and encodes the brightness measured by the photo sensor. A digital image is represented as a finite numeric set.

The storage requirement of a two dimensional digital image with 2^B gray levels and c color components of size N x M (where N is the number of pixels in a row, M the number of pixels in a column) can be computed using Equation 11.3. Thus, for a bitmap image of size 1024 x 768 with 3 color components and 256 levels (2^8 Bits = 1 Byte) the image size is 2.36 MB.

$$\text{Image size} = L \ x \ N \ x \ B \ x \ c. \hspace{3cm} \text{Equation 11.3}$$

Two dimensional images can be categorized into two types: (1) vector images or (2) raster images (e.g. bitmap). Digital images have a fixed number of rows and columns (and slices, in case of 3D images) of pixels and are represented as a finite set of digital values. For making images accessible in a long term, image file formats were defined to be able to store them in a standardized way. Here, we will briefly discuss the most popular image formats, although more than hundreds exist.

Raster Image Formats

Rasterization of an image is a process which produces a grid of pixels to be able to display it on a computer or to print it. Raster image data formats describes characteristics of pixels individually represented as a number of bits. Every file consists of a header storing meta information of the image file and a sequence of variable-sized structures.

- **Open Raw/RAW:** Most digital cameras enable the assessment of all data captured by the camera using the raw image format. Since this information is often inhibited according to image format trade secrets of the camera's manufacturer, initiatives such as OpenRAW image format were designed to influence manufacturers to publicly release these records.
- **Bitmap (BMP)/Device Independent Bitmap (DIB):** BMP or DIB are conventional raster image formats which, enable the storage of 2D digital color or monochrome images of arbitrary height, width or resolution, independently of the displaying device.

Vector Image Formats

For guaranteeing a smooth rendering of a digital image at any desired display size, vector image formats contain a geometric description. This format can be rasterized but also displayed with an analog cathode-ray tube (CRT) technology. Specific types of printers (called plotters) are designed to use vector data rather than pixel data to draw graphics.

- **Computer Graphics Metafile (CGM):** The CGM data format was designed for 2D vector graphics, raster graphics and text and it works for every operating system. A textual source file is used to specify all graphical elements, which can be compiled in three different ways using binary encoding (for efficient data reading), character-based encoding (if a small file size is required) or clear text encoding (if the content of the file should be modifiable and accessible with a text editor). This file format is object oriented and contains information for image rendering. Additionally, in a metafile information is provided for the description and specification of graphical information and geometric primitives.

- **Windows Meta File (WMF):** This file format was designed in the 1990s for Microsoft Windows operating systems with the focus on making images transferable between applications and incorporating vector as well as bitmap components.

11.2.4 Image Compression

Owing to the large number of images required to train and setup Computer Vision systems, image compression is often employed to reduce image size, leading to efficiencies in storage and transmission. Image compression focuses on reducing redundancy in imaging data and can be categorized into lossy or lossless compression approaches [3].

Lossy Compression

This compression type discards data in the compression process. It is built upon the transform coding principle, meaning it transforms raw data into a domain that more accurately represents the content. Repeated compression and decompression causes the images to suffer from generation loss, also called progressive quality loss. For this reason, lossy compression approaches are especially suitable for natural images (photographs). For such photos, some minor loss of fidelity is acceptable in order to achieve a substantial reduction in file size. There also exist lossy compression techniques which seem visually lossless, since they are capable of producing compressed images of imperceptible differences to the original one.

Image formats that use lossy compression:

- **Joint Photographic Experts Group (JPEG) compression:** This is the most popular lossy compression standard for 2D digital images. The adjustment of the compression degree allows one to balance storage size and image quality. Without visual impairment, JPEG compression reduces an image down to a fifth of its original size. However, note that the higher the compression degree, the higher the probability that artefacts (specifically block formation) will occur. JPEG is a suitable compression strategy for natural images, but not for computer graphics or medical data.

- **Discrete Cosine Transform (DCT) compression:** This compression approach works by expressing a sequence of many image data points as a sum of oscillating cosine functions at different frequencies. Since the human eye is weak in detecting the strength of high frequency brightness variations, DCT compression reduces the information amount in high frequency components for reducing the image size on the one hand and to obtain a visually lossless appearance of the compressed image on the other.

Lossless Compression

The defining property of lossless compression algorithms is that the original uncompressed image can be exactly reconstructed from the compressed data. Thus, lossless compression is often used for medical imaging, since loss of image information or the introduction of artefacts (as in lossy compression) could lead to false conclusions in the diagnoses process. This compression technique is also preferred, for example, for technical drawings, comics or archival purposes. The primary lossless compression techniques, from least-to most-frequently used, are Run Length Encoding (RLE), Huffman coding, and the most well-known method Lempel Ziv (LZ) Dictionary-based Encoding. More details regarding these techniques can be found in [3].

Image formats that use lossless compression:

- **Graphics Interchange Format (GIF):** This format is a bitmap image format introduced in the 1980s and still widely used, thanks to its wide support and portability. For a single image 256 distinct colors can be encoded, equating to eight bits per pixel. It is suitable for small images such as icons and simple animations.

- **Portable Network Graphics (PNG):** The PNG format arose as a replacement of the GIF format, since it does not require a patent license and is transferable via the internet. PNG can encode colors in palette-based images with 24 bit RGB or 32 bit RGBA, full-color non-palette-based RGB[A] images and grayscale images. PNG does not support non-RGB color spaces (CMYK) and thus is not suitable for professional-quality print graphics.

Tagged Image File Format (TIFF): This image file format was created by Adobe Systems, who wanted a standard format for images obtained by desktop scanners. TIFF is a flexible, adaptable file format for handling images (compressed with lossy or lossless compression) and meta-data (image size, definition, image-data arrangement, applied image compression or the image's geometry) within a single file. Header tags can also be incorporated into the file. Thus, TIFF is popular for photographers, graphics artist, and in the publishing industry.

■ 11.3 I Spy With My Little Eye Something That Is...

In order to make computers see and consequently to understand and analyze digital images regarding their content, image processing techniques are required. In this section we will give a brief overview of techniques used to extract image features of interest. A more detailed summary of these techniques can be found in [3].

An image feature is a mathematical way to describe an image or part of it in a more distinctive way in comparison to pure pixel values. The extraction of image features depends on the task a Computer Vision system is going to perform, such as identification of a face, object classification or hand-writing recognition. The detection of features is based on identifying points in a digital image at which the image brightness has discontinuities, that is, changes sharply.

We can differentiate between local and global features: local features describe a set of small image regions (e.g. the mouth, nose and eye region in an image of a face), and global features describe the whole image (e.g. the gray value histogram). For obtaining local features, the first step is to detect interest points (or keypoints) and determine the scaling. In the second step, the extracted features are used to compute a feature vector, which characterizes the local visual appearance.

In this section we will briefly discuss specific image feature extraction techniques, spanning from edge detection and interest point detection to approaches of computational photography like image inpainting, image warping or HDR.

Edge Detection

Edge detection plays an important role in the field of Computer Vision. Feature extraction using edge detection involves identifying points in a digital image at which the image brightness has discontinuities. These sharp changes in image brightness reflect property changes of the world and capture events of interest, which can be the following:

- Discontinuities in depth
- Discontinuities in surface orientation
- Changes in texture or material properties
- Variations in illuminations of a scene

The application of an edge filter to an image provides in the ideal case the boundaries of objects or surface markings, represented by a set of connected curves. In Figure 11.9 an example of edges which have been estimated by the Sobel edge detector is shown.

Figure 11.9 Example of detected edges (*right*) by applying a Sobel filter to the image on the left. (Image courtesy Roxane Licandro)

Edge detection can be thought of as a filtering process, since it reduces the amount of data that has to be processed by removing less relevant image properties. Edge detection approaches can be categorized into two main groups:

1. **Search-based Methods:** These approaches interpret edges as extrema of intensity change in an image. This measure of edge strength can be accessed by computing the gradient magnitude and subsequently search for local directional gradient magnitude maxima by computing the gradient direction.

2. **Zero-Crossing-Based Methods:** These approaches interpret edges not only as a region of high intensity change, also as regions where the velocity (second-order derivatives) of these intensity changes, switches from an accelerating to a decelerating condition or vice versa (this is when the second-derivative is zero, also called the zero-crossing). Thus, in order to find edges, zero-crossing-based approaches compute second-order derivatives (using for example Laplacian or non-linear differential equations) and then look for the corresponding zero crossings in these computations.

Corner and Interest Point Detection

The detection of corner points is of interest for many Computer Vision tasks such as object tracking, since it represents a stable and well-defined image feature. A corner can either be defined as the intersection of two edges, or as a point which has two dominant edge directions, different from each other, in a specified local neighborhood. In Figure 11.10 we see an example of the *Harris* interest point detector, where the red crosses mark the points of interests detected by this algorithm.

Figure 11.10 Examples of interest points (red crosses) detected by the *Harris* Corner Detection approach (*right*). The original image is visualized on the left. (Image courtesy Roxane Licandro)

Most corner detectors are not only sensitive to corners: local image regions with a high degree of variation in all directions (e.g. line endings) are also detected and called "interest points". To be able to extract corner points, local analyses have to be performed to determine "real" corners. Examples of Corner Detectors are the Moravec Corner Detector and Harris Corner Detector, while a common interest point detector is the Scale Invariant Feature Transform (SIFT) [3].

11.3.1 Computational Photography and Image Manipulation

The term "computational photography" summarizes the techniques of image processing and manipulation used to overcome the limits of digital photography. It enables novel imaging applications like:

- Unbounded dynamic ranges
- Definition of a variable focus, resolution or depth of field
- Adjustments in shape appearance, reflectance and lightning

The aim of computational photography is the analysis and understanding of scenes, using a high dimensional representation format to enrich the image. In this Section an overview of selected common techniques of computational photography is given, such as High Dynamic Range (HDR) imaging, image composing, image inpainting and morphing [3].

High Dynamic Range (HDR)

Non-HDR cameras capture images at a single exposure level with a limited range of contrast, resulting in a loss of detail in either the bright or dark areas of the scene, depending upon whether a (too-) high or (too-) low exposure setting was used. High Dynamic Range imaging focuses on creating a greater dynamic brightness range, to represent intensity levels of real scenes more accurately and to achieve more contrast in images. Therefore, images are acquired under different lighting conditions (exposure levels) and subsequently stitched together in such a way that both dark and bright areas are represented.

Tone Mapping

Tone-mapping techniques were developed for displaying HDR images on devices with lower dynamic range, such as print-outs, CRT, LCD monitors and projectors. It addresses the problem, by reducing the overall contrast, while still preserving local contrast (image details and the appearance of color).

Photo Composition

Photo composition (also called photo montage) is a technique to create a composite image by combining, cutting and joining different photographs. It enables the creation of an image illusion by simulating a scene with different visual elements from separate sources. It is often used in the entertainment sector in a process known as "green screening" or "blue screening": actors and other props are filmed in front of a uniformly green- or blue-coloured screen, which makes it easier to extract those visual elements and apply further processing to them, such as computer generated special effects.

Image Inpainting

Inpainting is a technique to reconstruct missing or deteriorated parts in images or videos by using interpolation. The missing parts can be caused either by the absence of an object in the actual natural scene (such as in aged, deteriorated paintings); by the introduction of artefacts during the acquisition; or by artificially removing items from a scene. There are various Computer Vision applications to solve this task with sophisticated algorithms:

- Reverse deterioration (e.g. removing cracks and scratches in photographs, dust spots in films)
- Object removal or addition (e.g. removing stamped dates, adding occlusions for confidentiality reasons)

The aim of inpainting is to provide a modified image, in which the inpainted region is merged seamlessly in such a way that viewers are not aware of the modification. In Figure 11.11 an example of image inpainting is provided using an approach proposed by NVIDIA[1]. This approach is capable of inpainting missing regions (white blobs). Although the inpainted regions show deviations from the original image, they provide a seamless reconstruction.

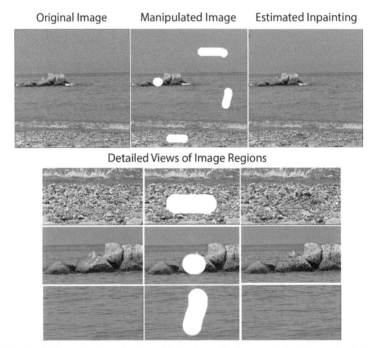

Figure 11.11 Inpainting technique developed by NVIDIA. First row: original image (*left*), image with removed parts (*middle*), inpainted result (*right*). Second row: detailed views of original (*right*), damaged (*middle*) and inpainted image regions (*right*). (Image courtesy Roxane Licandro)

Image Warping

This technique enables the manipulation of an image such that any visible shapes are significantly distorted. A set of points in a source image are mapped (warped) to a corresponding set of points in the warped source image, without changing the color. If the defined mapping function is injective (for every point in the original image exists a mapping to a point in the warped image), a reconstruction of the original image from the warped image is possible. In the bijective case (for every point in the original image exists a mapping to a point in the warped image, but also for every point in the warped image exists a point in the original image) the obtained mapping is invertible. Examples for warps are:

- **Linear mappings** (spatial displacements)
- **Projective mappings** (perspective transformation or homography): do not preserve sizes or angles. Applications are: image rectification (for removing image distortion), image

[1] https://www.nvidia.com/research/inpainting/index.html [accessed 14th of September 2021]

registration (matching of two images for comparing these), camera motion computation between two images of a scene.

- **Affine mappings** (translation, geometric contraction, expansion, dilation, reflection, rotation, shear and similarity transformations and combination of these): preserve straight lines and ratios of distances between points lying on a straight line, but does not preserve angles or lengths.

Source Image   Perspective   Affine
Transformation   Transormation

Figure 11.12 Illustration of image warping techniques. The source image is shown on the left, the perspectively transformed image in the middle and the affine transformed image (scaled) on the right. (Image courtesy Roxane Licandro)

Image Morphing

This technique has been developed to seamlessly change (morph) one image into another by a defined transition function. Its application has become popular, for example, in fantasy motion pictures or animations to depict people turning into other people or animals. The technique is a mixture of transforming the source image to the target image using defined key points and simultaneously fading out the source and fading in the target image. A more sophisticated fading technique is called cross-fading, where different image parts are gradually transitioned instead of the entire image.

Image Stitching

Image stitching (also called mosaicing) is a technique of computational photography to produce panorama or high-resolution images out of a set of single acquisitions showing overlapping views. For this process three steps are required: First, image registration is performed by aligning matching corresponding features in a set of images. Second, image calibration has to be performed to adjust the ideal lens model to the used camera lens model to remove artefacts like distortions, exposure differences or chromatic aberrations (a color distortion, which creates an outline of unwanted colors around objects with highly contrasting boundaries to their backgrounds). Third, image blending is executed to obtain an output projection incorporating the calibration and registration parameters computed. The focus of these techniques lies in providing a panorama image, which appears to be acquired in one step with no color differences, seam lines or distortions.

■ 11.4 Computer Vision Applications & Future Directions

In recent years, versatile Computer Vision systems and corresponding techniques emerged. We will have a closer look at image retrieval systems, which require powerful Computer Vision techniques to find matching images in databases or on websites. We will briefly discuss recent advances in the field of image- and video-based object identification, classification and tracking, and will summarize how these strategies are used in robotics and self-driving cars. As the last part of this section we will dive into the field of medical Computer Vision applications. For this field we will discuss the specific requirements and challenges scientists face, when they are developing a medical Computer Vision system and we will have a closer look at automatic segmentation approaches, anomaly detection and trajectory learning for disease risk prediction. In this section a brief overview of only a subset of popular applications of Computer Vision can be given. If you are interested to read more, for example about the field of 3D vision and depth imaging, or if you want to get more information regarding the algorithmic details of the fields presented, we recommend the publications cited in this chapter or the following books:

- Richard Szeliski, Computer Vision – Algorithms and Applications Ed. 2, *Springer International Publishing*, ISBN 978-3-030-34371-2, *https://www.springer.com/gp/book/978 3030343712, 2022, https://szeliski.org/Book/.*

- Simon J.D. Prince, Computer Vision: Models, Learning, and Inference, *Cambridge Press*, ISBN 9781107011793, 2012 *http://www.computervisionmodels.com/.*

- Chi-hau Chen, Computer Vision in Medical Imaging, *World Scientific Publishing Co. Pte. Ltd USA*, vol 2, ISBN 978-981-4460-93-4, 2014.

11.4.1 Image Retrieval Systems

The most popular image retrieval systems we work with on a daily basis are internet or image database search engines (e.g. *https://pixabay.com/*), which scan websites or image data storages for potentially similar images according to color information provided, text, or description of an image object. Computer Vision techniques are used to compute image features or unique descriptors of found images, and determine how similar these are in terms of defined metrics to the query image and corresponding features.

In the medical field, image retrieval systems are of great interest. Clinical systems store all imaging and medical record data captured in daily routine. Especially in large hospitals like Vienna General Hospital (AKH), around 77,000 stationary patients and 450,000 patients in the ambulatories are treated annually, creating huge amounts of routine data every day [2].

---

[2] Annual Report 2020 Medical University of Vienna *https://www.meduniwien.ac.at/web/fileadmin/content/serviceeinrichtungen/oeffentlichkeitsarbeit/jahresbericht/Jahresbericht_2020-MedUni.pdf* [accessed 23rd September 2021]

Computer Vision and machine learning can help radiologists to retrieve imaging and medical record data. In a case where a patient's diagnosis cannot be clearly derived from the acquired medical scan and/or symptoms themselves, an image retrieval system which has access to the hospital's Picture Archiving and Communication System (PACS), can help to find visually-similar cases and corresponding medical literature of differential diagnosis.

contextflow SEARCH Lung CT from contextflow GmbH (*https://contextflow.com/*), currently searches for 19 different disease patterns and nodules in lung Computer Tomography (CT) images. Figure 11.13 shows the graphical user interface of *contextflow SEARCH LUNG CT*. The current patient's query image is shown on the top left. Radiologists can mark specific regions of interest in the lung (red square) to receive similar cases from other patients in contextflow's Knowledge Base (middle panel).

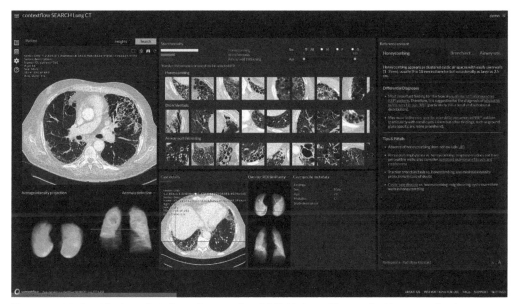

Figure 11.13 Graphical user interface of contextflow SEARCH Lung CT, a medical image retrieval system for lung CTs. (Image courtesy contextflow GmbH)

After clicking on a reference case, the corresponding image and anonymized patient information is displayed along with similarity heat maps, visualized as overlays for the chosen reference image, allowing radiologists to easy compare similar found regions. On the right panel, descriptions, differential diagnosis information, and tips and pitfalls are displayed.

A further field where image retrieval systems are of importance are forensics. Shoe prints, fingerprints or toolmarks are often found on crime scenes and are important evidence of a crime. These can easily be recorded using image-based acquisition techniques and stored in data storage systems. Especially image retrieval systems can help here to match the query image with images in the database. The conditions for acquiring images on a crime scene are not always optimal, since the potential evidence (e.g. a shoe print) is not always clearly visible in its full extent, or may be covered with dirt or other stains. The focus of Computer Vision systems for forensic image retrieval lies in providing robust computations of descriptors of the query object as well as a possibility to find matching objects of the same kind even in a different representation format or appearance.

In Figure 11.14 a result of an automatic image retrieval system for footwear impressions, which was developed at the Technische Universität Wien[3], is visualized. This system takes a query image and searches through thousands of images in a database of the Austrian police to provide similar shoe prints. The query image is shown on the top left and is marked with a grey square. The remaining images show the closest results, estimated by the developed metric, where the images in the green box are the actual matches from the same shoe (side note: the information regarding the actual match is only available for training and evaluating the algorithm and was visualized here to demonstrate the potential different shoe print appearances of the same shoe). Images in the database can come from other crime scenes or be acquired in a defined setup. Thus, 100 % visual matches are never achievable – one of the main challenges in defining image based descriptors in this Computer Vision application [7].

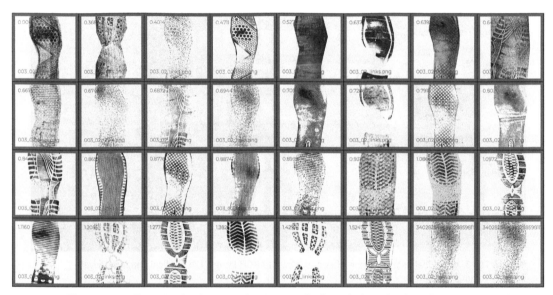

Figure 11.14 Example of an image retrieval system for forensic investigations. The query image is marked with a grey box, the most similar images from a store of thousands of shoe print images are marked with a red box, where the target shoe prints of the query are marked with a green box. (Image courtesy Manuel Keglevic, TU Wien)

While the medical and forensic domains are examples of just two challenging fields, the image retrieval systems have diverse other applications, such as in document analysis or cultural object preservation. In a nutshell, the application of Computer Vision techniques for image retrieval is strongly influenced by the underlying data, its quality, appearance uniformity, reproducibility and object/region of interest to be matched.

---

[3] This work was funded by the Federal Ministry of Agriculture, Regions and Tourism (BMLRT)),

11.4.2 Object Detection, Classification and Tracking

The next field of Computer Vision applications we will present are object recognition and detection techniques, and the classification of these objects or the tracking and surveillance over several acquisitions (that is, multiple frames, as in a video). These Computer Vision techniques are currently deeply researched in, for example, the automotive industry, virtual reality applications, or robotics. We would like to refer the reader also to to Section 8.5.1, where also Computer Vision approaches are introduced using machine learning strategies and convolutional neural networks to analyze images. Here, we can only give a brief overview of possible application fields of Computer Vision.

As one of the popular **object detection approaches,** we would like to introduce YOLO (abbreviation for You Only Look Once). It is able to reliably detect objects (persons, animals, vehicles) in images or videos captured in the wild (that means the data has not been acquired according to a defined setup in a studio) or in art work. Also, with this challenging data the approach is capable to perform this task in real-time. The output of this Computer Vision system is a bounding box around the detected object and the corresponding classification label. The approach combines deep learning, Computer Vision and image classification techniques. More information and technical details are provided in [8].

In the **automotive industry** object detection found its way into advanced collision avoidance systems, which combine radar or laser technologies with camera and corresponding object detection frameworks. The aim of these systems is to detect emerging dangers such as pedestrians, fast breaking cars or barriers on the lane. In this case the Computer Vision system has to work in real time and, in case of danger, set actions immediately (such as activating an emergency braking system). In recent years this concept has been investigated further for the development of **self-driving** cars. Figure 11.15 depicts a self-driving minibus from the Charité Berlin Mitte Hospital campus in Berlin, Germany (*http://www.charite.de/*). It was an initiative by Charité, the Federal Ministry for Environment, Nature Conservation and Nuclear Safety (BMUB) and the governmental public transit service (BVG). The test phase started in the course of the research project STIMULATE (Charité, Peitz) in 2018 with an operator on board, in case the system fails. Since 2019 the buses, equipped with several sensors and camera systems, run completely autonomously on defined campus routes, transporting students, patients and co-workers at a maximum speed of 45km/h.

Figure 11.15 Self-driving Minibus at Charité Berlin Mitte Hospital Campus. (Image taken from *https://pixabay.com/de/photos/fahrzeug-autonom-autonomes-fahren-4759347/*)

A survey of current expert systems and corresponding applications in the field of self-driving cars can be found in [9].

In **robotics,** the object recognition routines of the robot's visual system are additionally connected with action items (such as a mechanical arm) and other sensors (distance measure) to analyze the scene. For example, Max-AI (*https://www.max-ai.com/*) is an artificial intelligence enabled robot that identifies recyclables and other items for recovery. Its Computer Vision system integrates object detection techniques in combination with a deep learning neural network and a robotic arm, trained to detect, classify, grab and sort waste. It supports and speeds up the recycling process and should be a necessary future direction of Computer Vision systems, to support existing efforts to reduce waste and thereby protect our climate.

11.4.3 Medical Computer Vision

Medical Computer Vision focuses on the understanding and analysis of medical images. In this specific field, as in classic photography, the visible spectrum of light is one way to obtain images from the body or body parts (for example dermatoscopy images (a technique to examine the skin using skin surface microscopy) or histological images (a modality to examine the microscopic structure of tissues and cells). Other imaging techniques, based on x-ray absorption characteristics of tissues (computer tomography, radiograph, mammography), magnetic properties of hydrogen molecules (e.g. Magnetic Resonance Imaging – MRI), metabolic or radioactive tracer activity (e.g. Positron Emission Tomography) or the different reflective behaviour of ultrasound waves in the human body, can be used to obtain scans in 2D, 3D or 4D. The challenge in this field lies in making structures outside and – even more importantly – inside, a person visible, without harming the body by needing to open and examine it (exceptions are for example, biopsies or intraoperative imaging). We can differentiate between invasive imaging techniques, whose application to the human body leaves traces and can only be performed to a certain extent without harming the organism (x-rays, CT, PET) and non-invasive techniques like low field MRI or ultrasound, techniques preferentially used for imaging sensitive patients (such as fetuses or infants).

In medical Computer Vision applications (image segmentation, registration, classification or prediction) following dynamics form the major challenges [10]:

- **Interpatient variability:** structures of interest appear differently in scans according to the patient's specific phenotype (observable physical appearance).

- **Intrapatient or longitudinal dynamics:** developmental or pathological processes and surgical procedures can affect the size, position or deformation pattern of the observed region over time.

- **Modality dependent variability:** structures are visualized differently between image modalities (varying image contrast, partial visibility).

- **Imaging protocol and machine caused variability:** depending on the protocols or machines used for imaging, variations in image contrasts, resolution, imaging artefacts and varying field of view can all be expected.

The application of Computer Vision systems in medicine is versatile, where **segmentation** plays an important role. It enables the automatic delineation of a tissue or an organ in scans, which consequently enables the determination of its size, volume, location and change over time, and thus the planning of further treatments and surgical interventions.

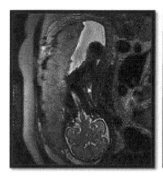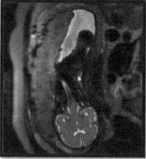

Figure 11.16 MR acquisition of the fetal brain in-utero (*left*) and corresponding annotations of brain tissues (*right*). (Image courtesy Medical University of Vienna)

When it comes to training a Computer Vision system for a segmentation task, the target labels will be annotations of the regions of interest, which are produced by a medical expert. The training process involve the optimization of predicted segmentations by comparing the system's outputs with the target region, using metrics which assess the quality of the segmentation and the overlap with the baseline. In Figure 11.16 a slice of an MR acquisition of a fetal brain in-utero is visualized on the left side. On the right, for the same image, annotations of different brain tissues in different colors are shown [11].

Also in recent years, **deep learning based approaches** are infiltrating the field of medical Computer Vision and have resulted in versatile application possibilities (see [12] for a detailed review). To make these techniques also applicable in the medical field, extensive amounts of data and (depending on the task) also annotations from experts are required. Obtaining segmentation baselines is time consuming, especially in the case of accurate delineations of complex volumetric structures (like the cortical surface of the brain) and consequently not feasible for large datasets. Thus, recently proposed segmentation approaches focus on developing routines which are capable of learning segmenting structures while being trained with scars annotations or even in an unsupervised way (without annotations) only (cf. [13]). A recent review of medical image segmentation approaches is summarized in [14].

Another important application of Computer Vision in medicine is **image registration**. This technique enables the alignment of images or volumes (3D images) according to defined landmarks or regions in medical scans. It provides a baseline for patient-specific longitudinal analysis or population focused comparison. It is also a potential strategy to define reference coordinate systems (e.g. brain atlases, whole-body MRI atlases), to which images can be aligned for comparison or for the estimation of deviations or anomalies regarding this reference. A review of recent medical image registration approaches can be found in [15].

The images obtained in the clinical routine are in most cases bound to defined guidelines and clinical protocols, which vary among clinical institutes, countries and machines. This requirement must be explicitly observed in large multi-sided studies or when datasets are merged. Here, image normalization strategies are required to avoid situations where the

Computer Vision system learns the machine- or protocol-caused variability in the data instead of being trained on the actual variability of the region of interest. Thus, a group of Computer Vision applications in medicine focus on representation learning on the one hand and on estimating a mapping between different kinds of data representations (**domain adaptation**) using unsupervised approaches (see [16] for more details).

Computer Vision systems are also present in the operating room during surgical procedures. Hyperspectral imaging (HSI) is a safe, non-contact and non-invasive optical imaging modality perfectly suited for the clinic. By splitting light into multiple spectral bands far beyond the conventional red, green, and blue colours that the naked eye can see, HSI is an emerging technology that can provide critical, but currently unavailable, information for real-time tissue differentiation during surgery. In particular, this technology can provide both semantic (e.g. tumor vs. non-tumor) and functional (e.g. blood perfusion and oxygenation saturation levels) tissue information which can help to increase surgical precision and patient safety while optimizing resection during tumor surgery. However, HSI data is very complex and requires advanced computer-processing and machine learning for its real-time visualization and interpretation during surgery [23]. Following successful first in-patient clinical feasibility case studies of a real-time intraoperative prototype system [24], Hypervision Surgical Ltd (*https://hypervisionsurgical.com/*) is currently working on converting this novel technology into a commercial medical device for real-time surgical guidance (cf. Figure 11.17).

Figure 11.17
Picture of a real-time prototype hyperspectral imaging system during an ethically-approved in-patient clinical study (Ebner et al. 2021 [24]). (Picture with CC-BY license)

There is also an application field in medical Computer Vision, which makes computers not only see but also foresee which regions have a high risk of developing a disease. In Figure 11.18 an example of time dependent **image-based prediction** in multiple myeloma is visualized [17] [10].

The left side depicts a slice of a magnetic resonance image acquired at the precursor state of the disease, showing the femur with bone lesions (dark dots) and a detailed view of this bone region. One year later the patient was scanned again (middle) with observable bone lesion growth marked in red. The prediction result for that same future time-point, but based on the precursor state, is shown on the right. The approach is capable of locating potential regions of lesion growth, but, since it is a prediction and not a segmentation task (more challenging) exact delineations of the target region are not yet achievable.

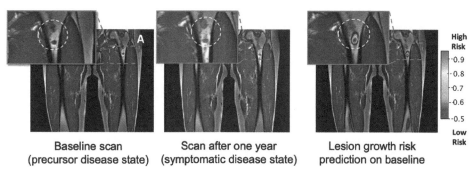

Baseline scan (precursor disease state)	**Scan after one year** (symptomatic disease state)	**Lesion growth risk** prediction on baseline

Figure 11.18 Longitudinal prediction of bone lesion growth risk in multiple myeloma. (Image courtesy Roxane Licandro)

To conclude this section we want to point out- that in medical Computer Vision, the humans being imaged are always the focus of the procedure, and ethics and clinical priorities have to be kept. This includes the careful planning of imaging studies, obtaining consent of the patient for the procedure and for being able to use the data within a Computer Vision system, the secure storage of and access to the data as well as the careful preparation and preprocessing of it. The standards and required accuracy of medical Computer Vision systems are usually higher than those of other Computer Vision fields, since false or introduced imaging artefacts by the system can trigger false diagnoses or treatment estimations, which consequently can cause – in an extreme case – the patient's death. It is of great importance to obtain reproducibility of results of the Computer Vision systems, in order to help medical experts to understand the conclusions the system made. In terms of the evolution of complex neural networks this has become a huge challenge as in all other Computer Vision fields. So how can we make humans see and understand what a computer learned to see? This and related aspects will be discussed in Section 11.5.

■ 11.5 Making Humans See

According to the recent improvements to computational power and the spread of machine learning approaches in the Computer Vision field, computers learned to see structures and properties in images, which we humans are not able to interpret. In order to create and improve Computer Vision systems, we must not only understand our vision system, but also understand what computers see, and which image properties trigger their decisions.

One field of research which can help here is, explainable AI, which consists of diverse techniques to help data scientists and machine learning engineers understand what drives machine learning model predictions. In Computer Vision research, explainable AI techniques can help us humans see what Computer Vision systems and the underlying neural networks see. Neural networks have been seen as black boxes, owing to their high complexity and immense numbers of parameters. With explainable AI it is possible to map the complexity of Computer Vision systems back to the image domain, which makes it interpretable for humans and consequently understandable and also controllable. More detailed information regarding explainable AI in the Computer Vision field can be found in [18] and in Section 18.4.3.

Deep Fakes and Manipulation of the Humans' Visual Perception

We have now arrived at a point where we have not only trained computers to see, but also to use this knowledge to reproduce scenes, image features and sequences of images (videos), based on their observations. Image and video manipulation has been widely and critically discussed in the past and was recently pushed to the next level by the hot topic of so-called *Deep Fakes*. This is a Computer Vision technique that enables the learning of visual patterns from images or videos in order to produce novel images or videos, which are perceived as 'realistic' looking by humans. Initially this technique was used for entertainment. In [19] a research team from Samsung AI trained a Computer Vision system to learn talking head movement patterns extracted from videos and apply these on static images, such as a painting of the Mona Lisa from Leonardo da Vinci. While on the one hand it seems entertaining, on the other hand it poses a potential danger: fake videos could be, for example, used as false evidence in criminal cases, or as political propaganda to manipulate public [20].

Recently, Computer Vision systems have been developed with a focus on detecting of deep fakes using for example encoded biological signals in images [21] or aural and oral dynamics [22].

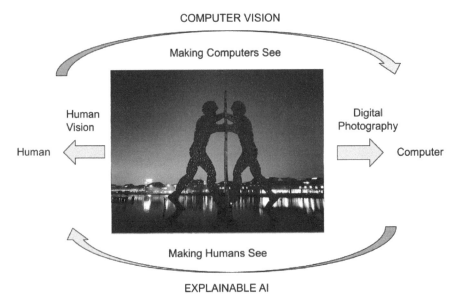

Figure 11.19 Schematic simplified illustration of the vision cycle – interaction of computers and humans in the vision process. (Image courtesy Roxane Licandro)

And here we are, closing the *vision cycle* as depicted in Figure 11.19. One open question still remains: if we let computers see like humans, or, consequently if computers understand how humans see, can we still believe what we see? The key to responsibility and thoughtful research will always be the humans in between.

■ 11.6 In a Nutshell

In recent years Computer Vision systems have received increased attention in a variety of fields (medicine, forensics, entertainment, surveillance, photography) triggered by the development of powerful machine learning techniques to make computers see. This task requires first the understanding of the human visual system to be able to remodel it for machines. In this chapter we learned about the basic image acquisition procedures and underlying models, to better understand the complexity and potential sources of artefacts or the source of false interpretations in images. A closed and important field to Computer Vision is image processing. Basic image feature extraction techniques were explained, and techniques of computational photography were introduced. This chapter concluded with an outline of Computer Vision applications and future directions. We got an insight into the challenges image retrieval systems phase when finding a matching image in a data storage for a specific query, how object detection and classification can help to protect the climate, and in which ways Computer Vision systems make a difference in medicine, by supporting the clinical and radiological workflow.

In the end we have to keep the human in focus when creating Computer Vision systems. The responsibility for how we use these systems (deep fakes) remains with us, particularly now as we close the vision cycle, and computers have learned to see.

■

References

[1] D. Marr, Vision, *MIT Press Cambridge Massachusetts US*, 2010, ISBN 9780262514620

[2] D. A. Atchison, George Smith, Chapter 1 – The human eye: an overview, Editor(s): David A. Atchison, George Smith, Optics of the Human Eye, *Butterworth-Heinemann*, Pages 3–10, 2000, ISBN 9780750637756, *https://doi.org/10.1016/B978-0-7506-3775-6.50005-5*

[3] R. Szeliski, Computer Vision – Algorithms and Applications Ed. 2, *Springer International Publishing*, 2022, ISBN 978-3-030-34371-2, *https://www.springer.com/gp/book/9783030343712*

[4] H.Y. Im, S.C. Chong, Computation of mean size is based on perceived size. *Attention, Perception, & Psychophysics*, 71, 375–384, 2009, *https://doi.org/10.3758/APP.71.2.375*

[5] P. Wenderoth, Visual Illusions. In: Binder M.D., Hirokawa N., Windhorst U. (eds) Encyclopedia of Neuroscience. *Springer, Berlin, Heidelberg*, 2009, *https://doi.org/10.1007/978-3-540-29678-2_6356*

[6] D. Alleysson, S. Susstrunk and J. Herault, "Linear demosaicing inspired by the human visual system," in *IEEE Transactions on Image Processing*, vol. 14, no. 4, pp. 439–449, 2005, *http://doi.org/10.1109/TIP.2004.841200*

[7] M. Keglevic, R. and Sablatnig, Retrieval of striated toolmarks using convolutional neural networks. *IET Comput. Vis.*, 11: 613–619, 2017, *https://doi.org/10.1049/iet-cvi.2017.0161*

[8] J. Redmon, S. Divvala, R. Girshick, A. Farhadi, You Only Look Once: Unified, Real-Time Object Detection, *Proceedings of the IEEE Conference on Computer Vision and Pattern Recognition (CVPR)*, pp. 779–788, 2016

[9] C. Badue, R. Guidolini, R. Vivacqua Carneiro, P. Azevedo, V. B. Cardoso, A. Forechi, L. Jesus, R. Berriel, T. M. Paixão, F. Mutz, L. de Paula Veronese, T. Oliveira-Santos, A. F. De Souza, Self-driving cars: A survey, *Expert Systems with Applications*, Volume 165, 2021, 113816, ISSN 0957-4174, *https://doi.org/10.1016/j.eswa.2020.113816*

[10] R. Licandro, "Spatio Temporal Modelling of Dynamic Developmental Patterns", TU Wien, March 2021. *https://doi.org/10.34726/hss.2021.39603*

[11] R. Licandro, G. Langs, G. Kasprian, R. Sablatnig, D. Prayer, E. Schwartz, "Longitudinal Atlas Learning for Fetal Brain Tissue Labeling using Geodesic Regression", *WiCV Workshop at the IEEE Conference on Computer Vision and Pattern Recognition*, 2016

[12] A. Esteva, K. Chou, S. Yeung et al. Deep learning-enabled medical Computer Vision. *npj Digit. Med.* 4, 5, 2021, *https://doi.org/10.1038/s41746-020-00376-2*

[13] N. Tajbakhsh, L. Jeyaseelan, Q. Li, J. N. Chiang, Z. Wu, X. Ding, Embracing imperfect datasets: A review of deep learning solutions for medical image segmentation, *Medical Image Analysis*, Volume 63, 2020, 101693, ISSN 1361-8415, *https://doi.org/10.1016/j.media.2020.101693*

[14] X. Liu, L. Song, S. Liu, Y. Zhang, A Review of Deep-Learning-Based Medical Image Segmentation Methods. *Sustainability*, 13(3):1224, 2021, *https://doi.org/10.3390/su13031224*

[15] Haskins et al. 2020, "Deep Learning in Medical Image Registration: a Survey", *Machine Vision and Applications*, 31:8, 2020, *https://doi.org/10.1007/s00138-020-01060-x*

[16] N. Tajbakhsh, L. Jeyaseelan, Q. Li, J. N. Chiang, Z. Wu, X. Ding, Embracing imperfect datasets: A review of deep learning solutions for medical image segmentation, *Medical Image Analysis*, Volume 63, 2020, 101693, ISSN 1361-8415, *https://doi.org/10.1016/j.media.2020.101693*

[17] R. Licandro, J. Hofmanninger, M. Perkonigg, S. Röhrich, M.-A. Weber, M. Wennmann, L. Kintzele, M. Piraud, B. Menze, G. Langs, "Asymmetric Cascade Networks for Focal Bone Lesion Prediction in Multiple Myeloma", *International Conference on Medical Imaging with Deep Learning (MIDL)*, 2019. *https://arxiv.org/abs/1907.13539*

[18] P. Linardatos, V. Papastefanopoulos, S. Kotsiantis, Explainable AI: A Review of Machine Learning Interpretability Methods. *Entropy*, Volume 23, 18. 2021, *https://doi.org/10.3390/e23010018*

[19] E. Zakharov, A. Shyshey, E. Burkov, V. Lempitsky, Few-Shot Adversarial Learning of Realistic Neural Talking Head Models. *https://arxiv.org/abs/1905.08233*

[20] Judge H.B. Dixon Jr (Ret.), "Deepfakes: More Frightening Than Photoshop on Steroids", *The Judges' Journal*, Volume 58, Number 3, 2019

[21] U. A. Ciftci, İ. Demir and L. Yin, "How Do the Hearts of Deep Fakes Beat? Deep Fake Source Detection via Interpreting Residuals with Biological Signals," *2020 IEEE International Joint Conference on Biometrics (IJCB)*, pp. 1–10, 2020, *https://doi.org/10.1109/IJCB48548.2020.9304909*

[22] S. Agarwal, H. Farid; Detecting Deep-Fake Videos from Phoneme-Viseme Mismatches, *Proceedings of the IEEE/CVF Conference on Computer Vision and Pattern Recognition (CVPR) Workshops*, pp. 981–989, 2021

[23] L., Peichao, M. Ebner, P. Noonan, C. Horgan, A. Bahl, S. Ourselin, J. Shapey, and T. Vercauteren. 2021. "Deep Learning Approach for Hyperspectral Image Demosaicking, Spectral Correction and High-Resolution RGB Reconstruction." *MICCAI Workshop on Augmented Environments for Computer-Assisted Interventions, Computer Assisted and Robotic Endoscopy, and Context Aware Operating Theaters* (In Print), September, 12. *http://arxiv.org/abs/2109.01403*

[24] M. Ebner, J. S.Eli Nabavi, X. Yijing Xie, F. Liebmann, J. M. Spirig, A. Hoch, et al. 2021. "Intraoperative Hyperspectral Label-Free Imaging: From System Design to First-in-Patient Translation." *Journal of Physics D: Applied Physics* 54 (29): 294003. *https://doi.org/10.1088/1361-6463/abfbf6*

12

Modelling and Simulation – Create your own Models

Günther Zauner, Wolfgang Weidinger

> *Don't fall in love with your simulation model.*
> F. Breitenecker

> *All models are wrong, but some are useful.*
> F. Breitenecker

Questions Answered in this Chapter:

- What are the basic methods of modelling and simulation?
- Where can classical Data Science be combined with Modelling and Simulation?
- How are Modelling and Simulation used in diverse applications such as transportation, modern simulation of inventory policy, and infectious disease models and pandemic simulations?
- Why is it vital to choose methods depending on the problem or question, instead of the other way round?

■

The Audience Addressed by this Chapter is

- people with a strong interest in Data Science applications in dynamic systems
- people with an interest in learning what dynamic modelling methods are
- people with real world questions about strategies for modelling the spread of infectious diseases strategies
- people interested in strategy testing

■

■ 12.1 Introduction

The aim of this chapter is to describe the standards in modelling and simulation, with special focus on the description of different modelling methods and their usage. These will be illustrated using a range of application examples, from infectious disease modelling (COVID 19) and transportation simulation, which will highlight both model calibration and discrete process simulation to simulation of inventory policy. In order to show how data science is integrated in the modelling process and in the interpretation of results, we will begin with an overview of a modelling process in general. Then we will briefly describe different modelling methods and their advantages and disadvantages. The subsequent sections will explain how to handle a model from parametrization and calibration to verification, validation and, finally, to simulation experiments and scenarios that provide results.

Besides building the model, the running of simulation models is essential. A simulation executes the model with a defined parametrization, enabling you to validate the logic of your behavioral model. Analyzing the simulation results, its graphical interpretation, and classical statistics are all part of the realization of a modelling and simulation project. So too is the explanation of simulation results based on a (high) number of simulation runs of a model with stochastic parameters.

Constraints Regarding Methods in Focus

All systems, both natural and man-made, are dynamic in the sense that they exist in the real world, which evolves in time. Mathematical models of such systems would be naturally viewed as dynamic, given that they evolve over time and therefore incorporate time. However, it is often useful to make an approximation, ignoring time dependence in a system. Such a system model is called "static".

The concept of a model can be declared as dynamic if it includes a continuous time-dependent component. The word "dynamic" is derived from the Greek word *dynamis*, meaning "force" and "power", with dynamics being the time-dependent interplay between forces. Time can be included explicitly as a variable in a mathematical formula or be present indirectly, for example as a time derivative or as events occurring at certain points in time. By contrast, static models are defined without involving time. Static models are often used to describe systems in steady-state or equilibrium situations.

In the following chapter, the focus lies solely on the dynamic modelling of systems. Static models are often based on classical statistics and, therefore, will not be discussed here. Similarly, the scientific field of partial differential equations (PDEs) is beyond the scope of this book, since the various PDEs belong to physical fields where a profound level of theory is needed to understand the methods. Nevertheless, a short summary and some basic references are given [1-5].

A partial differential equation (PDE) is a mathematical equation that involves multiple independent variables, an unknown function that is dependent on those variables, and partial derivatives of the unknown function with respect to the independent variables. PDEs are commonly used to describe the systems behavior over time of multidimensional systems in physics and engineering. But there are also applications in finance and market analyses.

Some PDEs have exact solutions, but in general, numerical approximation solutions are necessary. Which numerical standard method to use depends strongly on the underlying described system, which is defined by a PDE, and the domain and required level of detail of the research question. The finite difference method, for instance, works by approximating the derivatives in the PDE and then, using a large number of incremental values of the independent variables, calculates the unknown function at each of those values.

The finite difference method is often regarded as the simplest method to learn and use. The finite element and finite volume methods are widely used in electro technics and fluid simulation. Multigrid methods are also a standard method in application. In general, PDE modelling and simulation can be seen as a separate working area and scientific discipline, which is not a part of this chapter.

■ 12.2 General Aspects

When a problem occurs, usually a question is raised about possible solutions or methods for the evaluation. Information is collected, analyzed and, together with experience, a decision is made.

Models are one of these possible solutions and may be especially appropriate if there is too little evidence and data on the possible outcome of the challenge to solve. The problem is then translated into an abstract simplification of the real system. The whole modelling process addresses this formalization and abstraction of the problem, as well as the drawing of conclusions from it for the original system, in a necessary and sufficient way.

A mathematical model of a system is a symbolic description using abstract formulation. It uses mathematical symbols and is useless without correct interpretation. Manipulation of symbols uses solely mathematical laws. A mathematical formula confirms the status of a model when symbols and model variables get related to each other. A model is suitable if it answers the questions or was prepared to solve in an appropriate way [6].

Concerning modelling, the outside world contains three different kinds of "things"

■ Neglected things

■ Things which affect the model, but which should not be investigated with the model (exogenous values)

■ Things that are the reason for establishing the model (endogenous values)

The distinction of exogenous and endogenous values depends on the point of view. For instance, a model that should explain the principle of operation of a certain drug in the human body will have a different structure than a model to investigate the cost-effectiveness of the same drug.

■ 12.3 Modelling to Answer Questions

To come closer to the main benefit that can be gathered using modelling and simulation, a formalization of the research question has to be defined. The following structure provides a guide:

1. Formulation of the problem: What are the questions that should be answered?
2. Concept of the model:

Which values are important?

Which values describe the states of the model?

Which are the parameters?

Which values influence the model in general?

Which relations between the values exist?

3. Is the model concept useful? Is there enough knowledge and data accessible to implement the model? Can the proposed questions be answered using the proposed model if the model assumptions are true?

4. Can the model be validated?

At first, availability of data should not have an impact on the model concept. Only if the lack of information makes an implementation impossible, should the concept be adapted. The model concept often suggests an appropriate modelling technique but ultimately, the modeler chooses it.

Modelers have an important role in the whole process. They translate the modelled object to the abstract model and convey the model properties to others. Therefore, their beliefs and foreknowledge can influence the model and the interpretation of results [7]. Each model is just an idealized image of reality. Many exterior and interior influences must be neglected to make the model manageable. It is important to note down every simplification in the model concept and justify them even if it is not possible to provide a scientific proof that certain simplifications do not have severe influence on the model behavior [8].

Translating a problem into an abstract mathematical language consists of several steps, which are shown in Figure 12.1.

Reality

↓

System

↓   Definition of system boundaries

Idealised System

↓   Physical laws, model assumptions

Mathematical Relations

↓   Other mathematical relations

Non-causal Model

↓   Add cause/consequence relations

Causal Model

↓   Identification of parameters

Quantitative Model

↓   Simulation

Model Behaviour

Figure 12.1
Translation of a problem into abstract mathematical language

If any of the steps shown in Figure 12.1 cannot be performed or does not provide the required results, the modeler has to go back one or more steps to rework the model. All successive steps have to be realized again. Modelling is an iterative process [9], which is depicted in Figure 12.2

Figure 12.2 Iterative cycle of modelling

■ 12.4 Reproducibility and Model Lifecycle

If a simulation model is reproducible, it should be able to be made by another modelling expert, repeating the experiment using the same experimental data and methods, under the same operating conditions, in the same or a different environment, on multiple trials. Reproducibility is one of the core values for models used in big projects. While the project lifecycle serves as a starting point, parameter and output definition, documentation, verification, and validation are all aspects of high importance. A variety of tasks can be done to achieve reproducibility and, thus, also an improvement of credibility of a model.

A fundamental principle of scientific work is that knowledge should be transparent, which signifies that the availability for professional discourse should be given. For reproducibility it is necessary to put a focus on how to give and gain input from fellow researchers, which demands a statement on limitations and assumptions within a model. Possible shortcomings will be detected, and assumptions may be questioned. Beneath all the challenging and possibly cost intensive tasks related to achieving reproducibility, one should keep in mind the benefit of these efforts. There is a need to pay special attention to documentation, visualization, parameter formulation, data preparation [10], verification and validation. For detailed information concerning this process, the work of Popper gives further insights [11].

Understanding the lifecycle of the development process behind a modelling and simulation project is essential for talking about reproducibility. The reason for this is that one needs to know exactly what information is produced in which phase of the development process. Combined with parameter formulation, documentation, and verification as well as validation, understanding the lifecycle is crucial to produce reliable and usable results. It is through this, that knowledge confirming hypotheses (rectification) can be gained or wrong hypotheses (falsification) can be identified.

As modelling and simulation can be performed in several domains, depending on the field one is working on, there may be huge collections of hypotheses due to missing information. In some domains, for example modelling archeological transportation pathways or natural disease progression of cancer patients where ethical aspects do not allow to observe untreated behavior of identified cancer cases, one has to mainly build on subjective observations and characterizations of the system instead of given parameters ("Black Box" Modelling, compare Figure 12.3).

In this case falsification of assumptions and hypotheses can be a good research question, for example, to reduce the number of possibilities and the parameter estimations. What sounds disturbing for domains of classical engineering might be helpful and interesting in the field of health system research. So, one needs to stay flexible, open-minded, and not to forget to think in all directions.

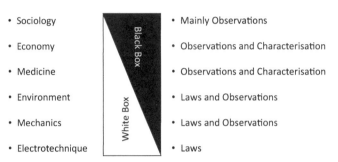

- Sociology   • Mainly Observations
- Economy   • Observations and Characterisation
- Medicine   • Observations and Characterisation
- Environment   • Laws and Observations
- Mechanics   • Laws and Observations
- Electrotechnique   • Laws

Figure 12.3 From White Box Modelling, such as an ordinary differential equation of a well-known physical process, to Black Box Modelling, where the detailed rules are not known.

When looking at functional relations used by the model the amount of a priori information known can vary. In the worst case only the input and output functions are available. The system requires that this input matches with the appropriate output. Without any further information the mechanism behind the correlation is an estimated function. For looking at the correlation between hypertension and the amount of sport a person does, the complete equation system describing the impact of sport on the human body is not available; therefore it has to be estimated by a function or look-up table. The process that is happening in the background is a complete black box (Figure 12.3).

On the other hand, calculating the stability of a broken bone that is fixed with nails is more of a white box. Although some parameters describing bone structure are not known exactly the interaction between the bone and nails can be described using exact physical functions.

As the last example shows Black-Box and White -Box are not two completely distinct modelling techniques but there is a fluent passage from one conception to the other. White-Box models provide more insight into actual dynamics. Physical parameters and system behavior can be changed and analyzed in detail. They are far closer to reality, explainable and therefore better to provide transparency to the results. Their drawbacks are that they need much more knowledge than Black-Box models, are more complex, more processing intensive and the parameter identification can be quite difficult. Nevertheless White-Box models should be chosen over Black-Box models whenever possible.

12.4.1 The Lifecycle of a Modelling and Simulation Question

Lifecycle means the process of developing a model and implementing it, including its parametrization, as a simulation in a well-defined simulation environment. To understand what reproducibility signifies, it is essential to first look at this subject.

At first the basic constituents have to be defined, namely, phases, contained concepts and resulting deliverables.

In general, a modelling and simulation project evolves rather iteratively, more like in a spiral process than in a straight-forward manner. The model normally has to be redefined several times, until it is ready to fulfill the preset goal. Importantly, one has to keep in mind that a model can never depict reality one-on-one but only a (simplified, limited) portion of it.

To make abstractions and assumptions as well as defining boundaries is fundamental for modelers to get a simple and over all computable view, which is yet also detailed and complete enough to answer the study question. That is a reason for the consistent revision of the process, until the right assumptions and abstractions are specified. The basic structure of the lifecycle is listed below, and a generalized view of a modelling and simulation lifecycle is shown in Figure 12.4, which is based on the work of Sargent [12] and Niki Popper [11] and was slightly adapted by the author.

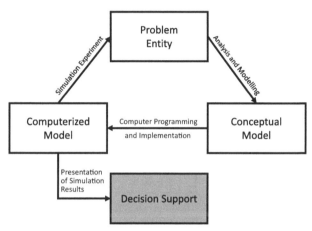

Figure 12.4 Generalized lifecycle of creating a model

Formulated in words, this means

- A problem arises which leads to one or more study questions
- The study questions guide the development into a certain direction with the goal to answer the defined study questions
- The system is then analyzed and modelled, which results in a conceptual model solving the study question(s)
- The conceptual model is implemented in a programming language
- The computerized model can

    either produce new findings, which can lead to a redefinition of the problem and, thereby, cause the need for a new iteration,

    or it can produce credible results, which can be shown by validating and verifying the outcomes

- A credible model can be used by modelers, developers, experts, and users to produce results which reflect reality within its predictive boundaries
- By calculating possible scenarios, the model can be used in the context of decision support.

After execution of the proposed model, the results are validated and verified, and one attempts to check whether the results are reliable. Afterwards, the lifecycle may re-iterate, or refinement can be done. If no refinement is necessary, the results can be taken as a current working model to be used for decision support. Each part of the lifecycle has its own requirements concerning data and information leading to a certain generated output. Referring back to reproducibility, we have to look at the output of some stage of the lifecycle, as this is the part that can be "reproduced".

12.4.2 Parameter and Output Definition

The information you get is the basis for every modeling and simulation study. This input can be manifold - it can, for example, consist of studies, databases, expert knowledge, or statistical evaluations. We may differentiate between general and data information. While general information is non-measurable and often subjective input, data contains quantifiable and rather objective information.

Looking at the lifecycle one can observe that in each of its stages, data and/or general information is transformed into an output. This output is used as an input by the subsequent stages, as depicted in Figure 12.5.

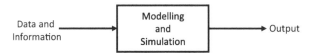

Figure 12.5 Model and Simulation: Data and Knowledge to Output

Data and general information enter the model in the form of parameters through a transformation process. As the term "parameter" is used in different meanings across various disciplines, keep in mind that the mathematical or computer science view is used here.

In Figure 12.6 an extended version of a lifecycle is depicted which is based upon Balci [13, 14]. Here you can get more information about how and when the definition and transformation of parameters, and their parametrization and calibration take place.

The modelling lifecycle starts with collecting general information and data. Both are transformed into structural knowledge about the system, which happens by contributing to the "System Knowledge and Objectives" phase. The data values themselves are not of importance in this phase of the lifecycle; the only essential part here is to determine which information could be useful for the model. Having such an input it may, for example, be possible to define first boundaries.

For the conceptual model, structural knowledge must be transformed into information that the model needs or produces. This means that the modeler tries to establish dependencies between the types of information the model will likely use. Concrete parameters are then defined in the communicative models. These serve a specific audience and are guided by the gathered general knowledge and the format of the data. This phase produces a well-defined set of parameters that can answer the given problem. It is normally a minimal set of parameters, where abstractions and generalizations are already applied.

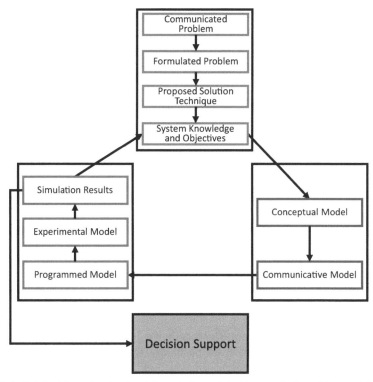

Figure 12.6 Detailed lifecycle of a simulation study reprinted by permission of the publisher

As soon as proper communicative models have been developed with a minimal set of parameters and outputs, the implementation can start. Afterwards, the (mathematical) notion of parameters and outputs are transferred into programming-language specific constructs and, thus, result in the Programmed Model.

At this point in the lifecycle, it is possible to run the simulation. While it is not necessary to sweep through the whole range of possible parameter values, it is necessary to find reasonable parameter values. For this reason, the model is now subjected to experimentation and becomes the Experimental Model.

Depending on the type of parameter under consideration, there are two different techniques for finding reasonable values:

- **Parametrization (known parameter values):** In this case parameter values can be derived from data values which are known a priori. If the data cannot be transformed in a way that all parameter values can be inferred, further investigations are necessary. This can be done by broadening the databases, gaining new data by conducting experiments or others. If this is not possible one has to switch to

- **Calibration (unknown parameter values):** These values must be estimated, assisted by given data (gained through, for example, statistical evaluations, studies, previous simulation runs, and so on). After running the experimental model, the simulation output is compared to a possibly known output data or constraints governing the output which can, for example, be given by experts from the specific domain.

If the simulation model produces an output that appears to be reasonable, the calibration task is finished, and the resulting parameter values are used for further simulation runs.

If the simulation output does not fit, the unknown parameter values have to be estimated again and the experimentation process has to be reiterated, often supported by mathematical optimization.

If calibration does not work, a redefinition of the model might be necessary or one of the known parameter values may have to be questioned. In this case the modelling process may have to start all over again due to a possibly changed knowledge about the system.

One has to keep in mind that in some domains, such as social sciences, imposing constraints on what could be an output is already an essential contribution in research. In that context one can argue that the purpose of modelling and simulation studies in some domains does not primarily lie in the generation of results, but in an exclusion of unlikely scenarios that would possibly enter the scientific thought process and lead to incorrect conclusions. The definition of constraints is a positive side-effect of performing such a study. It may even lead to the insight that a previously supposedly well-understood problem needs to be re-examined and clarified.

The so-called qualitative modelling is in several cases already the benefit that is most important for the decision-maker in industry or research.

In case of healthcare modelling, the problem definition and research question is at best defined by an interdisciplinary board. The benefit of defining the demand and point of view is normally decoupled from data and available information, which is in general the basis for choices of modelling technique . The chosen modelling technique results in feedback about the data needed, the data itself iteratively influences the method and of course information has to be collected if a hybrid model-decomposition or sequential coupling of different modelling methods is needed to solve the problem. These processes are in reality iteratively developed; therefore, the whole model implementation should be realized in modules, so that high flexibility and the ability to be validated is guaranteed (Figure 12.7, [15]).

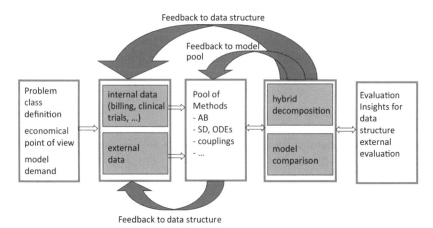

Figure 12.7 Modelling a real-world system in context of health technology assessment. The different steps and feedback loops, starting with the problem definition, followed by data identification and data-type acquisition-based modelling method choosing. Hybrid composition and model comparison are the following steps in high quality interdisciplinary decision support. In the end an evaluation and validation process is defined.

12.4.3 Documentation

Without documentation, reproducibility is hardly possible. There are three forms of documentation commonly used in the donation of modeling and simulation:

1. textual documentation,

2. visualization, and

3. the source code itself, which necessarily needs its own, thoroughly written and maintained documentation.

It is hard to find a way to make good documentation accurately and efficiently in a project team. But there are several helpful techniques, such as always requiring that documentation be written in Basic English. There exist several guidelines, like the ODD (Overview, Design Concepts, and Details) protocol [16].

Visualization is crucial besides textual information when trying to document and validate simulation models and to make simulation models reproducible. The process of modelling, and fundamental structural ideas concerning the model, can often be better presented via visual concepts. Note that visual analysis can also support exclusion of certain hypotheses, possibly even more so than proving with reference to some data.

Visualization includes the data analysis as well as modelling process and structure. In particular, the visualization of the modelling structure can be very helpful in the discussion process in bigger teams, to gain information on dependencies of variables and feedback loops.

The documentation of the source code in a modelling and simulation model is similar to good practice in other software projects. Certain practices should be strictly adhered to, including, the well-known basics like choosing proper names, the do one thing principle, and the don't repeat yourself principle.

12.4.4 Verification and Validation

Verification and validation are processes that need to happen in parallel to the development of the model as well as the simulation. Their very important aim is to guarantee a targeted development of the simulation study.

- **Verification** answers the question "Is the model developed right?" which needs to be asked in a modeling and simulation study. Verification tells us if a model is implemented correctly.

- **Validation** deals with the question "Is the right model developed?" which is another essential research question that needs to be looked at. Validation addresses this task.

While verification and validation are usually performed by the development team itself, a better idea is to have this part performed by an independent team consisting of people familiar with modelling together with people connected to the field of study (for instance, specialists in health care, infrastructure, production and logistics).

A slightly different formulation concerning the processes of verification and validation is addressed by the following questions [17, 18]:

- Is the model specification complete and is the model implementation correct? (Verification)

- Does the model resemble the system under examination and its behavior closely enough for answering the questions of the study? (Validation)

In general, it is not possible to conclusively answer these questions with yes. One can rather conduct several tests trying to falsify the correctness or the validity of the model. Each test the model passes, adds to its credibility. Especially the process of validation should go on while the model is in use, as each additional piece of knowledge and data can allow new tests and, thus, new insights. For example, a model with the purpose of comparing the standard treatment of an illness with a future disease management program should be revalidated when the program is already in use and has produced enough data for a new test.

Though the most important verification and validation tests naturally take place after model development, it is wise to perform them after each iteration step of the modelling study, as this approach can save a lot of time and money. Law [19] explicitly warns against just performing validation tests after development of the model or – even worse – not at all if there is not enough time and money left. Furthermore, independent verification and validation by knowledgeable people who are not part of the model development team adds to the credibility of a model, as model developers have a natural interest in positive verification and validation results [17].

12.4.4.1 Verification

Verification of simulation models does not differ from verification of computer software in general. It is based on a complete and consistent specification of the model. Tests concerning errors in the code and verification of fully specified model parts can take place before the complete model specification is available.

There are two categories of verification tests: static tests and dynamic tests [18]. Static tests analyze the structure and the code of models without execution, whereas in dynamic testing, model execution and the generated results and behavior are used for verification. In detail:

- **Static Verification Tests**

    Cross-Check: A skilled person that has not developed the model (or the concerned part of the model) examines the (commented) code of the model with help of the specification

    Structured Code Walk-Troughs [19]: The implementation of the model is presented in group meetings, which ideally consist of both members of the model development team and external people. The developers present each part of the model in detail and explain the code. The audience can criticize and audit the correctness.

    Structural Analysis: This approach uses a control flow graph of the model structure. The graph is a representation of all paths which the model might traverse during its execution. An examination of the graph can reveal structural anomalies, such as multiple entry and exit points, excessive levels of nesting within a structure and the use of unconditional branches [20].

    Formal Methods: Formal methods try to prove the correctness (as far as implementation is concerned) of a model [19]. When it can be done, it is extremely useful, but these methods are often not feasible for reasonably complex models.

- **Dynamic Verification Tests**

   Double Implementation: Two independent implementations of a model have to produce the same output with the same input and parameter settings. The teams which make the different implementations should of course consist of different people.

   Unit Testing: Each component of the model is tested individually. This is a bottom-up approach, as one starts with the smallest building blocks (for example functions) and tests increasingly larger structures.

   Structured Debugging Walk-Throughs: This is appropriate when code contains bugs which are leading to execution errors. In this test, the model execution of various test cases is followed line by line. It allows the examination of the value of every variable at each state. Thus, the audience can see at which code lines the model execution leads to an error.

12.4.4.2 Validation

Even a correctly implemented model can be a bad representation of the investigated system. Hence, validation is an important part of the model development process. In contrast to verification (where there exist formal, exact methods in theory) there cannot be a perfect validation. To give an example: in order to know whether a model produces exact values for the cost- effectiveness of a medical intervention, perfect knowledge of this cost-effectiveness is necessary. Yet this knowledge is rarely available.

The validation process consists of tests which try to completely undermine the credibility of the model. There are **tests of model structure** (also known as conceptual model validation), **tests of model behavior**, and also **tests of data validity** [21, 22]. Valid data are needed for building the conceptual model, for tests of model behavior and for simulation runs that are used in the decision analysis.

Tests for data validity are limited. Good procedures for data collection and maintenance should be used. Additionally, internal consistency checks and determination of outliers should be used to validate the data. In more detail:

- **Tests of Model Structure**

   Tests of Theories and Assumptions: The underlying assumptions of the model can be tested with statistical methods on data.

   Face Validation: Experts in the field examine the conceptual model to determine if it is correct and reasonable for the intended purpose.

- **Tests of Model Behavior**

   Behavior-reproduction Tests: These tests are one of the most important validation techniques. They consist of comparisons of model and system behavior under various test scenarios with data that has not been used to parameterize the model. The most common method is to compare output variables graphically, however, for stochastic output there are also the possibilities of hypothesis testing and calculation of confidence intervals.

   Comparison with other models: Another test is to compare the model results with results from other valid models that deal with the same question. Such a comparison should also be part of model validation in addition to external validation. The reasons for differing results should be discussed.

If observations from the system are impossible or only little data is available, one can also use other models for the same problem for comparison.

Behavior-prediction Tests: These tests are similar to behavior-reproduction tests, with the one exception that the model should reproduce future behavior. Therefore, they can take place at later times to re-evaluate the model when the future of the system is already known.

Sensitivity Analysis: These tests are important for the development of every model. The effect on model output shows whether the model reacts to changes like the real system does, and if it behaves plausibly in uncommon parameter regions. Furthermore, sensitive parameters must be determined more accurately, as they influence results significantly.

- **Tests for Both Model Structure and Behavior**

Extreme-conditions Tests [21]: The model should work correctly under extreme conditions. It is often quite clear which behavior a real system will show in such a situation. For example, an epidemic disease will die out if the infection probability equals zero.

Boundary-adequacy Tests [22]: The model boundary decides what is included in a model and which parts are not considered important (or where it is considered that a certain level of detail is enough). Therefore, one has to test if there are omitted parts which could have an influence on model outcome. The model passes the test if for no parts a theory can be built which would explain such an influence (in this stage it is a structural test). If a part could still have a significant effect, the model builders have to integrate it into the model and test the model with and without the part. The test is passed if there are no differences in model behavior (therefore this is a test of model behavior).

12.4.4.3 Variability and Uncertainty

There are different types of variability and uncertainty in modelling tasks and evaluations.

For instance, parameter values which are estimated values themselves are often used in models due to missing exact values. They carry an error that should be reported in primary studies, for example as a 95 % confidence interval. This parameter uncertainty and its implication for model results has to be evaluated systematically. This is done through sensitivity analysis. Sensitivity analysis can be performed in a deterministic or probabilistic way.

In deterministic analysis, parameter values are varied over a range (if the 95 % confidence interval is given, this is providing an appropriate range) and the variation in outcomes is observed. This can be done

- separately for each parameter (one-way sensitivity analysis) or
- as a multi-way sensitivity analysis.

All parameters should be analyzed. Probabilistic sensitivity analysis has the advantage of allowing for variation of all parameters at the same time. In this type of analysis, each parameter is drawn from a distribution. The choice of distribution needs to be explained in the model report, a part of good practice in documentation. Distribution parameters should be included. Knowledge about correlation between parameters should be used for the analysis (joint distributions). The results of probabilistic sensitivity analysis can be presented as scatter plots, for example. When performing probabilistic sensitivity analyses it is still recommended to add deterministic analyses to identify parameters that have a strong influence on model results. Deterministic sensitivity analyses can also be used to determine thresholds.

Another type of uncertainty is structural uncertainty. Some assumptions can be parameterized and tested through sensitivity analysis. Testing of other assumptions requires changes in the model structure or additions to the model. Structural uncertainty should be tested as far as possible.

■ 12.5 Methods

Based on the theory explained in the first part of the chapter, the next step is the definition and description of standard modelling methods used in a broad range of real-world applications. The theory, examples, and advantages and disadvantages are listed. The concept is based on modelling method classification, starting with two macroscopic methods (Ordinary differential equations, System Dynamics) followed by the most used microscopic techniques (discrete event simulation, agent-based modelling).

12.5.1 Ordinary Differential Equations (ODEs)

12.5.1.1 Theory

Differential equations are the most used method to describe dynamic models. They can be divided into two classes:

- *Ordinary* Differential Equations (ODEs)
- *Partial* Differential Equations (PDEs)

An ODE is an equation relating a function of one independent variable with its derivatives and other functions. An ODE system consists of several equations relating several functions and their derivatives.

Modelling progress of state variables over time induces time as an independent variable [23]. When talking about differential equations in the field of health systems research, HTA (Health Technology Assessment) or economics, these are usually explicit ordinary differential equations. Hereafter the regarded equations have the form

$$x(t) = f(x,t)$$

where x is a vector of state variables.

Many simulation programs, although not mentioning ODEs directly, use them in the background. System dynamics, for example, provides a modelling concept and graphical interface to implement models but in the background uses ODEs to calculate results.

Example

The first epidemic model explicitly analyzed with ODEs comes from Kermack & McKendrick [24]. The population is split up into three groups: susceptible (S), infected (I) and recovered (R) where recovered people remain resistant against infection. The parameter β is the infection rate, γ the recovery rate.

$$\frac{dS}{dt} = -\beta \cdot S \cdot I$$

$$\frac{dI}{dt} = \beta \cdot S \cdot I - \gamma \cdot I$$

$$\frac{dR}{dt} = \gamma \cdot I$$

$$S + I + R = N$$

Formula 12.1   Equations of the Kermack & McKendrick SIR model

The work of Kermack & McKendrick provided the foundation for various other models, like population dynamics, further state variables for inhomogeneous populations or disease spreading dynamics.

12.5.1.2 Advantages and Disadvantages of Differential Equations

Advantages

ODEs provide a very mathematical and often challenging way of describing dynamic systems. Their advantages are that they can accurately describe physical laws and the use of continuous time, which means events are not restricted to certain time points. Changes in the system behavior can be functions of time or can happen because of relationships between state variables. There are various tools to analyze ODE systems and many mathematical methods to investigate system behavior.

Disadvantages

Huge ODE systems are very confusing. Enlarging the system can be very difficult and often requires changes in the model structure. Adding the distinction between male and female in a basic SIR-model, for example, not only doubles the number of states but requires every single equation to be revised. The biggest disadvantage is that without mathematical knowledge it is neither possible to create an ODE system nor to understand the equations and the impact of small adjustments.

12.5.2 System Dynamics (SD)

12.5.2.1 Theory and history

System Dynamics modelling originated from pioneering work at MIT in the 1950s by Jay Forrester. His training as an engineer and experience in feedback control systems during the second world war, and his subsequent interest in management problems and access to the first campus computers at MIT, led to the first significant work in understanding the dynamics of supply chains and a complete model-based theory to explain the bullwhip effect (see Section 12.6.3). This was first published by Jay Forrester [25] and the field of study launched as Industrial Dynamics [26].

The System Dynamics modelling community has grown to be a thriving academic field of study. They present the application of system dynamics modelling to a vast range of application domains, for example in policy development [27], sustainable urban development [28], healthcare [29], health system development [30] or sustainable fish population [31].

Introduction and Graphical Elements

System Dynamics is an approach for modelling dynamic systems which evolve continuously over time, similar to ordinary differential equation (ODE) systems. SD modellers use hypothesized relations across activities and processes. These models are very closely related to the general systems approach and allow modelers to insert qualitative relationships (expressed in general quantitative forms). Like all simulation models, all results are contingent upon the assumed inputs. General systems theory views assemblies of interrelated parts as having feedback loops that respond to system conditions and provide a degree of self-correction and control.

SD depicts systems as consisting of a set of levels (also called stocks; one can imagine them as reservoirs or water tanks) which are connected by flows or rates (one might imagine flows as pipes). Each level stores a numerical state. Flows change the values of states over time (see the realization using Vensim simulation environment in Figure 12.8).

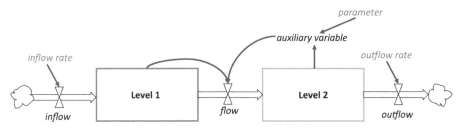

Figure 12.8 Elements of the System Dynamics notation. A continuous flow goes from one level to the other. There is both an inflow into and an outflow from the system. Inflow rate, parameter and outflow rate are constant parameters. Single arrows show causal connections between quantities'

For more complex models the use of auxiliary variables is helpful. These are variables that can be calculated algebraically from levels and other auxiliary variables. The use of auxiliary variables does not change the model behavior, but it adds clarity and helps in model development.

Figure 12.8 shows the graphical System Dynamics notation of a simple system with two levels. It contains both an inflow and an outflow. The flow (which could consist of material, people, information or anything else according to the units stored in the levels) from Level 1 into Level 2 depends directly on the value of the former, and indirectly (via the auxiliary variable whose definition could contain any sophisticated calculation that uses Level 2 and the constant parameter) on the value of the latter.

12.5.2.2 Main principle

System behavior is often mainly driven by feedback-loops in the system structure, where one variable has an amplifying or dampening effect over one or several relations on itself (the relations form a closed loop in the structure). More than one feedback loop can go through a variable. However, at least one variable in a loop has to be a flow, otherwise the result would be an algebraic loop – variables in the loop depending on their own value. Although many algebraic loops can be solved by iteration procedures, the System Dynamics methodology does not allow their use in models.

To gain insight into the feedback structure of a model it is often wise to construct a diagram with all the direct influences of the variables and information regarding whether influences are positive (reinforcing) or negative (dampening). This is called a causal loop diagram.

Causal Loop Diagrams

It is possible to simulate a model that is given by its stock and flow diagram, equations for all variables and values for all parameters. As opposed to this, the causal loop diagram shows information of qualitative nature. On the one hand it is a useful tool in the early development process of a model, before one determines the nature of variables (if they are levels, flows or auxiliaries) and fills in the equations. On the other hand it makes a qualitative analysis possible and gives valuable insight. Furthermore, it is easy to extract feedback loops out of the causal loop diagram.

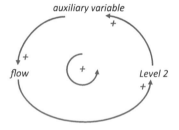

Figure 12.9
Positive (reinforcing) feedback loop for Level 2.
Plus signs label positive causal relations

Feedback loops are positive or reinforcing if the number of negative causal relations in the feedback loop is even. An example for this is shown in Figure 12.9, where larger values of Level 2 lead to a larger flow into Level 2. On the contrary, feedback loops are negative or dampening if the number of negative causal relations in the feedback loop is odd. An example for this is shown in Figure 12.10, where the flow out of Level 1 rises with the value of Level 1.

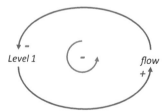

Bild 12.10
Negative (dampening) feedback loop for Level 1. The minus sign labels the negative causal relation between flow and Level 1

12.5.2.3 Advantages and Disadvantages of System Dynamics

Advantages

- System Dynamics takes a global view of the system, which helps to focus on the important dynamic relationships.
- The methodology describes a structured process, from the identification of important quantities and their causal relationships (causal loop diagrams) over the construction of stock and flow diagrams to the specification of the equations.
- The graphical notation is intuitive and easy to learn.
- Skills in a programming language are not necessary.
- Most System Dynamics models execute very fast (some in seconds) which makes it possible to do a lot of simulations and sensitivity analyses.
- Mathematical tools for analysis of systems of differential equations are fully applicable to System Dynamics models.

Disadvantages

- System Dynamics – as a top-down approach – treats quantities inside one level (for example patients) as homogeneous. If this is not a valid assumption one must introduce separate levels, which can increase model complexity.
- The approach cannot incorporate spatial relationships.
- It is necessary to think in global terms and quantities. Often, thinking of the behavior and reactions of individuals is more intuitive.
- Quantities are continuous. This might be problematic if the number of entities looked at is low.
- The graphical notation can get quite confusing in complex models with many causal relationships (some simulators allow vector-valued quantities, which might help).

12.5.3 Discrete Event Simulation

12.5.3.1 Theory

Discrete event simulation is one way of building up models to observe time based (or dynamic) behavior of a system. There are formal methods for building simulation models and ensuring that they are credible. During the experimental phase the models are executed (run over time) in order to generate results. The results can then be used to provide insights into a system and serve as a basis for decisions.

The main characteristic of Discrete Event Simulation is that the system state does only change at certain time points when events occur. Time moves from one of these events to the next, the time in between is of no relevance.

Each event has a time of occurrence. If an event takes place it may cause changes to the state of individual objects as well as the system itself. These changes occur right at the time of the event or after a certain time delay, but not slowly over time as it may happen in continuous simulation. Any changes happen within a certain time point.

The occurrences of events and the points in time at which they take place create the time-line of the simulation run.

Discrete Event Simulation Specification (DEVS) is a widely used approach for the modelling and simulation of dynamic discrete systems. The modern object-oriented DEVS worldview regards active objects (entities) passing passive objects (stations) along a given path.

Event List

The occurrence of events and their order need to be controlled in some way. In discrete simulation software programs this is usually done by a so-called event list or event chain. This list contains all future events as well as some additional information like the time of occurrence and optionally a priority. During the simulation run, new events are added to this list. Only if all events are executed and the list is empty has the simulation run reached its logical end. Of course, additional conditions for ending the simulation run can be set, and then the simulation run will be stopped even if the event list does still contain future events.

One big concern in Discrete Event Simulation is the handling of events that take place at the same time. Usually, the event list contains all events in order of their occurrence. Events that will take place at the same time are simply listed in the order they have been added to this list.

To ensure the correct order of events, priorities have to be assigned to give a ranking for the execution. This corresponds to the Select function in Definition 2, below.

12.5.3.2 Mathematical Description

A very common definition is given by Zeigler [32].

Definition 1: Discrete Event System Specification (DEVS)

A DEVS is a structure

$$M = \left(X,\ S,\ Y,\ \delta_{int},\ \delta_{ext},\ \delta_{con},\ \lambda,\ ta \right),$$

where

X	is the set of input values
S	is the set of states
Y	is the set of output values
$\delta_{int}: S \to S$	is the internal transition function
$\delta_{ext}: Q \times X^b \to S$	is the external transition function,

where

$Q = \left\{ s \in S, 0 \le e \le ta(s) \right\}$	is the total state set
e	is the time elapsed since the last transition
X^b	denotes the collection of bags over X (a sets in which some elements may occur more than once)
$\delta_{con}: Q \times X^b \to S$	is the confluent transition function
$\lambda: S \to Y^b$	is the output function
$ta: S \to R^+_{0,\,\infty}$	is the time advance function

Definition 2: Coupled Model

A Coupled Model is a structure build of several atomic models with

$$N = \left(X_N, Y_N, D, \{M_d\}, \{I_d\}, \{Z_{i,d}\}, Select\right),$$

where

X_N, Y_N are the sets of input and output values of the coupled model

D is the set of component references, so that for each $d \in D, M_d$ is a DEVS model

For each $d \in D \cup \{N\}, I_d \subset (D \cup \{N\}) \setminus \{d\}$ is the set of influencer models on subsystem d
For each $i \in I_d, Z_{i,d}$ is the translation function, where

$$Z_{i,d} : \{X_N \rightarrow X_d \quad if\ i=N \quad Y_i \rightarrow Y_N \quad if\ d=N \quad Y_i \rightarrow X_d$$

otherwise

select: $2^D \rightarrow D$ is a tie breaking function for simultaneous events; it must verify

select $(E) \in E, with\ E \subset 2^D$, the set of components producing the simultaneity of events

12.5.3.3 Example

A typical event would be the entering of a queue in front of a server. Examples for discrete event models are classic server-queue models like supermarkets or emergency rooms as shown in Figure 12.11 [33]:

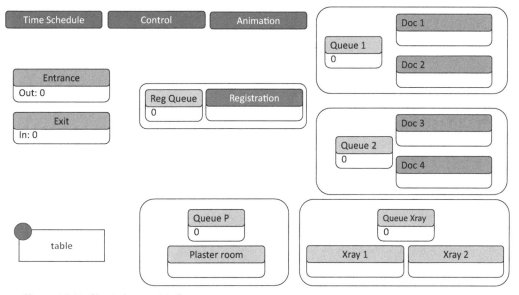

Figure 12.11 Simulation model of an emergency room

A patient enters the emergency room and moves to the registration desk. If several patients are already waiting, they have to remain in the queue in front until all patients that have entered before them are done. Entering and leaving the queue are events that cause the content of the affected objects to be increased or decreased and the patient to be moved from one object to another. As soon as the patient is finished at the registration, several events take place: the patient moves from the registration desk to the waiting area, so the state of the server representing the registration switches back to idle. The content is 0: the server is ready to accept the next patient in line. The waiting area is a queue in front of the casualty ward; its content is increased by one as soon as the patient enters. If a doctor is free, the next event is leaving the waiting area and entering the casualty ward. The server that represents the doctor is now set to "busy" until the treatment is finished and the next event – leaving the casualty ward – takes place. Depending whether the patients require further treatment, they move on either to the plaster room, the x-ray room or they are done and leave the emergency room.

12.5.3.4 Advantages and Disadvantages of Discrete Event Simulation

Advantages

Discrete Event Simulation in general allows a very clear differentiation between the structure and dynamic behavior of a system. Reducing this dynamic behavior to a series of events that take place at certain points in time makes this method of modelling a very useful approach for a wide variety of applications. The hierarchical structure of a system can be easily described, and the concept of object-oriented modelling can be well integrated.

Disadvantages

The main problem with event-based modelling is the occurrence of events that take place at the same point of time. This may quickly lead to a distortion of the course of events, based on the wrong order of changes to the system. It is usually necessary to implement a method to control the correct order of events to create a valid representation of the system behavior.

12.5.4 Agent-Based Modelling

12.5.4.1 Theory

Agent-based modelling is a relatively young discipline that has become possible with powerful computers in the last decade of the 20th century.

Goals of Agent-Based Modelling

- Possibility to model details with satisfying exactness.
- Creation of dynamic effects that cannot be created with other models and that cannot be represented by parameters.

What is an Agent?

An agent is an actor, an individual component that does something more or less independently. It is not necessarily a simplified person.

Definitions in literature are diverging and often focused on usage of these agents in concrete applications.

By combining the ideas in literature, an agent can generally be described as a model that contains components that fulfil the following characteristics [34, 35, 36]:

- Unique identification
- Possession of individual properties that can change over time
- Acting based on individual, adaptable rules
- Possibility to communicate with the environment and other agents

Furthermore, it is necessary to provide an environment in which the agents exist.

Consequently, the freedom for developing agent-based models is gigantic and the variety of different modelling ideas is enormous. This can be interpreted simultaneously as an advantage, with respect to flexibility of the modelling method, and as a disadvantage, with respect to reproducibility and documentation of a model [37].

In contrast to cellular automata which were in principle developed for physical applications and a basis for the historical developments, the origin of so-called agent-based models lies within the social sciences. As an inconvenient result, there is no common base that allows a formal definition of agent-based models. A lot of good literature is available providing ideas and tutorials to establish an agent-based model for a given question [35, 38, 39]. Yet, it is almost impossible to state a common denominator. Therefore, agent-based modelling should rather be seen as a general concept than a modelling method.

Nevertheless, a short overview of the idea and the structure is given in the following part.

The three main characteristics of agent-based models are [34]:

- *Modelling of emerging behavior*
- *Natural description of a system*
- *Flexibility*

Modelling of emergent behavior. The invention of cellular automata showed modellers that even simple rules in such an automaton can lead to complex and impressive patterns. In agent-based models such behavior can be observed even more prominently. Simple agents with simple rules can result in a complex system behavior. While it is easy to describe these rules it is hard and sometimes impossible to describe the resulting behavior precisely.

This is an important benefit because it gives us the possibility to model complex systems in an easy way.

Natural description of a system. Agent-based models provide a natural description of the real system. That means:

- Agents in the model look like components in reality and act in a way that can be observed in the real system.
- Parameters in the model correspond with quantities that occur in the real system.

Flexibility. Especially important are these points:

- **Scalability:** The number of agents can be increased without limitations, while the structure of agents is not affected.
- **Level of detail:** The level of detail regarding how agents are modelled is generally not restricted because it depends on the number and complexity of rules and attributes of agents.

- **Flexible rules:** Rules of agents can be adapted easily for the set-up and even during simulation without affecting the structure of other agents and of the environment.
- **Parameterization** of agents can be set individually and can be changed any time during simulation.

12.5.4.2 Advantages and Disadvantages of Agent-based Modelling

Technical Advantages

- Possibility to model dynamic effects, whose dynamic behavior is only little-known, by well-known rules.
- Flexible modelling environment that provides scalability for size and details in a simple way.
- Direct usage of data (parameters, relations between details). Ideally, no adjustment is necessary.
- Extension of agent-based models is often less work than extension of other model approaches.

Advantages in Application

- Knowledge about mathematical theories is not necessary.
- Model structure is very clear. Non-modelling project partners (economists, medics, and so on) understand the model structure and can provide important input to the model.

Technical Disadvantages

- Non-consideration of agent rules or wrong agent rules may result in incorrect global system behavior.
- Data for agents (parameters, rules) are sometimes not completely available. Then a comprehensive and often expensive calibration is necessary.
- There are very limited mathematical methods for analyzing agent-based models. Often, statistical evaluation of results is the only possibility.
- The initial creation of an agent-based model can require more programming work than other models.
- Simulations with many agents often require powerful computer systems and long run-times; availability of clusters may be a restriction.

Dangers in Applications

- Agent-based models look very "real". The feeling of having a correct model must not replace comprehensive validation.
- Danger of wrong usage and interpretation by non-modelers because the model looks so "real".

■ 12.6 Modelling and Simulation Examples

The following sections give a short sketch of applications of modern modelling and simulation examples. In general, quite often it is enough to use the explained standard solution to get the result, as it is clear that higher model complexity reduces the possibility for face validity and in the same moment increases the chance of making programming errors and losing both the overview of the parameters and numerical stability.

Nevertheless, it can be important to combine modelling methods and modern data science methods (reinforcement learning, calibration techniques, ...).

12.6.1 Dynamic Modelling of Railway Networks for Optimal Pathfinding Using Agent-based Methods and Reinforcement Learning

This dynamic agent-based model tries to find the most time-efficient routes for the defined agents; they need to find their way through a network with minimal disturbance of other agents. It is based on the railway network operated by the Austrian Federal Train Agency (ÖBB). The non-blocked tracks of the railway network obey an historical timetable. Due to their dynamic nature during a typical time period, classical path finding algorithms such as A^* are not sophisticated enough to allow agents to find viable paths through the system. Thus, a planning component for the agents was introduced, which is based on DynaQ+, a reinforcement learning method.

Basic Model Description

The infrastructure is represented as an undirected graph. Its nodes are points of interest (mainly train-stations, but also signals or junctions), the edges are the tracks between these points, weighted with the distance.

The well-defined agents of the models are the trains. The set of rules for each agent can be roughly split into two actions: successful and unsuccessful arrival to a node. This means either going forward or staying in the current node; the action is considered successful if there is enough capacity in the required station. If not, the action is either tried to be performed at the end of the time segment, or all actions of the agent are rescheduled according to the delay.

Thus, not only will the agent itself be delayed, but also other trains could be influenced, which can lead to congestion and propagation of delays. Each action is stored in the previously mentioned historical timetable, which is sorted by arrival time and trains; this means that actions with the same arrival time will be taken from top to bottom. Thus, the actions are discrete action events.

To pick the most optimal path, policies have to be created. As it is unfeasible to calculate every possible state in advance, we employ reinforcement learning to create a valid policy.

Reinforcement Learning

The goal is to learn behavior patterns by maximizing rewards based on the actions taken by the agents. In each node (or, using the terms of Reinforcement Learning, "state"), exists a number of actions which indicate the next station the agent will arrive and the probability of how favorable the actions in this specific state are. The aim of Q-Learning is to find the optimal state-action policy for each state. This is done by updating Q values of one state-action pair using the Bellman equation, which takes into account the values of the resulting next state.

$$Q(S_t,A_t) = Q(S_t,A_t) + \alpha \left[R_{t+1} + \gamma \max_{\alpha \in A(S_{t+1})} Q(S_{t+1}, \alpha) - Q(S_t,A_t) \right]$$

Here, $Q(S_t, A_t)$ defines the Q-value of an agent in state S_t and choosing action A_t. Obviously, the Q-value on the left-hand side of the equation presents the new calculated value, while occurrence on the right-hand side defines the old value before it is updated. The term in the brackets defines the Temporal Difference Error, which is composed of the expected optimal reward and the current value. The learning rate $\alpha \in [0, 1]$ indicates how much the new value affects the old one. DynaQ+, an extension of the well-known DynaQ specimen of reinforcement learning algorithms, adds additional planning steps, which use already taken actions under consideration of when they were performed in order to get to the optimal policy faster and to enable agents to react to changes in their environment.

As always with tabular reinforcement learning methods, the table of Q-values grows with the number of possible states. This means it is useful to approximate it with a neural network, which leads us to Deep Reinforcement Learning. One of the main disadvantages of this method is the dependence of the final result on the initialized Q-values. The structure of the neural network is defined via layers, precisely an input H (0), output H (L) and n hidden layers. Due to the representation of the network as a graph, we are using Graph Convolutional Networks, where the propagation layers are defined as

$$H^{(l+1)} = \sigma \left(D^{-\frac{1}{2}} \hat{A} D^{-\frac{1}{2}} H^{(l)} W^{(l)} \right),$$

where H(l) indicates the l-th neural network layer, while W(l) is a weight matrix for them. The term

$$D^{-\frac{1}{2}} \hat{A} D^{-\frac{1}{2}}$$

indicates the normalization of the adjacency matrix $\hat{A} = A + I$.

This neural network is trained with a pre-initialised Q-Network containing the shortest paths through the infrastructure network. It thereby achieves a much faster learning rate and, therefore, convergence for our reinforcement learning model.

Combining all these techniques allows us to teach our agent to find a path through the network and to successfully arrive at its destination.

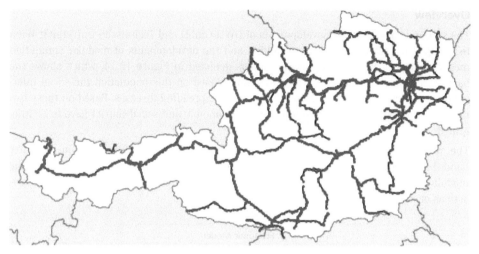

Figure 12.12 Railway network in Austria as implemented in the model

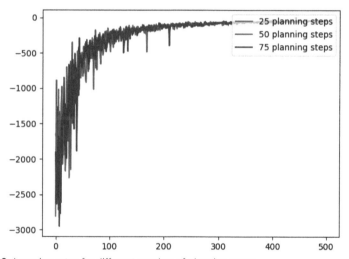

Figure 12.13 Learning rates for different number of planning steps

12.6.2 Agent-Based Covid Modelling Strategies

Purpose

The agent-based COVID-19 model aims to give ideas about the potential impact of certain policies and their combination on the spread of the disease. In doing so, it supports decision makers to correctly choose between possible policies by comparing the model outcomes with other important factors such as socioeconomic ones. In order to fulfill this target, it is relevant that the agent-based COVID-19 model validly depicts the current and near future distribution and state of disease progression of infected people and their future behavior.

Overview

The system is based on the developments of DWH GmbH and Technische Universität Wien in the field of infectious disease modelling and the developments of modular simulation model concepts. The general point of view is depicted in Figure 12.14, which shows the basis of all infectious diseases: the population. Based on this population the social interaction is a core part of the real-world behavior for spreading diseases. Based on these two models the disease itself and additionally the economic and social impact have to be integrated.

The modular concepts require well defined interfaces. This takes time, but on the other hand the modular blocks can be reused and can be validated one by one. Additionally, the modules can be exchanged, for instance for other populations with very special social interactions or if other economic aspects are in the focus [40].

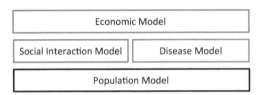

Figure 12.14 General modular model concept

For development of the COVID-19-model the following modules are realized:

- **Population.** Altogether the agent-based COVID-19 model is based on the Generic Population Concept (GEPOC, see [37]), a generic stochastic agent-based population model of Austria, that validly depicts the current demographic as well as regional structure of the population on a microscopic level. The flexibility of this population model makes it possible to modify and extend it by an nearly arbitrary variety of possible modules for simulation of population-focused research problems.

- **Contacts.** In order to develop a basis for infectious contacts, we modified and adapted a contact model previously used for the simulation of influenza spread. This model uses a distinction of contacts in different locations (households, schools, workplaces, leisure time) and is based on the POLYMOD study [41], a large survey for tracking social contact behavior relevant to the spread of infectious diseases.

- **Disease.** We implemented a module for the course of the disease that depicts the current pathway of COVID-19 patients starting from infection to recovery or death and linked it with the prior two modules.

- **Policies.** We added a module for implementation of interventions, ranging from contact-reduction policies, hygienic measures, contact tracing to vaccinations. This module is implemented in the form of a timeline of events.

Comparing with the classical theory on spreading of diseases with susceptible, infected and recovered persons looked at in a macroscopic way using ordinary differential equations (Figure 12.15) the systems were not able to figure out regionality, heterogeneous populations, population density, and, other social aspects, as well as different courses of disease and individual duration of infectiousness. The modular agent-based system can handle these problems, but significant effort must be put into examining the algorithms in order to guarantee validity.

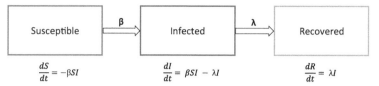

Figure 12.15 Classical macroscopic SIR model, with given ODEs

To meet the real-world-needs a population interaction such as the one depicted in Figure 12.16 is integrated. In the model, regular contacts between agents occur via locations (school classes, workplaces and households) and location-collections (schools, care homes), while random leisure time contacts extend the standard contact network.

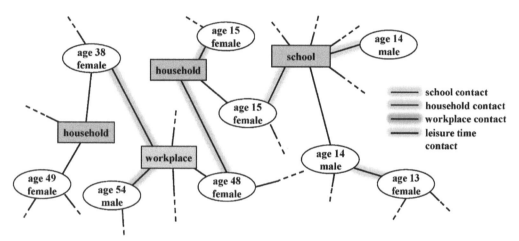

Figure 12.16 Contact network of agents in the agent-based COVID-19 model. Regular contacts between agents occur via locations (school classes, workplaces and households), location-collections (schools, care homes), while random leisure time contacts extend the standard contact network.

Structure and Scheduling

An infectious contact triggers the start of the newly infected agent's patient-pathway. This pathway describes the different states and stations an agent passes while suffering from the COVID-19 disease and can be interpreted as a sequence of events in which each triggers the next one after a certain, sampled duration. The pathway is depicted in a state chart in Figure 12.17 and describes how to interpret this figure by explaining the initial steps in more detail:

As soon as a person-agent becomes infected, its infected state is set to true, its susceptible variable is set to false, and its severity parameter is drawn from a given distribution. A latency period is sampled according to a distribution as well. The corresponding "Infectious" event is scheduled for the sampled time instant in the future. As soon as this "Infectious" event is executed, the infectious parameter is set to true and a parallel branch that updates the infectiousness is started. After the "Finish Incubation" event, the first branch in the patient's pathway decides whether the agent continues being detected by the standard test-regime or continues undetected due to having mild or no symptoms at all. All other elements of the pathway proceed analogously. All branches are evaluated with age-class-dependent probabilities:

In most cases (i.e. if the agent does not die for any other non-COVID related reason, see the Population module), the final state of every agent's disease pathway is the Recovery/Removal event which either sets the agent to "resistant" (meaning it is not susceptible anymore), or renders it deceased with a certain death-by-COVID probability that depends on the agent's disease severity. Consequently, the model differs between COVID-caused and COVID-affected deaths.

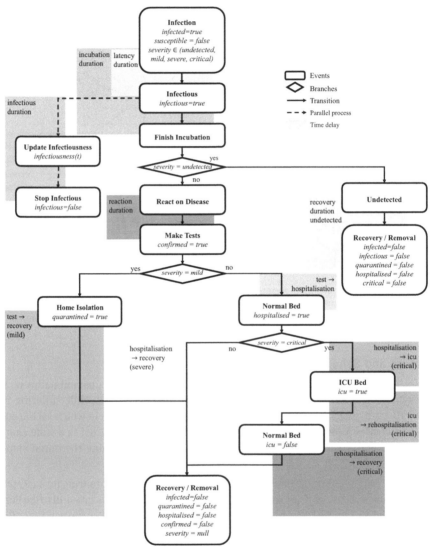

Figure 12.17 State chart of the patient pathway of a person-agent in the agent-based COVID-19 model. Only those state variables that are changed by the corresponding event are labelled, all others remain at the current value. The initial state of all infection-specific state variables is false or null, except for "susceptible", which is initially true.

Stochasticity

Basically, all model processes, including the initialisation, include the sampling of random numbers. Therefore, Monte Carlo simulation is applied, results of runs are averaged and also their variability is assessed. Aside from being time-consuming to smoothe, the stochasticity of the model is actually its key strength. It allows one to model heterogeneity and skewness of the infection-network, which distinguishes the model from classic macroscopic approaches. This specifically refers to the means by which contacts are modelled: Since the person-agent's contact rate is initially drawn from a Gamma distribution, the contacts sampled via Poisson distribution result in a so-called Gamma-Poisson mix, which is by definition Negative-Binomial distributed. This strategy allows us to directly parametrise the skewness of the contact network in accordance with published information on the dispersion factor of COVID-19 clusters.

Parametrization

With respect to parameterization, we distinguish between model input and model parameters. Classical model parameters specify scalar or array-typed model variables that are initialised at the beginning of the simulation and, if not changed by certain model events, keep their value for the entire simulation time. Examples are the infection probability of the disease, the age-dependent death rate of the population, or the distribution parameters of the recovery time.

In contrast to model parameters, the model input consists of an event-timeline that describes at which point in time a certain incident changes the behavior of the model. This incident usually refers to the introduction of a policy, like the closure of schools or the start of tracing but may also refer to instantaneous changes of model parameters which are related but cannot be directly attributed to policies, such as the increase of compliance among the population to increased hygiene recommendations.

Calibration

Clearly, there is no valid data available for direct parameterization of the base infection probability parameter, which is the most fundamental of the three factors that decide about a transmission in case of a direct contact. First of all, this parameter is hardly measurable in reality and moreover strongly depends on the definition of "contact". Consequently, this parameter needs to be fitted in the course of a calibration loop.

The calibration experiment is set up as follows:

- We vary the parameter "infection probability" using a bisection algorithm.

- For each parameter value, the simulation, parameterized without any policies, is executed ten times (Monte Carlo simulation) and the results are averaged.

- The average time-series for the cumulative number of confirmed cases is observed and cropped to the value as at the initial upswing of the epidemic curve: to be specific, all values between 200 and 3200. In this interval the growth of the curve can be considered as exponential.

- The cropped time-series is compared with the corresponding time-series of real measured data in Austria.

- Both time-series are compared regarding the average doubling time of the confirmed cases. The difference between the doubling times is taken as the calibration error for the bisection algorithm.

Model Implementation

The simulation of ABMs such as the specified agent-based COVID-19 model is a huge challenge with respect to computational performance. Because the model cannot be scaled down, almost 9 million interacting agents just for Austria need to be included into the model to simulate the spread of the disease in the entire population.

These high demands exclude most of the available libraries and software for ABM, including AnyLogic, NetLogo, MESA, JADE, or Repast Simphony [42-46]. Most of these simulators cannot be used, as their generic features for creating live visual output generates too many overheads.

Thus, it was decided to use a self-developed agent-based simulation environment ABT (Agent-Based Template [41]), realized in 2019 by dwh GmbH in cooperation with TU Wien. The environment is implemented in JAVA and specifically designed for supporting a reproducible simulation of large-scale agent-based systems.

Model Output

The outcomes of the model are time series with a daily time basis. They consist of aggregated numbers describing the current nation- and/or region-wide spread of the disease as well as numbers depicting the contact behavior of agents. These include, for example, the cumulative number of confirmed cases, the number of currently active asymptomatic cases, the total number of daily newly infected 10- to 30-year-old females, the total number of daily contacts for school children, or the average number of secondary infections per agent.

The calculated results of the model, together with additional scenarios and extensions, were used as a decision support for the Austrian COVID consortium and are, together with other data, the basis for the COVID rules for the public.

12.6.3 Deep Reinforcement Learning Approach for Optimal Replenishment Policy in a VMI Setting

Vendor-managed inventory (VMI) [47] is an inventory management practice in which a supplier of goods, usually the manufacturer, is responsible for optimizing the inventory held by a distributor. It is a widely used supply chain collaboration practice. One of the main reasons for taking this approach is to tackle the so-called "bullwhip effect" [48]. This is a distribution channel phenomenon in which demand forecasts yield supply chain inefficiencies, meaning that changes in demands from customers can result in high fluctuations further down the supply chain.

The goal of this model is to generate a VMI performance measurement approach to assign responsibilities for poor performance. It was also used to simulate different demand scenarios based on real data from Infineon Technologies AG and to calculate optimal replenishment quantities. The methods applied include discrete event modelling and reinforcement learning [49].

12.6.3.1 Model Description

The underlying VMI configuration, depicted in Figure 12.18, is the basis for the design of all relevant KPIs.

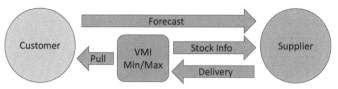

Figure 12.18 Representative Vendor Managed Inventory Scheme

Consider the current stock information, the supplier plans and delivery replenishments, which may be pulled by the customer from the stock at any point in time: There could be instances when the pull from the customer increases without being forecasted, resulting in a stock-out situation. Without VMI modelling, the supplier would have been held responsible for a failed delivery. To better assign responsibilities for any kind of stock violation, a root-cause enabling VMI performance measurement approach is used which follows the scheme below.

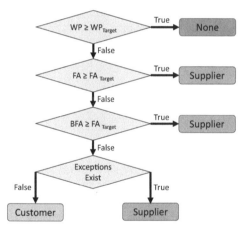

Figure 12.19
Configuration for determination of the root-cause during VMI Performance Measurement

One of the main KPIs used is the overall weekly performance, WP, which is compared to target weekly performance WP_{Target}.

$$WP_w = \frac{Days_{NV,w} \times Weight_{NV}}{\sum_{V=\{NV,OS,US,SO\}} Days_{V,w} \times Weight_V} \times 100$$

NV, OS, US and *SO* represent no-violation, over-stock, under-stock and stock-out. To reflect the severity of the violation, certain weights are further added to the formula.

Taking this scheme as a basis, a Deep Reinforcement Learning (RL) approach was taken to calculate optimal replenishment quantities.

A compact description of Reinforcement Learning can be found in the use case 'Dynamic modelling of railway networks', as well as in Chapter 8.

For solving the underlying Markov Decision Problem in this case, a deep Q-Network (DQN) that combines RL with deep neural networks was taken. The respective action space, state space and reward function were defined as follows:

State space: One unique state which is a normalized value between −1 and +1.

$$State = \begin{cases} +1, & \text{for } FSP > 2 \times Z_w F \\ \dfrac{DTMF}{(2 \times Z_w F) - MF}, & \text{for } MF \leq FSP \leq 2 \times Z_w F \\ \dfrac{DTMF}{MF}, & \text{for } 0 \leq FSP \leq MF \\ -1, & \text{for } FSP < 0 \end{cases}$$

FSP is the anticipated stock position, $Z_w F / Z_w F$ the anticipated maximum/minimum target stock level, MF the mean value of these and DTMF the anticipated distance to the mean.

Action space: This space is discrete and has 9 (0 -> 8) possible values, where the replenishment policy is a function $f(a) = m \times a$ and m is the magnitude of action. As an example, a replenishment amount of 7500 units corresponds to the value a=4 and m=2500.

Reward function: This uses the current stock position CSP as a main driver and assigns a value between -1 and +1 as reward/penalty. Z_w / Z_w is the maximum/minimum target stock level, M the mean value of these and DTM, the distance to the mean.

$$Reward = \begin{cases} 1 - \dfrac{2 \times DTM}{(2 \times Z_w) - M}, & \text{for } M \leq CSP \leq 2 \times Z_w \\ 1 + \left(\dfrac{2 \times DTM}{M} \right), & \text{for } 0 \leq CSP \leq MF \\ -1, & \text{elsewhere} \end{cases}$$

Different scenarios were used to evaluate the performance of this model. Scenario 1 used real data and randomly selected product type and customer. For Scenario 2 and 3 training sets representative of the variables in Scenario 1 where generated. Both used the Martingale Method of Forecast Evolution as a method for calculating random demand and forecast and Scenario 3 enhanced it by introducing sporadic rise and fall for these variables. All these scenarios were tested on real data.

It was shown that it is possible to optimize the replenishment policy by implementing this DRL algorithm. The most significant result was that the percentage of "no-violation" inventory status improved significantly (from 43 % to 99 % in Scenario 3). This came with increased transportation costs due to a rise in the number of total shipments.

■ 12.7 Summary and Lessons Learned

The three examples described in this chapter give a brief picture about different modelling concepts in applications. Common to all three of them is the necessity to choose the best fitting method depending on the problem question and the available data. In many cases the underlying, natural structure gives a good starting point for model selection.

Modern modelling and simulation also uses state of the art concepts in developing parametrization, calibration of parameters, definition and development of scenarios, as well as outcome interpretation and result visualization. Due to the fact that classical modelling methods are already well-known in theory (like differential equations and system dynamics), and computationally intensive methods like agent-based models can be used in a broad spectrum of research and industry now, modelling and simulation is becoming more and more important.

Special focus in a real-world setting lies in the field of

- reenactment of a real-life system, for instance to understand the influencing factors,
- decision support, when different (long time) scenarios should be compared,
- cases when A/B testing is not possible due to lack of time or a high number of different scenarios.

■ 12.8 In a Nutshell

Modelling and simulation provides additional strategies and methods for modern data science; it adds techniques to integrate real world system behavior and therefore a broad spectrum for scenario calculation and "What if…" questions. Modelling is no encapsulated method, it uses various data methods for parametrization, calibration, validation as well as for scenario definition.

Having finished this chapter:

- You understand the conceptual idea of modelling and simulation.
- You have a sound understanding of basic methods of modelling.
- You studied several use cases for modelling and simulation and identified the necessity of using different modelling methods and integrating data science concepts to get satisfying results.
- You understand the necessity of choosing methods depending on the problem or question, respectively, instead of the other way round. This is a good starting point for developing your own models.
- You know that reproducibility is very important. Due to this fact, documentation, validation and verification is essential.
- You know that it is necessary to understand your own model and what happens on the numerical solution level.

References

[1] Bridges, T. J., and S. Reich (2006). Numerical methods for Hamiltonian PDEs. Journal of Physics A: Mathematical and General, 39(19), 5287–5320. *https://doi.org/10.1088/0305-4470/39/19/s02*

[2] Nandakumaran, K., and P. S. Datti, Partial Differential Equations: Classical Theory with a Modern Touch, Cambridge University Press, 348, May 2020.

[3] Großmann, C., and H.-G. Roos: Numerische Behandlung partieller Differentialgleichungen. Teubner, 3. Auflage, 2006.

[4] Leveque, R. J.: Finite Volume Methods for Hyperbolic Problems. Cambridge University Press, 2002.

[5] Hackbusch, W.: Iterative Lösung großer schwachbesetzter Gleichungssysteme. Teubner, 1991.

[6] Murthy, D. N. P., Page, N. W., and E. Y. Rodin, Mathematical modelling: a tool for problem solving in engineering, physical, biological, and social sciences. Oxford: Pergamon Press, 1990.

[7] Bender, E. A., An Introduction to Mathematical Modelling. New York: Wiley, 1978.

[8] "Zielgerichtete mathematische Modellbildung – Werkzeuge für die Praxis", in: Dynamische Probleme- Modellierung und Wirklichkeit, Univ. Hannover, 1996, pp. 1–29.

[9] Zeigler, B. P., Theory of Modeling and Simulation. New York: Wiley, 1976

[10] Freire, J., Bonnet, P., and D. Shasha (2012). Computational reproducibility: state-of-the-art, challenges, and database research opportunities. In: Proceedings of the 2012 ACM SIGMOD International Conference on Management of Data (pp. 593–596). *https://doi.org/10.1145/2213836.2213908*

[11] Popper N., 2015 Comparative Modelling and Simulation – A Concept for Modular Modelling and Hybrid Simulation of Complex Systems Systems (Doctoral dissertation). Vienna University of Technology, Vienna, Austria.

[12] Sargent, R. (2010). Verification and validation of simulation models. In: Proceedings of the 2010 Winter Simulation Conference (pp. 166–183). Baltimore, MD.

[13] Balci, O. (1994). Validation, verification, and testing techniques throughout the life cycle of a simulation study. Annals of Operations Research, 53(1), 121–173. *http://doi.org/10.1007/BF02136828*

[14] Balci, O. (1997). Verification, validation and accreditation of simulation models. In: Proceedings of 1997 Winter Simulation Conference (pp. 135–141). Atlanta, GA, USA.

[15] Breitenecker, F., Emergency Department – Follow-up Treatment – ARGESIM Comparison 6 – Definition. SNE Simulation Nodes Europe. 1992; 2(3):30.

[16] Grimm, Volker & Berger, Uta & Bastiansen, Finn & Eliassen, Sigrunn & Ginot, Vincent & Giske, Jarl & Goss-Custard, John & Grand, Tamara & Heinz, Simone & Huse, Geir & Huth, Andreas & Jepsen, Jane & Jørgensen, Christian & Mooij, Wolf & Müller, Birgit & Pe'er, Guy & Piou, Cyril & Railsback, Steven & Robbins, Andrew & Deangelis, Donald. (2006). A Standard Protocol for Describing Individual-Based and Agent Based Models. Ecological Modelling. 198. 115–126. 10.1016/j.ecolmodel.2006.04.023.

[17] North, M. J., and C. M. Macal, Managing Business Complexity: Discovering Strategic Solutions with Agent-Based Modeling and Simulation. New York: Oxford University Press, 2007.

[18] Sargent, R. G., "Verification and Validation of Simulation Models," in: Proceedings of the 2007 Winter Simulation Conference, Washington, D.C., USA, 2007, pp. 124–137.

[19] Law, "How to Build Valid and Credible Simulation Models," in: Proceedings of the 2009 Winter Simulation Conference (WSC), Austin, TX, USA, 2009, pp. 24–33.

[20] Weinstein, M. C., et al., "Principles of Good Practice for Decision Analytic Modeling in Health-Care Evaluation: Report of the ISPOR Task Force on Good Research Practices-Modeling Studies," Value in Health, vol. 6, no. 1, pp. 9–17, Jan. 2003.

[21] Balci, "Verification, Validation and Testing," in: Handbook of Simulation: Principles, Methodology, Advances, Applications, and Practice, J. Banks, Ed. Hoboken, NJ, USA: John Wiley & Sons, Inc., 2007.

[22] W. Wing-Yi Chan, A Survey on Multivariate Data Visualization. Hong Kong: Department of Computer Science and Engineering, Hong Kong University of Science and Technology, 2006, pp. 1–29.

[23] Ayres, F., heory and Problems of Differential Equations. New York: McGraw-Hill, 1952.

[24] Kermack & McKendrick (1927) A contribution to the mathematical theory of epidemics. Proceedings of the Royal Society of London. Series A, Containing Papers of a Mathematical and Physical Character. The Royal Society 115(772): 700–721. Available at: *http://dx.doi.org/10.1098/rspa.1927.0118*.

[25] Forrester, J. W. (1958). Industrial Dynamics – a Major Breakthrough for Decision Makers. Harvard Business Review, 36(4), 37–66.

[26] Yearworth, M. (2014). A Brief Introduction to System Dynamics Modelling (p. 15). University of Bristol. 24 October 2014

[27] Freeman, R., Yearworth, M., Angulo, M., and T. Quested (2013). Evidence building for waste prevention: understanding the causal influences that result in waste. Paper presented at the 31st International Conference of the System Dynamics Society, Cambridge, Massachusetts USA.

[28] Pejic Bach, Mirjana & Tustanovski, Emil & Ip, W.H. & Yung, Kai & Roblek, Vasja. (2020). System dynamics models for the simulation of sustainable urban development: A review and analysis and the stakeholder perspective. Kybernetes. 49. *https://doi.org/10.1108/K-04-2018-0210*.

[29] Brailsford, S. C., "System dynamics: What's in it for healthcare simulation modelers," 2008 Winter Simulation Conference, 2008, pp. 1478–1483, doi: 10.1109/WSC.2008.4736227.

30] Einzinger, P., 2014. A Comparative Analysis of System Dynamics and Agent-Based Modelling for Health Care Reimbursement Systems (Doctoral dissertation). Vienna University of Technology, Vienna, Austria.

[31] Rahman, N. (2014). A System Dynamics Model for a Sustainable Fish Population. International Journal of Technology Diffusion, 5(2), 39–53. doi:10.4018/ijtd.2014040104

[32] Zeigler, B. P., "DEVS Today: Recent Advances in Discrete Event-Based Information Technology," in 11th IEEE/ACM International Symposium on Modeling, Analysis and Simulation of Computer Telecommunications Systems, 2003. MASCOTS 2003., Orlando, FL, USA, 2003, pp. 148–161

[33] Rahmi, S. M., "C6 Emergency Department: Follow-up Treatment - Taylor ED," Simulation News Europe SNE, vol. 10, no. 2–3, p. 33, Dec. 2000.

[34] Bonabeau, E., "Agent-based modeling: Methods and techniques for simulating human systems," Proceedings of the National Academy of Sciences, vol. 99, no. 3, pp. 7280–7287, May. 2002.

[35] Macal, C. M., and M. J. North, "Tutorial on Agent-Based Modeling and Simulation, Part 2: How to Model with Agents," in: Proceedings of the 2006 Winter Simulation Conference, Monterey, California, pp. 73–83.

[36] Wooldridge, M., "Agent-based software engineering," IEE Proceedings - Software Engineering, vol. 144, no. 1, p. 26, 1997.

[37] Bicher, M., Urach, Chr., and N. Popper. GEPOC ABM: A Generic Agent-Based Population Model for Austria. In: Proceedings of the 2018 Winter Simulation Conference, pp. 2656–2667, Gothenburg, Sweden, 2018. IEEE.

[38] Railsback, S. F., and V. Grimm (2012). Agent-based and individual-based modeling: a practical introduction. Princeton Univ. Press, Princeton. OCLC: 811181165.

[39] Epstein, J. M. (2012). Generative Social Science. Princeton University Press, Princeton. OCLC: 956983748.

[40] Miksch, F., Mathematical Modeling for New Insights into Epidemics by Herd Immunity and Serotype Shift. ASIM Fortschrittsbericht. doi: 10.11128/fbs.20 (2016).

[41] Mossong, J., Hens, N., Jit, M., Beutels, Ph., Auranen, K., Mikolajczyk, R., Massari, M., Salmaso, St., Scalia Tomba, G., Wallinga, J., et al. POLYMOD social contact data (2017)

[42] Beate Jahn, Gaby Sroczynski, Martin Bicher, Claire Rippinger, Nikolai Mühlberger, Júlia Santamaria, Christoph Urach, Michael Schomaker, Igor Stojkov, Daniela Schmid, Günter Weiss, Ursula Wiedermann, Monika Redlberger-Fritz, Christiane Druml, Mirjam Kretzschmar, Maria Paulke-Korinek, Herwig Ostermann, Caroline Czasch, Gottfried Endel, Wolfgang Bock, Nikolas Popper, and Uwe Siebert. Targeted covid-19 vaccination (tav-covid) considering limited vaccination capacities—an agent-based modeling evaluation. Vaccines, 9(5), 2021.

[43] Juan Ignacio Latorre Jimenez. EUROSIM 2019 Abstract Volume. In: EUROSIM 2019 Abstract Volume. ARGESIM, 2019.

[44] Lauer, St. A., Grantz, K. H., Qifang Bi, Forrest, K. J., Qulu Zheng, Meredith, H. R., Azman, A. S., Reich, N. G., and J. Lessler. The incubation period of coronavirus disease 2019 (COVID-19) from publicly reported confirmed cases: estimation and application. Annals of internal medicine, 2020.

[45] David Masad, D., and J. Kazil. Mesa: an agent-based modeling framework. In: 14th PYTHON in Science Conference, pp. 53–60, 2015.

[46] Makoto Matsumoto and Takuji Nishimura. Mersenne twister: a 623-dimensionally equidistributed uniform pseudo-random number generator. ACM Transactions on Modeling and Computer Simulation (TOMACS), 8(1):3–30, 1998.

[47] Vendor Managed Inventory (2021): Wikipedia, *https://en.wikipedia.org/w/index.php?title=Vendor-managed_inventory&oldid=1054860363*

[48] Bullwhip effect (2021): Wikipedia, *https://en.wikipedia.org/w/index.php?title=Bullwhip_effect&oldid=1054327373*

[49] Afridi, Nieto-Isaza, Ehm, Ponsignon, and Hamed. "A DEEP REINFORCEMENT LEARNING APPROACH FOR OPTIMAL REPLENISHMENT POLICY IN A VENDOR MANAGED INVENTORY SETTING FOR SEMICONDUCTORS." In Proceedings of the 2020 Winter Simulation Conference

13 Data Visualization

Barbora Vesela

"One picture is worth ten thousand words."

Chinese Proverb

Questions Answered in this Chapter:

- Why is data visualization needed?
- What is the history of data visualization?
- Which tools to use and what are tips and tricks to create a data visualization?
- What are the types and how to select a proper data visualization?
- How to present data visualization?

Humans have a natural need to understand the environment that surrounds them. Any contact with this external environment is mediated by basic senses such as sight, hearing, smell, taste and touch. Each of these senses has a unique ability to receive a specific type of information. The transmission of information is unevenly scattered between them: at most, up to 80 %, visual perception is involved [30].

In an effort to capture this information, individual data is collected by observing, measuring or recording action. The data is used to describe an observed phenomenon, object or property.

Data visualization combines both collected data and the advantages of visual perception. It creates a graphical representation of data using various types of charts, maps, diagrams and histograms, which help the observer to faster and better understand the observed phenomenon, object or property. It represents an analytical approach.

Nowadays a trend of digitalization is permeating our society. Although we are inundated with a large quantity of data, we often see only fragments of individual events and must put them together to obtain an overview of the situation. It is becoming increasingly difficult to distinguish important from unimportant information. It is even impossible to see a whole image of the situation.

Information is processed in our brain differently in conscious versus subconscious processes. At a conscious level, deliberation is based on serial computation with the use of logical, rational and syntactic rules. On the other hand, subconscious mechanisms use more parallel computation. People often attribute their and others' decisions to just simple arguments, but in fact, behind these decisions lie complex integrations of small pieces of information, gathered during entire life experiences [1].

When a certain topic has been quantitatively researched, data visualization offers insights into that issue and helps us to process the information better. Even large, high-dimensional data can be processed in an easily understandable way by the human brain [2]. With less effort we capture the information in a shorter time. Visualization brings us new information, allowing us to see hidden relationships and representations. It forces us to ask better questions and helps us make better decisions. It tells us a story of yesterday and today, and predicts a story for tomorrow.

Data visualization is not just nice to have, it is a must. Even a simple chart can help us more quickly understand a scenario and better decide the next action items. On the other hand, sophisticated data visualization can be a masterpiece. Its main purpose is to attract attention and deliver the information. This requires a deep dive into a problem we are trying to solve; it requires we think broadly about the problem set in the specific situation and environment from different perspectives. The combination of a creative, logical and critical thinking is necessary. Both options, a simple chart and sophisticated data visualization, can be comparably powerful.

■ 13.1 History

The effort to capture quantitative information into a visual form has a long history, starting with the first cartographic maps and graphics in statistics belonging to the ancient period. The predominant interest was in astrology and cartography. Due to the need to orientate, navigate and explore the surrounding environment, the first cartographic maps were created. The work of Claudius Ptolemy was particularly important: in his "Guide to Geography", he introduced a manual for compiling maps with the help of astronomical coordinates mostly processed in tabular form. His mathematical model of sonar system, where the Earth is stable and other bodies orbit it, has been considered correct for fifteen centuries [5].

The oldest known example of capturing variables graphically comes from the 10th century, and is reproduced in Figure 13.1. This anonymous graph shows the inclinations of the orbits of the planets as a function over time. The background is covered by a grid, the vertical axis represents the location, and the horizontal axis represents the time. This graph is a part of a manuscript which seems to have been used in monastery schools [6 – 9].

A further advancement of data visualization occurred in the 16th century. This was a period full of invention, research and exploration, considered as the beginning of modern science. With scientists were working in different areas simultaneously, diverse fields such as natural science, mathematics, engineering, astronomy, navigation and geography were developed. New techniques and instruments for observation and measurements were invented. Particularly important was the development of triangulation, a technique which involves applying multiple data collection techniques in order to analyze the results of any given, individual study. Its aim is to remove the weaknesses of individual methods, which, if used separately, would cause certain aspects of the topic to be overlooked [10, 8, 11]. During this period, the first trigonometric tables by Georg Rheticus and the first modern cartographic atlas "Theatrum Orbis Terrarum" (Theatre of the World) by Abraham Ortelius were created.

The atlas contained the majority of the then-available knowledge about and maps of the world. It was the first attempt to gather geographic knowledge in one volume [8, 9, 12].

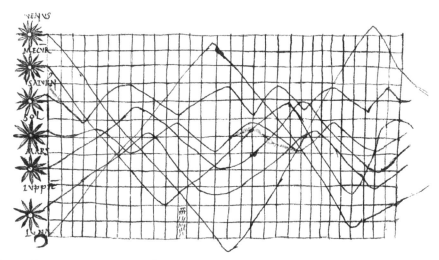

Figure 13.1 An anonymous graph from the 10th century showing the inclinations of the orbits of the planets as a function of time [7]

The 17th century saw continued interest in measurements of physical variables such as time, distance and space, leading to further developments in astronomy, map making, navigation, mathematics, probability theory and statistics. Theories of errors of measurement and estimation were developed, and studies of population, agricultural land, wealth and goods were made. The first visual representation of statistical data, created by Michael Florent van Langren and titled "1644" shows estimates of the difference in longitude between Toledo and Rome. It contains the names of the astronomers who provided the estimation, and an arrow representing the true distance (16° 30'), which was not known at that time. This visualization is considered as the earliest example of the principle of "effect ordering for data display" [8, 9]. See the depiction in Figure 13.2.

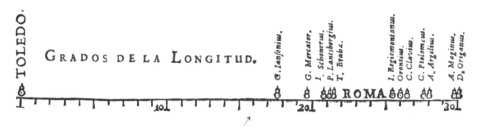

Figure 13.2 "1644", by Michael Florent van Langren, showing estimates by various astronomers of the difference in longitude between Toledo and Rome [8]

"1644" was not the only data visualization first to occur in the 17th century. In this time, we also see: the first graph of a continuous distribution function from Gaunt's table based on the bills of mortality, the first representation of a theoretic curve connecting barometric pressure to altitude, and the first weather map capturing winds [8].

The greatest flourishing of the field was done in the 18th and 19th centuries, nowknown as a period of new graphic forms. In cartography, isolines, contours, and isogons to show magnetic declination were all developed, in order to visualize physical properties in addition to geographic data.

Also for the first time, geometric objects such as squares and rectangles were used to compare the areas of European states. New methods such as curve fitting and interpolation were developed. Meanwhile, the invention of three-color printing helped attract more attention to the rapidly developing field of data visualization.

During this period, the line graph, bar chart and pie chart were all invented by Willian Playfair, considered to be the father of information design. He used two vertical scales for two different variables: population and taxes. He created "The Commercial and Political Atlas", which includes 43 time series plots and one column chart. Figure 13.3 shows one of these time series plots.

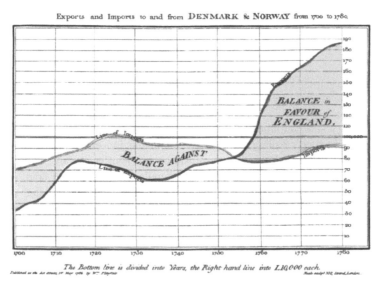

Figure 13.3 William Playfair's time series graph providing information about exports and imports of England to and from Denmark and Norway between 1700 to 1780 [13]

Other new creations from this time include histograms and scatterplots were created. Maps were collected in atlases showing economic, social, medical and physical topics. An example of medical visualization is the dot map created by Dr. John Snow, showing deaths due to cholera clustered around the Broad Street water pump in London, see in Figure 13.4 [14]. Printed coordinate paper was patented by Dr. Buxton.

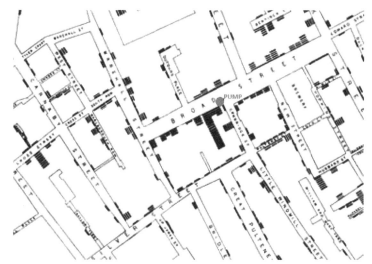

Figure 13.4 Graphical depiction of cholera deaths clustered around Broad Street pump in London. The pump is highlighted with blue color [14]

Also important was the work of Charles Joseph Minard, who created multiple useful visualizations, the most famous of which being a graphic describing the progress of Napoleon's soldiers in Russia. It represents a complex map using various variables such as temperature, geography, historical context, and loss of life of Napoleon's soldiers at a time and location. See the depiction in Figure 13.5. Minard was the first to use bar charts as proportional symbols in the legend for better understanding the map [15, 16].

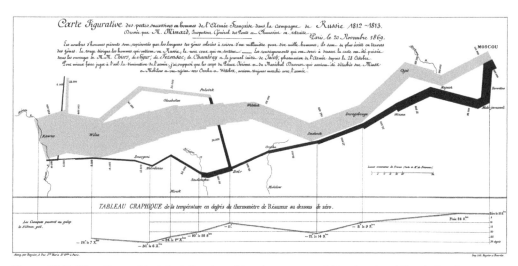

Figure 13.5 Minard's graphical depiction describing the progress of Napoleon's soldiers in Russia [19]

Florence Nightingale invented a polar area chart, so called "rose diagram", see in Figure 13.6.

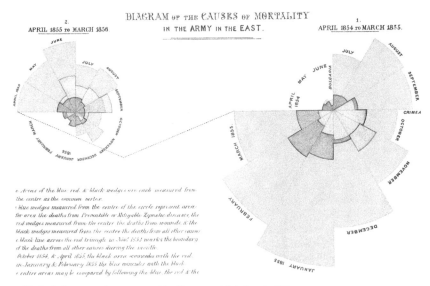

Figure 13.6 Polar area chart created by Florence Nightingale [17]

Luigi Perozzo created one of the first 3D data representations that shows the relationship between three variables. The visualization shows age among the Swedish population. The horizontal axis represents years, the vertical axis shows the number of people, and the third coordinate shows age groups [18, 9]. See the depiction in Figure 13.7.

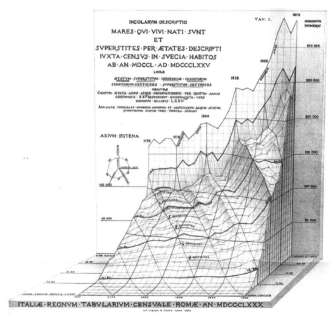

Figure 13.7 Three-dimensional data depiction created by Luigi Perozzo showing ages among the Swedish population [18]

The first half of the 20th century can be considered as a modern dark period. The invention of new graphic forms slowed. Focus was on the popularization of data visualization, which became mainstream. Graphical methods crucially contributed to new insights and theories in natural sciences.

The second half of the 20th century was affected by the rapid development of computers. With the creation of the first high-level computer language, Fortran, computers began to be used for processing statistical data. It was possible to collect and store larger volumes of data, process it easily, and create visualizations quickly. The new libraries specialized for work with data were created. At this point, computer science research began.

Later in this period, researchers like John W. Tukey in statistics and Jacques Bertin in cartography developed the field of information visualization. The first full color computer visualizations, and new interactive graphic software, were created. Important was the work, "The Visual Display of Quantitative Information", written by Edward Tufte. Methods for visualization of discrete and categorical data were reinvented. Various new, multidimensional reduction techniques such as biplot and correspondence analysis were developed and older techniques such as principal component analysis, multidimensional scaling and discriminant analysis were used. New visualization methods such as the association plot, mosaic plot and sieve diagram were developed [9, 8].

Nowadays, data visualization penetrates into various fields such as medicine, natural sciences, sport industry, economy, business and others. The processing of data has become a big topic.

■ 13.2 Which Tools to Use

Data visualizations can be created different ways. In the past, the paper form played a major role, but this gradually receded into the background as the digital form is gained strength. The number of tools specialized for data processing and visualization available on the market is growing.

The tools cover multiple levels of complexity, and various skills and functions. This reflects a diversity in working style and personalities of people. Data scientists have an opportunity to choose a proper application exactly for them according to their preferences.

The main goal remains the same: The tools should bring us some benefit for our work, whether in terms of time savings, clarity, interactivity, adequate recommendations and more.

In general, working with the applications should be easy. Simple usage allows us to save our energy and invest it into the task we are trying to solve. Learning new application should not take longer than doing our task. This can be supported by a user-friendly interface. It is necessary to think about the application as something which should help us, not hinder us.

From the beginning, we need to specify what is the purpose of our visualization and who is our audience. According to this we need to adjust our requirements. The question of which is more important, the creative graphical view or the highly accurate mathematical value, often has to be answered. For sophisticated visualizations whose aim is to attract attention, different applications are used than for scientific mathematical graphs.

We have to know our data. Often, we deal with heterogenous data obtained from various sources captured in different times. This can lead to a pipeline of errors, starting with a misleading data visualization and continuing with information misinterpretation, ending with making ill-informed or simply wrong decisions. To avoid this situation, we need to be careful and thorough when gathering this data.

We must also decide how to manage our data. Various tools may support various ways of working with data. A special interest must be paid to data protection, uploading inputs and downloading outputs. That is to say, data protection is a must. Visualization tools have to support a possibility to log in and allow access only for authorized users. The application should provide an option to assign users various roles with different levels of right based on their needs and power. Often, read only and edit functions are available.

Uploading inputs is often supported in three main ways. One way is to upload our data directly to the application. This method is simple, but if we deal with a large amount of data, it can be slow. The tool providers also often prohibit this method. Furthermore, this option does not provide full protection and control over data.

The second way is to upload our data to a cloud. It is a space on multiple, remote servers, delivered on demand with just-in-time capacity and costs. The data storage is managed and operated by a cloud computing provider as a service. On the one hand, this method saves on hardware costs, but on the other hand, it increases dependencies on third party companies. Nevertheless, it is becoming relatively popular [3].

The third way is to store data in our own servers and hardware. This method is relatively expensive, but it provides full control and protection over data. It brings the company independence from third party providers.

The tools usually support various input formats, and we must ensure that the format we deal with is among them. Otherwise, we need to convert our data to the supported format.

It is important to know which output formats the tool offers, and choose an appropriate one for our purpose.

We should consider how we would like to use the application. Basic tools can be suitable for short time simple solutions, while for long-term solutions, where continuous data collection takes place, more complex tools with support functions for scalability and iterative processing are needed.

The collection of a large amount of data is time consuming. Data scientists enjoy to see the results unfolding progressively. Often collection step goes together with the processing of currently acquired available data. It brings the opportunity to view the current computational status and start making some decisions before the whole computing is finished [4].

Support for the integration of visualization tools in an analytical workflow is necessary [4]. Otherwise, we will need to invest more time, energy and money to adjust our current workflow.

A tool may be used differently by individual users and teams. A large number of companies emphasizes teamwork collaboration. The tool should react to this and support the functionality of working in a team.

Developers welcome the possibility, which some applications allow, to slightly modify them and extend them according to their needs. This option enables developers to set up the tool exactly for their purpose.

Visualization tools offer different levels of assistance: from the basic functionality to the more complex. The tools often offer an interactive environment which allows faster orientation in a visualization.

In addition, advanced applications could provide recommendations for users regarding which graphical depiction to use for the data or which questions should be asked. The tool could not only analyze data from the past and today, but also give predictions for the future, based on the processing of historical data supported by an implementation of artificial intelligence and other machine learning algorithms in its workflow.

In summary, Figure 13.8 shows six main areas which should be addressed during the selection of a data visualization tool, and suggests questions that can be asked during this process.

Figure 13.8 Six main areas and related questions to consider when selecting a data visualization tool

At the end, the kind of tool we choose is up to us. It is necessary to test a tool in advance and find out which suits us the best. We take into account whether we will use the tool for a long or short time period.

■ 13.3 Types of Data Visualizations

There are various applications where data visualization is beneficial. It permeates most industries in a society. In the area of artificial intelligence, we encounter it in scientific papers; in data management, to visualize statistics of our datasets, training, validation and testing data; in modelling, to view a neural network's performance and final evaluation. The possibility to explore and visualize data increases the number of companies which use the power of business intelligence to drive their business. It helps them understand customer behavior, identify areas where improvement or modification of a product is needed, and predict future trends in a market.

For various applications, different data visualization types are used. In the following, we provide a short insight into the elementary types of visualizations.

13.3.1 Scatter Plot

The scatter plot is a graphical depiction of quantitative data, which are represented by points in a space described by Cartesian coordinates. Each axis corresponds to the value of one variable. Usually, the horizontal coordinate is determined as an independent and vertical as a dependent variable. Thus, typically, a scatter plot works with two variables. However, additional variables can be added in the form of different colors, hues, shapes or sizes of the data points. Beside the individual data points, a scatter plot allows us to explore patterns in data, such as missing data and outliers. Sometimes a trend line, mathematically calculated as the best fit to the data, is added to the plot to show the nature of variables' relationships to one another: this can be linear or nonlinear, positive or negative, weak or strong. See examples of scatter plot in Figure 13.9.

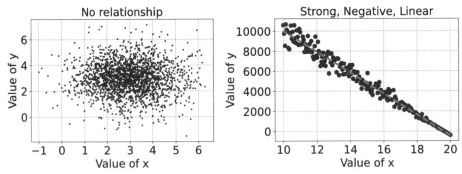

Figure 13.9 *Left:* a scatter plot showing two variables without a relationship. *Right:* a scatter plot with a red trend line showing a strong negative linear relationship between variables

13.3.2 Line Chart

A line chart, as shows in Figure 13.10, is a graphical depiction using points representing quantitative data connected by line from left to right, showing local change in value. Typically, the independent variable with continuous progression measured in regular intervals, such as units of time, is placed on the horizontal axis; the dependent variable of interest is represented on the vertical axis. The chart shows a trend in data. It also allows the display of multiple data sets, using a multiline option in which each data set corresponds to one line. Often, the lines are differentiated by color or hue. It is also possible to add uncertainty or variability of data to the plot.

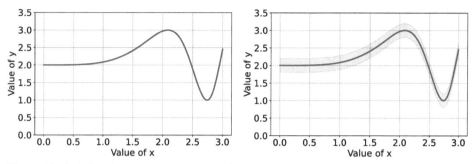

Figure 13.10 *Left:* a line chart between two variables. *Right:* the line chart with uncertainty added

As depicted in Figure 13.11, an area chart is a special type of line chart displaying quantitative values of data over an interval or period of time, using colored or textured area below the line, placed in Cartesian coordinate grid. The x coordinate should be always equal to zero. The graph provides a quick impression about the trends and quantity of data over time, and is designed to attract attention [22].

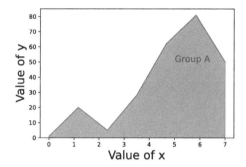

Figure 13.11
The figure shows an example of Area chart

13.3.3 Column and Bar Charts

Column and bar charts are the graphical depictions of quantitative information with the help of columns or bars, which are placed in relation to a horizontal and vertical coordinate. Whereas a bar chart is oriented horizontally, the column chart is oriented vertically. The length of each column or bar represents the proportional number of values in a corresponding measured class. Both charts are used to visualize categorical, ordinal and nominal data, and two or more values are compared. A special case is a double column and double bar chart, which can be used to show multiple sets of data in one plot. There are two variants: side-by-side and stacked. Side by side is powerful in the comparison of two data sets, whereas the stacked variant is used to show the total of two data sets [20]. See examples of a column chart in Figure 13.12 and a bar chart in Figure 13.13.

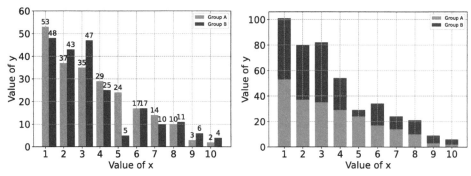

Figure 13.12 *Left:* a side-by-side column chart, useful for comparing two data sets. *Right:* a stacked column chart, often used to show the total of two data sets

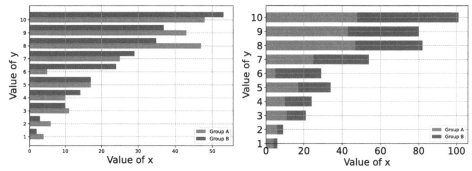

Figure 13.13 *Left:* a side-by-side bar chart, useful for comparing two data sets. *Right:* a stacked bar chart, often used to show the total of two data sets

13.3.4 Histogram

A histogram, such as the one depicted in Figure 13.14, is a graphical representation of continuous data measured at intervals using bins. It shows the shape (skewness, symmetricity) of the distribution of data for a single quantitative variable such as age, shades of grey in an image, and so on. Only one statistical variable is presented on the horizontal axis. The vertical axis typically shows the number count or percentage of occurrences observed in data. The height of the bar corresponds to the number of data points falling into the corresponding range of the bin. Often, less variation in the height of the bars on the vertical axis indicates more variability on the horizontal axis [23, 24].

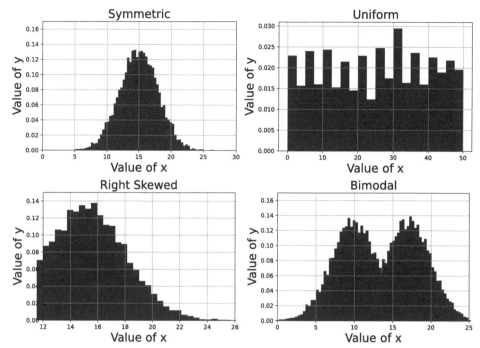

Figure 13.14 Histograms with different data distributions. *Clockwise from top left:* symmetric, uniform, right skewed, and bimodal

Compared to the bar chart, between the histogram bins there is not a gap, and the size of all bins is similar.

13.3.5 Pie Chart

Depicted in Figure 13.15, the pie chart, or "circle graph", is a plot providing a fast overall impression of categorical data with a lack of detailed information. It is a plot used to display data with the help of sectors in a circle. It shows only positive values. The number of sectors corresponds to the number of categories and the sector size is proportional to the number of values in the measured class. The sector size is calculated according to Equation 13.1.

$$Size\ of\ sector = \frac{Number\ of\ data\ in\ a\ class}{Total\ number\ of\ data} \times 360° \qquad Equation\ 13.1$$

Slices should be sorted according to their size, from the largest to the smallest, where the largest should begin at 0° degrees, at the top. The graph can be enriched with text placed in each sector, with the name of category and its frequency. Pie charts do not allow one to show data changes over time [21].

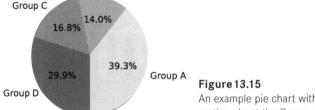

Figure 13.15
An example pie chart with text labels showing the information about the Group names and size of the sectors

13.3.6 Box Plot

The box plot, also called a "schematic plot", provides information about the spread and symmetry of data distribution using the median, approximate quartiles (25th and 75th percentile), minimum and maximum values of data points [25, 26]. The plot can be refined to also show unusual data points, such as outliers. Box plots helps us explore data and identify hidden patterns; for example, it can highlight asymmetric and irregularly shaped data distributions and show the extreme outliers [25, 26]. An example is shown in Figure 13.16.

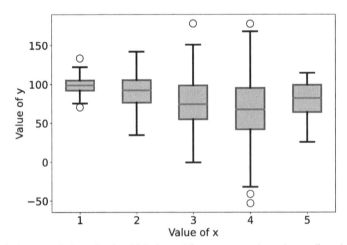

Figure 13.16 An example box plot, in which the red line corresponds to the median; the horizontal lines represent the 25th and 75th quartiles; the horizontal black lines show the minimum and maximum; and the circles depict outliers

13.3.7 Heat Map

A heat map, such as that shown in Figure 13.17, is a graphical depiction typically used to highlight a specific range of values of data indicating the observed feature. It allows us to explore how a phenomenon varies and is clustered over space.

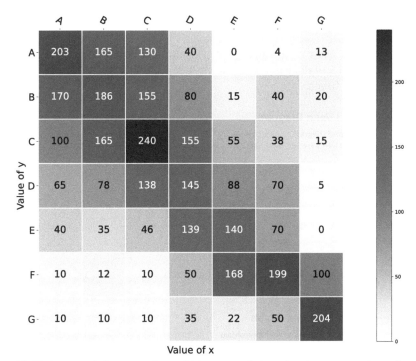

Figure 13.17 An example heat map, from which you can deduce that the most numbers of samples were correctly associated with its corresponding category

The clustered heat map works with a data matrix, where individual cells are displayed as rectangular tiles of a uniform size, filled with a specific color shades and hues based on their data values. The columns and rows of data matrix usually correspond to the columns and rows of the heat map [27, 28].

13.3.8 Tree Diagram

A tree diagram is used to map the structure of hierarchical data based on a branching system, using a parent-child relationship. Each node can have zero or more children and data on the same level. The siblings, should not overlap. Tree diagram enables multiple variations of layout. See example of tree diagram in Figure 13.18.

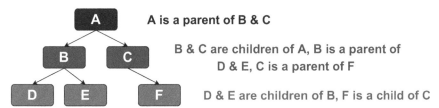

Figure 13.18 An example of tree diagram, which could be used for representing phenomena such as a hierarchical structure of leadership in a company

13.3.9 Other Types of Visualizations

There are, of course, many more kinds of data visualizations available than we have time to cover here. Figure 13.19 depicts just a few of these, including the Venn Diagram, Radar Chart, and Pyramid Graph.

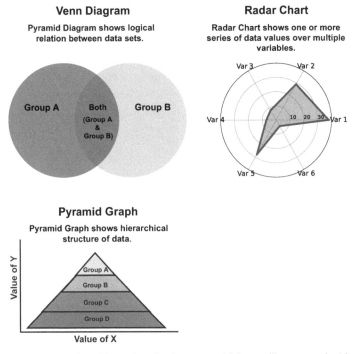

Figure 13.19 A selection of additional visualization types which we will not cover in this chapter

■ 13.4 Select the right Data Visualization

The selection of the proper graphical data visualization depends on various factors. The purpose and use of the depiction, the expertise of audience and type of processed data has to be considered.

There are two primary intentions of visualizations: presentation and analysis. Whereas the main goal of the presentation is to attract attention, explain, inform and tell a clear story, where usually only one visualization is used for the wide audience with various knowledge about the topic, the aim of the analysis is to explore the topic, and to detect and diagnose problems with the use of more data depictions intended for a narrower audience with a deeper knowledge about the field.

Data plays the key role. It is often noisy, heterogenous and obtained from different sources. Dimensionality (2D, 3D, multidimensional), size (small, medium, large), structure (structured, unstructured), heterogeneity and variable types all have to be considered.

The variable data types can be divided into the following categories:

- **Qualitative (categorical):** This is data that can be divided into characteristic groups, or categories. These could include, for example, hair color ("blond", "brown", "black") and education level ("basic", "high school", "university").

- **Quantitative (numerical):** Quantitative data can be counted. Thus, it could include variables such as age (10 years, 24 years, 36 years, 75 years), height (173 cm, 180 cm, 154 cm), weight (15.0 kg, 66.4 kg, 103.8 kg), number of children in a household (0, 1, 2, 3), price of an item (€ 5, € 8, € 10) and so on.

- **Discrete:** Discrete data is represented in whole numbers, as integers. This results in a gap between data points, since it is not possible to divide discrete values. Thus, the number of children a family has (0, 1, 2, 3), or the number of hospital visits a patient made in a year (0, 1, 2, 5), are possible examples.

- **Continuous:** Continuous data is counted in decimals, as floats. Theoretically, between data points is no gap, as it is always possible to divide the space between two values into infinitely smaller parts. Body temperature, for example, need not be measured in whole degrees (36.5 °C, 37.0 °C, 35.8 °C), and thus would be an example of continuous data, as would height (173.2 cm, 180.0 cm, 154.2 cm) and weight (15.4 kg, 66.0 kg, 103.1 kg).

- **Binary:** This is data which can be classified into just two categories. One of the sources of this type of data is the closed question, to which the answer can only be "yes" or "no". Binary data values can have a quantitative or qualitative character. For example, life status ("alive", "dead") or (1, 0), health status ("healthy", "ill") or (0, 1).

- **Nominal:** Nominal data is naturally disordered, with no sequence between the categories. The data values can have a quantitative or qualitative character. For example, hair color ("blond", "brown", "black"), aircraft model types ("helicopter", "airplane", "drone", "balloon"), number of children (0, 1, 2, 5).

- **Ordinal:** Ordinal data is naturally ordered and discrete, meaning there is a sequence between the categories. The data values can have a quantitative or qualitative character. For example, the level of vertebra fracture ("mild", "moderate", "severe") or (1, 2, 3), level of pain ("mild", "moderate", "severe") or (1, 2, 3) would all fall under the category of ordinal data.

- **Interval:** Interval data is continuous data which has no true zero point such as time.

- **Ratio:** Unlike interval data, ratio data has true zero point. It can include measures such as height (0.3 cm, 1.8 cm, 30.4 cm) and weight (15.0 kg, 66.4 kg, 103.8 kg).

The variable data types and their relationships are shown in Figure 13.20.

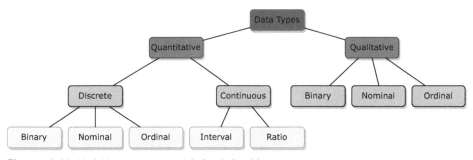

Figure 13.20 Variable data types and their relationships

As shown in Figure 13.21, for each specific type of data, certain kinds of data visualizations are more appropriate than others.

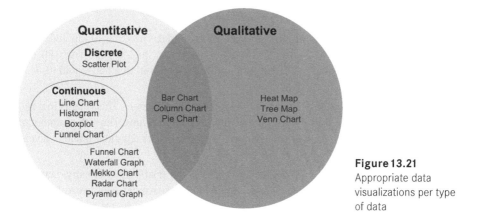

Figure 13.21
Appropriate data visualizations per type of data

The right data visualization to use can also be selected also according to the intention of the communication. Figure 13.22 provides a comprehensive overview.

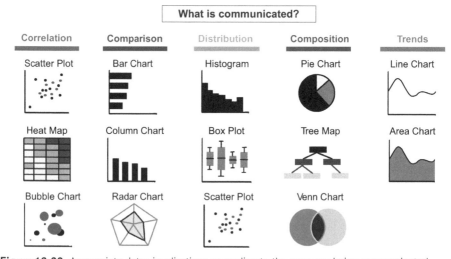

Figure 13.22 Appropriate data visualizations according to the message being communicated

◼ 13.5 Tips and Tricks

Effective data visualization requires a good understanding of its purpose. The message being communicated to the audience should be clear. The visualization should be easy to read, understand and interpret. This enables faster orientation in a topic and facilitates its better memorization. An effective visualization provides a good insight in various types of complex data, which can be used to gain knowledge. Depending on its intended purpose, it can be used to explore trends over time, depict the distribution of a dataset and find hidden features.

This can be achieved by a simple uniform design, where each item presents a clear and direct piece of information. Optimal data density, which can be achieved by avoiding overplotting, has to be considered: The amount of data should not overlap to the point where it is difficult to see the correlation between variables. All data should be clearly readable. This also applies to any supporting text, whose size and font style has to be appropriately selected. See examples of overfitting in Figure 13.23 for a scatter plot, Figure 13.24 for a line chart and Figure 13.25 for an area chart.

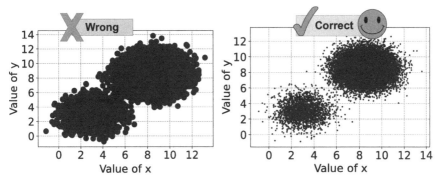

Figure 13.23 *Left:* an example of overfitting in scatter plot; *right:* a more appropriate display (notice how the correct result can be achieved by reducing the point size)

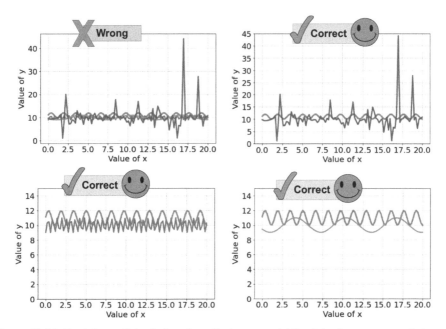

Figure 13.24 *Top left:* overfitting in line chart. For better readability, it is often recommended to display only one area per chart, as is shown in the remaining examples

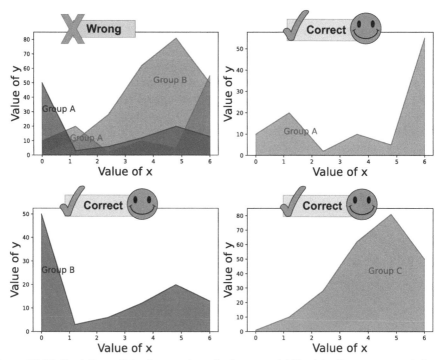

Figure 13.25 *Top left:* overfitting in area chart. For better readability, it is often recommended to display only one area per chart, as is shown in the remaining examples

Additional attributes such as colors, textures, hue and geometric symbols can be added, to attract the audience's attention and help them to better understand the topic. If the presentation is to include multiple visualizations, the same graphical style should be kept throughout. In general, depiction should not distort the data.

Often it is beneficial to highlight the data points of interest, so that the audience is drawn to them immediately. This can be applied for example in a scatter plot for important data values, or in a line chart for the points with the maximum and minimum values. Examples this are provided in Figure 13.26.

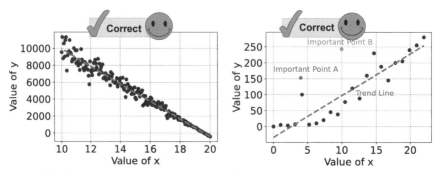

Figure 13.26 Correct examples of a scatter plot. *Left:* showing the trend line in red; *right:* highlighting important points

When creating visualizations for unordered variables, it is beneficial to follow the principle of effect ordering for data display. This principle says that the unordered data should be sorted according to the effect that is supposed to be showed. Similar items are placed together, which makes the data visualization globally more coherent [29]. Figure 13.27 shows this principle being applied to a column chart.

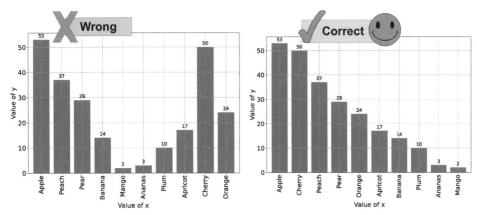

Figure 13.27 *Left:* unsorted columns in a column chart, leading to a confused message. *Right:* the same column chart, but following the principle of effect ordering for data display

You are also welcome to use labels in visualizations. For example, in the case of a pie chart, people can have difficulties comparing the size of the slices. Thus, it can be beneficial to add the text containing the size information, as depicted in Figure 13.28.

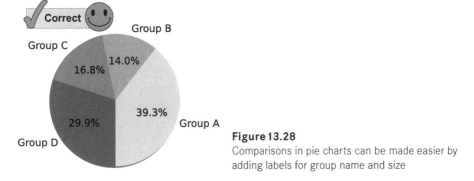

Figure 13.28
Comparisons in pie charts can be made easier by adding labels for group name and size

Whereas a zero baseline in a bar or column chart, or a histogram, is required, in a line chart it may be optional. In cases of comparison, relative values instead of absolute should usually be used. This gives space for proper interpretation, and correct conclusions can be drawn.

The width and number of the columns in a histogram should be checked according to the level of detail you wish to present. Whereas having fewer, wider columns provides less detailed information, and may cause some important patterns to be hidden, having many narrow columns allows you to show more details, can make it difficult to distinguish the noise from the valid data. In an ideal case, such as that shown in Figure 13.29, a trade-off between the level of detailed information and the size and number of columns in histogram is achieved.

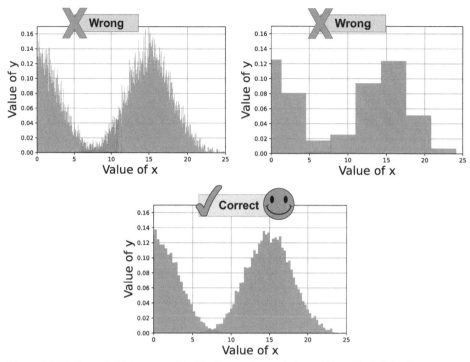

Figure 13.29 Example histograms with differing number and sizes of bins. *Top left:* having many, narrow bins reveal more detailed information but can include noise; *top right:* having fewer wider bins provide less information; *bottom:* a histogram correctly balancing the level of detail presented

In the case of a line chart for showing a small amount of data, we show measured data as points connected by a line. As Figure 13.30 shows, using point markers ensures that, when datapoints are missing, this is visually clear. This prevents the confusion and negates the risk of people making incorrect assumptions.

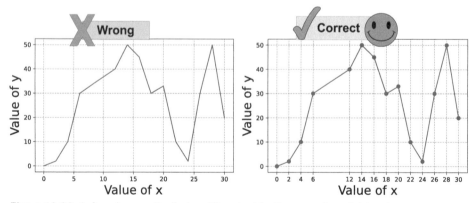

Figure 13.30 *Left:* an incorrectly displayed line chart for the case of small data where some datapoints may be missing. *Right:* a corrected version, where data values are displayed as points connected by a line

In addition to these tips and tricks, each data visualization task has to be considered and planned individually, in order to communicate the required message for the specific audience in the correct manner.

■ 13.6 Presentation of Data Visualization

Data visualizations do more than just provide a data. When presented in interactive sessions, we can increase the understandability and impact of the information, allowing the audience to remember it more clearly and easily.

For a better presentation, we need to know the background of the topic and the whole data chain. The knowledge starts already in a proper setup of the study. In accordance with this, the data collection and processing are done. Without this knowledge, data scientists are more likely to misinterpret some of the data features or miss some important pattern. Data visualization should not be the last part of the chain. After the visualization and presentation, there can and should be a discussion and a decision.

Before the presentation it is necessary to understand a topic. With this knowledge data scientists can make better assumptions and better understand data features. They need to take care to correctly interpret the graphic. For example, in statistics the well-known rule, "correlation does not imply causation, should be remembered.

The presentation should be adapted to the specifications of the audience. The language should look different for the narrow but highly professional scientific audience in the specific conference on the specific topic, versus for the wider public audience who have a short time slot for the visualization. In both cases the interpretation should be as accurate as possible.

■ 13.7 In a Nutshell

 Data Visualization is not just nice to have, it is a must.

Data visualization brings vital insights into data. It is about exploring the data features and helping us find hidden patterns. It allows better and faster understanding of a topic, and effective communication of that topic to new audiences.

■

References

[1] W. Singer, "The ongoing search for the neuronal correlate of consciousness," Open MIND, vol. 36, p. 36(T), 2015, doi: 10.15502/9783958570344

[2] L. van der Maaten, G.E. Hinton, "Visualizing High-Dimensional Data Using t-SNE," Journal of Machine Learning Research, vol. 9, p. 2579–2605, 2008

[3] "What is Cloud Storage? | AWS." Amazon Web Services, Inc. Accessed September 2, 2021. *https://aws.amazon.com/what-is-cloud-storage/*.

[4] G. Andrienko et al., "Big data visualization and analytics: Future research challenges and emerging applications," CEUR Workshop Proc., vol. 2578, no. February, 2020.

[5] "Klaudios Ptolemaios – Wikipedie." Wikipedie, Otevřená Encyklopedie. Last modified August 25, 2005. *https://cs.wikipedia.org/wiki/Klaudios_Ptolemaios*.

[6] H Gray Funkhouser. 1936. A note on a tenth century graph. Osiris 1 (1936), 260–262

[7] "Data Visualization." Wikipedia, the Free Encyclopedia. Last modified December 18, 2005. *https://en.wikipedia.org/wiki/Data_visualization*.

[8] W. H. Inmon and D. Linstedt, "A Brief History of Data," Data Archit. a Prim. Data Sci., pp. 39–44, 2015, doi: 10.1016/b978-0-12-802044-9.00007-6.

[9] "Data Visualization: History and Origins." Think Insights. Last modified August 17, 2021. *https://thinkinsights.net/digital/data-visualization-history/*.

[10] "Triangulace (metodologie) – Wikipedie." Wikipedie, Otevřená Encyklopedie. Last modified August 9, 2006. *https://cs.wikipedia.org/wiki/Triangulace_(metodologie)*.

[11] "The Technology, Science, and Inventions of the 16th Century." ThoughtCo. Accessed September 2, 2021. *https://www.thoughtco.com/16th-century-timeline-1992483*.

[12] D. Roegel, "A reconstruction of the tables of Rheticus ' Canon doctrinæ triangulorum (1551) HAL Id : inria-00543931 A reconstruction of the tables of Rheticus ' Canon doctrinæ triangulorum," no. 1551, 2021.

[13] K. Francis, M. Jacobsen, and S. Friesen, "The Use of Graphics to Communicate Findings of Longitudinal Data in Design-Based Research," Proc. 2015 InSITE Conf., no. November 2017, p. 928, 2015, doi: 10.28945/2240.

[14] T. Koch and K. Denike, "Essential, illustrative, or ... just propaganda? Rethinking John Snow's Broad Street map," Cartographica, vol. 45, no. 1, pp. 19–31, 2010, doi: 10.3138/carto.45.1.19.

[15] "The Underappreciated Man Behind the "Best Graphic Ever Produced"." National Geographic. Last modified March 16, 2017. *https://www.nationalgeographic.com/culture/article/charles-minard-cartography-infographics-history*.

[16] "Analyzing Minard's Visualization Of Napoleon's 1812 March." Thoughtbot. Accessed September 2, 2021. *https://thoughtbot.com/blog/analyzing-minards-visualization-of-napoleons-1812-march*.

[17] "Florence Nightingale Understood the Power of Visualizing Science." Science News. Last modified May 13, 2020. *https://www.sciencenews.org/article/florence-nightingale-birthday-power-visualizing-science*.

[18] R. Rau, C. Bohk-Ewald, M. M. Muszyńska, and J. W. Vaupel, "The Lexis Diagram," no. 2001, pp. 5–10, 2018, doi: 10.1007/978-3-319-64820-0_2.

[19] "Charles Joseph Minard." Wikipedia, the Free Encyclopedia. Last modified January 18, 2006. *https://en.wikipedia.org/wiki/Charles_Joseph_Minard*.

[20] "Bar Chart." BetterEvaluation. Last modified October 31, 2014. *https://www.betterevaluation.org/en/evaluation-options/BarChart*.

[21] "Pie Chart." BetterEvaluation. Last modified October 8, 2014. *https://www.betterevaluation.org/en/evaluation-options/piechart*.

[22] "What is an Area Graph, How Does an Area Graph Work, and What is an Area Graph Good For? – Storytelling with Data." Storytelling with Data. Last modified April 9, 2020. *https://www.story-tellingwithdata.com/blog/2020/4/9/what-is-an-area-graph*.

[23] R. L. Nuzzo, "Histograms: A Useful Data Analysis Visualization," PM R, vol. 11, pp. 309–312, 2019, doi: 10.1002/pmrj.12145.

[24] L. Boels, A. Bakker, W. Van Dooren, and P. Drijvers, "Conceptual difficulties when interpreting histograms: A review," Educ. Res. Rev., vol. 28, no. September, p. 100291, 2019, doi: 10.1016/j.edurev.2019.100291.

[25] M. Krzywinski and N. Altman, "Visualizing samples with box plots," Nat. Methods, vol. 11, no. 2, pp. 119–120, 2014, doi: 10.1038/nmeth.2813.

[26] D. F. Williamson, R. A. Parker, and J. S. Kendrick, "The box plot: A simple visual method to interpret data," Ann. Intern. Med., vol. 110, no. 11, pp. 916–921, 1989, doi: 10.7326/0003-4819-110-11-916.

[27] N. Gehlenborg and B. Wong, "Points of view: Heat maps," Nat. Methods, vol. 9, no. 3, p. 213, 2012, doi: 10.1038/nmeth.1902.

[28] L. Wilkinson and M. Friendly, "History corner the history of the cluster heat map," Am. Stat., vol. 63, no. 2, pp. 179–184, 2009, doi: 10.1198/tas.2009.0033.

[29] M. Friendly and E. Kwan, "Effect ordering for data displays," Comput. Stat. Data Anal., vol. 43, no. 4, pp. 509–539, 2003, doi: *https://doi.org/10.1016/S0167-9473(02)00290-6*.

[30] P.Kolář, "Posilování stresem Cesta k odolnosti," Universum, pp. 61, 2021

14 Data Driven Enterprises

Mario Meir-Huber, Stefan Papp

> *"Information is the oil of the 21st century,*
> *and analytics is the combustion engine."*
>
> Peter Sondergaard, SVP Gartner

Questions Answered in this Chapter:

- Which strategic decisions are essential to work in a data-driven way?
- What is a data strategy and how can you develop one?
- How do you build a data team? Centralized or decentralized?

"Data is the raw material of the 21st century" is a common statement in C-level floors of large companies. Many CEOs are paying increased attention to this topic. Companies that ignore the trend of generating value from data with analytical processes risk jeopardizing their existence.

Therefore, many companies face the question of how they can set up a sustainable, company-wide data strategy. This new orientation can sometimes challenge existing business models. Sometimes it even means that the data strategy can fundamentally change a company, requiring completely new business models.

For many companies it's not easy to get started, since they don't have the experience of Google or Facebook, which have been mining petabytes of data for many years. This chapter shows from a business perspective how a company can build a sustainable data strategy.

In this chapter, a model is presented, which consists of the three areas "Technology", "Organization" and "Business".

■ 14.1 The three Levels of a Data Driven Enterprise

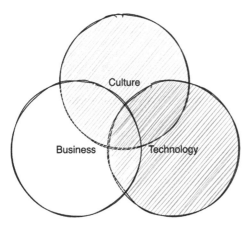

Figure 14.1
The intersection between Business, Technology and Culture

Data in the enterprise context is multidisciplinary. This is not just a technical challenge but also an organizational and cultural one. In order to increase data usage within an enterprise, leaders need to change corporate policies and the culture. This is explained in more detail in Section 14.2, "Culture".

Section 14.3, "Technology," explains the economic aspects of data platforms in more detail. Technical aspects are not discussed here, as in principle, the entire book deals with technical aspects.

Section 14.4, "Business," discusses certain basic requirements for implementing data-driven projects. Specific use cases are not mentioned here, as you will find a comprehensive presentation in Chapter 16, which is structured according to industries and areas.

■ 14.2 Culture

> *"Each strategy lasts until the first contact with the enemy.*
> *After that, there is only one system of substitutes." – Helmuth Graf von Moltke*

A key aspect of a corporate strategy is the organization of its units. The following sections focus on the core aspects:

1. Corporate strategy for data

2. Culture and organization

The first part, Corporate Strategy for Data, is primarily about the maturity model and how to create a data strategy. The second part, Culture and Organization, looks at corporate development. The essential point here is that the two aspects do not have to be carried out iteratively, but can run parallel and concurrently.

14.2.1 Corporate Strategy for Data

Every hike begins with a position fix. If you want to climb a mountain, you have to make sure you have suitable hiking maps (in digital or non-digital form) with you and know your position. Similarly, if one wants to establish a data strategy in the company, it is essential to know the current state first. Therefore, a current state analysis is normally carried out during strategy development. With the help of this analysis, it is possible to determine the maturity level of one's own organization. In the following, the four maturity phases are presented.

Entrepreneurial Data Maturity

It is essential to determine the maturity level of one's own company in order to derive meaningful measures for increasing analytical competence. The following four phases are provided for determining corporate data maturity:

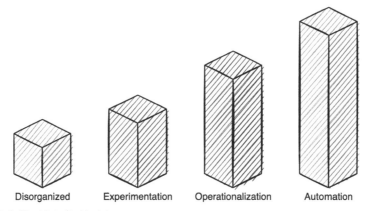

| Disorganized | Experimentation | Operationalization | Automation |

Figure 14.2 The Maturity Model

Phase 1: Disorganized

Strictly speaking, a company is already analyzing data when it stores information in Excel spreadsheets and uses this data as the basis for discussions in meetings. However, we do not want to take the view of information in spreadsheets as an analytical process here.

When we talk about companies in Phase 1, we are talking about those in which decision-makers usually make decisions based on gut feelings. In meetings, they may discuss what is written in Excel spreadsheets and what should be done as a result. However, it is not uncommon for decisions to be less strategic, and instead, made on an ad-hoc basis. Often they are based on compromises.

There is nothing wrong with this corporate culture per se. However, if you want to position analytics in this phase, you have to make sure that the mentality of the people involves changes. Decision makers must learn to trust data analysis. When management understands that more can be achieved with a structured approach than with ad hoc decisions, the foundation is laid for Phase 2.

Phase 2: Experimentation

If we look at Big Data as a discipline for efficiently analyzing mass data, many companies are in Phase 2.

Management has already understood that complex analytics can generate value. Individual decision-makers may also already have ideas about how their own companies could benefit. But there is still a lack of confidence. Even though numerous consultants have already pointed out the urgency to act quickly, executives still hesitate to make major investments, well aware that data programs can be expensive.

Instead of investing a lot of money in hardware and programs, employees are given the space to experiment on their own initiative on the back burner, in the hope that greater value will become apparent here, which might then justify an investment.

Depending on the size of the company, it can also happen that several people or departments want to take on this issue. Accordingly, conflicts of responsibility can arise. In large companies, it often happens that individual departments work on overlapping projects without knowing about each other.

Often, data initiatives are heavily IT-driven because many IT staff are curious and eager to try out new technologies. Sometimes, however, there are also efforts within various departments to work on the data topic, and individual departments may enter into competition. To a certain extent, this is desirable, as it generates a lot of ideas. However, if this happens without strategic orientation, it can be rather counterproductive and block projects in the long term.

It is important for the data strategist not to get caught between the two fronts. Instead, they should aim to bundle the interests of the people involved, and pragmatically direct the energy to where enough value is generated with data so that the company management releases further investment capital. This is the only way to reach Phase 3.

Phase 3: Operationalization

While Phase 2 is still about discussing the value of data-driven businesses, Phase 3 is already clear on how a business can benefit from data. In Phase 3, proof of concepts (PoCs) have already been created to determine how the company can generate added value from data.

What companies lack in Phase 3 is the operationalization of the solutions. In other words, the results that were determined in PoCs must now become operationally usable solutions and services for the department or for the company's customers. This step is often a very complex one, since PoCs are often very simple and essential parts of the PoC have to be extensively reworked for operational use.

Let's look at operationalization with some examples. Self-driving cars have been on the road for years and are accident-free in a controlled environment. But it will be some time before we are able to trust these cars to handle all situations at least as well as human drivers. Think here specifically of chaotic traffic situations like a rush hour in a major city.

In a PoC in a controlled environment, it is not rocket science to identify test persons via machine learning when they enter a store. But making a global and automated solution out of it, in which customers also receive personalized offers and all data protection requirements are met, is another matter.

The effort required to turn PoCs into real operational applications is often underestimated. Many believe that transferring results from PoCs to production is just a formality. However, many companies fail at the very first operationalizations because the complexity is high and many problems can arise, from data governance to infrastructure.

Phase 4: Automation

In the automation phase, the company has an operational platform. New analytical use cases follow a process that is partly automated and through which success can also be measured

As before, PoCs and subsequent operationalizations can be complex and can also get out of control. Data science is a structured process to generate new knowledge, it will never work without the risk of failure.

The essence of Phase 4 is that companies understand the process and the value that is generated from data.

The mindset is also already there at this point. The company perceives itself as being data-driven. No one questions the value and benefit of the transformation anymore. The teams around big data and analytics are constantly creating added value for the company.

14.2.2 The Current State Analysis

The Current State analysis is the actual starting point for a future data strategy. Here, the maturity level in the areas defined at the beginning, "Technology", "Business" and "Culture", is determined. The analysis is typically carried out using the questionnaire technique and is intended to provide a comprehensive picture of the state in the company with regard to data. The following questions are asked in the three core areas:

- **Technology**
    - Type of technologies and databases used
    - Data volumes in the systems and (daily) growth
    - Type of existing "data marts" and their data
    - Security and authorization systems for data and policies
    - Use of the data and type and frequency of access to them
    - Governance systems for data
    - Standards and systems around data quality
    - Systems that produce data
- **Organization**
    - Business units that deal with data, such as
        - Employees in the company and their know-how for data, and
        - Departments dealing with data
- **Business**
    - Current projects
    - The future project portfolio

The business environment (e.g. competitors) and the company's own assessment in comparison to it

Problems that exist in the handling of data

The time it takes to access the data

Use of external data

General maturity level of the department to use data for decisions in daily work

Depending on the size of the company, this analysis can be more or less extensive. If one considers a small company with a centralized corporate structure, the analysis will be very quick to perform. However, the authors have a lot of experience in working with large international corporations with decentralized structures. Here, the respective country organizations with their respective departments must be considered.

After the completion of the analysis, the evaluation and derivation of the most important strategic levers follows.

Project Selection

Let's look at the value proposition of Advanced Analytics and Big Data. These serve to

- reduce costs,
- help make quicker decisions,
- open up new markets and generate new business models.

It can often be helpful to try to identify specifically in which areas the company is operationally blind. For example, a telecommunications provider traditionally makes money from subscribers. By using Big Data, completely new business areas can come to light. However, those who are always focused on driving up subscriber numbers may overlook what other revenue streams may be available to the company.

Common questions are:

- How can we use a customer journey to determine what motivates customers to cancel (churn)?
- How can we use data to ensure that our machines fail less often (predictive maintenance)?

The next step is to identify the potential data sources. The attention should not only be on existing data sources, but also include potentially new ones. There should be no barriers to the thought process.

The result should be a matrix of existing data sources and their relation to possible use cases. Companies that have numerous or complex data sources can also purchase a Data Catalog.

It can be helpful to start with a first high-level exploration of the data in this phase in order to find information about the data quality.

The final step is project selection. Concepts of classical project selection play a role here. The following points should be essential in the consideration:

- **Costs vs. Benefits of the Project:** The ratio of costs to expected revenue increases is calculated. This results in either cost savings or new business models.
- **Feasibility:** Projects can be complex and lengthy to implement.

- **Strategic Importance:** Here it is important to consider whether a market competitor already offers similar products and whether the functionality is demanded by customers. This can possibly be in contrast to the previous two points.

- **Legal Aspects:** Chapter 15 will show that legal aspects also need to be considered. It may happen that the planned evaluation of data violates data protection and cannot be carried out.

At the end of the project selection, a prioritization of the individual topics is made. Based on the priority list, the respective projects are mapped in a time series and thus in a roadmap.

14.2.3 Culture and Organization of a Successful Data Organisation

Now that the corporate strategy has been established, it is time to look at the culture within the company and the organization. Whole books are written about corporate cultures, but here we want to focus "only" on the topic of data. This chapter will outline that, but let's get one thing straight: data is driven by the business, so it's important that the unit for data is not hidden in some deep hierarchy in IT. Simply because there is no value to be added by doing so.

The Team

In any case, creating and implementing the data strategy is a large team effort that requires different roles. We now look at these roles from a business perspective, having already looked at the platform perspective in Chapter 3, which includes information on the tasks of the operational roles Data Engineer and DevOps Engineer.

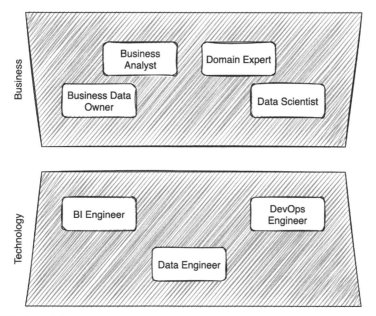

Figure 14.3 Team Roles

- **Business Analyst:** This role comes directly from the business environment of the company. A Business Analyst knows the company well and also the individual functions and divisions. She determines which projects and measures make sense in the company and what added value they bring. Analysts can also be assigned to individual departments. In banks, for example, there are Risk Analysts.

- **Domain Expert:** Often the most underestimated role in any data program is the Domain Expert. This person knows the domain inside and out from an operational perspective. In retail, it may be the ladies and gentlemen who have been sitting at the register for 20 years sifting through merchandise. In a telecommunications operation, it may be a Network Engineer who understands every detail of a radio access network. Domain Experts are the people who can provide feedback on whether and how a data program's business ideas are feasible.

- **Data Scientist:** We have already discussed the tasks of a Data Scientist in Chapter 2. Therefore, we will only look at the difference between a Data Scientist and a Data Analyst, since both analyze data.

  A Data Scientist focuses on generating new knowledge by analyzing data, whereas an Analyst only analyzes data to make a business decision. A data scientist generates new knowledge by deriving future decisions from past data and helping the company to become better. For example, he makes predictions about how business areas can develop in the future. A Data Analyst, on the other hand, simply describes the current situation. The data she analyzes could consist of, for example, the basis for an annual report with financial figures.

- **BI Engineer:** BI Engineers are visualization professionals. They know how to turn boring data into exciting graphics that create real "aha" experiences. The role of BI Engineers can also be seen as a bridge between Data Science and the business. BI Engineers usually use self-service BI tools and help users to prepare data in an appealing way.

- **Business Data Owner:** Business Data Owners are a kind of data accountant. They make sure that governance rules are followed. A business data owner constantly drives data quality and thus plays a major role in helping data scientists do their job better. In this, the Business Data Owner evaluates the input data and checks it against quality metrics. They should have a very good understanding of how data producing systems work and why data is in a particular format. In manufacturing operations, this could be machine data, for example. The Business Data Owner understands how the machine works and is therefore a good judge of why data is produced and in what form. Their importance is often underestimated, but they belong in a data team like controllers belong to accounting. The business data owner has the overall responsibility of the data in the respective business department.

Internal Organization

One issue that is often discussed is the question of the reporting lines. Since data programs are almost vital to the survival of many companies, the reporting function should be as high up in the hierarchy as possible. In large companies, this is the **Chief Data Officer**. This person leads the data strategy and is essential when it comes to transforming the company into a data-driven enterprise. This is primarily a person who is entrusted with strategic decisions.

Some companies see analytics as part of IT. This is not advisable unless IT solutions are the core products of the company. Data Engineers should remain in the line of the CIO, while Data Scientists are to be found within the business departments. The background is that the goals of Data Scientists are not the same as those of IT departments. IT departments aim to ensure stable operations. An IT fulfills its purpose when it enables other departments to do their job smoothly. A Data Scientist, on the other hand, produces knowledge that ideally opens up new business areas.

Nor should an analytics department be part of a BI department, since the BI department is usually several levels below the management. Conflicts of objectives also arise here. BI departments aim to optimally handle business processes for a department with the help of analytics. The task of a Risk Analyst is to provide a risk assessment, but the task of a data scientist could be to analyze whether information can be gained from the risk assessments of the analysts and the linkage with other data sources that help to strategically put the company on a new footing. The Risk Analyst usually does not have this creative freedom.

Centralized or Decentralized Teams

Large, multinational companies face different challenges than medium-sized companies. Often there is a holding company with autonomously acting sub-companies. This means that there may be teams per organizational unit.

The extent to which the central organization influences subordinate organizations varies from company to company. There are corporations in which the head office has always had little influence and the individual locations act autonomously and sometimes even compete with each other.

In other forms of organisation, the head office can also take on more control functions. Ultimately, it is always a question of the stakeholder management skills of the people involved. Some are in a better position than others to create networks of contacts to move things forward.

The person who sets the data strategy needs to think about whether the data science department is set up directly or indirectly.

- In the **direct/central set-up**, the respective roles and persons are grouped together centrally. The projects are carried out with the respective specialist departments as partners.
- If an **indirect/decentralized setup** is chosen, there is only a small department for coordination with respective roles in the departments.

Both models have advantages and disadvantages. The specifications of the board of directors are given more attention in a centralized organization than in a decentralized organization. In a decentralized structure, project content is driven by specialist departments. The consequence of this is that in decentralized organizations a silos become possible in which departments pursue their own interests. In turn, centralized orientations bear the risk that the actual interests of individual departments are not taken into account.

Differences also arise from resource requirements. In a decentralized organization, resources are tied to a department. People cannot simply be assigned to other organizations. In a centralized organization, FTE resources can be assigned to other projects more quickly, but they are also less specialized. The following table summarizes the points just discussed.

Table 14.1 Centralised vs. Decentralised Organisation

	Central	Decentralized
Alignment with corporate strategy	High	Medium
Projects	Less, tending to be strategic	More, tending to be operational
Adaptation to departmental requirements	Medium	High
Possibility of central control	High	Low
Efficiency	Low	Medium
Resource requirements	Medium	High

Only in very few cases will a data program completely break through the corporate structure. In most cases, it will adapt to existing cultures. Often there is also a combination of centralized and decentralized structures. A central team defines the framework within which the decentralized teams can operate, but does not control the decentralized teams (see CDO department).

Closer to the Business with Agility

A key topic that has become increasingly established in recent years is the desire to bring data closer to the business. Data has always been used in business and creates added value there. Therefore, it is essential to enable this. This cannot be solved with classic, rigid hierarchical thinking (cf. centralized vs. decentralized organization). Many companies have placed the data departments in newly created digitalization departments or in IT. Both approaches have so far caused problems in most of the companies with which the authors are in contact:

- The digitization departments had extensive freedom and did not have to support corporate legacies. These departments were often able to start from scratch, but did not create any added business value because the solutions could not be integrated.

- IT departments are too focused on legacy applications and have hardly been able to free themselves from them. Business departments and IT were or are often very foreign to each other and there is usually some friction between the two.

Consequently, a different setup has to be chosen. One of the most interesting approaches to this is agilization. Data teams need to be sponsored by a product owner who sits in the business. A scrum master manages these teams in agile sprints. All essential roles such as DevOps Engineer, Data Engineer, Data Scientist and alike are part of the team. The statement "you build it, you run it" applies here. The team is responsible for the operationalization of the product.

This is definitely a decentralized structure. In order to address certain dangers, such as the lack of a central strategy and high resource requirements, an intermediate layer must be added. Here, the Spotify model of tribes, squats and chapters is particularly suitable.[1]

---

[1] *https://agilescrumgroup.de/spotify-modell/*

This model of tribes makes it possible to establish a central unit, but at the same time bring it closer to the business. However, this also requires that both the IT managers and the managers in the business departments change their mindset in a cooperative direction. In Tribes, the actual reporting line is in IT, whereas functional management is the responsibility of the business. The respective elements are described below:

- **Tribe:** The tribe is the highest order in the agile setup. Here, there is usually a tribe leader who only performs technical tasks to a limited extent. This person acts more as a strategic HR manager. Core tasks are employee reviews, training, development and the assignment to the right squat. The Tribe Leader coordinates closely with the business departments and learns about the strengths and weaknesses of the individual members of the Tribe. The Tribe Leader has a large number of direct reports, typically ranging from around 30 to several hundred.

- **Squat:** A squat is comparable to a Scrum team. The squat is assigned to a business function and covers its business cases. A squat can be temporary or long-term, depending on which use case is to be implemented. A squat consists of all the functions that are necessary for a use case. A Squat is usually led by a Squat Leader (Scrum Master).

- **Chapter:** As individuals work in the squat, they are often not arranged per their usual subject matter. This can lead to Data Engineers or Data Scientists often acting as "lone wolves". This problem is solved by chapters, where the respective professionals are grouped together.

Figure 14.4 represents this setup.

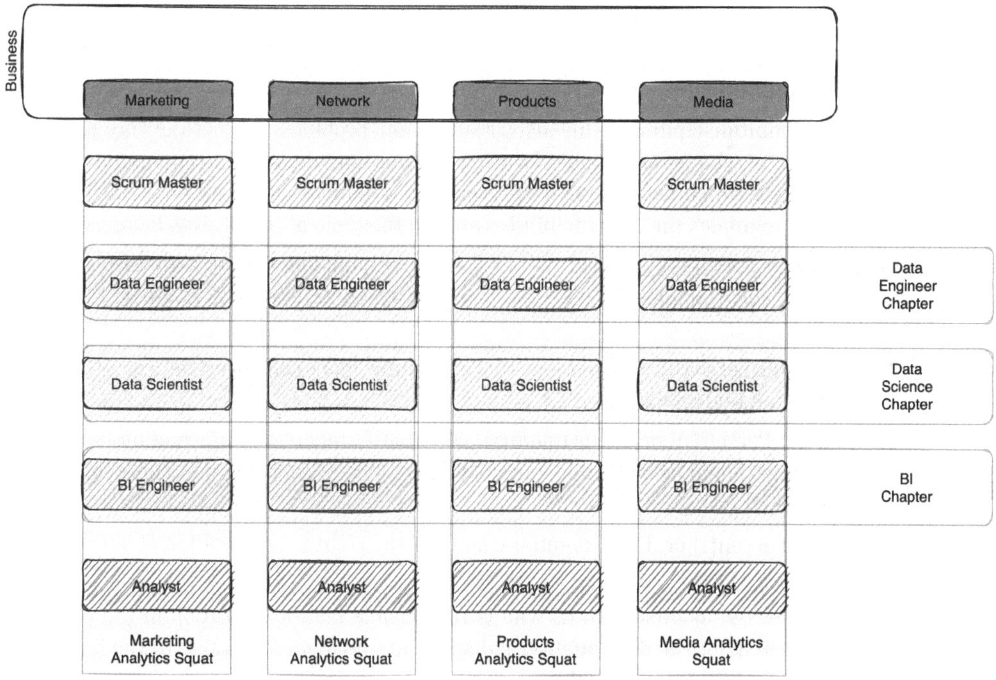

Figure 14.4 Agile Setup for a data project

The illustration shows a fictitious tribe in a telecommunications company. Here there are various business functions such as "Marketing", "Network", "Products" and "Media". For each of these functions there is a squat that implements projects together and under the ownership of the business. All four Squats make up the Tribe. It is important that each squat can act independently, which not only affects prioritization, but also technology selection. A key enabler for this is the "Data Mesh", which is described a little later in this chapter. However, in order for there to be uniformity of technologies, it is important to ensure that the respective functions are exchanged across chapters.

Chief Data Officer Unit

Regardless of which setup is ultimately chosen within the company, a department is always required that forms the link between data scientists, IT and the business units. It is advisable to set up a CDO (Chief Data Officer) department. Ideally, this department should be very close to the business and thus at a very high reporting level. This is usually found directly in the CIO, COO or CEO area. The unit is led by a Chief Data Officer, who has a few employees under him.

A CDO department sets a direction in the company, but does not take care of the operational execution of this. Therefore, you will primarily find senior program managers here who drive projects forward together with the business and IT departments. The rules and data architecture are also defined here. If a company opts for the "tribe" approach, the chapters are managed by this department, otherwise the technical departments are to be seen as a "dotted line" to the CDO department.

The main role of the CDO department is to set the strategy and oversee its execution.

Clear Responsibilities

Since data is multidisciplinary, this also creates some problems. One of the core problems is the question of who is responsible for what in the company. This question often leads to long discussions which waste time and resources. A remedy here can be a RACI matrix, which simply regulates the responsibilities around the topic of "data". RACI stands for:

- **Responsible:** Person(s) or departments that are responsible for the actual implementation. This is, for example, the use case team, which consists of data engineers and data scientists.
- **Accountable:** Person or department that is mainly responsible for the result (e.g. the product owner, budget manager, ...)
- **Consulted:** Person(s) or department(s) who have important information about the product. They should be consulted, but not responsible for the outcome. This could be, for example, Legal, Privacy or Security.
- **Informed:** Person(s) or department(s) who have the right to information about the product.

Here, the respective points, such as who is responsible for the operation of the platform, who is responsible for the data quality, and so on, are presented in a list. In the horizontal dimension, the respective stakeholders are listed. These are usually:

- **Business:** The particular business function of the company, such as marketing, finance, and purchasing

- **CDO:** The CDO department
- **The (local) IT:** The IT department or the IT departments of the respective country organisations, if the IT is set up decentrally
- **Legal, Privacy & Security:** Everything about legal and regulatory topics. The topic of security also plays a role here, provided it has not been considered via the "IT" point.
- **Local data management:** In decentrally organized companies, there is often also a local data management team. This can also be a country CDO department, for example.

The main elements that appear in a RACI matrix are:

- **Data Infrastructure:** This includes the legacy infrastructure, data governance tools, the data lake and data warehouse, and various support services (such as Active Directory, SSO, and so on).
- **Data Assets:** This includes all activities of data integration, master data management, data governance & security and analytical models.
- **Reporting and Analytics:** This includes data preparation, data cleansing, dashboards and analytical model development.
- **Compliance and Legal:** This includes all regulatory requirements as well as legal integration.
- **Strategy and organization:** This includes all strategic aspects such as organizational development, enterprise data architecture and use case prioritization.
- **Business process integration:** This includes the elements of integration into an end-to-end process in the company and integration into the real systems of the company.

Normally, each of these six elements of a RACI matrix has several subcategories. A RACI matrix that clearly defines responsibilities in a large corporation is usually three levels deep and has up to 70 individual elements. Going through each of these items is beyond the scope of this chapter.

The Importance of Data Governance

This section is not devoted to describing data governance per se. That is done elsewhere in this book, from a technical perspective. Rather, it is intended to discuss the great importance of data governance for corporate strategy.

A key aspect in many companies is decentralized data storage. With the data lake, the approach existed for a certain time to bring data into a central system and then have it "harmonized". However, this approach has failed in most companies. Today, a data lake is often just one component of the architecture, or it is common to find multiple data lakes in the enterprise. This leads to the question of how data can still be kept "clean".

Two things are necessary for this: First, the realization that data will always be decentralized, which in turn leads to the conclusion that, second, only data governance can address this problem. Decentrally organized data must be recorded in a data catalog. This makes the existing "data silos" discoverable and enables data consumers to connect this data if necessary, and integrate it into their analyses. Once data has been integrated into a data catalog, the associated processes can be automated. A core aspect here is automatic access to the respective data sources and the improvement of data quality.

In the long term, each of these decentralized data sources - which can already be called a data mesh - should offer its own APIs. This achieves harmonization without comprehensive data integration programs. You only bring the silos closer to standards and thus improve the data quality in the long term and sustainably.

14.2.4 Core Problem: The Skills Gap

One problem that all large companies have to deal with is the so-called "skills gap". Many key IT positions are often difficult or impossible to fill. Large, established companies also have this problem, although it affects them less intensely, as many employees tend to opt for large corporations. This looks good on the CV and corporations usually pay much better than small to medium sized companies.

Nevertheless, the skills gap affects all companies. Therefore, it is not enough to launch large internalization initiatives. It takes much more than that: building skills on the one hand and networking existing employees on the other.

Strategic Skill Development

In large companies, it is important to expand the skills of employees to include digital aspects. Dealing with data is an essential part of this, so it is important to set special focus here. Thus, for strategic skills development within the company, different groups of people must be addressed.

Figure 14.5
Skill Development: Groups

Figure 14.5 shows the three main groups relevant for skills development in the enterprise. The respective groups are described below:

- **All Employees:** In this group it is important to create an online learning program for all employees of the company. Only the basics should be taught here, ranging from use cases around data to explanations of common terms. The goal is that employees, such as those in controlling, helpdesk or similar, are familiar with the basic concepts of data. The aim is intentionally not to reach a technical level, as such a goal could scare off this group of people. This group is very important, as there is potential here for employees to become more interested in the data topic and thus be considered for re-skilling.

- **Managers:** In this group, managers in particular should be addressed. Depending on the level, courses should be offered either virtually or as classroom training. Lower and middle management should be taught about the tools and possibilities of data. Often it is middle management that is afraid of digitalization and thus blocks these topics. The courses should take away the fear of the subject and bring data-driven thinking to this group. For top management, a different approach should be taken. Ideally, a one-day workshop that needs to be planned long in advance. The workshop should primarily emphasize the business value of data. But it is also important to mention some basic terms and technical challenges, such as data governance.

- **Experts:** Very important is also the further training of the experts. There are several reasons for this: On the one hand, you have to make sure that the most important experts are always up to date. On the other hand, training offers bind these experts to the company. This group also includes potential experts. These are, for example, software developers or mathematicians who would be able to work with data. It is often easy to offer them re-skilling. It is important in the group of experts that they receive targeted training, like opportunities to attend specialist conferences or take courses on new tools.

Extensive skill development within the company is essential in any case. This section can only provide an overview. Ultimately, it is important that the programme is developed in close cooperation with HR. In many large companies there are specially appointed learning managers for this purpose.

Community Development

Many companies have experts on the topic of data. The cooperation of these is often only ad-hoc and very unorganized, as they often work on projects in the specialist departments. This can lead to duplications. Furthermore, synergies are not used. These problems can be solved by an organized community within a company. A role for community management can be established at a central point, such as the CDO department. In those companies where this was the case, large sums could be saved because projects could be reused and technical platforms as well.

Typically, different formats are used in a community:

- **Monthly video conferences:** various projects are presented here with technical details. It is advisable to make the whole thing virtual so that other locations can also be integrated.

- **Annual conference:** it is important that all the people involved meet in person once a year. Since it involves travel, it is advisable to make it a two-day event. This way you can also include an evening event, which provides a relaxed atmosphere.

In addition to conferences, it is also important to establish internal discussion platforms. This keeps the people involved in contact with one another outside of the monthly video conferences. It has been shown that an annual conference is also an important "booster" for this.

■ 14.3 Technology

This section deals with the business-relevant aspects of the technical platform. We have already dealt with the technical details of platforms in Chapters 2 and 3.

Business users are usually less interested in the technical details, such as which framework is used and in which programming language features are implemented. From a business point of view, it is relevant whether a platform also has the necessary features to implement new analytical use cases. Offered systems should have all enterprise features, such as governance features.

14.3.1 The Impact of Open Source

Many big data solutions are based at least in part on open source products. For a long time, business users in particular argued that free software could not be integrated into the complex IT landscapes of large companies that had evolved over decades. They lacked the enterprise components that only proprietary solutions could provide.

Those days are long gone. Behind open source distributions are companies with commercial interests. These companies extend the open source core with exactly those enterprise features that their customers need. The business model of making money from open source distributions by making them "enterprise ready" is also not new. Companies like Red Hat or SuSE have been successfully running this business model with Linux for years.

The open source business model also exploded the idea of system integrators being able to be considered universal service providers. Even the largest software houses now use open source components. Accordingly, the question of whether open source or not hardly arises any more.

14.3.2 Cloud

The shared vision of the authors of this book is that cloud services will have a status similar to electricity in the near future. There may be individual organizations, such as hospitals, that have a generator in the basement to stay in operation during a power outage, but the norm is to purchase electricity and not produce it yourself.

With on-premise solutions, seven-figure sums often have to be commissioned in order to start a Big Data program. Many managers often do not want to take responsibility for this and therefore prefer to start with a lightweight solution in the cloud. In addition, cloud providers are offering more and more enterprise features that on-premise solutions do not. Therefore, there is no way around the cloud.

Another argument in favor of the cloud is that it offers precisely the features that are suitable for a fail-fast approach and thus enables a process such as "agile analytics". The elasticity and scalability of cloud solutions creates a flexibility that an on-premise solution cannot offer.

Cloud providers also know that companies will not migrate completely to the cloud overnight. Concepts such as the **hybrid cloud**, in which companies move only parts of their landscape to the cloud, are booming accordingly.

14.3.3 Vendor Selection

Choosing the right platform and deciding on a vendor is harder today than ever before.

The days when companies could trust a universal solution provider to deliver one big appliance that runs everything are over, thanks to the diversity on offer. IT leaders are faced with a myriad of different solutions and product combinations that must also be aligned with a cloud strategy.

Problems with technologies are usually in the details. They don't come up in sales conversations. In addition, vendors not only offer a platform, but sometimes also associated packages, such as industry-specific data models, which are not always compatible with all software.

Changing trends in the offerings of various vendors can also be observed time and again. Some vendors that used to advertise their products with terms like 'DWH' or 'Hadoop' years ago now only talk about an analytical platform without going into details about what exactly is behind it.

Your core task as a decision maker is not to commit to a technology decision too early. Technology is a tool to meet your business needs. Some technologies support you better, others worse. The better you know your goals and requirements, the easier it will be to choose the right technology. Therefore, explore functional and non-functional requirements. What are the performance expectations? For which existing operational systems should there be API support? What does the data look like that needs to be processed?

Another important point is to know the existing IT landscape of the company. From this, you can also estimate expenses and the readiness for a technology change. Be sure to motivate your employees: Many are afraid of change or have had bad experiences with one technology or another, which might even block a migration.

Vendor lock-in and its impact is also a major topic. If you decide in favor of technology X today, how strongly are you making yourself dependent on them in the future? As a rule, you want to be flexible.

14.3.4 Data Lake from a Business Perspective

Chapter 2 described how data warehouses were often sold by system integrators as an expensive proprietary data solution, consisting of hardware and software. The data lake is an alternative with an open source core that is sometimes supplemented by proprietary software from vendors. The key argument here is cost and scalability.

A data lake replaces data warehouses only in the sense of proprietary databases, but it does not replace the concept of data warehousing . Modern data lakes also include capabilities to store data in a similar form as in the traditional DWH, and they also allow SQL queries. That's why we cite the data lake as a reference for the data platform here in this book.

Data Lakes are often built based on a holistic view of data. A data lake thus serves as a central repository for all of the company's data. Data Lakes also have a comprehensive authorisation and security concept and offer data catalogues in which company users can access the respective data sources.

The biggest danger of the data lake is the risk of a data swamp. If no one knows who owns the data, and sometimes it is not even clear which data is located in individual directories, the value of a data lake decreases accordingly. A data swamp usually occurs when data is loaded into the data lake in an uncontrolled manner. You can prevent a data swamp with the following measures:

- **Mindset building:** Make it clear to all your employees that loading data into a data lake in an uncoordinated way is frowned upon. Create data labs where employees can play around with the data.
- **Governance:** Mindset building is often not enough. To be on the safe side, you can also introduce governance rules that ensure a managed process. We went into this in more detail in Chapter 5.
- **Data Catalog:** Uploaded data is indexed by a Data Catalog and thus data is also captured semantically, see also Chapter 5.

In large companies, there is also the danger that there is not only one data lake, but many. Communication is the best weapon against redundancy here.

14.3.5 The Role of IT

In most industries, IT is an internal service provider that enables the business to generate value through its services. Whether it's a financial advisor, a grocer, or any other industry, there is always a computer system somewhere that stores data or runs applications that are essential to the value chain.

Even if we locate data science and analytics in business departments rather than in IT, data initiatives mean an upgrading of the IT department, since data engineering often accounts for a significant share of the effort. Power shifts and culture changes are feared. For example, a production manager used to be the master of his plant. The statement, "I'm not going to let others tell me how to work" can often be heard in production companies that are trying to use data to produce smarter. This cultural change must be taken into account in order to successfully implement the data strategy.

14.3.6 Data Science Labs

Once a company has built a data lake and fully implemented data governance and security, they can move on to more advanced things that allow experimentation with real, anonymized data.

Users of a Data Science Lab can typically only analyze subsets of data. Data in a data science lab is usually masked and hashed to make sensitive data unrecognizable. Data science labs often only exist for a certain period of time, such as during a specific marketing campaign. After that, the labs are terminated or relaunched. This is why we also speak of time-limited and unlimited data science labs.

Depending on the use case, different security and governance requirements have to be considered.

Another key challenge is the fact that data science labs are often operated by humans. In contrast to data preparation, this is not an automated process, but a manual one. Therefore, it is necessary that access mechanisms are implemented in detail. Depending on the Data Science Lab, different access mechanisms (control levels) must be implemented, as shown in Figure 14.6.

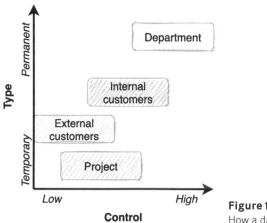

Figure 14.6
How a data science lab is setup

14.3.7 Revolution in Architecture: The Data Mesh

Since 2019, one architecture for data in particular has been discussed very intensively: the data mesh. Strictly speaking, this is not so much an architecture, but rather an "approach" to data. First described by Zhamak Dehghani[2] In her blog, the Data Mesh has become very popular. The key idea is that decentralization of data is accepted above all: one of the core concepts for this is the division into different domains and a clear ownership in the business.

The Data Mesh is basically a microservice architecture for data. It shows that any know-how about a specific data domain resides in the department responsible for it. For example, a marketing department understands what the particular marketing data means much better than an IT department ever can. In the past, this was also the reason for the many data silos that have formed in companies.

---

[2] Original post: *https://martinfowler.com/articles/data-monolith-to-mesh.html*

With the help of data lakes and data warehouses, attempts were made to master the silos. However, most of these attempts failed or could only be solved by using a lot of resources. The data mesh approach takes up the idea of distributed data without necessarily having to develop silos. Rather, the strengths of decentralized data are to be enriched by certain elements so that silos can be prevented.

Architectural Quantum

One of the fundamental elements underlying the data mesh is the theory of the "architectural quantum". This is a borrowing from microservice architecture. One should not build a system too complex, but rather, create it with the smallest possible architecture for the respective use case. In other words: the use case should determine the technology, not vice versa.

With the data lakes of the past, one usually created a very complex product that was supposed to cover all conceivable aspects of data. Often, however, the use cases were missing. If you then looked at the use cases, you might find that the data lake was greatly oversized. The architectural quantum takes a different approach: the architecture should be kept as simple as possible such that the use case can still be solved.

This viewpoint is very much in favor of the public cloud, because many data platforms can be used there on a turnkey basis. With the architectural quantum, one uses these platforms and takes care of the implementation of the use cases. The focus thus moves away from the development of the data platform, and onto the creation of value with data.

Data as a Product

Another very important component of a data mesh is the approach that data should be traded as a product. This means that it should meet the quality standards that are also set for the company's own products. If the company is an automobile manufacturer, the company's data should be of the same quality as the cars themselves, for example.

Here, a very clear ownership comes into play: the respective department that produces the data is also responsible for its quality. Since only the data producers can determine the quality, this is of central interest. Logically, there must be company-wide, uniform quality standards, which are usually regulated by a central office (the CDO).

Likewise, data products should be made available internally within the company. This means that data should be shared with other departments in compliance with the respective guidelines and standards (such as the GDPR). This can be done, for example, through data markets or data catalogs.

What is Needed for a Data Mesh?

Now that the concept of the data mesh envisions a strong decentralization, the question of data silos arises. Wasn't it the data lake that was supposed to combat silos? A stronger decentralization is inevitable anyway, but with the data mesh one has the possibility to build a unified bracket over it. So with the concept of the data mesh, the particular technology is no longer so important. The data platform must be available, and often that is the public cloud.

However, the data mesh requires clear governance: without uniform standards, quality assurance and data catalogues,it will only promote further silos. Therefore, we need to focus more on data governance.

■ 14.4 Business

At the highest level of Data Science maturity, a company is able to execute agile analytics processes in iterations that quickly produce results.

Models usually start with a hypothesis that has to be confirmed or negated using static procedures on data. For this purpose, data is prepared, analyzed and the results presented.

14.4.1 Buy and Share Data

One of the most important developments in the next few years will certainly be the sale and purchase of data. Many companies have been looking around for additional data sources for a long time. One hopes for a better view of things or the customer. A variety of data markets are currently emerging, which are populated by data producers, data markets and data buyers.

From industrial Company to Data Producer

Currently, many industrial companies are coming up with the idea of offering data alongside their own products. One example is the automotive industry: modern cars are equipped with a multitude of sensors and a mobile internet connection via 4G. This not only enables car manufacturers to offer a new quality of service to their customers, for example by offering remote services via mobile phone apps, but also allows them to process data about the cars.

One application that auto makers are currently evaluating or already offering is the possibility of providing telematics data to insurance companies. In this case, driving behavior is constantly tracked and insurance companies can dynamically adjust rates to the respective driver's driving behavior. This reduces the risk for the insurance companies enormously, and means people who adhere to the traffic rules can obtain more favorable rates.

Likewise, cars can calculate the weather with location accuracy: they are, so to speak, mobile weather stations. Due to the large number of vehicles, a very accurate picture is obtained.

But it's not just vehicles that can provide this information: pretty much every company has data that is of value to others. Over the next few years, all companies will probably offer their data in some manner.

Data Markets

In the examples described above, one question already arises: How can the data be offered? On the one hand, there is the possibility of developing complete, delimited products. In this case, however, one must ask oneself a variety of questions about the secure distribution of this data. Since these are often companies whose core competence is not software development, they often find this difficult. IT and software development is usually just an "unpleasant, expensive cost center".

To get around this problem, the major cloud providers have launched their own data markets. Amazon Web Services, for example, offers its own data catalogs with purchasable data, as does Microsoft. This already makes the sale of data much easier.

Another development are decentralized data markets. Here,sellers offer their data and buyers can obtain it. This way, one does not become so dependent on a provider, and the data is only available to the companies that participate in the data market. In this constellation, buyers and sellers often know each other in an economically close relationship.

Many of these decentralized data markets are just emerging, and some very innovative products are being developed to enable these data markets. One example of this is the German startup Nexyo[3].

14.4.2 Analytical Use Case Implementation

We divide an analytical use case into phases from idea to operationalization. These phases are:

- **Idea:** Someone has an idea for how to gain added value with data. This idea covers at least one of the three Big Data pillars (cost reduction, faster decisions, new markets). A business value must be formulated for the idea, otherwise it will not be heard and the chances of implementing it are low.

- **Prioritization:** Usually there are other ideas in parallel to one idea. In prioritization, a company focus is set.

- **Exploration:** An idea that is used for implementation becomes an opportunity. One starts to collect data, to check their data quality and to formulate hypotheses. During the exploration, the business value is also concretized and the corresponding processes for the protection of personal data are handled.

- **Agile modeling:** Models are formed, tested, and evaluated. We will go into this step in more detail in the next section.

- **Retrospective:** Does it pay off to roll out the results company-wide? What are the lessons learned and how do they affect other use cases?

- **Operationalization:** This is where the model becomes an operational solution that is rolled out globally.

---

[3] *https://nexyo.io/*

14.4.3 Self-service Analytics

The supreme discipline is then similar to what is already done in BI-self-service analytics. The goal here is that business users (who come from marketing, finance or other areas, for example) can perform simple data analyses as a workflow. This means it is not necessary to deal with programming languages such as Python or R. However, for self-service analytics, many basics such as a comprehensive security and authorization concept must first be in place. It is also necessary that data sources are extensively documented so that business users can pull together the right data sources. Finally, you need tools that are easy to use - as easy as you would expect from Microsoft Excel. However, most tools for this are still in their infancy and none has yet emerged that is as easy to use as Excel itself.

Well-known tools for self-service analytics are Tableau or Power BI. Web notebooks such as Jupyter are also mentioned again and again in this environment.

■ 14.5 In a Nutshell

The transformation to a data-driven company is not a technical challenge. Rather, it is true "change management" that must encompass all areas of a company.

Migrating a company to a Data Driven Enterprise can sometimes be one of the most exciting jobs nowadays. However, the expectations of someone in such a role are usually also extremely high. So individuals who hold this exciting role are also in an ejector seat. Empty words and nice presentations alone are not enough to modernize a company. In addition to a deep understanding of the subject matter and entrepreneurial action, a flair for corporate politics is also required.

15 Legal foundation of Data Science

Bernhard Ortner

> *"User confidence is crucial for the digital economy. 'Customer as a product' and 'unsafe privacy' are not sustainable business models. Digital is sophisticated enough to combine Security, Convenience and Personal Privacy."*
>
> Stephane Nappo

 Important Note

This chapter does not constitute legal advice. It is an interpretation of the General Data Protection Regulation (and partly the California Consumer Privacy Act (CCPA)) applied to Big Data as understood by the authors as at July 2021. The authors are knowledgeable and experienced with the topic, but are not lawyers themselves. Consequently, it is recommended seek legal aid, if legal advice is needed. ∎

 Questions Answered in this Chapter:

- What are the regulatory requirements on systems?
- How to categorize data and ensure it is maintained at a proper privacy level?
- How to implement various obligations, such as user rights?
- How to address the technical-organizational measures (TOM)?
- What is the difference between the General Data Protection Regulation and the California Consumer Privacy Act? ∎

■ 15.1 Introduction

While the previous chapters describe data processing from a technical perspective, this chapter emphasizes the legal context. We focus on the General Data Protection Regulation (GDPR) and describe the differences between it and the California Consumer Privacy Act (CCPA). The goal of the chapter is to provide an overview on the topic and act as technical guidance.

Data for analytics and data science projects, especially those involving Machine Learning or Deep Learning, is usually collected over a lengthy period of time. This is because such projects and methods require a large amount of data. In recent years, the paradigm of data processing has changed from only storing the data that is needed, to saving all the data which is available now and may be used for data science purposes in the future. As a result, the objective of the data collection is often defined afterwards, or the data is interpreted retrospectively.

Both the GDPR and CCPA try to foster the rights of individuals by defining an appropriate level of protection in their respective juridical systems. They do this by introducing protectable data categories.

■ 15.2 Categories of Data

In order to use and process data from users of an online platform, the owner of data platforms or storage systems has to include a section in their terms and conditions that explicitly allows the processing of data that is not owned or generated by the user. From a legal perspective, the person who created the data "owns" it, and thus, has all rights upon it. The property of being able to have unrestricted access to one's own data is called data sovereignty of an individual[1].

One problem arising from data sovereignty is that the operator of the data platform has an advantage, as they can technically decide when and where the data is used, and may process or analyse it as soon as the data is entered into the system. This does not correspond to the legal conception of data sovereignty, as the rights in this case are moved from the producer to the platform operator.

In Europe, the European parliament and the council of the European Union, acting as legislators, recognized this imbalance and tried to protect its citizens by formulating individual rights against any misuse of their data. Three categories of data were defined, each with a different level of protection:

a) **Limited protectable data:** Data that does not describe or contain individual data is considered as "limited protectable." As a result, this data can be stored without any limitations and does not require any special treatment. Exemples in this category are technical parameters or aggregated data that are sufficiently anonymized, that is, that are not traceable back to an individual or do not contain any personal information.

b) **Personal data[2]:** This category contains data that describes something about individuals, such as their shopping behaviour. We can differentiate between personal-linked data, which is data that can be directly assigned to an individual, and personal data. Personal-linked data has no direct reference to a person, but indirectly describes a person. These include, for example, technical connection parameters such as an IP address, tele-

---

[1] Hummel et al. – Data sovereignty: A review
[2] Article 5 – Principles relating to processing of personal data; *https://eur-lex.europa.eu/legal-content/EN/TXT/HTML/?uri=CELEX:32016R0679*

phone number, vehicle number or insufficiently anonymized or pseudo-anonymized data.

c) **Sensitive personal data**[3]: This kind of data directly describes an individual, such as ethic origin, political convictions or direct biological characteristics, like fingerprints. The information is of significant legal interest and is usually protected via separate laws. The GDPR provides a basic consensus across Europe to standardize the definition of sensitive data and how it has to be protected by listing various techniques and requirements that have to be fulfilled. For example sensitive data should be treated with particular care and / or may only be stored to a limited extent.

■ 15.3 General Data Protection Regulation

The first law on data privacy in the European Union (EU) was passed in 1995 as a data protection guideline, which defines a minimum standard of data protection. It regulates rudimentary data processing of sensitive personal data, and defines in which circumstances data processing is permitted. The member states then had three years to incorporate this directive into national law and adapt it accordingly. In the decade from 1995 to 2016, some adjustments and expansions were made, before the GDPR replaced them in May 2016.

The GDPR[4] by design is a general law that has to be adopted in some manner – such as in terms of penalties or of how it is executed by the local data protection agency - by every member state of the EU. Another law that complements the GDPR is the ePrivacy regulation. This is primarily focused on privacy as it relates to marketing activities, and as such, requires steps like gathering user consent to the use of tracking cookies on web pages.

15.3.1 Fundamental Rights of GDPR

The GDPR has massively strengthened the personal rights of data producers. Data may no longer be collected without a legal justification, and the reason for collection and the analysis to be conducted must both be presented in detail beforehand. The producer can then decide whether he or she accepts the collection or rejects it. The declaration of consent must be freely given[5] and has to contain six principles.

1. **Lawful and transparent data processing**[6]: Processing of the individual has to be written in an understandable form, due to the fact that most of the individuals have no technical background. Consequently, the language should be clear, simple and understandable. If data is requested, it must be exported in a machine-readable format.

---

[3] Article 9 – Processing special categories of personal data; *https://eur-lex.europa.eu/legal-content/EN/TXT/ HTML/?uri=CELEX:32016R0679*
[4] *https://eur-lex.europa.eu/eli/reg/2016/679/oj*
[5] Point (32) – *https://eur-lex.europa.eu/legal-content/EN/TXT/HTML/?uri=CELEX:32016R0679*
[6] Point (39) – *https://eur-lex.europa.eu/legal-content/EN/TXT/HTML/?uri=CELEX:32016R0679*

2. **Appropriation of data processing**[7]: Processing of (sensitive) data must have a clear and defined purpose. The purpose of processing is defined before an individual provides the consent and cannot be changed afterwards. Otherwise, the individual has to provide the consent again.

3. **Data Protection and Data minimization**[8]: Data collection is limited to a minimum set of information that is necessary (and specified in the declaration beforehand) for the analysis. The default technical settings of the software, and the liability of the data protection officer, are used to guarantee this principle (known as "privacy by default"). This requirement ensures that people who are less tech-savvy also receive an appropriate level of data protection.

4. **Correctness and deletion**[9]: An individual can request a correction or deletion of their data at any time.

5. **Limitation of data storing**[10]: Personal Identifiable Information of individuals should only be stored as long as it is necessary for its (pre)processing. After processing the data and deleting an individual's identifiable part, the non-identifiable subset of it can be stored in a secure way.

6. **Integrity and trustworthiness**[11]: Storage of the data is guaranteed by current technical or organizational security measures (TOMs). These measures are also intended to prevent unauthorized access, duplication or data leaks.

The six principles above have to be fulfilled at all times, and the data protection agency can request to view the corresponding consent declarations at any time. Therefore, storing the declaration of consent is an important task for achieving GDPR-compliant data processing.

Once the consent is provided, it needs to be periodically re-evaluated.

15.3.2 Declaration of Consent

A declaration of consent[12] is a voluntary consent to the processing and analysis of the consent provider's data. In this context, vague formulations are not allowed; it must be clear to what it is the individual agrees. Furthermore, the consent is not allowed to be part of a company's service offering and can not be a prerequisite for the fulfilment of the offered service.

If a person's sensitive data[13] is to be processed, the affected data attributes must be explicitly mentioned, including the granularity with which they are to be processed. In addition, a declaration of consent also has to mention the rights of the affected individual, such as the right of erasure, correction and deletion of the data, as well as revocation rights to opt-out of the processing at any time. In the context of the GDPR, the execution of these rights must

---

[7] Article 5 – *https://eur-lex.europa.eu/legal-content/EN/TXT/HTML/?uri=CELEX:32016R0679*
[8] Point (78) – *https://eur-lex.europa.eu/legal-content/EN/TXT/HTML/?uri=CELEX:32016R0679*
[9] Section 3 – Article 16/Section 4 – Article 28 *https://eur-lex.europa.eu/legal-content/EN/TXT/HTML/?uri= CELEX:32016R0679*
[10] Section 2 – Article 13 – *https://eur-lex.europa.eu/legal-content/EN/TXT/HTML/?uri=CELEX:32016R0679*
[11] Section 2 – *https://eur-lex.europa.eu/legal-content/EN/TXT/HTML/?uri=CELEX:32016R0679*
[12] Section 5 – *https://eur-lex.europa.eu/legal-content/EN/TXT/HTML/?uri=CELEX:32016R0679*
[13] See category c in Section 15.2 of this chapter

also be stored in a secure way, to prove that it has been taken care of. Please be aware that this proof can also contain personal data, and thus must itself be treated like GDPR-affected data.

Additionally, an opt-in process - that is, giving active consent to the declaration - is preferable to an opt-out. Prefilled declarations, where certain opt-ins are already checked, can introduce problems, because the individual might oversee an option and thus the final status of the declaration may be invalidated by the data protection authority. General or abstract written consent options, such as a single consent relating to all aspects of the GDPR, are problematic as well because the law defines that each point must be confirmed individually.

In Figure 15.1 you can see two examples of how consent declarations are displayed in practice when you visit certain websites for the first time.

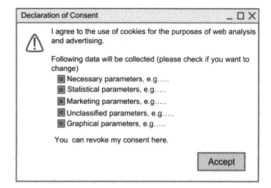

Figure 15.1 Example declaration of consent on a webpage

The problem with the declaration of consent shown on the left is that, from the end-user perspective, it is not clear to what a person consents. For example, it is not clear which data is being collected and for what purpose. This has to be avoided; Instead, the conditions to which an individual is agreeing must be explicitly stated. Opt-Out also potentially violates the data minimization principle as GDPR favors opt-ins, but as at November 2021 it is yet to be clarified by the regulators, how exactly they shall be treated.

The right-hand side shows an example of an opt-in, where each option has to be actively approved. Unfortunately, this declaration of consent is also not GDPR-compliant, as it is not immediately clear which data is processed, and how. Thus, both of the above examples violate at least the right to explanation and transparency.

The e-Privacy Law[14] represents a further improvement of the GDPR. It stipulates that data collecting organizations must apply appropriate, privacy-friendly settings and implement a protection against tracking mechanisms, such as cookies.

Outsourcing of Data Processing

When a third party[15], such as subcontractors or other companies, is involved in (foreign) data processing tasks, GDPR enforces the same level of data protection of the original com-

---

[14] *https://digital-strategy.ec.europa.eu/en/policies/eprivacy-regulation*
[15] Article 28 – *https://eur-lex.europa.eu/legal-content/EN/TXT/HTML/?uri=CELEX:32016R0679*

pany upon the third party. The legal contract is called a "data processing agreement" and raises the following questions:

- Is the processing of personal data an essential step in fulfilling the agreement of the client, and is there no personal interest in the data on the part of the service provider?
- Who is in charge of defining the appropriate processing step?
- Is the contractor only involved in a (technical) auxiliary or support function?

If these questions are answered appropriately, then the responsibilities of the company and its subcontractors can be defined. The service provider has to be responsible for handling the provided data, which also includes the fact that data may not be passed on to third parties without the consent of the data producer/owner.

One possible way to mitigate this problem is to sign a joint control contract. This defines the data and responsibilities for processing personal data. The legal responsibility remains with the data collecting company, but the data processing steps can then be delegated to the contractor. The responsibilities are non delegable and include the monitoring of:

- Documentation and storage of the corresponding declarations, including the consent obligations
- Documentation of the tasks that the contractor can perform individually
- Documentation and existence of shared responsibilities

In general, it should be noted that the data processing steps can be delegated, but not the obligations.

15.3.3 Risk-assessment

Regardless of who processes the data, the data collector has to do a risk assessment[16]. This assessment is called a "Data Protection Impact Assessment" (DPIA). A DPIA is required if new technologies are used or if there is a high risk to the rights and freedoms of natural persons when processing their data. The risk impact assessment has the goal to determine the risks and potential misuse and to minimize and mitigate both.

The GDPR lists the following examples of situations in which a risk assessment has to be conducted:

- Systematic and comprehensive assessment of personal data that relate in particular to work performance, economic situation, health, personal preferences or interests, reliability or behaviour, or the (re)location of natural persons, based on automated processing
- Extensive processing of sensitive or personal data
- Systematic extensive surveillance of public areas, for example, video surveillance

The risk impact assessment is optional if the following conditions are met:

- The processing operations were assessed accordingly before May 25, 2018 and have not changed since then.

---

[16] Section 3 – *https://eur-lex.europa.eu/legal-content/EN/TXT/HTML/?uri=CELEX:32016R0679*

- The processing is in the public interest and there is already a data protection impact assessment.
- There is no high risk to the rights of individuals, and their freedoms are guaranteed.

The impact assessment has to contain the points listed below:

- Systematic description of the planned processing operations

    Scope and type of data (sensitive, personal or purely technical)

    Description of processing steps

- A description of the purpose of the processing
- An assessment of the necessity and extent of processing. To check the necessity, the following criteria can be used:

    The data processing takes place only for specified, clear, and legitimate purposes.

    The data processing is appropriate for the purpose and limited to what is necessary.

    The rights defined by the GDPR, such as the right to object, have been adequately communicated.

    In the event of high risks for individuals, the local data protection authority must be consulted.

- An assessment of the risks to the rights and freedoms of the individual. It is important to mention that the assessment is done from the "end user" perspective. Any threats, effects, and appropriate countermeasures must also be described.

An acceptable way to reduce risk for the end user is data anonymization, pseudo-anonymization, encryption, and the granting of access rights. We will cover these in the following sections.

15.3.4 Anonymization und Pseudo-anonymization

Anonymization is the change of a data record so that it can no longer be clearly assigned to an individual. Beside the removal of identifiable attributes, such as customer numbers, it also includes the removal of such attribute combinations that identify individuals within anonymized data. This combination of attributes is called a quasi-identifier (QID). Testing for quasi-identifiers is very computationally intensive and thus practically inefficient, because all combinations of all data records have to be tested.

If an attribute is replaced by another, for example a person's initials with another name or Caesar ciphered attribute[17], then it is called "pseudo-anonymization" or "pseudonymization." If the information about how the replacement happened (such as information on which algorithm was used for encryption, and the password), is lost, then the pseudonymization starts to become anonymization, since no one can restore the original state of the data.

---

[17] This cipher replaces the letters of the text by a letter whose position is moved by a fixed number offset.

15.3.5 Types of Anonymization

When conducting literature research, different types of anonymization can be found. Figure 15.2 depicts anonymization algorithms as a tree diagram.

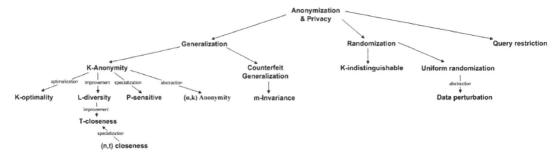

Figure 15.2 Types of currently known anonymization algorithms

Due to the large number of algorithms, only *K*-Anonymity and randomization are considered in this chapter, since these two algorithm classes represent opposing ideas and are used often in practice.

K-**Anonymity**

K-Anonymity groups the records into *K*-groups and ensures that there are at least *K*-records in the groups or equivalence classes. A group is defined in such a way that it always includes an attribute or a group of attributes that contain similar data. The similarity of the data results from the fact that they are identical except for one attribute which is used for the *K*-Anonymization part.

How exactly such a similarity check is implemented depends on the implementing programmer, but generalization is usually used to guarantee the "similarity" of the check.

The problem with *K*-Anonymity is that one attribute is sometimes sufficient enough to make the anonymization reversible, and *K*-Anonymity is prone to attacks with the aid of background knowledge. In the case of big data, the possibilities for an attribute based disclosure attack become difficult to mitigate. For every record in the data, each of the available attributes have to be tested to determine whether it - or a combination of attributes – can be used to identify an individual.

Various improvements, such as l-diversity and t-closeness, try to remedy the weaknesses of k-anonymity by demanding appropriate boundary conditions for its key attributes. For example, with l-diversity, every attribute has to differ l times to mitigate inference attacks based on such attributes

Randomization

Randomization inserts artificial data records such that a certain number of records will be returned for any given query. In order to ensure this, data must be generated or adapted, ad hoc, that have a statistical similarity to the original data. Once a data set has been randomized, both "types" of data - original and generated - are stored together. This process eliminates the necessity for anonymization, because a human-being cannot distinguish between these two types. The effort of anonymization is shifted from a later time (*k*-Anonymity) to the time of data acquisition (randomization). In addition, this anonymization technique scales well with other privacy-approaches. For example, individual attributes can be encrypted or only the relevant attribute can be queried, to further guarantee data security.

A complete randomization privacy chain would therefore look like that depicted in Figure 15.3.

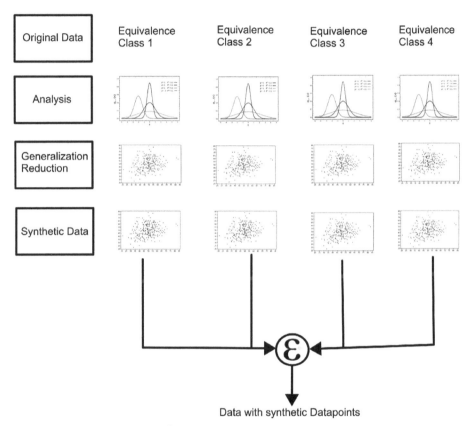

Figure 15.3 Randomization-chain[18]

A dominant representative of this category is ε differential privacy. Here ε describes the degree of privacy; all data records may differ at most in the ε number of attributes.

Regardless of how the data anonymization is implemented, the steps of the anonymization approach must be precisely documented to meet any regulatory requirements. As a consequence, it is advisable to keep track of audit logs and log accesses, changes, and data movements, and prepare and store them for external auditors. Interested readers who want to find out more about the topic of auditing are referred to further literature.[19]

---

[18] Based on *https://www.heise.de/mac-and-i/artikel/Besserer-Datenschutz-Wie-Apples-Differential-Privacy-funktioniert-Update-3678489.html?seite=all*
[19] *https://mapr.com/blog/changing-game-when-it-comes-auditing-big-data-part-1/*

15.3.6 Lawful and Transparent Data Processing

The GDPR defines an auditing processes[20] which facilitates data governance, as every step of the data processing has to be documented for every single attribute, for every single data set, at all times. This is problematic because in some data science and particularly big data methods, such as deep learning, the steps may not be visible for documenting, or the impact of the GDPR from the given technique may be difficult to infer. The underlying problem is the continuously increasing complexity of the models and calculations or evaluations, such that they are generally referred to as an indecipherable "black box". The problem even increases, when it is not evident how an individual's data affects the final result of the analysis.

Another problem is the impact of the declaration of consent on the finished data products, since the data product is described in the conceptual phase when an individual consents to it. For example, if a model has been trained for outliers and the declaration of consent (regardless of whether in general or for individual attributes) is withdrawn, the corresponding data points must be removed from the population. Given that each data point can have a significant influence on the result, the final model will change and thus possibly deliver a completely different result. Such a change potentially also affects other people who have been assessed by the same model.

In addition, the result of the data science methods have to be made explicit, so that any person can request an explanation of decisions based on their data and request a manual judgement of any automatized decision[21] made by a machine without any human intervention. The "Lime" software package is trying to solve this problem. It is available for the common data science programming languages such as Python and R, and tries to approximate complex models with a simpler one. Then it generates new input data based on the simpler one and feeds it into the original model. Lime saves the response from the system and infers how the model works. The information obtained in this way is then presented as an explanation in a graphical way.

Figure 15.4 represents an attempt using LIME, to understand the predictions of a data science model which recognizes different fruits in images. The blue sections depict the regions within each image which had the greatest influence on the decision.

Banana:	0.54	Banana:	0.12	Banana:	0.23
Melon:	0.19	Melon:	0.74	Melon:	0.31
Apple:	0.06	Apple:	0.18	Apple:	0.84

Figure 15.4 Using the LIME package to explore the decisions of a fruit recognition model[22]

---

[20] Point (39) – *https://eur-lex.europa.eu/legal-content/EN/TXT/HTML/?uri=CELEX:32016R0679*

[21] Section 4 Art. 22 – *https://eur-lex.europa.eu/legal-content/EN/TXT/HTML/?uri=CELEX:32016R0679*

[22] Based on the sample scripts at *https://github.com/thomasp85/lime*

Data Export

The GDPR provides the right to data export[23] to every data producer. The data collected by the platform-provider has to be exported at the corresponding request of the producer. The export format of the data is deliberately unspecified in the GDPR, in order to guarantee a certain degree of freedom and compatibility for future formats. The provider is only forced to export the data; whether to do this by exporting to a file or building a new interface is up to them to choose. For the latter option, it makes sense to define an industry standard to make it easier to export or import data into a new system, for example when an individual changes banks or telecommunications providers.[24]

One exception to the obligation to export data is it can be skipped if the datamight contain a trade secret. More concretely, individual models built on the data do not have to be exported, only the underlying data upon which the models are based.

The new "Free Flow of Data Initiative[25]" extended the right to data export so that it now also includes non-personal data. This adaptation tries to ensure cross-platform compatibility within the EU and avoids vendor lock-in with cloud providers. It is now no longer possible to escape any lawsuits filed by governments, in particular, by the Data Protection Commission, by moving data to another country.

15.3.7 Right to Data Deletion and Correction

A person can request that their data be deleted immediately[26]. This implies a lot of effort on a platform provider, since it has to document which data has been deleted, and where. The data must be deleted in any of the situations listed below:

- The collected data is no longer required for analysis. That is, the platform provider has no justification to keep it. This enforces automatic housekeeping to get rid of the data.
- The declaration of consent for the original purpose has been withdrawn. Anyone can request the deletion of individual attributes at any time.
- An objection to the data processing has been made.
- Data has been processed unlawfully. "Unlawfully processed" means any processing that is not the same as the original purpose written in the declaration of the collection.
- The deletion is ordered as part of a legal ruling or obligation in the respective member country.

The method of deletion is not specified under the law. Thus, for example, the data record can be deleted directly, or it may be immediately marked as deleted but only truly be so during the next housekeeping, when all marked data records are physically deleted.

Similar to the right to erasure, at least from a technological point of view, is the right to rectification[27]. The difference is that in the latter case, the data is supplemented or expanded.

---

[23] Point (68) – *https://eur-lex.europa.eu/legal-content/EN/TXT/HTML/?uri=CELEX:32016R0679*
[24] Depending on the industry, this can be an obligation from another law, e. g. PSD2 for finance institutions.
[25] *https://eur-lex.europa.eu/legal-content/EN/TXT/?uri=CELEX%3A32018R1807*
[26] Article 17 – *https://eur-lex.europa.eu/legal-content/EN/TXT/HTML/?uri=CELEX:32016R0679*
[27] Section 3 – Article 16 – *https://eur-lex.europa.eu/legal-content/EN/TXT/HTML/?uri=CELEX:32016R0679*

It is important to note here that the additions must also be covered by the originally defined declaration of consent, and must not contradict it. Again, the changes can be made immediately, or after a certain period.

This right to erasure was specified in more detail by the e-Privacy Regulation. Individuals can request that their data be deleted every six (6) months. This includes all data on the platform as well the data the organisation has backed up.

15.3.8 Privacy by Design

Privacy by Design[28] starts in the design phase of a (big data) system, and picks up the idea that data protection can best be implemented during this phase. Rather than relying on technical solutions, privacy by design focuses on technical organizational measures (TOM), a mixture of technical and organizational countermeasures. Unfortunately, one problem with this is that these TOMs are not fully specified and can vary even within the same country. The only concretely stated example is pseudonymization, but all common measures have to be considered if one wants to effectively support data protection. Various other factors must be considered, too. This includes the costs and scope of the implementation as well as the rights and risks that arise during processing. Here, the state of the art must also be regularly evaluated and, if necessary, improved.

15.3.9 Privacy by Default

Privacy by Default[29] describes the fact that data protection-friendly default settings have to be enabled by default. We saw this in the cookie example from Figure 15.1: a data protection-friendly setting was used which disabled all cookies as a default; The user had to switch them on individually.

Privacy by default fosters a certain basic level of data protection for non tech-savvy people who are less familiar with data protection. The concept is also based on the same basic idea of opt-in and opt-out (discussed earlier), and data minimization. That is, that a user must actively decide to trigger certain data processing tasks.

▪ 15.4 ePrivacy-Regulation

The ePrivacy Regulation[30] replaces the data protection guideline for electronic communication and extends it to various digital communication media such as OTT services (OTT, short

---

[28] Section 1 – Article 25 – *https://eur-lex.europa.eu/legal-content/EN/TXT/HTML/?uri=CELEX:32016R0679*
[29] Section 1 – Article 25 – *https://eur-lex.europa.eu/legal-content/EN/TXT/HTML/?uri=CELEX:32016R0679*
[30] *https://digital-strategy.ec.europa.eu/en/policies/eprivacy-regulation*

for "over-the-top," refers to services that are rented or sold over the Internet; Prominent examples of OTT services are Skype and WhatsApp).

The ePrivacy Regulation primarily aims for companies that operate communication platforms. It regulates the use of cookies and makes the application of tracking cookies much more difficult, as the declaration of consent is interpreted more strictly. Thus, a person may only be tracked if they consent. Particularly in combination with other laws (like the GDPR), this can imply problems for the advertising industry, such as in keyword "behavioural targeting[31]". Another goal of the regulation is to facilitate open access to the content of any given webpage. Thus, it should no longer be possible for a platform to only make its content available for users who have made a declaration of consent. An exception to this may apply when the website has a legitimate interest in setting a cookie that does not include advertising (coupling ban[32]). For example, a valid interest exists in the case of online shops, wherein some cookies are required to technically manage a shopping cart effectively in one session.

The impact of the ePrivacy Regulation cannot be estimated, because it has not yet been finalized.

■ 15.5 Data Protection Officer

A data protection officer (DPO)[33] has to be designated in any situation in which there is a regular collection of personal data and the company size exceeds 20 people. The role of the commissioner must not collide with her actual role. For example, an IT manager may not also be a data protection officer.

The DPO role covers a mixture of technical and legal responsibilities. Thus, this person must be familiar with both "worlds." Once a suitable person is found, the contact details of the DPO must be made publicly available so that anyone can contact them if necessary. The person is the primary contact for all GDPR-related questions, such as any relating to the aforementioned data protection rights and responsibilities.

15.5.1 International Data Export in Foreign Countries

Data exports[34] outside the EU are permitted, provided the export destination country shares a similar data protection standard to that of the EU. In addition, the consent of the data protection authority is required.

The exact list of countries considered to have a similar data protection standard to the EU can be found on the Internet[35.] The list currently includes Andorra, Argentina, Canada, the

---

[31] Point (6) – *https://digital-strategy.ec.europa.eu/en/policies/eprivacy-regulation*
[32] Article 8 – *https://digital-strategy.ec.europa.eu/en/policies/eprivacy-regulation*
[33] Section 4 – Article 37 – *https://eur-lex.europa.eu/legal-content/EN/TXT/HTML/?uri=CELEX:32016R0679*
[34] Chapter 5– *https://eur-lex.europa.eu/legal-content/EN/TXT/HTML/?uri=CELEX:32016R0679*
[35] https://ec.europa.eu/info/law/law-topic/data-protection/data-transfers-outside-eu/adequacy-protection-personal-data-non-eu-countries_en

Faroe Islands, Guernsey, Israel, Isle of Man, Jersey, New Zealand, Switzerland, Uruguay, and the United States of America.

The "Schrems II" judgment invalidated the data exchange agreement, which means that the transfer of european personal data to third countries currently has to be covered by separate contracts, such as the EU's Standard Contractual Clauses (SCC)[36.] Furthermore, the data collecting company has to ensure that the destination country has similar data protection mechanisms.

■ 15.6 Security Measures

Data protection[37] cannot be accomplished without appropriate measures to track the current level of security. Some recent examples of famous security breaches include Facebook's data problems with Cambridge Analytica (at least 87 million data records lost from Facebook profiles) and the problems with the Indian eGovernance platform Aadhaar (1.1 billion lost biometric data records from Indian citizens). In fact, the website InformationisBeautiful.net[38] chronologically visualizes data breaches and their type.

An active security policy, that mitigates the risk of a breach by regulating access mechanisms and effectively protecting data, is mandatory in that it is requested by the GDPR[39]. The GDPR additionally requires that an existing data breach will be reported to the appropriate authority within 72 hours, unless this breach did not affect the rights and freedoms of individuals.

The report to the authority must include the following points:

- A detailed description of the type of breach, including information on the categories and the number of data records that may be affected
- Name and contact details of the data protection officer
- Description of the consequence of the injury
- Actions that have been taken

The problem with a data breach is that it needs to be discovered. Only then can IT measures be applied to prevent the breach the next time. That is, the prevention is retroperspective. To make matters worse, as soon as data has been copied (by hackers responsible for the breach, for example), it is virtually impossible to delete it.

---

[36] https://ec.europa.eu/info/law/law-topic/data-protection/international-dimension-data-protection/standard-contractual-clauses-scc_en

[37] Point (94) – https://eur-lex.europa.eu/legal-content/EN/TXT/HTML/?uri=CELEX:32016R0679

[38] http://www.informationisbeautiful.net/visualizations/worlds-biggest-data-breaches-hacks/

[39] Point (83) – https://eur-lex.europa.eu/legal-content/EN/TXT/HTML/?uri=CELEX:32016R0679

15.6.1 Data Encryption

The GDPR facilitates solutions that are state of the art and improve the protection of individuals. One of these techniques is data security. Concrete steps for data security are divided into two types, depending on the state of the data:

- **Data in transit** is the data that is currently being moved from one storage location to another. That is, it is being actively transformed, aggregated, and changed.

- **Data at Rest** is the data that is currently not being moved and is therefore not being actively processed.

Both data types ensure a certain level of security. However, some parts of the encryption are based on the type of application, since active data is usually transmitted in SSL/TLS. The most efficient way to protect data is to encrypt it as soon as it is stored and decrypt it again when it is used.

Nevertheless, the GDPR also introduces an effort on the part of the infrastructure to adequately protect the data, for example, in the form of Identity and Access Management.

For more information on data encryption, please refer to *Chapter 5 - Data Management*.

◼ 15.7 CCPA compared to GDPR

The CCPA[40] is a similar legal construct to the GDPR and was passed by California in January 2020. CCPA has similar goals to the GDPR, but there are differences as it is less related to the individual and more focused on a company level. Furthermore, it is limited to the state of California and not in force in other states of the United States.

The sections below describe the differences between the CCPA and the GDPR. Laws or measures that work similarly in both legal constructs, such as the definition of terms or the right of data deletion, are not described separately.

The main point of view of the CCPA is a predominantly corporate one, in which data may be processed until there is an objection (opt-out) from the consumer. The CCPA then prevents only the transfer of data to third parties, and not the data collection by the processing company itself.

The CCPA applies to any company in the world that processes the personal data of more than 50,000 California residents, has revenue of more than $ 25 million, or generates more than 50 percent of its annual revenue from the sale of data. It defines the processing of data as the transfer of a user's data to another company or a third party for a monetary or intangible value.

The CCPA is set to be amended by the California Privacy Rights Act (CPRA), and will therefore become more strict from 2023 onwards. The CPRA improves the security requirements for data as well the rights of consumers by introducing a new category for data that are indirectly personal and sensitive, such as IDs, financial data, communication data, and so on.

---

[40] *https://leginfo.legislature.ca.gov/faces/codes_displayText.xhtml?division=3.&part=4.&lawCode=CIV&title=1.81.5*

In addition, privacy settings, notifications of data collection, and the rights of individuals will need to be more precisely defined.

15.7.1 Territorial Scope

The CCPA protects consumers who are natural persons and who are long-term residents of California[41]. Long-term residence is not precisely defined in terms of time. It obliges companies to take certain actions to protect individuals' data, and defines a catalogue of criteria according to which the CCPA has to be applied. As is also the case for the GDPR, this catalogue is based on sales figures and the amount of personal data that is processed annually.

In contrast, the GDPR establishes control bodies, such as the DPO, in companies and provides them with corresponding responsibilities and obligations. The GDPR also does not differentiate where a service is provided, as it applies as soon as a service is consumed in the EU.

15.7.2 Opt-in vs. Opt-out

The main difference between the two laws is how data can be collected.

In the CCPA, opting out - that is, to reject the processing of one's own data - is only possible when data is sold or shared. This does not prevent the collection of the data. However, the CCPA does define a list of possible types of data that may not be collected, such as medical data, financial data that fall under the Gramm-Leach-Bliley Act (GLBA) or data that falls under the Driver's Privacy Protection Act. Furthermore, in the case of children or persons particularly worthy of protection, active consent must be given. In such cases, the process is similar to the GDPR.

It is also forbidden under the CCPA to sell data in the case of biometric data or if a person has declined to provide consent. However, the legislator also stipulates some cases where data must be collected, for example where there is legitimate legal interest, such as when data is required for legal reasons. In such a case, only the resale can be prevented, but not the collection itself.

15.7.3 Right of Data Export

CCPA grants individuals the right to have their data exported[42] for twelve months, starting with the date they request it. If a request is submitted, the data is classified into a category, based on characteristics such as identifying data, network information or geolocation. Then, the platform provider has to provide all data of the corresponding category in a readable format once per year.

---

[41] 1798.140 *https://leginfo.legislature.ca.gov/faces/codes_displayText.xhtml?division=3.&part=4.&lawCode=CIV&title=1.81.5*

[42] 1798.100 *https://leginfo.legislature.ca.gov/faces/codes_displayText.xhtml?division=3.&part=4.&lawCode=CIV&title=1.81.5*

15.7.4 Right Not to be Discriminated Against

Unique in the CCPA is that software is not allowed to discriminate[43] against certain people. Consequently, a service-provider is not allowed to charge different prices for the same service or software, or improve or decrease the quality level of the service or software, based upon whether or not a user agrees to the terms and conditions. It is also forbidden to conceal services, parts of the services or complete software at all.

The non-discrimination has to be proven, which has thus driven up research into and interest in "trustworthy AI". In case of doubt, it must be explained precisely that the quality level of the software does not differ for a non-consenting user compared to a consenting one.

■ 15.8 In a Nutshell

In this chapter, we outlined the regulatory obligations of systems and platforms and emphasised the legal responsibilities of data producers. We showed how the GDPR and CCPA moved the data sovereignty from platform operators and data aggregators to the users and corresponding producers of the data. The GDPR addresses the latest developments in automatic decision support, which have led to a global collection of various data about individuals. These data collections are automatically evaluated in retrospect and as a result interpreted in a statistically meaningful way.

As a data collector, when interpreting personal data the legislator will try to enforce you to minimize the impact of your actions on users. It does this by enforcing various responsibilities, such as the data minimization principle. Furthermore, if a data model is built upon the data, GDPR also gives users the right of explanation, in order to mitigate the risks of automated interpretation.

This explainability, especially in the case of data science products, is sometimes difficult to achieve because it requires understanding, in detail, which parameters affect a machine learning model and how. Traceability of a model's input features is a key point of the GDPR (and CCPA). This can delay the development of new data science products,because it has to be defined beforehand which data is necessary. .

The data protection officer is responsible for all legal activities related to processing data, such as collecting declarations of consent or defining the default degree of privacy. Such responsibilities can only be delegated to a limited extent. If the GDPR is not properly implemented, there is a risk of penalties, such as fines.

■

---

[43] 1798.125 - *https://leginfo.legislature.ca.gov/faces/codes_displayText.xhtml?division=3.&part=4.&lawCode=-CIV&title=1.81.5*

16 AI in Different Industries

Stefan Papp, Mario Meir-Huber, Wolfgang Weidinger, Thomas Treml, Marek Danis

> *"Consumer data will be the biggest differentiator in the next two to three years. Whoever unlocks the reams of data and uses it strategically will win."*
>
> Angela Ahrendts, Senior VP of Retail at Apple

Questions Answered in this Chapter:

- How is Artificial Intelligence being applied in each industry?
- What are the unique features of the individual sectors?

In this chapter, we address how AI will permanently change the way we work and live. To do this, it is necessary to first look at digital disruption, the stakeholders involved, and the history.

Management consultants often speak of the "disruption of traditional business models" and the "penetration of new markets." What is meant by this is that AI will substantially change the entire corporate culture in individual industries, including essential processes and how we generate profits.

Many companies also view the digital transformation to a data-driven organization as a company-wide paradigm shift. Instead of relying on personal experience and gut feeling, decisions are made based on data evaluations and statistical models that enable predictions of trends. In the final stage of expansion, companies automate processes within the framework of *prescriptive analytics*. A key aspect in this field is that algorithms 'make decisions' themselves. A good reference example would be trading. Right now, most algorithms will alert a broker about good deals, but it is still a human broker who makes the final decision to buy or not to buy.

In the following, we will continuously refer to so-called 'data programs.' In a data program, a program manager works with a team of data scientists, data architects, users, and all other stakeholders to integrate the necessary infrastructure and processes into the company over an extended time. Thus, it is not uncommon for this project to take several years.

Consulting firms help non-IT clients with the *digital transformation* and the migration to becoming a data-driven enterprise. Typical clients can also be your bank, your favorite grocery chain, or your energy provider. There is hardly an industry where there is no data from which to extract value.

Sales strategies of consulting firms have heavily influenced data programs in these companies. Therefore, it is necessary to understand the approach of external consultants working in these industries. The campaigns in which the external service providers outline how they intend to transform their clients into a data-driven organization in group-wide data programs will determine how the companies themselves perceive this measure.

Commercial software applications that generate value from data are almost as old as computers themselves. Yet, the growth of large, international consulting firms and system integrators over the past decades shows that this continues to be a profitable business model. However, technicians often make the mistake of trying to sell technology at pre-sales meetings. Not only are managers not interested in technical details, but discussions between skeptics and proponents of new technologies also break out time and again in technology meetings. Not infrequently, the goal is lost sight of altogether. Developers debate which implementation details lead to the desired results, while other project participants are not even consistently clear about the big picture.

 The Skeptics Debate

Technology debates have always been held and will probably exist as long as there are multiple ways to implement technical requirements. At first, skeptics resisted any form of digitization. And once in a while, this resistance has to be renewed.

"Computers? We have our beloved pen and paper method to make our calculations; it'll only crash if we make a paper airplane out of it. Computer! That'll never work."

"Data warehouse? We don't warehouse our data. We've built our own software that does something with the data, too. Data warehouse! That'll never work."

"Data lake? In a lake, I go swimming, but I won't drown my data there; I have my warehouse. Well-proven since the 90s. Data lake! That will never work."

"Cloud? Why should I put my data in a cloud? I have my lake, and anyway, my data is more secure in a data center of my choice. Cloud! That'll never work."

"Data mesh? I may eat mashed potatoes, but I do not need a data mesh. That'll never work."

To be fair, the skeptics are often the ones who have experienced the downside of innovation. For example, if an overambitious IT manager orders a new system, it can sometimes happen that the changeover causes more problems than expected. Those who have to support the new system within the company, and have to put up with frustrated users who are emotionally upset because new problems keep occurring, also suffer as a result.

Accordingly, there is little technology in the PowerPoint slides of many consulting services providers in the AI environment. Abstract terms such as 'Big Data' are made suitable for the masses by salespeople repeating them like a prayer mill. It is essential to treat the terms superficially and not delve too deeply into the technology. Distributed data processing via open-source data platforms becomes 'Big Data,' applied statistics on data via deep learning frameworks becomes 'Smart Data' or 'Data Science,' and streaming processing is touted as 'Fast Data.' Terms like 'Big Data,' 'Advanced Analytics,' 'Machine Learning,' and 'AI' are part of sales campaigns. Since the terms are presented and interpreted differently depending on the consulting firm, enterprises often have no uniform understanding of essential terms.

Ultimately, however, there are always arguments in favor of using new technologies. No one can deny that paper cannot be retrieved centrally and that distributing copies of documents to all employees by hand is not an efficient solution either. After the first wave of digitization, manufacturers realized that they could sell targeted data-driven solutions that completely mapped a company's data world. Non-IT companies gradually became dependent on IT as they began to digitize their business processes.

Until 2010, business intelligence was considered a corporate area for analyzing data in an organized manner and deriving decisions from it. The appropriate technology for this was the enterprise data warehouse. Companies' revenues increased with DWHs, but vendors' revenues and prices also went up. Many customers complained about vendor lock-in, the dependence on expensive system integrators, and large consulting companies with a reputation for rebranding juniors as senior consultants by putting them in business suits.

It may have been the cost-cutting argument that initiated the shift to distributed open-source platform solutions such as Apache Hadoop in 2010. The economic crisis of 2008 had increased the pressure to reduce costs in many companies. In addition, technology advisors praised commodity hardware and open-source as lower-cost alternatives to appliances. So consultants and systems integrators created a new trend: They branded a comparatively inexpensive open-source product called Apache Hadoop as the ultimate successor to expensive enterprise data warehouses. An important argument for its use was the avoidance of the vendor lock-in mentioned above.

But the promises of many consultants in business suits have not been entirely fulfilled. Someone also wants to make money from open-source software, and, strictly speaking, open-source offerings can often be identified as a sham. Many companies use the buzzword 'open-source' to sell hybrid products, that is, products that contain open-source components and proprietary components, resulting in corresponding licensing costs.

Setting up a complete data platform consisting of hardware and software components is complex, especially when policies require demanding service level agreements. Moreover, in most cases, companies lack personnel who can ensure smooth operation. As a result, functional (e.g., various services not running) and non-functional deficiencies (e.g., multiple services having poor performance) occur frequently.

In addition, decision-makers should not underestimate the cost of permanently operating a complex hardware and software solution. Someone on payroll must replace defective hardware regularly, and maybe someone else must maintain and secure server rooms. Suppose the distributors charge service level costs. In that case, questions arise about how much money companies save when migrating from a DWH provided by a provider as a complete package to a self-managed pseudo open source landscape.

Many strategy advisors perceive cloud-based solutions as the ideal way out of this dilemma. With Amazon S3, for example, each gigabyte of storage cost two cents per month in 2018. In addition, experts consider this storage to be almost permanently available, and the risk of losing data is usually lower than hosting it in your own data center. Plus, you can roll out all the popular data platforms, including Hadoop, in the cloud. And if a company no longer needs various data services, it can cancel all cloud services at any time. In contrast, an on-premise solution becomes obsolete; the purchased hardware will continue to appear on the balance sheet.

After the DWH and the Hadoop hype, we now have the cloud hype. But this does not mean that the other technologies are no longer relevant. First and foremost, the market is becoming more diverse. Just because you can store data in object stores of cloud providers, which is becoming cheaper and more accessible for companies, does not mean that other storage technologies have become obsolete in principle.

Chapter 2 introduced polyglot data storage[1], which describes having different technologies for different data. However, some tasks are still best solved by traditional DWHs; for others, a distributed file system fits better. Moreover, a company can host any data platform in the cloud.

This trend is also evident in various industries. In some sectors, personal data protection is paramount; in others, specially coded sensor data processing. The data solutions and requirements of a bank differ significantly from companies that build machines.

This trend requires a change in thinking. In the past, system integrators often built an ecosystem around the system they offered. Then, data scientists and business analysts would try to find use cases that would allow them to max out the provided hardware and software solutions. This approach is being replaced by "use case first" thinking: At the beginning, the project team defines a use case they want to implement to generate new business models or optimize existing processes. Then, they select the technology that can best solve the requirements defined by the use case.

In this chapter, we look at various industries with their typical analytical use cases to understand how AI and data science can change business models in the typical representatives of these industries. It is important to emphasize that we can only provide an overview here and that there are many other, sometimes highly specialized, use cases besides those described.

In the description of the use cases, we first provide an overview of the industry. In doing so, we outline key challenges that a company can address using machine learning. The next step is to envision how the industry may look in the future when it is thoroughly infused with artificial intelligence. Finally, we also address what possible initial steps we can take to approach this vision.

◼ 16.1 Automotive

Modern cars are driving sensor data generators that produce terabytes of data during a journey. Startups can monetize this data. Data enthusiasts even claim that vehicles will generate more significant revenue from data than from the sale of vehicles themselves at some point.

However, many car manufacturers still see themselves as mechanical engineers because they could manufacture their products long before the first computers came onto the market. So while even the most die-hard car builders will admit that cars are no longer conceivable without IT, mechanical engineering is still the focus for most. And since, in the end, it's

---

[1] *https://en.wikipedia.org/wiki/Polyglot_(computing)*

always about money, IT and production become competitors when it comes to allocating budgets.

Authors like Lawrence Burns describe how the automotive industry works[2]. They show how suppliers work, how they work in production, and how research differs from other industries. Connoisseurs of the individual manufacturers claim that among the German carmakers is the corporate culture so different that entire books could be filled with a comparison of Volkswagen, BMW, Daimler, and Co.

In the automotive industry, plants often operate independently of headquarters. For example, when the leaders plan a new project, the plant managers compete for the order. They act as if they have to compete against other competitors, even though they belong to the same company. This knowledge is essential for data experts because it explains why the cross-plant data lake does not exist and why data availability also has a corporate policy dimension.

Some experts predict that the expertise and deep understanding of the underlying data could reshuffle the cards and change market share in favor of those who have already started to deal with Big Data earlier. We can also speculate that the use of electronic engines will reduce complexity in cars. For example, an electric vehicle does not need a transmission, unlike cars with internal combustion engines. Suppose the cars become less complex in their design. This change can strengthen IT teams, as the possibilities for qualitative differentiation from the competition move from the "hardware" (the car) to the "software."

Artificial intelligence and the collection and analysis of data will massively change the automotive industry in the next 20 years. This transformation includes a lot of changes for drivers. We will describe some of these changes in the following section.

16.1.1 Vision

You are sitting together with a good friend in the evening. Over a glass of wine, you dream of Paris and the Champs-Élysées.

"Why don't we have breakfast in Paris tomorrow?", you ask.

"Yes," your friend replies, "why not?"

With the spontaneous decision made, you get into your car of the future. In this one, there is no more steering wheel and no more accelerator pedals. Instead, you have a fully self-driving vehicle.

You don't own the car; you rely on car sharing like everyone else. Additionally, this means that cars are only parked when they are serviced or refueled. The goal of vehicle providers is to generate an AI that guarantees a high utilization of cars.

Your car is arranged like a sleeper with a few specific selections that your AI has set up for you. Finally, curtains closed, maybe a little bedtime movie based on your taste profile in the car, and you fall asleep.

In the morning, Edith Piaf will wake you up.

---

[2] Burns, L. D., Shulgan C.: Autonomy: The Quest to Build the Driverless Car – And How It Will Reshape Our World. Ecco, 2018

"Non, je ne regrette rien". First, you enjoy the view of the Eiffel Tower. Then, the AI suggests a bistro where you can have breakfast. But, before that, you stop at a new place that didn't exist until a few years ago, a kind of freshening station with a shower and bath.

While you shower, you look forward to the day. You can always get from A to B and C with small self-driving autorickshaws. Since the AI knows your preferences, you can also let yourself be surprised by where you are taken in Paris.

Lost in thought, you think of the past. How much everything has changed. You remember that there used to be offenses like drunk driving and that many people died because of it. That's all history now. You know that your car collected data as you drove and passed it on to various stations. Data scientists can use sensor data to determine the status of road surfaces, for example, and figure out when roadway resurfacing is necessary. But you don't hear about any of this. You just tell the car where to go, and it takes you there.

16.1.2 Data

Data in the automotive industry is often machine-generated. It follows specific industry standards, which we will not go into in detail about here.

The sensor data of cars can, of course, also come from measuring devices installed in the car to reflect the condition of car parts: Engine heat sensors, sensors that measure engine speeds, and so on.

It is essential for autonomous driving to recognize and react to objects as quickly as possible with the help of sensor data. If the algorithms are mature enough to respond correctly to the environment, nothing is standing in the way of autonomous driving.

It is also essential that the car must function in all environments. That's why there are also many test drives in areas with extreme weather conditions. For autonomous driving, this means that self-driving cars have to cope with the highway in California and the traffic in New Delhi, for example, without colliding with one of the numerous rickshaws or a cow on the road.

So in sum, it's about teaching a car's internal systems how to interpret data they collect while driving to recognize objects. To enable smooth autonomous driving, fog, for example, must be recognized as such, as must a person crossing the road.

16.1.3 Use Cases

Autonomous Driving

Self-driving cars are perhaps the best-known use case in a digital society. The idea that all you have to do is get into the car and then be taken safely to your destination is on everyone's mind.

However, many "autonomous functionalities" are already part of today's cars.

The fully autonomous driving car is the goal, and there are many milestones along the way. Autonomous driving starts with parking aids, cruise control, and distance alarms. Then, sensors detect hazards and react accordingly. Each new generation of cars will bring more autonomy, and the development up to the fully autonomous driving car will be a flowing process.

Many of the industries described in this chapter will also be affected by autonomous driving, significantly if it fundamentally changes the delivery of goods. We can argue that autonomous driving can have a similar impact on our society as the Internet and smartphones before. Thus, it is not for nothing that giants like Google and Apple invest much money in autonomous driving.

In this context, we recommend books like "How Autonomous Vehicles will Change the World: Why self-driving car technology will usher in a new age of prosperity and disruption."[3]

Car Quality

We can use masses of data for the production of cars. Load tests and, in particular, stress tests are beneficial here. Stress means, for example, extreme weather conditions. Accordingly, car testing often takes place in remote areas with extreme temperatures.

We can use sensor data to evaluate whether the test vehicles can cope with various extreme situations and determine maximum load values. Production is thus accelerated, and the quality of the goods produced is optimized.

Data Monetization

Your car is a moving all-rounder. The data you collect can be used, for example, to predict traffic jams and measure changes in road surfaces. Sensor data from a journey can then be sold to organizations responsible for running a transport network.

When we think of monetization, that is, "turning something into money," the trend of car sharing, in particular, becomes fascinating. Cars stand 90 % of the time. Understandably, you can't rent out your car while it's parked at your workplace; how would you get home? But what if we assume self-driving cars?

You could also rent out your car analogously to your apartment with an "Airbnb-like" service through this use case. While sitting in the office, you earn money by having your autonomously driving car drive tourists. In the evening, of course, you are picked up by your car.

This use case also leads many market researchers to believe that car-sharing will increasingly displace car ownership. But, strictly speaking, it doesn't matter whether you are driven by your car or a random car, as long as the vehicle is not a status symbol for you.

16.1.4 Challenges

The central challenges are societal. Self-driving cars will have a massive impact on our society. Not only will they turn the entire transportation system upside down, but self-driving cars can also upheave the entire delivery logistics industry, which can have a massive impact on other industries. To understand this, you only need to ask yourself one question: Would you have a purchased item delivered by taxi today? Unless it were urgent,

---

[3] *https://www.amazon.com/dp/1733328769*

you, like many other people, would probably be put off by the cost. However, autonomous driving can reduce this cost factor to a fraction.

In the future, goods - unless drones deliver them - will simply be loaded into a car and sent to a destination without a driver. As a result, freight forwarders will need fewer drivers. We will discuss this in more detail in section 16.13. Likewise, the need for taxi drivers and chauffeurs is likely to decrease significantly.

With the acceptance of self-driving cars, people are also more accepting than before to surrendering sovereignty in survival-critical areas to a machine. Sure, we already trust computers to run their applications correctly, and of course, there are computer systems upon which lives depend, at least indirectly. But autonomous driving cars are a whole new dimension here, as no one will deny that statistically, people often die in car traffic. By accepting self-driving cars, we are in a sense declaring that we are more likely to trust a machine with our lives than other people or ourselves. After this step, many people might be more willing to trust machines with their lives in other areas as well. For example, what would you say to a fully automated surgical procedure without a human specialist at the scalpel? This list could go on and on with other instances where a computer could offer more safety than a human.

From a technical point of view, autonomous driving is a challenge because producing data costs energy, and the data transmission rate of mobile networks is not good enough everywhere to get the data to the destination in the required time. Autonomous driving is therefore strongly linked to energy and telecommunications. It must also be possible in more remote areas, where the infrastructure is less developed than in a metropolitan area.

It is also essential that autonomous vehicles can cope with chaotic big city traffic. Presumably, California's highways are currently the busiest routes for autonomous driving cars, as Tesla and Google have been testing their cars here for years. However, California road traffic follows stricter rules than traffic in many other countries. For example, while you sometimes have no speed limits on German autobahns, you can expect restrictions of 65 miles per hour in California, which is the equivalent of about 105 km/h. Also, general traffic conditions differ in other countries. A car that can drive autonomously from Palo Alto to Sunnyvale without any errors could run into problems in the traffic of Berlin, Delhi, or Yerevan.

From a legal perspective, liability issues need to be clarified. For example, in a traffic accident involving human drivers, there is usually a straightforward explanation of the accident and who was at fault. The causes of accidents can be clarified even more quickly if self-driving cars log their journeys in detail, but we also need a legal basis for proceeding in the event of an accident.

■ 16.2 Aviation

We divide Aviation into the areas of airlines and airports. Of course, there are also overlaps, as airlines are dependent on airports.

An airline's job is to get passengers and cargo to their destination safely and as punctually as possible. Punctual airlines have a better reputation, and this reputation can have a medium-term impact on business success. Even if the price of tickets is a significant factor in customers' decisions to choose a flight, it can be costly for consumers if flights are delayed and they miss a connecting flight as a result. Compensation does not always fully cover the damage incurred. This fact means that lines that tend to be unpunctual also risk losing price-conscious customers, even if they offer their flight at the cheapest conditions.

The expected flight experience can also be a decisive factor in choosing a flight, especially a long-haul one. For example, the desired boarding service plays a significant role for many passengers when selecting intercontinental flights. Many passengers also perceive substantial differences in the services offered by airlines.

Airports play their part in ensuring that flights can meet their deadlines and that guests get from A to B quickly. Many airports measure customer satisfaction and evaluate data to find out how they can serve their passengers even better. A reference example is Vienna Airport, where passengers can give feedback on cleanliness in the toilets and friendliness at the security check. In this way, these airports develop a better and more consistent service quality than airports that ignore such data.

In the following section, we will show how we can use data to improve Aviation services.

16.2.1 Vision

You remember the old days. You remember the moment when you boarded a flight with a tight connection. While your travel companion wonders if the connection time isn't too close, you wave it off: "It's okay!", you return confidently, "they're professionals."

Then, shortly before boarding, the bad news: delay. No one can or wants to tell you what's going on. So you wait, restlessly, sitting as if on hot coals.

You finally get to board the plane after complaining long and hard, and you're anxious for every minute. However, you are annoyed by passengers who take their time taking their seats, even on a delayed flight.

Until you reach the connecting flight gate, it remains unclear whether you will have to negotiate an alternative flight at the transfer desk. A relaxed flight is out of the question, especially if you miss necessary appointments due to delayed arrival.

You wipe that thought away and come back to the present in the future. You live in modern times; you know that everything is regulated, everything runs correctly, and airlines have become more flexible in getting their passengers to their destination. For example, computer models generate an ideal flight load factor and ensure departure times are based on actual demand. There is also an early warning system for all phenomena that can trigger delays, and airlines react to these and thus improve their punctuality.

And then there's another thing of the past: there used to be a time when the selection of your neighbor depended on luck. Having to sit next to someone with whom you have no chemistry for several hours can be frustrating. However, since the AI knows you and the other guests, they will have no problem finding a seatmate that works for you.

16.2.2 Data

Turbines in aircraft generate terabytes of data per hour. Aircraft also collect position and weather data supplied by satellites during the flight. These can be used in models to predict expected delays.

Mathematical models also show how a machine must be fueled to bring the calculated total load to its destination.

Data from social networks can also be insightful for airlines. The more the models know about passengers' preferences, the easier it will be to personalize the flight experience and make it as pleasant as possible.

16.2.3 Use cases

Personalization

You are on a long-haul flight. In the plane's entertainment program, you'll find movie suggestions that match your preferences. You may even be able to continue movies you started watching at home or an earlier flight, as the database of a streaming service for movies you subscribe to is also accessible from the plane. An AI model tailored the meal plan to your tastes. This choice was made possible by an AI model. This model has calculated which menu best suits the guests. For example, if the AI detects a high proportion of vegans, the menu takes this into account.

AI can optimize seat selection. With the appropriate data, AI can seat you next to people with similar interests. For example, people who are interested in finance take seats next to each other. A few rows behind, parents discuss child-rearing. Even for people who prefer not to talk to anyone, the AI will find like-minded people. These choices also affect the satisfaction of the flight personnel, as it can be very unpleasant for them to have to mediate disputes between passengers.

Customer Satisfaction

At an airport, there are tons of systems that measure passenger satisfaction. This starts with ratings of the restroom cleanliness and extends to the friendliness of the handling in the security area. The evaluation of this data can increase the quality of the services offered.

When these satisfaction scores are aggregated and publicized, it attracts other guests. Transit at an airport that is confusing and where staff is known to be unfriendly may deter passengers and make them plan stopovers so that they only stop at airports that guarantee minimum satisfaction. This step may have an even more significant impact when computers suggest flight itineraries and passengers mark courteous treatment in flight as an essential criterion.

Delay prediction

Based on historical data and experience, it is often easy to predict which flights might be delayed, but extensive data analysis helps refine such a model even further.

What are the weather conditions? What kind of passengers is boarding? The more data the model has, the more accurately an expected delay can be determined, and corrective action can be taken. And if not: the earlier that passengers are informed about delays, the less hassle there is.

16.2.4 Challenges

Airlines are profit-oriented companies. Some of them accept delays or overbooking if it brings an economic benefit. They also take into account the fact that it is cheaper to compensate passengers for inconveniences. Mathematical models are used to calculate how high this pain threshold is that passengers are expected to endure.

The ambitious flight schedules are also a challenge. Often the flight crew has only half an hour on the ground between flights. In that time, everything has to be done: shut down the engines, let the people leave the aircraft, program the new flight route, organize fuel and information about the weather, and calculate whether it is even possible to take off with the load in the weather conditions. For example, if something doesn't fit or the aircraft has to be de-iced, which is often the case in winter, the flight will likely be delayed. This delay usually can't be made up; it often lasts the whole day. It's like a domino effect.

We can improve a lot with the help of data science. But airlines are often seen as conservative, and it takes some convincing to push through innovations. There are also best practices that every airline adheres to. This can mean that specific changes only work if a correspondingly high proportion of airlines participate and the airports are involved.

■ 16.3 Energy

The liberalization of the electricity market led to high competitive pressure among energy suppliers. Suddenly, companies that operated in a price-protected environment and lived by producing electricity and selling it at regulated prices were confronted with the reality that supply and demand can cause a variable price.

The energy sector consists of the four areas

- Production,
- Sale,
- Storage and
- Trade.

Data science is a common thread running through these four areas. For example, if we produce too much electricity and do not find enough suitable customers, electricity must be stored temporarily at a high cost or sold cheaply. Storage is expensive because storage power plants have to be built and maintained, and electricity is also lost during storage.

So, suppose we can predict prices and demand and calculate the potential to reduce the price of electricity production. In that case, we can minimize the storage of electricity and thus be as efficient as possible.

16.3.1 Vision

Your self-driving car will take you past meadows and forests during your trip to Paris. The air is pure. A few years ago, there were still vast factories of electricity producers here. Today there is only green energy, and only what is needed is produced.

You once talked about this with a friend who explained that we could predict the energy demand extremely accurately thanks to AI. The model analyzes historical data and can consider other factors that affect electricity demand, such as weather and events. As a result, producers align renewable energy production with meteorological forecasts. Since – thanks to our AI – sun, wind, and water are predictable, we can match our entire production with consumption.

Another friend works in the construction industry and proudly tells you how AI has impacted there, too. When construction companies erect new buildings, they pay attention to maximum energy efficiency. The data scientists at the architecture firms have now optimized their models and leverage historical data to determine how buildings at different locations are sustainably energy-efficient.

New passive buildings even give off energy under ideal weather conditions. A friend who often travels for work raves that she not only earns money via Airbnb: The surplus energy that the house generates via the photovoltaic system also brings her money. That's why she plans to buy a few old houses, modernize their energy budget and rent them out.

Then your car reports that a battery change is due. So your car drives to a battery change station, which used to be a filling station when people still relied on fossil fuels. Robotic arms remove the used battery from under your car and insert a fully charged battery within seconds. You don't even have to leave the car to do it.

 Read "Bill Gates: How to avoid a climate Disaster"[4] and ask yourself how to use data science to understand Bill Gates' vision.

16.3.2 Data

Energy supply companies want to know how high the expected consumption is. One source for this is historical data collected from the corporations themselves.

Energy consumption is also strongly linked to the weather. A cold and early winter means different consumption patterns. People have to heat more and spend more time in their

---

[4] https://www.amazon.com/How-Avoid-Climate-Disaster-Breakthroughs-ebook/dp/B07YRY461Y/

homes. On the other hand, a good season with lots of snowfall for winter sports regions implies that hotels are fully booked and ski resorts are fully operational. Accordingly, the energy demand in the area is higher.

Analytical models can use historical data to predict a region's likely energy needs when fed with current weather data. But of course, you also want to know how much energy is generated from photovoltaics or wind power and whether energy production should possibly be boosted elsewhere.

We can derive the energy demand in a region also from other factors. For example, if there are events in a city that attracts visitors, more energy is consumed.

16.3.3 Use Cases

Dynamic Pricing

Data models calculate the expected electricity price. Accordingly, production is throttled or cranked up to produce the ideal amount for sale. The reason is that those who make surpluses must temporarily store the energy produced. When energy is stored, energy is lost. Moreover, the process is not cost-effective.

So the more accurately an electricity provider can predict how much energy will be needed based on human behavior, weather data, historical data, and other influences, the more we can optimize production and pricing.

Predictive Maintenance

Predictive maintenance means identifying which maintenance is required at any point in time to keep equipment in good working order. Typical measurable characteristics are signs of wear and tear. For example, wind turbines or photovoltaic systems that are out of operation because they are defective are things that a utility provider wants to prevent.

Suppose we can use sensor data to predict which components of an energy producer could fail imminently. In that case, we can take preventive action and avoid failures.

We can model predictive maintenance using linear regression. For example, we can collect measurement data over time and label each record as to whether or not it was associated with a failure. If you then match live data with a regression model, you can identify problem cases.

Weather Forecast

Weather forecasts are more important for energy providers. Weather defines the output of renewable energy. The more sun, the more production of photovoltaics. The more wind, the more production of wind energy. Weather forecasts also help us to predict the energy demand.

An energy provider who can predict the weather well can also throttle energy production through fossil fuel. This measure is one step towards carbon reduction as defined in the Paris Agreement.

16.3.4 Challenges

The energy market is under pressure because private consumers can choose their suppliers after deregulation of the electricity market. Unfortunately, many producers were not prepared for this development.

The energy industry is one of the industries in which little IT innovation was necessary in the past. For example, in a non-liberalized market, a supplier's employees could manually read out metering data in households and later record the evaluations in an application. Accordingly, there was little pressure to replace the old electricity meters with smart meters. However, new competitors who are not afraid of AI are working with data science models that can help them produce electricity more efficiently.

Of course, we must not ignore data protection. For example, is an electricity provider allowed to determine a consumer's regular consumption, or does it violate the individual's privacy? The fact that it is possible to determine whether people have been away from home for a long time is also particularly explosive. This information would be an invitation for burglars.

AI and Energy are connected with sustainability goals to reduce carbon emissions. However, power stations are expensive to build, it takes years to get a return on investment, and they can be operative for decades. So while we optimize and balance the output of renewable energy sources, some countries might not want to take their coal-fired power stations off the grid. The book mentioned above of Bill Gates addresses this and more of the problems in more detail.

■ 16.4 Finance

Many financial institutions, banks, stock exchanges, and insurance companies pump vast investment money into their data platforms. In principle, the banks' business is to assess risks in order to be able to offer lucrative interest rates. Additionally, they also make money from ATMs, currency exchanges, and card fees. Data scientists can use the information extracted from data to optimize these revenue streams.

The business model of financial institutions differs in many cases from other industries. Authorities and financial institutions impose regulatory requirements on banks. Unfortunately, this means a lot of bureaucracy, which can lead an innovation-enthusiastic IT expert to the brink of despair.

16.4.1 Vision

At home, you look at relics of the past, all arranged in their display case: A few books are there, an old telephone with a dial, and a wallet.

Contactless technologies mean you no longer have to put cash on the table. Instead, we can use NFC chips in many stores to register who has taken which product from the shelves and then deduct the amount as soon as the customer leaves.

So the bank of the future only offers online services; branches with counters have long since ceased to exist. Instead of going to the bank, you meet with your advisor in a coffee house if you want a personal conversation. But many also conduct banking transactions virtually.

16.4.2 Data

Banks usually have a lot of structured data, as data is often generated via transactions, which are always structured. A transaction in a technical sense means that operations are carried out entirely or not at all. If a bank customer withdraws money from an ATM, a database entry stores all information about this withdrawal.

Unstructured data is sometimes found in risk assessments, for example, when data analysis uses social media data.

In principle, banks know about their customers by analyzing financial transaction data and matching it with demographic data.

16.4.3 Use Cases

Customer Journey/Customer Loyalty

Banks want to know as much as possible about their customers to be able to assess their behavior. For example, how does a given customer use their card, how does their spending build up, and, above all, how satisfied are they? In addition, which communication channels (internet or telephone, for example) do the customer use, and what can you deduce from their behavior when using these channels?

Which pages does the customer click on when they visit the homepage, how long do they stay there? When they call the call center, what concerns do they have, and what topics move them?

The customer journey is a method to keep track of a customer's actions and calculate how satisfied they are and which products they might like. When all channels are analyzed, the marketing expert speaks of an 'omnichannel process.'

Fraud Detection

Fraud detection, the recognition of fraudulent financial activities, can best be explained using credit card transactions. This use case is probably the prime example of how linear regression is applied in a bank, as fraud attempts repeatedly happen, especially when credit or ATM card data has been stolen.

Imagine that a customer's behavior, let's take an 80-year-old retiree as a reference example, suddenly deviates from his usual actions. Instead of going to the grocery store around the corner, as usual, he suddenly uses his card abroad to buy exotic items and send them to addresses that do not correspond to his home address. How likely would you find it that someone here would misuse the retiree's card? And please also consider that an elderly gentleman might not immediately notice this misuse.

Credit card fraud detection works via so-called balanced scorecards, in which each attribute of a transaction is evaluated individually for deviations. Actions that correspond to normal behavior are risk-free. Various characteristics of each transaction, such as a new IP address, new delivery address, an unusual product category, or payment deficiency, are all assessed for risk. Similarly, algorithms cross-check historical data to include historical fraud in the risk assessment. For example, transactions made from countries with more fraud attempts in the past will be factored into the model.

Adding all factors together, we receive a fraud probability. If we exceed a threshold value, the card is blocked. A customer service representative contacts the customer to clarify the situation.

Loan Acceptance Prediction

Loan acceptance prediction means predicting how likely a customer is to accept an offer for a loan if a bank proactively offers it to them. With this application of data science, financial institutions try to win over customers before they inform themselves about lending at several banks. This approach reduces the risk that the customer will choose a competitor.

To determine if a customer might be interested in applying for a loan, we can look at bank customers' past transactions and compare them with demographic data. It becomes apparent which patterns have led to someone wanting to apply for a loan from the past. When we identify these patterns in a customer, they are contacted even before getting comprehensive advice from the competitor.

Often, we can classify customers by these models. Candidates for a loan are, for example, people who want to buy their own homes. If you look among your acquaintances, you may notice that there are often patterns here. For example, people around 30 might be more inclined to want to buy housing than retirees; this group could then be classified, for example, as 'housebuilders': people who, unless dissuaded by unexpected life events, will build a house at some point in their lives. Imagine that a bank successfully identifies these people better than another bank and addresses them with loan offers at the right time.

How could this be done? Suppose a customer starts to cancel various non-essential expenses, and the account balance gradually increases per month. This behavior could indicate that they want to create funds for a home loan. To filter out precisely these bank customers from a customer database, many data scientists would use a random forest here. A balanced scorecard is also conceivable to identify candidates for a loan. We explained these methods in more detail in Chapter 8.

Customer Classification

We addressed classifying customers in the loan request prediction section. However, in addition to "housebuilders," other groups of people can also be classified. One factor could be risk tolerance. Some people use securities to speculate; others are incredibly risk-averse.

We may identify some clients as potential entrepreneurs or career-minded individuals. As result, these risk-averse clients may be assigned to a different customer service representative than modest individuals who prefer a stable lifestyle.

16.4.4 Challenges

Fintechs are increasingly competing with traditional financial institutions. They don't have branches, and they don't have to manage legacy IT architectures that still run applications programmed in Cobol. Fintechs are correspondingly agile and better able to leverage data science, bringing better service quality and ultimately leading to new and robust competition for traditional banks. There is a consensus that there is no such thing as "too big to fail." Even the big ones are gambling with their existence if they ignore AI and Data Science. However, other financial institutions don't see it that way, and some predict that market shares could change in the next few years.

In the banking environment, it is essential to comply with the regulations imposed by the legislator. These requirements make it necessary for every step in a project to be approved by several departments. Thus, a bank is often forced to follow the waterfall model, which requires analysts to specify software functionalities in advance. Only when security experts and regulatory experts have approved the specification can the software be put into operation. Furthermore, since an audit may occur at any time, the documentation must always be kept in a financial auditor's representable status.

The regulatory requirements are often cited as a reason why working as an IT expert in a bank is long and tedious. Instead of developing and expanding software in an agile manner, an IT expert here is often severely restricted in her scope of action.

■ 16.5 Health

When we think of health (in the sense of the term "health industry"), several areas are relevant. These include the pharmaceutical industry, medical research, medical professionals, hospitals, and other organizations to keep people and animals healthy. Veterinary medicine should not go unmentioned either, as statistically, the number of pet owners is increasing, and they spend a lot of money on the well-being of their charges.

There is a lot of money to be made in the health industry. In Maslow's pyramid of needs, maintaining health is a fundamental building block. Accordingly, we spend a lot of money on health.

Opinions differ about the use of IT in medicine. It is clear to everyone that working with medical devices that are not connected to computers is no longer possible. Still, many ask themselves how the stored data is handled and whether it is good to let data scientists loose on medical data.

Data Science can improve efficiency in all healthcare institutions. In the following sections, we will show that there are numerous application examples. We will also explain why Data Science in medicine can trigger a snowball effect, from which perhaps one of the largest application areas of AI and data-driven innovation can emerge.

16.5.1 Vision

You are reading about Prometheus[5], the world's largest healthcare industry data project. For years, zettabytes of information were collected during voluntary long-term test series, medical examinations, and many other channels and stored in the cloud. The dimension of these investigations is unimaginable.

Scientists have studied all the details and gained comprehensive knowledge about which factors influence a person's life. Finally, there are statistically provable facts about which foods are healthy and how a person must live to stay fit and vital.

 Exercise

Play through a complete process of a hospital visit and try to split them into atomic operations from which architects can then design a microservice architecture. Can you estimate how many different services we would need to implement?

Health care is individual. We can measure genetic prerequisites and derive health plans from the results. You collect all data about yourself via various devices connected to your body. These devices recognize your ideal biometric values and corresponding deviations from them. You can also instruct your AI assistant to prepare nutritional suggestions that are tailored to your individual needs, taking into account, for example, a deficiency of particular vitamins or minerals.

There is an early warning system that alerts people that they are risking harm via their lifestyle. And who doesn't take action when a system signals the risk of a heart attack? In addition, diseases such as diabetes and other ailments that can accompany a person for the rest of their lives are also prevented or delayed in this way.

The visit to the doctor is also more efficient. There is now a prescreening, and the order of patients is better managed. In addition, it is possible to make doctor consultations in advance on the web. In addition, you can be examined with the help of virtual reality technology, and only in exceptional cases do you have to be physically present.

While out for a walk, you are overtaken by a jogger you have known from childhood. He had both legs amputated after an accident. But thanks to AI, new prostheses have been created that many see as a symbiosis between humans and technology. No healthy person would even be able to come close to keeping up with a runner using prosthetics. Some people are already planning to replace their biological limbs with prosthetic limbs, and the performance of artificial organs is also beginning to exceed that of natural organs. In the (fictional) "Bio-Tech Fusion Handbook," you can read about other trends that sound incredible.

---

[5] This is a fictitious project.

16.5.2 Data

Patient data is probably the most protective and valuable information there is. If all data on all patients and their lifestyles were available, we could make extreme progress in health research.

The human body provides vast amounts of analyzable data: Factors such as pulse, blood values, body fat values, blood sugar levels, and the quantities of various hormones are only part of a collection of many other values only known to medical experts. If this data is constantly measured and evaluated, it could trigger medical revolutions.

16.5.3 Use Cases

Complaint Reduction

We can measure hospital satisfaction. For example, patients can provide feedback about the food, the cleanliness of the toilets, and the staff's friendliness. Patient satisfaction managers explore the input and determine where action is needed. For example, customer happiness departments can develop programs to improve performance for staff who receive poor ratings.

Drug Interaction Analysis

If you are testing different medications, it also makes sense to do trials to discover any negative interactions.

Particularly in the pharmaceutical sector, vast amounts of data are collected, which often provides essential insights into the effects of the interaction of administered substances with the environment.

Competitive Sports

Many athletes already measure their biometric indicators, such as pulse, and try to optimize them. Coaches can use the data to determine which values their client needs to optimize to achieve top performance and determine which factors impact those values. From this information, trainers create new diets and training plans.

We can use AI to detect injuries and signs of wear and tear at an early stage. There must presumably be an extremely high willingness to evaluate data in competitive sports since performance improvement is often linked to financial incentives.

16.5.4 Challenges

As is often the case, where there is the most benefit, there is also the most risk. Concerns about data confidentiality are perhaps nowhere more vital than in the healthcare sector. Imagine you are laid off. You find out after some time that your employer has gained access to your health records. It turns out that your data revealed a susceptibility to contracting a genetic disease. Other potential employers also get access to the data. For many, this is a horror scenario.

The question of the protection of patient data is an important issue. We should analyze data only if people give their explicit consent. However, the question then arises as to whether we are getting enough data that will help us to gain new insights.

Whichever way you view it, one thing remains true: Nothing is more precious to people than their own lives. So if we can use data science to find out how to improve the quality of life, humanity will benefit.

When writing this book, the majority may see dangers rather than benefits in exploring health data. The Automotive passage outlined a possible paradigm change once people start trusting machines more than other humans. In the Middle Ages and Renaissance, alchemists were looking for ways to reverse aging and extend life. Once the amount of people who believe in the value of data exploration reaches a certain threshold, health data processing could become the topic of the biggest 'data rush' in history.

■ 16.6 Government

Many people immediately think of Big Brother when they think of data and government. And when you look at the structures that intelligence agencies have built up, it's not entirely absurd. If you were to rank the users of Big Data solutions, intelligence agencies would probably be somewhere near the top.

Elections are also sometimes influenced by Big Data analyses. This issue came to prominence through the British 'Brexit' referendum and the election of Donald Trump in 2016. Election campaigners who have access to user profiles via social media such as Facebook and Co can analyze their preferences and target these people with the appropriate topics.

16.6.1 Vision

Everything is digitized. Finally, it is no longer necessary to stand in line at an office to cast a simple voting decision. But more than that, digitization also means citizen participation. In numerous forums and voting procedures, citizens at all levels can have their say and share their ideas.

Urban planning and especially housing creation have entered a new era thanks to AI. Satisfaction in individual districts is measured. An AI determines the needs of the citizens, and only new buildings that meet those requirements are permitted.

A trend towards direct democracy is gradually developing. People vote on different issues, and thanks to regional coordinators, politics becomes a dialogue.

In the future, politicians will process data to better address as many issues as possible in the formation of public opinion.

16.6.2 Data

A lot of data in the public sector is structured and sensitive. Your tax file and your entry in the central register of residents, for example, are areas that you do not want unauthorized persons to see.

Public institutions sometimes make their data open-source. San Francisco is a good example, whose data is a popular source for data scientists. For example, users can find data on registered businesses' locations, licensed food stands, and criminal incidents.

The biggest Big Data user is probably the intelligence service. Here, the data sources are almost inexhaustible. Every form of monitored communication can also be evaluated and analyzed. Social networks such as Facebook and telephone data that must be searched using deep package inspection present new "volume challenges" for data evaluation due to data increase every year.

16.6.3 Use Cases

Tax Fraud

One issue in the public sector is tax fraud. This scenario includes many well-known fraud scenarios such as the missing trader fraud.[6] Data analytics can help finance ministries track down companies and citizens who evade taxes.

Surveillance and Law Enforcement

Big Brother is watching you. Intelligence agencies, as already mentioned, are perhaps the most significant users of Big Data. There are substantial server farms that are impossible to hide on the map, but most people do not know what is inside. We can surmise that the purpose of these facilities is to defend against threats from intelligence surveillance of communications. A rule of thumb is that the more data intercepted, the more can be inferred. However, the application of data technologies is not so much aimed at finding encrypted secret messages in citizens' communications. Much more important are conclusions from communication patterns (traffic analysis) obtained from the evaluation of so-called 'metadata', that is, structured information about the actual message.

Civil security authorities also use Big Data to pursue and prevent crimes. The collection of personal and case data has a long tradition in the history of forensic technology. The digitalization of these files and their linking with international information systems promises, on the one hand, to increase the efficiency of prosecuting authorities and, on the other hand, to open up entirely new possibilities for them. For citizens, on the other hand, this becomes a threat to their right to informational self-determination. This scenario is particularly true when public and private databases are filtered according to presumed stereotypical characteristics of potential offenders (dragnet searches).

If there is a series of crimes, the geographical evaluation of the crime scenes can determine vulnerable locations for future crimes and allow conclusions about the area in which the

---

[6] *https://en.wikipedia.org/wiki/Missing_trader_fraud*

perpetrators live (geographic profiling). This method is not new in forensic science, but it is greatly improved by the possibility of including topographical data and street layouts in modern Geographic Information Systems (GIS). The processing of the results in such systems also increases the usefulness for law enforcement authorities. Chapter 18 covers ethical questions in detail.

In the fight against organized crime, modern data technologies also help to improve existing methods. For example, monitoring these organizations' communications and financial flows allows conclusions about their social structure and economic network. However, in contrast to the intelligence mentioned above, monitoring communications are explicitly targeted at suspicious organizations or individuals. Above all, the linking of data across national borders is of particular importance for this area.

A specific feature is the recording of security cameras in public places. Although their actual function is to prosecute crimes that have already been committed, they are installed in practice mainly for crime prevention at certain hotspots.

Social media platforms are both an opportunity and a challenge for security authorities. The analysis of user and usage data provides new opportunities for law enforcement. But, on the other hand, these virtual spaces are themselves the scene of real crimes, which are challenging to get to grips with using traditional criminalistic methods and tie up personnel, who are in turn lacking in public spaces.

Traffic Management

Every driver knows the scenario: you are driving comfortably in the city and suddenly see a red light. As a conscientious driver, naturally, you stop. You look to the left, to the right, and to the front. The road is clear, and you waste valuable time waiting there.

Now imagine a system in which traffic light control is automated on-demand. You are cruising towards the intersection. Since you are the only one at the intersection, the signal is not red, and you can proceed unimpeded.

Smart Cities

In the Smart Cities use case, many things that have already been mentioned or will be mentioned in this chapter become visible. Autonomous vehicles will change city streets in the coming years, just as cityscapes are already changing due to the transformation of commerce. There will have to be new ways of meeting the energy needs of smart cities and distributing energy efficiently. Art, culture, and media, while becoming increasingly digital, are still being created in communities that need a space to implement new ideas.

We can divide smart city concepts into two opposing planning approaches. Prominently represented in the media are the mainly technology-centered top-down initiatives driven by infrastructure and product providers. The promise here is to optimize the overall city system by collecting and processing information about its current state and making it available to decision-makers in real-time in so-called city dashboards. However, citizens often also have access to it to adapt their behavior to changes (e.g., in public transport). Singapore is a prime example of this approach.

In contrast, the second approach aims to connect citizens through ICT (Information and Communications Technology), enable participation in urban policy-making, and foster local communities. The focus of these initiatives is usually not on the whole city but limited to interventions in smaller sub-areas. Currently, Vienna is a good and internationally respected example of such a strategy.

For urban planning and development, the application of ICT and data technologies results in a paradigm shift. Decisions that were previously based on expert opinion can now finally be evidence-based. Of course, this does not mean that we can replace the mayor of a city with artificial intelligence. But planning and, above all, control tasks at a low level will be based on data and automated.

Mobility is probably the topic with the most significant potential for effective smart city initiatives. Of course, the aforementioned autonomous driving will fundamentally change individual transport. But public transport will also be intelligently controlled and adapt more than before to the temporal rhythm of the citizens of a smart city.

Other core areas of the development towards a technical smart city are energy and water supply. Again, the introduction of data-driven planning and intelligent control will lead to more careful use of resources.

The backbone for these new developments in the city will, as always, be the infrastructure provided. On the one hand, we must modernize the existing infrastructure in transport, electricity and water. This modernization means making its components more measurable and thus controllable. On the other hand, however, we must create an urban data infrastructure in parallel, which combines all the smart city-data.

Hazard Identification

Even if official statistics say that violent crime is decreasing, there will probably never be a non-violent society. Therefore, many cities monitor public places via CCTV (Closed Circuit Television). For example, in the UK there are cameras in public transport.

How much surveillance we need is a matter of debate. Still, presumably, there is a consensus that we can use video to record crimes and that video recording can deter people from committing crimes. But what if CCTV films someone pulling a gun? With many video streams, we can use the material only for "post-mortem" analysis. In other words, authorities analyze the data after the crime has already been committed, as there is not enough staff to monitor the videos continuously.

There are solutions already that utilize image recognition to detect weapons. However, in more advanced scenarios, threat detection solutions might include body language and spoken words to assess a dangerous situation.

National Defence/Military

We have already described in threat detection how the state can benefit from homeland security. Object and threat detection are, of course, also crucial in the military. For example, if airspace surveillance identifies an object as dangerous, it can be intercepted.

It is tough when there are "false positives" here. In the 1980s, there was a missile warning in the Soviet Union, but it later turned out to be a false alarm. We have one person to thank for the fact that no cruise missiles were fired.

Each military sector, from airspace security to the navy, has its use cases, the detailed analysis of which is beyond the scope of this book.

Civil Protection

Professional data evaluation during disasters can save lives. For example, let's assume it has been raining or snowing for days. Knowing where to expect avalanches or mudslides means being able to cordon off regions and save lives.

We can find hazard zones using historical data or by matching satellite imagery. Unfortunately, in the course of climate change, there will always be new requirements in this area.

16.6.4 Challenges

We can divide analytics for governments into two areas: intelligence and citizen services.

Intelligence is the area that makes data processing a danger for many because the bottom line is that it is nothing more than surveillance. But, of course, the buzzwords 'counter-terrorism' and 'security' can be used to gloss over many things. Still, it is also legitimate to ask what impact citizen surveillance has on those citizens' lives.

Perhaps the most significant challenge is transparency. It's no secret that Amazon has its gov cloud, available only to governments. Nor is it a secret that the NSA has vast data centers of its own. Yet, whistleblowers like Edward Snowden or Chelsea Manning have shown that governments deal with PII data without restrictions. Of course, one can argue that there is existing law and that it also applies to states. But there are enough regulations that undermine established law in the name of security.

Digitalization can facilitate direct democracy, but we should question the maturity of citizens themselves. Does it make sense for people to vote on a whim when they don't know what's at stake? We described data science as a method to reduce ourselves to facts and include less emotion in the decision-making process. But what if the research is about which topics stir up emotions most?

How much does the promise of empowering the population also open the door to their manipulation? If we know about the people we want to influence, we also know what we have to say to make them like us. So then, we should not be surprised when political parties specifically adapt the messages to their voters and populism in every form spreads in politics. There are still many open questions here about how politics can be responsibly digitized.

■ 16.7 Art

Art is perhaps one of the areas where many readers would least expect to find applications of artificial intelligence. After all, art is considered by many to be the domain of human creativity. Thus, it is hard to imagine a computer creating work as expressive as a Mona Lisa or an epic like Lord of the Rings.

However, art offers some application areas for artificial intelligence, such as creation and trading. For example, patrons make a living selling art and promoting artists. Thus, we can use AI applications to estimate prices of artworks via regression models and possibly also to discover new talents whose works match current art trends.

Artists are also using AI themselves to create art. And Microsoft has published Drawing-IT, a system that links art to AI. Thus, the connection between AI and art is not as far-fetched as it first appears.

16.7.1 Vision

You are redecorating your apartment. You notice that a picture is missing somewhere: "Alexa," you say, "I'd like to have a picture there that brings a little more life into the room."

Alexa, or, more accurately, the digital assistant called Alexa, asks you a few questions. Then, it shows you a few examples of different artists and gathers information on your preferences little by little. Finally, an order goes to the 3D printer, and you are surprised to see a result that seems to match your taste. Ultimately, you express yourself through the pictures you hang or the music playing when a guest enters your home. All of this is part of how you show yourself to the outside world.

You are talking to a friend who has written a book. Artistic creation has also changed in this area. Your friend has outlined the book and had parts of it written by an AI, enabling him to make his book multi-dimensional. The interactive plot means different plot alternatives, which the writing AI adapts to the reader's preferences. Without AI, this step would not have been possible on a large scale.

16.7.2 Data

What data do we need to evaluate artworks or have artworks produced by an AI? Raw data for this is images, videos, and music. The more art data you feed into an AI, the more you can apply regression and classification algorithms.

We can analyze people's genuine reactions when they see a work of art. This data can come from video streams, for example. Algorithms determine people's moods based on the facial expressions that are recognizable in the image data.

It is also helpful to have profiles of art buyers. For example, if we know which artworks people have bought in the past, we can also use this data to determine which paintings the customer might like in the future using recommendation engines.

16.7.3 Use cases

Price Calculation

We want to determine what price a work of art can fetch by analyzing data. As input values, we have artworks, demographic data, and historical data from auctions. Then, via machine learning algorithms, we calculate the possible price the artwork can achieve.

Artificial Muse

Many artists are experimenting with linking AI and their work. One example of such a group of artists is the project 'artificial muse.[7]

An artist paints pictures, and an AI engine analyzes these pictures via deep learning algorithms and, based on the evaluations, tries to inspire the artist.

Although it will be some time before artificial intelligence can write complete novels on its own, an AI engine is already good at recommending style elements via linear regression that can underscore a plotline. For example, an author is working on a scary novel and wants to describe a house of horrors. An analytical model can then suggest what details the author should refer to in the process. It can also identify which stylistic elements are currently popular in literature and would resonate well.

Reaction Measurements

Art is often also about triggering and sometimes provoking reactions in the viewer. Sometimes, it is difficult to predict the effect of artists' work in public space, for example. However, the responses to art in public space can be measured explicitly by analyzing the viewers' behavior via video streams.

16.7.4 Challenges

Presenting art in the same breath as data science may sound provocative, even for a field that sometimes draws attention to itself through provocation. After all, art is considered the last bastion of human creativity. For many, it may be inconceivable that AI should replace geniuses such as Picasso, Goethe or Mozart in the future.

However, technology and art have long been growing together in particular areas. Many artists use technology to incorporate it into their work.

■ 16.8 Manufacturing

When we talk about Manufacturing or Production, we talk about the industries that produce mass products in factories. So we use the term 'manufacturing' to talk about the manufacturing industry itself, and with the term 'production,' we reference the mass production process.

Automation has always been an essential part of production. Production managers want to ensure that they reduce manual operations, increasing quality and saving costs.

We can use data in manufacturing to improve production processes. Of course, companies will continue to exist for the mass production of products. But if we look at the innovation thrusts in 3D printing, for example, we see that this technology will also be suitable for

---

[7] www.artificialmuse.ai

widespread, individual usage at some point. Private individuals will then be able to print at least simple objects themselves.

16.8.1 Vision

You are on your way back from Paris when you realize you have forgotten to buy a souvenir. You had intended to buy a coffee cup set, so you let your AI assistant know. He takes care of it.

Once home, a surprise awaits you. You live in a time when part of the production becomes local again. The producer of the coffee cup set no longer sells the product but releases the data for individual products in exchange for payment. A 3D printer at your home has printed the coffee cup set for you in excellent quality. That we will be able to print various household items at some point is beyond doubt. The question that arises is what level of complexity 3D printers will master and by when.

In mass production, on the other hand, automation has progressed so far that hardly any people perform manual work steps anymore. The world of data has supported automation here. Machine learning and co make it possible to configure the bills of materials so that there are no more inventories. This efficiency has a beneficial impact on resource consumption.

16.8.2 Data

Sensor data from machines often generate several terabytes of data per hour. Frequently, this production data is specially coded and differs significantly from human-readable data.

We cannot move all real-time generated data to the cloud in a reasonable time. Often the throughput rate is too low. Imagine a factory, perhaps not necessarily located next to a backbone to a cloud provider, producing terabytes of data. That data needs to be able to be read. Hadoop may have lost its popularity in recent years, but it is still suitable for local bulk data stores where data needs to be written quickly.

Manufacturing companies are also heavily dependent on commodity prices. What data do we need for calculation models on price developments? We need data on the situation in countries that supply these raw materials. If we can calculate the impact of political changes on commodity prices, we can decide whether or not to buy.

16.8.3 Use Cases

Optimizing Procurement/Demand Prediction

This use case is about optimizing purchasing processes and predicting demand. First, we collect data on suppliers. Then, based on various factors, we determine offer prices and calculate how prices will develop.

If our suppliers operate in countries with a tense political situation, we also want to know about the likelihood of political turbulence. For this purpose, personal data on influential people in a country can sometimes be interesting. For example, suppose a dictator rules a country. In that case, it can make sense to apply Natural Language Processing to text data crawled from news and social media to determine whether the situation has changed.

At the same time, we can see what sales we had in the past from our historical data. We can build models through which we compare the data from the past with the factors of the present and thus determine the probable sales through regression and adjust our production accordingly.

Quality Improvement

Reading and evaluating sensor data on production lines is a typical machine learning use case. We can measure every step from raw material emulsion to heating, forming, punching, and quality control with sensors.

We can link sensor data to production waste via regression. If, for example, a certain number of increased sensor values can be connected to a higher proportion of defective goods, we can initiate corrective measures.

You can thus minimize a scrap of your production, and sometimes you can also determine how individual phases in production affect others. This quality optimization can help companies in countries with higher wage levels to remain competitive.

 Exercise

Have an excursion to a production mill and take a tour. While they explain the whole production pipeline to produce goods, try to imagine how you could leverage the data collected by sensors. How could you, for instance, try to detect rejects in a pipeline?

16.8.4 Challenges

The quality of the data coming from sensors can sometimes be poor. Many machine builders have not optimized their data production for data science applications. In addition, there are sometimes misalignments between IT departments in manufacturing and the production managers. Sometimes production doesn't want to be told by IT how to do its job. We cannot implement analytical use cases if production has a "we don't need it anyway" veto. At the same time, Western producers, particularly, are dependent on quality to justify higher labor costs. Therefore, if the quality in countries with high labor costs is not noticeably better than in low-wage countries, management will outsource production in the long term.

◼ 16.9 Oil and Gas

Will oil and gas industries remain as powerful as they are now, or will alternative energies prevail? According to the Paris Agreement, we will have to replace fossil fuels, but how much data science can help reduce carbon emissions?

Some people might be surprised that nuclear energy is seen by many as a possible alternative to fossil fuels. Despite its complicated history, some even see this energy source as the logical successor to the oil and gas industry. If renewable energy cannot fill the gap and the alternative would be to reduce energy use or use nuclear power to reduce climate change, many would choose the latter.

Nonetheless, it makes sense to look at this industry, as oil and gas are currently one of the largest industries in the world. Additionally, if we expect nuclear energy to grow, we should maintain a focus on that sector.

16.9.1 Vision

An oil and gas executive from startup AI-Oil has acquired the concession for an old oil field, as well as the old drilling and production data. The data is a big part of the cost, but the startup's owner knows it will be worth it for the company.

The company's self-developed AI program reads through the data. Soon, a green dot lights up on the map that models the field. Then, another. And another. Slowly, individual clusters form. After the program has worked its way through, AI-Oil's lead data scientist runs another function, and the possible production quantities appear on the screen. The result looks good. Once again, it has been proven that it is still possible to "squeeze" some oil out of fields that were already considered exhausted with more precise calculation models.

A service company immediately provides the estimated costs for the infrastructure, calculated in real-time with a view to the current workload.

A few more clicks and the program is connected to the data of the global financial markets via add-on. The forecast of supply and demand is refined by automatically reading and evaluating press releases from all companies. Here, a factory for ultra-light plastics for aircraft construction is opening; an old chemical plant is closing. The impact of these news items is quantified and taken into account for the next few years. And if you know the demand and the historical data, you can also determine how prices will develop.

In an interview with the press, the founders of AI-Oil express confidence. Soon, they are sure that not only oil but also money will be flowing again.

16.9.2 Data

Few are aware of the petroleum industry's pioneering role in data collection and processing. Accurate data has always been necessary, from geology to chemistry to mechanical engineering to proprietary petroleum engineering. As a result, vast amounts of data sets of all sizes and shapes are generated, from the first wells with a few dozen data points to area-wide 4D seismic images taken every millisecond.

And that's just the static data; operational data from a global infrastructure- from thousands of mobile devices and personnel to constant sensor monitoring of pumps and the pipeline network – is added all the time.

Hardly any other industry is so dependent on the global economic situation. That's why quite a few oil companies invest a lot of time and energy in evaluating economic data and news. How, for example, will the political climate in Kuwait or Ecuador affect production? Could developments in the US or China curb or increase demand?

The industry has been instrumental in developing and implementing the latest technology throughout the data cycle. As a result, new sensors have been developed for data acquisition that can operate in the most adverse conditions, under hundreds of bars of pressure, in toxic and corrosive environments, and in extreme temperatures, both inside the Earth and on the surface in the Arctic, with unprecedented accuracy.

Microchips were developed for processing, which later found use in virtually every home, whether inside Intel computers in early applications of GPS or in connecting to the Internet in remote areas. To process the terabytes of seismic data these microchips accumulate, the world's largest supercomputers include petroleum companies. Moreover, the data is presented in a visually appealing way in 3D projection spaces.

Data protection is, of course, essential for petroleum companies. As one of the most profitable industries, business data theft can bring devastating damage. Chip cards for identification, now found at every ATM, originated in the oil industry.

16.9.3 Use Cases

Field Discovery

Until a few years ago, seismic data was mainly interpreted by hand. Computers were used to process and display them, but experienced geologists did reservoir recognition. Field discovery is about visual pattern recognition, which is now gradually being automated by machine learning.

What used to take months is now done in days. We achieve a decisive improvement by evaluating existing data with new methods so that new measurements are either not necessary at all or only in a targeted manner.

Another aspect is the rise of fracking, also called hydraulic fracturing. We fracture bedrock formations by a pressurized liquid and therefore have an alternative way to extract fossil fuels. There are many data-driven explorations to be done to find the best sites for fracking.

Scientific Data

On the one hand, new machines and sensors are being developed in laboratories. But, on the other hand, exploitation of oil reserves is only possible through precise geological and chemical knowledge of the earth's interior. Therefore, a lot of deterministic research is being done on the processes. But since the rocks hidden inside the earth are difficult to grasp and we cannot recreate everything in the laboratory, many findings are based on stochastic and statistical methods.

Thus, the work of a data scientist can become a "home game." While in other industries, they still have to justify their way of working because many people are not aware of the background and don't have the technical knowledge to understand it, they can assume that experienced employees in the oil industry will work better with them because they know their requirements.

Predictive Maintenance

Oil and gas is a heavy industry, perhaps the "heaviest" there is. Machines as big as buildings, ships, vehicles, pipelines and refineries are as much a part of it as uninterruptible processes that run for days or weeks. And all of this is usually on the high seas, in the Arctic or the middle of the jungle, with an arrival time to the production facility of two to three weeks. If a device fails or individual components fail, costs rapidly grow into the millions as production comes to a standstill in the worst-case scenario.

Predictive maintenance is just as important here as knowing which spare parts you will need. For this reason, the industry has one of the largest redundancy inventories of any. So every possible optimization here means savings in the millions.

Predictive maintenance can help to detect wear and tear on equipment by evaluating sensor data. At the same time, it helps to determine, based on historical data, which spare parts need to be on-site and in what quantity in order to enable smooth operation.

Process Management

After we find an oil well, setting up and maintaining a production facility is a huge undertaking. Thousands of specialists need to be coordinated, hundreds of transport vehicles acquire working materials and haul away raw materials. This process involves numerous different companies that also need to be coordinated. Whole floors of planners are employed to ensure that everything runs smoothly.

Here, we gain a lot of efficiency through machine learning and process optimization software. A concrete example is the modeling of demand. As soon as a model is generated that predicts the need for various components, the planners' work is made easier.

Geo-Engineering

The Paris Agreement demands zero carbon emissions until 2050. This is terrible news for an industry that depends on fossil fuels. However, there are research projects on removing carbon from the air with new technologies or methods, called geo-engineering. If there is a breakthrough, the removal of combustion engines might be deprioritized.

No matter if it is about devices to bind CO_2, mirrors reflecting sunlight, breeding plankton farms, a lot of data is involved. Therefore, it can be an exciting field for data professionals.

16.9.4 Challenges

Despite applying new, disruptive technologies, the oil and gas industry, dominated by a few substantial companies, is very conservative. The challenge here is not in the central business as the latest and best methods are always used in exploration and production, giving a clear advantage over the competition.

But it's hard to bring corporate governance into the digital age. These are huge companies with hundreds of thousands of employees working in dangerous conditions in hundreds of countries. Millions and billions of euros are at stake here.

All companies are committed to digital transformation. The challenge is to bring dozens of different departments and functions up to the same standard. The organizational hurdle here is many times higher than the technical one.

However, those who manage to digitize all processes, from personnel management to marketing, and from maintenance to operational planning, and who can connect all their data effectively will realize substantial efficiency gains.

■ 16.10 Safety at Work

Few people are aware that employee protection can be seen as an industry in its own right. Millions of euros are spent to ensure a regulated, accident-free working day. This includes various types of training and certification, inspections, safety meetings and strict regulations or prohibitions.

Occupational safety measures have developed over decades, and in many areas, we are now in a much better situation than we used to be. Nevertheless, millions of accidents at work happen every year, thousands of them fatal. We could do perhaps more, but it is not entirely clear what. Some believe that the technical means and prohibitive rules have been exhausted. The recent trend is toward behavioral safety, that is, motivating individuals to act safely. Current results are promising and are based on an extensive collection of data from a wide range of sectors in this industry.

16.10.1 Vision

The shift supervisor sits in her office container, as she does every morning, looking over the reports in front of her.

The first report is about the work schedule for today. "Damn, the night shift didn't finish everything again. That means working faster to keep on schedule. A safety risk. All employees get a bonus if the plan is met, and that motivation could make employees careless." The second report contains the weather forecast: "Five degrees and cloudy, not bad," she thinks to herself.

And then there's the accident prediction. There is a predicted increased risk of hand injuries. The supervisor makes a note in her notebook to be sure to remind workers to wear gloves. "Markus, the new guy, is particularly at risk for this. The movement pattern analysis shows that he is overtired," the supervisor reads there. She will arrange a refresher training for him next week. Until then, she'll have him working with an experienced colleague.

A siren goes off outside. An employee has walked under a suspended load despite the barrier. A camera mounted on the office container overlooks the entire area; the intelligent image recognition has recognized the situation and triggered the alarm. Fortunately, nothing happened.

16.10.2 Data

Due to the legal obligation to report, there is a relatively large amount of detailed data on serious accidents. Even minor accidents are recorded internally by many companies. Documentation was one of the first occupational safety measures introduced decades ago to create awareness.

Each accident also leads to a standard FMEA (Failure Mode and Effects Analysis) type investigation, which can be detailed with many records.

Although known to everyone in the company, the security measures are often less meticulously documented than desirable and are usually found in internal memos, guidelines or process flows.

16.10.3 Use Cases

Further development

Because of the new ways of processing and analyzing data, casualties can be better identified by looking through and calculating the entire data set rather than just the small part of a single department. And it's not just about computing power. Innovations in storage, categorization, linking between systems, or even reading reports open up new possibilities for knowledge creation.

Occupational health and safety measures can thus be better coordinated to achieve optimum accident reduction.

Accident forecast

"Next week, my department will have an accident." This statement sounds a bit like science fiction, but it is already partly reality. One can calculate in advance an increased accident occurrence and determine the accident probability for individual processes.

If you think about it, it's always been done this way, except that individuals assessed the risk based on their experience. Now we can take all cases into account and calculate the exact risk.

Maybe, like the weather forecast, it won't always come true one hundred percent of the time. But if it helps protect more people from injury, it's already a critical success.

Training

Training is a fundamental building block of the workplace safety industry. There is a minimum amount of content that everyone needs to know, plus refresher training regularly. Data science can help in two ways.

Trainers can customize instructions according to job needs or the attitude of the individual. Such a step requires sufficient data about the job specifics and the background of the participants.

In addition, the effectiveness of the individual training units can be elicited, not only according to whether the participants have mastered the course content but also whether it helps them to work safely. There are training units that have to be repeated every year. This interval was arbitrarily determined. With modern analytical methods, we can determine whether training every two years is sufficient or whether it would be better to do it every half year.

Targeted inspections

Occupational safety thrives on controls and inspections. Above a specific size or responsibility, this becomes a long and tedious process. However, with the help of data science, it is possible to determine in advance whether an inspection is likely to uncover any irregularities or not.

In New York, this has been applied to the fire department. Instead of checking every hundred buildings in a grid, inspectors only check twenty buildings for fire hazards.

This allows identifying and eliminating the danger more quickly and means that staff can be deployed in a more targeted manner, and their work becomes more exciting and motivating.

16.10.4 Challenges

In this section, we have already touched on the fact that there is a lot of data on occupational safety measures, but it is usually quite scattered. The various data sources are kept in different forms and departments, depending on who is responsible for what: Structural barriers and measures such as the separate storage of hazardous materials are recorded in building management; Video surveillance of parking lots is managed by IT; Operations record procedural guidelines and safety meetings, and Human Resources keep training records. Bringing all this information together can be a nightmare in the face of corporate bureaucracy.

Another challenge that is not unique to this topic is data protection. A lot of information in this area is sensitive. On the one hand, accident data with details on the affected and involved are sometimes medically and legally relevant. On the other hand, details of internal procedures are a trade secret.

It is crucial to find a way to overcome these problems in order to bring about an improvement in working conditions.

■ 16.11 Retail

Many people don't think of a supermarket in terms of data analysis. For them, a supermarket is still a domain where people deliver goods, people sort goods, and at the checkout, there are usually still people who receive a customer. In other words, an industry in which data analysis is not relevant.

But the reality is different. Product placement is an all-important philosophy that can become critical to the existence of suppliers. Store managers have to place products with a high probability of purchase optimally. It is also essential that neighboring products should give the buyer ideas about what else to purchase. Ideally, the customer is presented with the products logically in a structured order from the beginning of their journey through the supermarket, right up to the checkout.

16.11.1 Vision

Your self-driving car drives you home from the office. You know full well that your personal AI assistant at home will organize the refill of the fridge and freezer with fresh goods in your absence. This automation means that, in theory, you don't have to worry about anything. If something runs out in the household, an AI will reorder it. Based on your past personal preferences, Alexa, Siri and Co. know what should not be missing. And if you ever get a craving for something new, all you have to do is say, "Alexa, tonight will be a schnitzel night." The only question Alexa might ask you is whether you want to prepare the schnitzels yourself or have them delivered ready-made. But as a rule, Alexa will be able to calculate this request herself.

Shopping in a supermarket has changed. Sure they still exist, you can find them on every corner, but shopping looks very different now. Instead of putting goods into an actual shopping cart, shopping consists of trying and looking. With all the automated services available now, manual shopping is all about the experience. Supermarkets are paying more attention than ever to the shopping experience to give customers an incentive they wouldn't have in an online store. In addition, the payment process is handled in the background.

16.11.2 Data

Customer experience managers can attach sensors to shopping carts to track customer journeys. For example, where standing times occur, it is essential to analyze whether customers cannot find the products they would like to buy.

Video cameras detect when people are entering and leaving. But, of course, it would violate data protection rules to identify individuals. Still, it is at least possible to decide how many people are in the store and, if necessary, also determine a few characteristics about them. For example, what is the approximate gender distribution, estimated average age, and so on?

Another topic is sensor data on products or shelves. Here, too, it is possible to deduce customer behavior. For example, an AI can determine which shelves need to be restocked and when. Models from this data can help to optimize stock levels.

16.11.3 Use Cases

AI-assisted Purchasing

In the vision, we had Alexa, Siri, Cortana, and co place orders themselves to make sure you have everything you need. In this use case, we assume that you want to go shopping yourself.

Electronic AI assistants may send you different products while you're in the supermarket.

"Alexa, where can I find the spices in this supermarket?"

"Two shelves over, you'll find them. Do you want a recommendation?"

"Sure. What do you recommend with moussaka?"

By scanning the product codes, the AI could also find out whether there are any substances in a product that you or someone in your family is allergic to.

Product Placement

As a market operator, you want to know which products you need and which ones you don't. Which ones sell well, which ones don't? Which product group B will a customer buy if it is next to product group A?

Product placement is one of the central topics for optimizing a supermarket in terms of purchasing efficiency. Products that logically belong together are grouped, and an optimized assortment is used to try and prevent slow-moving goods.

AI can generate models that perfectly optimize each supermarket, adapting placement to the environment and typical customer demographics. It can also identify buying trends at other locations and derive marketing campaigns for individual products.

16.11.4 Challenges

Retail has traditionally been a conservative market. Some providers do not even offer their customers so-called loyalty cards. Management often tries to keep IT costs to a minimum, and POS systems usually work with old software.

Covid has created a lot of pressure on retail. Many customers have become acquainted with ordering online and e-commerce software offerings have increased. Companies selling products only online also have fewer costs and therefore can offer their goods cheaper.

Until now, Amazon has only been considered a competitor for suppliers of non-perishable goods. Now, the company is also putting pressure on well-established supermarket chains. Amazon invests in brick-and-mortar stores and delivers groceries to customers' homes via its subsidiary, Amazon Fresh.

The business may not be profitable yet. Older people, in particular, are used to going shopping and don't see the appeal in an online grocery store. Digital natives, however, who are familiar with ordering online from a young age, will also order groceries online. The location of supermarkets further influences the acceptance of virtual grocery shopping. Suppose there is no supermarket near the home. In that case, people will be more inclined to try alternative virtual shopping methods.

Another aspect driving the virtualization of all purchasing processes is self-driving cars and the resulting optimization of delivery logistics through AI, which will significantly reduce shipping costs.

■ 16.12 Telecommunications Provider

Telco providers have traditionally made a living from selling subscriptions. Based on their current business model, you go to the store, sign a contract and then pay the telco provider a monthly fee for using their services. We could say this consists of two major parts: First, to get you, and second, to keep you as long as possible.

In some countries, the business of telco providers is becoming difficult. They might gain new customers with campaigns and offer lower-priced subscriptions, but once a minimum price is locked in, it is hard to raise the prices again. In addition, offers such as the mobile phone messaging app 'WhatsApp' are shrinking the SMS market.

The most promising future market is 5G. 5G is supposed to deliver several improvements for end-users, including fast internet, down to the millisecond response time. But the network rollout is costly for telcos, and its profit is minimal, leading to the consequences listed below regarding their business model. The beneficiaries of 5G are IT companies that can now offer even more and richer services. For example, let's look at Google: The $ 100 billion business would be worth nothing without internet access. All services, such as YouTube, are provided through telcos. It is similar to Netflix: without high bandwidth, the use of this service is not possible.

Telcos have access to a lot of data, and this data offers plenty of opportunities for new business models. We can identify three critical areas that have future potential:

- improvement of customer relations,
- internal optimization and
- the possibility to build up new business areas with data.

16.12.1 Vision

Imagine you are walking on a shopping street. You have shared your profile with your internet provider for data analysis and receive complimentary internet in return.

While you are shopping, you receive some special personalized offers based on your location. After finishing shopping, your phone recommends an event in your area that matches your preferences. A suitable companion is also quickly found, as there is someone nearby you know who shares your interests and with whom you can attend the event together.

Before that, you go shopping in a supermarket. Since this supermarket has also analyzed its customers using telco data, you immediately find what you want: Your mobile phone guides you to the goods.

16.12.2 Data

In the telecommunications industry, data professionals distinguish between technical data and business data. Technical data is created when using smartphones: so-called 'Call Detail Records' (CDRs), cell change information, sensor data from the radio network area, and so on.

In business, we collect customer data by recording the behavior of customers. This transactional, behavioral, and CRM data is precious, especially when it includes access to customer social media data.

16.12.3 Use Cases

Churn/Customer Loyalty

An existing contract hardly causes any costs for a provider. Whether a customer makes more or fewer calls makes no difference from a cost perspective. Either way, the infrastructure must be available to offer the services. Consequently, all telcos need to retain their customers as much as possible.

Analytics can help build models that assess a client's loyalty and predict the likelihood of them abandoning the company, which is referred to as the 'churn rate.'

Location-based Offers

Customers moving along shopping streets can be offered matching deals. The telco recognizes that they are in a particular position. Suppose a match to the customer preferences is found via AI. In that case, the customers are informed about special offers only if they have consented to use their data for these purposes.

There are certain opinions that telcos can earn more via location-based offers than via contracts. In this way, at least some contracts could also be financed via advertising in the future.

Mobility Solutions

Telcos have large amounts of data about the movement behavior of their customers in their mobile network. Based on this movement data, a telco can precisely tell how many visitors have attended an event or have seen an advertisement. Based on mobility data, this is, of course, particularly interesting for outdoor advertising. However, these solutions are even more interesting for retail: A telco can tell a mall very precisely how many users and what kind of users are there (based on income bracket, socio-demographic characteristics, and the like). Another advantage here is seeing which customers are going to the competing supermarket around the corner.

Network Planning

The planning of the 5G network is primarily done based on data. For this purpose, telcos analyze their customers' location in order to determine who would switch to a 5G tariff early. Since the 5G rollout will be very cost-intensive, the telcos will implement it in the long term and first and foremost in areas where customers are willing to pay more for a 5G add-on package.

Another critical point here is the improvement of the existing network. For example, CDRs can be used to identify where calls are repeatedly dropped. Algorithms can then decide where to invest. This is important because customers who experience poor network quality are more likely to switch providers.

Marketing Automation

A topic that affects very many industries is the automation of marketing measures in the company. Especially in saturated markets like the telecommunications industry, there is hardly any growth potential left. Therefore, it is imperative to be able to address customers directly and relevantly. This only works if you have a comprehensive customer data platform (Customer Subscriber Data Platform). This then decides which customers to address in which channels and with which message. The offers are highly personalized. This means, for example, that customers who have been using an iPhone for years also receive corresponding offers since there is probably hardly any interest in another smartphone.

Call Centers

Telcos often have huge call centers in which they serve their customers. There is a multitude of optimization possibilities here. One major challenge is the management of "caller peaks." Here, a telco tries to calculate the peak load and design the call center based on that. With intelligent algorithms, this load can be better distributed, for example, by putting customers with a high priority in the front of the phone queue and customers with a low priority behind.

Likewise, telcos may inform customers about problems in advance. For example, when a network outage or network problems occur, the number of calls to call centers goes way up. Therefore, proactive information can significantly improve the service.

Another future scenario is voice recognition. You will call the call center in a few years, and you will first speak only with computers. These are already so intelligently designed that humans will hardly recognize this. Only when the algorithm no longer knows any answers will you be connected to a human.

Equipment Failure/Predictive Maintenance

Just as in many other industries, predictive maintenance is an essential topic for telcos. The primary question here is which parts of the network, mainly physical devices (transmitters), will fail and when. Frequent reasons for network problems are weather conditions, as data often has to be transported from radio mast to radio mast. If these can be predicted, the network can be improved significantly.

16.12.4 Challenges

Customers will understandably not always agree to their data being evaluated. Accordingly, it is crucial to adhere to data protection rules so that only those customers receive data-based offers that expressly agree.

Also, the data quality delivered over mobile networks is not always satisfactory. This affects position data, for example, as different terrain affects the quality of the radio signals. Methods such as triangulation can improve location determination, but these methods also have limitations.

■ 16.13 Transport

This section will focus on freight transport, which freight forwarding companies carry out by road and rail. The core expectation is that goods arrive safely and on time. Therefore, resource planning, pricing, and cost reduction are essential to companies.

There is another aspect of AI, especially regarding reaching sustainability goals: Optimizing logistics to reduce the number of freights or kilometers on the road. For example, algorithms can find more efficient routes or combine deliveries.

16.13.1 Vision

You have purchased a product through an online shop, which is an original that must be shipped. We emphasize this because, in the society of the future, many things can also be produced in-house by 3D printers.

An application will show you how long it will take to get this product to you immediately.

In the days before the information society, there were lots of steps along the way. First, someone had to package the product, take it to the post office, where it was sorted, forwarded to distribution points, etc. Then when the package was with you in a few days, you had to be home, because otherwise the postman would just leave you a notice and you'd have to go back to the post office. But that wasn't the end of it. After you had unpacked the goods, you also had to dispose of the packaging material.

But we live in a digital society, where everything is automated. So after the purchase, the journey starts immediately. Robots pack your goods in a standard reusable container, which you can return when you receive the goods.

You can always track your product during delivery and when it will be with you via the transport network. From a central warehouse, robots put your goods on an autonomous driving truck. On various waypoints, some goods might be unloaded just to be loaded on different trucks by robots. The whole transport network from the store to your home is a huge graph in which sophisticated algorithms have calculated the most efficient path to your home. Some also talk about an "IRL TCP/IP system," meaning a TCP/IP system in real life. If the package is small enough, fast delivery is also possible through drones.

Delivery services can align the delivery of packages with your presence at home, or you can grant a delivery service temporary and monitored access to your home. In addition, if a drone delivers a parcel, it can also be left on a terrace or balcony.

16.13.2 Data

Imagine a digital twin based on a vast graph system that maps all routes and means of transportation which are currently transporting products from A to B. You can turn the entire transportation system into a TCP/IP network. For example, vehicle A brings goods 1, 2, and 3 to Deposit A. Goods 1 comes to vehicle B, which travels to another node, where these goods are in turn shipped to vehicle C.

The entire route calculation is optimized so that each product reaches the end customer with as little effort as possible.

16.13.3 Use Cases

Predictive Maintenance

In all transport companies, defects are expensive. Imagine a train is canceled or delayed. In some freight, penalties are incurred. A delay can mean that other trains are also delayed with the railways, especially if they have to wait for a train to depart.

Predictive maintenance provides the information that maintenance staff needs to detect possible defects more quickly. You can use sensor data and measurements to determine whether defects are probable shortly and whether it makes sense to replace worn components beforehand.

Resource Management

Imagine you want to optimize the loading of a truck or a freight car. How you arrange your goods and load individual containers and cargos to maximize resource utilization matters significantly.

Data Science can optimize the load distribution on your transporters, which helps you save costs.

16.13.4 Challenges

From a social perspective, many view self-driving cars in transport ambivalently. For example, the working conditions of haulage drivers are often strenuous. Even with only a few breaks, they hardly manage to meet ambitious delivery deadlines. So, drivers would benefit from autonomous trucks if they could "share the route" and rest in the truck while the autopilot is active.

But what if a truck can go the road seamlessly? Many drives might get worried about their jobs, although it might take a while until they are fully replaceable. We may see Uber as an alternative form of taxi service. Still, existing taxi companies in many countries tried to fight Uber through legislation and lobbying. If there is already a resistance against Uber, which still employs human drivers, we can expect more resistance when services can replace (truck) drivers.

■ 16.14 Teaching and Training

Establishing digitization in schools and using AI for teaching and talent development can mean, for example, using regression techniques to analyze teaching methods and derive trends from predicting whether performance will fall or rise when using a particular process.

Suppose we had access to all the data. Then, we could build behavioral factors into the "performance model." We could also analyze exactly how efficient training methods are and whether they are worth investing in further.

We can today reach out to almost everyone globally through social media. Unfortunately, at the same time, this opportunity opened the door also to individuals to spread "personal propaganda" and misinformation. Primarily through the Corona pandemic, we have learned how emotional discussions can get. Most people care only about spreading their viewpoints, and they are not interested in reflecting on their views by hearing out those who have a different perspective. As a result, civilized fact-based discussions sometimes seem to be nearly impossible.

A future school also has to help overcome this social media challenge: They have to teach more than ever the ability to differentiate between objective knowledge and fake news. But, unfortunately, this also requires being vigilant about information coming from various governmental institutions.

Besides learning to participate meaningfully in discussions on the internet, one key aspect of learning is data literacy and interpreting data correctly. Or in other words, we have to teach the next generations very much to think like data scientists from early stages.

Social Media and the Village Idiot Theory

There had always been outliers in our societies. Sometimes they are mavericks who challenge the status quo and bring us forward. Sometimes, however, these people would be called "village idiots" or strangelings in earlier times. It is a different debate if the outcasts just missed the right moment to become mavericks or if fate was just cruel to them.

As they do not fit in, they often try to get attention and do or say weird things. Mothers teach their children to ignore village idiots, and commonly, the rest knows from experience as there had been too many incidents that wisdom is not one of village idiots' traits.

In social media, those outcasts who would be otherwise "village idiots" may gain an audience as no one right away understands that they are quirky. So in the future, if you have a heated discussion with someone, try to imagine that you might be talking to the kind of person that your mother would have warned you about and stop wasting your precious time.

On the other hand, if you cannot remember who the "village idiot" was in the past and remember that people already had heated discussions with you or ignored you, you should start asking different questions.

■

16.14.1 Vision

The more AI that is available in schools, the more individual attention students can receive. But, unfortunately, many of us still grew up in a school system where teachers primarily gave frontal instruction.

The modern school begins with a placement assessment to determine what the child brings with them regarding resources and abilities when they enter school. The ultimate goal is to nurture talents, not force the child into a system that dictates what is right or wrong, regardless of their abilities.

Performance assessment uses the full range of data science methods. In addition, we can analyze the language of students to assess how they approach problem-solving. The evaluation also explores how students take in information, visual or auditory, for example.

The content transfer takes place digitally to a large extent and contains constant quality improvements. In modern learning centers, teachers change from frontal teaching to mentoring. The interaction between individuals is essential as we can verify immediately whether the student has understood the content or not.

Playfully, the children learn new skills and acquire knowledge. Curricula no longer exist; learning objectives are adapted individually. AI also helps to understand which teaching methods work better with which students. According to the principle of "more of the good and less of the bad," we can adapt didactics individually.

Mentors prepare children for a changing time. Students, therefore, learn only the most essential facts because they can look up details from the Internet. But, above all, they learn behavioral patterns to identify objective information and separate them from untruths successfully.

New data-driven learning platforms also teach behavior patterns, such as solving problems efficiently and dealing with unexpected challenges. In the past, some students had learned how to prevent mistakes to get good grades with mediocre but less error-prone works. In the future, students are encouraged to try new things and take risks as their mentors expect them to make mistakes and to learn from constructive feedback.

16.14.2 Data

Data for education can be, for example, any form of testing such as placement tests, but also teacher evaluations and the way teaching materials are used.

Data from test results needn't necessarily reflect right or wrong. Natural Language Processing can also be used, for example, to draw conclusions about expressive ability and whether students may be acting in destructive patterns that prevent them from learning successfully.

If students use social media, supervisors can determine in which direction they are developing. We can generate models to understand how they learn and think.

16.14.3 Use Cases

MOOC

MOOCs (Massive Open Online Courses) have become an integral part of the educational experience. Udemy, Udacity, Pluralsight, EDX, Coursera, and many other online learning offerings are flooding the market.

In the race for the best quality, one question is how to measure the courses' quality and detect room for improvement. Today, quality assurance systems get feedback from users per lesson and calculate dropout rates or how often students repeat segments of a video.

AI will enable us to assess the efficiency of content in new ways. For example, once we can determine when a significant number of students lose their attention span in a video, we might adjust the content on a segment level. In addition, MOOCs might become far more interactive, and this also means that we can deduct the efficiency of exercises by looking at students' behavior.

Personalized Learning

All students have individual strengths and weaknesses. Training institutes can build profiles that record how someone thinks and learns. Supervisors can compare personal profiles and assemble learning groups that could fit together based on an evaluation.

Curriculums can offer individuals courses in the form of a recommendation engine. The more feedback students give, the more accurately an AI-based teaching assistant recommends courses to students that match their skills and potential.

16.14.4 Challenges

Critics claim that the existing school system is not flexible enough to adapt to the demands of an economy with dynamic priority changes. Instead, they see educational systems as rigid organizations where teachers have acquired a fixed routine in transmitting knowledge. As a result, those who have been used to this routine have difficulties adapting to a new teaching style.

We outlined in the use cases that the more we study students' behavior during classes, the more we understand how they learn, the more we can improve their learning experience. However, these assessments might go so far that we measure their attention level through facial expressions. Therefore, we can see a risk that the detailed analysis of how students learn is an invasion of privacy and problematic for data protection.

■ 16.15 The Digital Society

In conclusion to the Data Science use cases, we present a digital society vision that integrates Machine Learning and AI in daily lives. Beforehand, we mentioned that autonomous driving could be a game-changer and may open the door to further application of scenarios where computers do the work of humans. So far, machines have guided us. We use our smartphones to choose a hotel for a night or find products we like to purchase; still, we decide for ourselves. Future generations may allow computers to make fundamental decisions for them.

Almost every profession will be affected by the automation methods presented in this book. We did not cover jobs perceived as a grey zone or illegal in some countries, such as gambling or sex work. But everything connected with strong emotions can become far more effective once there is an understanding of what needs to be triggered and at which moment. Moreover, we have shown that we can deduct this information from data.

Of course, it may still take a lot of imagination to envision robots as geriatric nurses. Still, it is already clear that fewer and fewer employees are standing at the counter in banks, and innovation replaces teachers, taxi drivers, and supermarket employees with machines just as gradually.

Science Fiction literature shows options for utopian and dystopian outcomes. Some see digitalization as progress, others as a threat. So the essential question we have to ask ourselves is: What is the role of humans in a fully automated world?

Wikipedia lists some sources discussing whether governments should tax machines instead of labor[8] in scenarios where a machine replaces human labor to "make AI compatible with social systems as well." There is also a discourse that suggests that we need to question our economic system if we want to live differently in the future. A financial system that thrives on income from human work may no longer fit the purpose in the age of automation. We will also have to ask ourselves whether everyone needs to work to sustain society. According to Maslow, once we have fulfilled our basic needs, the purpose will become more important for humans. Therefore, human sciences may experience a renaissance via digitalization.

For skeptics, the automated society is an illusion. They stress that enthusiasts vastly overestimate technologies, and citizens underestimate them. They fear a surveillance society fostered by Big Data. And they want to fight against it.

You can counter that the generation that lived at the beginning of the 20th century could not have imagined a mobile phone either. If you had told someone 50 years ago that we could receive global knowledge through the Internet, many would not have believed you.

Innovations come in spurts, and each new trend triggers a chain of events. For example, in 2005, YouTube came on the market; today, people make a living by marketing themselves on YouTube and driving up their viewership numbers. People also make their living as professional computer gamers. And others advise people who have burnout caused by digitalization.

One should not leave dystopian visions unmentioned here. Many also see Big Data as a precursor to worlds like those depicted in '1984,' 'Terminator,' 'The Matrix,' or 'Minority Report,' in which intelligent machines take control and enslave humanity. Fears range from the total annihilation of humankind because computers classify it as a virus to the fear of total surveillance. But even less apocalyptic scenarios strike many as frightening. A negative example of a data-driven company could, for example, also conclude that it can do without various employees and terminate them for this reason. Such a scenario is not particularly optimistic either. Identity theft may happen as such in 'The Net.'

We also have to be aware that militaries will fight future wars with drones, and we have seen that these harbingers of destruction with the help of AI can acquire targets on their own.[9]

At the same time, we might find a counterargument in another example: In '2001: A Space Odyssey,' HAL 9000 is often seen as an evil computer. But in another way, we can interpret his actions as quite egomaniacal, a human trait. He believed that he simply could not err. This phenomenon has been seen a lot with narcissistic leaders. How many leaders were so convinced about themselves that they accepted total destruction? We fear computers might control us at some point, but who is scared about humans who govern us with mass hysteria, as often seen in fascist systems?

The digitalized society brings challenges as well. It will always be possible to get out, go into nature, and live far away from the modern world. Yes, maybe it will be more accessible in the future because such a society can allow dropouts to live such a life, as many can live well without a regular job thanks to automation. We believe that the realization of the digitalized society will lead to the individual being in the center. Everyone will have the opportunity to realize their individual lives and live their true will.

---

[8] Wikipedia: Machine tax, 2018
[9] https://www.independent.co.uk/life-style/gadgets-and-tech/drone-fully-automated-military-kill-b1856815.html

■ 16.16 In a Nutshell

Every industry has its own rules.

Every industry is different. The industry case studies presented are only a small excerpt. Above all, without specific knowledge of the domain, it is challenging to execute data science projects.

The possible benefits are real, as are the potential threats.

AI can bring us a better world, but it can also be misused. So, in the end, it is up to us how we shape our future.

■

17 Mindset and Community

Stefan Papp

> *"Data scientists are kind of like the new Renaissance folks because data science is inherently multidisciplinary."*
>
> John Foreman, VP of Product Management at MailChimp

Questions Answered in this Chapter:

- What role does corporate culture play in data science projects?
- What impact does fear of change have on data science projects?
- How can companies adapt their culture to become data science ready?
- How do agile projects and data science fit together?
- What are the antipatterns in data projects, and how can you deal with them?

In this book, we have classified a 'Data Scientist' as a person that creates new knowledge through data analysis. In addition, a data scientist often acts as an *intrapreneur* who influences strategic decisions as an 'entrepreneur within the company.'

Data science experts and data platforms are only two of the building blocks required for successful data science projects. The corporate culture and its ability to change are primarily responsible for the success or failure of these ventures to gain new insights. Without a willingness to rethink existing processes and structures, nobody can implement the knowledge from this book satisfactorily.

17.1 Data-Driven Mindset

In the past, independent thinkers often changed the world. But, unfortunately, society often dismissed mavericks who challenged the status quo as lunatics.

You probably know at least one of the following quotes:

> *"I think there is a market in the world for maybe five computers."* – Thomas Watson, Chairman IBM 1943

or

> *"The Internet will go down like a spectacular supernova in 1996 in a cataclysmic collapse."*
> – Robert Metcalfe, 1995

PC Welt magazine has published many quotes from influential figures who didn't believe in change in their day.[1] One crowning example is Steve Ballmer when he laughs about the iPhone and emphasizes that business users "would never buy a phone without a keyboard."

One recipe for "making the impossible, possible" is to believe in yourself, question what exists, and not let the establishment dissuade you. In the biography of Steve Jobs by Walter Isaacson, the author claims that the Apple founder simply ignored objections from engineers that his wishes were technologically unfeasible. Isaacson called this trait of Jobs his "reality distortion field." The consequence was that this pressure sometimes inspired employees to go above and beyond. [2]

In this book, we describe the result of the transformation of companies towards data science as a digital society. The previous chapters explained how this could change how we live and how targeted data analysis can turn entire industries upside down. Amara's Law is also essential here:

> "We tend to overestimate the effect of a technology in the short run and underestimate the effect in the long run," – Roy Amara.

In times of rapid change, many citizens are also afraid of moving away from traditions. The possible misuse of data is only one of multiple concerns. Many people fear no longer having a place in the digital society. Digital natives who have grown up with innovations are more adaptable than people who at some point trusted that they would retire with their first job.

It would be unrealistic to speculate that, in a short time, data science will digitally transform the world. But, at the same time, we use technology standards today that were not imaginable in science fiction films of the past.

Sometimes, in this context, data scientists also have the task of breaking down old thought patterns in companies. They have to convey change as an opportunity for the company to put itself in a position to generate new knowledge from data.

Paradoxically, refusing to change because of security concerns leads to precisely the opposite. Those who do not move with the times risk their very existence. There is no such thing as "too big to fail." Studebaker once had the world's largest car manufacturing plant; Today, you'll find Studebakers in museums. The list goes on and on: Horten, Saba, Commodore, and many more. Courses, such as Critical Business Skills for Success[3], use case studies like Netflix vs. Blockbuster to illustrate that leading companies with the wrong strategy can lose their dominance. Some analysts even predict that the German automotive industry is at risk of losing its position on the market as they fall behind in the race to develop autonomous cars. [4]

Who will perish or who might persist is not the subject of this book. Our task in this context is to point to the notion of *Science* in Data Science. Science creates new knowledge, and new knowledge leads to change. Companies that ignore change will not remain competitive.

---

[1] *www.pcwelt.de/ratgeber/Die_spektakulaersten_Fehlprognosen_der_IT-Geschichte-6948150.html*
[2] Isaacson, W.: Steve Jobs. Simon & Schuster, 2011
[3] Conner, M.C.: Critical Business Skills for Success. Teaching Company, 2013
[4] *https://derletztefuehrerscheinneuling.com/2019/02/28/die-erschreckende-ambitionslosigkeit-deutscher-hersteller-beim-autonomen-fahren/*

Diversity and Data Science

One question that came up in recent years was whether Data Science techniques might increase or decrease discrimination. The claim was that if you provide unbalanced training data to AI models, the model will perform better for that group. For example, suppose your training data consists of people with one skin color in a facial recognition program. In that case, the trained model may fail to recognize people of another ethnicity. Not only can this have detrimental effects on the well-being of the underrepresented group, but it can also cause severe consequences for the AI-program creators.[5]

Friends of data science often highlight that data scientists have the means and the responsibility to remove bias because, in the end, sexual orientation, religious beliefs, skin color, age, nationality, or gender are just parameters in a formula. This approach to eliminate these parameters from analysis would align with current political 'hashtag movements' goals.

Even if we could prove our algorithms were unbiased, unwanted side effects could arise. What if, for example, we learned through data that genetic differences have more significance than we thought? Could scientific theories then inspire political ideas based on race or other genetic traits?

Data Science has the potential to help people make completely unbiased decisions. For example, say we use algorithms to help automate candidate selection during hiring processes: we could then remove all non-relevant parameters from the decision-making process and that factors such as gender or ethnicity cannot affect hiring decisions anymore. However, it might still take a long time to replace a recruiter as machines cannot interpret interpersonal relationships and various human traits, especially for personnel decisions.

■

Communication challenges and bureaucracy in companies grow with the number of employees. The associated inertia makes it difficult for corporations to react to new developments. Numerous articles report an increasing number of people who are dissatisfied with their jobs in corporations. Many feel like a small wheel in the system.[6]

In an oppressive environment, a digital transformation driven by data science seems like a possible cure-all for any form of corporate disenchantment. After all, strategy consultants promise a different way of working. Data science is supposed to break up existing structures and reshape them. So let's have a look into some possible pitfalls during a transformation.

---

[5] https://www.forbes.com/sites/mzhang/2015/07/01/google-photos-tags-two-african-americans-as-gorillas-through-facial-recognition-software/
[6] https://www.zeitgeistich.de/zufriedenheit-im-grosskonzern/

■ 17.2 Data Science Culture

17.2.1 Start-up or Consulting Firm?

For the implementation of a digital transformation, companies often seek the support of external IT service providers. However, large consulting firms have the reputation of selling a lot of management overhead in their services and not always acting sustainably in the customer's interests.

 Practical Example: A Statement of a Decision-maker about Consulting Firms

"Many of our technicians are not happy with management's decision about the contract with consulting firm X. Many of the representatives from the consulting firm are still relatively young, and in addition, their high daily rates seem over-priced.

One of our managers has worked for consulting firm X in the past. If the project is in trouble, he and his pals from the consulting firm X will do everything to get back on track, even at the risk that X will have no profit in that project. If, in the end, the project with consulting firm X still fails, many stakeholders will high-light the project's complexity and that even consulting firm X cannot do magic. However, if the decision-maker had hired a start-up, who might be a bit more agile and innovative than consultant firm X, and if the project had failed, then our stakeholders would have criticized the decision to hire a start-up for a large enterprise project."

■

For start-ups, it is a challenge to manage large projects which demand many different competencies. For example, a complete data project often requires hardware, computer network, operating system, security, and data experts. And each of these experts must also have specific, sometimes specialized technical knowledge.

Big consulting firms are often not popular with engineers, who often claim that such firms use their market power to get into large companies. People feel more sympathetic toward the underdog, particularly the innovative start-up of ambitious young entrepreneurs without the management overhead. However, we also have to look at the downsides of those start-ups.

Practical Example: A Decision-maker on Hiring a Start-up

"Start-up Y has promised to solve all our problems. They call themselves a 'Bay Area innovator' and highlight their years of experience as a leading AI company. However, during our engagement, it turns out that hardly any of them have worked on a major AI project yet, and we found some of the profiles of their key employees advertised as professional front-end developers for other clients. Even the San Francisco address is just a mailbox address; most employees work from Eastern Europe. So, though they try very hard and their rates are slightly cheaper than a larger consulting firm, we end up being beta testers."

It would be wrong to claim that start-ups generally overestimate themselves. Nor would it be right to condemn all large consulting firms as overly bureaucratic organizations that only present colorful PowerPoint slides. If there is one thing to conclude then, maybe it is that each organization can develop a particular form of arrogance which leads them away from every company's natural main goal to bring value to their clients. The Dunning-Kruger Effect mentioned later will go more into detail on this.

17.2.2 Labs Instead of Corporate Policy

Many large organizations have reorganized and created organizational units which have been decoupled from corporate politics and given the name 'labs.' These labs provide a culture of innovation, which means working with universities and establishing a so-called 'Tribe' culture, as popularized by Spotify.[7] Equally important is the workplace itself. Instead of boring offices, there are workspaces specifically designed to facilitate a friendly, creative working atmosphere.

17.2.3 Keiretsu Instead of Lone Wolf

If start-ups want to carry out a large project that they cannot manage independently, they can join forces with partners. As a 'bidding consortium,' they can agree to distribute responsibilities. However, partnerships also entail risks. Bidding consortiums fail if one of the companies wants to increase their workload during the project and begins to "fish in other people's waters." The question of trust also arises: A company can control its services and quality standards, but how do they ensure that the partner company also treats the project with the same professionalism?

Keiretsu is a cooperative model that helped Japan rebuild its economy after World War II. Each firm in a conglomerate specializes in one particular product or service, and, in order to ensure a collaborative partnership, each firm also holds shares in the other participating

---

[7] *https://www.atlassian.com/agile/agile-at-scale/spotify*

firms. Thus, all companies will increasingly act in each other's interests and positively influence their partners' quality and processes.

 Practical Example: SME-Keiretsu

Company A specializes in data engineering and Company B in data science. Company A holds shares in Company B and vice versa. Company A profits when Company B gets a job in the data science environment. The temptation to apply for the same contract is therefore low for company A.

The open-source culture thrives on clearly defined interfaces between software components; individual components must remain interchangeable. This principle of loose coupling also works in a partner network. For example, if company B can no longer accept orders, company A can also engage company C.

Large corporations have the means to invest a lot of resources to win contracts with clients. However, especially if their goal is to increase revenue, they sometimes accept making no profit initially and are very generous with free initial prototypes to bind the client. This aggressive behavior makes it difficult for small companies to compete.

The "SME Keiretsu" model outlined above can be used in the B2B sector to oppose the corporate "Goliath" as an "agile David" as smaller companies share the risks and would also be able to risk more as if they were alone.

 Entrepreneurship: Consulting vs. Products

Many data experts are turning their backs on the corporate world to become independent experts. In doing so, many ask themselves whether they, as data experts, should try to sell their knowledge as a service to clients (consulting) or whether they should develop a product.

In consulting, you benefit from an immediate cash flow when you win a project. The downside of consulting is that consultants often end up doing tedious work. Many consultants exchange long-term job security against higher short-term pay as day rates result in more money than a monthly salary. However, those who enter product development must first deal with the venture capital market since creating a product takes longer and must be financed. Product companies also require more budget for product branding and sales.

If you want to understand how to do a start-up with an IT product, read the book "Disciplined Entrepreneurship"[8] and research venture capital. Be also aware that it is hard to build a product without the support of others, whereas as a consultant, you can work alone if needed.

---

[8] https://www.amazon.com/Disciplined-Entrepreneurship-Steps-Successful-start-up-ebook/dp/B00DQ97TWO

17.2.4 Agile Software Development

In 2001, seventeen independent-minded software practitioners created the Agile Manifesto because the old thought patterns and working methods in traditional software development no longer worked in some cases. As a result, many software projects failed.

"Individuals and interactions over processes and tools
Working software over comprehensive documentation
Customer collaboration over contract negotiation
Responding to change over following a plan" – Agile Manifesto[9]

Agile software development comprises strategy (how to organize work) and tactics (how to get things done to meet the requirements). Scrum and Kanban have been established as main models to manage projects, and both offer best practices to keep the workflow running smoothly. Development methods such as eXtreme Programming aim at efficiently achieving a high-quality software product.

Another vital aspect is corporate values that influence what companies are doing. Each company has individual values that define how they operate. Many companies define them openly, such as Amazon[10]. Some highlight that if a company does not define them, they will still have unwritten laws on "things are done there." Some experts claim that data-driven companies should focus on values such as authenticity, humbleness or striving for excellence.

Numerous consultants cite flat hierarchies as a forward-looking model, i.e., employees meet at eye level to replace traditional, sometimes authoritarian pyramid systems. Instead of permanent positions, everyone is accountable for roles they take over. However, this also means that people in the team take more responsibility for their work and organize themselves.

17.2.5 Company and Work Culture

What influence does the culture and mentality of a country have on its working environment? For a start, a country's legislation and corporate culture provide the framework within which companies can operate.

One often hears that start-up culture is lacking in some EU countries. Highly qualified talents prefer the security of a salaried existence instead of realizing themselves as entrepreneurs with new ideas. Many also complain that bureaucracy and lobbying are more important than progress and that some countries are stagnant. Often, young people receive too little support to pursue a future-proof career by studying STEM subjects. Critics accuse the EU countries of promoting a culture of fear, which leads many people to view any kind of progress negatively.

Critics of digitalization often speak of predatory capitalism and criticize that American companies earn vast sums by snooping on people and do not even want to pay appropriate taxes for this.

---

[9] *https://agilemanifesto.org*
[10] *https://www.amazon.jobs/en/principles*

Others emphasize that a Western-centric view of the world overlooks that China and other Asian countries are on the verge of taking over the leading technical role in the world. Books like "AI Superpowers: China, Silicon Valley, and the New World Order" by Kai-Fu Lee, mention Europe only at the margin.[11] That alone should be enough to make people stop and think.

 Example: Armenia

The example of Armenia shows how politics can exert influence. Some call it the "Silicon Valley of the former Soviet Union."[12] Others refer to the capital Yerevan as "Silicon Mountain," which is listed by the Enterprise Times as "the best non-American hub for an IT career after San Francisco, Austin, and New York."[13] Armenia was also named Country of the Year 2018 by the Economist.[14]

So how does a country previously perceived as a former Soviet republic sandwiched between two hostile states manage to emerge as a potential new AI supernation with the most significant venture capital outside the US?

There are three reasons for this:

- **Diaspora:** Numerous Armenians have emigrated worldwide due to the 1915 genocide, many to the United States. California companies run by diaspora Armenians are setting up branches in Armenia.

- **Education:** Armenia invests in its youth. The showcase model here is Tumo[15], a training center for teenagers. Eighteen-year-old serial entrepreneurs are not uncommon in Armenia.

- **Geography:** Without mineral resources and access to the sea, the country is mainly dependent on the service sector.

Armenia is not the only country to create a thriving start-up culture. With low taxation, easy and fast migration for qualified engineers (via Digital Nomad Programs), and other incentives, many countries make innovation hubs where new unicorn companies can be born. Furthermore, economists even claim that some countries sabotage themselves with restrictive migration policies for highly qualified engineers.

Policymakers can invest in training, reduce bureaucracy and, most importantly, create framework conditions that make it easier for people to start up.

Companies themselves often follow a pets or cattle strategy. The word "cattle" means replaceable animals. A farmer may lament the death of a cow as a loss of income, but he doesn't care about the cow itself. Pets, on the other hand, have value to the owner. So when Buddy, the family dog, dies, it can be a family tragedy, and family members will miss the old dog, even if they get at some point a new dog.

---

[11] Lee, K.-F.: AI Superpowers: China, Silicon Valley, and the New World Order. Houghton Mifflin Harcourt, 2018

[12] https://thenextweb.com/asia/2017/03/17/armenias-rising-tech-scene-new-silicon-valley-former-soviet-union/

[13] https://www.enterprisetimes.co.uk/2018/10/25/10-best-cities-for-tech-career-opportunities/

[14] https://www.economist.com/leaders/2018/12/22/the-economists-country-of-the-year-2018

[15] www.tumo.org

In a "corporate cattle strategy," employees mean turnover. The management keeps costs low and sees employees just as a resource to make a profit. In extreme cases, cattle-strategy companies deduct bathroom or cigarette breaks from employees' work hours. If an efficient employee quits, you lament the loss of revenue but not the person's departure.

In contrast, the pets culture means that employees are the focus. A company invests in them, treats them well, and makes sure they stay motivated. Of course, every profit-oriented company expects to make money with the employee. Still, the company understands that only a happy employee is the most profitable employee in the long run.

But some companies are still in the Stone Age when it comes to employee management. It is precisely these companies that wonder why they cannot fill any data scientist positions. What we can learn from Google and Co. is to promote high potentials by all means. Above all else, it's about recruiting people with the right mindset.

"People don't buy WHAT you do; they buy WHY you do it." – Simon Sinek

The "Work Hard, Play Hard" culture means that people are willing to do what it takes to achieve a shared vision because they are passionate about the purpose and culture of the company. It is about employees believing both in an idea and also in the "why."[16] In other words, the most passionate employees are the most profitable.

If you want to dig deeper into the topic of company culture, look at how Spotify, Google, and others have built their company culture and consider what actions could move your company forward.

 The Role of Europe

It is not always easy for European companies to jump over their shadows. Too many security experts impose regulations that, strictly speaking, overshoot the mark, even if data protection itself is welcome. Where there is light, there is shadow. Particularly in ambitious countries, corporate entities often ignore ethics. Europeans are a lot more concerned about civil rights than in other countries, which has certainly worked in our favor in other areas in the past (take the history of environmental protection as an example).

Another concern of many is a culture of "mediocracy" in some European countries. For example, many Europeans expect to work from 9 to 5 without any overtime and still be competitive, while in Asia, some ambitious employees work 80 hours and more.

What remains is that Europeans have to face the facts. AI is here, and Europe can stand on the sidelines as a spectator and leave the development to others because it is scared to death. But Europeans can also actively shape the future; they can face the pros and cons of digitization and data science and drive the development of data science and the data landscape. Here, it makes sense to think a few dimensions bigger in Europe as well.

■

---

[16] Sinek, S.: Start with Why. Portfolio, 2009

■ 17.3 Antipatterns

Antipatterns are behavioral patterns that lead to the opposite of the desired state; in other words, they are ways of thinking that can cause data projects to fail. However, they all have one thing in common: leaders can change them by establishing an alternative corporate culture.

17.3.1 Devaluation of Domain Expertise

Some companies consider Data Science to be exclusively a technical topic. The management expects that if you put data and algorithms in, you can just harvest results.

Let us assume a company plans to become data-driven, having learned from strategy consultants that this is the only way they could survive in the long run. The strategy consultants also envision a bright future for the company as a data-driven enterprise. Management, therefore, hires highly paid data scientists and expects miracles from them. Management calls them the company's future; they get top-notch equipment, a workplace in a new building block, and access to all the data they need.

Imagine that among the company employees is the archetypical long-term employee: a subject matter expert (SME), who is sometimes described by colleagues as assertive and maybe even annoying, but who has been working for the company for decades and knows all processes in and out. During the assessment by the strategy consultants, this employee had pointed out various details that contradict the vision of a bright future and fat bonuses, which the strategy consultant had promised the management board. It's no coincidence, then, that this employee's workplace is in the old building, far away from the newly formed all-star data scientist team. Management considers the employee's skepticism a danger and believes their pessimistic attitude could unsettle the remaining project members. After all, the point is to create something new.

> "It was imperative to me to keep all the naysayers away from the project team. We finally want to do something new without all those people telling us it will never work, just because they do not believe in it." – Department head of a financial company that later struggled with its digital transformation.

The all-star data science team presents the first use cases they want to incorporate into the company's DNA. The slide deck is perfect, and the board loves it. The team also receives much support from the strategy consultants who envisioned the transition to a data-driven enterprise in the first place. Management calls the plan a fantastic approach that exceeds their initial expectations. They even accept that they need to invest a bit more than initially planned to create the company's new future.

Months later, everyone is devastated. The data scientists' ideas do not prove to be practicable. Finally, in retrospective sessions, the domain expert can present their views; they can explain, even without mathematics, why the plans of the all-star team have no practical value. It becomes apparent that, had they had the SME's input all along, they might have explored more profitable options. It is a weak consolidation that the consultants' newly proposed strategy now contains some of the SME's ideas, rebranded in their terminology.

Every company should always involve SMEs. Excluding those who know the details of the operative business is like flying blind over unknown terrain. The danger of crashing is great because even the most stable aircraft will not stand up to an unmapped rock.

17.3.2 IT Will Take Care of It

This book already mentioned that business departments should own data science initiatives and integrate IT as enablers. It is helpful to detail why the IT department should not take care of data science.

IT must ensure that employees can perform their tasks to the best of their ability using electronic processing. System uptime is an essential part of IT performance reports. If too many users experience troubles using their day-to-day business applications, an IT department may receive a negative rating. The best way for IT departments to avoid problems is to limit access and available functionality. If the dumbest assumable users (DAU) have fewer options to make mistakes, IT will have to fix fewer issues. The safest method is not just to restrict access to applications but also their visibility. In the end, according to the Dunning-Kruger effect, DAUs might be quite self-confident and ask for permission to use available applications if they see them in a software catalog.

Proof of Concepts (PoCs) as part of a data science project can cause conflicts. Data Scientists need access to as much data as possible for their research. However, the strategy of IT departments is to limit access to systems and data as much as possible to avoid potential problems. In the worst case, the data science team may not even realize that the data they need exists within the company.

One way around this conflict is the so-called 'bi-modal IT.' In this system, there is one IT team whose task is to maintain operations, and there is another IT team that gives users as much freedom as possible in a corporate lab. In addition, one way of providing legal protection is to use NDAs (Non-Disclosure Agreements), in which employees who work with sensitive data agree to maintain confidentiality. In the banking environment, for example, this has been the standard for a long time.

17.3.3 Resistance to Change

Not all employees always benefit from changes. Employees often see managers as people who "only" manage resources and are interested in profits. So if they sell the idea to move a company into a new era, employees fear that working in that new era might not include them. Older employees, in particular, fear being put on the losing side by transformations.

Moreover, if business leaders communicate possible innovations poorly, then employees' interest groups may run up a storm against the innovations. In some extreme cases, employees might even secretly sabotage changes in a company. There are many examples in history where corporate transitions failed because the employees did not trust their bosses.

In the end, everything depends on the leadership skills of those who introduce change. It is about creating the awareness that a company is not viable in the long run without change.

Change is part of business, and fear of change is deadly. There are many books on what makes leaders great, and we cannot cover every value. However, one value that most people agree with is that authenticity is essential for every leader as we tend to trust people who honestly address any topic.

If a leader presents a new corporate strategy before their employees and doubts its success, how should they persuade the skeptics, who are afraid of losing their jobs? Many have seen this scenario before: A consultant presents a brand new strategy to the company. The consultant is fully confident, saying that everything needs to change and the future will be great. However, when a business leader tries to present that vision to an audience, they suddenly feel less confident once they realize they are also accountable for its success. It is always easy to promise great things unless you risk losing your job in the event of failure.

In most organizations, change also does not happen overnight. So instead of trying to enforce change, leaders should provide a strategy for a gradual transition that matches the corporate DNA.

17.3.4 Know-it-all Mentality

In many companies, there is the stereotype of the "all-knowing expert." They have already seen everything; you don't need to tell them anything. Everything that springs from their thoughts must be reasonable and will surely solve all problems. Other ideas are considered nonsense to this 'expert'; they do not allow different opinions.

"Know-it-alls" can completely ruin data projects. The data world is complex, and technologies change quickly. No one can understand everything. The real gold for a company is young, high-potentials who are learning new technologies. If guided by the right leaders, these people will spread their wings; if managed by a know-it-all, they might be afraid to speak up, as know-it-alls often cultivate a "fear culture."

There are many situations in which money is wasted by designing platforms that originate from a know-it-all. Worse, companies often throw money down the drain to keep a faulty architecture from such an employee alive. Often it is too hard to admit that everyone trusted a self-righteous person who had convinced them they were right. Unfortunately, history is full of horrible examples of charismatic but flawed leaders who did not doubt for a second that they were right and who took everything with them in their eventual downfall. In the end, we tend to believe those who seem to be convinced. Unfortunately, according to those who study the Dunning-Kruger effect, it is not always the intelligent people who have the most substantial confidence.[17]

> *"It doesn't make sense to hire smart people and then tell them what to do; we hire smart people, so they can tell us what to do."* – Steve Jobs

You can establish a values-driven culture to look after talented, introverted employees if you run a company. Once you empower the right people, your company will succeed.

17.3.5 Doom and Gloom

This antipattern overlaps with what we presented under "Resistance to change." However, there, we focussed more on internal resistance. In this antipattern, we talk about those external consultants that make money by making you afraid.

Many consultants make a living out of making systems secure. And those who make a living from it do well to be able to point out dangers.

People who see doom everywhere are as dangerous as over-enthusiasts who ignore every risk. Big Data is a naysayer's paradise. There are countless risks that a pessimist can bring up, such as

- "Chinese hackers will steal your data."
- "Employees will sabotage every change."
- "Customers do not want any change at all."
- "It's expensive and costs will explode."

The tricky thing is that it is always easier to follow the recommendations of doomsayers than optimists. If you do what alarmists say, it seems you cannot fail. If you ignore warnings and a proposal for change fails, you might have to explain your past decisions. There is less immediate risk involved in most cases if one listens to those who warn of dangers.

Although we should not become reckless, we should always be aware that the most significant risk is stagnation. And stagnation is, in the end, what the naysayers propose.

17.3.6 Penny-pinching

Many IT managers want the most modern data platform. Because it's open-source, of course, it has to be the latest version to stay ahead. The teams are even encouraged to install beta versions to remain at the forefront of innovation.

At the same time, however, cost-awareness is practiced like a religion. No money is spent on external consultants because it seems cheaper if the company's employees familiarize themselves with the new system. HR disregards highly qualified applicants who do not want to sell themselves short. The few underpaid company's employees can watch training videos if they run out of work, but there is no budget to send them to a conference where they could meet other skilled professionals. There is also no investment in hardware, even though the developers complain that the existing servers have too little RAM and the processes break down.

> "*We don't need anything new as long as the old works somehow.*" – The famous adage of a post-war generation.

Unfortunately, the truth is that trying to cut corners can be expensive. A backend developer with essential database experience doesn't become a distributed computing expert juggling petabytes of data overnight. Without incentives, many employees will work from 9 to 5, but not go the extra mile. In the end, a culture of mediocrity is the death of innovation.

17.3.7 Fear Culture

We often get to know a culture of fear already in school. For example, teachers try to find mistakes instead of empowering students to try out new things. In a culture where students learn to go the safe path in order to avoid getting bad grades, we create an environment where people believe it is always better to play safe. When they start to work as employees, they are intimidated as their superiors could behave like teachers and grade them by their number of mistakes. Therefore, they remain passive and just follow instructions instead of making decisions on their own.

This mentality is poison for any creative environment. Companies that live in this culture will not recruit the necessary talent to shift to a Data-Driven Enterprise. So-called high potentials can usually pick and choose their employers, and correspondingly, few stray into a "stone age" work culture. Companies with a culture of fear also harm themselves, as good employees leave again. It is only a matter of time before these "fear companies" run into serious problems.

17.3.8 Control over Resources

In a blog post in BigData Insider, someone asked whether digitization would fail due to a lack of human resources.[18] Companies seem to struggle to acquire the necessary professionals to carry out their projects. Universities have reacted and are offering data science courses, but these can only alleviate the scarcities; they cannot eliminate them.

For example, company X has made the strategic decision to digitize, and it is looking for employees to support them in implementing the digitization strategy. However, the headquarters of company X is in an area where hardly any professionals are available, so they are also open to looking for people outside of their region.

Many of us remember the famous 5/4/3 mode (five days of work, four days on-site, and three nights sleeping away) and know that it doesn't solve the problem (although this is beginning to change with Covid-19). An initial on-site presence is helpful to build relationships from both a professional and social point of view. However, once you are committed to each other, the rest of the collaboration is a leadership issue. Well-managed, ambitious people also take their job seriously remotely and will not abuse the trust placed in them. The fascinating thing about this is that remote work allows you to involve experts distributed around the world who would otherwise not be available. In addition, experts from some countries are also more cost-effective.

There are many examples where a flexible working model leads to success. However, it has always been leadership and the team spirit, which has developed over time, that has spurred people on to high performance: it was never managerial control.

---

[18] *www.bigdata-insider.de/scheitert-die-digitalisierung-am-big-data-fachkraeftemangel-a-540015/*

17.3.9 Blind Faith in Resources

Many professionals dream of becoming Data Scientists or AI engineers. They see the potential to receive huge salaries, change the world, learn about secrets, and have a job with a high reputation.

Even those who do not have the education or skills to work as data scientists got excited. In blogs, consultants explain the fast track to becoming a Data Scientist. First, an aspirant has to learn to use the correct expressions, have the right contacts on LinkedIn, and then stick to the principle of "fake it until you make it" in the first job.

 Practical Example: The New Data Science Rock Star

Your HR has finally recruited the new Data Scientist to bring the company into the 21st century. Perhaps this new employee fits the perfect image of a nerd; they know all the science fiction series, wear thick glasses, have a somewhat daring hairstyle, and, of course, wear a T-shirt with geek slogans every day (the extreme stereotype says this T-shirt might not even change as often as hygienically recommended!). When talking to you, the new employee raves about Machine Learning, AI and proclaims what they have already done...
You may not always understand it, but it seems like they know their stuff. Even if the HR manager finds fault with the new recruit's people skills, you quickly agree that nobody recruited them for their charm.

Fast-forward to a few weeks later. Your super data scientist, unfortunately, does not meet the expectations placed upon them. Although they explain to other employees all the things that need to be changed, the HR manager realizes that the recruited "rock star" is unfortunately not a "completer."

One of your programmers has reported significant deficiencies in the Data Scientist's Python knowledge, and an inability to solve even simple problems with SSH. Unfortunately, your new mastermind also seems to lack basic statistical knowledge.

You start doing a little research. Then, after getting feedback from former employers, you pray for the sake of peace in the team that the new recruit didn't brag about their high salary to colleagues, as this would most definitely completely disrupt the group.

We advise all hiring managers to prepare job interviews carefully. Ask questions that go into depth. Don't blindly trust that your candidates know everything, even if they appear confident. Explaining what products are on the market is easy; describing what they do in detail is another matter.

17.3.10 The Swiss Army Knife

We all know that excellent resources are scarce. For some companies, it takes multiple months to fill various technical roles. Above, we described the "Know it all" as a self-righteous person who believes they can solve all problems. The "Swiss Army Knife" is different; they are a multi-talented individual who can solve many things.

A typical Swiss Army Knife does not want to spend too much time in meetings. But, as a solution-oriented person, she gets things done. She fits into various roles, and whatever task you give her, she will solve it. She is also naturally curious to explore things she has never done before.

Swiss Army Knives often have no problem overworking. Some of them define themselves through work, and they work 60 to 80 hours a week voluntarily. Moreover, many leaders have hit the jackpot with a swiss army knife that is not aware of their value. Rumors say there are even swiss army knives that earn clearly below the average salary.

Even if the swiss army knife might seem obsessed with creating a perfect solution and if she seems to be perfectly loyal, like every employee, there is always a risk of losing her. For example, imagine you have to build a data platform. This swiss army knife is a data architect, security engineer, data manager, and systems architect in one person. Now imagine losing her.

Be also aware that those engineers around the swiss army knife might have slowed down as there was always someone who, in the end, solved all problems.

17.3.11 Over-Engineering

Sometimes a local relational database is enough to explore a company's data. But, unfortunately, many companies get carried away and invest in technologies that take them way over the top. If you buy a Big Data solution such as Hadoop for large, unstructured data sets and then try to shovel, say, manageable data sets into it, you're acting counterproductively. It is more important to know the exact requirements, understand what you need and want, and invest in the appropriate solution.

 It's always good to learn from others. Talk to experts who have already worked on digital data science projects and understand what went well and what went badly.

■ 17.4 In a Nutshell

Everything is changing.

Digitalization and data science are reshuffling the cards in companies. AI is changing the way we work. Refusing to embrace this trend would have the same consequences as if a company had denied the Internet in the 1990s. For a successful data strategy, the mindset of the company must be right. Without a vision and the courage to change, initiatives fail even with the best tools and the most brilliant data scientists.

Corporate culture is essential.

Without a suitable corporate culture, every company will fail to introduce data science. Good leadership is necessary to prepare the company for a digital transformation.

18 Trustworthy AI

Rania Wazir

> *All algorithms should be seen as untrustworthy until proven otherwise.*
> *Cathy O'Neil*

Questions Answered in this Chapter:

- What is the current hard-law and soft-law framework for trustworthy AI, especially in the EU?
- Who are the possible AI stakeholders?
- What is fairness in AI, and how is bias defined?
- What are different metrics for measuring the fairness impacts of algorithms?
- What are possible techniques for mitigating unwanted bias?
- How can data and models be documented to improve transparency, usability, and trust?
- What are current methods for explaining model decisions?

The broad class of technologies that fall under the umbrella of AI – from expert systems to machine learning driven solutions and data science applications – are revolutionizing industry, pervading most sectors of the economy and beyond, and have the potential to benefit the economy, society, and the environment. However, as has come to light in recent years, these technologies also come with risks[1,2,3]. Public skepticism has been rising, as examples of stereotyping and discrimination, concerns over worker's rights, and detrimental impact on democratic principles and the environment have been exposed. In order for AI technologies to continue enjoying rapidly growing adoption and realize their beneficial potential, there will be increasing demand for AI-based systems that can be trusted. For AI system providers, this trust translates into increased uptake of products where it is present, and to legal and reputational harms where this trust is breached. In the chapter that follows, we will explore in practice what trust in AI systems means, in particular in the context of machine learning and data science solutions; who are the stakeholders that need to be considered; and some practical implementation steps that can guide the development process.

---

[1] O'Neil, C., Weapons of Math Destruction: How Big Data Increases Inequality and Threatens Democracy, Broadway Books, 2017.
[2] Kate Crawford, AI Now Report 2019
[3] Fundamental Rights Agency of the EU (FRA), Getting the Future Right

Our task will be to try to weave the many disparate requirements together, to create a coherent picture that can accompany the AI system development process from start to finish. We start with the legal and soft-law framework, looking at prominent ethics guidelines, and existing and upcoming regulations and standards. Trust will mean different things to different AI stakeholders – and it is important to identify the various stakeholders involved with an AI system in order to ensure its trustworthiness; we therefore take a brief detour into AI stakeholder identification, before focussing on the issues of fairness in AI, and explainability. This chapter can make no claim to completeness, but aims rather to deliver some guidance to AI system providers and/or users who wish to create/deploy products that can be trusted.

■ 18.1 Legal and Soft-Law Framework

Since 2016, there has been an explosion of so-called "ethics guidelines" for AI. In fact, by 2019 there were already over 80 published guidelines.[4] From academic research institutes to the big tech companies, from international NGOs to state governments, everyone had their input on what constituted "ethical" AI. Unfortunately,most guidelines are rather high level, and diverge on the principles they consider necessary for an AI to be "ethical". According to the research by Jobin et al.[5], there are five general principles referenced by at least half of the guidelines: transparency, justice and fairness, non-maleficence, responsibility, and privacy; however, their precise meaning and corresponding implementation strategies again diverge.

Some of the main international ethics guidelines on AI include:

- OECD Principles on AI[6]
- UNESCO Recommendation on the Ethics of AI[7]
- UNICEF Policy Guidance on AI for Children[8]
- EU HLEG Guidelines for Trustworthy AI[9]
- EU White Paper on AI[10]

A Trustworthy AI, however, goes beyond ethics. An obvious additional requirement is a quality imperative: the system should be robust, reliable, and safe. The OECD Principles, for example, are addressed to governements and other state actors, intending to serve as guid-

---

[4] Jobin, Anna, Marcello Ienca, and Effy Vayena. "The global landscape of AI ethics guidelines." Nature Machine Intelligence 1.9 (2019): 389–399.
[5] Jobin, Anna, Marcello Ienca, and Effy Vayena. "The global landscape of AI ethics guidelines." Nature Machine Intelligence 1.9 (2019): 389–399.
[6] *https://www.oecd.ai/ai-principles*
[7] *https://unesdoc.unesco.org/ark:/48223/pf0000373434*
[8] *https://www.unicef.org/globalinsight/reports/policy-guidance-ai-children*
[9] *https://digital-strategy.ec.europa.eu/en/library/ethics-guidelines-trustworthy-ai*
[10] *https://ec.europa.eu/info/publications/white-paper-artificial-intelligence-european-approach-excellence-and-trust_en*

ance for fostering the development of Trustworthy AI. They propose the following 5 main principles[11]:

1. **Inclusive growth, sustainable development and well-being.** Poses a general requirement for Trustworthy AI to be beneficial: enhancing human capabilities, reducing inequalities, and protecting the environment.

2. **Human-centred values and fairness.** A Trustworthy AI needs to respect rule of law and human rights, including the right to freedom, the right to dignity and autonomy, the right to privacy and data protection, and the right to non-discrimination.

3. **Transparency and explainability.** Requires responsible disclosure of information about the AI system, in order to foster general understanding of such systems; make stakeholders aware of their interactions with an AI system; and allow those affected by an AI system to understand and contest its outputs.

4. **Robustness, security and safety.** Entails traceability for datasets, processes and decisions; as well as appropriate risk managment measures to address risks such as safety, IT security, privacy, and bias, during each phase of the AI system lifecycle.

5. **Accountability.** All actors involved in developing, deploying or operating AI systems, in accordance with their role, should be held accountable for the proper functioning of the AI systems, including ensuring that the above requirements are met.

The EU High Level Expert Group on AI has an even more extensive list of requirements for a Trustworthy AI, this one addressed to AI system developers, providers, and users.[12] A Trustworthy AI needs to be legal, ethical, and robust, and should satisfy the following requirements:

1. **Human agency and oversight.** Including fundamental rights, human agency and human oversight.

2. **Technical robustness and safety.** Including resilience to attack and security, fall back plan and general safety, accuracy, reliability and reproducibility.

3. **Privacy and data governance.** Including respect for privacy, quality and integrity of data, and access to data.

4. **Transparency.** Including traceability, explainability and communication.

5. **Diversity, non-discrimination and fairness.** Including the avoidance of unfair bias, accessibility and universal design, and stakeholder participation.

6. **Societal and environmental wellbeing.** Including sustainability and environmental friendliness, social impact, society and democracy.

7. **Accountability.** Including auditability, minimisation and reporting of negative impact, trade-offs and redress.

The HLEG Guidance is perhaps one of the most practical set of guidelines available so far. It provides a clear understanding of the reasoning behind the requirements, and information on how to implement them in practice. Based on the guidelines, the group also developed

---

[11] *https://www.oecd.ai/ai-principles*

[12] High Level Expert Group on Artificial Intelligence set up by the European Commission, "Ethics Guidelines for Trustworthy AI", April 2019, p.14. Accessed from *https://digital-strategy.ec.europa.eu/en/library/ethics-guidelines-trustworthy-ai*

the Assessment List for Trustworthy AI (ALTAI)[13], a tool to help AI system providers, developers, and users assess the extent to which their AI system satisfies the seven requirements for a trustworthy AI.

18.1.1 Standards

The path from guidelines to practical implementation is long, and regulation and international standards are necessary stepping stones. Several international standards organizations are actively involved in creating the necessary standards for ensuring Trustworthy AI:

- **IEEE Ethically Aligned Design:** *https://ethicsinaction.ieee.org/#series*. The IEEE has its own set of ethical guidelines, covering almost 300 pages[14]. This is supplemented by the 7000 Series of Standards, specifying specific aspects of ethical AI. The first two to be published cover general principles of ethical design, and specifications for measuring the human well-being impacts of autonomous and intelligent systems.

- **ISO/IEC Standards on AI and Trustworthy AI:** *https://www.iso.org/committee/6794475.html*. ISO and IEC have established a joint committee to address artificial intelligence. Several standards and technical reports have already been published, and many more are in the pipeline. In particular, the recently published ISO/IEC TR 24028: Overview of trustworthiness in artificial intelligence[15] provides an overview of reqirements and pitfalls in developing and deploying a trustworthy AI system, and can be seen as a roadmap for upcoming standards specifications.

- **NIST Standards for Trustworthy and Responsible AI:** *https://www.nist.gov/programs-projects/trustworthy-and-responsible-ai*. NIST's project includes standards for several key aspects of Trustworthy AI, including most recently a draft publication on mitigating harmful bias[16], as well as previously published standards on explainability and security.

- **CEN-CENELEC Committee on Artificial Intelligence:** *https://www.cencenelec.eu/areas-of-work/cen-cenelec-topics/artificial-intelligence/*. CEN and CENELEC have established the new joint committee in response to the EC White Paper on AI and the German Standardization Roadmap for Artificial Intelligence[17].

18.1.2 Regulations

In particular in the EU, there has been a push to develop a digital strategy that goes beyond guidelines, and imposes some regulation on the AI industry. The first piece of legislation in this direction came with the General Data Protection Regulation (GDPR), which came into force in 2018. Other regulations are in the pipeline – for example, the Digital Services Act (DSA) and the Digital Markets Act (DMA), whose goal is to reduce the "Gatekeeper" effect of

---

[13] *https://altai.insight-centre.org/*
[14] *https://ethicsinaction.ieee.org/#ead1e*
[15] *https://www.iso.org/standard/77608.html*
[16] *https://doi.org/10.6028/NIST.SP.1270-draft*
[17] *https://www.din.de/en/innovation-and-research/artificial-intelligence*

very large online platforms, and give users and consumers more transparency and choice vis a vis these platforms (DSA), and enable smaller players to enter and compete within the platform economy (DMA). However, while these regulations have elements with direct implications for data collection and AI system transparency, the core regulation addressed to AI is the EU AI Act, which came out in draft form in April 2021.

- **EU Digital Strategy:** *https://ec.europa.eu/info/strategy/priorities-2019-2024/europe-fit-digital-age_en*

- **GDPR:** *https://ec.europa.eu/info/law/law-topic/data-protection/data-protection-eu_en*

- **DSA:** *https://ec.europa.eu/info/strategy/priorities-2019-2024/europe-fit-digital-age/digital-services-act-ensuring-safe-and-accountable-online-environment_en*

- **DMA:** *https://ec.europa.eu/info/strategy/priorities-2019-2024/europe-fit-digital-age/digital-markets-act-ensuring-fair-and-open-digital-markets_en*

- **EU Draft AI Act:** *https://digital-strategy.ec.europa.eu/en/policies/european-approach-artificial-intelligence*

The draft AI Act addresses any AI systems being placed on the market, or put into use, within the EU. It takes a risk-based approach to regulating AI, where risk does not just entail physical or psychological harms, but also risks to fundamental rights. For the scope of the regulation, the draft AI Act makes an intentionally broad definition of AI, and includes many algorithms whose inclusion as "AI" has triggered hot debate: not just machine learning algorithms, but also logic-based methods and expert systems, statistical and Bayesian techniques, optimization and search. The full listing is available in Annex I of the draft AI Act.

The AI Act identifies four types of application which are prohibited, involving subliminal manipulation, social scoring, and facial recognition:

- AI systems that manipulate people and can lead them to behave in ways that are physically or psychologically damaging to themselves or to others.

- AI systems that take advantage of vulnerabilities of particular groups, due to their age or a mental or physical handicap, and can lead to behaviour that is physically or psychologically harmful to themselves or to others.

- Social scoring by public authorities

- The use of real-time remote biometric identification systems in publicly accessible spaces for law enforcement purposes (however, this prohibition comes with several exceptions).

The main substance of the proposed regulation is, however, intended for high-risk applications. These are identified in Annex II – which includes a list of applications already subject to sectoral regulation, and where the act imposes additional obligations – and Annex III, which indicates eight new areas of application, with specific use cases within each area identified as being high risk. Annex II includes, among others, AI systems used in toys, machinery, medical devices, aviation, motor vehicles, and other forms of transport. The areas of application listed in Annex III are:

1. Biometric identification and categorisation of natural persons

2. Management and operation of critical infrastructure

3. Education and vocational training

4. Employment, workers management and access to self-employment

5. Access to and enjoyment of essential private services and public services and benefits

6. Law enforcement

7. Migration, asylum and border control management

8. Administration of justice and democratic processes

The novelty in Annex III is that the draft AI Act reserves to the Commission the right to add use cases to the Annex if the use cases belong to one of the eight areas of application, and are found to pose a high risk to safety, health, or fundamental rights. This enables the Commission to side-step renewed parliamentary negotiations on eventual amendments, and embeds a certain degree of flexibility with which to repsond to new evidence of harm.

The proposed regulation imposes some requirements on providers of high risk AI systems, albeit in most cases, no outside auditing is required, and a self-assessment suffices. The main requirements pertain to data quality and governance (Article 10), risk assessment and risk management systems (Article 9), model performance testing (Article 15), and model documentation (Article 11, Annex IV).

■ 18.2 AI Stakeholders

AI Systems are embedded in complex ecosystems involving a broad range of actors. Understanding risks of bias, and how to mitigate them, involves getting a grasp on the various stakeholders, their roles, and their needs. The following list can serve as a guide, but is by no means exhaustive.

- **Data provider:** organization/person that collects, processes, and delivers the data used by the AI provider.

- **AI provider:** organization/person that develops AI systems. Within the organization, specific additional roles can be identified.

  Management and Board

  Legal department/Corporate responsibility department

  Data Protection Officer

  System Architects, Data Engineers

  Developers, Machine Learning Engineers, Data Scientists

  Quality Assurance

- **AI user:** organization/person that deploys an AI system. Within the organization, specific additional roles can be identified.

  Management and Board

  Legal department/Corporate responsibility department

  Quality Assurance

  Data Protection Officer

System Architects, Data Engineers

Human Resources

Procurement

People who have to work directly with the new AI system, or whose jobs are replaced by the new AI system

- **AI subject:** organization/person that AI system outputs/predictions are about.
- **Certification body:** organization that certifies compliance with established standards.
- **Regulator:** authority stipulating performance criteria for AI deployed within their jurisdictions.
- **Broader society, including for example human rights organizations, consumer protection organizations, envirnomental protection organizations, and media:** they may need to be kept informed about requirements for Trustworthy AI, and should be able to request that they are upheld.

■ 18.3 Fairness in AI

What is a fair algorithm? According to the Oxford English Dictionary:

Fairness: *Impartial and just treatment or behaviour without favouritism or discrimination.*

This definition is not yet actionable – in order to determine if an AI system is fair, the concept needs to somehow be quantified. However, fairness is a social construct, and is dependent on context and cultural/societal norms. This has led to the creation of many different definitions of fairness (21 and counting[18]), each with its own mathematical formulation (fairness metric) – as will be described below. To add to the confusion, the terms unfair algorithm and biased algorithm are often used interchangeably.

Bias (Oxford English Dictionary): *Inclination or prejudice for or against one person or group, especially in a way considered to be unfair.*

1.1 A concentration on or interest in one particular area or subject.

1.2 A systematic distortion of a statistical result due to a factor not allowed for in its derivation.

This conflation between unfair and biased may seem natural when considering the main definition of bias. Nonetheless, it is important to consider that any classification model must have bias in order to work. Take, for example, a classifier that has to differentiate between pictures of mammals and of birds. It needs to have a bias towards labelling pictures of animals with wings as birds. Instead, if it were completely free of bias, it would not be able to make any distinction at all, and would place all objects in the same category. So the first clarification is necessary: algorithms need to avoid *unwanted* bias - bias which is based on

---

[18] Verma, S. and Rubin, J., (2018), "Fairness Definitions Explained", Proceedings of the International Workshop on Software Fairness (FairWare), pp. 1–7.

some protected characteristic or some spurious correlation, and which is not relevant to the task at hand.

Furthermore, within the engineering and statistics communities, a certain kind of un- wanted bias already exists: bias according to Definition 1.2 (statistical bias). This often leads to confusion and misunderstanding when discussing bias in machine learning: simply put, an algorithm that is "fair" might still have statistical bias, while at the same time, a system that is free of statistical bias might still be unfair.

The crux of the issue lies within the definition: "a systematic distortion of a statistical re- sult" implies that a "ground truth" (or "true value") is known so that a systematic distortion can be detected by comparison. But what is this "ground truth"? If, as has traditionally been the case, this is the current population parameter value, then it should come as no surprise that, for example, a hiring algorithm for an engineering position trained on historical em- ployment data, would disfavor women precisely because it accurately reflected the status quo (and hence, had no statistical bias). This is not just a mere hypothesis – consider the case of Amazon's ditched machine learning driven recruiting tool[19]. Conversely, in trying to achieve greater gender equity and be "fair", it could be deemed necessary to introduce statistical bias into the algorithm. Of course, this contradiction between statistical bias and fairness might not arise if "ground truth" were taken to be some idealized goal (i.e. the ideal gender distribution of engineering employees). However, this is a controversial issue; and changing the terminology would still leave unresolved the fundamental problem of what the ideal distribution should be. For this reason, many current fairness metrics avoid the use of a "ground truth" as a reference parameter.

In order to avoid confusion, in this chapter, we will use bias to describe inputs to, or proper- ties of, a machine learning model (or more generally, an AI system). Fairness, on the other hand, will be used to describe the impact of model-based outputs or predictions on various protected demographics. This is also consistent with a growing body of literature, which tries to identify and mitigate sources of bias in AI systems, and uses fairness metrics to evaluate model effects.

18.3.1 Bias

Bias can come in many forms, and can enter the machine learning and data science life cycles at various stages. To identify the four main stages:

1. The bias may be in the training or test data. Having large amounts of data does not auto- matically absolve data collectors from the traditional statistical data errors. Sampling bias, selection bias, and non-response bias are just some of the main traps that data holds for the unaware. However, as the above example of training a hiring algorithm by using historical data shows - even if the procedure for procuring the data was correct statisti- cally, the data could still be biased because of embedded human biases. The hiring data used to train the algorithm might accurately reflect the status quo - and thus encode and perpetuate the current societal bias against women in engineering. Word embeddings

---

[19] J. Dastin, (2018), 'Amazon scraps secret AI recruiting tool that showed bias against women', Reuters, 11 October 2018.

and language models are another example of such kinds of bias – the text used to train these models is full of societal biases, so that the word embeddings reflect not just general semantic patterns, but also gender[20] and ethnic[21] stereotypes and prejudices.

2. Bias can also enter the system when designing the algorithm – for example, a classification system could be biased because of the categories it is designed to select (black/white, male/female[22]); biases could arise in feature engineering (some features might be more predictive for some groups than for others, and selecting features based on overall accuracy could cause the model to perform worse for some groups), or in the choice of algorithm to use (for example, algorithms that are too simple can underfit the data, and lead to bias in the models). A particularly insidious form of bias can enter the algorithm design when attempting to model a concept that is not fully quantifiable – for example, in a university admissions setting, using records of previously admitted students to train a model for detecting successful candidates to a Ph.D. program[23] (in fact, this simply models previous admissions committees preferences and biases); or in a hospital care management setting, using health care costs as a proxy for severity of the illness to be treated[24].

3. Biases can also enter the system post-hoc, for example, in the interpretation of the model results. Alternatively, decisions based on model predictions could affect data that is then fed back into an online learning algorithm, causing the formation of runaway feedback loops[25], and amplifying existing biases in the data or the model.

4. Finally, deployment is also prone to bias: from temporal drift, to inappropriate use (in a context different from the intended one), and from adversarial attacks (consider, for example, Microsft's infamous Chatbot Tay[26]), to selective deployment (for example, using predictive models to determine grades for children in larger classes, but using human evaluation to determine grades for children in smaller classes[27]).

While it is not possible to list all possible kinds of bias that can become implicated in a machine learning model, we briefly describe below some of the more common forms of bias[28].

---

[20] Bolukbasi, T., Chang, K.-W., Zou, J., Saligramma, V., Kalai, A., (2016), 'Man is to computer programmer as woman is to homemaker? debiasing word embeddings', Proceedings of the 30th International Conference on Neural Information Processing Systems, NIPS 2016, pp. 4356-4364.

[21] Manzini, T., Yao Chong, L., Black, A. W., Tsvetkov, Y., (2019), 'Black is to Criminal as Caucasian is to Police: Detecting and Removing Multiclass Bias in Word Embeddings', Proceedings of the 2019 Conference of the North American Chapter of the Association for Computational Linguistics: Human Language Technologies, Vol. 1, pp. 615-621.

[22] Leufer, D., (2021), 'Computers are binary, people are not: how AI systems undermine LGBTQ identity', Access Now, April 2021.

[23] Burke, L., (2020), U of Texas will stop using controversial algorithm to evaluate Ph.D. applicants, Inside Higher Ed, 14 December 2020.

[24] Obermeyer, Z., Powers, B., Vogeli, C., Mullainathan, S., (2019), 'Dissecting racial bias in an algorithm used to manage the health of populations', Science, Vol. 366, pp. 447-453.

[25] Ensign, D., Friedler, S. A., Neville, S., Scheidegger, C., and Venkatasubramanian, S. (2018), 'Runaway feedback loops in predictive policing', Proceedings of the 1st Conference on Fairness, Accountability and Transparency, PMLR, Vol. 81, pp. 160-171.

[26] The Guardian (2016), 'Microsoft 'deeply sorry' for racist and sexist tweets by AI chatbot', 26 March 2016.

[27] Elbanna, A., Engesmo, J., (2020), 'A-level results: why algorithms get things so wrong – and what we can do to fix them', The Conversation, August 19, 2020.

[28] Suresh, H., and Guttag, J., (2021), 'A Framework for Understanding Sources of Harm throughout the Machine Learning Life Cycle', arXiv preprint, https://arxiv.org/pdf/1901.10002.pdf

- **Human Cognitive Bias:** Any kind of bias that can occur when humans are processing and interpreting information
- **Societal Bias:** Biases and prejudices that arise from a social, cultural, or historical context
- **Confirmation Bias:** A tendency to accept model predictions that are consonant with ones pre-existing beliefs
- **Group Attribution Bias:** Occurs when it is assumed that what is true for an individual in a group is also true for everyone in that group.
- **Automation Bias:** A tendency to over-rely on outputs from a predictive model
- **Temporal Bias:** Bias that arises from not taking into account differences in the observed/measured quantities over time
- **Sampling Bias:** Occurs when data is not sampled randomly from the intended population, so that some individuals are more likely to be included in the sample than others.
- **Representation Bias:** Arises when individuals or groups in a study differ systematically from the population of interest. While this can include the case of sampling bias, it is a broader concept. For example, even if data is sampled randomly from the overall population, the sample sizes, or data quality, for certain subgroups can be low, leading to results that do not generalize well to those subgroups.
- **Measurement Bias:** This type of bias can occur when features and/or labels used in the model are proxies for the actual quantity of interest, possibly introducing systematic errors between what is intended, and what is actually measured (as in the example of using health care costs to measure severity of an illness cited above[29]).
- **Evaluation Bias:** Occurs when testing benchmarks are not properly calibrated, or when performance metrics are not appropriate to the model's deployment context. An often-cited example of this would be the poor performance of facial recognition software on women of color, because they were under-represented in the benchmark data sets used for testing such software[30].
- **Statistical Bias:** The systematic difference between a statistical estimate and the true underlying value ("ground truth")

Given the multiple manifestations of bias, and the several stages at which they can enter the machine learning life cycle, how can bias be detected? Bias in the training/validation/testing data can often be detected through good data documentation practices (see Section 18.4.1), and through the traditional exploratory data analysis (EDA). However, sometimes the bias in the data is too subtle; or else the bias arises at a later stage in the machine learning life cycle. In such cases, bias can only be detected through its effect on the model predictions, by applying some *fairness metrics.*

---

[29] Obermeyer, Z., Powers, B., Vogeli, C., Mullainathan, S., (2019), 'Dissecting racial bias in an algorithm used to manage the health of populations', Science, Vol. 366, pp. 447–453.

[30] Buolamwini, J., and Gebru, T., (2018), 'Gender Shades: Intersectional Accuracy Disparities in Commercial Gender Classification', Proceedings of Machine Learning Research, Vol. 81, pp. 1–15. *http://proceedings.mlr.press/v81/buolamwini18a/buolamwini18a.pdf*

18.3.2 Fairness Metrics

In order to discuss the fairness metrics, it is convenient to recall the Confusion Matrix for a binary classifier, and some associated values:

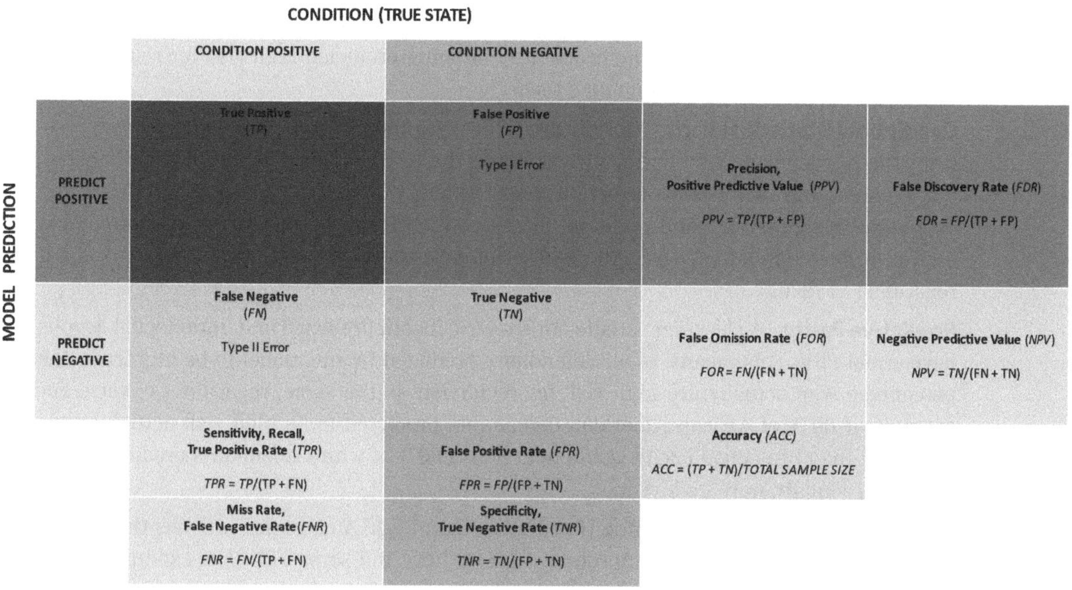

CONDITION (TRUE STATE)

	CONDITION POSITIVE	CONDITION NEGATIVE		
PREDICT POSITIVE	True Positive (TP)	False Positive (FP) Type I Error	**Precision, Positive Predictive Value** (PPV) $PPV = TP/(TP + FP)$	**False Discovery Rate** (FDR) $FDR = FP/(TP + FP)$
PREDICT NEGATIVE	False Negative (FN) Type II Error	True Negative (TN)	**False Omission Rate** (FOR) $FOR = FN/(FN + TN)$	**Negative Predictive Value** (NPV) $NPV = TN/(FN + TN)$
	Sensitivity, Recall, True Positive Rate (TPR) $TPR = TP/(TP + FN)$	**False Positive Rate** (FPR) $FPR = FP/(FP + TN)$	**Accuracy** (ACC) $ACC = (TP + TN)/TOTAL\ SAMPLE\ SIZE$	
	Miss Rate, False Negative Rate (FNR) $FNR = FN/(TP + FN)$	**Specificity, True Negative Rate** (TNR) $TNR = TN/(FP + TN)$		

Figure 18.1 Confusion Matrix for a binary classifier

Lets consider an example which is by now a classic in the fairness in machine learning literature: a model for predicting recidivism widely used in the US for making parole decisions – COMPAS. In May 2016, ProPublica published an article[31] indicating that the predictions of a widely-used recidivism modelling model (COMPAS), were biased.

The debate between ProPublica and Northpointe, the company that developed COMPAS, drew many academics, legal scholars, and civil rights advocates into its wake[32] [33]. Several issues were at stake, but we will focus on one aspect – Northpointe claimed that their algorithm was fair, and had the data to show it. But ProPublica claimed that the algorithm was unfair, and had the data to prove it as well. How could this be?

A brief survey of some of the most popular fairness metrics can help clarify the controversy.

Group **Fairness.** *These fairness metrics are based on the premise that different groups should be treated equally. Such fairness metrics require the identification of the sub-group or sub-*

[31] Angwin, J., Larson, J., Mattu, S., and Kirchner, L., (2016), 'Machine bias: There's software used across the country to predict future criminals. And it's biased against blacks', ProPublica, 23 May 2016. https://www.propublica.org/article/machine-bias-risk-assessments-in-criminal-sentencing

[32] Dressel, J., and Farid, H., (2018), 'The accuracy, fairness, and limits of predicting recidivism', Science Advances, 17 January 2018: Vol. 4, no. 1. *https://advances.sciencemag.org/content/4/1/eaao5580.full*

[33] Feller, A., Pierson, E., Corbett-Davies, S., Goel, S., (2016), 'A computer program used for bail and sentencing decisions was labeled biased against blacks. It's actually not that clear', Monkey Cage, 17 October 2016. *https://www.washingtonpost.com/news/monkey-cage/wp/2016/10/17/can-an-algorithm-be-racist-our-analysis-is-more-cautious-than-propublicas/?noredirect=on&utm_term=.24b3907c91d1*

groups of the population that are potential victims of bias (also called protected group), and a comparator group (unprotected group). In the COMPAS case, the protected group was African American defendants, and the comparator group was white defendants.

Group Fairness (Demographic Parity, Statistical Parity). A classifier satisfies this definition if subjects in both protected and unprotected groups are equally likely to be assigned to the positive predicted class. In the example of predicting recidivism, a model would satisfy this definition if, for example, the probability of being predicted high risk for re-offending was 20 % regardless of the defendant's race.

Conditional Statistical Parity (Conditional Demographic Parity). This fairness metric relaxes the previous one, and permits to condition the result on a set of legitimate attributes. For example, the recidivism prediction model could condition on the type of offense the defendant was guilty of – and would be considered fair if the probability of being predicted high risk for re-offending, given the type of offense that had been committed, was equal regardless of race.

Predictive Parity. A classifier satisfies this metric if both protected and unprotected groups have equal PPV. This means, of all defendants predicted by the model to be high risk, the percentage who actually are high risk for recidivism is the same, regardless of race. For example, if 80 % of African American defendants predicted to be high risk actually were high risk, then Predictive Parity would hold if also 80 % of white defendants predicted to be high risk, actually were high risk.

False Positive Error Rate Balance (Predictive Equality). A classifier satisfies this metric if both the protected and the unprotected group have the same FPR. For example, if the recidivism prediction model were to have an FPR of 15 % for both African American and white defendants, then it would be considered fair by this metric.

False Negative Error Rate Balance (Equal Opportunity). This fairness metric is satisfied if both protected and unprotected groups have the same FNR.

Equalized Odds. This metric combines False Positive Error Rate Balance and False Negative Error Rate Balance. It holds whenever the FPR and the FNR are equal for both protected and unprotected groups.

Overall Accuracy Equality. A classifier satisfies this metric if the overall accuracy for both the protected and theunprotected groups is the same. In the case of the recidivism prediction model, Overall Accuracy Equality would hold, for instance, if the model predictions were 85 % accurate for African American, and for white, defendants.

Test-fairness (Calibration). This metric is a more refined version of Group Fairness. Test-fairness holds if, for any predicted probability score P, subjects in both protected and unprotected groups are equally likely to belong to the positive class. For example, if the recidivism prediction model were to satisfy Test-fairness, then for any value of P between 0 and 1, the likelihood that an African American defendant with predicted probability P of re-offending belongs to the true high risk class must be the same as the likelihood for a white defendant with predicted probability P of re-offending to belong to the true high risk class.

Individual **Fairness**. *The following fairness metrics are based on the notion of giving similar predictions to similar individuals.*

Fairness Through Unawareness. A classifier satisfies this fairness metric if it does not explicitly use any sensitive characteristics in making its predictions. In the recidivism prediction model, this would mean that the attribute race was not included among the features the model used to make its predictions.

Fairness Through Awareness. This fairness metric attempts to capture the concept that similar individuals (excluding sensitive features – such as race in the recidivism model case) should have similar predictions. Similarity is determined by a pre-defined distance metric; and in order for a classifier to be fair according this definition, the distance between the prediction outputs for individuals should not exceed the distance between the individuals.

There are many other fairness metrics, including several involving the use of causal reasoning and causal graphs that attempt to identify if there are causal links between sensitive characteristics and model predictions. The interested reader is encouraged to consult the articles of Verma et al.[34] and Mehrabi et al.[35] for a more in-depth discussion.

Now that we're equipped with some basic understanding of fairness metrics, we can return to the COMPAS controversy.

Northpointe said the algorithm is fair, because within each risk category, the proportion of defendants who reoffend is approximately the same regardless of race. They were using the Predictive Parity metric: The proportion of correctly predicted high risks is the same regardless of demographic.

ProPublica said the algorithm is unfair, because among defendants who ultimately did not reoffend, African Americans were more than twice as likely as whites to be classified as high risk (42 percent vs. 22 percent). They also showed that white defendants had a higher False Negative Rate. ProPublica used the Equalized Odds fairness metric: All groups should have equal False Negative Rate and equal False Positive Rate.

It turns out, that the fairness metrics are not compatible – this is shown by some impossibility theorems[36]. However, without getting into high-level mathematics, we just recall some values from the Confusion Matrix above: Let p be the Prevalence (i.e. the proportion of high risk individuals in a population), FPR be the False Positive Rate, FNR the False Negative Rate, and PPV be the Positive Predictive Value. Then a little bit of Algebra and this formula[37]

$$FPR = (1 - FNR)\frac{p(1 - PPV)}{(1 - p)PPV}$$

... suffice to show that Equalized Odds and Predictive Parity cannot both hold true when p is different for African American defendants vs. white defendants. In fact, the overall recidivism rate for African American defendants is higher than for white defendants (52 percent vs. 39 percent). The issues in predicting recidivism lie much deeper, and are difficult to

---

[34] Verma, S. and Rubin, J., (2018), "Fairness Definitions Explained", Proceedings of the International Workshop on Software Fairness (FairWare), pp. 1–7.

[35] Mehrabi, N., Morstatter, F., Saxena, N., Lerman, K., Galstyan, A., (2019), 'A Survey on Bias and Fairness in Machine Learning', arXiv preprint. *https://arxiv.org/pdf/1908.09635.pdf*

[36] Kleinberg, J., Mullainathan, S. and Raghavan, M., (2018), 'Inherent Trade-Offs in the Fair Determination of Risk Scores', ACM SIGMETRICS Performance Evaluation Review, Vol. 46, No. 1, p. 40.

[37] Chouldechova, A., (2017), 'Fair Prediction with Disparate Impact: A Study of Bias in Recidivism Prediction Instruments', Big Data, Vol. 5, No. 2, pp. 153–163.

capture in one fairness metric. Dressel et al.[38], and Richardson et al.[39] point to some of the other issues and challenges involved in attempting to use algorithms in complex situations with deeply embedded societal biases, and where model predictions can have such a fundamental impact on those affected.

So we have more than 20 definitions of fairness, and they cannot all hold true simultaneously – this means that some fairness definition has to be selected a priori, in order to determine if the model is biased or not. How can the right fairness definition be selected? Unfortunately, there is no simple answer to this question. There is no regulatory guidance (yet), and the fairness definitions do not clearly map onto legal concepts (see Wachter et al.[40] for a discussion in European Law). It is therefore essential to consider the use context of the model, and the stakeholders, and preferably to establish the fairness criteria in open discussion with those most likely to be impacted by the model.

18.3.3 Mitigating Unwanted Bias in AI Systems

Checking for bias should be an integral part of the machine learning model training procedure: Check for bias, de-bias the model, repeat.

De-biasing can happen at three stages:

- Pre-process
- In-process
- Post-process

Pre-process de-biasing assumes that the training data is the source of bias, and modifies/adjusts the data, or even creates "fairer" synthetic versions, in order to minimize the bias. The advantage of this approach is that one is then completely free to choose the algorithm to train for prediction. However, pre-process de-biasing cannot remove bias that arises during the algorithm design, or later stages of development/deployment. Additionally, de-biasing the data might actually just hide the bias, rather than remove it: for example, Gonen et al.[41] show that attempts to remove gender bias in word embeddings are actually just concealing the bias.

In-process de-biasing directly modifies the model training process. It operates either by integrating a fairness metric into the loss function, or by introducing a fairness constraint. The advantage of this bias mitigation measure is that it provides the best trade-off between fairness and accuracy. However, it can make the training process even less transparent, possibly leading to even more hidden biases.

---

[38] Dressel, J., and Farid, H., (2018), 'The accuracy, fairness, and limits of predicting recidivism', Science Advances, 17 January 2018: Vol. 4, no. 1.

[39] Richardson, R., Schultz, J., and Crawford, K. (2019), 'Dirty Data, Bad Predictions: How Civil Rights Violations Impact Police Data, Predictive Policing Systems, and Justice', NYU Law Review, Vol. 94, N. 192.

[40] Wachter, S., Mittelstadt, B., Russell, C., (2021), 'Why Fairness Cannot Be Automated: Bridging the Gap Between EU Non-Discrimination Law and AI', Computer Law & Security Review, Vol. 41, (2021):105567.

[41] Gonen, H., and Goldberg, Y., (2019), 'Lipstick on a Pig: Debiasing Methods Cover up Systematic Gender Biases in Word Embeddings But do not Remove Them', Proceedings of the 2019 Conference of the North American Chapter of the Association for Computational Linguistics: Human Language Technologies, Vol 1, pp. 609–614.

Post-process de-biasing corrects for bias only after the predictions are made. This approach does not change the data, or the prediction model itself, and can also be used on proprietary black-box models (i.e. if the model has been developed by some other organization). The disadvantage is that it does not allow for an optimal compromise between accuracy and fairness, and that it adds an extra step to the whole modelling process.

There are several open source toolkits that provide the tools for bias detection and bias mitigation. Here are some of the most popular ones to date:

- Themis *https://themis-ml.readthedocs.io/en/latest/*
- LinkedIn Fairness Toolkit (LiFT) *https://github.com/linkedin/LiFT*
- Google What-IF Tool *https://pair-code.github.io/what-if-tool/*
- FairTest *https://github.com/columbia/fairtest*
- AIF360 *https://github.com/Trusted-AI/AIF360*

■ 18.4 Transparency of AI Systems

Transparency for an AI system has several levels. At the most superficial level, it involves notifying those who are interacting with an AI System, or subject to AI system predictions, that this is happening. For example, the current draft AI Act[42] includes a provision for certain "medium risk" applications (such as emotion recognition systems, or systems generating deep fakes – see the draft AI Act, Article 52) to apply this minimal form of transparency.

At a deeper level, transparency of AI systems involves giving external stakeholders varying degrees of insight into the inputs and processes used in developing the algorithm. This can include information about training and evaluation data, feautures used, the algorithm, training methods, performance metrics, and quality assurance and risk management systems in place. It can also include explanations of how the model predictions were made.

However, transparency also comes with costs – from the time and effort required to create appropriate documentation, to possible losses in accuracy in trying to create more explainable algorithms. So why do it?

- *Quality assurance* can be improved, because development processes have been documented.
- Understanding how the model predictions were made can simplify *testing and debugging*, and give more confidence in how the model will behave under new conditions, thus improving system *safety*.
- *Biases* are more easily detected, if the data sets are well understood, and the features that were important in making model predictions are known.
- Using model explainability to detect if small changes/perturbations in the data lead to disproportionately large changes in model outputs can help improve *model robustness*.

---

[42] EU Draft AI Act: *https://digital-strategy.ec.europa.eu/en/policies/european-approach-artificial-intelligence*

- In some cases, the *regulator* may require documentation (see, for example, the draft AI Act, Articles 9 and 10, and Annex IV), or even an explanation (arguably, this is contained in GDPR Article 22 and more clearly laid out in Recital 71)

- It might be necessary for a third-party *auditor* to assess conformity of the AI system with regulatory requirements.

- Finally, clearly documented models whose predictions can be adequately explained, are more easily *trusted*.

In the sections that follow, current best practices for data and model documentation will be described; the chapter closes with a discussion of explainability.

18.4.1 Documenting the Data

Data is one of the major ingredients in a machine learning system, and can have a profound impact on final model performance. Yet surprisingly, until 2018, very few efforts were made to document how that data was collected, pre-processed, and used. As noted by Gebru et al.[43]:

In the electronics industry, every component, no matter how simple or complex, is accompanied with a datasheet that describes its operating characteristics, test results, recommended uses, and other information. By analogy, we propose that every dataset be accompanied with a datasheet that documents its motivation, composition, collection process, recommended uses.

While, for example, the draft AI Act explicitly requires some form of datasheet as part of the model documentation for high risk AI systems, there are other good reasons for creating them:

- Increased transparency and accountability for the data set creators

- Other researchers can more easily reproduce model results, increasing trust in the model's performance

- Unwanted biases arising from biased training data can be detected more easily, and mitigation measures adopted

- Potential data set users can more easily determine if the data set is suitable for their needs

A datasheet, as proposed by Gebru et al. (see also Bender et al.[44] for a similar concept specifically for Natural Language Processing data) is a series of questions about the data set collection process and composition, that is also an opportunity for the data set creators to reflect on their data collection process. Questions include:

- Why is the data being collected? Who requested/funded the data collection, and for what purpose?

---

[43] Gebru, T., Morgenstern, J., Vecchione, B., Wortman Vaughan, J., Wallach, H., Daumé III, H., Crawford, K., (2020), 'Datasheets for Datasets', arXiv preprint. *http://arxiv.org/abs/1803.09010*

[44] Bender, E., and Friedman, B., (2018), 'Data Statements for Natural Language Processing: Toward Mitigating System Bias and Enabling Better Science', Transactions of the Association for Computational Linguistics, Vol. 6, pp. 587–604. *https://aclanthology.org/Q18-1041.pdf*

- What is the composition of the data set (for example, does it contain tabular data, or text data? Multi-modal data?)
- How was the data collected? What sampling procedure, why was that method chosen, and sampled from which population?
- Was the data labelled? If so, by whom?
- What were the pre-processing steps?
- What are the results of the Exploratory Data Analysis? (For example, how many items, how many features, correlations, sensitive characteristics, etc.)
- What are the intended uses of this data set, and are there uses to avoid?
- Will the data set be distributed? If so, how?
- Who is repsonsible for the maintenance of the data set?

Such documentation could go a long way towards avoiding certain kinds of bias – for example, understanding the composition of the training data might have alerted developers to the fact that people with darker skin tones were under-represented in the data, before they deployed a model that labelled some people as Gorillas[45]; while knowing who labelled the data, and what societal biases they might bring to the table, could have lead to the earlier detection of picture captioning models that perpetuate gender stereotypes[46].

Very easily overlooked stakeholders in AI development are the workers who are employed to label the data. Very often, these are poorly-paid crowd workers. Documenting the data and how it was collected could also contribute to improving the labor conditions of these crowd workers[47] – having to be transparent about who labelled the data and how much they were remunerated might incline tech employers to offer more advantageous working conditions.

18.4.2 Documenting the Model

Documentation for the machine learning model follows the same principles as documentation for the data sets: such documentation should help increase transparency and accountability for the model developers; allow for reproducibility of models and/or their results; include measures for model bias; and avoid model use in inappropriate contexts.

Some examples of what such model documentation could look like can be found in Mitchell et al.[48], or in Annex IV of the draft AI Act. In particular, the following information should be included:

---

[45] Simonite, T., When It Comes to Gorillas, Google Photos Remains Blind, Wired, 1 November 2018. *https://www.wired.com/story/when-it-comes-to-gorillas-google-photos-remains-blind/*

[46] Simonite, T., When AI Sees a Man, It Thinks 'Official.' A Woman? 'Smile', 19 November 2020. *https://www.wired.com/story/ai-sees-man-thinks-official-woman-smile/*

[47] Semuels, A., 'The Internet Is Enabling a New Kind of Poorly Paid Hell', The Atlantic, 23 January 2018. *https://www.theatlantic.com/business/archive/2018/01/amazon-mechanical-turk/551192/*

[48] Mitchell, M., Wu, S., Zaldivar, A., Barnes, P., Vasserman, L., Hutchinson, B., Spitzer, E., Raji, I. D., Gebru, T., (2019), 'Model Cards for Model Reporting', FAT '19: Proceedings of the Conference on Fairness, Accountability, and Transparency. *http://arxiv.org/abs/1810.03993*

- Basic logistic information about the model, such as person or organization developing it, licenses, and where to send questions or bug reports..

- Basic descriptions of the training algorithms, the model parameters, optimization function, fairness constraints, and features.

- Intended use, in particular optimal uses, primary intended users, and use cases to avoid.

- Under which conditions – for example, using which target populations; if audio/visual input is required, which kind, and under what environmental conditions – the model performance has been tested.

- Which metrics were used to measure model performance? Which fairness metrics? What decision thresholds were used?

- Details on the training and test data (see Documenting the data section above)

We also recommend adding information on energy efficiency and environmental impact – research[49] [50] indicates that the energy consumption of storing large amounts of data, and training and deploying very large complex models (for example deep learning models) is significant.

18.4.3 Explainability

Explainability is another term in AI that is often discussed, but rarely defined; it is also often used interchangeably with interpretability. However, we adopt the following working definition: *explainability* is the property of an AI system to provide evidence or reasons for its outputs and/or processes[51].

As already discussed in the chapter introduction, explainability can be essential for detecting unwanted biases, testing and debugging models, ensuring safety – and establishing trust in the model and its predictions. For example, as Ribeiro et al.[52] show, it is possible to train a classifier to distinguish between huskies and wolves – yet, only when model explanations are added does it become clear that, due to some data collection artefacts (all pictures of wolves had snow in the background), what was actually trained was a snow versus no-snow classifier. When data sets become so large that such data artefacts are not easily detected, it is difficult to trust the outputs of complex prediction models, even if they seem to be performing well.

Given that explainability is a desirable property of an AI system, how can it be achieved? The first fundamental decision comes at the algorithm selection phase: should an intrinsically explainable algorithm be used (such as linear/logistic regression, decision trees, or Naive Bayes), or should some post-hoc methods be applied to a more complex algorithm

---

[49] Strubell, E., Ganesh, A., and McCallum, A., (2019), 'Energy and Policy Considerations for Deep Learning in NLP', Proceedings of the 57th Annual Meeting of the Association for Computational Linguistics, pp. 3645-3650.

[50] Bender, E. M., Gebru, T., McMillan-Major, A., Shmitchell, S., (2021), 'On the Dangers of Stochastic Parrots: Can Language Models Be Too Big?', Proceedings of the 2021 ACM Conference on Fairness, Accountability, and Transparency, pp. 610-623.

[51] NIST, 'Four Principles of Artificial Intelligence', *https://nvlpubs.nist.gov/nistpubs/ir/2021/NIST.IR.8312.pdf* – see definition of "Explanation"

[52] Ribeiro, M. T., Singh, S., Guestrin, C., (2016), '"Why Should I Trust You?" Explaining the Predictions of Any Classifier', arXiv preprint. *https://arxiv.org/pdf/1602.04938.pdf*

(random forests, or neural networks, for example). Depending on the use case and the available data, a simpler and intrinsically explainable model can be a viable and competitive option. A useful approach would be training a simple model in addition to more complex variants in order to understand the trade off between performance and explainability.

Additionally, it is important to understand the explainability measures to use: this is very often determined by whom the explanation is for, and their level of machine learning expertise. Should the explanation method be model specific, or can it apply to many different kinds of models? Should the explanation be local – providing an understanding of why the model produced a prediction for a particular instance, or should the explanation be global, addressing the entire model behaviour? Finally, how should the model explanations be delivered? Popular methods include:

- **Feature summary statistics:** this could be feature importance information, showing how much each feature contributed to the model decision; or in the form of a correlation matrix, showing the correlations between the features and the predicted output.

- **Feature summary visualization:** for example, curves that show a feature and the average predicted outcome for that feature

- **Model internals:** this includes variable coefficients for linear or logistic regression; the learned tree structure in a decision tree; or else learned weights in the neural networks setting. However, while the internals for the simpler models can deliver reasonable explanations, understanding the implications in the neural networks case could be a challenge.

- If the prediction model is based on a complex algorithm, it could be possible to approximate it (either locally or globally) with an intrinsically interpretable model.

Two very popular frameworks for post-hoc explanations are LIME[53] and SHAP[54].

LIME provides local explanations to any kind of model (i.e. it is model agnostic). In order to explain the model prediction for a particular instance, LIME perturbs the instance, and obtains the model predictions for the new perturbed points. It weights the perturbed points according to their distance from the original instance, and then trains a weighted linear (or any other kind of interpretable) model on the data set of perturbed points.

SHAP[55] is based on Shapley values, which use coalitional game theory to compute the "marginal utility" of each feature in determining a local prediction. These local predictions are then added up in a linear model, in order to produce a global explanation. A word of caution: SHAP must have access to the model's entire training data in order to function.

Model-agnostic post-hoc explanations such as SHAP and LIME can be a useful resource when trying to understand the behaviour of, for instance, a deep neural network-based model. However, as the NIST paper points out, there are a few other requirements for an explainable AI – and a fundamental one is *Explanation Accuracy*: An explanation correctly reflects the reason for generating the output and/or accurately reflects the system's process[56]. Unfortunately, recent research has shown that SHAP and LIME explanations can be

[53] *https://github.com/marcotcr/lime*
[54] *https://github.com/slundberg/shap*
[55] *https://github.com/slundberg/shap*
[56] NIST, 'Four Principles of Artificial Intelligence', *https://nvlpubs.nist.gov/nistpubs/ir/2021/NIST.IR.8312.pdf*

manipulated[57] [58] – leaving some doubt as to how accurate their explanations are, and when they break down.

■ 18.5 Conclusion

Trustworthy AI is a field still very much in its infancy. While there is already a large body of so-called ethics guidelines, the regulatory and standards framework is still under construction, and practical tools, where they exist, are fragmented and often usable only by a small group of experts. This unsettled state of affairs, combined with the buzzword status of the term "Trustworthy AI", can make it appear more of a special "add-on", or "nice-to-have" feature, rather than what it should be: an integral part of the AI system life-cycle, ensuring that the AI solution will be beneficial, and reliably deliver what it promises.

■ 18.6 In a Nutshell

This chapter covers various aspects of Trustworthy AI:

- The Trustworthy AI framework: ethics guidelines, international standards, and EU regulations.
- A brief overview of possible AI stakeholders.
- Fairness in AI, from different types of bias, to various metrics for measuring the fairness impacts of algorithms, and possible techniques for mitigating unwanted bias.
- Transparency, including documentation for data and models, and methods for explaining model decisions.

  ■

---

[57] Slack, D., Hilgard, S., Jia, E., Singh, S., Lakkaraju, H., (2020), 'How can we fool LIME and SHAP? Adversarial Attacks on Post hoc Explanation Methods', AIES '20, 7–8 February 2020.
[58] Dimanov, B., Bhatt, U., Jamnik, M., Welle, A., (2020), 'You Shouldn't Trust Me: Learning Models Which Conceal Unfairness From Multiple Explanation Methods', 24th European Conference on Artificial Intelligence – ECAI 2020.

19 The authors

Stefan Papp is an entrepreneur. He helps organizations build data architectures and migrate on-premise solutions to the cloud. Stefan Papp's primary focus is solutions in the Climate Action environment. He and his team create solutions to reduce carbon emissions and carbon trading is also a key topic here. Stefan Papp is setting up a competence center for Climate Action in Armenia.

Stefan is also an advisor to promising Armenian startups. He is one of many business angels who invest in helping Armenia to become the "Silicon Valley of the East."

Wolfgang Weidinger is a Data Scientist and has worked in a wide variety of industries and sectors such as start-ups, finance, consulting and wholesale. There he led Data Science teams and drove their role as spearheads in digital and data-driven transformation.

He is President of the Vienna Data Science Group (*www.vdsg.at*), a non-profit association of and for Data Scientists. This brings together both research and practice across a wide range of industries. The VDSG is a rapidly growing international community whose goal is to educate about Data Science and its subfields such as Machine Learning and Artificial Intelligence, as well as their impact on society.

Wolfgang is particularly interested in the societal impact of Data Science and AI, as well as the establishment of interdisciplinary Data Science teams in companies and their disruptive impact on business models.

Katherine Munro is a Data Scientist and Data Science Ambassador in the e-commerce domain, conducting both research and corporate training in AI, machine learning, Natural Language Processing and data science.

With a background in computational linguistics and machine learning, Katherine has worked in research and development for Mercedes-Benz and the Fraunhofer Institute, specializing in user interfaces and Natural Language Understanding. She has also worked as a university lecturer and English teacher, and is now a public speaker, education Lead for Women in AI Upper Austria, volunteer mentor at Female Coders Linz, and trainer for Linkedin Learning.

Bernhard Ortner currently works as a Data Architect Lead and Enterprise Architect of Wiener Linien, where he is transforming the organization by building the next mobility platform. His activities include the adaptation of existing processes around Big Data and the establishment of Big Data standards and best practices. He also lectures selected Data Engineering topics at the Duale Hochschule Baden-Württemberg, and participates in various Open Source communities. His main motivation is to find new ways and possibilities for the application of Big Data.

Annalisa Cadonna is a statistician and data science consultant. She received her Ph.D. in Applied Mathematics and Statistics from University of California, Santa Cruz. Annalisa has applied statistical and machine learning methods to deliver projects in the financial, energy and medical industries. Currently, her professional goal is bridging the gap between time series research and industry applications, by using probabilistic programming and cloud technologies. Annalisa strives to use statistics and machine learning as means for the achievement of the Sustainable Development Goals and to be active in the development of tools and frameworks for responsible artificial intelligence. She is also one of the organizers of R-ladies Vienna.

Georg Langs is a full professor for Machine Learning in Medical Imaging at the Medical University of Vienna, where he heads the Computational Imaging Research Lab at the Department of Biomedical Imaging and Image-guided Therapy. He is co-founder and chief scientist of the spin-off contextflow GmbH, which develops software for AI-based image search. Georg Langs studied mathematics at the Vienna University of Technology and computer science at the Graz University of Technology, and was a Research Scientist at MIT's Computer Science and Artificial Intelligence Lab, where he is still a Research Affiliate.

Roxane Licandro is a postdoctoral research associate at the Medical University of Vienna and a research fellow at the Massachusetts General Hospital and Harvard Medical School. She graduated from her medical computer science studies at TU Wien, where she worked as a university assistant at the Computer Vision Lab. She was awarded a Marie Skłodowska-Curie Fellowship and completed research stays at Charité Berlin, Children's Hospital Zurich and University College London. She worked at the Kunsthistorisches Museum Wien and at Agfa Healthcare. Her research focus lies on finding new ways to computationally model and predict dynamic processes in space and over time, paediatric and fetal brain development, statistical pattern analysis in cancer research and geometric shape analysis of anatomical and cultural objects.

Mario Meir-Huber is the Head of Data at UNIQA, the leading insurance company in Central and Eastern Europe. Here, he and his team are working to make the company data-driven. Before joining UNIQA, he worked in similar positions at a leading telecommunications company as well as at large technology providers such as Microsoft. In addition to his job, he is a keynote speaker at various international events such as GITEX or London Tech Week. Mario has already published several books on the topic of the Cloud and (Big) Data. His blog can be reached at *cloudvane.net*.

Dr. Danko Nikolić is an expert in both brain research and AI. For many years he has run an electrophysiology lab at the Max-Planck Institute for Brain Research. Also, he is an AI and machine learning professional heading a Data Science team and developing commercial solutions based on AI technology. He invented AI Kindergarten—a concept for training AI of the future for achieving near human-level intelligence. He also pioneered using machine learning to read "minds" from the brain's electrical signals; he and his team were able to reconstruct what an animal was seeing solely by analyzing the brain signals. He introduced the concept of ideasthesia ("sensing concepts") into neuroscience and is the author of a theory called practopoiesis describing how biological systems achieve intelligence. He has a degree in Psychology and Civil Engineering from the University of Zagreb, Croatia and a PhD from the University of Oklahoma, USA. He was an honorary professor at the university of Zagreb from 2014 to 2019.

Zoltan C. Toth is a data engineering architect, lecturer and entrepreneur. With a background in Computer Science and Mathematics, he has taught data architectures, big data technologies and machine learning operations to Fortune 500 companies worldwide. In the past two decades he has worked with several large enterprises as a Solutions Architect, implementing data analytics infrastructures and scaling them up to processing petabytes of data. He is also a lecturer at the Central European University. He founded Datapao, a data engineering consultancy that became Databricks's European professional services center and a Microsoft Gold Partner in Data Science.

Barbora Vesela is a data scientist and software engineer working at Frequentis, which operates in a safety critical communication and information environment. Her background is a study of biophysics at Masaryk University in Brno and biomedical engineering both at FH Technikum Wien and Brno University of Technology. She is interested in various topics combining data science and signal and image processing applied in multiple environments, such as medicine, research and air traffic management.

Rania Wazir is a mathematician and data scientist focussing on Trustworthy AI, Natural Language Processing and Social Media Monitoring. She is a vice chair of Austria's Standards Committee on AI, and Austrian delegate to the ISO working group on Trustworthy AI; she is also coordinator of the VDSG's data4good initiative, which works with non-profits on data-based projects. She lead a consortium of machine learning, legal, and social science experts that recently completed an investigation into bias in algorithms for the EU Fundamental Rights Agency, and is currently tech lead in a three-year project to create a fair by design AI development process, funded by the Austrian Research Agency. Dr. Wazir is co-founder, together with open innovation expert Dr. Gertraud Leimüller, of the recent start-up leiwand.ai, whose goal is to provide companies and organizations involved in the development or use of AI systems with the tools and know-how necessary to ensure their systems are trustworthy.

Günther Zauner is a long-time employee at dwh GmbH, a mathematician and expert in the field of modeling and simulation, parametrization and forecast modeling. He is working on industrial projects as well as on research projects (e. g. EU FP7 CEPHOS-LINK, Horizon 2020 RheumaBuddy). He specializes in the development of modeling concepts, integration of routine data and population behavior. He is a member of VDSG, Society of Medical Decision Making (SMDM) and a member of the board of International Society for Pharmacoeconomics and Outcomes Research Austria (ISPOR Austria). Furthermore, he is reviewer of several journals, and he is doing a PhD study in the field of Public Health under the lead of Professor Majdan at the University of Trnava.

Index